Les voyelles anglaises / English vowels

[ɑ:]	far	âme
[æ]	man	salle
[e]	get	sec
[ə]	utter	le
[ɜ:]	absurd	beurre
[ɪ]	stick	i très court
[i:]	need	si
[ɒ]	in-laws	phase
[ɔ:]	more	essor
[ʌ]	mother	entre à et eux
[ʊ]	book	bouquin (très court)
[u:]	hoot	sous

Les diphtongues anglaises / English diphthongs

[aɪ]	time	aïe
[aʊ]	cloud	ciao
[eɪ]	name	nez suivi d'un y court
[ɔɪ]	point	cow-boy
[ov]	so	eau

['] indique que la syllabe suivante est accentuée: *ability* [ə'bɪlətɪ]

Some French words starting with h have ' before the h. This ' is not part of the French word. It shows i) that a preceding vowel does not become an apostrophe or elision takes place. (This is called an aspirated h).

'hanche la hanche, les hanches [no z sound between *les* and *hanches*]

habit l'habit, les habits [a z sound between *les* and *habits*]

Langenscheidt Universal Dictionary

French

**French – English
English – French**

edited by the
Langenscheidt editorial staff

Langenscheidt
Munich · Vienna

Compiled by LEXUS with: / Réalisé par LEXUS:

Sandrine François · Jane Goldie
Claire Guerreau · Julie Le Boulanger
Peter Terrell

Neither the presence nor the absence of a designation
indicating that any entered word constitutes a trademark
should be regarded as affecting the legal status thereof.

Les mots qui, à notre connaissance, sont considérés comme des
marques ou des noms déposés sont signalés dans cet ouvrage
par la mention correspondante. La présence ou l'absence de
cette mention ne peut pas être considérée comme ayant valeur
juridique.

15060 (98194)

© 2011 Langenscheidt GmbH & Co. KG, Munich
Printed in Germany

Contents / Table des matières

Abbreviations / Abréviations

and	&	et
see	→	voir
registered trademark	®	marque déposée
adjective	*adj*	adjectif
adverb	*adv*	adverbe
agriculture	AGR	agriculture
anatomy	ANAT	anatomie
architecture	ARCH	architecture
astronomy	ASTR	astronomie
astrology	ASTROL	astrologie
attributive	*atr*	devant le nom
motoring	AUTO	automobiles
aviation	AVIAT	aviation
biology	BIOL	biologie
botany	BOT	botanique
British English	*Br*	anglais britannique
chemistry	CHIM	chimie
commerce, business	COMM	commerce
computers, IT term	COMPUT	informatique
conjunction	*conj*	conjonction
cooking	CUIS	cuisine
economics	ÉCON	économie
education	EDU	éducation
education	ÉDU	éducation
electricity	ÉL	électricité
electricity	ELEC	électricité
especially	*esp*	surtout
euphemism	*euph*	euphémisme
familiar, colloquial	F	familier
feminine	*f*	féminin
figurative	*fig*	figuré

finance	FIN	finance
formal	*fml*	langage formel
feminine plural	*fpl*	féminin pluriel
geography	GEOG	géographie
geography	GÉOGR	géographie
geology	GÉOL	géologie
geometry	GÉOM	géométrie
grammar	GRAM	grammaire
historical	HIST	historique
IT term	INFORM	informatique
interjection	*int*	interjection
invariable	*inv*	invariable
law	JUR	juridique
law	LAW	juridique
linguistics	LING	linguistique
literary	*litt*	littéraire
masculine	*m*	masculin
nautical	MAR	marine
mathematics	MATH	mathématiques
medicine	MED	médecine
medicine	MÉD	médecine
masculine and feminine	*m/f*	masculin et féminin
military	MIL	militaire
motoring	MOT	automobiles
masculine plural	*mpl*	masculin pluriel
music	MUS	musique
noun	*n*	nom
nautical	NAUT	marine
plural noun	*npl*	nom pluriel
singular noun	*nsg*	nom singulier
oneself	o.s.	se, soi
popular, slang	P	populaire
pejorative	*pej*	péjoratif

pejorative	*péj*	péjoratif
pharmacy	PHARM	pharmacie
photography	PHOT	photographie
physics	PHYS	physique
plural	*pl*	pluriel
politics	POL	politique
preposition	*prep*	préposition
preposition	*prép*	préposition
pronoun	*pron*	pronom
psychology	PSYCH	psychologie
something	*qch*	quelque chose
someone	*qn*	quelqu'un
radio	RAD	radio
railroad	RAIL	chemin de fer
religion	REL	religion
singular	*sg*	singulier
someone	s.o.	quelqu'un
sports	SP	sport
something	*sth*	quelque chose
subjunctive	*subj*	subjonctif
noun	*subst*	substantif
theater	THEA	théâtre
theater	THÉÂT	théâtre
technology	TECH	technique
telecommunications	TÉL	télécommunications
telecommunications	TELEC	télécommunications
typography, typesetting	TYP	typographie
television	TV	télévision
vulgar	V	vulgaire
auxiliary verb	*v/aux*	verbe auxiliaire
intransitive verb	*v/i*	verbe intransitif
transitive verb	*v/t*	verbe transitif
zoology	ZO	zoologie

A

à *lieu* in; *direction* to; **au bout de la rue** at/to the end of the street; **~ 2 heures d'ici** 2 hours from here; **~ cinq heures** at five o'clock; **~ Noël** at Christmas; **~ demain** until tomorrow; **c'est ~ moi** it's mine, it belongs to me; **aux cheveux blonds** with blonde hair; **~ pied** on foot; **~ dix euros** at *ou* for ten euros

abaissement *m* lowering; *(humiliation)* abasement; **abaisser** lower; *fig (humilier)* humble; **s'~** drop; *fig* demean o.s.

abandonner abandon; *pouvoir* give up; SP withdraw from; **s'~** *(se confier)* open up; **s'~ à** give way to

abasourdi amazed

abat-jour *m* (lamp)shade

abattre *arbre* fell; AVIAT shoot down; *animal* slaughter; *péj (tuer)* kill; *fig (épuiser)* exhaust; *(décourager)* dishearten; **s'~** collapse

abbaye *f* abbey

abcès *m* abscess

abdomen *m* abdomen

abeille *f* bee

aberrant F absurd

abêtir make stupid

abîmer spoil, ruin; **s'~** be ruined; *d'aliments* spoil

aboiement *m* barking

abolir abolish; **abolition** *f* abolition

abominable appalling

abondance *f* abundance

abonné, ~e *m/f* subscriber; **abonnement** *m* subscription; *de transport, de spectacles* season ticket; **abonner: s'~ à** subscribe to

abord *m*: **d'~** first; **au premier ~** at first sight; **~s** surroundings; **aborder 1** *v/t (prendre d'assaut)* board; *(heurter)* collide with; *fig: question* tackle; *personne* approach **2** *v/i* land (*à* at)

aboutir *d'un projet* succeed; **~ à** end at; *fig* lead to; **aboutissement** *m (résultat)* result

aboyer bark

abréger abridge

abréviation *f* abbreviation

abri *m* shelter; **être sans ~** be homeless

abricot *m* apricot; **abricotier** *m* apricot (tree)

abriter *(loger)* take in, shel-

ter; ~ **de** (*protéger*) shelter
from; **s'~** take shelter
abrupt abrupt; *pente* steep
abruti stupid; **abrutir:** ~ *qn* be
bad for s.o.'s brain; (*surmener*) exhaust s.o.
absence *f* absence; **absent**
absent; *air* absent-minded;
absenter: **s'~** leave, go away
absolu absolute; **absolument** absolutely
absorber absorb; *nourriture*
eat; *boisson* drink; **s'~ dans**
be absorbed in
abstenir: **s'~** POL abstain; **s'~**
de faire qc refrain from doing sth; **abstention** *f* POL abstention
abstrait abstract
absurdité *f* absurdity; ~**(s)**
nonsense
abus *m* abuse; ~ **de confiance** breach of trust; **abuser**
overstep the mark; ~ **de qc**
misuse ou abuse sth; **s'~** be
mistaken; **abusif, -ive** excessive; *emploi d'un mot* incorrect
académie *f* academy
acajou *m* mahogany
accabler: *être accablé de* be
weighed down by; ~ *qn de*
qc heap sth on s.o.
accalmie *f aussi fig* lull
accaparer ÉCON, *fig* monopolize
accéder: ~ *à* reach, get to;
INFORM access; *à l'indépendance, au pouvoir* gain;
d'un chemin lead to

accélérateur *m* AUTO gas pedal, *Br* accelerator; **accélérer**
aussi AUTO accelerate
accent *m* accent; (*intonation*)
stress; *mettre l'~ sur qc fig*
put the emphasis on sth; **accentuer** *syllabe* stress, accentuate
acceptable acceptable; **accepter** accept; (*reconnaître*)
agree; ~ **de faire** agree to do
sth
accès *m aussi* INFORM access;
MÉD fit
accessoire 1 *adj* incidental **2**
m detail; ~**s** accessories;
THÉÂT props
accident *m* accident; *événement fortuit* mishap; *par ~*
by accident, accidentally;
accidentel, ~le accidental
acclamation *f* acclamation;
~**s** cheers, cheering; **acclamer** cheer
acclimater: **s'~** become acclimatized
accolade *f* embrace; *signe*
brace, *Br* curly bracket
accommodation *f* adaptation; **accommoder** adapt;
CUIS prepare; **s'~ à** adapt
to; **s'~ de** make do with
accompagnateur, -trice *m/f*
guide; MUS accompanist; **accompagner** accompany
accomplir accomplish; *souhait* realize
accord *m* agreement; MUS
chord; *d'~* OK, alright; *être*
d'~ agree; *tomber d'~* come
to an agreement; **accordé-**

(bien) ~ in tune

accordéon accordion

accorder *crédit* grant; GRAM make agree; MUS tune; **s'~** get on; GRAM agree; **s'~ qc** allow o.s. sth

accouchement *m* birth; **accoucher** give birth (*de* to)

accouder: s'~ lean (one's elbows); **accoudoir** *m* armrest

accoupler connect; **s'~** BIOL mate

accourir come running

accoutumance *f* MÉD dependence; **accoutumer: s'~ qn à qc** get s.o. used to sth; **s'~ à qc** get used to sth

accrocher *manteau* hang up; AUTO collide with; **s'~ à** hang on to; *fig* cling to

accroître increase; **s'~** grow

accroupir: s'~ crouch, squat

accueil *m* reception, welcome; **accueillir** greet, welcome

accumulation *f* accumulation; **accumuler** accumulate; **s'~** accumulate

accusation *f* accusation; JUR prosecution; *plainte* charge; **accusé, ~e** *m/f* **1** JUR: **l'~** the accused **2** COMM: **accusé** *m de* réception acknowledgement (of receipt); **accuser** (*incriminer*) accuse (*de* of); (*faire ressortir*) emphasize

acerbe caustic

acéré sharp

acharnement *m* grim determination; **acharner: s'~ à faire qc** be bent on doing sth; **s'~ sur ou contre qn** pick on s.o.

achat *m* purchase; **faire des ~s** go shopping

acheter buy

achever finish; **s'~** finish

acide 1 *adj* sour; CHIM acidic **2** *m* CHIM acid

acier *m* steel

acné *f* acne

à-coup *m* jerk; **par ~s** in fits and starts

acoustique acoustic

acquéreur *m* purchaser; **acquérir** acquire; *droit* win

acquiescer: ~ à agree to

acquis acquired; *résultats* achieved

acquisition *f* acquisition

acquitter *facture* pay; JUR acquit; **s'~ de** carry out; *dette* pay

âcre acrid; *goût*, *fig* bitter; **âcreté** *f* bitterness

acrobate *m/f* acrobat; **acrobatie** *f* acrobatics *pl*

acte *m* (*action*) action, deed; (*document officiel*) deed; THÉÂT act; **~ de mariage** marriage certificate

acteur, -trice *m/f* actor; actress

actif, -ive 1 *adj* active **2** *m* COMM assets *pl*

action *f* action; COMM share; **~s** stock, shares *pl*; **actionnaire** *m/f* shareholder

actionner operate; *alarme* set

activate

activer (*accélérer*) speed up

activité f activity

actualiser update

actualité f current events *pl*; **~s** TV news *sg*

actuel, **~le** current, present; (*d'actualité*) topical; **actuellement** currently, at present

adaptation f adaptation; **adapter** adapt; **s'~ à** adapt to

addition f addition; *au restaurant* check, *Br* bill; **additionner** add

adéquat suitable; *montant* adequate

adhérent, **~e** m/f member; **adhérer** stick, adhere (**à** to)

adhésif, **-ive 1** *adj* sticky, adhesive **2** m adhesive

adieu m goodbye; **faire ses ~x** say one's goodbyes (**à qn** to s.o.)

adjectif m GRAM adjective

adjoint, **~e** m/f & *adj* assistant, deputy

admettre (*autoriser*) allow; (*accueillir*) admit, allow in; (*reconnaître*) admit

administrateur, **-trice** m/f administrator; **administratif**, **-ive** administrative; **administration** f administration; (*direction*) management, running

admirateur, **-trice 1** *adj* admiring **2** m/f admirer; **admiration** f admiration; **admirer** admire

admissible *candidat* eligible; *ce n'est pas ~* that's unacceptable

admission f admission

adolescence f adolescence; **adolescent**, **~e** m/f adolescent, teenager

adopter adopt; **adoption** f adoption

adorable adorable; **adorer** REL worship; *fig* (*aimer*) adore

adosser lean; **s'~ contre** ou **à** lean against ou on

adoucir soften; **s'~ du temps** become milder

adrénaline f adrenalin

adresse f address; (*habileté*) skill; **~ électronique** email address

adresser *lettre* address (**à** to); *remarque* direct (**à** at); **~ la parole à** address, speak to; **s'~ à qn** apply to s.o.; (*être destiné à*) be aimed at s.o.

adroit skillful, *Br* skilful

adulte 1 *adj* adult; *plante* mature **2** m/f adult, grown-up

adultère 1 *adj* adulterous **2** m adultery

adverbe m GRAM adverb

adversaire m/f opponent, adversary

adversité f adversity

aération f ventilation; **aérer** ventilate; *literie*, *pièce* air

aérien, **~ne** atr; *vue* aerial

aérobic m aerobics

aérodynamique aerodynamic

aéronautique aeronautical
aéroport *m* airport
aérosol *m* aerosol
affable affable
affaiblir weaken; **s'~** weaken
affaire *f* (*question*) matter, business; (*entreprise*) business; *marché* deal; (*bonne occasion*) bargain; JUR case; (*scandale*) affair, business; **~s** biens personnels things, belongings; **les ~s étrangères** foreign affairs; **affairer:** **s'~** busy o.s.
affaisser: **s'~** *du terrain* subside; *d'une personne* collapse
affamé hungry (**de** for)
affectation *f d'une chose* allocation; *d'un employé* assignment; MIL posting; (*pose*) affectation; **affecter** (*destiner*) assign; MIL post; (*émouvoir*) affect
affectif, -ive emotional
affection *f* affection; MÉD complaint
affectueux, -euse affectionate
affermir strengthen
affichage *m* billposting; INFORM display; **affiche** *f* poster; **afficher** *affiche* stick up; *attitude*, INFORM display
affilier: **s'~ à** *club* join; **être affilié à** be a member of
affiner refine
affinité *f* affinity
affirmatif, -ive affirmative;

personne assertive; **affirmation** *f* statement; **affirmer** (*prétendre*) maintain; *autorité* assert
affligeant distressing, painful; **affliger** distress
affluence *f:* **heures** *fpl* **d'~** rush hour *sg*; **affluent** *m* tributary; **affluer** come together
affolement *m* panic; **affoler** (*bouleverser*) madden, drive to distraction; *d'une foule, d'un cheval* panic; **s'~** panic
affranchir free; *lettre* meter, *Br* frank
affreux, -euse horrible; *peur, mal de tête* terrible
affront *m* insult, affront; **affronter** confront, face; SP meet; **s'~** confront ou face each other; SP meet
afin: ~ de faire in order to do, so as to do; **~ que** (+ *subj*) so that
africain, ~e African; **Africain, ~e** *m/f* African; **Afrique** *f:* **l'~** Africa
agaçant annoying; **agacement** *m* annoyance; **agacer** annoy; (*taquiner*) tease
âge *m:* **Moyen-Âge** Middle Ages *pl*; **personnes** *fpl* **du troisième ~** senior citizens; **quel ~ a-t-il?** how old is he?, what age is he?; **âgé** elderly; **~ de deux ans** aged two, two years old
agence *f* agency; *d'une banque* branch; **~ immobilière**

realtor's, *Br* estate agent's; ~ **matrimoniale** marriage bureau

agenda *m* diary; ~ **électronique** (*personal*) organizer

agenouiller: *s'~* kneel (down)

agent *m* agent; ~ **de change** stockbroker; ~ **immobilier** realtor, *Br* real estate agent; ~ **de police** police officer

agglomération *f* built-up area; *concentration de villes* conurbation

aggraver make worse; *s'~* worsen

agile agile; **agilité** *f* agility

agios *mpl* ÉCON bank charges

agir act; ~ *sur* affect s.o.; *il s'agit de* it's about

agitation *f* hustle and bustle; POL unrest; (*nervosité*) agitation; **agiter** *bouteille* shake; *mouchoir, main* wave; (*préoccuper, énerver*) upset; *s'~ d'un enfant* fidget; (*s'énerver*) get upset

agneau *m* lamb

agonie *f* death throes *pl*

agrafer *vêtements* fasten; *papier* staple; **agrafeuse** *f* stapler

agrandir enlarge; **agrandissement** *m* enlargement; *d'une ville* expansion

agréable pleasant (*à* to)

agrément *m* approval, consent; *les ~s* (*attraits*) the delights

agresser attack; **agresseur** *m* attacker; *pays* aggressor;

agressif, -ive aggressive; **agression** *f* attack; PSYCH stress

agriculteur *m* farmer; **agriculture** *f* agriculture, farming

agrumes *mpl* citrus fruit

ahuri astounded; **ahurissant** astounding

aide 1 *f* help, assistance; *à l'~ de qc* with the help of sth; *avec l'~ de qn* with s.o.'s help 2 *m/f* (*assistant*) assistant; **aider** 1 *v/t* help; *s'~ de qc* use sth 2 *v/i* help; ~ *à qc* contribute to sth

aïeul, ~e *m/f* ancestor; **aïeux** ancestors

aigle *m* eagle

aigre sour; *vent* bitter; *critique* sharp; *voix* shrill

aigu, ~ë sharp; *son* high-pitched; *conflit* bitter; *intelligence* keen; MÉD, GÉOM, GRAM acute

aiguille *f* needle; *d'une montre* hand; *tour* spire

aiguiser sharpen; *fig: appétit* whet

ail *m* garlic

aile *f* wing; AUTO fender, *Br* wing

ailier *m* SP wing, winger

ailleurs somewhere else, elsewhere; *d'~* besides; *par ~* moreover

aimable kind

aimant *m* magnet

aimer like; *parent, enfant, mari etc* love; ~ **mieux** prefer

aine *f* groin

aîné, ~e 1 *adj* elder; *de trois ou plus* eldest **2** *m/f* elder/eldest; *il est mon ~ de deux ans* he is two years older than me

ainsi this way, thus *fml;* **~ que** and, as well as

air *m* air; *aspect* look; MUS tune; *se donner des ~s* give o.s. airs; **airbag** *m* airbag

aire *f* area; **~ de jeu** playground

aisance *f* ease; *(richesse)* wealth

aise *f* ease; *être à l'~* be comfortable; *être mal à l'~* be uncomfortable; *prendre ses ~s* make o.s. at home

aisselle *f* armpit

ajourner postpone *(de* for); JUR adjourn

ajouter add; *s'~ à* be added to

ajuster adjust; *vêtement* alter; *(viser)* aim at; *(joindre)* fit *(à* to)

alarme *f* alarm; *donner l'~* raise the alarm; **~ antivol** burglar alarm; **alarmer** alarm; *s'~* be alarmed by

album *m* album

alcool *m* alcohol; **alcoolique** *adj & m/f* alcoholic; **alcoolisme** alcoholism; **alco(o)-test** *m* Breathalyzer®, *Br* Breathalyser®

aléatoire uncertain; INFORM, MATH random

alentour *m* *mpl* surroundings *pl;* **aux ~s** in the vi-

cinity of; *(autour de)* about

alerte 1 *adj* alert **2** *f* alarm; **~ à la bombe** bomb scare; **alerter** alert

algèbre *f* algebra

Algérie *f:* **l'~** Algeria; **algérien, ~ne** Algerian; **Algérien, ~ne** *m/f* Algerian

algue *f* BOT seaweed

aligner TECH align *(sur* with); *(mettre sur une ligne)* line up; *s'~* line up; *s'~ sur qc* align os.h with sth

aliment *m* foodstuff; **~s** food; **alimentation** *f* food; *en eau, en électricité* supply; **~ de base** staple diet; **alimenter** feed; *en eau, en électricité* supply **(en** with); *conversation* keep going

alinéa *m* paragraph

allaiter breast-feed

allécher tempt

allée *f (avenue)* path; **~s et venues** comings and goings

allégé *yaourt* low-fat; *confiture* low-sugar; **alléger** lighten; *impôt, tension* reduce

allègre cheerful

Allemagne *f:* **l'~** Germany; **allemand, ~e 1** *adj* German **2** *m langue* German; **Allemand, ~e** *m/f* German

aller 1 *v/i* go; **~ en voiture** go by car; **~ chercher** go for, fetch; **comment allez-vous?** how are you?; *je vais bien* I'm fine; **ça va?** is that OK?; *(comment te portes-tu?)* how are you?; **ça va**

bien merci fine, thanks; **~ bien avec** go well with; **on y va!** F let's go!; **allez!** go on!; **allons!** come on!; **allons donc!** come now!; **s'en ~** leave; *d'une tâche* disappear; *cette couleur te va* **bien** that color really suits you 2 *v/aux*: *je vais partir* **demain** I'm going to leave tomorrow, I'm leaving tomorrow 3 *m*: **~ et retour** round trip; *Br* return trip; *billet* round-trip ticket, *Br* return (ticket); **~ simple** one-way ticket, *Br* single; **match** *m* ~ away game

allergie *f* allergy; **allergique** allergic (**à** to)

alliance *f* POL alliance; (*mariage*) marriage; (*anneau*) wedding ring; **allié**, **~e** 1 *adj* allied; *famille* related by marriage 2 *m/f* ally; *famille* relative by marriage

allô hello

allocation *f* allowance; **~ chômage** workers' compensation, *Br* unemployment benefit

allonger lengthen, make longer; *jambes* stretch out; **s'~** get longer; (*s'étendre*) lie down

allumage *m* AUTO ignition; **allumer** 1 *v/t* light; *chauffage*, *télévision etc* turn on 2 *v/i* turn the lights on; **allumette** *f* match

allure *f* (*démarche*) walk; (*vi-*

tesse) speed; (*air*) appearance; **avoir de l'~** have style

allusion *f* allusion

alors then; (*par conséquence*) so; **~ que** *temps* when; *opposition* while

alouette *f* lark

alourdir make heavy

Alpes *fpl*: **les ~** the Alps

alphabet *m* alphabet

alpinisme *m* mountaineering; **alpiniste** *m/f* mountaineer

altercation *f* argument

altérer *denrées* spoil; *couleur* fade; *vérité* distort; *texte* alter

alternance *f* alternation; *de cultures* rotation; **alternative** *f* alternative; **alterner** alternate

altitude *f* altitude

alto *m* alto; **à cordes** viola

altruisme *m* altruism

aluminium *m* aluminum, *Br* aluminium

amabilité *f* kindness

amadouer softsoap

amaigrir thinner; **amaigrir**: **~ qn** cause s.o. to lose weight; **s'~** lose weight, get thinner

amalgame *m* mixture, amalgamation

amande *f* almond

amant *m* lover

amarrer MAR moor

amas *m* pile; **amasser** amass

amateur *m* lover; *non professionnel* amateur; **en ~** as a hobby

ambassade f embassy; **ambassadeur, -drice** m/f ambassador

ambiance f (atmosphère) atmosphere

ambigu, ~ë ambiguous; **ambiguïté** f ambiguity

ambitieux, -euse 1 adj ambitious **2** m/f ambitious person; **ambition** f ambition

ambivalence f ambivalence

ambulance f ambulance; **ambulancier** m paramedic, Br ambulance man

ambulant traveling, Br travelling

âme f soul; **état** m d'~ state of mind; ~ **charitable** do-gooder

amélioration f improvement; **améliorer** improve; **s'~** improve, get better

aménager appartement arrange, lay out; terrain develop; vieille maison convert

amende f fine

amender improve; projet de loi amend

amener bring; (causer) cause; **s'~** turn up

amer, -ère bitter

américain, ~e 1 adj American **2** m LING American English; **Américain, ~e** m/f American; **américaniser** Americanize

amérindien, ~ne Native American; **Amérindien, ~ne** m/f Native American

Amérique f: **l'~** America; **l'~**

centrale Central America; **l'~ latine** Latin America; **l'~ du Nord** North America; **l'~ du Sud** South America

amertume f bitterness

ameublement m (meubles) furniture

ameuter rouse

ami, ~e m/f friend; (amant) boyfriend; (maîtresse) girlfriend; **devenir ~ avec qn** make friends with s.o. **2** adj friendly; **amiable: à l'~** amicably; JUR out of court; arrangement amicable, friendly; JUR out-of-court

amical, ~e 1 adj friendly **2** f association

amincir 1 v/t make thinner; d'une robe make look thinner **2** v/i get thinner

amiral m admiral

amitié f friendship; **~s** best wishes

amnésie f amnesia

amnistie f amnesty

amoindrir diminish, lessen; **s'~** diminish

amollir soften

amonceler pile up

amont: en ~ upstream (de from)

amoral amoral

amorcer begin; INFORM boot up

amorphe sans énergie listless

amortir choc cushion; bruit muffle; douleur dull; dettes pay off; **amortisseur** m AUTO shock absorber

amour *m* love; ~**s** love life;
faire l'~ make love; **amou-**
reux, -euse *regard* loving;
vie love *atr*; *personne* in love
(**de** with); **tomber** ~ fall in
love; **amour-propre** *m* pride

amphithéâtre *m* amphithe-
ater, *Br* amphitheatre;
d'université lecture hall

ample *vêtements* loose; *sujet*
broad; *ressources* ample;
ampleur *f d'un désastre etc*
scale

amplification *f* TECH amplification; *fig* growth; **amplifier**
TECH amplify; *fig: problème*
magnify; *idée* expand

ampoule *f sur la peau* blister;
de médicament ampoule;
lampe bulb

amputate; *fig* cut

amusant funny, amusing

amuse-gueule *m* appetizer

amuser amuse; s'~ have a
good time, enjoy o.s.; s'~ à
faire qc have fun doing
sth, enjoy doing sth; faire
qch pour s'~ do sth for fun

amygdale *f* ANAT tonsil; *fig*
amygdalite *f* tonsillitis

an *m* year; le jour ou le premier de l'~ New Year's
Day; elle a 15 ~s she's 15
(years old)

analogie *f* analogy; analogique INFORM analog; **analo-**
gue analogous (**à** with)

analphabète illiterate; analp-
habétisme *m* illiteracy

analyse *f* analysis; *de sang*
test; **analyser** analyze, *Br*
analyse; *sang* test; **analyti-**
que analytical

ananas *m* BOT pineapple

anarchie *f* anarchy; **anar-**
chiste *m* anarchist

anatomie *f* anatomy

ancêtres *mpl* ancestors

anchois *m* anchovy

ancien, -nne old; *de l'Antiqui-*
té ancient; **anciennement**
formerly

ancre *f* anchor

Andorre *f* l'~ Andorra

âne *m* donkey; *fig* ass

anéantir annihilate

anecdote *f* anecdote

anémie *f* MÉD anemia, *Br*
anaemia

anesthésie *f* MÉD anesthesia,
Br anaesthesia

ange *m* angel

angine *f* MÉD throat infection;
~ **de poitrine** angina

anglais, -e 1 *adj* English 2 *m*
langue English; **Anglais, -e**
m/f Englishman; English-
woman; **les** ~ the English

angle *m* angle; *(coin)* corner;
~ **mort** blind spot

Angleterre *f* l'~ England

anglophone English-speak-
ing

angoisse *f* anguish; **angois-**
ser distress

anguille *f* eel

anguleux, -euse angular

animal 1 *m* animal; ~ **domes-**
tique pet 2 *adj* animal *atr*

animateur, -trice *m/f* d'une

émission host, presenter; *d'une discussion* moderator; *d'activités culturelles, d'une entreprise* leader; *de dessin animé* animator; **animation** f (*vivacité*) liveliness; *de mouvements* hustle and bustle; *de dessin animé* animation; **animé** *rue, quartier* busy; *conversation* lively, animated; **animer** *fête* liven up; (*stimuler*) animate; *discussion, émission* host; **s'~** come to life; *d'une personne, discussion* become animated

animosité f animosity

anneau m ring

année f year; **les ~s 90** the 90s; **bonne ~!** happy New Year!

annexe f *d'un bâtiment* annex; *d'un document* appendix; *d'une lettre* enclosure

anniversaire m birthday; *d'un événement* anniversary

annonce f announcement; *dans journal* ad (vertisement); (*présage*) sign; **petites ~s** classified ads; **annoncer** announce; **s'~ bien/mal** be off to a good/bad start

annotation f annotation

annuaire m: **~ du téléphone** phone book

annuel, ~le annual, yearly

annulaire m ring finger

annulation f cancellation; *d'un mariage* annulment; **annuler** cancel; *mariage an-*

nul

anodin harmless; *personne* insignificant; *blessure* slight

anomalie f anomaly

anonyme anonymous; **société** f **~** incorporated *ou* Br limited company

anorak m anorak

anorexie f anorexia; **anorexique** anorexic

anormal abnormal

anse f *d'un panier etc* handle; GÉOGR cove

antagonisme m antagonism

antarctique 1 *adj* Antarctic **2** m **l'Antarctique** Antarctica, the Antarctic

antécédents mpl history

antenne f ZO antenna, feeler; TV, *d'une radio* antenna, Br aerial

antérieur (*de devant*) front; (*d'avant*) previous, earlier; **~ à** prior to, before

anthropologie f anthropology

antibiotique m antibiotic

antibrouillard m fog lamp

anticipation f anticipation; **payer par ~** pay in advance; **d'~** *roman* science-fiction

anticiper anticipate; **~ un paiement** pay in advance

anticonstitutionnel, ~le unconstitutional

antidater backdate

antidérapant m AUTO non-skid tire *ou* Br tyre

antidote m MÉD antidote

antigel m antifreeze

antipathie f antipathy
antipelliculaire: shampoing m ~ dandruff shampoo
antiquaire m antique dealer; **antique** ancient; **meuble** antique; péj antiquated; **antiquités** fpl antiques
antisémite 1 adj anti-Semitic **2** m/f anti-Semite
antiseptique m & adj antiseptic
antisocial antisocial
antiterroriste anti-terrorist
antivol m anti-theft device
anxiété f anxiety; **anxieux**, **-euse** anxious
août m August
apaiser personne calm down; douleur soothe; soif, faim satisfy
apathie f apathy
apercevoir see; **s'~ de qc** notice sth
apéritif m aperitif
à-peu-près m approximation
apitoyer: ~ qn move s.o. to pity; **s'~ sur qc** feel sorry for s.o.
aplanir flatten, level; fig: différend smooth over
aplatir flatten; **s'~ (s'écraser)** be flattened; **s'~ devant** kowtow to
aplomb m self-confidence; (audace) nerve; **d'~** vertical, plumb; **je ne suis pas d'~** fig I don't feel a hundred percent
apostrophe f (interpellation) rude remark; signe apostro-

phe
apparaître appear; **faire ~** bring to light
appareil m device; AVIAT plane; **qui est à l'~?** TÉL who's speaking?; **~ ménager** household appliance; **~ photo** camera
apparemment apparently
apparence f appearance; **en ~** on the face of things; **sauver les ~** save face; **apparent** visible; (illusoire) apparent
apparenté related (à to)
apparition f appearance
appartement m apartment, Br flat
appartenir belong (à to); **il ne m'appartient pas d'en décider** it's not up to me to decide
appauvrir impoverish; **s'~** become impoverished; **appauvrissement** m impoverishment
appel m call; MIL (recrutement) draft, Br call-up; JUR appeal; ÉDU roll-call; **faire ~ à qc (nécessiter)** require; **faire ~ à qn** appeal to s.o.; **appeler** call; (nécessiter) call for; **en ~ à qn** approach s.o.; **comment t'appelles-tu?** what's your name?, what are you called?
appendice m appendix; **appendicite** f MÉD appendicitis
appétissant appetizing; **appétit** m appetite; **bon ~!** en-

joy (your meal)!

applaudir applaud, clap; **applaudissements** *mpl* applause, clapping

applicateur *m* applicator; **application** *f* application; **appliquer** apply; **s'~** *d'une personne* work hard; **~ Y sur X** smear X with Y

apport *m* contribution; **apporter** bring

appréciation *f* estimate; (*jugement*) opinion; COMM appreciation; **apprécier** estimate; *personne, musique, la bonne cuisine* appreciate

appréhender ~ qc be apprehensive about sth; **~ qn** JUR arrest s.o.; **appréhension** *f* apprehension

apprendre learn; *nouvelle aussi* hear (*par qn* from s.o.); **~ qc à qn** (*enseigner*) teach s.o. sth; (*raconter*) tell s.o. sth

apprenti, ~e *m/f* apprentice; *fig* beginner; **apprentissage** *m* learning; *d'un métier* apprenticeship

apprivoiser tame

approbateur, -trice approving; **approbation** *f* approval

approcher 1 *v/t* bring closer (*de* to) **2** *v/i* approach; **s'~ de** approach

approfondir deepen; (*étudier*) go into in detail

approprié appropriate, suitable (*à* for); **approprier: s'~ qc** appropriate sth

approuver *loi* approve; *personne, manières* approve of

approvisionnement *m* supply (*en* of)

approximatif, -ive approximate; **approximation** *f* approximation

appui *m* support; *d'une fenêtre* sill; **prendre ~ sur** lean on; **appuyer 1** *v/t* lean; (*tenir debout*) support; *fig* candidat, idée support, back **2** *v/i:* **~ sur** bouton press, push; *fig* stress; **s'~ sur** lean on; *fig* rely on

après 1 *prép* after; **d'~ les journaux** going by what the papers say **2** *adv* afterward **3** *conj:* **~ que** after

après-demain the day after tomorrow

après-midi *m ou f* afternoon

apr. J.-C. (= *après Jésus-Christ*) AD (= anno Domini)

aptitude *f* aptitude

aquarelle *f* watercolor, *Br* watercolour

aquarium *m* aquarium

arabe 1 *adj* Arab **2** *m langue* Arabic; **Arabe** *m/f* Arab; **Arabie** *f:* **l'~ Saoudite** Saudi (Arabia)

araignée *f* spider

arbitrage *m* arbitration

arbitre *m* referee; **libre ~ m** free will; **arbitrer** arbitrate

arbre *m* tree; TECH shaft

arbuste *m* shrub

arc *m* ARCH arch; GÉOM arc

arc-en-ciel *m* rainbow

arche *f* arch; *Bible* Ark

archéologie *f* archeology; **archéologue** *m/f* archeologist, *Br* archaeologist

archet *m* archer; MUS bow

archevêque *m* archbishop

architecte *m/f* architect; **architecture** *f* architecture

arctique 1 *adj* Arctic **2** *m* l'Arctique *m* the Arctic

ardent *soleil* blazing; *désir* burning; *défenseur* fervent; **ardeur** *f fig* ardor, *Br* ardour

ardoise *f* slate

ardu arduous

arène *f* arena; **~s** arena

arête *f* d'un poisson bone; d'une montagne ridge

argent *m* silver; (*monnaie*) money; **~ liquide** *ou* **comptant** cash

argot *m* slang

argument *m* argument; **argumenter** argue

aride arid, dry

aristocrate *m/f* aristocrat; **aristocratie** *f* aristocracy

armateur *m* shipowner

arme *f* weapon (*aussi fig*); **~ à feu** firearm; **armée** *f* army; **~ de l'air** airforce; **armement** *m* arming; **~s** armaments; **armer** arm (*de* with); *fig* equip (*de* with)

armistice *m* armistice

armoire *f* cupboard; *pour les vêtements* closet, *Br* wardrobe

arnaque *f* F rip-off F; **arnaquer** F rip off F

aromate *m* herb; (*épice*) spice; **arome, arôme** *m* flavor, *Br* flavour; (*odeur*) aroma

arracher pull out; *pommes de terre* pull up; **~ qc à qn** snatch sth from s.o.; **s'~ à** *ou* **de qc** free o.s. from sth; **s'~ qc** fight over sth

arrangement *m* arrangement; **arranger** arrange; *objet* fix; *différend* settle; *cela m'arrange* that suits me; **s'~ avec qn pour faire qch** come to an arrangement with s.o. about sth; **s'~ pour faire qch** manage to do sth

arrestation *f* arrest; *en état d'~* under arrest

arrêt *m* (*interruption*) stopping; *d'autobus* stop; JUR judgment; **sans ~** constantly; **arrêter 1** *v/i* stop **2** *v/t* stop; *moteur* turn off; *voleur* arrest; *jour, date* set; **~ de faire qch** stop doing sth; **s'~** stop

arrière 1 *adv* back; *en ~* backward; *regarder* back; (*à une certaine distance*) behind; *en ~ de* behind **2** *adj inv* rear **3** *m* AUTO, SP back; *à l'~* in back, at the back

arrière-goût *m* aftertaste; **arrière-grand-mère** *f* great-grandmother; **arrière-grand-père** *m* great-grandfather; **arrière-pensée** *f* ul-

terior motive; **arrière-petit-
-fils** m great-grandson

arrivée f arrival; SP finish line;
arriver arrive; *d'un événement* happen; ~ **à faire qch**
manage to do sth; ~ **à qn**
happen to s.o.; **j'arrive!**
(I'm) coming!

arrogance f arrogance; **arrogant** arrogant

arrondir *vers le haut* round
up; *vers le bas* round down;
arrondissement m *d'une
ville* district

arroser water; ~ **qch** fig have
a drink to celebrate sth; **ar-
rosoir** m watering can

art m art; **avoir l'~ de faire
qch** have a knack for doing
sth

artère f ANAT artery; (*route*)
main road

arthrite f arthritis

artichaut m artichoke

article m article, item; JUR article, clause; *de presse*, GRAM
article; **~s de luxe** luxury
goods

articulation f ANAT joint; *d'un
son* articulation; **articuler**
son articulate

artificiel, **~le** artificial

artisan m craftsman; **artisa-
nal** hand-made; *fromage*,
pain etc traditional

artiste m/f artist; *comédien*,
chanteur performer **2** adj artistic

as m ace

ascenseur m elevator, Br lift

ascension f ascent; fig (*progrès*) rise; **l'Ascension** REL
Ascension

asiatique Asian; **Asiatique**
m/f Asian; **Asie** f: **l'~** Asia

asile m shelter; POL asylum; **~
de vieillards** old people's
home; **demandeur** m **d'~**
asylum seeker

aspect m (*vue*) look; (*point
de vue*) angle, point of view;
d'un problème aspect; (*air*)
appearance; **à l'~ de** at the
sight of

asperge f BOT stalk of asparagus; **~s** asparagus

asperger sprinkle; **~ qn de
qch** spray s.o. with sth

asphyxie f asphyxia

aspirateur m vacuum (cleaner); **aspirer** *de l'air* breathe
in, inhale; *liquide* suck up;
~ **à (faire) qch** aspire to (doing) sth

aspirine f aspirin

assagir: **s'~** settle down

assaillir *vedette* mob; **être as-
sailli de** be assailed by; *de
coups de téléphone* be bom-
barded by

assainir (*nettoyer*) clean up;
eau purify

assaisonnement m seasoning

assassin m murderer; *d'un
président* assassin; **assassinat** m assassination; **assassiner** murder; *un président*
assassinate

assemblée f gathering; (*réu-*

nion) meeting; **~ générale**
annual general meeting; **assembler** assemble; **s'~** assemble, gather

asseoir: s'~ sit down

assez enough; (*plutôt*) quite;
~ d'argent enough money; **~
grand** big enough

assidu *élève* hard-working

assiette *f* plate; **ne pas être
dans son ~** *fig* be under
the weather

assigner assign

assimiler (*comparer*) compare; *connaissances, étran-
gers* assimilate

assis: *être ~* be sitting; **assise**
f fig basis

assistance *f* (*public*) audience; (*aide*) assistance; **assistant, ~e** *m/f* assistant;
~e sociale social worker;
assister 1 *v/i:* **~ à qc** attend
sth, be (present) at sth **2** *v/t:*
~ qn assist s.o

association *f* association; **associé, ~e** *m/f* partner; **associer** associate (**à** with); **s'~**
join forces; COMM go into
partnership; **s'~ à** *douleur*
share in

assoiffé thirsty

assombrir: s'~ darken

assommant F deadly boring;
assommer stun; F bore to
death

Assomption *f* REL Assumption

assorti matching; **~ de** ac-
companied by; **assortiment**

m assortment

assoupir send to sleep; *fig:
douleur, sens* dull; **s'~** doze
off; *fig* die down

assourdir deafen; *bruit* muffle

assumer take on, assume

assurance *f* assurance; (*contrat*) insurance

assuré, ~e 1 (*sûr*) confident **2**
m/f insured party; **assuré-
ment** certainly; **assurer** *succès* ensure; *par une assurance* insure; **s'~** take out insurance; **s'~ de qc** (*vérifier*)
make sure of sth, check sth

asthme *m* asthma

astiquer *meuble* polish; *casserole* scour

astre *m* star

astrologie astrology

astronaute *m/f* astronaut

astronomie *f* astronomy; **astronomique** astronomical
(*aussi fig*)

astuce *f* (*ingéniosité*) astute-
ness; (*truc*) trick; **astucieux,
-euse** astute

atelier *m* workshop; *d'un artiste* studio

athée *m/f* atheist; **athéisme**
m atheism

athlète *m/f* athlete; **athlétisme** *m* athletics *sg*

Atlantique *m:* **l'~** the Atlantic

atlas *m* atlas

atmosphère *f* atmosphere

atome *m* atom

atout *m fig* asset

atroce dreadful, atrocious;

atrocité f atrocity

attachant captivating

attaché-case m executive briefcase

attacher 1 ~*e* v/t attach, fasten; *animal* tie up; *prisonnier* secure; *chaussures* do up **2** v/t CUIS (coller) stick; **s'~ à** become attached to

attaquant, ~e m/f sp striker; **attaque** f attack; **~ à la bombe** bomb attack; **attaquer** attack; *travail, sujet* tackle; **s'~ à** attack; *problème* tackle

attarder: s'~ linger

atteindre reach; *d'un projectile* strike, hit; *d'une maladie* affect

atteinte f fig attack; **porter ~ à** qc undermine sth; **hors d'~** out of reach

attendant: en ~ in the meantime; **en ~ qu'il arrive** (subj) while waiting for him to arrive; **attendre** wait; **~ qn** wait for s.o.; **s'~ à qc** expect sth; **~ un enfant** be expecting a baby

attendrir fig: *personne* move; *cœur* soften; **s'~** be moved (*sur* by); **attendrissement** m tenderness

attentat m attack; **~ à la bombe** bombing, bomb attack; **~ à la pudeur** indecent assault

attente f wait; (*espoir*) expectation

attentif, -ive attentive (*à* to); **attention** f attention; (**fais**) **~!** look out!, (be) careful!;

faire ~ à qc pay attention to sth

atténuer reduce; *propos, termes* tone down

atterrir AVIAT land; **~ en catastrophe** crash-land

attestation f certificate; **attester** certify; (*prouver*) confirm

attirance f attraction; **attirer** attract; **s'~ des critiques** come in for criticism

attitude f attitude; *d'un corps* pose

attraction f attraction

attrait m attraction

attraper catch; (*duper*) take in

attrayant attractive

attribuer attribute; *prix* award; *part, rôle* allot; *valeur* attach; **s'~** take; *attribution* f allocation; *d'un prix* award; **~s** (*compétence*) competence

attrister sadden

attroupement m crowd; **attrouper: s'~** gather

aube f dawn; **à l'~** at dawn

auberge f inn; **~ de jeunesse** youth hostel

aubergine f BOT eggplant, *Br* aubergine

aucun ~ **1** adj avec négatif no, not …any; avec positif, interrogatif any **2** pron avec négatif none; **~ des deux** neither of the two; avec positif, interrogatif anyone, anybody

audace f daring, audacity; *péj* audacity; **audacieux, -euse** (*courageux*) daring, audacious; (*insolent*) insolent

au-delà beyond; **~ de** above; **au-dessous: ~ (de)** below; **au-dessus: ~ (de)** above; **au-devant: aller ~ de** meet; *désirs* anticipate

audible audible

audience f d'un tribunal hearing

audiovisuel, ~le audiovisual; **auditeur, -trice** m/f listener; FIN auditor; **audition** f audition; (*ouïe*) hearing; de témoins examination

augmentation f increase; de salaire raise, Br rise; **augmenter 1** v/t increase; salarié give a raise ou Br rise to **2** v/i increase, rise

aujourd'hui today

auparavant beforehand; **deux mois ~** two months earlier

auprès: ~ de beside, near

auquel → lequel

auriculaire m little finger

aurore f dawn

ausculter MÉD sound

aussi 1 adv too, also; **il est ~ grand que moi** he's as tall as me **2** conj therefore

aussitôt immediately; **~ que** as soon as

austère austere

Australie f: **l'~** Australia; **australien, ~ne** Australian; **Australien, ~ne** m/f Austral-

ian

autant (*tant*) as much (*que* as); *avec pluriel* as many (*que* as); *comparatif:* **~ de ... que ...** as much ... as ...; *avec pluriel* as many ... as ...; (*pour*) **~ que je sache** (*subj*) as far as I know; **en faire ~** do the same

auteur m/f author; d'un crime perpetrator

authenticité f authenticity; **authentique** authentic

autiste autistic

auto f car, automobile

autobiographie f autobiography

autocollant 1 adj adhesive **2** m sticker

autodéfense f self-defense, Br self-defence

autodidacte self-taught

auto-école f driving school

autographe m autograph

automatique adj & m automatic; **automatiquement** automatically; **automatiser** automate

automne m fall, Br autumn

automobile f car, automobile; **automobiliste** m/f driver

autonomie f independence; POL autonomy

autoradio m car radio

autorisation f authorization, permission; **autoriser** authorize, allow; **autoritaire** authoritarian; **autorité** f authority

autoroute f highway, Br motorway

auto-stop m: **faire de l'~** hitchhike

autour: ~ (de) around

autre 1 adj other; **un/une ~** another ...; **nous ~s Américains** we Americans; **rien d'~** nothing else; **~ part** somewhere else; **~ part** on the other hand **2** pron: **un/une ~** another (one); **l'~** the other (one); **les ~s** the others; (autrui) other people; **les ~s, les uns les ~s** each other, one another

autrefois in the past

autrement (différemment) differently; (sinon) otherwise

Autriche f: **l'~** Austria; **autrichien, ~ne** Austrian; **Autrichien, ~ne** m/f Austrian

autrui other people pl, others pl

auxquelles, auxquels → lequel

av. (= **avenue**) Ave (= avenue)

aval 1 adv: **en ~** downstream (**de** from) **2** m FIN guarantee

avalanche f avalanche

avaler swallow

avance f advance; **d'une course** lead; **d'~** in advance; **en ~** ahead of time; **avancement** m progress; (promotion) promotion; **avancer 1** v/t chaise, date bring forward; main put out; argent

advance; thèse put forward **2** v/i make progress; MIL advance; **d'une montre** be fast; **s'~ vers** come up to

avant 1 prép before; **~ tout** above all; **~ de faire qch** before doing sth **2** adv temps before; espace in front of; **en ~** forward **3** conj: **~ que** (+ subj) before **4** adj: **roue** f **~** front wheel **5** m front; **d'un navire** bow; sp forward

avantage m advantage; **~s sociaux** fringe benefits; **avantager** suit; (favoriser) favor, Br favour

avant-dernier, -ère last but one

avant-hier the day before yesterday

avant-première f preview

avant-propos m foreword

avant-veille f: **l'~** two days before

avare 1 adj miserly **2** m miser; **avarice** f miserliness

avarié nourriture bad

avec with

avenir m future; **à l'~** in future; **d'~** promising

Avent m Advent

aventure f adventure; (liaison) affair; **aventurer: s'~** venture (**dans** into)

avenue f avenue

avérer: s'~ (+ adj) prove

averse f shower

aversion f aversion (**pour** ou **contre** to); **prendre qn en ~** take a dislike to s.o.

avertir inform (*de* of); (*mettre en garde*) warn (*de* of); **avertissement** *m* warning; **avertisseur** *m* AUTO horn

aveu *m* confession

aveuglant blinding; **aveugle 1** *adj* blind **2** *m/f* blind man; blind woman; **aveugler** blind

aviateur, -trice *m/f* pilot; **aviation** *f* aviation, flying

avide greedy, avid (*de* for); **avidité** *f* greed

avilissant degrading

avion *m* (air)plane, *Br* (aero-)plane; **aller en ~** fly, go by plane; **par ~** (by) airmail

aviron *m* oar; SP rowing

avis *m* opinion; (*information*) notice; **à mon ~** in my opinion; **changer d'~** change one's mind; **sauf ~ contraire** unless otherwise stated

aviser: ~ qn de qc advise *ou* inform s.o. of sth; **s'~ de qc** notice sth; **s'~ de faire qch** take it into one's head to do sth

av. J.-C. (= **avant Jésus-Christ**) BC (= before Christ)

avocat, ~e 1 *m/f* lawyer; (*défenseur*) advocate **2** *m* BOT avocado

avoir 1 *v/t* (*posséder*) have, have got; (*obtenir*) get; **j'ai froid/chaud** I am cold/hot; **~ 20 ans** be 20; **il y a** there is; *avec pluriel* there are; **qu'est-ce qu'il y a?** what's the matter?; **il y a un an** a year ago **2** *v/aux* have; **j'ai déjà parlé** I have *ou* I've already spoken; **je lui ai parlé hier** I spoke to him yesterday **3** *m* COMM credit; (*possessions*) possessions *pl*

avoisiner: ~ qc border on sth

avortement *m* miscarriage; **provoqué** abortion; **avorter 1** *v/t* **femme** terminate the pregnancy of; **se faire ~** have an abortion **2** *v/i* miscarry; *fig* fail

avouer: ~ (avoir fait qc) confess (to having done sth)

avril *m* April

axe *m* axle; GÉOM axis; *fig* basis

B

babiller babble

bâbord *m* MAR: **à ~** to port

bac¹ *m* **bateau** ferry; *récipient* container

bac² *m* F, **baccalauréat** *m* *exam that is a prerequisite for university entrance*

bâche *f* tarpaulin

bâcler F botch F

badaud *m* onlooker

badiner joke

baffe *f* F slap

bafouiller 1 *v/t* stammer **2** *v/i* F talk nonsense

bagages *mpl* baggage, luggage; *fig* (*connaissances*) knowledge; *faire ses ~* pack

bagarre *f* fight; **bagarrer** F: *se ~* fight

bagnole *f* F car

bague *f* ring; *~ de fiançailles* engagement ring

baguette *f* stick; MUS baton; *pain* French stick; *~s pour manger* chopsticks

baie[1] *f* BOT berry

baie[2] *f* (*golfe*) bay; *Baie d'Hudson* Hudson Bay

baigner *enfant* bathe, Br bath; *se ~* go for a swim; **baignoire** *f* (*bath*) tub

bail *m* lease

bâiller yawn; *d'un trou* gape; *d'une porte* be ajar

bain *m* bath; *salle f de ~s* bathroom; *être dans le ~ fig* (*au courant*) be up to speed; *~ de bouche* mouthwash; **bain-marie** *m* CUIS double boiler

baiser 1 *m* kiss **2** *v/t* kiss; V screw V

baisse *f*: *être en ~* be falling; **baisser 1** *v/t* lower; *radio, chauffage* turn down **2** *v/i* *de forces* fail; *de lumière* fade; *d'une température, d'un prix* drop, fall; *de vue* deteriorate; *se ~* bend down

bal *m* dance; *formel* ball

balade *f* walk, stroll; **balader** walk; *se ~* go for a walk *ou* stroll

baladeur *m* Walkman®

balai *m* broom; *donner un coup de ~ à qch* give sth a sweep

balance *f* scales *pl*; COMM balance; ASTROL *Balance* Libra; **balancer** *jambes* swing; F (*lancer*) chuck F; F (*jeter*) chuck out F; *se ~* swing; **balançoire** *f* swing

balayer sweep; *fig: gouvernement* sweep from power; *soucis* sweep away

balbutier stammer

balcon *m* balcony

baleine *f* whale

ballade *f* ballad

balle *f* ball; *d'un fusil* bullet; *de marchandises* bale

ballet *m* ballet

ballon *m* ball; *pour enfants*, AVIAT balloon

ballotter 1 *v/t* buffet **2** *v/i* bounce up and down

balnéaire: *station f ~* seaside resort

balourd clumsy

balte Baltic; **Baltique**: *la* (*mer*) *~* the Baltic (Sea)

balustrade *f* balustrade

bambou *m* bamboo

banal (*mpl* -als) banal; **banalité** *f* banality

banane *f* banana; **bananier** *m* banana tree

banc *m* bench, seat; *~ de sable* sandbank

bancaire bank *atr*

bancal (*mpl* -als) *table* wobbly

bandage *m* MÉD bandage

bande f de terrain, de tissu strip; MÉD bandage; (rayure) stripe; (groupe) group; péj gang, band; **bander** MÉD bandage; **~ les yeux à qn** blindfold s.o.
bandit m bandit; (escroc) crook
banlieue f suburbs pl; **de ~** suburban
bannière f banner
bannir banish
banque f bank; **~ du sang** blood bank
banquet m banquet
banquette f seat
banquier m banker
baptême m baptism; **baptiser** baptize
bar m bar; meuble cocktail cabinet
baraque f shack
barbant F boring
barbare 1 adj barbaric **2** m/f barbarian
barbe f beard; **~ à papa** cotton candy, Br candy floss
barbecue m barbecue
barber F bore rigid F
barbu bearded
barder m: **ça va ~** there's going to be trouble
baromètre m barometer
barque f MAR boat
barrage m dam; (barrière) barrier
barre f bar; MAR helm; (trait) line; **~ des témoins** JUR witness stand
barreau m bar; d'échelle rung

barrer (obstruer) block, bar; mot cross out; **se ~** F leave
barrette f barrette, Br hairslide
barrière f barrier; (clôture) fence; **~s douanières** customs barriers
bar-tabac m bar-cum-tobacco store
bas, ~se 1 adj low; GÉOGR lower; instrument bass; voix deep **2** adv low; parler à low voice, quietly; **en ~** downstairs; **là-~** there **3** m bottom; (vêtement) stocking; **au ~ de** at the bottom of
basané weatherbeaten; naturellement swarthy
bas-côté m d'une route shoulder
basculer topple over
base f base; d'un édifice foundation; fig: d'une science basis; **de ~** basic; **à ~ de lait** milk-based
base f de données database
base-ball m baseball
baser base (**sur** on); **se ~ sur** draw on; d'une idée be based on
basilic m BOT basil
basket(-ball) m basketball; **baskets** fpl sneakers, Br trainers
basque 1 adj Basque **2** m langue Basque; **Basque** m/f Basque
basse-cour f AGR farmyard; animaux poultry
bassine f bowl

bataille f battle; **livrer ~** give battle; **batailler** fig battle

bâtard m bastard; **chien** mongrel

bateau m boat; **faire du ~** go sailing; **mener qn en ~** fig put s.o. on, Br have s.o. on

bâti 1 adj Built on; **bien ~** well-built **2** m frame

bâtiment m building; **secteur** construction industry; MAR ship

bâtir build

bâton m stick; **parler à ~s rompus** make small talk; **~ de rouge** lipstick; **~ de ski** ski pole ou stick

battant 1 adj **pluie** driving **2** m **d'une porte** leaf; **personne** fighter

batte f de base-ball bat

battement m **de cœur** beat; **de temps** interval

batterie f ÉL battery; MUS drums pl; **dans un orchestre** percussion; **batteur** m CUIS whisk; **électrique** mixer; MUS drummer; **en base-ball** batter; **battre 1** v/t beat; **cartes** shuffle **2** v/i beat; **d'un volet** bang; **se ~** fight

bavard, ~e 1 adj talkative **2** m/f chatterbox; **bavarder** chatter; **(divulguer un secret)** talk

baver drool, slobber; **bavure** f fig blunder, blooper F; **sans ~** impeccable

Bd (= **boulevard**) Blvd (= Boulevard)

B.D. f (= **bande dessinée**) comic strip

béant gaping

béat péj: **sourire** silly

beau, bel, belle (mpl **beaux**) beautiful, lovely; **homme** handsome; **il fait beau** (**temps**) it's lovely weather; **il a beau dire ...** it's no good him saying ...

beaucoup a lot; **~ de** lots of, a lot of; **~ de gens** lots ou a lot of people, many people; **je n'ai pas ~ d'argent** I don't have a lot of ou much money; **~ trop cher** much too expensive

beau-fils m son-in-law; **d'un remariage** stepson; **beau--frère** m brother-in-law; **beau-père** m father-in-law; **d'un remariage** stepfather

beauté f beauty

beaux-arts mpl: **les ~** fine art

beaux-parents mpl parents--in-law

bébé m baby

bec m **d'un oiseau** beak; **d'un récipient** spout; MUS mouthpiece; F mouth

bedaine f (beer) belly

bégayer stutter, stammer

béguin m fig F: **avoir le ~ pour** have a crush on

beige beige

beignet m CUIS fritter

belge Belgian; **Belge** m/f Belgian; **Belgique: la ~** Belgium

bélier m ZO ram; ASTROL **Bé-**

lier Aries

belle → *beau*

belle-famille *f* in-laws *pl*

belle-fille *f* daughter-in-law; *d'un remariage* stepdaughter; **belle-mère** *f* mother-in-law; *d'un remariage* stepmother; **belle-sœur** *f* sister-in-law

belliqueux, -euse warlike

bémol *m* MUS flat

bénédiction *f* blessing

bénéfice *m* benefit; COMM profit; **bénéficier:** *~ de* benefit from; **bénéfique** beneficial

Bénélux: *le ~* the Benelux countries *pl*

bénévolat voluntary work; **bénévole 1** *adj* travail voluntary **2** *m/f* volunteer

bénin, -igne *tumeur* benign; *accident* minor

bénir bless; **bénit** consecrated; *eau f ~e* holy water

béquille *f* crutch; *d'une moto* stand

berceau *m* cradle; **bercer** rock; *se ~ d'illusions* delude o.s.

béret *m* beret

berger *m* shepherd; *chien ~* German shepherd, *Br aussi* Alsatian

berline *f* AUTO sedan, *Br* saloon

bermuda(s) *m* (*pl*) Bermuda shorts *pl*

berner fool

besogne *f* job, task

besoin *m* need; *avoir ~ de (faire) qch* need (to do) sth; *au ~* if need be

bestial bestial

bétail *m* (*sans pl*) livestock

bête 1 *adj* stupid **2** *f* animal; (*insecte*) insect; *chercher la petite ~* nitpick; **bêtement** stupidly; **bêtise** *f* stupidity; *dire des ~s* talk nonsense; *une ~* a stupid thing to do/ say

béton *m* concrete

betterave *f* beet, *Br* beetroot

beugler *de bœuf* low; *F d'une personne* shout

beurre *m* butter; *~ de cacahuètes* peanut butter

bévue *f* blunder

biais 1 *adv:* *en ~* diagonally; *de ~ regarder* sideways **2** *m* fig (*aspect*) angle; *par le ~ de* through

biberon *m* (baby's) bottle

Bible *f* bible

bibliothèque *f* library; *meuble* bookcase

bic® *m* ballpoint (pen)

bicentenaire *m* bicentennial, *Br* bicentenary

biceps *m* biceps

biche *f* ZO doe

bicyclette *f* bicycle; *aller en ou à ~* cycle

bidon *m:* *~ à essence* gas *ou Br* petrol can

bidonville *m* shanty town

bidule *m* F gizmo F

bien 1 *m* good; (*possession*) possession; *le ~ ce qui est* *juste* good; **faire le ~** do good; **faire du ~ à qn** do s.o. good; **~s** (*possessions*) property; (*produits*) goods **2** *adj* good; (*beau, belle*) good-looking; **être ~** feel well; (*à l'aise*) be comfortable; **ce sera très ~ comme ça** that will do very nicely; **se sentir ~** feel well; **avoir l'air ~** look good; **des gens ~** respectable people **3** *adv* well; (*très*) very; **des fois ~** lots of times; **eh ~** well; **oui, je veux ~** yes please **4** *conj* **~ que** (+ *subj*) although

bien-être *m* welfare; **sensation agréable** well-being

bienfait *m* benefit

bien-fondé *m* legitimacy

bienheureux, -euse happy; REL blessed

bienséance *f* propriety

bientôt soon; **à ~!** see you (soon)!

bienveillance *f* benevolence

bienvenu, ~e 1 *adj* welcome **2** *m/f* **être le/la ~(e)** be welcome **3** *f* **souhaiter la ~e à** welcome

bière *f* beer; **~ blanche** wheat beer; **~ brune** dark beer; *Br* bitter; **~ pression** draft (beer), *Br* draught (beer)

bifteck *m* steak

bifurquer: ~ (vers) fork (off onto); *fig* branch out (into)

bigame 1 *adj* bigamous **2** *m/f* bigamist; **bigamie** *f* bigamy

bijou *m* jewel; **~x** jewelry, *Br*

jewellery; **bijouterie** *f* jewelry store, *Br* jeweller's; **bijoutier, -ère** *m/f* jeweler, *Br* jeweller

bikini *m* bikini

bilan *m* balance sheet; *fig* (*résultat*) outcome; **faire le ~ de** take stock of

bilingue bilingual

billard *m* billiards *sg*; **table ~** billiard table; **~ américain** pool

bille *f* marble; **billard** (*billiard*) ball; **stylo m (à) ~** ball-point (pen)

billet *m* ticket; (*petite lettre*) note; **~ (de banque)** bill, *Br* (bank)note; **billeterie** *f* ticket office; *automatique* ticket machine; FIN ATM, *Br aussi* cash dispenser

biochimie *f* biochemistry

biodégradable biodegradable

biodiversité *f* biodiversity

biographie *f* biography

biologie *f* biology; **biologique** biological; **aliments** organic

biotechnologie *f* biotechnology

bis *adj*: **24~** 24A **2** *m* encore

biscornu *fig* weird

biscotte *f* rusk

biscuit *m* cookie, *Br* biscuit

bise *f*: **faire la ~ à** kiss

bisexuel, ~le bisexual

bisou *m* F kiss

bissextile: année *f* ~ leap year

bistro(t) m bistro

bit m INFORM bit

bitume m asphalt

bizarre strange, bizarre

blafard wan

blague f joke; **sans ~!** no kidding!; **blaguer** joke

blaireau m badger; **pour se raser** shaving brush

blâme m blame; (sanction) reprimand

blanc, blanche 1 adj white; **page** blank; **nuit f blanche** sleepless night **2** m white; **textile** (household) linen; **par opposé aux couleurs** whites pl; **dans un texte** blank **3** m/f **Blanc, Blanche** white, White

blancheur f whiteness; **blanchir 1** v/t whiten; **mur** whitewash; **linge** launder, wash; **du soleil** bleach; **fig: innocenter** clear **2** v/i go white

blasé blasé

blasphème m blasphemy; **blasphémer** blaspheme

blé m wheat, Br corn

blêmir turn pale

blesser hurt (aussi fig); **dans un accident** injure; **à la guerre** wound; **se ~** injure ou hurt o.s.; **blessure** f d'accident injury; **d'arme** wound

bleu 1 adj blue; **viande** very rare **2** m blue; **fromage** blue cheese; **sur la peau** bruise; **fig (novice)** rookie F

blindage m armor, Br armour; **blinder** armor, Br ar-

mour; **fig F** harden

bloc m block; **POL** bloc; **de papier** pad; **faire ~** join forces

bloc-notes m notepad

blocus m blockade

blond, ~e 1 adj blonde; **tabac** Virginian; **sable** golden **2** m/f blonde **3** f **bière** beer, Br aussi lager

bloquer block; **mécanisme** jam; **roues** lock; **compte** freeze

blouson m jacket, blouson

bluff m bluff; **bluffer** bluff

bobard m F tall tale ou Br story

bocal m (glass) jar

bock m: **un ~** a (glass of) beer

bœuf m steer; **viande** beef

bohémien, ~ne m/f gipsy

boire drink; (absorber) soak up

bois m matière, forêt wood; **en ~** wooden

boisson f drink; **~s alcoolisées** alcohol

boîte f box; **en tôle** can, Br aussi tin; **F (entreprise)** company; **~ (de nuit)** nightclub; **en ~** canned, Br aussi tinned; **~ à gants** glove compartment; **~ aux lettres** mailbox, Br letterbox

boiter limp; **fig: de raisonnement** be shaky; **boiteux, -euse** table etc wobbly; **fig: raisonnement** shaky; **être ~** d'une personne have a limp

boîtier m case, housing

bol m bowl

bombardement *m* bombing; *avec obus* bombardment; **bombarder** bomb; *avec obus, questions* bombard; **bombe** *f* bomb; *(atomiseur)* spray; **à retardement** time bomb; **bombé** bulging

bon, **~ne 1** *adj* good; *route, moment* right; *de **~ne foi** personne* sincere; **être ~ en qch** be good at sth; **à quoi ~?** what's the use?; witticism; **~ anniversaire!** happy birthday!; **~ voyage!** have a good trip!, bon voyage!; **~ne chance!** good luck!; **~ne année!** Happy New Year!; **~ne nuit!** good night!; *ah* **~** really **2** *adv*: *sentir* **~** smell good; *tenir* **~** not give in; *trouver* **~** *de faire qch* think it right to do sth **3** *m* COMM voucher; *avoir du* **~** have its good points; **~ d'achat** gift voucher; **~ du Trésor** Treasury bond

bonbon *m* candy, *Br* sweet; **~s** candy, *Br* sweets

bond *m* leap; *d'une balle* bounce

bondé packed

bondir jump, leap (*de* with)

bonheur *m* happiness; *(chance)* luck; *par* **~** luckily; *au* **petit** **~** at random

bonhomme *m* *(type)* guy F

boniment *m* battage spiel F, sales talk; F *(mensonge)* fairy story

bonjour *m* hello

bonne *f* maid

bonnet *m* hat; *gros* **~** *fig* F big shot F; **~ de douche** shower cap

bonsoir *m* hello, good evening

bonté *f* goodness

bonus *m* no-claims bonus

bord *m* edge; *(rive)* bank; *d'une route* side; *d'un verre* brim; *au* **~** *de la mer* at the seaside; *être au* **~** *des larmes* be on the verge of tears; *monter à* **~** go on board

bordel *m* F brothel; *(désordre)* mess F

bordélique F chaotic

border *(garnir)* edge (with); *(être le long de)* border; *enfant* tuck in

bordure *f* border, edging; *en* **~** *de forêt, ville* on the edge of

borne *f* boundary marker; ÉL terminal; **~s** *fig* limits; *dé-passer les* **~s** go too far; **borné** narrow-minded; **borner**: *se* **~** *à (faire)* restrict o.s. to (doing)

bosse *f* *(enflure)* lump; *d'un bossu, d'un chameau* hump; *du sol* bump

bosser F work hard

bossu, **~e** *m/f* hunchback

botanique 1 *adj* botanical **2** *f* botany

botte *f* *chaussure* boot

bouc *m* billy-goat; **~ émissaire** *fig* scapegoat

bouche f mouth; de métro entrance; ~ **d'aération** vent; ~ **d'incendie** (fire) hydrant

bouché blocked; temps overcast

bouche-à-bouche m MÉD mouth-to-mouth resuscitation

bouchée f mouthful

boucher[1] v/t block; trou fill (in); **se** ~ **d'un évier** get blocked; **se** ~ **le nez** hold one's nose

boucher[2], **-ère** m/f butcher (aussi fig)

boucherie f magasin butcher's; fig slaughter

bouchon m top; de liège cork; fig: trafic hold-up

boucle f loop; de ceinture buckle; de cheveux curl; ~ **d'oreille** earring; **bouclé** cheveux curly; **boucler** ceinture fasten; porte fasten; MIL surround; en prison lock away

bouddhisme m Buddhism; **bouddhiste** m Buddhist

bouder 1 v/i sulk **2** v/t: ~ **qn/qc** give s.o./sth the cold shoulder

boudin m: ~ **(noir)** blood sausage, Br black pudding

boue f mud

bouée f MAR buoy

bouffée f de fumée, vent puff; de parfum whiff

bouffer F eat

bouffi bloated

bouger move; de prix change

bougie f candle; AUTO spark plug

bouillie f baby food

bouillir boil; fig be boiling (with rage); **faire** ~ boil; **bouilloire** f kettle

bouillon m (bulle) bubble; CUIS stock; **bouillonner** bubble; fig: d'idées seethe

bouillotte f hot water bottle

boulanger, **-ère** m/f baker; **boulangerie** f bakery

boule f ball; **jeu** m **de** ~**s** bowls sg

bouleau m BOT birch (tree)

boulevard m boulevard

bouleversement m upheaval; **bouleverser** (mettre en désordre) turn upside down; traditions overturn; émotionnellement shatter

boulimie f bulimia

boulot m F work

bouquet m bouquet

bouquin m F book; **bouquiner** read

bourde f blunder, blooper F

bourdon m ZO bumblebee; **bourdonner** d'insectes buzz; de moteur hum; d'oreilles ring

bourgeois, ~**e 1** adj middle-class **2** m/f member of the middle classes

bourgeoisie f middle classes pl

bourgeon m BOT bud

bourrasque f gust

bourratif, **-ive** stodgy

bourré crammed (**de** with); F

(*ivre*) drunk, sozzled F

bourrer *cousin* stuff; *pipe* fill; **se ~ de qc** F stuff o.s. with sth

bourru surly

bourse f d'études grant; (*porte-monnaie*) coin purse, *Br* purse; **Bourse (des valeurs)** Stock Exchange

boursouf(f)lé swollen

bousculer (*heurter*) jostle; (*presser*) rush; *fig: traditions* overturn

bousiller F *travail* screw up F; (*détruire*) wreck

boussole f compass

bout m end; (*morceau*) piece; **au ~ de** at the end of; **d'un ~ à l'autre** right the way through; **être à ~** be at an end; **venir à ~ de** overcome

bouteille f bottle; *de butane* cylinder

boutique f store, *Br* shop; *de mode* boutique

bouton m button; *de porte* handle; ANAT spot, zit F; BOT bud; **bouton-d'or** m BOT buttercup; **boutonner** button; BOT bud; **boutonneux, -euse** spotty

bovin 1 *adj* cattle *atr* **2** *mpl* **~s** cattle *pl*

bowling m bowling, *Br* ten-pin bowling; *lieu* bowling alley

boxe f boxing; **boxer** box; **boxeur** m boxer

boycott m boycott; **boycotter** boycott

B.P. (= *boîte postale*) PO Box (= Post Office Box)

bracelet m bracelet

braconnier m poacher

braguette f fly

brailler bawl

braiser CUIS braise

brancard m (*civière*) stretcher

branche f branch; *de céleri* stick

brancher connect up (*sur* to); *à une prise* plug in; **branché** F (*informé*) clued up; (*en vogue*) trendy

brandir brandish

braquer 1 *v/t*: **~ sur** aim *ou* point at **2** *v/i* AUTO turn the wheel; **se ~ contre** *fig* turn against

bras m arm; **avoir le ~ long** *fig* have influence

brasse f stroke

brasser *bière* brew; **brasserie** f *usine* brewery; *établissement* restaurant

brave *adj* brave; (*before the noun*) good **2** m: **un ~** a brave man; **braver** (*défier*) defy; **bravoure** f bravery

break m AUTO station wagon, *Br* estate (car)

brebis f ewe

bredouiller mumble

bref, -ève 1 *adj* brief, short **2** *adv* briefly, in short

Brésil: **le ~** Brazil; **brésilien, ~ne** Brazilian; **Brésilien, ~ne** n/f Brazilian

Bretagne: **la ~** Britanny

bretelle f *de lingerie* strap;

d'autoroute ramp, *Br* slip road; **~s** *de pantalon* suspenders, *Br* braces

brevet *m* diploma; *pour invention* patent; **breveter** patent

bric-à-brac *m inv* bric-a-brac

bricolage *m* do-it-yourself, DIY; **bricole** *f* little thing; **bricoler** do odd jobs

brièvement briefly; **brièveté** *f* briefness, brevity

brigade *f* MIL brigade; *de police* squad; *d'ouvriers* gang

brillamment brilliantly; **brillant** shiny; *couleur* bright; *fig* brilliant; **briller** shine (*aussi fig*); **faire ~ meuble** polish

brin *m d'herbe* blade; *de corde* strand

brindille *f* twig

brioche *f* CUIS brioche; F (*ventre*) paunch

brique *f* brick

briquet *m* lighter

brise *f* breeze

brisé broken

briser 1 *v/t* break; *vie, bonheur* destroy; (*fatiguer*) wear out **2** *v/i de la mer* break; **se ~ de verre etc** break; *des espoirs* be shattered

britannique British; **Britannique** *m/f* Briton, Britisher, Brit F; **les ~s** the British

broc *m* pitcher

brocante *f magasin* second--hand store

broche *f* CUIS spit; *bijou* brooch

brochet *m* pike

brochette *f* CUIS skewer; *plat* shish kebab

brochure *f* brochure

brocolis *mpl* broccoli *sg*

broncher *sans ~* without batting an eyelid

bronches *fpl* ANAT bronchial tubes

bronchite *f* MÉD bronchitis

bronze *m* bronze

bronzé tanned; **bronzer 1** *v/t peau* tan **2** *v/i* get a tan; **se ~** sunbathe

brosse *f* brush; *coiffure* crew-cut; **~ à dents/cheveux** toothbrush/hairbrush; **brosser** brush; **se ~ les dents** brush one's teeth

brouhaha *m* hubbub

brouillard *m* fog; **il y a du ~** it's foggy

brouille *f* quarrel; **brouiller** *œufs* scramble; *cartes* shuffle; *papiers* muddle; *radio* jam; *involontairement* cause interference to; *amis* cause to fall out; **se ~** *du ciel* cloud over; *de vitres* mist up; *d'idées* get muddled; *d'amis* fall out

brouillon *m* draft; **papier** *m* **~** scratch paper, *Br* scrap paper

broussailles *fpl* undergrowth

broyer grind; **~ du noir** *fig* be down

bru f daughter-in-law
brugnon m BOT nectarine
bruine f drizzle
bruit m sound; *qui dérange* noise; *(rumeur)* rumor, *Br* rumour; **faire du ~** make a noise; *fig* cause a sensation
brûlant burning *(aussi fig)*; *(chaud)* burning hot; *liquide* scalding; **brûlé** burnt; **brûler 1** v/t burn; *d'eau bouillante* scald; *électricité* use; **~ un feu rouge** go through a red light **2** v/i burn; **se ~** burn o.s.; *d'eau bouillante* scald o.s.; **brûleur** m burner; **brûlure** f *sensation* burning; *lésion* burn; **~s d'estomac** heartburn
brume f mist
brun, ~e 1 *adj* brown; *cheveux, peau* dark **2** m/f dark-haired man/woman; **une ~e** a brunette **3** m *couleur* brown
brushing® m blow-dry
brusque abrupt, brusque; *(soudain)* abrupt, sudden; **brusquement** abruptly, suddenly; **brusquer** rush
brut, ~e 1 *adj* raw; *poids, revenu* gross; *pétrole* crude; *sucre* unrefined; *champagne* very dry **2** m crude (petroleum) **3** f *brute* brute; **brutal** brutal; **brutalement** brutally; **brutaliser** ill-treat; **brutalité** f brutality
Bruxelles Brussels
bruyant noisy

buanderie f laundry room
bûcher[1] m woodpile; *(échafaud)* stake
bûcher[2] v/i work hard; ÉDU F hit the books, *Br* swot
budget m budget
buée f steam, condensation
buffet m buffet; *meuble* sideboard
buisson m shrub, bush
bulbe f BOT bulb
bulgare 1 *adj* Bulgarian **2** m *langue* Bulgarian; **Bulgare** m/f Bulgarian; **Bulgarie: la ~** Bulgaria
bulle f bubble
bulletin m *(formulaire)* form; *(rapport)* bulletin; *à l'école* report card; **~ (de vote)** ballot (paper); **~ de salaire** paystub, *Br* payslip
bureau m office; *meuble* desk; **~ de change** exchange office, *Br* bureau de change; **~ de poste** post office; **~ de tabac** tobacco store, *Br* tobacconist's
bureaucratie f bureaucracy; **bureautique** f office automation
bus m bus
buste m bust
but m *(cible)* target; *(objectif)* aim, goal; *d'un voyage* purpose; sP goal; **sans ~** aimlessly; **buteur** m goalscorer
buté stubborn
buter: ~ contre qch knock into sth; **~ sur un problème** hit a problem; **se ~** *fig* dig

one's heels in

butin *m* booty; *de voleurs* haul

butte *f* (*colline*) hillock; *être*

en ~ à be exposed to

buvable drinkable; **buvette** *f* bar; **buveur, -euse** *m/f* drinker

C

c' → **ce**

ça that; **~ va?** how are things?; (*d'accord?*) ok?; **~ y est** that's it; **c'est ~!** that's right

cabale *f* (*intrigue*) plot

cabane *f* (*baraque*) hut

cabaret *m* (*boîte*) night club

cabine *f* cabin; *d'un camion* cab; **~ téléphonique** phone booth

cabinet *m* petite pièce small room; *d'avocat* office; *de médecin* office, *Br* surgery; (*clientèle*) practice; POL Cabinet

câble *m* cable

cabosser dent

cabrer: **se ~** *d'un animal* rear

cabriolet *m* AUTO convertible

cacah(o)uète *f* BOT peanut

cacao *m* cocoa; BOT cocoa bean

cache-cache *m*: **jouer à ~** play hide-and-seek; **cache-nez** *m* scarf; **cacher** hide; **se ~ de** hide from

cachet *m* seal; *fig* (*caractère*) style; PHARM tablet; (*rétribution*) fee; **~ de la poste** postmark

cachette *f* hiding place; **en ~**

secretly

cachotterie *f*: **faire des ~s** be secretive; **cachottier, -ère** secretive

cactus *m* cactus

cadavre *m* (dead) body, corpse; *d'un animal* carcass

caddie® *m* cart, *Br* trolley

cadeau *m* present, gift; **faire un ~ à qn** give s.o. a present

cadenas *m* padlock

cadence *f* tempo rhythm; *de travail* rate

cadet, ~te *m/f* younger; *de plus de deux* youngest; **il est mon ~ de trois ans** he's three years younger than me

cadran *m* dial; **~ solaire** sundial

cadre *m* frame; *fig* framework; *d'une entreprise* executive; (*environnement*) surroundings *pl*

cafard *m* ZO cockroach; **avoir le ~** F be feeling down

café *m* coffee; *établissement* café; **~ crème** coffee with milk, *Br* white coffee

cafeteria *f* cafeteria

cafetière *f* coffee pot; **~ électrique** coffee maker

campagne

cage f cage

cagibi m F box room

cagneux, -euse knock-kneed

cagoule f hood; (passe-montagne) balaclava

cahier m notebook; ÉDU exercise book

cahoter jolt

cahoteux, -euse bumpy

caille f quail

cailler du lait curdle; du sang clot

caillou m pebble, stone

caisse f chest; pour le transport crate; de champagne, vin case; (argent) cash; (guichet) cashdesk; dans un supermarché checkout; caissier, -ère m/f cashier

cajoler (câliner) cuddle

calamité f disaster, calamity

calcium m calcium

calcul[1] m calculation

calcul[2] m MÉD stone; ~ rénal kidney stone

calculatrice f: ~ (de poche) (pocket) calculator; calculer calculate; calculette f pocket calculator

calé F: être ~ en qch be good at sth

caleçon m d'homme boxer shorts pl; de femme leggings pl

calembour m pun

calendrier m calendar; emploi du temps schedule, Br timetable

caler moteur stall; TECH wedge

califourchon: à ~ astride

câlin 1 adj affectionate 2 m (caresse) cuddle

calmant 1 adj soothing; contre douleur painkilling 2 m tranquilizer, Br tranquilliser; contre douleur painkiller

calme 1 adj calm; Bourse, vie quiet 2 m calmness; MAR calm; (silence) peace and quiet; calmement calmly; calmer personne calm down; douleur relieve; se ~ calm down

calomnie f slander; écrite libel; calomnier insult; par écrit libel

calorie f calorie

calquer trace

calvitie f baldness

camarade m/f friend; POL comrade

cambriolage m break-in, burglary; cambrioler burglarize, Br burgle

cambrioleur, -euse m/f house-breaker, burglar

camelote f F junk

caméra f camera

caméscope m camcorder

camion m truck, Br aussi lorry

camionnette f van

camomille f BOT camomile

camoufler camouflage; fig: intention hide; faute cover up

camp m camp (aussi MIL, POL); ficher le ~ F get lost P

campagne f country, countryside; MIL, *fig* campaign; **à la ~** in the country

camper camp; **se ~ devant** plant o.s. in front of; **campeur, -euse** *m/f* camper

camping *m*: (**terrain** *m* **de**) campground, campsite; **faire du ~** go camping

Canada le ~ Canada; **canadien, ~ne** Canadian, **Canadien, ~ne** *m/f* Canadian

canal *m* channel; (*tuyau*) pipe; (*bras d'eau*) canal

canalisation *f* (*tuyauterie*) pipes *pl*, piping; **canaliser** *fig* channel

canapé *m* sofa; GASTR canapé

canapé-lit *m* sofa-bed

canard *m* duck; F newspaper

canari *m* canary

cancans *mpl* gossip

cancer *m* MÉD cancer; ASTROL **Cancer** Cancer

candeur *f* ingenuousness

candidat, ~e *m/f* candidate; **candidature** *f* candidacy; **à un poste** application

candide ingenuous

cane *f* (female) duck; **caneton** *m* duckling

canette *f* (*bouteille*) bottle

caniche *m* poodle

canicule *f* heatwave

canif *m* pocket knife

canin dog *atr*, canine

canine *f* canine

canne *f* cane, stick; **~ à pêche** fishing rod

cannelle *f* cinammon

canoë *m* canoe; *activité* canoeing

canon *m* MIL gun; HIST cannon; *de fusil* barrel

canot *m* small boat; **~ pneumatique** rubber dinghy; **~ de sauvetage** lifeboat

cantine *f* canteen

canular *m* hoax

caoutchouc *m* rubber; (*bande élastique*) rubber band

cap *m* GÉOGR cape; AVIAT, NAUT course

capable capable (**de faire** of doing)

capacité *f* (*compétence*) ability; (*contenance*) capacity

cape *f* cape

capitaine *m* captain

capital 1 *adj* essential **2** *m* capital; **capitaux** *pl* capital **3** *f* *ville* capital (city); *lettre* capital (letter)

capitalisme *m* capitalism

capituler capitulate

capot *m* AUTO hood, Br bonnet

capote *f* *vêtement* greatcoat; AUTO top, Br hood; **~** (**anglaise**) F condom

caprice *m* whim; **capricieux, -euse** capricious

Capricorne *m* ASTROL Capricorn

capter *regard* catch; RAD, TV pick up

capteur *m*: **~ solaire** solar panel

captif, -ive *m/f* & *adj* captive; **captivant** *personne* captivating; *lecture* gripping;

captiver *fig* captivate; **captivité** *f* captivity

capture *f* capture; (*proie*) catch; **capturer** capture

capuche *f* hood

car[1] *m* bus, *Br aussi* coach

car[2] *conj* for

carabine *f* rifle

carabiné F: **un ... carabiné** one hell of a ... F

caractère *m* character; **avoir bon ~** be good-natured; **caractériel** *troubles* emotional; *personne* emotionally disturbed

caractériser be characteristic of; **caractéristique** *f & adj* characteristic

carambolage *m* AUTO pile-up

caramel *m* caramel

caravane *f* AUTO trailer, *Br* caravan

carboniser burn

carburant *m* fuel

carburateur *m* TECH carburet(t)or

cardiaque MÉD **1** *adj* cardiac, heart *atr* **2** *m/f* heart patient

cardinal: **les quatre points** *mpl* **cardinaux** the four points of the compass

cardiologue *m/f* cardiologist, heart specialist

carême *m* REL Lent

carence *f* (*incompétence*) inadequacy; (*manque*) deficiency

caresse *f* caress; **caresser** caress; *idée* play with; *espoir* cherish

cargaison *f* cargo; *fig* load

caricature caricature

carie *f* MÉD: **une ~** a cavity

carié *dent* bad

caritatif, ~ive charitable

carnage *m* carnage

carnassier, ~ère carnivorous

carnaval *m* carnival

carnet *m* notebook; *de tickets, timbres* book

carnivore 1 *adj* carnivorous **2** *m* carnivore

carotte *f* carrot; **poil de ~** ginger

carpe *f* ZO carp

carpette *f* rug

carré 1 *adj* square; *fig: réponse* straightforward **2** *m* square

carreau *m de fenêtre* pane; *cartes* diamonds; **à ~x** checked

carrefour *m* crossroads *sg* (*aussi fig*)

carrelage *m* (*carreaux*) tiles *pl*

carrément bluntly, straight out

carrière *f* quarry; *profession* career; **militaire** *m* **de ~** professional soldier

carrosserie *f* AUTO bodywork

carrure *f* build

cartable *m* schoolbag; *à bretelles* satchel

carte *f* card; *dans un restaurant* menu; GÉOGR map; NAUT, *du ciel* chart; **~ bancaire** debit card, banker's card; **~ de crédit** credit card;

~ **d'embarquement** boarding pass; ~ **d'identité** identity card; ~ **postale** postcard; ~ **téléphonique** phonecard

carton m cardboard; **boîte** cardboard box; ~ **jaune/rouge** en football yellow/red card

cartouche f cartridge; **de cigarettes** carton

cas m case; **en aucun** ~ under no circumstances; **dans ce** ~-**là** in that case; **en tout** ~ in any case; **en** ~ **de** in the event of

casanier, -ère m/f stay-at-home

cascade f waterfall

case f (**hutte**) hut; (**compartiment**) compartment; **dans formulaire** box; **dans mots-croisés, échiquier** square

caser put; (**loger**) put up; **se** ~ (**se marier**) settle down

caserne f barracks; ~ **de pompiers** fire station

casier m **courrier** pigeon-holes pl; **bouteilles, livres** rack; ~ **judiciaire** criminal record

casino m casino

casque m helmet; **de radio** headphones pl; **casquette** f cap

cassable breakable

casse-cou m inv daredevil; **casse-croûte** m snack; **casse-noisettes** m nutcrackers pl; **casse-pieds** m/f inv F pain in the neck F

casser 1 v/t break; **noix** crack; JUR quash; ~ **les pieds à qn** F (**embêter**) get on s.o.'s nerves F; **se** ~ break **2** v/i break

casserole f (sauce)pan

casse-tête m fig: **problème** headache

cassette f cassette; ~ **vidéo** video

cassis m BOT blackcurrant; (**crème** f **de**) ~ blackcurrant liqueur

castrer castrate

cataclysme m disaster

catalogue m catalog, Br catalogue; **cataloguer** catalog, Br catalogue; F péj label

catalytique: pot m ~ catalytic converter

cataracte f waterfall; MÉD cataract

catastrophe f disaster, catastrophe; **en** ~ in a rush; **catastrophique** disastrous, catastrophic

catch m wrestling

catéchisme m catechism

catégorie f category; **catégorique** categorical

cathédrale f cathedral

catholique 1 adj (Roman) Catholic **2** m/f Roman Catholic

cauchemar m nightmare (aussi fig)

cause f cause; JUR case; **à** ~ **de** because of; **être en** ~ **d'honnêteté** be in question

causer 1 v/t (**provoquer**) cause **2** v/i (**s'entretenir**) chat

(*avec qn de* with s.o. about);
causette *f* chat; **faire la ~**
have a chat
caustique CHIM, *fig* caustic
caution *f* security; *pour loge-*
ment deposit; JUR bail; *fig*
(*appui*) backing; **cautionner**
stand surety for; JUR bail; *fig*
(*se porter garant de*) vouch
for; (*appuyer*) back
cavaler F: **~ après qn** chase
after s.o.
cavalier, -ère 1 *m/f pour che-*
val rider; *pour bal* partner 2
m aux échecs knight 3 *adj*
offhand, cavalier
cave *f* cellar; **~ (à vin)** wine
cellar
caverne *f* cave
caviar *m* caviar
cavité *f* cavity
CD *m* (= *compact disc*) CD;
CD-Rom *m* CD-Rom
ce *m* (**cet** *m*, **cette** *f*, **ces** *pl*) 1
adj this; **~ livre-ci**
this book; **~ livre-là** that
book; **ces jours-ci** these
days 2 *pron* **c'est pourquoi**
that is *ou* that's why; **c'est**
triste it's sad; **~ sont mes**
enfants these are my children; **c'est un acteur** he is
ou he's an actor; **c'est que**
tu as grandi! how you've
grown!; **ce que tu fais** what
you're doing; **ce qui me**
plaît what I like; **ce qu'il**
est gentil! isn't he nice!;
sur ~ with that
ceci this

cécité *f* blindness
céder 1 *v/t* give up; **cédez le**
passage AUTO yield; *Br* give
way 2 *v/i* give in (**à** to); (*se*
casser) give way
cédille *f* cedilla
cèdre *m* BOT cedar
ceinture *f* ANAT waist; **~**
de sécurité seatbelt
cela that; **à ~ près** apart from
that
célèbre famous
célébrer celebrate
célébrité *f* fame; *personne* celebrity
céleri *m* BOT: **~ (en branche)**
celery; **~(-rave)** celeriac
célibat *m* single life; *d'un prê-*
tre celibacy; **célibataire** 1
adj single, unmarried 2 *m*
bachelor 3 *f* single woman
celle, celles → **celui**
cellophane *f* cellophane
cellule *f* cell
cellulose *f* cellulose
Celsius Celsius
celui *m* (**celle** *f*, **ceux** *mpl*,
celles *fpl*) the one, *pl* those;
~ qui ... personne he who ...;
chose the one which; **celle**
de Claude Claude's; **celui-**
ci this one; **celui-là** that one
cendre *f* ash; **~s de cigarette**
cigarette ash; **cendrier** *m*
ashtray
cène *f* REL: **la ~** (Holy) Communion; **la Cène** *peinture*
the Last Supper
censé: **il est ~ être malade**
he's supposed to be sick

censure f censorship; *organe*
board of censors; **censurer**
censor

cent 1 *adj* hundred **2** *m* a hundred, one hundred; *monnaie*
cent; *pour ~* per cent; **cen-
taine** f: *une ~ de* a hundred
or so; *des ~s de* hundreds
of; **centenaire 1** *adj* hund-
red-year-old **2** *m* *fête* cen-
tennial, *Br* centenary; **centième** hundredth; **centilitre**
m centiliter, *Br* centilitre;
centimètre *m* centimeter,
Br centimetre; *ruban* tape
measure

central, ~e **1** *adj* central **2** *m*
TÉL telephone exchange **3** *f*
power station; **centraliser**
centralize

centre *m* center, *Br* centre; ~
d'accueil temporary accommodations *pl*; **centrer** center, *Br* centre

centre-ville *m* downtown area, *Br* town centre

cep *m* vine stock

cèpe *m* BOT cèpe, boletus

cependant yet, however

cercle *m* circle; ~ *vicieux* vicious circle

cercueil *m* casket, *Br* coffin

céréales *fpl* (breakfast) cereal

cérébral cerebral

cérémonie f ceremony; *sans
~ repas* informal; *se présenter etc* informally; *mettre
à la porte* unceremoniously

cerf *m* deer

cerf-volant *m* kite

cerise f cherry; **cerisier** *m*
cherry (-tree)

cerne *m*: *avoir des ~s* have
bags under one's eyes; **cerner** *(encercler)* surround;
fig: *problème* define

certain 1 *adj* certain; *être ~
de qc* be certain of sth;
d'un ~ âge middle-aged **2**
pron: *certains*, *-aines* some
(people)

certainement certainly; *(sûrement)* probably

certes certainly

certificat *m* certificate; ~ *de
mariage* marriage certifi-
cate; **certifier** guarantee; ~
qc à qn assure s.o. of sth

certitude f certainty

cerveau *m* brain

cervelle f brains *pl*; *se brûler
la ~* fig blow one's brains out

ces → **ce**

cesser stop; ~ *de faire qch*
stop doing sth; **cessez-le-
-feu** *m* ceasefire

cession f disposal

c'est-à-dire that is, that is to
say

cet, cette → **ce**

ceux → **celui**

chacun, ~e each (one); *c'est ~
pour soi* it's every man for
himself

chagrin *m* grief; *faire du ~ à*
upset

chahut *m* F racket, din; **cha-
huter** heckle

chaîne f chain; *radio*, TV

channel; **~s** AUTO snow chains; **~ hi-fi** hi-fi

chair f flesh; **avoir la ~ de poule** have goosebumps

chaise f chair; **~ longue** (transatlantique) deck chair

chalet m chalet

chaleur f heat; plus modérée warmth (aussi fig); **chaleureusement** warmly

chamailler F: **se ~** bicker

chambre f (bed)room; JUR, POL chamber; **~ à air** de pneu inner tube; **~ à coucher** bedroom; **~ à un lit** single (room); **~ à deux lits** twin-bedded room; **~ d'amis** spare room

chambré vin at room temperature

chameau m camel

champ m field (aussi fig); **~ de courses** racecourse

champagne m champagne

champêtre country atr

champignon m fungus; nourriture mushroom

champion, ~ne m/f champion; **championnat** m championship

chance f luck; (occasion) chance; **bonne ~!** good luck!; **avoir de la ~** be lucky; **c'est une ~ que** (+ subj) it's lucky that

chanceler stagger; d'un gouvernement totter

chanceux, ~euse lucky

chandail m sweater

change m exchange; **taux m**

de ~ exchange rate; **donner le ~ à qn** deceive s.o.; **changeant** changeable; **changement** m change; **~ de vitesse** gear shift; **changer 1** v/t change (**en** into); (échanger) exchange (**contre** for) **2** v/i change; **~ d'avis** change one's mind; **se ~** change

chanson f song

chant m song; action de chanter singing; d'église hymn

chantage m blackmail

chanter sing; d'un coq crow; **faire ~ qn** blackmail s.o.

chanteur, -euse m/f singer

chantier m building site; **~ naval** shipyard

chaos m chaos; **chaotique** chaotic

chaparder F pinch F

chapeau m hat; **chapeauter** fig head up

chapelet m REL rosary

chapelle f chapel

chapelure f CUIS breadcrumbs pl

chapitre m chapter; division de budget heading; fig subject

chaque each

charbon m coal; **~ de bois** charcoal

charcuterie f CUIS cold cuts pl, Br cold meats; magasin pork butcher's; **charcutier** m pork butcher

charge f load; fig burden; ÉL, JUR, MIL charge; (responsabilité) responsibility; **avoir des enfants à ~** have dependent children; **~s** charges; (*impôts*) costs; **~s fiscales** taxation

chargement *m* loading; *ce qui est chargé* load; **charger 1** *v/t* navire, arme load; batterie, JUR charge; (*exagérer*) exaggerate; **~ qn de qc** put s.o. in charge of sth; **se ~ de** look after 2 *v/i* charge

chariot *m pour bagages, achats* cart, *Br* trolley; (*charrette*) cart

charisme *m* charisma

charitable charitable; **charité** *f* charity; **faire la ~ à qn** give s.o. money

charmant charming, delightful; **charme** *m* charm; **charmer** charm

charnière *f* hinge

charnu fleshy

charognard *m* scavenger

charpente *f* framework; **charpentier** *m* carpenter

charte *f* charter

charter *m* charter

chasse¹ *f* hunting; (*poursuite*) chase; **prendre en ~** chase (after); **~ privée** private game reserve

chasse² *f:* **~ d'eau** flush

chasser gibier hunt; (*expulser*) drive away; employé dismiss; **chasseur** *m* hunter; AVIAT fighter; *dans un hôtel* bellhop, *Br* bellboy

châssis *m* frame; AUTO chassis

chaste chaste

chat¹ *m* cat

chat² *m* INFORM chatroom; conversation (online)

châtaigne *f* chestnut; **châtaignier** *m* chestnut (tree); **châtain** *inv* chestnut

château *m* castle; **~ fort** (fortified) castle; **~ d'eau** water tower

châtier punish; **châtiment** *m* punishment

chaton *m* kitten

chatouiller tickle

chatte *f* cat

chatter INFORM chat (online)

chaud 1 *adj* hot; *plus modéré* warm; **il fait ~** it's hot/warm **2** *m* heat; *plus modéré* warmth; **j'ai ~** I'm hot/warm

chaudière *f* boiler

chauffage *m* heating; **~ central** central heating

chauffard *m* F roadhog

chauffer 1 *v/t* heat (up), warm (up); *maison* heat; **se ~** warm o.s.; *d'un sportif* warm up 2 *v/i* warm *ou* heat up; *d'un moteur* overheat

chauffeur *m* driver; *privé aussi* chauffeur; **~ de taxi** taxi *ou* cab driver

chaussée *f* pavement, *Br* roadway

chausser bottes put on; **se ~** put one's shoes on; **chaussette** *f* sock; **chausson** *m* slipper; **chaussure** *f* shoe; **~s de marche** hiking boots;

~s de ski ski boots

chauve bald; **chauve-souris** f bat

chauvinisme m chauvinism

chef m (meneur), POL leader; (patron) boss; d'une entreprise head; d'une tribu chief; CUIS chef; **au premier ~** first and foremost; **de propre mon ~** on my own initiative

chef-d'œuvre m masterpiece

chemin m way; (route) road; (allée) path; **~ de fer** railroad, Br railway

cheminée f chimney; (âtre) fireplace; (encadrement) mantelpiece; de bateau funnel

cheminot m rail worker

chemise f shirt; (dossier) folder; **~ de nuit** de femme nightdress; **chemisier** m blouse

chêne m BOT oak (tree)

chenil m kennels pl

chenille f ZO caterpillar

chèque m COMM check, Br cheque; **~ de voyage** traveler's check, Br traveller's cheque; **chéquier** m checkbook, Br chequebook

cher, -ère 1 adj dear (**à qn** to s.o.); coûteux dear, expensive **2** adv: **payer qch ~** pay a high price for sth **3** m/f **mon cher, ma chère** my dear

chercher look for; **~ à faire qch** try to do sth; **aller ~** fetch, go for; **venir ~** collect,

come for; **envoyer ~** send for

chéri darling

chétif, -ive puny

cheval m horse; AUTO horsepower; **aller à ~** ride; **être à ~ sur qch** straddle sth; **chevalier** m HIST knight; **chevalière** f signet ring

chevelu personne long-haired; **chevelure** f hair

chevet m bedhead; **table f de ~** nightstand, Br aussi bedside table

cheveu m hair; **~x** hair; **aux ~x courts** short-haired

cheville f ANAT ankle; TECH peg

chèvre f goat

chevreau m kid

chevreuil m deer; CUIS venison

chez: ~ lui at his place; direction to his place; **Marcel** at Marcel's; **quand nous sommes ~ nous** when we are at home; **rentrer ~ soi** go home; **aller ~ le coiffeur** go to the hairdresser ou Br hairdresser's; **~ Molière** in Molière

chez-soi m home

chiant F boring

chic 1 m style **2** adj chic; (sympathique) decent

chicaner quibble (**sur** over)

chicorée f BOT chicory

chien m dog; **temps de ~** fig F filthy weather; **~ d'aveugle** seeing-eye dog, Br guide dog; **chienne** f dog; **le chien et la ~** the dog and the bitch

chier V shit; *ça me fait ~* P it pisses me off P

chiffon m rag; *(à poussière)* duster; **chiffonner** crumple; *fig* F bother

chiffre m number; *(code)* cipher

Chili: **le ~** Chili; **chilien,** **~ne 1** adj Chilean; **Chilien,** **~e** m/f Chilean

chimie f chemistry

chimiothérapie f chemotherapy

chimique chemical

Chine: **la ~** China; **chinois,** **~e 1** adj Chinese **2** m langue Chinese; **Chinois,** **~e** m/f Chinese

chiot m pup

chips mpl chips, Br crisps

chirurgie f surgery; **~ esthétique** plastic surgery; **chirurgien,** **~ne** m/f surgeon; **~ dentiste** dental surgeon

choc m shock; *d'opinions, intérêts* clash

chocolat m chocolate

chœur m choir **en ~** in chorus

choisir choose; **~ de faire** decide to do; **choix** m choice; *(assortiment)* range; **de (premier) ~** choice

cholestérol m cholesterol

chômage m unemployment; **être au ~** be unemployed; **~ partiel** short time; **chômeur, -euse** m/f unemployed person; **les ~s** the

unemployed pl

chope f beer mug

choquant shocking; **choquer:** **~ qc** knock sth; **~ qn** shock s.o.

chorale f choir

chose f thing; **autre ~** something else; **c'est ~ faite** it's done

chou m BOT cabbage; **~x de Bruxelles** Brussels sprouts

chouette 1 fowl **2** adj F great

chou-fleur m cauliflower

chrétien, **~ne** adj & m/f Christian

christianisme m Christianity

chrome m chrome

chronique 1 adj chronic **2** f *d'un journal* column; *reportage* report; **chroniqueur** m *pour un journal* columnist

chronologique chronological

chronométrer time

chuchoter whisper

chut: **~!** hush

chute f fall; **~ des cheveux** hair loss

ci: **à cette heure-~** at this time; **comme ~ comme ça** F so-so; **par-~ par-là** here and there

cible f target; **cibler** target

ciboulette f BOT chives pl

cicatrice f scar *(aussi fig)*; **cicatriser: (se) ~** heal

ci-contre opposite; **ci-dessous** below; **ci-dessus** above

cidre m cider

ciel *m* sky; REL heaven

cigale *f* cicada

cigare *m* cigar

cigarette *f* cigarette

ci-inclus enclosed; **ci-joint** enclosed, attached

cil *m* eyelash

ciment *m* cement

cimetière *m* cemetery

ciné *m* F movie theater, *Br* cinema; **cinéma** *m* movie theater, *Br* cinema; *art* cinema, movies *pl*

cinglé F mad, crazy

cinq five; **le ~ mai** May fifth, *Br* the fifth of May; **cinquantaine** *f* about fifty; **elle approche la ~** she's getting on for fifty; **cinquante** fifty; **cinquantième** fiftieth **cinquième** fifth

cintre *m* arch; *pour vêtements* coathanger

cirage *m pour parquet* wax, polish; *pour chaussures* polish

circonférence *f* circumference

circonspect circumspect

circonstance *f* circumstance

circuit *m* circuit; *de voyage* tour; SP track

circulaire *adj & f* circular

circulation *f* circulation; *voitures* traffic; **circuler** circulate; **faire ~** *nouvelles* spread

cire *f* wax; **cirer** polish; *parquet aussi* wax

cirque *m* circus

cirrhose *f*: **~ du foie** cirrhosis of the liver

ciseaux *mpl* scissors *pl*

citadin, **~e 1** *adj* town *atr*, city *atr* **2** *m/f* town-dweller, city--dweller

citation *f* quotation; JUR summons *sg*

cité *f* city; **~ universitaire** fraternity house, *Br* hall of residence

citoyen, **~ne** *m/f* citizen; **citoyenneté** *f* citizenship

citron *m* lemon; **~ vert** lime; **citronnier** *m* lemon (tree)

civière *f* stretcher

civil 1 *adj* civil; *non militaire* civilian; *état m* ~ marital status **2** *m* civilian; **en ~** in civilian clothes; *policier* in plain clothes; **civilisation** *f* civilization

civique civic

civisme *m* public-spiritedness

clair 1 *adj* clear; *couleur* light; *chambre* bright **2** *adv voir* clearly; *dire, parler* plainly **3** *m*: **~ de lune** moonlight

clairière *f* clearing

clairvoyant perceptive

clandestin secret, clandestine; *passager m* ~ stowaway

claque *f* slap; **claquer 1** *v/t porte* slam; *argent* F blow; **~ des doigts** snap one's fingers **2** *v/i d'un fouet* crack; *des dents* chatter; *d'un volet* slam

clarifier clarify

clarinette f clarinet

clarté f (lumière) brightness; (transparence) clarity

classe f class; **il a de la ~** he's got class; **~ économique** economy class

classement m position, place; BOT, ZO classification; de lettres filing; **classer** classify; actes, dossiers file; **~ une affaire** consider a matter closed

classique 1 adj classical; (traditionnel) classic **2** m en littérature classical author; MUS classical music; film, livre classic

clause f clause; **~ pénale** penalty clause

clavicule f collarbone

clavier m keyboard

clé f key; TECH wrench; **~ de fa** MUS bass clef; **fermer à ~** lock; **sous ~** under lock and key

clef f → **clé**

clément merciful

clergé m clergy

clic m bruit, INFORM click

client, **~e** m/f (acheteur) customer; d'un médecin patient; d'un avocat client; **clientèle** f customers pl, clientèle; d'un médecin patients pl; d'un avocat clients pl

cligner: **~** (des yeux) blink; **~ de l'œil à qn** wink at s.o.

clignotant m turn signal, Br indicator; **clignoter** d'une lumière flicker

climat m climate (aussi fig)

climatisation f air conditioning; **climatisé** air conditioned

clin m: **~ d'œil** wink; **en un ~ d'œil** in a flash

clinique 1 adj clinical **2** f clinic

cliquer INFORM click (**sur** on)

clochard, **~e** m/f hobo, Br tramp

cloche f bell f; F (idiot) nitwit F; **clocher 1** m steeple **2** v/i F: **ça cloche** something's not right

cloison f partition

cloîtrer fig: **se ~** shut o.s. away

clonage m cloning; **clone** m clone; **cloner** clone

clope m ou f F cigarette, Br F fag; (mégot) cigarette end

cloque f blister

clôture f d'un débat closing; d'un compte closing; (barrière) fence

clou m nail; fig main attraction; MÉD boil; **clouer** nail; **être cloué au lit** be confined to bed

clown m clown

club m club; **~ de gym** gym

coaguler du lait curdle; du sang coagulate

cobaye m ZO, fig guinea pig

coca m Coke®

coccinelle f ladybug, Br ladybird; F AUTO Volkswagen® beetle

cocher sur une liste check, Br

aussi tick off

cochon 1 *m* ZO, *fig* pig **2** *adj* cochon, *~ne* F dirty; **cochonnerie** *f* F: *des ~s* filth; *nourriture* junk food

coco *m*: *noix f de ~* coconut

cocotte *f* CUIS casserole; F darling; *figu* tart; *~ minute* pressure cooker

code *m* code; *~ confidentiel* PIN number; *~ pénal* penal code; *se mettre en ~* switch to low beams; *~ postal* zip-code, *Br* postcode

cœur *m* heart; *de bon ~* gladly; *par ~* by heart; *j'ai mal au ~* I feel nauseous

coffre *m meuble* chest; FIN safe; AUTO trunk, *Br* boot; **coffre-fort** *m* safe

cogérer co-manage

cognac *m* brandy, cognac

cogner *d'un moteur* knock; *~ à ou contre qc* bang against sth; *se ~ à ou contre qc* bump into sth

cohabiter cohabit

cohérent *théorie* consistent, coherent

cohue *f* crowd, rabble

coiffer: *~ qn* do s.o.'s hair; *se ~* do one's hair; **coiffeur** *m* hairdresser, hair stylist; **coiffeuse** *f* hairdresser, hair stylist; *meuble* dressing table; **coiffure** *f de cheveux* hairstyle

coin *m* corner; *cale* wedge

coincer squeeze; *porte, tiroir* jam; *coincé dans un em-*

bouteillage stuck in a traffic jam

coïncidence *f* coincidence

col *m* collar; *d'une bouteille, d'un pull* neck; GÉOGR col; *~ blanc/bleu* white-collar/ /blue-collar worker

colère *f* anger; *se mettre en ~* get angry

colique *f* colic; *(diarrhée)* diarrhea, *Br* diarrhoea

colis *m* parcel, package

collaborateur, -trice *m/f* collaborator ((*aussi* POL péj); **collaboration** *f* collaboration, cooperation, POL péj collaboration; **collaborer** collaborate, cooperate (*avec* with; *à* on); POL péj collaborate

collant 1 *adj* sticky; *vêtement* close-fitting; F *personne* clingy **2** *m* pantyhose *pl*, *Br* tights *pl*

colle *f* glue; *fig* P question tough question; *(retenue)* detention

collecte *f* collection; **collectif, -ive** collective; *voyage m ~* group tour

collection *f* collection; **collectionner** collect; **collectionneur, -euse** *m/f* collector

collège *m école* junior high, *Br* secondary school; **collégien, ~ne** *m/f* junior high student, *Br* secondary school pupil

collègue *m/f* colleague, co-worker

coller 1 v/t stick, glue **2** v/i stick (**à** to); **se ~ contre** mur press o.s against; personne cling to

collier m bijou necklace; de chien collar

colline f hill

collision f collision; **entrer en ~ avec** collide with

colocataire m/f roommate, Br flatmate

colombe f dove (aussi fig)

Colombie: la ~ Colombia; **colombien, ~ne** Colombian; **Colombien, ~ne** m/f Colombian

colonie f colony; **~ de vacances** summer camp

colonne f column

colorant 1 adj shampoing color atr; Br colour atr **2** m dye; dans la nourriture coloring, Br colouring; **colorer** color, Br colour

coma m coma

combat m fight; MIL aussi battle; **mettre hors de ~** put out of action; **combattant 1** adj fighting **2** m combatant; **combattre** fight

combien adv quantité how much; avec pl how many **2** m: **tous les ~** how often; **on est le ~ aujourd'hui?** what date is it today?

combinaison f combination; (astuce) scheme; de mécanicien coveralls pl, Br boiler suit; lingerie (full-length)

slip; **~ de plongée** wet suit

combiner combine; voyage, projet plan

comble 1 m fig: sommet height; **~s** pl attic; **de fond en ~** from top to bottom **2** adj full (to capacity); **combler** trou fill in; déficit make good; personne overwhelm; **~ qn de qch** shower s.o. with sth

combustible 1 adj combustible **2** m fuel

comédie f comedy; **~ musicale** musical; **comédien, ~ne** m/f actor; qui joue le genre comique comic actor

comestible 1 adj edible **2** mpl **~s** food

comique 1 adj THÉÂT comic; (drôle) funny, comical **2** m comedian; acteur comic (actor); genre comedy

comité m committee

commande f COMM order; TECH control; INFORM command; **commander 1** v/t COMM order; (ordonner) command, order; MIL be in command of; TECH control **2** v/i (diriger) be in charge; COMM order

comme 1 adv like; **noir ~ la nuit** as black as night; **~ ci ~ ça** F so-so; **~ vous voulez** as you like; **~ si** as if; if; **il travaillait ~** he was working as a ...; **moi, ~ les autres, je ...** like the others, I ... **2** conj as

commencement *m* beginning, start; **commencer** begin, start; **~ qc par qc** start sth with sth; **~ par faire qc** start by doing sth

comment how; **~?** (*qu'avez-vous dit?*) pardon me?, *Br* sorry?; **~!** *surpris* what!

commentaire *m* comment; RAD, TV commentary; **commenter** comment on; RAD, TV commentate on

commerçant, ~e **1** *adj*: **rue** *f* **~e** shopping street **2** *m/f* merchant, trader

commerce *m* trade, commerce; (*magasin*) store, *Br* shop; *fig* (*rapports*) dealings *pl*; **commercial** commercial; **commercialiser** market

commettre commit; *erreur* make

commis *m*: **~ voyageur** commercial traveler *ou Br* traveller

commissaire *m* commission member; *de l'UE* Commissioner; SP steward; **commissariat** *m* commissioner; **~** (**de police**) police station

commission *f* commission; (*message*) message

commode 1 *adj* handy; *arrangement* convenient; **pas ~** *personne* awkward **2** *f* chest of drawers; **commodité** *f* convenience

commotion *f* MÉD: **~ cérébrale** stroke

commun 1 *adj* common; *œu-*vre joint; **mettre en ~** *argent* pool **2** *m*: **hors du ~** out of the ordinary

communal (*de la commune*) local

communauté *f* community; *de hippies* commune

communication *f* communication; (*message*) message; **~ téléphonique** telephone call

communion *f* REL Communion

communiquer 1 *v/t* communicate; *maladie* pass on, give (**à qn** to s.o.) **2** *v/i* communicate

communisme *m* communism; **communiste** *m/f* & *adj* Communist

commutateur *m* switch

compact compact

compagne *f* companion; *dans couple* wife

compagnie *f* company; **~ aérienne** airline

compagnon *m* companion; *dans couple* husband; *employé* journeyman

comparaison *f* comparison; **par ~ à** compared with; **comparer** compare (**à** to, **avec** with)

compartiment *m* compartment; *de train* car, *Br* compartment

compas *m* compass

compassion *f* compassion

compatible compatible

compatir: **~ à** sympathize

with

compatriote *m/f* compatriot

compenser compensate for

compétence *f* (*connaissances*) ability, competence; JUR jurisdiction; **compétent** competent, skillful, *Br* skilful; JUR competent

compétitif, -ive competitive; **compétition** *f* competition

compiler compile

complaire: **se ~ dans/à faire** delight in/in doing

complet, -ète 1 *adj* complete; *hôtel, description, jeu de cartes* full; *pain* whole wheat, *Br* wholemeal **2** *m* suit; **complètement** completely; **compléter** complete; **se ~** complement each other

complexe *adj & m* complex

complication *f* complication

complice 1 *adj* JUR: **être ~ de** be an accessory to **2** *m/f* accomplice

compliment *m* compliment; **mes ~s** congratulations

compliqué complicated; **compliquer** complicate; **se ~** become complicated

comporter (*comprendre*) comprise; (*impliquer*) involve; **se ~** behave (o.s)

composer 1 *v/t* (*former*) make up; MUS compose; *livre, poème* write; *numéro* dial **2** *v/i transiger* come to terms (**avec** with); **se ~ de** be consist of

compositeur, -trice *m/f* composer

composter *billet* punch

compote *f*: **~ de pommes** stewed apples

compréhension *f* understanding

comprendre understand, (*inclure*) include; (*comporter*) comprise

compresse *f* MÉD compress

comprimé *m* tablet

compris (*inclus*) included; **y ~** including

compromettre compromise

comptabilité *f* accountancy; (*comptes*) accounts *pl*; **comptable** *m/f* accountant

comptant: **au ~** cash

compte *m* account; (*calcul*) calculation; **~s** accounts; **en fin de ~** when all's said and done; **se rendre ~ de** realize; **tenir ~ de qc** take sth into account; **~ courant** checking account, *Br* current account; **~ rendu** report; *de réunion* minutes *pl*; **compter 1** *v/t* count; (*prévoir*) allow; (*inclure*) include; **~ faire** plan on doing **2** *v/i* count; **~ sur** rely on; **à ~ de** starting (from); **compteur** *m* meter

comptoir *m* *d'un café* bar; *d'un magasin* counter

con, ~ne F **1** *adj* damn stupid F **2** *m/f* damn idiot F

concentration *f* concentration; **concentrer** concentrate; **se ~** concentrate

(**sur** on)

concept m concept

conception f (idée) concept; (planification) design; BIOL conception

concernant concerning, about; **concerner** concern

concert m MUS concert; **de ~ avec** together with

concession f concession; AUTO dealership

concevable conceivable; **concevoir** (comprendre) understand, conceive; (inventer) BIOL, plan, idée conceive

concierge m/f superintendent, Br caretaker; d'école janitor, Br aussi caretaker; d'un hôtel concierge

concis concise

concitoyen, ~ne m/f fellow citizen

conclure conclude; **~ de** conclude from; **conclusion** f conclusion

concombre m cucumber

concours m competition; (assistance) assistance

concret, -ète concrete

concurrence f competition; **faire ~ à** compete with; **concurrent, ~e 1** adj rival **2** m/f competitor

condamnation f sentence; action sentencing; fig condemnation

condamner JUR sentence; malade give up; (réprouver) condemn; porte block up

condescendance f péj condescension

condition f condition; **~ préalable** prerequisite; **à (la) ~ que** (+ subj) on condition that; **conditionner** (emballer) package; PSYCH condition

condoléances fpl condolences

conducteur, -trice 1 m/f driver **2** m PHYS conductor

conduire 1 v/t take (mener) lead; voiture drive; EL conduct; **se ~** behave **2** v/i AUTO drive; (mener) lead

conduit m d'eau, de gaz pipe; **~ d'aération** ventilation shaft

conduite f (comportement) behavior, Br behaviour; direction management; d'eau, de gaz pipe; AUTO driving

cône m cone

confection f making; industrie clothing industry

conférence f conference; (exposé) lecture; **être en ~** be in a meeting

confesser confess; **~ qn** REL hear s.o.'s confession; **se ~** REL go to confession; **confession** f confession; (croyance) faith

confiance f confidence; **faire ~ à** trust; **confiant** confident; (crédule) trusting

confidence f confidence; **faire une ~** confide in; **confident, ~e** m/f confidant; **con-**

fidentiel, **~le** confidential

confier: **~** *qc à qn* (*laisser*) entrust s.o. (with sth); **se ~ à** confide in

confirmation *f* confirmation (*aussi* REL); **confirmer** confirm (*aussi* REL)

confiserie *f* confectionery; *magasin* confectioner's; **~s** candy, *Br* sweets

confisquer confiscate (*à* from)

confiture *f* jelly, *Br* jam

conflit *m* conflict; *d'idées* clash

confondre confuse; (*déconcerter*) take aback; **se ~** (*se mêler*) merge

conforme: **~ à** in accordance with; **conformiste** *m/f* conformist

confort *m* comfort; **confortable** comfortable; *somme* sizeable

confronter confront; (*comparer*) compare

confusion *f* confusion; (*embarras*) embarrassment

congé *m* vacation, *Br* holiday; MIL leave; *avis de départ* notice; *prendre* **~** *de* take one's leave of; **~** *de maladie* sick leave

congélateur *m* freezer; **congelé** *aliment* frozen; **congeler** freeze

congénital congenital

congestion *f* MÉD congestion; **~** *cérébrale* stroke; **congestionné** *visage*
flushed

congrès *m* convention, conference; *Congrès aux États-Unis* Congress

conique conical

conjecture *f* conjecture

conjoint, **~e 1** *adj* joint **2** *m/f* spouse

conjonctivite *f* MÉD conjunctivitis

conjugaison *f* GRAM conjugation

conjugal conjugal; *vie* married

conjuguer *efforts* combine; GRAM conjugate

connaissance *f* knowledge; (*conscience*) consciousness; *personne connue* acquaintance; **~s** *d'un sujet* knowledge; **connaisseur** *m* connoisseur; **connaître** know; (*rencontrer*) meet; *s'y* **~** *en* be an expert on

connecter TECH connect; **se~** INFORM log on

connerie *f* V: *une* **~** a damn stupid thing to do/say

connexion *f* connection; *hors* **~** INFORM off-line

connu well-known

conquérir conquer

conquête *f* conquest

consacrer REL consecrate; (*dédier*) dedicate; *temps, argent* spend; **se ~** *à* dedicate *ou* devote o.s. to

conscience *f* moral conscience; *physique,* PSYCH consciousness; *prendre* **~**

de become aware of

consécutif, -ive consecutive; *~ à* resulting from

conseil *m* advice; (*conseiller*) adviser; (*assemblée*) council; *un ~* a piece of advice; *~ d'administration* board of directors

conseiller *personne* advise; *~ qc à qn* recommend sth to s.o.

consentir 1 *v/i* consent, agree (*à* to) **2** *v/t prêt, délai* agree

conséquence *f* consequence; *en ~* consequently

conservation *f* preservation; *des aliments* preserving

conserve *f* preserve; *en boîte* canned food, *Br aussi* tinned food; **conserver** keep; *aliments* preserve

considérable considerable; **considération** *f* consideration; **considérer** consider

consigne *f* orders *pl; d'une gare* baggage checkroom, *Br* left luggage office; *pour bouteilles* deposit; ÉDU detention

consistance *f* consistency; **consistant** *liquide, potage* thick; *mets* substantial; **consister:** *~ en/dans* consist of; *~ à faire* consist in doing

consolation *f* consolation

console *f* console; *jouer à la ~* play computer games

consoler console*t; se ~ de* get over

consolider consolidate

consommateur, -trice *m/f* consumer; *dans un café* customer; **consommation** *f* consumption; *dans un café* drink; **consommer 1** *v/t* consume, use **2** *v/i dans un café* drink

consonne *f* consonant

conspiration *f* conspiracy; **conspirer** conspire

constamment constantly

constance *f* (*persévérance*) perseverance; *en amour* constancy

constant constant; *ami* staunch; *efforts* persistent

constater observe

consternation *f* consternation; **consterner** fill with consternation, dismay

constipation *f* MÉD constipation

constituer constitute; *comité, société* form; *rente* settle (*à* on); *se ~ fortune* build up

constitution *f* (*composition*) composition; ANAT, POL constitution; *d'un comité, d'une société* formation

construction *f* construction, building; **construire** construct, build; *théorie, roman* construct

consul *m* consul; **consulat** *m* consulate

consultation *f* consultation; **consulter 1** *v/t* consult **2** *v/i* be available for consultation

contact *m* contact; *se mettre*

en ~ avec contact; **mettre/ couper le ~** AUTO switch the engine on/off

contagieux, -euse contagious; *rire* infectious

contaminer contaminate; MÉD *personne* infect

conte m story, tale

contempler contemplate

contemporain m & adj contemporary

contenir *foule* control; *larmes* hold back; *peine* suppress; **se ~** contain o.s.

content pleased, content (**de** with)

contenu m content

contestation f discussion; *(opposition)* protest; **contester** challenge

contexte m context

continent m continent

contingent m *(part)* quota

continu continuous; ÉL *courant* direct; **continuer 1** v/t continue; *rue, ligne* extend **2** v/i continue, go on; *de route* extend; **~ à** ou **de faire** continue to do, go on doing; **continuité** f continuity; *d'une tradition* continuation

contorsion f contorsion

contour m contour; *d'une fenêtre, d'un visage* outline; **~s** *(courbes)* twists and turns

contourner get around

contraceptif, -ive contraceptive; **contraception** f contraception

contracter *dette* incur; *mala-*

die aussi contract; *obligation, engagement* enter into; *assurance* take out; *habitude* acquire

contradiction f contradiction

contraindre: ~ qn à faire qc force s.o. to do sth; **contrainte** f constraint; **sans ~** freely, without restraint

contraire 1 adj sens opposite; *principes* conflicting; *vent* contrary **2** m: **le ~ de** the opposite ou contrary of; **au ~** on the contrary

contrarier *personne* annoy; *projet* thwart

contraster contrast

contrat m contract

contravention f infringement; *(procès-verbal)* ticket

contre 1 prép against; *(en échange)* (in exchange) for; **tout ~** qch right next to sth; **par ~** on the contrary; **quelque chose ~ la diarrhée** something for diarrhea **2** m: **le pour et le ~** the pros and the cons pl

contrebande f smuggling; *marchandises* contraband; **contrebandier** m smuggler

contrebasse f double bass

contrecœur: **à ~** reluctantly

contrecoup m after-effect

contredire contradict

contrée f country

contrefaire counterfeit; *signature* forge; *personne, gestes* imitate; *voix* disguise

contre-nature unnatural

contrepartie f compensation;
  en ~ in return
contre-plaqué m plywood
contrer counter
contresens m misinterpretation; **prendre une route à ~**
  go down a road the wrong
  way
contretemps m hitch
contribuable m taxpayer;
  contribuer contribute (**à**
  to); ~ **à faire** help to do
contrôle m (**vérification**)
  check; (**domination**) control;
  (**maîtrise de soi**) self-control;
  ~ **douanier** customs inspection; ~ **radar** radar speed
  check; **contrôler** identité,
  billets etc check; (**maîtriser**,
  dominer) control; **se ~** control o.s.
controversé controversial
contusion f MÉD bruise
convaincre (**persuader**) convince; ~ **qn de faire qch** persuade s.o. to do sth
convalescent, **~e** m/f convalescent
convenable suitable; (**correct**) personne respectable;
  salaire adequate; **convenance** f: **les ~s** the propri-
  eties
convenir (**persuader**) con~**à**
  qc be suitable for sth; ~ **de**
  qc (**décider**) agree on sth;
  ~ **que** (**reconnaître que**) admit that; **comme convenu**
  as agreed
convention f convention

converger converge
conversation f conversation;
  ~ **téléphonique** telephone
  conversation, phonecall
conversion f conversion
convertir convert
conviction f conviction
convive m/f guest; **convivia-
  lité** f conviviality, friendliness; INFORM user-friendli-
  ness
convocation f d'une assemblée convening; JUR summons sg
convoi m convoy
convoquer assemblée con-
  vene; JUR summons; candidat notify; employé, écolier
  call in
convoyer MIL escort
convulsion f convulsion
coopération f cooperation;
  coopérer cooperate (**à** in)
coordination f coordination
coordonnées fpl MATH coor-
  dinates pl; de personne contact details
copain m F pal
copie f copy; ÉDU paper; **copier** copy (**sur qn** from s.o.)
copieux, **-euse** copious
copine f F pal
copropriétaire m/f co-owner,
  part owner
coq m rooster
coquelicot m BOT poppy
coquetier m eggcup
coquetterie f flirtatiousness;
  (**élégance**) stylishness
coquillage m shell; **des ~s**

shellfish

coquille f shell; *erreur* misprint, typo

coquin, **~e 1** adj *enfant* naughty **2** m/f rascal

corbeau m zo crow

corbeille f basket; *au théâtre* circle

corbillard m hearse

corde f rope; mus, *de tennis* string

cordialité f cordiality

cordon m cord; **~ littoral** offshore sand bar

cordonnier m shoe repairer

Corée: **la ~** Korea; **coréen**, **~e 1** adj Korean **2** m langue Korean; **Coréen**, **~ne** m/f Korean

corne f horn

cornée f cornea

corneille f crow

corner m *en football* corner

cornet m *sachet* (paper) cone; mus cornet

cornichon m gherkin

corporation f body; hist guild

corporel, **~le** hygiène personal; *châtiment* corporal; *art* body atr

corps m body; *mort aussi* corpse; mil corps; **prendre ~** take shape

corpulence f stoutness, corpulence

correct correct; *tenue* suitable; F *(convenable)* acceptable, ok F

correcteur m: **~ orthographi-**

que spellchecker

correction f qualité correctness; *(modification)* correction; *(punition)* beating

correspondance f correspondence; *de train etc* connection; **correspondre** correspond; **~ à réalité** correspond with, *preuves* tally with; *idées* fit in with

corridor m corridor

corriger correct; *épreuve* proof-read; *(battre)* beat

corrompre corrupt; *(soudoyer)* bribe

corrosion f corrosion

corruption f corruption; *(pot-de-vin)* bribery

corsage m blouse

corse vin Corsican; **Corse 1** m/f Corsican **2** f **la Corse** Corsica

corsé vin full-bodied; *sauce* spicy; *café* strong; *facture* stiff; *problème* tough

cortège m cortège; *(défilé)* procession

cortisone f cortisone

corvée f chore; mil fatigue

cosmétique m & adj cosmetic

cosmopolite m & adj cosmopolitan

costaud F sturdy

costume m costume; *pour homme* suit

cote f *en Bourse* quotation; *d'un document* identification code

côte f ANAT rib; (*pente*) slope; *à la mer* coast; *viande* chop; **~ à ~** side by side

côté m side; *à ~* (*près*) nearby; *à ~ de* next to; *de ~* aside; *de l'autre ~ de* on the other side of; *du ~ de* in the direction of; *sur le ~* on one's/its side; *mettre de ~* put aside

côtelette f CUIS cutlet

cotisation f contribution; *à une organisation* subscription

coton m coton

côtoyer rub shoulders with; **~ qc** border sth

cottage m cottage

cou m neck

couchant 1 m west **2** *adj:* **soleil m ~** setting sun

couche f layer; (*étendre aussi* coat; *de bébé* diaper, *Br* nappy

coucher 1 v/t (*mettre au lit*) put to bed; (*héberger*) put up; (*étendre*) put *ou* lay down **2** v/i sleep; **se ~** go to bed; (*s'étendre*) lie down; *du soleil* set, go down **3** m: **~ du soleil** sunset

coucou m cuckoo; (*pendule*) cuckoo clock

coude m ANAT elbow; *d'une route* turn

coudre sew; *bouton* sew on; *plaie* sew up

couette f comforter, *Br* quilt

couler 1 v/i flow, run; *d'eau de bain* run; *d'un bateau* sink **2** v/t *liquide* pour; (*mouler*)

cast; *bateau* sink

couleur f color, *Br* colour

coulisse f: **~s** THÉÂT wings; *dans les ~s* fig behind the scenes

couloir m passage, corridor; *d'un bus, avion* aisle

coup m blow; *dans jeu* move; **boire un ~** F have a drink; *du ~* and so; *après ~* after the event; *tout d'un ~, tout à ~* suddenly, all at once; *coup de couteau* stab; *coup de foudre: ce fut le ~* it was love at first sight; *coup de main: donner un ~ à qn* give s.o. a hand; *coup d'œil: au premier ~* at first glance; *coup de pied* kick; *coup de poing* punch; *donner un ~ à* punch; *coup de téléphone* (phone) call; *coup de soleil: avoir un ~* have sun stroke

coupable 1 *adj* guilty **2** *m/f* culprit, guilty party

coupe[1] f *de cheveux, d'une robe* cut

coupe[2] f (*verre*) glass; SP cup; *de fruits, glace* dish

coupe-ongles m inv nail clippers *pl*

couper 1 v/t *morceau, eau* cut off; *robe, chemise* cut out; *vin* dilute; *animal* castrate **2** v/i **~ au court** take o.s.; (*se trahir*) give o.s. away

couple m couple

coupon m *de tissu* remnant; COMM coupon; (*ticket*) ticket

coupure f cut; de journal cutting; (billet de banque) bill, Br note; **~ de courant** power outage, Br power cut

cour f court; ARCH courtyard; **Cour internationale de justice** International Court of Justice

courage m courage, bravery; **courageux, -euse** brave, courageous

couramment fluently

courant 1 adj current; eau running; langage everyday **2** m current (aussi ÉL); **~ d'air** draft, Br draught; **être au ~ de qch** know about sth

courbature f stiffness; **avoir des ~s** be stiff

courbe 1 adj curved **2** f curve; **courber** bend; **se ~** (se baisser) stoop, bend down

coureur m runner; péj skirt-chaser

courge f BOT squash, Br marrow

courgette f BOT zucchini, Br courgette

courir 1 v/i run (aussi d'eau); d'un bruit go around **2** v/t risque, danger run; **~ les magasins** go around the stores

couronne f crown; de fleurs wreath; **couronnement** m coronation

courrier m mail, Br aussi post; (messager) courier; **~ électronique** electronic mail, e-mail

courroie f belt

cours m course; ÉCON price; de devises rate; (leçon) lesson; à l'université class, Br aussi lecture; **donner libre ~ à** give free rein to; **en ~ de route** on the way

course f à pied running; SP race; en taxi ride; (commission) errand; **~s** (achats) shopping; **faire des ~s** go shopping

court[1] m (aussi **~ de tennis**) (tennis) court

court[2] adj short; **à ~ de** short of

court-circuit m ÉL short circuit

courtier m broker

courtiser femme court

courtoisie f courtesy

cousin, ~e m/f cousin

coussin m cushion

coût m cost; **coûter** **1** v/t cost; **combien ça coûte?**, how much is it?, how much does it cost? **2** v/i cost; **~ cher** be expensive

couteau m knife

coûteux, -euse expensive, costly

coutume f custom; **avoir ~ de faire** be in the habit of doing

couture f sewing; d'un vêtement, bas etc seam

couvée clutch; fig brood

couvent m convent

couver **1** v/t hatch; personne pamper **2** v/i d'un feu smolder, Br smoulder; d'une révolution be brewing

couvercle m cover

couvert 1 adj ciel overcast; ~ **de** covered with ou in 2 m à table place setting; **~s** flatware, Br cutlery; **mettre le ~** set the table; **couverture** f cover; sur un lit blanket

couvrir cover (**de** with ou in); ~ **qn** fig (protéger) cover (up) for s.o.; **se ~** (s'habiller) cover o.s. up; du ciel cloud over

covoiturage m carpooling; **faire du ~** carpool

crabe m crab

cracher spit

crachin m drizzle

craie f chalk

craindre fear, be frightened of; **de faire** be afraid of doing; ~ **que (ne)** (+ subj) be afraid that

crainte f fear; **de ~ de** for fear of

craintif, -ive timid

cramoisi crimson

crampe f MÉD cramp

crampon m crampon

cran m notch; **il a du ~** F he's got guts?

crâne m skull

crâner F (pavaner) show off

crapaud m zo toad

crapule f villain

craquelé cracked

craquement m crackle; **craquer** crack; d'un parquet creak; de feuilles crackle; d'une couture split; d'une personne (s'effondrer) crack up

crasse 1 adj ignorance crass **2** f dirt

cravate f necktie, Br tie

crayon m pencil; ~ **à bille** ballpoint pen; ~ **de couleur** crayon

créance f COMM debt; **créancier, -ère** m/f creditor

création f creation; de mode, design design; **créativité** f creativity

créature f creature

crèche f day nursery; de Noël crèche, Br crib

crédibilité f credibility; **crédit** m credit; (prêt) loan; (influence) influence; **acheter à ~** buy on credit; **faire ~ à qn** give s.o. credit

créditeur, -trice m/f creditor **2** solde credit atr; **être ~** be in credit

crédule credulous

créer create; institution set up; COMM produit design

crématorium m crematorium

crème 1 f cream; ~ **anglaise** custard; ~ **dépilatoire** hair remover; ~ **solaire** suntan cream **2** m coffee with milk, Br white coffee **3** adj inv cream

créneau m AUTO space; COMM niche

crêpe f CUIS pancake

crépiter crackle

crépu frizzy

crépuscule m twilight

crétin, ~e m/f idiot, cretin

creuser hollow out; *trou* dig; *fig* look into

creux, -euse 1 *adj* hollow; *assiette f creuse* soup plate **2** *adv:* *sonner* ~ ring hollow **3** *m* hollow

crevaison f flat, *Br* puncture

crevant F (*épuisant*) exhausting; (*drôle*) hilarious

crevasser crack; *se* ~ crack

crever 1 *v/t ballon* burst; *pneu* puncture **2** *v/i* burst; F (*mourir*) kick the bucket; F AUTO have a flat *ou Br* puncture

crevette f shrimp

cri m shout, cry; *c'est le dernier* ~ *fig* it's all the rage

cribler sieve; *criblé de fig* riddled with

cric m jack

crier 1 *v/i* shout; ~ *au scandale* protest **2** *v/t* shout

crime m crime; (*assassinat*) murder; **criminel**, ~le **1** *adj* criminal **2** *m/f* criminal; (*assassin*) murderer

crinière f mane

criquet m zo cricket

crise f crisis; MÉD attack; ~ *cardiaque* heart attack

crisper *muscles* tense; *visage* contort; *fig* F irritate; *se* ~ tense up

crisser squeak

cristal m crystal

critère m criterion

critique 1 *adj* critical **2** *m* critic **3** *f* criticism; *d'un film etc* review; **critiquer** criticize

croc m (*dent*) fang; *de boucherie* hook

crochet m hook; *ouvrage* crochet; *d'une route* sharp turn; ~*s en typographie* square brackets

crochu *nez* hooked

crocodile m crocodile

croire *v/t* believe; (*penser*) think; ~ *qc de qn* believe sth about s.o. **2** *v/i:* ~ *à qc* believe in sth; ~ *en Dieu* believe in God **3:** *il se croit intelligent* he thinks he's intelligent

croisade f crusade

croisement m crossing (*aussi* BIOL); *animal* cross; **croiser 1** *v/t* cross (*aussi* BIOL); ~ *qn dans la rue* pass s.o. in the street **2** *v/i:* ~ *fig* MAR cruise; *se* ~ *de routes* cross; *de personnes* meet

croisière f MAR cruise

croissance f growth

croissant m *de lune* crescent; CUIS croissant

croître grow

croix f cross; *mettre une* ~ *sur qc fig* give sth up

croquer 1 *v/t* crunch; (*dessiner*) sketch **2** *v/i* be crunchy

croquis m sketch

crotte f droppings pl

crouler collapse (*aussi fig*)

croupir stagnate (*aussi fig*)

croustillant crusty

croûte f *de pain* crust; *de fromage* rind; MÉD scab

croûton *m* crouton

croyance *f* belief; **croyant,** **~e** *m*/*f* REL believer

cru 1 *adj* raw; *lumière, verité* harsh; *paroles* blunt **2** *m* (*domaine*) vineyard; *de vin* wine

cruauté *f* cruelty

cruche *f* pitcher

crucial crucial

crucifier crucify; **crucifix** *m* crucifix

crudité *f* crudeness; *de paroles* bluntness; *de lumière* harshness; *de couleur* garishness; **~s** CUIS raw vegetables

cruel, ~le cruel

crustacés *mpl* shellfish *pl*

Cuba CUBA, **~e** Cuban; **Cubain, ~e** *m*/*f* Cuban

cube MATH *m* cube **2** *adj* cubic; **cubisme** *m* ART cubism

cueillir pick

cuiller, cuillère *f* spoon; **cuillerée** *f* spoonful

cuir *m* leather; **~ chevelu** scalp

cuirasse *f* armor, *Br* armour

cuire cook; *au four* bake; *rôti* roast

cuisine *f* cooking; *pièce* kitchen; **la ~ italienne** Italian cooking *ou* cuisine; **cuisiner** cook; **cuisinière** *f* cook; (*fourneau*) stove

cuisse *f* ANAT thigh; CUIS *de poulet* leg

cuisson *f* cooking; *du pain* baking; *d'un rôti* roasting

cuit cooked, done; *rôti, pain*

done

cuivre *m* copper; **~ jaune** brass; **~s** brasses

cul *m* ∨ ass P, *Br* arse P

cul-de-sac *m* blind alley; *fig* dead end

culminer *fig* peak

culotte *f* short pants *pl, Br* short trousers *pl*; *de femme* panties *pl*

culpabilité *f* guilt, culpability

culte *m* worship; (*religion*) religion; (*service*) church service; *fig* cult

cultivateur, -trice *m*/*f* farmer; **cultiver** cultivate (*aussi fig*); *légumes, tabac* grow; **se ~** improve one's mind

culture *f* culture; AGR cultivation; *de légumes, fruits etc* growing

culturel, ~le cultural

cumuler: ~ des fonctions have more than one position

cupidité *f* greed, cupidity

cure *f* MÉD course of treatment; **~ de repos** rest cure

curé *m* curate

cure-dent *m* tooth pick

curiosité *f* curiosity; *objet rare* curio

curry *m* curry

curseur *m* INFORM cursor

cuvée *f* *de vin* vatful; *vin* wine, vintage; **cuver 1** *v*/*i* mature **2** *v*/*t*: **~ son vin** *fig* sleep it off

cuvette *f* (*bac*) basin; *de cabinet* bowl

CV *m* (= *curriculum vitae*) ré-

sumé, *Br* CV (= curriculum vitae)
cybercafé *m* Internet café
cycle *m* cycle; **cyclisme** *m* cycling; **cycliste** *m/f* cyclist
cyclone *m* cyclone

cygne *m* swan
cylindre *m* cylinder
cynique 1 *adj* cynical **2** *m/f* cynic
cystite *f* MÉD cystitis

D

dactylo *f* typing; *personne* typist
daigner: ~ *faire qch* deign to do sth
daim *m* ZO deer; *peau* suede
dalle *f* flagstone
daltonien, ~ne colorblind, *Br* colourblind
dame *f* lady; *aux échecs, cartes* queen; *jeu m de ~s* checkers *sg*, *Br* draughts *sg*
damner damn
Danemark: le ~ Denmark
danger *m* danger; *courir un ~* be in danger
dangereux, -euse dangerous
danois, ~e 1 *adj* Danish **2** *m langue* Danish; **Danois, ~e** *m/f* Dane
dans in; *boire ~ un verre* drink from a glass
danse *f* dance; *action* dancing; ~ *folklorique* folk dance; **danser** dance; **danseur, -euse** *m/f* dancer
dard *m d'une abeille* sting
date *f* date; *de longue ~ amitié* long-standing; ~ *limite* deadline; ~ *limite de conservation* use-by date; da-

ter **1** *v/t* date **2** *v/i* ~ *de* date from; *à ~ de ce jour* from to-day
datte *f* date
davantage more
de 1 *prép origine* from; *possession* of; *il vient ~ Paris* he comes from Paris *la maison ~ mon père* my father's house; *un film ~ Godard* a movie by Godard; ~ *jour* by day; *trembler ~ peur* shake with fear; *cesser ~ travailler* stop working **2** *partitif: du pain* (some) bread; *des petits pains* (some) rolls; *je n'ai pas d'argent* I don't have any money, I have no money; *est-ce qu'il y a des disquettes?* are there any diskettes?
dé *m jeu* dice; *(à coudre)* thimble
dealer *m* dealer
déambuler stroll
débâcle *f de troupes* rout; *d'une entreprise* collapse
déballer unpack
débandade *f* stampede
débarbouiller: ~ *un enfant*

wash a child's face

débardeur *m vêtement* tank top

débarquement *m de marchandises* unloading; *de passagers* landing, disembarkation; **débarquer 1** *v/t marchandises* unload; *passagers* land, disembark **2** *v/i* land, disembark; ~ **chez qn** *fig* F turn up at s.o.'s place

débarrasser *table etc* clear; ~ **qn de qc** take sth off s.o.; **se ~ de** get rid of

débat *m* debate; *(polémique)* argument

débattre: ~ *qc* discuss *ou* debate sth; **se ~** struggle

débauche *f debauchery;* **débaucher** *(licencier)* lay off; F lead astray

débile 1 *adj* weak; F idiotic **2** *m:* ~ **mental** mental defective

débit *m (vente)* sale; *d'un stock* turnover; *d'une usine* output; *(élocution)* delivery; FIN debit; **débiter** *marchandises* sell (retail); *péj: fadaises* talk; *texte étudié* deliver, *péj* recite; *d'une pompe* deliver; *d'une usine, de produits* output; *bois, viande* cut up; FIN debit **(de** with); **débiteur, -trice 1** *m/f* debtor **2** *adj compte* overdrawn; *solde* debit

déblayer *endroit* clear; *débris* clear (away)

débloquer 1 *v/t* TECH release;

prix, compte unfreeze; *fonds* release **2** *v/i* F be crazy; **se ~** *d'une situation* get sorted out

déboguer debug

déboires *mpl* disappointments

déboisement *m* deforestation

déboîter 1 *v/t* MÉD dislocate **2** *v/i* AUTO pull out; **se ~ l'épaule** dislocate one's shoulder

débonnaire kindly

débordé snowed under **(de** with); ~ *par les événements* overwhelmed by events; **déborder** *d'une rivière* overflow its banks; *du lait, de l'eau* overflow

débouché *m d'une vallée* entrance; COMM outlet; ~*s d'une profession* prospects; **déboucher 1** *v/t tuyau* unblock; *bouteille* uncork **2** *v/i:* ~ **de** emerge from; ~ **sur** lead to *(aussi fig)*

débourser *(dépenser)* spend

debout standing; *objet* upright, on end; *être* ~ stand; *(levé)* be up; *du lit, de bed;* **se mettre ~** stand up, get up

déboutonner unbutton

débraillé untidy

débrancher ÉL unplug

débrayer AUTO declutch; *fig* down tools

débris *mpl* debris *sg; fig* remains

débrouillard resourceful; **débrouiller** disentangle; *fig: affaire* clear up; **se ~** cope

début *m* beginning, start; **~s** THÉÂT, POL debut; **débutant, ~e** *m/f* beginner

décacheter *lettre* open

décadent decadent

décaféiné *café m* ~ decaffeinated coffee, decaff ⊦

décalage *m dans l'espace* moving; *(différence)* difference; *fig* gap; **décaler** *rendez-vous* change the time of; *dans l'espace* move

décamper F clear out

décaper *surface* clean; *meuble vernis* strip

décapiter decapitate

décapotable *f (voiture f)* ~ convertible

décapsuleur *m* bottle opener

décarcasser: se ~ F bust a gut F

décéder die

déceler *(découvrir)* detect; *(montrer)* point to

décembre *m* December

décemment decently; *(raisonnablement)* reasonably

décennie *f* decade

décent decent

décentralisation *f* decentralization

déception *f* disappointment

décerner *prix* award

décès *m* death

décevoir disappointment

déchaîner *fig* provoke; **se ~**

d'une tempête break; *d'une personne* fly into a rage

décharge *f* JUR acquittal; *dans fusillade* discharge; **~ électrique** electric shock; **décharger** unload; *batterie* discharge; *arme* fire; *accusé* acquit; *colère* vent (**contre** on); **~ qn de qch** relieve s.o. of sth

décharné skeletal

déchausser: se ~ take one's shoes off

déchéance *f* decline; JUR forfeiture

déchets *mpl* waste

déchiffrer decipher

déchiqueté *côte* jagged; **déchiqueter** *corps, papier* tear to pieces

déchirant heart-breaking; **déchirer** *tissu* tear; *papier* tear up; *fig: silence* pierce; **se ~** *d'une arme* tear; **~ un muscle** tear a muscle

décidé *(résolu)* determined (**à faire qc** to do sth); **décidément** really; **décider** 1 *v/t* decide on; *question* settle, decide; **~ qn à faire qc** convince s.o. to do sth; **~ de faire qch** decide to do sth 2 *v/i* decide; **se ~** make one's mind up, decide (**à faire qch** to do sth)

décimal decimal

décimer decimate

décimètre *m:* **double ~** ruler

décisif, -ive decisive; **décision** *f* decision; *(fermeté)* determination

déclaration f declaration, statement; *d'une naissance* registration; *de vol, perte* report; **déclarer** declare; *naissance* register; **se ~** declare o.s.; *en amour* declare one's love; *d'un feu, d'une épidémie* break out

déclencher trigger; **se ~** be triggered

déclic m bruit click

déclin m decline

décliner 1 v/i *du soleil* go down; *du jour, des forces, du prestige* wane; *de la santé* decline **2** v/t *offre* decline

décoder decode; **décodeur** m decoder

décoiffer *cheveux* ruffle

décollage m AVIAT take-off; **décoller 1** v/t peel off **2** v/i AVIAT take off; **se ~** peel off

décolleté 1 adj *robe* low-cut **2** m neckline

décolorer *tissu, cheveux* bleach; **se ~** fade

décombres mpl rubble

décommander cancel; **se ~** cancel

décomposer *produit* break down (**en** into); CHIM decompose; **se ~** *d'un cadavre* decompose; *d'un visage* become contorted

décompresser F unwind, chill out F

décompte m deduction; *d'une facture* breakdown

déconcentrer: ~ qn make it

hard for s.o. to concentrate

déconcertant disconcerting

déconfit disheartened

déconfiture f collapse

décongeler *aliment* thaw out

décongestionner *route* decongest; *nez* clear

déconnecter unplug, disconnect; **se ~** INFORM log off, log out

déconner P *actions* fool around; *paroles* talk crap P

déconseiller advise against

décontenancer disconcert

décontracter relax; **se ~** relax

décor m decor; fig (*cadre*) setting; **~s** de théâtre sets, scenery; **décorateur, -trice** m/f decorator; THÉÂT set designer; **décorer** decorate (**de** with)

découler: ~ de arise from

découper cut up; *photo* cut out (**dans** from); **se ~ sur** fig stand out against

décourager discourage (**de faire qc** from doing sth); **se ~** lose heart, become discouraged

découvert, ~e 1 adj *tête, épaules* bare, uncovered; **à ~** FIN overdrawn **2** m overdraft **3** f discovery; **découvrir** uncover; (*trouver*) discover; *ses intentions* reveal; (*comprendre*) find (*que* that); **se ~** *d'une personne* take off a couple of layers; (*enlever son chapeau*) take

off one's hat; *du ciel* clear
décret *m* decree
décrire describe; **~ une orbite autour de** orbit
décrocher *tableau* take
down; *fig* F *prix, bonne situation* F; **~ le téléphone** pick up the receiver;
pour ne pas être dérangé
take the phone off the hook
décroître decrease, decline
déçu disappointed
décupler increase tenfold
dédaigner 1 *v/t* scorn; *personne* treat with scorn **2**
v/i: **~ de faire qch** disdain
to do sth; **dédaigneux, -euse** disdainful; **dédain** *m* disdain
dedans inside
dédicace *f* dedication; **dédier** dedicate
dédommager compensate
(**de** for)
dédouanement *m* customs
clearance; **dédouaner** *qch* clear sth through customs; **~ qn** *fig* clear s.o.
dédoublement *m:* **~ de personnalité** split personality;
dédoubler split in two; **se
~** split
dédramatiser play down,
downplay
déduction *f* deduction; **déduire** COMM deduct; (*conclure*) deduce (**de** from)
déesse *f* goddess
défaillance *f* weakness; *fig*
shortcoming; *technique* fail

ure; **défaillir** weaken; (*se
trouver mal*) feel faint
défaire undo; (*démonter*)
take down, dismantle; *valise*
unpack; **se ~** come undone;
se ~ de qn/qc get rid of s.o./
sth; **défait** *visage* drawn;
chemise, valise undone; *armée, personne* defeated; **défaite** *f* defeat; **défaitisme** *m*
defeatism
défaut *m* (*imperfection*) defect; *morale* shortcoming,
failing; (*manque*) lack; *par*
default; **faire ~** be lacking;
par ~ INFORM default *atr*
défavorable unfavorable, *Br*
unfavourable; **défavorisé**
disadvantaged; **les milieux
~s** the underprivileged
classes
défectueux, -euse defective
défendre defend; **~ à qn de
faire qc** forbid s.o. to do sth
défense *f* defense, *Br* defence *f; d'un éléphant* tusk;
~ de fumer no smoking; **défenseur** *m* defender; *d'une
cause* supporter; JUR defense attorney, *Br* counsel
for the defence; **défensif,
-ive** *adj* & *f* defensive
déférent deferential; **déférer:
~ qn à la justice** prosecute
s.o.
défi *m* challenge; (*bravade*)
defiance
défiance *f* distrust, mistrust
déficience *f* deficiency; **~ immunitaire** immune deficien

cy

déficit *m* deficit; **déficitaire** *balance* showing a deficit; *compte* in debit

défier *(provoquer)* challenge; *(braver)* defy; **~ qn de faire qch** dare s.o. to do sth

défigurer disfigure; *fig: réalité* misrepresent

défilé *m* parade; GÉOGR pass; **~ de mode** fashion show; **défiler** parade, march

défini definite; **bien ~** well defined; **définir** define; **définitif, -ive** definitive; **en définitive** in the end; **définition** definition; **définitivement** definitely; *(pour de bon)* for good

déflagration *f* explosion

défoncer *voiture* smash up, total; *porte* break down; *terrain* break up

déformer deform; *chaussures* stretch (out of shape); *visage, fait* distort; *idée* misrepresent; **se ~ chaussures** lose their shape

défouler: **se ~** give vent to one's feelings

défroisser *vêtement* crumple

défunt, ~e 1 *adj* late **2** *m/f:* **le ~** the deceased

dégagement *m* *d'une route* clearing; *de chaleur* release; **dégager** *(délivrer)* free; *route* clear; *odeur, chaleur* give off; **se ~** free o.s.; *d'une route, du ciel* clear

dégât *m* *d'une route* clearing; **~s** damage

dégel *m* thaw *(aussi* POL*)*

dégeler 1 *v/t* *frigidaire* defrost; *crédits* unfreeze **2** *v/i* *d'un lac* thaw

dégénérer degenerate *(en* into*)*

dégivrer defrost; TECH de-ice

déglutir swallow

dégonfler let the air out of, deflate; **se ~** deflate; *fig* F lose one's nerve

dégourdi resourceful; **dégourdir** *membres* loosen up; **se ~ les jambes** stretch one's legs

dégoût *m* disgust; **dégoûtant** disgusting; **dégoûter** disgust; **~ qn de qc** put s.o. off sth; **se ~ de qc** take a dislike to sth

dégrader MIL demote; *édifice* damage; *(avilir)* degrade; **se ~** deteriorate; *d'un édifice* fall into disrepair

degré *m* degree; *(échelon)* level

dégressif, -ive *tarif* tapering

dégringoler fall

dégriser sober up

déguerpir clear off

dégueulasse P disgusting; **dégueuler** F vomit

déguisement *m* disguise; *pour bal masqué etc* costume; **déguiser** disguise; *enfant* dress up (en as); **se ~** disguise o.s.; *pour bal masqué etc* dress up

dégustation *f* tasting; **déguster** taste

dehors 1 *adv* outside **2** *prép:*
en ~ de outside **3** *m* exterior

déjà already; **c'est qui déjà?**
F who's he again?

déjeuner 1 *v/i midi* (have)
lunch; *matin* (have) breakfast **2** *m* lunch; *petit ~* breakfast

déjouer thwart

DEL *f* (= **diode électrolumi-
nescente**) LED (= light-
emitting diode)

délabré dilapidated

délacer loosen, unlace

délai *m* (*temps imparti*) time
allowed; (*date limite*) deadline; (*prolongation*) extension; **sans ~** without delay

délaisser (*abandonner*)
leave; (*négliger*) neglect

délassement *m* relaxation;
délasser: se ~ relax

délateur, -trice *m/f* informer;
délation *f* denunciation

délayer dilute, water down;
fig: discours pad out

délecter: se ~ de take delight
in

délégué, ~e *m/f* delegate; **déléguer** delegate

délibération *f* deliberation;
(*décision*) resolution; **délibéré** deliberate; **délibérer**
deliberate

délicat delicate; *problème*
tricky; (*plein de tact*) tactful;
délicatesse *f* delicacy; (*tact*)
tact; **délicatement** deli-
cately

délicieux, -euse delicious

délier loosen, untie; **~ la langue à qn** loosen s.o.'s
tongue

délimiter define

délinquance *f* crime, delinquency

délire *m* delirium; *enthousiasme* frenzy; **foule en ~** ecstatic crowd; **délirer** be deliri-
ous; **être fou** be stark rav-
ing mad

délit *m* offence, *Br* offence;
commettre un ~ de fuite
leave the scene of an accident

délivrance *f* release; (*soulagement*) relief; (*livraison*)
delivery; *certificat* issue

délivrer release; (*livrer*) deliver; *certificat* issue

délocaliser relocate

déloyal disloyal; **concurrence** *f* **~e** unfair competition

deltaplane *m* hang-glider;
faire du ~ go hang-gliding

déluge *m* flood

demain tomorrow; **à ~!** see
you tomorrow!

demande *f* (*requête*) request;
écrite application; ÉCON demand; **sur** *ou* **à la ~ de** at
the request of; **demandé**
popular, in demand; **de-
mander** ask for; *somme
d'argent* ask; (*nécessiter*) call
for; **~ qch à qn** ask s.o. for
sth; (*vouloir savoir*) ask
s.o. sth; **~ à qn de faire qc**
ask s.o. to do sth; **se ~ si**
wonder if

démanger: *le dos me démange* my back itches; *ça me démange depuis longtemps* I've been itching to do it for ages

démanteler dismantle

démaquillant *m* cleanser; *lait m* ~ cleansing milk; **démaquiller**: *se* ~ take off one's make-up

démarcation *f* demarcation

démarchage *m* selling

démarche *f* step (*aussi fig*); *faire des ~s* take steps

démarquer: *se* ~ stand out (*de* from)

démarrage *m* start; **démarrer** start (up)

démasquer unmask

démêlé *m* argument; *avoir des ~s avec la justice* have problems with the law; **démêler** disentangle; *fig* clear up

déménager move; **déménageurs** *mpl* movers, removal men

démence *f* dementia; **dément** demented; *c'est* ~ *fig F* it's unbelievable

démener: *se* ~ struggle; (*s'efforcer*) make an effort

démenti *m* denial

démentir (*nier*) deny; (*infirmer*) belie

démerder: *se* ~ F manage, sort things out

démesuré enormous; *orgueil* excessive

démettre *poignet* dislocate;

se ~ *de ses fonctions* resign one's office

demeure *f* residence; **demeurer** (*habiter*) live; (*rester*) stay, remain; **demeuré** retarded

demi 1 *adj* half; *une heure et* ~*e* an hour and a half; *il est quatre heures et* ~*e* it's four thirty, it's half past four **2** *adv* half; *à* ~ 3 *m* half; *bière à* ~ a pint; *en football, rugby* halfback

demi-cercle *m* semi-circle

demi-finale *f* semi-final

demi-frère *m* half-brother

demi-heure *f* half-hour

démilitariser demilitarize

demi-litre *m* half liter *ou Br* litre

demi-mot: *il nous l'a dit à* ~ he hinted at it to us

demi-pension *f* American plan, *Br* half board

demi-pression *f* half-pint of draft *ou Br* draught beer

demi-sel *m* slightly salted butter

demi-sœur *f* half-sister

démission *f* resignation; *fig* renunciation; **démissionner 1** *v/i* resign; *fig* give up **2** *v/t* sack

demi-tarif *m* half price

demi-tour *m* AUTO U-turn; *faire* ~ *fig* turn back

démocrate democrat; **démocratie** *f* democracy

démodé old-fashioned

démographique demographic; **poussée** f ~ population growth

demoiselle f (*jeune fille*) young lady; ~ **d'honneur** bridesmaid

démolir demolish (*aussi fig*); **démolition** f demolition

démon m demon

démonstration f demonstration

démonter dismantle; *fig* disconcert

démontrer demonstrate, prove; (*faire ressortir*) show

démoraliser demoralize

démordre: *il n'en démordra pas* he won't change his mind

démotiver demotivate

démuni penniless

dénaturer distort

dénicher find

dénier deny

dénigrer denigrate

dénivellation f difference in height

dénombrer count

dénomination f name

dénoncer denounce; *à la police* report; *contrat terminate*; *se ~ à la police* give o.s. up to the police; **dénonciateur, -trice** m/f informer; **dénonciation** f denunciation

dénoter indicate, denote

dénouement m ending; **dénouer** loosen; *se ~ fig d'une scène* end; *d'un mystère* be cleared up

denrée f: ~**s** (*alimentaires*) foodstuffs

dense dense; **densité** f density; *du brouillard, d'une forêt* denseness

dent f tooth; *j'ai mal aux ~s* I've got toothache; *avoir une ~ contre qn* have a grudge against s.o.; **dentaire** dental

dentelle f lace

dentier m false teeth *pl*; **dentifrice** m toothpaste; **dentiste** m/f dentist

dénuder strip

dénué: ~ *de qc* devoid of sth; ~ *de tout* deprived of everything; **denuement** m destitution

déodorant m deodorant

dépannage m AUTO *etc* repairs *pl*; (*remorquage*) recovery; **dépanner** repair; (*remorquer*) recover; ~ *qn fig* f help s.o. out; **dépanneur** m repairman; *pour voitures* mechanic; **dépanneuse** f wrecker, *Br* tow truck

départ m departure; SP, *fig* start; *au ~* at first

départager decide between

départemental departmental; *route ~* e secondary road

dépassé out of date, old-fashioned; **dépasser** *personne* pass; AUTO pass, *Br* overtake; *but etc* overshoot; *fig* exceed; *se ~* surpass o.s.

dépaysement m disorienta-

dépression

tion; *changement agréable* change of scene

dépêcher dispatch; *se ~ de faire qch* hurry to do sth; *dépêche-toi!* hurry up!

dépendance *f* dependence; *~s bâtiments* outbuildings; *entraîner une (forte) ~* be (highly) addictive; **dépendre**: *~ de* depend on; *moralement* be dependent on

dépens *mpl*: *aux ~ de* at the expense of

dépense *f* expenditure; *d'essence, d'électricité* consumption, use; **dépenser** spend; *son énergie, ses forces* use up; *essence* consume, use; *se ~* exert o.s., be physically active; **dépensier, -ère 1** *adj* extravagant **2** *m/f* spendthrift

dépérir waste away; *fig d'une entreprise* go downhill

dépeuplement *m* depopulation

dépilatoire: *crème f ~* hair remover, depilatory cream

dépistage *m d'un criminel* tracking down; *MÉD* screening

dépit *m* spite; *en ~ de* in spite of

dépité crestfallen

déplacé out of place; *(inconvenant)* uncalled for; *POL* displaced; **déplacer** move; *personnel* transfer; *problème* shift the focus of; *se ~* move; *(voyager)* travel

déplaire: *~ à qn (fâcher)* offend s.o.; *cela lui déplaît de faire ...* he dislikes doing ...

déplaisant unpleasant

dépliant *m* leaflet; **déplier** unfold

déploiement *m* MIL deployment; *de forces, courage* display

déplorable deplorable

déporter POL deport; *se ~ d'un véhicule* swing

déposer 1 *v/t* put down; *armes* lay down; *passager* drop; *roi* depose; *argent, boue* deposit; *projet de loi* table; *ordures* dump; *plainte* lodge **2** *v/i d'un liquide* settle; JUR testify; *se ~ de la boue* settle; **dépôt** *m* deposit; *chez le notaire* lodging; *d'un projet de loi* tabling; *des ordures* dumping; *(entrepôt)* depot

dépouiller *animal* skin; *(voler)* rob *de* of; *(examiner)* go through; *~ le scrutin ou les votes* count the votes

dépourvu: *~ de* devoid of; *prendre qn au ~* take s.o. by surprise

dépoussiérer dust; *fig* modernize

dépraver deprave

déprécier *chose* decrease the value of; *personne* belittle; *se ~* depreciate, lose value; *d'une personne* belittle o.s.

dépression *f* depression; **fai-**

re une ~ be depressed
déprime f depression; **déprimer** depress
dépuceler deflower
depuis 1 prép since; *espace* from; *j'attends ~ une heure* I have been waiting for an hour; ~ *quand permettent--ils que …?* since when do they allow …? **2** adv since **3** conj: ~ *que* since
député m POL MP, Member of Parliament; ~ *européen* m Euro MP
déraciner uproot; (*extirper*) root out, eradicate
dérailler go off the rails; *fig* F: *d'un mécanisme* go on the blink; (*déraisonner*) talk nonsense; **dérailleur** m *d'un vélo* derailleur
déraisonnable unreasonable
dérangement m disturbance; **déranger** disturb
déraper AUTO skid
déréglé *vie* wild
déréglementer deregulate
dérégler *mécanisme* upset
dérision f derision; *tourner en* ~ deride
dérisoire derisory, laughable
dérivatif m diversion; **dériver 1** v/t MATH derive; *cours d'eau* divert **2** v/i MAR, AVIAT drift; ~ *de d'un mot* be derived from
dermatologue m/f dermatologist
dernier, -ère last; (*le plus récent*) *mode, roman etc* latest;

extrême utmost; *ce* ~ the latter; **dernièrement** recently, lately
dérobée: *à la* ~ furtively; **dérober** steal; ~ *qch à qn* rob s.o. of sth, steal sth from s.o.; *se* ~ *à discussion* shy away from; *obligations* shirk
déroger JUR: ~ *à* make an exception to, depart from
déroulement m unfolding; *le* ~ *du projet* the running of the project; **dérouler** unroll; *bobine, câble* unwind; *se* ~ take place; *d'une cérémonie* go (off)
dérouter (*déconcerter*) disconcert
derrière 1 adv behind **2** prép behind **3** m back; ANAT bottom; *de* ~ *patte etc* back *atr*
dès from, since; ~ *lors* from then on; (*par conséquent*) consequently; ~ *lundi* as of Monday; ~ *que* as soon as
désabuser disillusion
désaccord m disagreement
désaffecté disused; *église* deconsecrated
désagréable unpleasant, disagreeable
désappointement m disappointment
désapprobateur, -trice disapproving
désapprouver disapprove of
désarmement m MIL disarmament; **désarmer** disarm (*aussi fig*)
désarroi m disarray

désastre *m* disaster

désavantage *m* disadvantage; **désavantager** put at a disadvantage

désaveu *m* disowning; *d'un propos* retraction; **désavouer** disown; *propos* retract

descendance *f* descendants *pl*; **descendant**, **~e** *m/f* descendant

descendre 1 *v/i* go/come down; *d'un bus* get off; *d'une voiture* get out; *de température, prix* go down; *d'un chemin* drop; AVIAT descend; ~ *chez qn* stay with s.o.; ~ *de qn* be descended from s.o. 2 *v/t* (*porter vers le bas*) bring down; (*emporter*) take down; F (*abattre*) shoot down; *vallée, rivière* descend; ~ **les escaliers** come/go downstairs; **descente** *f* descent; (*pente*) slope; *en parachute* jump; ~ **de lit** bedside rug

description *f* description

désemparé at a loss

déséquilibré PSYCH unbalanced

désert 1 *adj* deserted; **une île ~e** a desert island 2 *m* desert; **déserter** desert; **déserteur** *m* MIL deserter

désertification *f* desertification

désertion *f* desertion

désespérant depressing

désespérer 1 *v/t* drive to despair 2 *v/i* despair

désespoir *m* despair; **en ~ de cause** in desperation

déshabillé *m* negligee; **déshabiller** undress; **se ~** get undressed

déshériter disinherit

déshonorer disgrace, bring dishnor *ou* Br dishonour on

déshydraté dehydrated; dessicated; *personne* dehydrated; **déshydrater**: **se ~** become dehydrated

design *m*: ~ **d'intérieurs** interior design

désigner (*montrer*) point to, point out; (*appeler*) call; (*nommer*) appoint (**pour** to), designate

désillusion *f* disillusionment

désinfectant *m* disinfectant

désintéressé disinterested, impartial; (*altruiste*) selfless; **désintéresser**: **se ~** de lose interest in

désintoxication *f*: **faire une cure de ~** go into detox

désinvolture *f* casualness

désir *m* desire; (*souhait*) wish

désirer want; *sexuellement* desire; ~ **faire qch** want to do sth; **désireux, -euse** eager (**de faire** to do)

désister POL: **se ~** withdraw, stand down

désobéir disobey; ~ **à** disobey; **désobéissant** disobedient désobligeant disagreeable

désodorisant *m* deodorant

désolé upset (*de* about, over); *je suis ~* I am so sorry

désopilant hilarious

désordre *m* untidiness; *en ~* untidy

désorganisé disorganized

désormais now, *à partir de maintenant* from now on

désosser remove the bones from

despote *m* despot; **despotique** despotic

dessécher dry out; *de fruits* dry

dessein *m* intention; *à ~* intentionally; *dans le ~ de faire qc* with the intention of doing sth

desserrer loosen

dessert *m* dessert

desservir *des transport publics* serve; (*s'arrêter à*) stop at; *table* clear; *~ qn* do s.o. a disservice

dessin *m* drawing; (*motif*) design; **dessiner** draw

dessoûler *V* sober up

dessous 1 *adv* underneath; *en ~* underneath 2 *m* underside; *ci~* below; *les voisins du ~* the downstairs neighbors

dessous-de-plat *m inv* table mat

dessus 1 *adv* on top; *sens ~ dessous* upside down; *en ~* on top; *par~* over; *ci~* above 2 *m* top; *les voisins*

du ~ the upstairs neighbors; *avoir le ~ fig* have the upper hand; **dessus-de-lit** *m inv* bedspread

déstabilisant unnerving; **déstabiliser** destabilize

destin *m* destiny, fate

destinataire *m* addressee; **destination** *f* destination; **destinée** *f* destiny; **destiner** mean, intend (*à* for)

destituer dismiss; MIL discharge

destructeur, -trice destructive; **destruction** *f* destruction

désuet, -ète obsolete; *mode* out of date

détachable detachable; **détacher** detach; *ceinture* undo; *chien* release; *employé* second; (*nettoyer*) clean; *~ sur* stand out against

détail *m* detail; COMM retail trade; *vendre au ~* sell retail; *prix m de ~* retail price; *en ~* detailed

détaillant *m* retailer

détartrage *m* descaling

détecteur *m* sensor

détective *m* detective

déteindre fade; *~ sur* come off on; *fig* rub off on

détendre slacken; *~ d'une corde* slacken; *fig* relax

détenir *m* JUR detain, hold

détente *f d'une arme* trigger; *fig* relaxation; POL détente

détention *f* holding; JUR detention

détenu, **~e** *m/f* inmate

détergent *m* detergent

détériorer damage; **se~** deteriorate

déterminant decisive; **déterminer** establish, determine

déterrer dig up

détester detest, hate

détonation *f* detonation

détour *m* detour; *d'un chemin, fleuve* bend; **sans ~** *fig*: dire qch straight out

détourné *fig* indirect; **détourner** trafic divert; *avion* hijack; *tête, yeux* turn away; *de l'argent* embezzle; **se ~** turn away

détresse *f* distress

détriment *m*: **au ~ de** to the detriment of

détritus *m* garbage, *Br* rubbish

détroit *m* strait

détromper put right

détruire destroy; *(tuer)* kill

dette *f* debt

deuil *m* mourning; *il y a eu un ~ dans sa famille* there's been a bereavement in the family

deux 1 *adj* two; **les ~** both; **nous ~** the two of us, both of us; **~ fois** twice 2 *m* two; **en ~** in two, in half; **à ou par ~** in twos, two by two; **deuxième** second; *étage* third; *Br* second; **deux-pièces** *m inv* bikini two-piece swimsuit; *appartement* two-room apartment; **deux-**

-points *m inv* colon

dévaliser banque rob, raid; *maison* burglarize, *Br* burgle; *personne* rob; *fig*: frigo raid

dévalorisant demeaning; **dévalorisation** *f* drop in value; *fig* belittlement; **dévaloriser** devalue; *fig* belittle

dévaluation *f* devaluation; **dévaluer** devalue

devancer be ahead of; *désir, objection* anticipate

devant 1 *adv* in front; **droit ~** straight ahead 2 *prép* in front of; **passer ~ l'église** go past the church; **~ Dieu** before God 3 *m* front

devanture *f* shop window

dévaster devastate

développement *m* development; **développer** develop; **se ~** develop

devenir become; *il devient vieux* he's getting old; *que va-t-il ~?* what's going to become of him?

dévergondé *sexuellement* promiscuous

déverser ordures dump; *passagers* disgorge

dévêtir undress

déviation *f* d'une route detour; *(écart)* deviation

dévier 1 *v/t* divert, reroute 2 *v/i* deviate (**de** from)

deviner guess

devis *m* estimate

dévisager stare at

devise *f* FIN currency; *(moto,*

règle de vie motto; **~s étrangères** foreign currency

dévisser unscrew

dévoiler unveil; *secret* reveal, disclose

devoir 1 *v/t de l'argent* owe **2** *v/aux:* **il doit le faire** he has to do it, he must do it; **il aurait dû me le dire** he should have told me; **tu devrais l'acheter** you should buy it; **ça doit être cuit** it should be done **3** *m* duty; *pour l'école* homework

dévorer devour

dévouement *m* devotion; **dévouer: se ~ pour** dedicate one's life to

dextérité *f* dexterity, skill

diabète *m* diabetes *sg*

diable *m* devil; **diabolique** diabolical

diagnostic *m* MÉD diagnosis; **diagnostiquer** MÉD diagnose

diagonal, ~e 1 *adj* diagonal **2** *f* diagonal (line); **en ~e** diagonally

diagramme *m* diagram

dialogue *m* dialog, *Br* dialogue

diamant *m* diamond

diamètre *m* diameter

diapositive *f* slide

diarrhée *f* diarrhea, *Br* diarrhoea

dictateur *m* dictator; **dictature** *f* dictatorship

dictée *f* dictation

dictionnaire *m* dictionary

diesel *m* diesel

diète *f* diet

Dieu *m* God; **~ merci!** thank God!

diffamer slander

différence *f* difference; **différencier** differentiate

différend *m* dispute

difficile difficult; *(exigeant)* hard to please; **difficulté** *f* difficulty

difformité *f* deformity

diffusion *f* spread; RAD, TV broadcast; *de chaleur etc* diffusion

digérer digest

digestion *f* digestion

digital digital; **empreinte** *f* **~e** fingerprint

digne *(plein de dignité)* dignified; **~ de** worthy of; **dignité** *f* dignity; *(charge)* office

digue *f* dyke

dilapider squander

dilater expand; *pupille* dilate

dilemme *m* dilemma

diluer dilute

dimanche *m* Sunday

dimension *f* dimension; *(taille)* size; *d'une faute* magnitude

diminuer 1 *v/t nombre, prix* reduce; *joie, forces* diminish; *mérites* detract from; *souffrances* lessen, decrease **2** *v/i* decrease

diminutif *m* diminutive; **diminution** *f* decrease, decline; *d'un nombre, prix* reduction

dinde f turkey; **dindon** m turkey

dîner 1 v/i dine **2** m dinner

dingue F crazy, nuts F

diplomate m diplomat; **diplomatie** f diplomacy

diplôme m diploma; *universitaire* degree; **diplômé** diploma holder; *de l'université* graduate

dire say; (*informer, réveler, ordonner*) tell; **~ à qn de faire qch** tell s.o. to do sth; **à vrai ~** to tell the truth; **cela va sans ~** that goes without saying

direct direct; **en ~** *émission* live; **directement** directly; **directeur, -trice** *adj comité* management **2** m/f manager; *plus haut dans la hiérarchie* director; ÉDU principal, Br head teacher; **direction** f (*sens*) direction; (*gestion, directeurs*) management; AUTO steering; **~ assistée** power steering; **directive** f instruction; *de l'UE* directive

dirigeant m leader; **diriger** manage, run; *pays* lead; *orchestre* conduct; *voiture* steer; *arme, critique* aim (*contre* at); *regard, yeux* turn (*vers* to); *personne* direct; **se ~ vers** head for

discerner make out; **~ le bon du mauvais** tell good from bad

discipline f discipline

disc-jockey m disc jockey,

DJ

discontinu *ligne* broken; *effort* intermittent

discorde f discord

discothèque f (*boîte*) discotheque, disco; *collection* record library

discours m speech

discréditer discredit

discret, -ète (*qui n'attire pas l'attention*) unobtrusive; *couleur* quiet; *robe* simple; (*qui garde le secret*) discreet; **discrétion** f discretion

discrimination f discrimination

disculper clear, exonerate; **se ~** clear o.s.

discussion f discussion; (*altercation*) argument; **discuter** discuss; (*contester*) question

disjoncter 1 v/t ÉL break **2** v/i F be crazy; **disjoncteur** m circuit breaker

disparaître disappear; (*mourir*) die; *d'une espèce* die out; **faire ~** get rid of

disparition f disappearance; (*mort*) death; **espèce en voie de ~** endangered species

dispenser: **~ qn de (faire) qc** excuse s.o. from (doing) sth

disperser disperse; **se ~** (*faire trop de choses*) spread o.s. too thin

disponibilité f availability; **disponible** available

disposer (*arranger*) arrange;

~ de qn/qc have s.o./sth at one's disposal; **se ~ à faire qc** get ready to do sth

dispositif *m* device

disposition *f* (*arrangement*) arrangement; *d'une loi* provision; (*humeur*) mood; (*tendance*) tendency; **être à la ~ de qn** be at s.o.'s disposal; **avoir des ~s pour qch** have an aptitude for sth

disputer match play; **~ qc à qn** compete with s.o for sth; **se ~** quarrel, fight

disqualifier disqualify

disque *m* disk; SP discus; **~ compact** compact disc; **disquette** *f* diskette, disk; **~ de sauvegarde** backup disk

dissertation *f* ÉDU essay

dissimuler conceal, hide (**à** from)

dissiper dispel; *brouillard* disperse; *fortune* squander; **se ~ du brouillard** clear

dissoudre dissolve

dissuader: **~ qn de faire qc** dissuade s.o. from doing sth; persuade s.o. not to do sth; **dissuasion** *f* dissuasion

distance *f* distance; *prendre ses ~s avec qn* distance o.s. from s.o.; **distancer** outdistance

distiller distill; **distillerie** *f* distillery

distinct distinct; **~ de** different from; **distinctif, -ive** distinctive; **distinguer** (*percevoir*) make out; (*différen-*

cier) distinguish (**de** from); **se ~** (*être différent*) stand out (**de** from)

distraction *f* (*passe-temps*) amusement; (*inattention*) distraction

distraire *du travail, des soucis* distract (**de** from); (*divertir*) amuse, entertain; **se ~** amuse o.s.; **distrait** absent-minded

distribuer distribute; *courrier* deliver; **distributeur** *m* distributor; **~ automatique** vending machine

dit (*surnommé*) referred to as; (*fixé*) appointed

divaguer talk nonsense

divan *m* couch

diverger diverge; *d'opinions* differ

divers (*différent*) different, varied; *au pl* (*plusieurs*) various

diversifier diversify

diversion *f* diversion

diversité *f* diversity

divertir amuse, entertain; **divertissement** *m* amusement, entertainment

divin divine; **divinité** *f* divinity

diviser divide; **se ~** be divided (**en** into); **division** *f* division

divorce *m* divorce; **demander le ~** ask for a divorce; **divorcé, ~e** *m/f* divorcee; **divorcer** get a divorce (**d'avec** from) dix ten; **dix-huit** eighteen; **dixième** tenth; **dix-neuf** nineteen; **dix-sept** seventeen; **dizaine** *f*: *une ~ de* about ten, ten or so

D.J. *m/f* (= *disc-jockey*) DJ, deejay (= disc jockey)

docile docile

docteur *m* doctor; **doctorat** *m* doctorate, PhD

doctrine *f* doctrine

document *m* document; **documentation** *f* documentation; **documenter**: *se ~* collect information

dodu chubby

dogmatique dogmatic

doigt *m* finger; *~ de pied* toe; *croiser les ~s* keep one's fingers crossed

dollar *m* dollar

domaine *m* estate; *fig* domain

dôme *m* dome

domestique 1 *adj* domestic **2** *m* servant

domicile *m* place of residence; **domicilié**: *~ à* resident at

domination *f* domination; **dominer 1** *v/t* dominate **2** *v/i* (*prédominer*) be predominant; *se ~* control o.s.

dommage *m*: (**quel**) *~!* what a pity!; *c'est ~ que* (+ *subj*) it's a pity (that); *~s et intérêts* JUR damages

dompter *animal* tame; *rebelle* subdue; **dompteur** *m* trainer

DOM-TOM *mpl* (= *département-*

ments et territoires d'outre-mer) overseas departments and territories of France

don *m* donation; (*cadeau, aptitude*) gift; *~ du ciel* godsend; **donation** *f* donation

donc *conclusion* so; *écoutez ~!* do listen!; *comment ~?* how (so?)!; *allons ~!* come on!

données *fpl* data *sg* (*aussi* INFORM), information; **donner 1** *v/t* give **2** *v/i*: *~ sur la mer* look onto the sea

dont whose; *le film ~ elle parlait* the movie she was talking about; *la manière ~ elle me regardait* the way (in which) she was looking at me

doré *bijou* gilded; *couleur* golden

dorénavant from now on

dorer gild

dormeur, -euse *m/f* sleeper; **dormir** sleep

dortoir *m* dormitory

dos *m* back; *~ d'âne m* speed bump; *pont* hump-backed bridge

dose *f* MÉD dose; PHARM proportion; **doser** measure out

dossier *m* d'une chaise back *f*; *de documents* file, dossier; *~ médical* medical record

douane *f* customs *pl*; **douanier, -ère 1** *adj* customs *atr* **2** *m/f* customs officer

double 1 *adj* double **2** *m*

deuxième exemplaire duplicate; *au tennis* doubles (match); *le ~* double, twice as much; **doubler 1** *v/t* double; *auto* pass, *Br* overtake; *film* dub; *vêtement* line **2** *v/i* double; **doublure** *f d'un vêtement* lining

doucement gently; *(bas)* softly; *(lentement)* slowly; **douceur** *f d'une personne* gentleness; *~s (jouissance)* pleasures; *(sucreries)* sweet things

douche *f* shower; **prendre une ~** shower, take a shower

doué gifted; *~ de qc* endowed with sth

douleur *f* pain

douloureux, -euse painful

doute *m* doubt; **sans ~** without doubt; **sans aucun ~** undoubtedly; **douter:** *~ de qn/qch* doubt s.o./sth; *se ~ que* suspect that; **douteux, -euse** doubtful

doux, douce sweet; *temps* mild; *personne* gentle; *au toucher* soft

douzaine *f* dozen; **douze** twelve; **douzième** twelfth

dragée *f* sugared almond

draguer *rivière* dredge; *F femmes* try to pick up; **dragueur** *m* F ladies' man

dramatique dramatic; **dramatiser** dramatize; **drame** *m* drama

drap *m de lit* sheet

drapeau *m* flag

drap-housse *m* fitted sheet

dresser put up; *contrat* draw up; *animal* train; *~ qn contre qn* set s.o. against s.o.; *se ~* straighten up; *d'une tour* rise up; *d'un obstacle* arise

drogue *f* drug; *~ douce* soft drug; *~ récréative* recreational drug; **drogué, ~e** *m/f* drug addict; **droguer** drug; *se ~* take drugs; *MÉD (traiter)* give medication to; *se ~* take drugs; *MÉD péj* pop pills; **droguerie** *f* hardware store

droit 1 *adj côté* right; *ligne* straight; *(debout)* erect; *(honnête)* upright **2** *adv* **tout ~** straight ahead **3** *m* right; *(taxe)* fee; *JUR* law; *être en ~ de faire qch* be entitled to do sth; *~s d'auteur* royalties

droite *f* right; *côté* right-hand side; *à ~* on the right(-hand side)

drôle funny; *une ~ d'idée* a funny idea

dubitatif, -ive doubtful

duc *m* duke

duchesse *f* duchess

duel *m* duel

dûment *adv* duly

dune *f* (sand) dune

Dunkerque Dunkirk

duper dupe

duplex *m* duplex

duquel → **lequel**

dur 1 *adj* hard; *climat* harsh;

viande tough **2** *adv* travailler, frapper hard

durable durable, lasting; *croissance, utilisation de matières premières* sustainable

durant during; *des années ~* for years

durcir 1 *v/t* harden **2** *v/i*: *se ~* harden

durée *f* duration; *~ de vie* life; *d'une personne* life expectancy

durement harshly; *être frappé ~ par* be hard hit by

durer last

duvet *m* down; *(sac de couchage)* sleeping bag

DVD *m* DVD (= digitally versatile disk)

dynamique 1 *adj* dynamic **2** *f* dynamics

dynamo *f* dynamo

dyslexique dyslexic

E

eau *f* water; *tomber à l'~* fall in the water; *fig* fall through; *~ courante* running water; *~ gazeuse* carbonated water, *Br* fizzy water; *~ de Javel* bleach

eau-de-vie *f* brandy

ébahi dumbfounded

ébaucher *tableau, roman* rough out; *texte* draft; *~ un sourire* smile faintly

ébéniste *m* cabinetmaker

éblouir dazzle *(aussi fig)*

éboueur *m* garbageman, *Br* dustman

éboulement *m* landslide

ébouriffé tousled; **ébouriffer** *cheveux* ruffle

ébranler shake; *s'~* move off

ébriété *f* inebriation

ébruiter *nouvelle* spread

ébullition *f* boiling point; *être en ~* be boiling

écaille *f de coquillage, tortue*

shell; *de poisson* scale; *de peinture, plâtre* flake; *matière ~* tortoiseshell; **écailler** *poisson* scale; *huître* open; *s'~ de peinture* flake (off); *de vernis à ongles* chip

écart *m (intervalle)* gap; *(différence)* difference; *(indiscrétion)*; *à l'~* at a distance *(de* from)

écarter *jambes* spread; *fig: idée* reject; *danger* avert; *s'~ (s'éloigner)* stray from

écervelé scatterbrained

échafaudage *m* scaffolding

échancré low-cut

échange *m* exchange; *~s extérieurs* foreign trade; *en ~* in exchange *(de* for); **échanger** exchange *(contre* for); **échangeur** *m* interchange

échantillon *m* comm sample

échappement *m* AUTO exhaust; *tuyau m d'~* tail pipe;

échapper *d'une personne* ~ **à qn** escape from s.o.; ~ **à qc** escape sth; *l'*~ **belle** have a narrow escape; *s'*~ escape

écharde *f* splinter

écharpe *f* scarf; *de maire* sash; **en** ~ MÉD in a sling

échauffer heat; *s'*~ SP warm up; ~ **les esprits** get people excited

échéance *f d'un contrat* expiration date, *Br* expiry date; *de police* maturity

échec *m* failure; **essuyer un** ~ meet with failure

échecs *mpl* chess; **jouer aux** ~ play chess

échelle *f* ladder; *d'une carte, des salaires* scale; **à l'**~ **mondiale** on a global scale

échelonner space out; *paiements* spread, stagger (**sur un an** over a year)

échevelé disheveled, *Br* dishevelled

échiner F: *s'*~ **à faire qch** go to great lengths to do sth

échiquier *m* chessboard

écho *m* echo

échotier, -ère *m/f* gossip columnist

échouer fail; (*s'*)~ *d'un bateau* run aground

éclabousser spatter

éclair *m* flash of lightning; CUIS eclair; **comme un** ~ in a flash; **éclairage** *m* lighting

éclaircie *f* clear spell; **éclaircir** lighten; *fig*: *mystère* clear up; *s'*~ *du ciel* clear

éclairer light; ~ **qn** light the way for s.o.; *fig* enlighten s.o.

éclat *m de verre* splinter; *de métal* gleam; *des yeux* sparkle; *de couleurs, fleurs* vividness; ~ **de rire** peal of laughter; **un** ~ **d'obus** a piece of shrapnel; **éclatant** dazzling, *couleur* vivid; *rire* loud; **éclater** *d'une bombe* blow up, explode; *d'un ballon, pneu* burst; *d'un coup de feu* ring out; *d'une guerre, d'un incendie* break out; *fig*: *d'un groupe, parti* break up; ~ **en sanglots** burst into tears

éclipser eclipse (*aussi fig*); *s'*~ F vanish, disappear

éclore *d'un oiseau* hatch out; *de fleurs* open

écluse *f* lock

écœurement *m* disgust; (*découragement*) discouragement; **écœurer** disgust, sicken; (*décourager*) dishearten; ~ **qn** *d'un aliment* make s.o. feel nauseous

école *f* school; ~ **maternelle** nursery school; ~ **primaire** elementary school, *Br* primary school ~ **publique** state school; ~ **qn** schoolboy; **écolière** *f* schoolgirl

écologie *f* ecology; **écologique** ecological

économe economical, thrifty

économie *f* economy; *science*

economics *sg*; **~ souterraine** black economy; **~s** savings; **économiser** save; **~ sur qc** save on sth; **économiseur** *m* **d'écran** INFORM screen saver

écorce *f* *d'un arbre* bark; *d'un fruit* rind

écorcher *animal* skin; (*égratigner*) scrape; *fig: nom, mot* murder

écossais, ~e Scottish; **Écossais, ~e** *m/f* Scot; **Écosse** *f*: **l'~** Scotland

écoulement *m* flow; COMM sale; **écouler** COMM sell; **s'~** flow; *du temps* pass; COMM sell

écourter shorten; *vacances* cut short

écoute *f*: **être à l'~** be always listening out; **aux heures de grande ~** RAD at peak listening times; TV at peak viewing times; **écouter 1** *v/t* listen to **2** *v/i* listen; **écouteur** *m* TÉL receiver; **~s** RAD headphones

écran *m* screen; **porter à l'~** TV adapt for television; **~ tactile** touch screen; **~ total** sunblock

écrasant overwhelming; **écraser** crush; *cigarette* stub out; (*renverser*) run over; **s'~ au sol** *d'un avion* crash

écrémé: **lait** *m* **~** skimmed milk

écrevisse *f* crayfish

écrier: **s'~** cry out

écrire write; **comment est-ce que ça s'écrit?** how do you spell it?; **écrit** *m* document; **l'~** *examen* the written exam; **par ~** in writing; **écriteau** *m* notice; **écriture** *f* writing; COMM entry; **les (Saintes) Écritures** Holy Scripture

écrivain *m* writer

écrou *m* nut

écrouler: **s'~** collapse

écru *couleur* natural

écueil *m* reef; *fig* pitfall

éculé *chaussure* worn-out; *fig* hackneyed

écume *f* foam

écureuil *m* squirrel

écurie *f* stable

édenté toothless

édifice *m* building; **édifier** erect; *fig* build up

éditer *livre* publish; *texte* edit; **éditeur, -trice** *m/f* publisher; (*commentateur*) editor; **édition** *f* publishing; *action de commenter* editing; (*tirage*) edition; **maison** *f* **d'~** publishing house; **éditorial** *m* editorial

édredon *m* eiderdown

éducatif, -ive educational; **education** *f* education; (*culture*) upbringing

éduquer educate; (*élever*) bring up

effacer erase; **s'~** *d'une inscription* wear away; *d'une personne* fade into the background

effarement *m* fear; **effarer**

frighten

effectif, -ive 1 *adj* effective **2** *m* manpower, personnel; **effectivement** true enough

effectuer carry out

efféminé *péj* effeminate

effervescent effervescent; *fig:* **foule** excited

effet *m* effect; COMM bill; **en ~** sure enough; **faire de l'~** have an effect; **~s** (personal) effects

efficace *remède* effective; *personne* efficient; **efficacité** *f* effectiveness; *d'une personne* efficiency

effleurer brush against; (*aborder*) touch on

effondrement *m* collapse; **effondrer: s'~** collapse

efforcer: s'~ de faire qch try very hard to do sth

effort *m* effort; **faire un ~** make an effort, try a bit harder

effraction *f* JUR breaking and entering

effrayant frightening; **effrayer** frighten; **s'~** be frightened (**de** at)

effroi *m* fear

effronterie *f* impertinence, effrontery

effroyable terrible, dreadful

égal 1 *adj* equal; *surface* even; *vitesse* steady; **ça lui est ~** it's all the same to him **2** *m* equal; **sans ~** unequaled, *Br* unequalled; **également** (*pareillement*) equally; (*aus-*

si) as well, too; **égaler** equal; **égaliser 1** *v/t haies, cheveux* even up; *sol* level **2** *v/i* SP tie the game, *Br* equalize; **égalité** *f* equality; *en tennis* deuce; **être à ~** be level; *en tennis* be at deuce

égard *m:* **à cet ~** in that respect; **à l'~ de qn** to(ward) s.o.; **par ~ pour** out of consideration for; **~s** respect

égarer *personne* lead astray; *chose* lose; **s'~** get lost; *du sujet* stray from the point

égayer cheer up

église *f* church

égocentrique egocentric

égoïsme *m* selfishness, egoism; **égoïste 1** *adj* selfish **2** *m/f* egoist

égorger: ~ qn cut s.o.'s throat

égout *m* sewer

égoutter drain

égratignure *f* scratch

Égypte *f:* **l'~** Egypt; **égyptien; ~ne** Egyptian; **Égyptien; ~ne** *m/f* Egyptian

éjecter eject; F *personne* kick out

élaborer *projet* draw up

élan *m* momentum; F SP run-up; *de tendresse* upsurge; *de générosité* fit; (*vivacité*) enthusiasm

élancer *v/i:* **ma jambe m'élance** I've got shooting pains in my leg; **s'~** dash; SP take a run-up

élargir widen, broaden; *vêtement* let out; *débat* widen

élastique 1 *adj* elastic **2** *m* elastic; *de bureau* rubber band

électeur, -trice *m/f* voter; **élection** *f* election; **électorat** *m* droit franchise; *personnes* electorate

électricien, ~ne *m/f* electrician; **électricité** *f* electricity; *~ statique* (electricity); **électrique** electric; **électriser** electrify

électrocuter electrocute

électroménager: appareils *mpl* ~s household appliances

électronique 1 *adj* electronic; *livre* ~ e-book, electronic book **2** *f* electronics

élégance *f* elegance; **élégant** elegant

élément *m* element; (*composante*) component; *d'un puzzle* piece; *~s* (*rudiments*) rudiments; **élémentaire** elementary

éléphant *m* elephant

élevage *m* breeding; *~ (du bétail)* cattle farming

élève *m/f* pupil

élevé high; *esprit* noble; *style* elevated; *bien/mal ~* well/badly brought up; **élever** raise; *prix, température* raise, increase; *statue* put up, erect; *enfants* bring up, raise; *animaux* breed; *s'~* rise; *d'une tour* rise up; *d'un cri* go up; *s'~ contre* rise up against; *s'~ à* amount

to; **éleveur, -euse** *m/f* breeder

élimination *f* elimination; *des déchets* disposal; **éliminatoire** *f* qualifying round; **éliminer** eliminate; *difficultés* get rid of

élire elect

elle *f* she; *après prép* her; *chose* it

elle-même herself; *chose* itself

elles *fpl* they; *après prép* them

elles-mêmes themselves

éloigné remote

éloigner move away; *soupçon* remove; *s'~* move away (*de* from); *s'~ de qn* distance o.s. from s.o.

éloquence *f* eloquence; **éloquent** eloquent

élu, ~e 1 *adj*: *le président ~* the President elect **2** *m/f* POL (elected) representative

élucider *mystère* clear up; *question* clarify

émacié emaciated

e-mail *m* e-mail

émanciper emancipate; *s'~* become emancipated

emballage *m* packaging; **emballer** package; *fig* F thrill; *s'~ d'un moteur* race; *fig* F get excited; **emballé sous vide** vacuum packed

embargo *m* embargo

embarquer 1 *v/t* load **2** *v/i ou s'~* embark; *s'~ dans* F get involved in

embarras m difficulty; (gêne) embarrassment; *être dans l'~* be in an embarrassing position; *sans argent* be short of money; **embarrassant** embarrassing; (encombrant) cumbersome; **embarrasser** embarrass; (encombrer) escaliers clutter up

embaucher take on, hire

embellir 1 v/t make more attractive; fig embellish **2** v/i become more attractive

embêtant F annoying; **embêter** F (ennuyer) bore; (contrarier) annoy; *s'~* be bored

emblème m emblem

emboîter insert; *~ le pas à qn* fall into step with s.o. (aussi fig); *s'~* fit together

embolie f embolism

embonpoint m stoutness

embouchure f GÉOGR mouth; MUS mouthpiece

embouteillage m traffic jam

emboutir crash into

embranchement m branch; (carrefour) intersection, Br junction

embrasser kiss; période, thème take in, embrace; métier take up; *~ du regard* take in at a glance

embrayage m AUTO clutch; action letting in the clutch

embrouiller muddle; *s'~* get muddled

embryon m embryo

éméché F tipsy

émeraude f & adj emerald

émerger emerge

émerveiller amaze; *s'~* be amazed (*de* by)

émetteur m RAD, TV transmitter

émettre radiations etc give off, emit; RAD, TV broadcast, transmit; opinion voice; action, nouveau billet issue; *emprunt* float

émeute f riot

émietter crumble

émigration f emigration; **émigré, ~e** m/f emigré; **émigrer** emigrate

émincer cut into thin slices

éminent eminent

émission f emission; RAD, TV program, Br programme; COMM, FIN issue

emmagasiner store

emmêler fils tangle; fig muddle

emménager: *~ dans* move into

emmener take away

emmerder F: *~ qn* get on s.o.'s nerves; *s'~* be bored rigid

emmitoufler wrap up; *s'~* wrap up

émotion f emotion; F (frayeur) fright

émouvant moving; **émouvoir** (toucher) move; *s'~* be moved

emparer: *s'~ de* seize; clés, héritage grab; des doutes, de la peur overcome

empâter: *s'~* thicken

empêchement m: *j'ai eu un* ~ something has come up; **empêcher** prevent; ~ *qn de faire qc* prevent *ou* stop s.o. doing sth; (*il*) *n'empêche que* nevertheless

empereur m emperor

empiéter: ~ *sur* encroach on

empiffrer F: *s'~* stuff o.s.

empiler pile (up)

empire m empire; *fig* (*maîtrise*) control

empirer get worse, deteriorate

emplacement m site

emplette f purchase; *faire des ~s* go shopping

emplir fill; *s'~* fill (*de* with)

emploi m (*utilisation*) use; ÉCON employment; ~ *du temps* schedule, *Br* timetable; *chercher un* ~ be looking for work *ou* for a job

employé, ~*e* m/f employee; **employer** use; *personnel* employ; *s'~ à faire qc* strive to do sth; **employeur, -euse** m/f employer

empocher pocket

empoigner grab, seize

empoisonner poison

emporter take; *prisonnier* take away; (*entraîner, arracher*) carry away; *du courant* sweep away; *d'une maladie* carry off; *l'~ sur qn/qc* get the better of s.o./sth; *s'~* fly into a rage

empreinte f impression; *fig* stamp; ~ *génétique* genetic fingerprint

empresser: *s'~ de faire qc* rush to do sth; *s'~ auprès de qn* be attentive to s.o.

emprise f hold

emprisonnement m imprisonment; **emprisonner** imprison

emprunt m loan; **emprunter** borrow (*à* from); *chemin, escalier* take

ému moved, touched

en¹ *prép* in; *direction* to; *agir ~ ami* act as a friend; ~ *voiture* by car; ~ *or* of gold; *en même temps* while, when; *mode* by

en² *pron*: *qu'~ pensez-vous?* what do you think about it?; *il y ~ a deux* there are two (of them); *j'~ ai* I have some; *j'~ ai cinq* I have five; *je n'~ ai pas* I don't have any; *il ~ est mort* he died of it

encadrer *tableau* frame; *encadré de deux gendarmes* *fig* flanked by gendarmes

encaisser COMM take; *chèque* cash; *fig* take

en-cas m CUIS snack

encastrer build in

enceinte¹ *adj* pregnant

enceinte² f enclosure; ~ (*acoustique*) speaker

encens m incense

encercler encircle

enchaîner chain up; *fig*: *pensées, faits* link (up)

enchanté enchanted; ~*!* how do you do?; **enchanter** (*ra-*

vir) delight; (*ensorceler*) enchant

enchère f bid; *vente f aux ~s* auction

enchevêtrer tangle; *fig: situation confuse*; *s'~ de fils* get tangled up; *d'une situation* get muddled

enclin *être ~ à faire qch* be inclined to do sth

encoche f notch

encolure f neck; *tour de cou* neck (size)

encombrant cumbersome; *être ~ d'une personne* be in the way; **encombrer** *maison* clutter up; *rue, passage* block; *s'~ de* load o.s. down with

encore *de nouveau* again; (*toujours*) still; *pas ~* not yet; *~ une bière?* another beer?; *~ plus rapide* even faster

encourageant encouraging; **encourager** encourage; *projet, entreprise* foster

encrasser dirty; *s'~* get dirty

encre f ink

encyclopédie f encyclopedia

endetter *s'~* get into debt

endeuillé bereaved

endive f chicory

endolori painful

endommager damage

endormi asleep; *fig* sleepy; **endormir** send to sleep; *douleur* dull; *s'~* fall asleep

endosser *vêtement* put on; *responsabilité* shoulder; *chè-*

que endorse

endroit m (*lieu*) place; *d'une étoffe* right side

enduire *~ de* cover with; **enduit** m *de peinture* coat

endurance f endurance

endurcir harden

endurer endure

énergie f energy; **énergique** energetic; *protestation* strenuous

énervant irritating; **énerver** *~ qn* (*agacer*) get on s.o.'s nerves; (*agiter*) make s.o. edgy; *s'~* get excited

enfance f childhood

enfant m ou f child

enfer m hell (*aussi fig*)

enfermer lock up; *champ* enclose; *s'~* shut o.s. up

enfiler *aiguille* thread; *perles* string; *vêtement* slip on; *rue* turn into

enfin (*finalement*) at last; (*en dernier lieu*) lastly, last; (*bref*) in a word

enflammer set light to; *allumette* strike; MÉD inflame; *fig: imagination* fire; *s'~* catch; *imagination* become inflamed; *fig: de l'imagination* take flight

enfler swell; **enflure** f swelling

enfoncer 1 *v/t clou, pieu* drive in; *couteau* thrust, plunge (*dans* into); *porte* break down **2** *v/i dans sable etc* sink (*dans* into); *s'~* sink

enfreindre infringe

enfuir: **s'~** run away

engagement *m* (*obligation*) commitment; *personnel* recruitment; THÉÂT booking; (*mise en gage*) pawning

engager (*lier*) commit (**à** to); *personnel* hire; TECH (*faire entrer*) insert; *discussion* begin; (*entraîner*) involve (**dans** in); THÉÂT book; (*mettre en gage*) pawn; **s'~** (*se lier*) commit o.s. (**à faire qc** to doing sth); (*commencer*) begin; MIL enlist

engelure *f* chillblain

engendrer fig engender

engin *m* machine; MIL missile; F *péj* thing

englober include

engloutir (*dévorer*) devour, wolf down; fig engulf

engouffrer devour, wolf down; **s'~ dans** *de l'eau* pour in; fig: *dans un bâtiment* rush in; *dans une foule* be swallowed up by

engourdir numb; **s'~** go numb

engraisser fatten

engrenage *m* gear

engueuler F bawl out; **s'~** have an argument

énigme *f* enigma; (*devinette*) riddle

enivrer intoxicate; fig exhilarate

enjamber step across; *d'un pont* span

enjeu *m* stake

enjoliveur *m* AUTO wheel trim, hub cap

enjoué cheerful, good humored, Br good-humoured

enlèvement *m* (*rapt*) abduction, kidnap; **enlever** take away, remove; *vêtement* take off, remove; (*kidnapper*) abduct, kidnap; **~ qc à qn** take sth away from s.o.

enneigé *route* blocked by snow; *sommet* snow-capped

ennemi, ~e 1 *m/f* enemy **2** *adj* enemy *atr*

ennui *m* boredom; **~s** problems; **ennuyer** (*contrarier, agacer*) annoy; (*lasser*) bore; **s'~** be bored; **ennuyeux, -euse** (*contrariant*) annoying; (*lassant*) boring

énoncé *m* statement; *d'une question* wording; **énoncer** state; **~ des vérités** state the obvious

énorme enormous; **énormément** enormously; **~ de** F an enormous amount of

énormité *f* enormity

enquête *f* inquiry; *policière aussi* investigation; (*sondage d'opinion*) survey; **enquêter**: **~ sur** investigate

enraciné deep-rooted

enregistrement *m* registration; *de disques* recording; AVIAT check-in; **enregistrer** register; *disques* record; *bagages* check in

enrhumer: **s'~** catch (a) cold

enrichir enrich; **s'~** get richer

enrouer: *s'~* get hoarse

enrouler *tapis* roll up; ~ **qc autour de qch** wind sth around sth

enseignant, **~e** *m/f* teacher

enseignement *m* education; *d'un sujet* teaching; **enseigner** teach (*qc à qn* s.o. sth)

ensemble 1 *adv* (*simultanément*) together **2** *m* (*totalité*) whole; (*groupe*) group, set; MUS, *vêtement* ensemble; MATH set; *dans l'~* on the whole

ensevelir bury

ensoleillé sunny

ensommeillé sleepy

ensuite then; (*plus tard*) after

entacher smear

entaille *f* cut; (*encoche*) notch; **entailler** notch; *s'~ la main* cut one's hand

entamer start; *économies* make

entasser *choses* pile up; *personnes* cram

entendre hear; (*comprendre*) understand; (*vouloir dire*) mean; **~ faire qc** intend to do sth; **~ dire que** hear that; *s'~* (*avec qn*) get on (with s.o.); (*se mettre d'accord*) come to an agreement (with s.o.); *entendu regard* knowing; *bien ~* of course; **entente** *f* agreement

enterrement *m* burial; *cérémonie* funeral; **enterrer** bury

en-tête *m* heading; INFORM

header; COMM letterhead; *d'un journal* headline

entêtement *m* stubbornness; **entêter**: *s'~* persist (*dans* in; *à faire qc* in doing sth)

enthousiasme *m* enthusiasm; **enthousiasmer**: *s'~ pour* be enthusiastic about

enticher: *s'~ de personne* become infatuated with; *activité* develop a craze for

entier, **-ère** whole, entire; (*intégral*) intact; *confiance*, *satisfaction* full

entonnoir *m* funnel

entorse *f* MÉD sprain

entortiller (*envelopper*) wrap

entourage *m* entourage; (*bordure*) surround; **entourer**: ~ **de** surround with; *s'~ de* surround o.s. with

entraide *f* mutual assistance; **entraider**: *s'~* help each other

entrailles *fpl* intestines

entrain *m* liveliness; **entraînement** *m* SP training; TECH drive; **entraîner** (*charrier*, *emporter*) sweep along; SP train; *fig* result in; *frais entail*; *personne* drag; TECH drive; *s'~* train

entrave *f fig* hindrance; **entraver** hinder

entre between; *le meilleur d'~ nous* the best of us; ~ **autres** among other things

entrebâiller half open

entrechoquer: *s'~* knock against one another

envoyer

entrecôte f rib steak

entrée f entrance, way in; *ac-cès au théâtre, cinéma* admission; (*billet*) ticket; (*vestibule*) entry(way); cuis starter; inform *touche* enter (key); *de données* input; ~ **interdite** no admittance

entrejambe m crotch

entrelacer interlace

entremets m cuis dessert

entremise f: *par l'~ de* through (the good offices of)

entreposer store; **entrepôt** m warehouse

entreprenant enterprising; **entreprendre** undertake; **entrepreneur, -euse** m/f entrepreneur; **entreprise** f enterprise; (*firme*) company, business

entrer 1 v/i come/go in, enter; ~ *dans* come/go into, enter; *voiture* get into; *pays* enter; *catégorie* fall into; *l'armée, le parti etc* join 2 v/t bring in; inform input, enter

entre-temps in the meantime

entretenir *maison, machine etc* maintain; *famille* keep, support; *amitié* keep up; *s'~ de qc* talk to each other about sth

entretien m maintenance, upkeep; (*conversation*) conversation

entrevoir glimpse; *fig* foresee

entrevue f interview

entrouvrir half open

énumérer list, enumerate

envahir invade; *d'un sentiment* overwhelm; **envahissant** *personne* intrusive; *sentiments* overwhelming

enveloppe f *d'une lettre* envelope; **envelopper** wrap; **enveloppé de brume**, *mystère* enveloped in

envenimer poison (*aussi fig*)

envergure f *d'un oiseau, avion* wingspan; *fig* scope; *d'une personne* caliber, *Br* calibre

envers 1 *prép* toward, *Br* towards 2 *d'une feuille* reverse; *d'une étoffe*: wrong side; *à l'~* pull inside out; (*en désordre*) upside down

envie f (*convoitise*) envy; (*désir*) desire (*de* for); *avoir ~ de (faire) qc* want (to do) sth; **envier** envy; ~ *qc à qn* envy s.o. sth

environ 1 *adv* about 2 *mpl*: ~*s* surrounding area; *dans les* ~*s* in the vicinity

environnement m environment

envisager (*considérer*) think about; (*imaginer*) envisage

envoi m shipment; *d'un fax* sending

envoler: *s'~* fly away; *d'un avion* take off; *fig*: *du temps* fly

envoyé m envoy; *d'un journal* correspondent; **envoyer** send; *gifle* give

éolienne f wind turbine

épais, **~se** thick; *foule* dense; **épaisseur** f thickness; **épaissir** thicken

épancher: s'~ pour out one's heart (**auprès de** to)

épanouir s'~ blossom

épargne f saving; **~s** (*économies*) savings; **épargner 1** v/t save; *personne* spare; **~ qc à qn** spare s.o. sth **2** v/i save

éparpiller scatter

épars sparse

épatant F great, terrific; **épater** astonish

épaule f shoulder

épave f wreck (*aussi fig*)

épée f sword

épeler spell

éperdu *besoin* desperate; **~ de** beside o.s. with

épi m ear

épice f spice; **épicer** spice; **épicerie** f grocery store, *Br* grocer's; **épicier**, **-ère** m/f grocer

épidémie f epidemic

épier spy on; *occasion* watch for

épilepsie f epilepsy; **crise f d'~** epileptic fit

épiler remove the hair from

épinards mpl spinach

épine f *d'une rose* thorn; *d'un hérisson* spine, prickle; **épineux**, **-euse** *problème* thorny

épingle f pin; **~ de sûreté** safety pin; **tiré à quatre ~s**

fig well turned-out

Épiphanie f Epiphany

épisode m episode

éploré tearful

éplucher peel; *fig* scrutinize; **épluchures** fpl peelings

éponge f sponge; **éponger** sponge down; *flaque* sponge up; *déficit* mop up

époque f age, epoch, period; **meubles** mpl **d'~** period *ou* antique furniture

époumoner: s'~ F shout o.s. hoarse

épouse f wife; **épouser** marry; *principe etc* espouse

épousseter dust

époustouflant F breathtaking

épouvantable dreadful

épouvantail m scarecrow

épouvanter horrify; *fig* terrify

époux m husband; **les ~** the married couple

éprendre: s'~ de fall in love with

épreuve f trial; *SP* event; *imprimerie* proof; *photographie* print; **à toute ~** confiance *etc* never-failing; **à l'~ du feu** fireproof

éprouver test, try out; (*ressentir*) experience

épuisé exhausted; *livre* out of print; **épuiser** exhaust; **~ les ressources** be a drain on resources; **s'~** tire o.s. out (**à faire qch** doing sth); *d'une source* dry up

épurer purify
équateur *m* equator
équilibre *m* balance, equilibrium; **équilibrer** balance
équipage *m* crew
équipe *f* team; *d'ouvriers* gang; **~ de nuit** night shift; **~ de secours** rescue party; **équipement** *m* equipment; **équiper** equip (*de* with)
équitable just, equitable
équitation *f* riding
équivalent 1 *adj* equivalent (*à* to) **2** *m* equivalent
équivoque 1 *adj* equivocal, ambiguous **2** *f* ambiguity; (*malentendu*) misunderstanding
érable *m* BOT maple
érafler scratch; **éraflure** *f* scratch
ère *f* era
érection *f* erection
éreinter exhaust; **s'~** exhaust o.s. (*à faire qch* doing sth)
ériger erect; **s'~ en** set o.s. up as
érosion *f* erosion
érotisme *m* eroticism
errer roam; *des pensées* stray
erreur *f* mistake, error; **~ de calcul** miscalculation
érudit erudite; **érudition** *f* erudition
éruption *f* eruption; MÉD rash
escabeau *m* (*tabouret*) stool; (*marchepied*) stepladder
escalade *f* climbing; **~ de violence etc** escalation in; **escalader** climb

escalator *m* escalator
escale *f* stopover; **faire: ~ à** MAR call at; AVIAT stop over in
escalier *m* stairs *pl*, staircase; **dans l'~** on the stairs; **~ de secours** fire escape
escalope *f* escalope
escamoter (*dérober*) make disappear; *antenne* retract; *fig: difficulté* get around
escapade *f*: **faire une ~** get away from it all
escargot *m* snail
escarpement *m* slope
esclaffer: **s'~** guffaw, laugh out loud
esclavage *m* slavery; **esclave** *m/f* slave
escompte *m* discount; **escompter** discount; *fig* expect
escorter escort
escrime *f* fencing; **escrimer**: **s'~** fight, struggle (*à* to)
escroc *m* crook
espace *m* space; **espacer** space out; **s'~** become more and more infrequent
Espagne *f* Spain; **espagnol, ~e 1** *adj* Spanish **2** *m langue* Spanish; **Espagnol, ~e** *m/f* Spaniard
espèce *f* kind, sort (*de* of); BIOL species; **~ d'abruti!** *péj* idiot!; **en ~s** comm cash
espérer 1 *v/t* hope for; **~ que** hope that; **~ faire qc** hope to do sth **2** *v/i* hope; **~ en** trust in
espiègle mischievous

espion, ~ne *m/f* spy; **espionnage** *m* espionage, spying; **espionner** spy on

espoir *m* hope

esprit *m* spirit; *(intellect)* mind; *(humour)* wit

esquisse *f* sketch; *fig: d'un roman* outline; **esquisser** sketch; *fig: projet* outline

esquiver dodge; **s'~** slip away

essai *m* (test) test, trial; *(tentative)* attempt, try; *en rugby* try; *en littérature* essay; **à l'~** on trial

essaim *m* swarm

essayage *m:* **cabine** *f* **d'~** changing cubicle; **essayer** try; *(mettre à l'épreuve, évaluer)* test; *vêtement* try on; **~ de faire qc** try to do sth; **s'~ à qc** try one's hand at sth

essence *f* essence; *carburant* gas, *Br* petrol; *bot* species sg

essentiel, ~le 1 *adj* essential **2** *m:* **l'~** the main thing; *de sa vie* the main part

essieu *m* axle

essor *m fig* expansion

essorer wring out; *d'une machine à laver* spin

essoufflé out of breath

essuie-glace *m* (windshield) wiper, *Br* (windscreen) wiper; **essuie-mains** *m* hand-towel; **essuyer** wipe; *fig* suffer

est 1 *m* east **à l'~ de** (to the) east of **2** *adj* east, eastern

est-ce que: **~ c'est vrai?** is it true?; **est-ce qu'ils se por-**

tent bien? are they well?

esthéticienne *f* beautician

esthétique esthetic, *Br* aesthetic

estimatif, -ive estimated; **devis** *m* **~** estimate; **estimation** *f* estimation; *des coûts* estimate

estime *f* esteem; **estimer** *valeur* estimate; *(respecter)* have esteem for; *(croire)* feel, think; **s'~ heureux** consider o.s. lucky

estival summer *atr*

estomac *m* stomach

Estonie *f* Estonia

estrade *f* podium

estropier cripple

estuaire *m* estuary

et and; **~ ... ~ ...** both ... and ...

étable *f* cowshed

établi *m* workbench

établir *entreprise* establish, set up; *, contact, ordre* establish; *salaires, prix* fix; *facture, liste* draw up; *record* set; *culpabilité* establish, prove; *raisonnement, réputation* base (**sur** on); **s'~** *(s'installer)* settle; **établissement** *m* establishment; *de salaires, prix* setting; *d'une facture, liste* drawing up; *d'un record* setting; *d'une loi, d'un impôt* introduction

étage *m* floor, story, *Br* storey; *d'une fusée* stage

étagère *f meuble* bookcase,

shelves *pl*; *planche* shelf
étain *m* pewter
étalage *m* show; **faire ~ de
qch** show sth off; **étaler** *carte* spread out; *peinture, paiements* spread (**sur** over); *vacances* stagger; *marchandises* display; *fig* (*exhiber*)
show off; **s'~ de peinture**
spread; *de paiements* be
spread out (**sur** over); (*se
vautrer*) sprawl; *par terre* fall
flat
étanche watertight; **étancher**
make watertight
étang *m* pond
étape *f* lieu stopover, stopping place; *d'un parcours*
stage, leg; *fig* stage
état *m* state; (*liste*) statement,
list; **en tout ~ de cause** in
any case, anyway; **hors d'~**
out of order
États-Unis *mpl*: **les ~** the
United States
été *m* summer
éteindre *incendie, cigarette*
put out; *électricité, radio,
chauffage* turn off; *de
feu, lumière* go out; *de télé
etc* go off; *euph* (*mourir*)
pass away
étendre *malade, enfant* lay
(down); *beurre, enduit*
spread; *peinture* apply; *bras*
stretch out; *linge* hang up;
vin dilute; *sauce* thin; *influence* extend; **s'~** extend,
stretch (**jusqu'à** as far as,
to); *d'une personne* lie

down; *d'un incendie, d'une
maladie* spread; *d'un tissu*
stretch; **étendue** *f* extent;
d'eau expanse; *de connaissances, d'une catastrophe* extent
éternel, **~le** eternal; **éternité** *f*
eternity
éternuer sneeze
éthique 1 *adj* ethical **2** *f* ethics
étinceler sparkle; **étincelle** *f*
spark
étiqueter label (*aussi fig*)
étiquette *f* label; (*protocole*)
etiquette
étirer: **s'~** stretch
étoffe *f* material; **étoffer** *fig*
flesh out
étoile *f* star (*aussi fig*); **~ filante** falling star; *Br* shooting star; **~ de mer** starfish
étonnement *m* astonishment, surprise; **étonner** astonish, surprise; **s'~ de** be
astonished *ou* surprised at;
s'~ que (+ *subj*) be suprised
that
étouffant stifling, suffocating; **étouffée** CUIS: **à l'~**
braised; **étouffer** suffocate;
avec un oreiller smother, suffocate; *fig: bruit* quash; *révolte* put down, suppress;
cri smother; *scandale* hush
up
étourderie *f* foolishness; *action* foolish thing to do
étourdi foolish, thoughtless;
étourdir daze; **~ qn** *d'alcool,
de succès* go to s.o.'s head;

étourdissement m (vertige) dizziness, giddiness

étrange strange

étranger, -ère 1 adj strange; de l'étranger foreign **2** m/f stranger; de l'étranger foreigner **3** m: à l'~ abroad; investissement foreign, outward

étrangler strangle; fig: critique, liberté stifle

être 1 v/i he: **nous sommes lundi** it's Monday; **nous avons été éliminé** we were eliminated; **~ à qn** appartenir à belong to s.o. **2** v/aux have; **elle n'est pas encore arrivée** she hasn't arrived yet; **elle est arrivée hier** she arrived yesterday **3** m being; personne person

étreindre grasp; ami embrace, hug; de sentiments grip; **étreinte** f hug, embrace; de la main grip

étrenner use for the first time

étrennes fpl New Year's gift

étroit narrow; tricot tight, small; amitié close; **être ~ d'esprit** be narrow-minded

étroitesse f narrowness

étude f study; salle à l'école study room; de notaire office; activité practice; **faire des ~s** study; **~ de marché** market research; **étudiant, ~e** m/f student; **étudier** study

étui m case

étuvée CUIS: à l'~ braised

euphorique euphoric

euro m euro

Europe f: l'~ Europe; **européen, ~ne** European; **Européen, ~ne** m/f European

eux mpl they; après prép them

eux-mêmes mpl themselves

évacuation f evacuation

évadé m escaped prisoner, escapee; **évader: s'~** escape

évaluer (estimer) evaluate; tableau, meuble value; coût, nombre estimate

évanouir: s'~ faint; fig vanish, disappear

évaporer: s'~ evaporate

évasif, -ive evasive; **évasion** f escape

éveil m awakening; **en ~** alert; **éveiller** wake up; fig arouse; **s'~** wake up; fig be aroused

événement m event

éventail m fan; fig: de marchandises range

éventé boisson flat; **éventer** fan; fig: secret reveal

éventualité f eventuality, possibility; **éventuel, ~le** possible

évêque m bishop

évertuer: s'~ à faire qc try one's hardest to do sth

évident obvious

évier m sink

éviter avoid; **~ qc à qn** spare s.o. sth; **~ de faire qc** avoid doing sth

évoluer develop, evolve; **évolution** f development; BIOL evolution

évoquer *esprits* conjure up; ~ *un problème* bring up a problem

exact *nombre, poids* exact, precise; *reportage* accurate; *calcul, date, solution* right, correct; *personne* punctual; **exactitude** *f* accuracy; (*ponctualité*) punctuality

ex æquo: *être* ~ tie, draw

exagération *f* exaggeration; **exagérer** exaggerate

exalter excite; (*vanter*) exalt

examen *m* exam; MÉD examination; *passer un* ~ take an exam; *être reçu à un* ~ pass an exam; **examiner** examine

exaspérer exasperate

excédent *m* excess; *budgétaire, de trésorerie* surplus; ~ *de bagages* excess baggage; **excéder** exceed; (*énerver*) irritate

excellence *f* excellence; *Excellence* Excellency; **excellent** excellent; **exceller** excel (*dans* in; *en* in, at; *à faire qch* at doing sth)

excepté 1 *adj*: *la Chine* ~*e* except for China **2** *prép* except; ~ *que* except for the fact that; ~ *si* unless, except if; **excepter** exclude, except; **exception** *f* exception; *à l'* ~ *de* with the exception of; *exceptionnel*, ~*le* exceptional

excès *m* excess; *à l'* ~ to excess, excessively; ~ *de vitesse* speeding; **excessif, -ive**

excessive

excitation *f* excitement; (*provocation*) incitement (*à* to); *sexuelle* arousal; **exciter** excite; (*provoquer*) incite (*à* to); *sexuellement* arouse; *appétit* whet; *imagination* stir

exclamation *f* exclamation; **exclamer:** *s'*~ exclaim

exclure exclude

exclusion *f* expulsion; *à l'* ~ *de* to the exclusion of; (*à l'exception de*) with the exception of

exclusivité *f* COMM exclusivity, sole rights *pl*; *en* ~ exclusively

excursion *f* trip, excursion

excuse *f* excuse; ~*s* apology; **excuser** excuse; *s'*~ apologize (*de* for); *excusez-moi* excuse me

exécuter *ordre, projet* carry out; MUS perform; *loi, jugement* enforce; *condamné* execute; **exécution** *f* *d'un ordre, projet* carrying out; MUS performance; *d'une loi, un jugement* enforcement; *d'un condamné* execution

exemplaire 1 *adj* exemplary **2** *m* copy; (*échantillon*) sample; *en deux* ~*s* in duplicate

exemple *m* example; *par* ~ for example; *donner l'* ~ set a good example

exempt exempt (*de* from); *souci* free (*de* from); **exempter** exempt (*de* from);

exemption f exemption

exercer corps exercise; *influence* exert, use; *pouvoir* use; *profession* practice, Br practise; *mémoire* train; MIL drill; **s'~** (s'entraîner) practice, Br practise; **exercice** m exercise (*aussi* ÉDU); *d'une profession* practice; COMM fiscal year, Br financial year; MIL drill

exhiber exhibit; *document* produce; **s'~** make an exhibition of o.s.; **exhibitionniste** m exhibitionist

exigeant, ~e demanding; **exigence** f demand; **exiger** demand

exigu, ~ë tiny

exil m exile; **exilé, ~e** m/f exile; **exiler** exile; **s'~** go into exile

existence f existence; **exister** exist

exonérer exempt

exorbitant exorbitant

exotique exotic

expansion f expansion

expatrier *argent* move abroad *ou* out of the country; **s'~** settle abroad

expédier send; COMM ship, send; *travail* do quickly

expéditeur, -trice m/f sender; COMM shipper, sender; **expédition** f sending; COMM shipment; (*voyage*) expedition

expérience f experience; *scientifique* experiment

expérimenté experienced;

expérimenter (*tester*) test

expert, ~e adj & m/f expert; **expertise** f (*estimation*) valuation; JUR expert testimony

expier expiate

expiration f *d'un délai* expiration, Br expiry; *de souffle* exhalation; **expirer** *d'un contrat, délai* expire; (*respirer*) exhale; (*mourir*) die, expire fml

explication f explanation; **expliquer** explain; **s'~** explain o.s.; **s'~ avec qn** talk things over with s.o.

exploit m sportif, médical feat; *amoureux* exploit

exploitant, ~e m/f agricole farmer

exploitation f *d'une ferme, ligne aérienne* running; *du sol* farming; *de richesses naturelles péj*: des ouvriers exploitation; (*entreprise*) operation

exploiter ferme, ligne aérienne run; *sol* farm; *richesses naturelles* exploit (*aussi* péj)

explorateur, -trice m/f explorer; **explorer** explore

exploser explode (*aussi fig*); **~ de rire** crack up F; **explosif, -ive** adj & m explosive; **explosion** f explosion (*aussi fig*)

exportateur, -trice 1 adj exporting **2** m exporter; **exportation** f export; **exporter** export

exposé *m* account, report; ÉDU presentation; **exposer** *art, marchandise* exhibit, show; *problème, programme* explain; *à l'air, à la chaleur* expose (*aussi* PHOT); **exposition** *f d'art, de marchandise* exhibition; *d'un problème* explanation; *au soleil* exposure (*aussi* PHOT)

exprès[1] *adv* (*intentionnellement*) deliberately, on purpose; (*spécialement*) expressly

exprès[2], **-esse 1** *adj* express **2** *adj inv* **lettre f exprès** express letter

express 1 *adj inv* express **2** *m train* express; *café* espresso

expressément expressly

expression *f* expression

exprimer express; **s'~** express o.s.

expulser expel; *d'un pays* deport; **expulsion** *f* expulsion; *d'un pays* deportation

exquis exquisite

extase *f* ecstasy

extension *f des bras, jambes* stretching; (*prolongement*) extension; *d'une épidémie* spread; INFORM expansion

exténuer exhaust

extérieur 1 *adj* external; *mur aussi* outside **2** *m* (*partie externe*) outside, exterior; **à l'~ de** outside; **extérioriser** express, let out; **s'~** *d'un senti-*

ment find expression; *d'une personne* express one's emotions

exterminer exterminate

externaliser COM outsource

externe external

extincteur *m* extinguisher

extinction *f* extinction (*aussi* fig)

extirper *mauvaise herbe* pull up; MÉD remove; *fig renseignement* drag out

extorquer extort

extorsion *f* extortion

extraction *f* extraction

extrader extradite

extraire extract

extrait *m* extract

extraordinaire extraordinary

extraterrestre *m/f* extraterrestrial, alien

extravagance *f* extravagance; *d'une personne, d'une idée* eccentricity

extraverti extrovert

extrême 1 *adj* extreme **2** *m* extreme; **à l'~** to extremes

Extrême-Orient *m*: **l'~** the Far East

extrémiste *m/f* POL extremist; **extrémité** *f d'une rue* (very) end; *d'un doigt* tip; (*situation désespérée*) extremity; **~s** ANAT extremities

exubérant exuberant

exulter exult

eye-liner *m* eyeliner

F

fable f fable

fabricant, ~e m/f manufacturer, maker; **fabrication** f making; *industrielle* manufacture; **fabriquer** make; *industriellement aussi* manufacture; *histoire* fabricate

fabuleux, -euse fabulous

fac f (= **faculté**) uni, university

façade f façade

face f face; *d'une pièce* head; **en ~ (de)** opposite; **faire ~ à** face up to; **face-à-face** m inv face-to-face (debate)

fâché annoyed; **fâcher** annoy; **se ~** get annoyed; **se ~ avec qn** fall out with s.o.; **fâcheux, -euse** annoying; *(déplorable)* unfortunate

facile easy; *personne* easy-going; **facilement** easily; **facilité** f easiness; *à faire qch* ease; **~s de paiement** easy terms; **faciliter** make easier, facilitate

façon f *(manière)* way, method; **de ~ (à ce) que** (+*subj*) so that; **de toute ~** anyway, anyhow; **de cette ~** (in) that way; **à la ~ de** like, in the style of

facteur m mailman, *Br* postman; MATH, *fig* factor

factrice f mailwoman, *Br* postwoman

facture f bill; COMM invoice; **facturer** invoice

facultatif, -ive optional

faculté f faculty

fade insipid

faible 1 *adj* weak; *bruit, lumière, espoir* faint; *avantage* slight **2** m *pour personne* soft spot; *pour chocolat* ~ weakness; **faiblesse** f weakness; **faiblir** weaken

faille f GÉOL fault; *dans théorie* flaw

faillible fallible; **faillir**: **il a failli gagner** he almost won

faim f hunger; **avoir ~** be hungry; **mourir de ~** starve (*aussi fig*)

fainéant, ~e 1 *adj* idle, lazy **2** m/f idler

faire 1 v/t do; *robe, meuble, repas, liste* make; **~ de la natation/du ski** swim/ski, go swimming/skiing; **cinq plus cinq font dix** five and five are *ou* make ten; **ça ne fait rien** it doesn't matter; **~ rire qn** make s.o. laugh; **~ peindre la salle de bain** have the bathroom painted **2** v/i: **~ vite** hurry up, be quick *impersonnel*: **il fait chaud/froid** it's *ou* it's warm/cold **4**: **ça ne se fait pas** it's not done; **se ~ rare** become rarer; **se ~ à qc** get used to sth; **je ne m'en fais pas** I'm not worried

faisable feasible

faisan *m* pheasant

faisceau *m* bundle; *de lumière* beam

fait[1] *m* fact; *(action)* act; *(événement)* development; **au ~** by the way; **de ce ~** consequently; **en ~** in fact; **tout à ~** absolutely; **un ~ divers** a brief news item

fait[2] *adj*: **être ~ pour qn/qch** be made for s.o./sth; **c'est bien ~ pour lui** serves him right!

falaise *f* cliff

falloir: **il faut un visa** you need a visa, you have to have a visa; **il faut l'avertir** we have to warn him; **il me faut sortir, il faut que je sorte** *(subj)* I have to go out, I must go out; **s'il le faut** if necessary; **il aurait fallu prendre le train** we should have taken the train; **comme il faut** respectable; **il ne faut pas que je sorte** *(subj)* I mustn't go out

falsifier *argent* forge; *document* falsify; *vérité* misrepresent

famélique starving

fameux, -euse *(célèbre)* famous; *(excellent)* wonderful

familiariser familiarize; **familiarité** *f* familiarity; **familier, -ère** familiar

famille *f* family

famine *f* famine

fanatique 1 *adj* fanatical **2** *m/f* fanatic; **fanatisme** *m* fanaticism

faner: **se ~** fade

fanfare *f* *(orchestre)* brass band; *(musique)* fanfare; **fanfaron, ~ne 1** *adj* boastful **2** *m* boaster

fantaisie *f* imagination; *(caprice)* whim

fantasme *m* fantasy; **fantasmer** fantasize

fantasque strange, weird

fantastique 1 *adj* fantastic; *(imaginaire)* imaginary **2** *m*: **le ~** fantasy

fantôme *m* ghost

farce *f au théâtre* farce; *(tour)* joke; CUIS stuffing; **farceur, -euse** *m/f* joker; **farcir** CUIS stuff; *fig* cram

fard *m* make-up; **~ à paupières** eye shadow

fardeau *m* burden *(aussi fig)*

farder: **se ~** make up

farine *f* flour; **~ de maïs** corn starch, *Br* cornflour

farouche *(timide)* shy; *volonté, haine* fierce

fascination *f* fascination; **fasciner** fascinate

faste *m* pomp

fast-food *m* fast food restaurant

fastidieux, -euse tedious

fastueux, -euse lavish

fatal fatal; *(inévitable)* inevitable; **fatalisme** *m* fatalism;

fataliste 1 adj fatalistic **2** m/f fatalist; **fatalité** f fate

fatigant tiring; (agaçant) tiresome; **fatigue** f tiredness; **fatiguer** tire; (importuner) annoy; **se ~** get tired

faubourg m (working-class) suburb

fauché F broke F; **faucher** fig mow down; F (voler) pinch F

faufiler: se ~ dans une pièce slip into a room

faune f wildlife, fauna

faussaire m forger; **fausser** calcul, vérité distort; clef bend

faute f mistake; (responsabilité) fault; **par sa ~** because of him; **~ de** for lack of; **sans ~** without fail

fauteuil m armchair; **~ roulant** wheelchair

fauve 1 adj tawny **2** m félin big cat

faux, fausse 1 adj false; incorrect aussi wrong; bijoux imitation, fake; **fausse couche** f miscarriage; **~ témoignage** perjury **2** adv: **chanter ~** sing out of tune **3** m copie forgery, fake

faux-filet m CUIS sirloin

faux-monnayeur m counterfeiter, forger

faux-semblant m pretense, Br pretence

faveur f favor, Br favour; **de ~** traitement preferential; prix special; **en ~ de** in favor of

favorable favorable, Br fa-

vourable; **favori, ~te** m/f & adj favorite, Br favourite; **favoriser** favor, Br favour; faciliter, avantager promote; **favoritisme** m favoritism, Br favouritism

fax m fax; **faxer** fax

féconder fertilize; **fécondité** f fertility

fédéral federal; **fédération** f federation

fée f fairy

feeling m feeling; **avoir un bon ~ pour qc** have a good feeling about sth

feindre: ~ l'étonnement pretend to be astonished, feign astonishment; **~ de faire qch** pretend to do sth; **feinte** f feint

fêler: se ~ crack

félicitations fpl congratulations; **féliciter** congratulate (de on)

fêlure f crack

femelle f & adj female

féminin 1 adj feminine; sexe female; problèmes, magazines, mode women's **2** m GRAM feminine; **féministe** m/f & adj feminist; **féminité** f femininity

femme f woman; (épouse) wife; **~ battue** battered wife; **~ au foyer** homemaker, Br housewife

fendre split; (fissurer) crack; cœur break; **se ~** split; (se fissurer) crack

fenêtre f window

fenouil m BOT fennel

fente f crack; d'une boîte à lettres, jupe slit; pour pièces de monnaie slot

fer m iron; **à cheval** horseshoe; **à repasser** iron

férié: jour m **~** (public) holiday

ferme¹ 1 adj firm; terre f**~** dry land, terra firma **2** adv travailler hard; s'ennuyer **~** be bored stiff

ferme² f farm

fermé closed, shut; robinet off; club exclusive

fermenter ferment

fermer 1 v/t close, shut; eau, gaz, robinet turn off; manteau fasten; **ferme-la!** shut up! **2** v/i close, shut; d'un manteau fasten; **se ~** close, shut

fermeté f firmness

fermeture f closing; définitive closure; mécanisme fastener; **~ éclair** zipper, Br **~ zip** (fastener)

fermier 1 adj œufs, poulet free-range **2** m farmer

féroce fierce, ferocious; **férocité** f fierceness, ferocity

ferré, ~e: voie f **~e** (railroad ou Br railway) track

ferroviaire railroad atr, Br railway atr

fertile fertile; **~ en** full of; **fertilité** f fertility

fervent fervent

fesse f buttock; **~s** butt, Br

bottom; **fessée** f spanking

festin m feast

festival m festival

festivités fpl festivities

fêtard m F reveler, Br reveller; **fête** f festival; (soirée) party; publique holiday; REL feast (day), festival; jour d'un saint name day; **les ~s (de fin d'année)** the holidays, Christmas and New Year; **faire la ~** party; **~ foraine** fun fair; **Fête des mères** Mother's Day; **Fête nationale** Bastille Day; **fêter** celebrate; (accueillir) fête

feu m fire; AUTO, MAR light; de circulation (traffic) light, Br (traffic) lights pl; d'une cuisinière burner; fig (enthousiasme) passion; **coup** m **de ~** shot; **prendre ~** catch fire; **vous avez du ~?** got a light?; **~ arrière** AUTO taillight

feuillage m foliage; **feuille** f leaf; de papier sheet; **~ d'impôt** tax return; **~ de paie** payslip; **feuilleter** livre etc leaf through

feuilleton m serial; TV soap opera

feutre m felt; stylo felt-tipped pen; chapeau fedora

février m February

fiable reliable

fiançailles fpl engagement; **fiancé, ~e** m/f fiancé; **fiancer: se ~ avec** get engaged to

fibre f fiber, Br fibre; **avoir la ~ paternelle** fig be a born father; **la ~ patriotique** patriotic feelings

ficeler tie up; **ficelle** f string; pain thin French stick

fiche f pour classement index card; formulaire form; ÉL plug

ficher F (faire) do; (donner) give; (mettre) stick; **fiche-moi la paix!** leave me alone!; **je m'en fiche** I don't give a damn

fichier m INFORM file; **~ joint** attachment

fichu F (inutilisable) kaput F; (sale) filthy; **être mal ~ santé** be feeling rotten

fictif, -ive fictitious; **fiction** f fiction

fidèle 1 adj faithful **2** m/f REL, fig: **les fidèles** the faithful pl; **fidélité** f faithfulness

fier[1]: **se ~ à** trust

fier[2], **-ère** adj proud (**de** of); **fierté** f pride

fièvre f fever; **avoir de la ~** have a fever; **fiévreux, -euse** feverish

figer congeal; **se ~** fig: d'un sourire become fixed

figue f fig; **figuier** m fig tree

figurant, ~e m/f de théâtre walk-on; de cinéma extra; **figure** f figure; (visage) face; **figuré** figurative; **figurer** figure; **se ~ qc** imagine sth

fil m thread; de métal, ÉL, TÉL wire; **coup ~ de ~** TÉL

(phone) call

filature f spinning; usine mill; **prendre qn en ~** fig tail s.o.

file f line; d'une route lane; (d'attente) line, Br queue

filer 1 v/t spin; F (donner) give; (épier) tail **2** v/i F (partir vite) race off; du temps fly past

filet m d'eau trickle; de pêche, tennis net; CUIS fillet

filial, ~e 1 adj filial **2** f COMM subsidiary

fille f girl; parenté daughter; **vieille ~** old maid; **fillette** f little girl

filleul m godson; **filleule** f goddaughter

film m movie, Br aussi film; **couche** film; **~ policier** detective movie ou Br aussi film; **filmer** film

fils m son; **~ à papa** (spoilt) rich kid

filtre m filter; **filtrer 1** v/t filter; fig screen **2** v/i filter through; fig leak

fin[1] f end; **à la ~** in the end; **mettre ~ à qc** put an end to sth; **sans ~** endless; **parler** endlessly

fin[2] **1** adj fine; (mince) thin; taille, cheville slender; esprit refined; (rusé, malin) sharp **2** adv fine(ly)

final, ~e 1 adj final **2** m: **~e** MUS finale **3** f SP final; **finale 1** m MUS finale **2** f SP final

finaliser finalize; **finaliste** m/f finalist

finance f finance; **financer** fund, finance; **financier, -ère 1** adj financial **2** m financier

finesse f (délicatesse) fineness

fini 1 adj finished **2** m finish; **finir 1** v/t finish **2** v/i finish; **~ de faire qc** finish doing sth; **~ par faire qc** finish up doing sth

finlandais, ~e 1 adj Finnish **2** m langue Finnish; **Finlandais, ~e** m/f Finn; **Finlande** f: **la ~** Finland

firme f firm

fisc m tax authorities pl

fissure f crack

fixe 1 adj fixed; adresse, personnel permanent **2** m basic salary; **fixer** fasten; (déterminer) fix, set; PHOT fix; (regarder) stare at; **se ~** (s'établir) settle down

flageolet m flageolet bean

flagrant flagrant; **en ~ délit** red-handed

flair m sense of smell; fig intuition; **flairer** smell (aussi fig)

flambant: **~ neuf** brand new; **flamber 1** v/i blaze **2** v/t CUIS flambé

flamme f flame; fig fervor, Br fervour

flan m flan

flancher quail

flâner stroll

flanquer flank; F (jeter) fling; coup give

flaque f puddle

flasque flabby

flatter flatter; **se ~ de qc** congratulate o.s. on sth; **flatterie** f flattery; **flatteur, -euse 1** adj flattering **2** m/f flatterer

flèche f arrow; d'un clocher spire; **monter en ~** de prix skyrocket

fléchir 1 v/t bend; (faire céder) sway **2** v/i d'une poutre bend; fig (céder) give in; (faiblir) weaken; d'un prix, de ventes fall

flegmatique phlegmatic

flemme f F laziness; **j'ai la ~ de le faire** I can't be bothered

flétrir: **se ~** wither

fleur f flower; d'un arbre blossom; **fleurir** flower, bloom; fig flourish; **fleuriste** m/f florist

fleuve m river

flexibilité f flexibility; **flexible** flexible

flic m F cop F

flinguer F gun down

flipper 1 m pinball machine; jeu pinball **2** v/i F freak out F

flirter flirt

flocon m flake; **~ de neige** snowflake

Floride f Florida

florissant fig flourishing

flot m flood (aussi fig); **~s** waves; **remettre à ~** refloat (aussi fig)

flottant floating; vêtements baggy

flotte f fleet; F (*eau*) water; F (*pluie*) rain; **flotter** d'un *bateau* float; d'un *drapeau* flutter; d'un *sourire*, *air* hover; *fig* waver

flou blurred, fuzzy; *robe* loose-fitting

fluctuation f fluctuation; **fluctuer** COMM fluctuate

fluide 1 adj fluid; *circulation* moving freely **2** m PHYS fluid; **fluidité** f fluidity

fluorescent fluorescent

flûte f MUS, *verre* flute; *pain* thin French stick

fluvial river atr

flux m MAR flow

fœtus m fetus, Br foetus

foi f faith; **être de bonne/ mauvaise ~** be sincere/insincere

foie m liver; **une crise de ~** a stomach upset

foire f fair

fois f time; **une ~** once; **deux ~** twice; **trois ~** three times; **il était une ~ ...** once upon a time there was ...; **quatre ~ six** four times six; **à la ~** at the same time

foisonner be abundant

folie f madness; **faire des ~s** *achats* go on a spending spree

folk m folk (music)

folklore folklore

follement madly

fomenter foment

foncé *couleur* dark; **foncer** de *couleurs* darken; AUTO speed

along; **~ sur** rush at

foncier, -ère COMM land

foncièrement fundamentally

fonction f function; (*poste*) office; **faire ~ de** act as; **en ~ de** according to; **prendre ses ~s** take up office

fonctionnaire m/f public servant

fonctionnement m functioning; **fonctionner** work; *du système* function

fond m bottom; d'une *salle, armoire* back; d'une *peinture* background; (*contenu*) content; d'un *problème* heart; d'un *pantalon* seat; **à ~** thoroughly; **au ~, dans le ~** basically

fondamental fundamental

fondateur, -trice m/f founder; **fondation** f foundation; **fondé 1** adj well-founded **2** m: **~ de pouvoir** authorized representative; **fondement** m fig basis; **sans ~** groundless; **fonder** found; **~ qch sur** base sth on; **se ~ sur** d'une *personne* base o.s. on; d'une *idée* be based on

fondre **1** v/t *neige* melt; dans *l'eau* dissolve; *métal* melt down **2** v/i de la *neige* melt; dans *l'eau* dissolve; **~ sur** *proie* pounce on

fonds m **1** sg fund; d'une *bibliothèque* collection; **~ de commerce** business **2** pl (*argent*) funds

fondu melted

fouiller

fondue f CUIS fondue; **~ bour-**
guignonne beef fondue
fontaine f fountain; (source)
spring
fonte f métal cast iron; **~ des**
neiges spring thaw
football m soccer, Br aussi
football; **~ américain** football, Br American football;
footballeur, -euse m/f soccer player, Br aussi football-
er
footing m jogging; **faire du ~**
jog, go jogging
force f strength; (violence)
force; **à ~ de travailler** by
working; **de ~** by force; **~s**
armées armed forces
forcené, -e m/f maniac
forcer force; **se ~** force o.s.
forestier, -ère 1 adj forest atr
2 m ranger, Br forest warden
forêt f forest
forfait m (COMM package;
(prix) all-in price; **déclarer**
~ withdraw
formaliser: se ~ de take offense ou Br offence at; **for-**
malité f formality
format m format; **formater**
format
formation f formation; (éducation) training; **~ continue**
continuing education
forme f form; **en ~ de** in the
shape of; **être en ~** be in
form, be in good shape; **for-**
mel, ~le formal; (explicite)
categorical; **formellement**
adv: **~ interdit** strictly for-

bidden; **former** form; (instruire) train; **se ~** form
formidable enormous; F
great F
formulaire m form
formulation f wording
formule f formula; **formuler**
formulate; **vœux, jugement**
express
fort 1 adj strong; (gros) stout;
coup, pluie heavy; somme
big; **être ~ en qch** be good
at sth **2** adv parler loudly;
pousser, frapper hard; (très)
extremely; (beaucoup) a
lot **3** m strong point; MIL
fort; **fortement** pousser
hard; (beaucoup) greatly
fortifier strengthen
fortuit chance
fortune f luck; **de ~** makeshift
fosse f pit; (tombe) grave;
fossé m ditch; fig gulf; **fos-**
sette f dimple
fossile m & adj fossil
fou, folle 1 adj mad; (incroyable) incredible; **être ~ de**
qn/qc be mad ou crazy
about s.o./sth.; **~ de joie** etc
beside o.s. with **2** m/f madman; madwoman
foudre f lightning; **coup** m **de**
~ fig love at first sight
foudroyer strike down; **~ qn**
du regard give s.o. a wither-
ing look
fouet m whip; CUIS whisk
fougueux, -euse fiery
fouiller 1 v/i dig; (chercher)
search **2** v/t et police search;

en archéologie excavate

fouiner nose around

foulard *m* scarf

foule *f* crowd; *une ~ de* masses of

fouler trample; *sol* set foot on; *se ~ la cheville* twist one's ankle; **foulure** *f* sprain

four *m* oven; TECH kiln; *fig* F (*insuccès*) flop F

fourchette *f* fork; (*éventail*) bracket; **fourchu** forked; *cheveux mpl ~s* split ends

fourgon *m* baggage car, *Br* luggage van; *camion* van; **fourgonnette** *f* small van

fourmi *f* ant

fourmillements *mpl* pins and needles; **fourmiller** swarm (*de* with)

fournaise *f fig* oven; *fourneau m* furnace; CUIS stove

fourni: *bien ~* well stocked; **fournir** supply (*de*, *en* with); *occasion* provide; *effort* make; *~ qc à qn* provide s.o. with sth; **fournisseur** *m* supplier; *~ d'accès (Internet)* Internet service provider, ISP; **fourniture** *f* supply; *~s scolaires* school stationery and books

fourré[1] *m* thicket

fourré[2] *adj* CUIS filled; *vêtement* lined

fourrer stick, shove; (*remplir*) fill; *se ~ dans* get into

fourrière *f* pound

fourrure *f* fur

fourvoyer: *se ~* go astray

foutre F do; (*mettre*) stick; *coup* give; *se ~ de qn* make fun of s.o.; *indifférence* not give a damn about s.o.; *je m'en fous!* I don't give a damn!

foyer *m* fire; *d'une famille* home; *de jeunes* club; (*pension*) hostel; *d'un théâtre* foyer; *d'un incendie* seat; *d'une infection* source

fracas *m* crash; **fracasser** shatter

fractionner divide (up) (*en* into)

fracture *f* MÉD *m* fracture; **fracturer** *coffre* break open; *jambe* fracture

fragile fragile; *santé* frail; *cœur* weak; **fragiliser** weaken; **fragilité** *f* fragility

fragment *m* fragment

fraîcheur *f* freshness; (*froideur*) coolness (*aussi fig*); **fraîchir** *du vent* freshen; *du temps* get cooler

frais[1], fraîche 1 *adj* fresh; (*froid*) cool; *peinture* wet; *nouvelles* recent; *servir ~* serve chilled; *il fait ~* it's cool **2** *adv* freshly, newly **3** *m*: *prendre le ~* get a breath of fresh air

frais[2] *mpl* expenses *pl*; COMM costs *pl*; *faire des ~* incur costs; *à mes ~* at my (own) expense; *~ bancaires* bank charges; *~ généraux* overhead, *Br* overheads

fraise *f* strawberry

framboise f raspberry

franc¹, franche adj frank; regard open; COMM free

franc² m franc

français, ~e 1 adj French **2** m langue French; **Français, ~e** m/f Frenchman; **Française, ~e** m/f Frenchwoman; **les ~** the French pl; **France** f: **la ~** France

franchir cross; obstacle negotiate

franchise f caractère frankness; (exemption) exemption; COMM franchise; d'une assurance deductible, Br excess

franco adv: **~ (de port)** carriage free; **y aller ~** fig F go right ahead

francophone 1 adj French-speaking **2** m/f French speaker

franc-parler m outspokenness

frange f bangs pl, Br fringe

frappant striking; **frappe** f INFORM keying; **faute f de ~** typo, typing error; **frapper 1** v/t hit, strike; (impressionner) strike **2** v/i (agir) strike; **à la porte** knock (**à** at); **~ dans ses mains** clap (one's hands)

fraternel, ~le brotherly, fraternal; **fraternité** f brotherhood

fraude f fraud; ÉDU cheating; **passer en ~** smuggle; **frauduleux, -euse** fraudulent

frayer: **se ~ chemin** clear

frayeur f fright

fredonner hum

frein m brake; **sans ~** fig unbridled; **~ à main** parking brake, Br hand brake; **freiner 1** v/i brake **2** v/t fig curb, check

frêle frail

frelon m hornet

frémir shake; de feuilles quiver; de l'eau simmer; **frémissement** m shiver; de feuilles quivering

frénésie f frenzy; **avec ~** frenetically

fréquemment frequently; **fréquence** f frequency; **quelle est la ~ des bus?** how often do the buses go?; **fréquent** frequent; situation common

fréquentation f d'un théâtre etc attendance; **tes ~s** (amis) the company you keep; **fréquenter** endroit go to regularly, frequent; personne see; groupe go around with

frère m brother

fret m freight

frétiller wriggle

friable crumbly

friand: **être ~ de qc** be fond of sth; **friandises** fpl sweet things

fric m F money, dosh F

friche f AGR: **en ~** (lying) fallow

friction f friction; de la tête scalp massage; **frictionner** massage

frigidaire *m* refrigerator

frigide frigid

frigo *m* F icebox, fridge; **frigorifier** refrigerate

frileux, -euse: être ~ feel the cold

frimer show off; **frimeur, -euse** show-off

fringues *fpl* F clothes, gear F

frire 1 *v/i* fry 2 *v/t:* **faire ~** fry

frisé curly; **friser** *cheveux* curl; *fig: le ridicule* verge on

frissonner shiver

frit fried; **(pommes) frites** *fpl* (French) fries, *Br aussi* chips; **friteuse** *f* deep fryer; **friture** *f poissons Br* whitebait, *small fried fish*; *huile* oil; *à la radio*, TÉL interference

frivole frivolous; **frivolité** *f* frivolity

froid 1 *adj* cold (*aussi fig*); *j'ai* **~** I'm cold; **prendre ~** catch (a) cold 2 *m* cold; **humour** *m* **à ~** dry humor; **froidement** *fig* coldly; (*calmement*) coolly; *tuer in cold blood*; **froideur** *f* coldness

froissement *m bruit* rustle; **froisser** crumple; *fig* offend; **se ~** crumple; *fig* take offense *ou Br* offence

fromage *m* cheese; **~ blanc** fromage frais; **~ à tartiner** cheese spread

froncer gather; **~ les sourcils** frown

front *m* front; ANAT forehead; **de ~** from the front; *fig*

head-on; **marcher de ~** walk side by side

frontière *f* frontier, border

frotter 1 *v/i* rub 2 *v/t* rub (*de* with); *meuble* polish; *sol* scrub; *allumette* strike

frousse *f* F fear; **avoir la ~** be scared

fructifier BOT bear fruit; *d'un placement* yield a profit

fructueux, -euse fruitful

fruit *m* fruit; **~s** fruit; **~s do mer** seafood

frustrant frustrating; **frustration** *f* frustration

fugitif, -ive 1 *adj* runaway; *fig* fleeting 2 *m/f* fugitive

fugue *f d'un enfant* escapade; MUS fugue; **faire une ~** run away

fuir 1 *v/i* flee; *du temps* fly; *d'un tuyau* drip; *d'un robinet* drip; *d'un liquide* leak out 2 *v/t: question* avoid; *fuite* *f* flight (*devant* from); *d'un tuyau etc* leak; **prendre la ~** take flight

fulgurant dazzling; *vitesse* lightning

fumé smoked; *verre* tinted

fumée *f* smoke; **fumer** smoke; **fumeur, -euse** *m/f* smoker

funèbre funeral *atr*; (*lugubre*) gloomy

funérailles *fpl* funeral

funeste fatal

fur: **au ~ et à mesure** as I/you *etc* go along; **au ~ et à mesure que** as

fureter ferret around

fureur *f* fury; **faire** ~ be all the rage

furie (*colère*) fury; *femme* shrew; **furieux, -euse** furious (**contre qn** with s.o.; **de qch** with *ou* at sth)

furtif, -ive furtive, stealthy

fuseau *m*: ~ **horaire** time zone

fusée *f* rocket

fusible *m* ÉL fuse

fusil *m* rifle; ~ **de chasse** shotgun; **fusiller** execute by firing squad

fusion *f* COMM merger; PHYS fusion; **fusionner** COMM merge

futé cunning, clever

futile futile; *personne* frivolous

futur *m* & *adj* future

fuyant *menton* receding; *regard* evasive

G

gabarit *m* size; TECH template

gâcher *fig* spoil; *travail* bungle; *temps, argent* waste

gâchis *m* (*désordre*) mess; (*gaspillage*) waste

gadget *m* gadget

gaffe *f* F blooper F, blunder; **faire** ~ à F be careful of

gaffer F make a gaffe *ou* blooper F

gage *m* forfeit; (*preuve*) token; **tueur** *m* à ~**s** hitman; **mettre en** ~ pawn

gagnant, ~e 1 *adj* winning **2** *m/f* winner

gagne-pain *m* livelihood

gagner win; *salaire, amitié etc* earn; *place, temps, endroit* reach; *de peur etc* overcome; ~ **sa vie** earn one's living

gai cheerful; *un peu ivre* tipsy; **gaieté** *f* cheerfulness

gain *m* (*avantage*) bene-

fit; ~**s** profits; *d'un employé* earnings

gaine *f* sheath

galant galant; **homme** ~ gentleman

galaxie *f* galaxy

galère *f*: **il est dans la** ~ *fig* he's in a mess; **galérer** F sweat

galerie *f* gallery; AUTO roofrack; ~ **d'art** art gallery; ~ **marchande** mall

galet *m* pebble

Galles *fpl*: **le pays** *m* **de** ~ Wales; **gallois, ~e 1** *adj* Welsh **2** *m langue* Welsh; **Gallois, ~e** *m/f* Welshman; Welsh woman

galop *m* gallop; **galoper** gallop

galopin *m* urchin

galvaniser galvanize

gambader gambol, leap

gamin, ~e 1 *m/f* kid **2** *adj*

childlike

gamme f MUS scale; fig range; **bas de ~** downscale, Br downmarket

gang m gang

gangster m gangster

gant m glove; **~ de toilette** washcloth, Br facecloth

garage m garage; **garagiste** m auto mechanic; propriétaire garage owner

garant, ~e m/f guarantor; **garantie** f guarantee; **garantir** guarantee

garce f F bitch

garçon m boy; (serveur) waiter; **~ d'honneur** best man; **~ manqué** tomboy; **garçonnière** f bachelor apartment ou Br flat

garde¹ f care (**de** of); MIL guard; **prendre ~** be careful; **être de ~** be on duty; **mettre qn en ~** put s.o. on their guard; **~ à vue** police custody

garde² m guard; **~ forestier** (forest) ranger

garde-boue m AUTO fender, Br wing

garde-fou m railing

garde-malade m/f nurse

garder objet keep; vêtement keep on; (surveiller) guard; malade, enfant look after; **se ~ de faire qch** be careful not to do sth

garderie f daycare center, Br daycare centre

gardien, ~ne m/f de prison

guard, Br warder; d'un musée attendant; d'immeuble, d'école janitor; fig guardian; **~ (de but)** goalkeeper; **~ de la paix** police officer

gare¹ f station; **~ routière** bus station

gare²: **~ à toi!** watch out!; ça va mal se passer you'll be for it!

garer park; **se ~** park; pour laisser passer move aside

gargariser: **se ~** gargle

gargouiller gurgle; de l'estomac rumble

garnement m rascal

garnir (fournir) fit (**de** with); (orner) trim (**de** with); **garniture** f légumes vegetables pl

gars m F guy F

gasoil m gas oil, Br diesel

gaspillage m waste; **gaspiller** waste; **gaspilleur, -euse 1** adj wasteful **2** m/f waster

gastroentérite f gastroenteritis

gastronome m/f gourmet; **gastronomie** f gastronomy

gâteau m cake; **~ sec** cookie, Br biscuit

gâter spoil; **se ~** d'un aliment spoil; du temps deteriorate

gauche 1 adj left; manières gauche **2** f left; **à ~** on the left (**de** of); **gaucher, -ère 1** adj left-handed **2** m/f left-hander

gaufre f waffle; **gaufrette** f wafer

gaver *oie* force-feed; **~ qn de qch** *fig* stuff s.o. full of sth

gaz *m* gas; **mettre les ~** step on the gas; **~ à effet de serre** greenhouse gas

gaze *f* gauze

gazeux, -euse *boisson* carbonated, *Br* fizzy

gazinière *f* gas cooker

gazole *m* gas oil, *Br* diesel

gazon *m* grass

gazouiller twitter

géant, ~e 1 *adj* gigantic, giant *atr* **2** *m/f* giant

geindre groan

gel *m* frost; *fig: des prix* freeze; *cosmétique* gel

gélatine *f* gelatine

gelée *f* frost; *cuis* aspic; *confiture* jelly, *Br* jam; **geler 1** *v/t* freeze **2** *v/i d'une personne* freeze; **il gèle** there's a frost

Gémeaux *mpl* ASTROL Gemini

gémir groan; **gémissement** *m* groan

gênant (*embarrassant*) embarrassing

gencive *f* gum

gendarme *m* policeman; **gendarmerie** *f* police force; *lieu* police station

gendre *m* son-in-law

gêne *f* (*embarras*) embarrassment; (*dérangement*) inconvenience; *physique* difficulty; **sans ~** shameless; **gêner** bother; (*embarrasser*) embarrass; (*encombrer*) be in the way

général, ~e 1 *adj* general; **en ~** generally **2** *m* MIL general **3** *f* THÉÂT dress rehearsal; **généraliser** generalize; **se ~** spread; **généraliste** *m* MÉD generalist; **généralités** *fpl* generalities

générateur *m* generator; **générer** generate

généreux, -euse generous; **générosité** *f* generosity

génétique genetic; **génétiquement** genetically; **~ modifié** genetically modified, GM

génétiquement genetically; **~ modifié** genetically modified, GM

Genève Geneva

génial *de génius*; (*formidable*) terrific; **génie** *m* genius; TECH engineering; **avoir du ~** be a genius; **~ civil** civil engineering

genou *m* knee; **à ~x** on one's knees

genre *m* kind, sort; GRAM gender; **bon chic, bon ~** preppie *atr*

gens *mpl* people *pl*

gentil, ~le nice; *enfant* good; **gentillesse** *f* (*amabilité*) kindness

géographie *f* geography

géologie *f* geology; **géologue** *m/f* geologist

géomètre *m/f* geometrician; **géométrie** *f* geometry

gérance *f* management; **gé-**

rant, ~e m/f manager

gerbe f de blé sheaf

gercé lèvres chapped

gérer manage

gériatrie f geriatrics

germain: *cousin* m ~, *cousine* f ~e (first) cousin

gorme m germ (aussi fig)

germer germinate

gestation f gestation

geste m gesture; **gesticuler** gesticulate

gestion f management; **gestionnaire** m/f manager

ghetto m ghetto

gibier m game

giboulée f wintry shower

gicler spurt

gifle f slap (in the face); **gifler** slap (in the face)

gigantesque gigantic

gigaoctet m gigabyte

gigot m d'agneau leg

gigoter f fidget

gilet m vest, Br waistcoat; (chandail) cardigan; ~ *de sauvetage* lifejacket

gin m gin; ~ *tonic* gin and tonic

gingembre m BOT ginger

girafe f giraffe

giratoire: *sens* m ~ traffic circle, Br roundabout

gisement m GÉOL deposit; ~ *pétrolifère* ou *de pétrole* oilfield

gitan, ~e m/f gypsy

gîte m holiday home

givre m frost; **givré** covered with frost; avec du sucre

frosted; F (fou) crazy

glace f ice; (miroir) mirror; AUTO window; (crème glacée) ice cream; d'un gâteau frosting, Br icing; d'une tarte glaze; **glacer** freeze; (intimider) petrify; gâteau frost, Br ice; tarte glaze; **se** ~ freeze; du sang run cold; **glacial** icy (aussi fig); **glacière** f cool bag; fig icebox; **glaçon** m icicle; artificiel icecube

glaise f (aussi **terre** f ~) clay

gland m acorn

glande f gland

glander F hang around F

glaner fig glean

glapir shriek

glauque eau murky; couleur blue-green

glissade f slide; accidentelle slip; **glissant** slippery; **glissement** m ~ *de terrain* landslide; **glisser 1** v/t slide (**dans** into) **2** v/i slide; sur l'eau glide (**sur** over); (déraper) slip; être glissant be slippery; **se** ~ **dans** slip into

global global; prix, somme total, overall; **globalisation** f globalization; **globe** m globe; ~ *oculaire* eyeball

gloire f glory; **glorieux**, -euse glorious; **glorifier** glorify

glousser cluck; rire giggle

gluant sticky

glycine f wisteria

gnangnan F film, livre sloppy F

goal m goalkeeper

grain

gobelet m tumbler; *en carton, plastique* cup

gober gobble; F *mensonge* swallow

godet m récipient pot; *de vêtements* flare

gogo F: *à ~* galore

goinfrer: se ~ péj stuff o.s.

golf m SP golf; *terrain* golf course

golfe m GÉOGR gulf

gomme f gum; *pour effacer* eraser; **gommer** (*effacer*) erase

gond m hinge; *sortir de ses ~s* fly off the handle

gondole f gondola

gonflable inflatable; **gonfler 1** v/i swell **2** v/t blow up; (*exagérer*) exaggerate

gonzesse f F péj chick F

gorge f throat; (*poitrine*) bosom; GÉOGR gorge; *avoir mal à la ~* have a sore throat; **gorgée** f mouthful; **gorger: se ~** gorge o.s. (*de* with)

gosier m throat

gosse m/f F kid F

goudron m tar

gouffre m abyss; *fig* depths *pl*

goujat m boor

goulot m neck; *boire au ~* drink from the bottle

goulu greedy

gourd numb (with the cold)

gourde f récipient water bottle; *fig* F moron F

gourer F: *se ~* goof F

gourmand F: ~**e 1** *adj* greedy **2** m/f gourmand; **gourmandi-** se f greediness; ~**s** mets delicacies; **gourmet** m gourmet

gourmette f chain

gourou m guru

gousse f pod; ~ *d'ail* clove of garlic

goût m taste; *de bon ~* tasteful, in good taste; *de mauvais ~* tasteless, in bad taste; *avoir du ~* have taste; **goûter 1** v/t taste; *fig* enjoy **2** v/i *prendre un goûter* have an afternoon snack **3** m afternoon snack

goutte f drop; ~ *de pluie* raindrop; **goutte-à-goutte** m MÉD drip; **goutter** drip; **gouttière** f gutter

gouvernement m government; **gouverner** pays govern; *passions* master, control; MAR steer; **gouverneur** m governor

grâce f grace; (*bienveillance*) favor, *Br* favour; JUR pardon; *faire ~ à qn de qc* spare s.o. sth; *~ à* thanks to; **gracier** reprieve; **gracieux, -euse** graceful; *à titre ~* free

grade m rank; **gradé** m MIL noncommissioned officer

gradins mpl SP bleachers, *Br* terraces

graduellement gradually

graduer (*augmenter*) gradually increase; *instrument* graduate

graffitis mpl graffiti *sg ou pl*

grain m grain; MAR squall; ~ *de*

beauté mole, beauty spot; ~ **de raisin** grape

graine f seed

graissage m lubrication, greasing; **graisse** f fat; TECH grease; **graisser** grease, lubricate; (*salir*) get grease on; **graisseux, -euse** greasy

grammaire f grammar; **grammatical** grammatical

gramme m gram

grand 1 *adj* big; (*haut*) tall; (*adulte*) grown-up; (*long*) long; (*important, glorieux*) great; **il est ~ temps** it's high time; **~e surface** f supermarket; **les ~es vacances** *fpl* the summer vacation, *Br* the summer holidays; **~ ensemble** new development, *Br* (*housing*) estate **2** *adv* **ouvrir ~** wide **3** *m* giant, great man

grand-chose: pas ~ not much

Grande-Bretagne: la ~ Great Britain

grandeur f (*taille*) size; ~ **nature** lifesize

grandiose magnificent

grandir 1 *v/i* grow **2** *v/t:* ~ **qn** make s.o. look taller; **de l'expérience** strengthen s.o.

grand-mère f grandmother

grand-père m grandfather

grands-parents *mpl* grandparents *pl*

granit(e) m granite

granuleux, -euse granular

graphique 1 *adj* graphic **2** m

chart; MATH graph; INFORM graphic

grappe f cluster; ~ **de raisin**, bunch of grapes

grappin m: **mettre le ~ sur qn** get one's hands on s.o.

gras, ~se 1 *adj* fatty, fat; (*personne*) fat; *cheveux, peau* greasy; **faire la ~se matinée** sleep late **2** m CUIS fat

gratification f (*prime*) bonus; PSYCH gratification; **gratifier:** ~ **qn de qc** present s.o. with sth

gratiné CUIS with a sprinkling of cheese; *fig* F addition colossal

gratitude f gratitude

gratte-ciel m skyscraper; **gratter** scrape; (*griffer, piquer*) scratch; (*enlever*) scrape off; *mot* scratch out; *se* ~ scratch; **grattoir** m scraper

gratuit free; *fig* gratuitous

gravats *mpl* rubble

grave serious; *son* deep; *ce n'est pas* ~ it's not a problem

graver engrave; *disque* cut

gravier m gravel

gravillon m grit; ~**s** gravel, *Br* loose chippings *pl*

gravir climb

gravité f seriousness; PHYS gravity

gravure f ART engraving; (*reproduction*) print

gré m: **bon ~, mal ~** like it or not; **contre mon ~** against my will; **de bon ~** willingly; **de son plein ~** of one's own free will

grec, ~que 1 adj Greek **2** m langue Greek; **Grec, ~que** m/f Greek; **Grèce: la ~** Greece

greffe graft; **~ du cœur** MÉD heart transplant; **greffer** graft; cœur, poumon transplant

greffier m clerk of the court

grêle[1] adj jambes skinny; voix shrill

grêle[2] f hail; **grêler: il grêle** it's hailing; **grêlon** m hailstone

grelotter shiver

grenade f BOT pomegranate; MIL grenade

grenadine f grenadine, pomegranate syrup

grenier m attic

grenouille f frog

grès m sandstone; poterie stoneware

grésiller sizzle; RAD crackle

grève[1] f strike; **être en ~, faire ~** be on strike; **se mettre en ~** go on strike; **~ de la faim** hunger strike

grève[2] f (plage) shore

gréviste m/f striker

gribouillage m scribble; (dessin) doodle; **gribouiller** scribble; (dessiner) doodle

grief m grievance

grièvement blessé seriously

griffe f claw; COMM label; fig (empreinte) stamp; **griffer** scratch

griffonner scribble

grignoter 1 v/t nibble on; économies nibble away at **2** v/i nibble

grill m broiler, Br grill; **grillade** f broil, Br grill

grillage m wire mesh; (clôture) fence

grille f d'une fenêtre grille; (clôture) railings pl; d'un four rack; (tableau) grid; **grille-pain** m inv toaster; **griller 1** v/t viande broil, Br grill; pain toast; café, marrons roast **2** v/i d'une ampoule burn out; **~ un feu rouge** go through a red light

grillon m cricket

grimace f grimace; **faire des ~s** pull faces

grimper climb

grincement m de porte squeaking; **grincer** d'une porte squeak; **~ des dents** grind one's teeth

grincheux, -euse grouchy

grippe f MÉD flu; **prendre qn en ~** take a dislike to s.o.; **grippé** MÉD: **être ~** have flu

gris gray, Br grey; temps, vie dull; (ivre) tipsy

grisant exhilarating

grisâtre grayish, Br greyish

griser: ~ qn go to s.o.'s head; **se laisser ~ par** get carried away by

grisonner go gray ou Br grey

grognement m (plainte)

grumbling; *d'un cochon etc* grunt; **grogner** (*se plaindre*) grumble; *d'un cochon* grunt; **grognon**, **~ne: être ~** be grumpy

grommeler mutter

gronder 1 *v/i* growl; *du tonnerre* rumble; *d'une révolte* brew **2** *v/t* scold

gros, **~se 1** *adj* big; (*corpulent*) fat; *lèvres* thick; *rhume, souliers* heavy; *chaussures* thick; *plaisanterie* coarse; *vin* rough; **~ mots** *mpl* bad language **2** *adv*: **gagner ~** win a lot; **en ~** (*globalement*) on the whole; COMM wholesale **3** *m personne* fat man; COMM wholesale trade

groseille *f* BOT currant; **~ à maquereau** gooseberry

grossesse *f* pregnancy

grosseur *f* (*corpulence*) fatness; (*volume*) size; (*tumeur*) growth

grossier, **-ère** (*rudimentaire*) crude; (*indélicat*) coarse; (*impoli*) rude; *erreur* big

grossir 1 *v/t au microscope* magnify; *nombre, rivière* swell; (*exagérer*) exaggerate; **~ qn** *d'une robe etc* make s.o. look fatter **2** *v/i d'une personne* put on weight

grotesque grotesque

grotte *f* cave

grouiller: **~ de** be swarming with; **se ~** F get a move on

groupe *m* group; **~ sanguin** blood group; **grouper**

group; **se ~ autour de qn** gather around s.o.

grue *f* ZO, TECH crane

grumeleux, **-euse** lumpy

gué *m* ford

guenilles *fpl* rags

guêpe *f* wasp

guère: **ne ... ~** hardly

guéridon *m* round table

guérir 1 *v/t cure* (**de** of) **2** *v/i* heal; *d'un malade* get better; **guérison** *f* (*rétablissement*) recovery

guerre *f* war; **en ~** at war; **faire la ~** be at war (**à** with); **~ civile** civil war; **~ des gangs** gang warfare; **guerrier**, **-ère 1** *adj* warlike **2** *m* warrior

guet *m*: **faire le ~** keep watch; **guet-apens** *m* ambush; **guetter** keep an eye open for; (*épier*) watch

gueule *f* F mouth; (*visage*) face; **ta ~!** F shut it! F; **~ de bois** hangover; **gueuler** F yell

gueuleton *m* F enormous meal

guichet *m de banque, poste* wicket; *Br* window; *de théâtre* box office; **~ automatique** ATM, *Br aussi* cash dispenser

guide 1 *m* guide **2** *f* girl scout, *Br* guide **3**: **~s** *fpl* guiding reins; **guider** guide

guidon *m de vélo* handlebars *pl*

guillemets *mpl* quote marks

guindé stiff

guirlande f garland; **~s de Noël** tinsel

guise f: **agir à sa ~** do as one likes; **en ~ de** as, by way of

guitare f guitar; **guitariste** m/f guitarist

guttural guttural

Guyane: **la ~** Guyana

gym f gym; **gymnase** m SP gym; **gymnaste** m/f gymnast; **gymnastique** f gymnastics sg; **corrective, matinale** exercises pl

gynécologue m/f MÉD gynecologist, Br gynaecologist

gyrophare m flashing light

H

habile skillful, Br skilful; **habileté** f skill; **habilité** JUR authorized

habillé (élégant) dressy; **habiller** dress; **s'~** get dressed, dress; **élégamment** get dressed up

habit m: **~s** clothes

habitable inhabitable; **habitant, ~e** m/f inhabitant; **habitation** f living; (domicile) residence; **habiter 1** v/t live in **2** v/i live

habitude f habit, custom; **d'~** usually; **par ~** out of habit; **habitué, ~e** m/f regular; **habituel, ~le** usual; **habituer: ~ qn à qch** get s.o. used to sth; **s'~ à** get used to

'**hache** f ax, Br axe; '**hacher** chop; **viande ~ée hachée** ground beef, Br mince

'**hachisch** m hashish

'**hachoir** m appareil meat grinder, Br mincer; **couteau** cleaver; **planche** chopping board

haddock m smoked haddock

'**haie** f hedge; SP hurdle; **pour chevaux** fence, jump; **une ~ de policiers** fig a line of police

'**haillons** mpl rags

'**haine** f hatred; '**haineux, -euse** full of hatred

'**haïr** hate

'**hâle** m (sun)tan

haleine f breath; **hors d'~** out of breath

'**haleter** pant

'**hall** m d'hôtel, immeuble foyer; de gare concourse

'**halle** f market

halloween f Halloween

hallucination f hallucination

halogène m: (**lampe** f) **~** halogen light

'**halte** f stop; **faire ~** halt, make a stop

haltère m dumbbell; **faire des ~s** do weightlifting

haltérophilie f weightlifting

'**hamac** m hammock

'**hameau** m hamlet

hameçon m hook

'**hamster** m hamster

'hanche *f* hip

'handicap *m* handicap; 'handicapé, ~e 1 *adj* disabled, handicapped 2 *m/f* disabled *ou* handicapped person

'hangar *m* shed; AVIAT hangar

'hanter haunt

'hantise *f* fear, dread

'happer catch; *fig: de train, bus* hit

'haras *m* stud farm

'harassant *travail* exhausting

'harceler harass

'hard *m* hardcore; MUS hard rock

'hardi bold

'hareng *m* herring

'hargne *f* bad temper; 'hargneux, -euse *euse euse; chien* vicious

'haricot *m* BOT bean; *c'est la fin des ~s* F that's the end

harmonie *f* harmony; harmoniser match (up); MUS harmonize; *s'~ de couleurs* go together; *s'~ avec* go with

'harpe *f* MUS harp

'harpon *m* harpoon

'hasard *m* chance; *au ~* at random; *par ~* by chance; 'hasarder hazard; *se ~ à faire qc* venture to do sth

'hâte *f* hurry, haste; *en ~* in haste; *avoir ~ de faire qc* be eager to do sth; 'hâter hasten; *se ~* hurry

'hausse *f* increase; rise; 'hausser increase; ~ *les épaules* shrug (one's shoulders)

'haut 1 *adj* high; *immeuble* tall, high; *cri, voix* loud; *fonctionnaire* high-level 2 *adv* high; *de ~* from above; *de ~ en bas* from top to bottom; *regarder qn* up and down; *en ~* above; *en ~ de* at the top of 3 *m* top; *du ~ de* from the top of; *des ~s et des bas* ups and downs

'hautain haughty

'hauteur *f* height; *fig* haughtiness; *être à la ~ de qc* be up to sth

hebdomadaire *m & adj* weekly

hébergement *m* accommodations *pl*, *Br* accommodation; héberger: ~ *qn* put s.o. up; *fig* take s.o. in

hébreu *m*: *l'~* Hebrew

hectare *m* hectare (approx 2.5 acres)

'hein F eh?; *c'est joli, ~?* it's pretty, isn't it?

'hélas alas

'héler hail

hélice *f* MAR, AVIAT propeller; *escalier m en ~* spiral staircase

hélicoptère *m* helicopter

hémisphère *m* hemisphere

hémorragie *f* hemorrhage, *Br* haemorrhage

'hennir neigh

hépatite *f* hepatitis

herbe *f* grass; CUIS herb; *mauvaise ~* weed; *fines ~s* herbs

héréditaire hereditary; hérédité *f* heredity

hérésie f heresy; **hérétique 1** adj heretical **2** m/f heretic

'hérissé ruffled

'hérisson m hedgehog

héritage m inheritance; **hériter 1** v/t inherit **2** v/i: **~ de qc** inherit sth; **~ de qn** receive an inheritance from s.o.; **héritier, -ère** m/f heir

'hernie f MÉD hernia; **~ discale** slipped disc

héroïne[1] f drogue heroin

héroïne[2] f heroine

héroïque heroic

héroïsme m heroism

'héron m heron

'héros m hero

herpès m herpes

hésitation f hesitation; **hésiter** hesitate

hétérogène heterogeneous

hétérosexuel, ~le heterosexual

heure f hour; **arriver à l'~** arrive on time; **de bonne ~** early; **à tout à l'~!** see you soon!; **quelle ~ est-il?** what time is it?; **il est six ~s** it's six (o'clock); **~ locale** local time; **~s d'ouverture** opening hours

heureusement luckily, fortunately; **heureux, -euse** happy; (chanceux) fortunate

'heurt m de deux véhicules collision; fig (friction) clash; **'heurter** collide with; fig offend; **se ~** collide (à with); fig (s'affronter) clash (**sur** over)

hiberner hibernate

'hibou m owl

'hideux, -euse hideous

hier yesterday

'hiérarchie f hierarchy

high-tech inv high tech, hitech

hilare grinning

hippique SP equestrian; **concours** m **~** horse show; **hippodrome** m race course

hirondelle f swallow

hirsute hairy

hispanique Hispanic

'hisser drapeau, voile hoist; (monter) lift, raise; **se ~** pull o.s. up

histoire f history; (récit, conte) story; **faire des ~s** make a fuss

historique 1 adj historic **2** m chronicle

hiver m winter

H.L.M. m ou f (= **habitation à loyer modéré**) low cost housing

'hocher: **~ la tête** approbation nod (one's head); désapprobation shake one's head

'hockey m **sur gazon** field hockey, Br hockey; **sur glace** hockey, Br ice hockey

'holding m holding company

'hold-up m holdup

'hollandais, ~e 1 adj Dutch **2** m langue Dutch; **~, ~e** m/f Dutchman; Dutchwoman; **'Hollande: la ~** Holland

'homard m lobster

homéopathie f homeopathy

homicide m homicide; ~ **involontaire** manslaughter; ~ **volontaire** murder

hommage m homage; **rendre ~ à** pay homage to

homme m man; ~ **d'affaires** businessman; ~ **d'État** statesman

homologue m counterpart, opposite number; **homologuer** record ratify; **tarif** authorize

homophobe homophobic

homosexuel, ~**le** m/f & adj homosexual

'**Hongrie** f: **la ~** Hungary; '**hongrois**, ~**e** 1 adj Hungarian 2 m langue Hungarian; **Hongrois**, ~**e** m/f Hungarian

honnête honest; (convenable) decent; (passable) reasonable; **honnêteté** honesty

honneur m honor, Br honour; **en l'~ de** in honor of; **faire ~ à** qc honor sth; **honorable** honorable, Br honourable; **honoraire** 1 adj honorary 2 ~**s** mpl fees; **honorer** honor, Br honour; **honorifique** honorific

'**honte** f shame; **avoir ~ de** be ashamed of; '**honteux, -euse** (déshonorant) shameful; (déconfit) ashamed

'**hooligan** m hooligan

hôpital m hospital; **à l'~** in the hospital, Br in hospital

'**hoquet** m hiccup; **avoir le ~** have (the) hiccups

horaire 1 adj hourly 2 m emploi du temps timetable, schedule; des avions, trains etc schedule, Br timetable

horizon m horizon

horizontal horizontal

horloge f clock

'**hormis** but

hormonal hormonal; **hormone** f hormone

horodateur m dans parking pay and display machine

horoscope m horoscope

horreur f horror; (monstruosité) monstrosity; **avoir ~ de qc** detest sth; (quelle) ~! how awful!

horrible horrible

horrifiant horrifying

'**hors**: ~ **de** (à l'extérieur de) outside; ~ **de danger** out of danger; ~ **sujet** beside the point; **être ~ de soi** be beside o.s.

'**hors-bord** m outboard

'**hors-d'œuvre** m CUIS appetizer, starter

'**hors-jeu** offside

horticulture f horticulture

hospice m REL hospice; (asile) home

hospitalier, -ère hospitable; MÉD hospital atr

hospitaliser hospitalize

hospitalité f hospitality

hostile hostile; **hostilité** f hostility

'**hot-dog** m hot dog

hôte m host; (invité) guest

'hôtel *m* hotel; ~ *de ville* town hall

hôtellerie *f:* *l'~* the hotel business

hôtesse *f* hostess; ~ *de l'air* air hostess

'houblon *m* BOT hop

'houille *f* coal

'houle *f* MAR swell; 'houleux, -euse *fig* stormy

'housse *f* protective cover

'houx *m* BOT holly

'hublot *m* NAUT porthole; AVIAT window

'huer boo, jeer

huile *f* oil; ~ *solaire* suntan oil; huiler oil

'huis *m:* *à ~ clos* behind closed doors; JUR in camera; huissier *m* JUR bailiff

'huit eight; ~ *jours* a week; *demain en* ~ a week tomorrow; 'huitaine *f:* *une* ~ *de* about eight, eight or so; *une* ~ *(de jours)* a week; 'huitième eighth

huître *f* oyster

humain human; *traitement* humane; humaniser humanize; humanitaire humanitarian; humanité *f* humanity

humble humble

humecter moisten

'humer breathe in

humeur *f* mood; (*tempérament*) temperament; *être de bonne/mauvaise* ~ be in a good/bad mood

humide damp; (*chaud et* ~)

humid; humidifier moisten; *atmosphère* humidify; humidité *f* dampness; humidity

humiliation *f* humiliation; humiliant humiliating; humilier humiliate

humour *m* humor, *Br* humour; *avoir de l'~* have a (good) sense of humor

'huppé exclusive

'hurlement *m d'un loup* howl; *d'une personne* scream; 'hurler *d'un loup* howl; *d'une personne* scream; ~ *de rire* roar with laughter

hydratant *cosmétique* moisturizing

hydraulique hydraulic

hydroélectrique hydroelectric

hydrogène *m* CHIM hydrogen

hydroglisseur *m* jetfoil

hygiène *f* hygiene; *avoir une bonne* ~ *de vie* have a healthy lifestyle; hygiénique hygienic; *papier* ~ toilet paper; *serviette* ~ sanitary napkin, *Br* sanitary towel

hymne *m* hymn; ~ *national* national anthem

hyperactif, -ive hyperactive

hypersensible hypersensitive

hypertension *f* MÉD high blood pressure

hypertexte: *lien m* ~ hypertext link

hypnotiser hypnotize

hypocrisie *f* hypocrisy; hypocrite 1 *adj* hypocritical 2 *m/f* hypocrite

hypothèque *f* COMM mortgage

hypothèse *f* hypothesis; **hypothétique** hypothetical

hystérie *f* hysteria; **hystérique** hysterical

I

ici here; *jusqu'*~ to here; (*jusqu'à maintenant*) so far; *par* ~ this way; (*dans le coin*) around about here; *d'*~ *là* by then, by that time

icône *f* icon

idéal *m & adj* ideal; **idéaliser** idealize; **idéalisme** *m* idealism; **idéaliste 1** *adj* idealistic **2** *m/f* idealist

idée *f* idea; (*opinion*) view; *avoir dans l'*~ *de faire qch* be thinking of doing sth; *tu te fais des* ~*s* (*tu te trompes*) you're imagining things; ~ *fixe* obsession

identifier identify (*avec, à* with); *s'*~ *avec ou à* identify with

identique identical (*à* to)

identité *f* identity; *pièce f d'*~ identity, ID

idéologie *f* ideology

idiomatique idiomatic

idiot, ~e 1 *adj* idiotic **2** *m/f* idiot; **idiotie** *f* idiocy; *dire des* ~*s* talk nonsense

idole *f* idol

idylle *f* romance

ignare *péj* **1** *adj* ignorant **2** *m/f* ignoramus

ignoble vile

ignorance *f* ignorance; **ignorant** ignorant; **ignorer** not know; *personne, talent* ignore

il he; *chose* it; *impersonnel* it; ~ *va pleuvoir* it is *ou* it's going to rain

île *f* island; *les* ~*s britanniques* the British Isles

illégal illegal

illégitime *enfant* illegitimate

illettré illiterate

illicite illicit

illimité unlimited

illisible illegible; *mauvaise littérature* unreadable

illogique illogical

illuminer light up, illuminate; *par projecteur* floodlight

illusion *f* illusion; *se faire des* ~*s* delude o.s.; **illusoire** illusory

illustration *f* illustration; **illustrer** illustrate; *s'*~ distinguish o.s. (*par* by)

îlot *m* (small) island; *de maisons* block

ils *mpl* they

image *f* picture; *dans un miroir* reflection, image; (*ressemblance*) image

imaginaire imaginary; **ima-**

gination *f* imagination; **imaginer** imagine; (*inventer*) devise; **s'~ que** imagine that

imbattable unbeatable

imbécile 1 *adj* idiotic **2** *m/f* idiot, imbecile

imbiber soak (**de** with)

imbu: **~ de** *fig* full of

imitation *f* imitation; THÉÂT impersonation; **imiter** imitate; THÉÂT impersonate

immaculé immaculate

immangeable inedible

immatriculation *f* registration; **plaque f d'~** AUTO license plate, *Br* number plate; **immatriculer** register

immature immature

immédiat 1 *adj* immediate **2** *m*: **dans l'~** for the moment; **immédiatement** immediately

immense immense

immerger immerse; **s'~ d'un sous-marin** submerge

immeuble *m* building

immigrant, **~e** *m/f* immigrant; **immigration** *f* immigration; **immigrer** immigrate

imminent imminent

immiscer: **s'~ dans qc** interfere in sth

immobile immobile

immobilier, **-ère 1** *adj*: **biens** *mpl* **~s** real estate **2** *m* property

immobiliser immobilize; *train*, *circulation* bring to a standstill; *capital* tie up; **s'~**

(*s'arrêter*) come to a standstill

immonde foul

immoral immoral; **immoralité** *f* immorality

immortaliser immortalize; **immortalité** *f* immortality; **immortel**, **~le** immortal

immuniser immunize; **immunisé contre** *fig* immune to; **immunité** *f* JUR, MÉD immunity

impact *m* impact

impair 1 *adj* odd **2** *m* blunder

impardonnable unforgiveable

imparfait imperfect

impartial impartial

impasse *f* dead end; *fig* deadlock, impasse

impassible impassive

impatience *f* impatience; **impatient** impatient; **impatienter**: **s'~** get impatient

impayé unpaid

impeccable impeccable

impénétrable impenetrable

impératif, **-ive 1** *adj* imperative **2** *m* (*exigence*) requirement; GRAM imperative

impératrice *f* empress

imperceptible imperceptible

imperfection *f* imperfection

impérieux, **-euse** *personne* imperious; *besoin* urgent

impérissable immortal; *souvenir* unforgettable

imperméabiliser waterproof; **imperméable 1** *adj* *tissu* waterproof **2** *m* raincoat

impersonnel, ~le impersonal
impertinence f impertinence; **impertinent** impertinent
imperturbable imperturbable
impétueux, -euse impetuous
impitoyable pitiless
implacable implacable
implanter fig introduce; usine set up; **s'~** become established; d'une industrie set up
implicite implicit
impliquer personne implicate; (entraîner) mean, involve; (supposer) imply
implorer aide beg for; ~ qn de faire qch implore ou beg s.o. to do sth
impoli rude, impolite
impopulaire unpopular
importance f importance; d'une ville size; d'une somme, catastrophe magnitude; **important 1** adj important; ville, somme large, sizeable 2 m: **l'~, c'est que ...** the important thing is that ...
importateur, -trice f adj importing 2 m importer; **importation** f import; **importer 1** v/t import; mode, musique introduce 2 v/i matter, be important (**à** to); **n'importe quand** any time; **n'importe quoi!** nonsense!
importun troublesome; importuner bother
imposable taxable

imposant imposing; **imposer** impose; marchandise tax; **s'~** (être nécessaire) be essential; (se faire admettre) gain recognition
impossible 1 adj impossible 2 m: **faire l'~ pour faire qch** do one's utmost to do sth
imposteur m imposter
impôt m tax; **déclaration f d'~s** tax return
impotent crippled
impraticable projet impractical; rue impassable
imprécis vague, imprecise
imprégner impregnate (**de** with); **imprégné de** fig full of
impression f impression; imprimerie printing; **impressionnant** impressive; (troublant) upsetting; **impressionner** impress; (troubler) upset; **impressionniste** m/f & adj impressionist
imprévisible unpredictable
imprévu 1 adj unexpected 2 m: **sauf ~** all being well
imprimante f INFORM printer; **~ laser** laser printer; **~ à jet d'encre** ink-jet (printer); imprimé m (formulaire) form; tissu print; poste **~s** printed matter; **imprimer** print; INFORM print out; édition publish
improbable unlikely, improbable
improductif, -ive unproduc-

tive

impropre *mot, outil* inappropriate; **~ à la consommation** unfit for human consumption

improviste: à l'~ unexpectedly

imprudence *f* imprudence; **imprudent** imprudent

impudence *f* impudence; **impudent** impudent

impudique shameless

impuissance *f* powerlessness; MÉD impotence; **impuissant** powerless; MÉD impotent

impulsif, -ive impulsive; **impulsion** *f* impulse; *à l'économie* boost

impuni unpunished

impur *eau* dirty, polluted; *(impudique)* impure

imputer attribute (**à** to); FIN charge (**sur** to)

inabordable *prix* unaffordable

inacceptable unacceptable

inaccessible inaccessible; *personne* unapproachable; *objectif* unattainable

inachevé unfinished

inactif, -ive idle; *population* non-working; *remède, méthode* ineffective; *marché* slack

inadéquat inadequate; *méthode* unsuitable

inadmissible unacceptable

inadvertance *f*: **par ~** inadvertently

inanimé inanimate; *(mort)* lifeless; *(inconscient)* unconscious

inaperçu: passer ~ pass unnoticed

inapproprié inappropriate

inapte *à* unsuited to; MÉD, MIL unfit for

inattendu unexpected

inattention *f* inattentiveness; **erreur d'~** careless mistake

inaudible inaudible

inaugurer inaugurate

inavouable shameful

incapable incapable (**de faire** of doing)

incapacité *f* (*inaptitude*) incompetence; *de faire qch* inability

incarcérer imprison

incassable unbreakable

incendiaire incendiary; *discours* inflammatory; **incendie** *m* fire; **~ criminel** arson; **incendier** set fire to

incertain uncertain; *temps* unsettled; *(hésitant)* indecisive; **incertitude** *f* uncertainty

incessamment any minute now

inchangé unchanged

incident *m* incident; **~ de parcours** mishap

incinérer incinerate; *cadavre* cremate

incisif, -ive incisive; **incision** *f* incision

inciter encourage (**à faire qch** to do sth); *péj* egg on, incite

inclinable tilting; **inclinaison** f slope

inclination f fig inclination (**pour** for); **~ de tête** (salut) nod; **incliner** tilt; **s'~** bend; pour saluer bow; **s'~ devant qc** (céder) yield to sth; **s'~ devant qn** aussi fig bow to s.o.

inclure include; dans une lettre enclose; **inclus: ci-inclus** enclosed; **jusqu'au 30 juin ~** to 30th June inclusive

incohérence f de comportement inconsistency; de discours incoherence

incolore colorless, Br colourless

incomber: il vous incombe de le lui dire it is your duty to tell him

incommoder bother

incomparable incomparable

incompatibilité f incompatibility; **incompatible** incompatible

incompétence f incompetence; **incompétent** incompetent

incomplet, -ète incomplete

incompréhensible incomprehensible; **incompréhension** f lack of understanding

incompris misunderstood (**de** by)

inconcevable inconceivable

inconditionnel, ~le 1 adj unconditional **2** m/f fan, fanatic

inconfortable uncomforta- ble

inconnu, ~e 1 adj (ignoré) unknown; (étranger) strange **2** m/f stranger

inconscient unconscious; (irréfléchi) irresponsible

inconsidéré rash, thoughtless

inconsistant inconsistent; fig: raisonnement flimsy

inconsolable inconsolable

incontestable indisputable; **incontesté** outright

incontournable: être ~ be a must

inconvénient m disadvantage m; **si vous n'y voyez aucun ~** if you have no objection

incorporer incorporate (**à** with, into); MIL draft

incorrect wrong, incorrect; tenue, langage improper

incorrigible incorrigible

incrédule (sceptique) incredulous; **incrédulité** f incredulity

incriminer personne blame; JUR accuse; paroles, actions condemn

incroyable incredible, unbelievable

inculpé, ~e m/f: **l'~** the accused, the defendant; **inculper** JUR charge, indict (**de, pour** with)

inculquer: qc à qn instill ou Br instil sth into s.o.

inculte terre waste atr, uncultivated; (ignorant) uneducated

incurable incurable

incursion f MIL raid, incursion; *fig: dans la politique etc* venture (**dans** into)

Inde f: l'~ India

indécent indecent; (*incorrect*) inappropriate, improper

indécis undecided; *personne, caractère* indecisive

indéfini indefinite; (*imprécis*) undefined

indéfinissable indefinable

indélicat *personne, action* tactless

indemne unhurt; **indemniser** compensate (**de** for); **indemnité** f (*dédommagement*) compensation; (*allocation*) allowance

indéniable undeniable

indépendance f independence; **indépendant** independent (**de** of); *travailleur* freelance; **indépendantiste** (pro-)independence *atr*

indescriptible indescribable

indésirable undesirable

indéterminé unspecified

index m index; *doigt* index finger

indicateur, -trice m (*espion*) informer; TECH gauge, indicator

indicatif m TÉL code

indication f indication; (*information*) piece of information; **~s** instructions

indice m (*signe*) sign, indica-

tion; JUR clue

indien, ~ne Indian; *d'Amérique aussi* native American; **Indien** m/f Indian; *d'Amérique aussi* native American

indifférence f indifference; **indifférent** indifferent

indigène adj & m/f native

indigeste indigestible; **indigestion** f MÉD indigestion

indignation f indignation

indigne unworthy; *parents* unfit

indigner make indignant; **s'~ de qc/contre qn** be indignant about sth/with s.o.

indiqué appropriate; **ce n'est pas ~** it's not advisable; **indiquer** indicate; show; *d'une pendule* show; (*recommander*) recommend

indirect indirect

indiscipline f indiscipline; **indiscipliné** undisciplined; *cheveux* unmanageable

indiscret, -ète indiscreet; **indiscrétion** f indiscretion

indispensable indispensable

indistinct indistinct

individu m individual; **individualisme** m individualism; **individuel, ~le** individual; *secrétaire* private, personal; *liberté* personal; *chambre* single; *maison* detached

indivisible indivisible

indolent lazy, indolent

indolore painless

indomptable *fig* indomitable

indu: **à une heure ~e** at some

ungodly hour

indubitable indisputable

induire: ~ *qn en erreur* mislead s.o.

indulgence *f* indulgence; *d'un juge* leniency; **indulgent** *juge* lenient

industrialisé industrialized; **industrialiser** industrialize; **industrie** *f* industry; **industriel**, **~le 1** *adj* industrial **2** *m* industrialist

inébranlable solid (as a rock)

inédit (*pas édité*) unpublished; (*nouveau*) original, unique

inégal unequal; *surface* uneven; *rythme* irregular; **inégalité** *f* inequality; *d'une surface* unevenness

inepte inept; **ineptie** *f* ineptitude; **~s** nonsense

inépuisable inexhaustible

inerte *corps* lifeless, inert; PHYS inert; **inertie** *f* inertia

inespéré unexpected, unhoped-for

inestimable *tableau* priceless; *aide* invaluable

inévitable inevitable; *accident* unavoidable

inexact inaccurate

inexcusable inexcusable, unforgiveable

inexistant non-existent

inexplicable inexplicable

inexprimable inexpressible

infaillible infallible

infantile *mortalité* infant *atr*; *péj* infantile; *maladie* children's

infarctus *m* MÉD: ~ *du myocarde* coronary (thrombosis)

infatigable tireless, indefatigable

infect disgusting; *temps* foul; **infecter** infect; *air, eau* pollute; **s'~** become infected; **infectieux**, **-euse** infectious; **infection** *f* MÉD infection

inférieur, **~e 1** *adj* lower; *qualité* inferior **2** *m/f* inferior; **infériorité** *f* inferiority

infernal infernal

infidèle unfaithful; REL pagan *atr*; **infidélité** *f* infidelity

infiltrer: **s'~** *dans* get into; *fig* infiltrate

infime tiny, infinitesimal

infini 1 *adj* infinite **2** *m* infinity

infirme 1 *adj* disabled **2** *m/f* disabled person; **infirmerie** *f* infirmary; ÉDU sickbay; **infirmier**, **-ère** *m/f* nurse; **infirmité** *f* disability

inflammation *f* MÉD inflammation

inflation *f* inflation

inflexible inflexible

infliger *peine* inflict (*à* on); *défaite* impose

influence *f* influence; **influencer** influence; **influent** influential

influer: ~ *sur* affect

info *f* F RAD, TV news item; **les ~s** the news *sg*

informaticien, **~ne** *m/f* com-

inodore

puter scientist

information f information; JUR inquiry; **une ~** a piece of information; **les ~s** RAD, TV the news sg; **traitement** m **de l'~** data processing

informatique 1 adj computer atr **2** f information technology, IT; **informatiser** computerize

informe shapeless

informer inform; **s'~** find out (**de qc auprès de qn** about sth from s.o.)

infraction f infringement (**à** of)

infranchissable impossible to cross; obstacle insurmountable

infrarouge infrared

infrastructure f infrastructure

infroissable crease-resistant

infructueux, **-euse** unsuccessful

infusion f herb tea

ingénierie f engineering; **ingénieur** m engineer

ingéniosité f ingeniousness

ingrat ungrateful; tâche thankless; **ingratitude** f ingratitude

ingrédient m ingredient

ingurgiter gulp down

inhabitable uninhabitable; **inhabité** uninhabited

inhalateur m MÉD inhaler; **inhaler** inhale

inhérent inherent (**à** in)

inhibé inhibited; **inhibition** f

PSYCH inhibition

inhospitalier, **-ère** inhospitable

inhumain inhuman

ininflammable non-flammable

ininterrompu uninterrupted; pluie, musique non-stop

initial, **~e 1** adj initial **2** f initial (letter)

initiation f initiation; **~ à** fig introduction to

inimitié f enmity

initiative f initiative

initié, **~e** m/f insider; **initier** initiate (**à** in); fig introduce (**à** to)

injecté: **~** (**de sang**) bloodshot; **injecter** inject; **injection** f injection

injoignable unreachable, uncontactable

injure f insult; **~s** abuse; **injurier** insult, abuse

injuste unfair, unjust; **injustice** f injustice; d'une décision aussi unfairness

inlassable tireless

inné innate

innocence f innocence; **innocent** innocent; **innocenter** clear

innombrable countless; auditoire, foule vast

innovant innovative; **innovation** f innovation

inoccupé personne idle; maison unoccupied

inodore odorless, Br odourless

inoffensif, -ive harmless; *humour* inoffensive

inondation f flood; **inonder** flood; **~ de** fig inundate with

inopiné unexpected

inopportun ill-timed

inorganique inorganic

inoubliable unforgettable

inouï unheard-of

inoxydable stainless

inquiet, -ète anxious, worried (*de* about); **inquiéter** worry; **s'~** worry (*de* about); **inquiétude** f anxiety

insaisissable elusive; *différence* imperceptible

insatiable insatiable

insatisfaisant unsatisfactory; **insatisfait** unsatisfied; *mécontent* dissatisfied

inscription f inscription; (*immatriculation*) registration; **inscrire** (*noter*) write down, note; *dans registre* enter; à *examen* register; (*graver*) inscribe; **s'~** put one's name down; à *l'université* register; à *un cours* enroll, Br enrol (à for)

insecte m insect; **insecticide** m insecticide

insécurité f insecurity; POL security problem

insensé mad, insane

insensibiliser numb; **insensible** ANAT numb; *personne* insensitive (à to)

insérer insert; *annonce* put; **insertion** f insertion

insigne m (*emblème*) insig-

nia; (*badge*) badge

insignifiant insignificant

insinuer insinuate; **s'~ dans** worm one's way into

insipide insipid

insistance f insistence; **insistant** insistent; **insister** insist; F (*persévérer*) persevere; **~ pour faire qch** insist on doing sth; **~ sur qc** (*souligner*) stress sth

insolation f sunstroke

insolence f insolence; **insolent** insolent

insolite unusual

insolvable insolvent

insomnie f insomnia

insonoriser soundproof

insouciant carefree

insoumis rebellious

insoutenable (*insupportable*) unbearable; *argument* untenable

inspecter inspect; **inspecteur, -trice** m/f inspector; **inspection** f inspection

inspiration f fig inspiration; **inspirer 1** v/i breathe in, inhale **2** v/t inspire; **s'~ de** be inspired by

installation f installation; **~ électrique** wiring; **~s** facilities; **installer** install; *appartement*: fit out; (*loger, placer*) put; **s'~** (*s'établir*) settle down; à *la campagne etc* settle; *d'un médecin, dentiste* set up

instant m instant, moment; **à l'~** just this minute; **dans un**

~ **in a minute**; *pour l'*~ **for the moment**; **instantané 1** *adj* **immediate**; *café* **instant**; *mort* **instantaneous 2** *m* PHOT **snap(shot)**

instaurer **establish**

instinct *m* **instinct**; **instinctif, -ive** **instinctive**

instituer **introduce**; **institut** *m* **institute**; ~ *de beauté* **beauty salon**; **instituteur, -trice** *m/f* **(primary) school teacher**; **institution** *f* **institution**

instructeur *m* MIL **instructor**; **instructif, -ive** **instructive**; **instruction** *f* (*enseignement, culture*) **education**; MIL **training**; JUR **preliminary investigation**; INFORM **instruction**; ~*s* **instructions**; **instruire** ÉDU **educate, teach**; MIL **train**; JUR **investigate**; **instruit** **(well-)educated**

instrument *m* **instrument**

insu: *à l'*~ *de* **unbeknownst to**

insubordination *f* **insubordination**

insuffisance *f* **deficiency**; ~ *respiratoire* **respiratory problem**; **insuffisant** *quantité* **insufficient**; *qualité* **inadequate**

insulaire 1 *adj* **island** *m* **at 2** *m/f* **islander**

insuline *f* **insulin**

insulte *f* **insult**; **insulter** **insult**

insupportable **unbearable**

insurger: *s'*~ *contre* **rise up**
against

insurrection *f* **insurrection**

intact **intact**

intégral **full, complete**; *texte* **unabridged**

intégration *f* (*assimilation*) **integration**

intègre **of integrity**

intégrer (*assimiler*) **integrate**; (*incorporer*) **incorporate**; **intégriste** *m/f* & *adj* **fundamentalist**

intégrité *f* (*honnêteté*) **integrity**

intellectuel, ~**le** *m/f* & *adj* **intellectual**

intelligence *f* **intelligence**; **intelligent** **intelligent**

intempéries *fpl* **bad weather**

intempestif, -ive **untimely**

intenable *situation, froid* **unbearable**

intense **intense**; **intensif, -ive** **intensive**; **intensification** *f* **intensification**; *d'un conflit* **escalation**; **intensifier** **intensify**; *s'*~ **intensify**; *d'un conflit* **escalate**; **intensité** *f* **intensity**

intenter: ~ *un procès contre* **start proceedings against**

intention *f* **intention**; *avoir l'*~ *de faire qch* **intend to do sth**; *à l'*~ *de* **for**; **intentionné**: *bien* ~ **well-meaning**; *mal* ~ **ill-intentioned**; **intentionnel**, ~**le** **intentional**

interactif, -ive **interactive**

intercéder: ~ *pour qn* **intercede for s.o.**

intercepter intercept; *soleil* shut out

interchangeable interchangeable

interdiction f ban; **interdire** ban; **~ à qn de faire qc** forbid s.o. to do sth; **interdit** forbidden; *(très étonné)* taken aback

intéressant interesting; *(avide)* selfish; *prix* good; *situation* well-paid; **intéressé** interested; *(concerné)* concerned; **intéresser** interest; *(concerner)* concern; **s'~ à** be interested in; **intérêt** m interest; *(égoïsme)* self-interest; **~s** COMM interest

interface f interface

intérieur 1 *adj poche* inside; *porte, vie* inner; *politique, vol* domestic; *mer* inland **2** m inside; *d'une auto etc* interior; **à l'~ (de)** inside

intérim m interim; *travail* temporary work; **intérimaire 1** *adj travail* temporary **2** m/f temp

interlocuteur, -trice m/f: **mon/son ~** the person I/ she was talking to

intermédiaire 1 *adj* intermédiate **2** m/f intermediary; COMM middleman

interminable interminable

intermittence f: **par ~** intermittently

international, ~e m/f & adj international

interne 1 *adj* internal; *oreille* inner; *d'une société* in-house **2** m/f *élève* boarder; *médecin* intern, Br houseman; **interner** intern

Internet m Internet; **sur ~** on the Internet

interpeller call out to; *de la police*, POL question

interphone m intercom; *d'un immeuble* entry phone

interposer interpose; **s'~** *(intervenir)* intervene

interprète m/f interpreter; *(porte-parole)* spokesperson; **interpréter** interpret; *rôle*, MUS play

interrogation f question; *d'un suspect* questioning, interrogation; **interrogatoire** m *par police* questioning; *par juge* cross-examination; **interroger** question; *de la police* question, interrogate; *d'un juge* cross-examine

interrompre interrupt; **s'~** break off

interrupteur m switch; **interruption** f interruption; **sans ~** without stopping

intersection f intersection

intervalle m space, gap; *de temps* interval

intervenir intervene; *d'une rencontre* take place; **intervention** f intervention; MÉD operation; *(discours)* speech

interview f interview; **interviewer** interview

intestin 1 *adj* internal **2** m intestin

intime 1 *adj* intimate; *ami* close; *pièce* cozy, *Br* cosy; *vie* private **2** *m/f* close friend
intimider intimidate
intimité *f* intimacy; *vie privée* privacy
intituler call; *s'~* be called
intolérable intolerable; **intolérance** *f* intolerance; **intolérant** intolerant
intoxication *f* poisoning; *~ alimentaire* food poisoning; **intoxiquer** poison; *fig* brainwash
intransigeant intransigent
intrépide intrepid
intrigue *f* plot; *~s* scheming, plotting; **intriguer 1** *v/i* scheme, plot **2** *v/t* intrigue
introduction *f* introduction; **introduire** introduce; *visiteur* show in; (*engager*) insert; *s'~ dans* gain entry to
introuvable impossible to find
introverti, ~e *m/f* introvert
intrus, ~e *m/f* intruder
intuitif, -ive intuitive; **intuition** *f* intuition; (*pressentiment*) premonition
inusable hard-wearing
inutile *qui ne sert pas* useless; (*superflu*) pointless, unnecessary; **inutilisable** unuseable
invalide 1 *adj* (*infirme*) disabled **2** *m/f* disabled person; **invalider** JUR, POL invalidate; **invalidité** *f* disability
invariable invariable

invasion *f* invasion
invendable unsellable
inventaire *m* inventory; COMM *opération* stocktaking
inventer invent; *histoire* make up; **inventeur, -trice** *m/f* inventor; **invention** *f* invention
inverse 1 *adj* MATH inverse; *sens* opposite; *dans l'ordre ~* in reverse order **2** *m* opposite, reverse; **inverser** invert; *rôles* reverse
investigation *f* investigation
investir FIN invest; (*cerner*) surround; **investissement** *m* FIN investment
invétéré inveterate
investisseur, -euse *m* investor
invincible invincible; *obstacle* insuperable
invisible invisible
invitation *f* invitation; **invité, ~e** *m/f* guest; **inviter** invite; *~ qn à faire qch* urge s.o. to do sth
invivable unbearable
involontaire unintentional; *témoin* unwilling; *mouvement* involuntary
invoquer *Dieu* call on, invoke; *aide* call on; *texte, loi* refer to; *solution* put forward
invraisemblable unlikely, improbable
Iran *m*: *l'~* Iran; **iranien, ~ne** Iranian; **Iranien, ~ne** *m/f* Iranian

Iraq

Iraq m: l'~ Iraq; **iraquien, ~ne** Iraqi; **Iraquien, ~ne** m/f Iraqi

irascible irascible

irlandais, ~e 1 adj Irish **2** m langue Irish (Gaelic); **Irlandais, ~e** m/f Irishman; Irishwoman; **Irlande** f: l'~ Ireland

ironie f irony, **ironiser** be ironic

irraisonné irrational

irrationnel, ~le irrational

irréalisable projet impracticable; rêve unrealizable

irréaliste unrealistic

irréconciliable irreconcilable

irrécupérable beyond repair; personne beyond redemption; données irretrievable

irréductible indomitable; ennemi implacable

irréel, ~le unreal

irréfléchi thoughtless, reckless

irréfutable irrefutable

irrégulier, -ère irregular; surface, terrain uneven; étudiant, sportif erratic

irrémédiable maladie incurable; erreur irreparable

irremplaçable irreplaceable

irréparable faute, perte irreparable; vélo beyond repair

irréprochable irreproachable

irrésistible irresistible

irrésolu personne indecisive; problème unresolved

irrespirable unbreathable

irresponsable irresponsible

irrigation f AGR irrigation

irritable irritable; **irritation** f irritation; **irriter** irritate; s'~ get irritated

islam, Islam m REL Islam; **islamique** Islamic; **islamiste** Islamic fundamentalist

islandais, ~e 1 adj Icelandic **2** m langue Islandic; **Islandais, ~e** m/f Icelander; **Islande**: l'~ Iceland

isolation f insulation; contre le bruit soundproofing; **isolé** isolated; TECH insulated; **isolement** m isolation; **isoler** isolate; prisonnier place in solitary confinement; ÉL insulate

Israël m Israel; **israélien, ~ne** Israeli; **Israélien, ~ne** m/f Israeli

issu: être ~ de parenté come from; résultat stem from

issue f way out (aussi fig), exit; (fin) outcome; à l'~ de at the end of

Italie f: l'~ Italy; **italien, ~ne 1** adj Italian **2** m langue Italian; **Italien, ~ne** m/f Italian

itinéraire m itinerary

IVG f (= interruption volontaire de grossesse) termination, abortion

ivoire m ivory

ivre drunk; ~ de joie, colère wild with; **ivresse** f drunkenness; **ivrogne** m/f drunk

J

jacasser chatter

jacinthe f BOT hyacinth

jade m jade

jaillir shoot out (*de* from)

jalousie f jealousy; (*store*) Venetian blind; **jaloux, -ouse** jealous

jamais ◇ *positif* ever; **à ~** for ever, for good; ◇ *négatif* never; **ne ... ~** never; **je ne lui ai ~ parlé** I've never spoken to him

jambe f leg

jambon m ham

jante f rim

janvier m January

Japon: **le ~** Japan; **japonais, ~e** 1 *adj* Japanese 2 m *langue* Japanese; **Japonais, ~e** m/f Japanese

jappement m yap

jaquette f d'un livre dust jacket

jardin m garden; **~ botanique** botanical gardens pl; **~ public** park; **jardinage** m gardening; **jardiner** garden; **jardinier** m gardener; **jardinière** f à fleurs window box; **femme** f gardener

jargon m jargon; *péj* (*charabia*) gibberish

jarret m back of the knee; CUIS shin

jaser gossip

jatte f bowl

jauge f gauge; **jauger** gauge

jaunâtre yellowish; **jaune 1** *adj* yellow **2** m: **~ d'œuf** egg yolk; **jaunir** go yellow; **jaunisse** f MÉD jaundice

jazz m jazz; **jazzman** m jazz musician

je I

jean m jeans pl; **veste** f **en ~** denim jacket

jeep f jeep

Jésus-Christ Jesus (Christ)

jet m (*lancer*) throw; (*jaillissement*) jet; *de sang* spurt; **~ d'eau** fountain

jetable disposable

jetée f MAR jetty

jeter throw; (*se défaire de*) throw away; **~ un coup d'œil à qch** glance at sth

jeton m token; *de jeu* chip

jeu m play (*aussi* TECH); *activité, en tennis* game; (*série, ensemble*) set; *de cartes* deck, *Br* pack; MUS playing; THÉÂT acting; **le ~** gambling; **être en ~** be at stake; **~ de mots** play on words

jeudi m Thursday

jeun: **à ~** on an empty stomach

jeune 1 *adj* young; **~s mariés** newly-weds **2** m/f: **un ~** a young man; **les ~s** young people pl, the young

jeûne m fast; **jeûner** fast

jeunesse f youth; *caractère jeune* youthfulness

J.O. mpl (= *Jeux Olympiques*) Olympic Games

joaillerie f *magasin* jewelry store, *Br* jeweller's; *articles* jewelry, *Br* jewellery; **joaillier, -ère** m/f jeweler, *Br* jeweller

jogging m jogging; (*survêtement*) sweats pl, *Br* tracksuit; **faire du** ~ go jogging

joie f joy; **débordant de** ~ jubilant

joindre join; *efforts* combine; *à un courrier* enclose (*à* with); *personne* contact, get in touch with; *mains* clasp; **se** ~ **à qn pour faire qch** join s.o. in doing sth

joint m joint; *d'étanchéité* seal, gasket; *de robinet* washer

joli pretty

joncher strew (*de* with)

jonction f junction

jongler juggle; **jongleur** m juggler

joue f cheek

jouer 1 v/t play; *argent, réputation* gamble; THÉÂT *pièce* perform; *film* show; **la comédie** put on an act **2** v/i play; *d'un acteur* act; *parier* gamble; ~ **au football** play football; ~ **d'un instrument** play an instrument; ~ **sur cheval etc** put money on

jouet m toy

joueur, -euse m/f player; *de*

jeux d'argent gambler; **être beau/mauvais** ~ be a good/bad loser

jouir have an orgasm, come; ~ **de qc** enjoy sth; (*posséder*) have sth; **jouissance** f enjoyment; JUR possession

jour m day; (*lumière*) daylight; (*ouverture*) opening; **au grand** ~ in broad daylight; **de nos** ~**s** these days; **du** ~ **au lendemain** overnight; **être à** ~ be up to date; **se faire** ~ **de problèmes** come to light; **deux ans** ~ **pour** ~ two years to the day; **il fait** ~ it's (getting) light; **au petit** ~ at first light

journal m (*news*)paper; *intime* diary; TV, *à la radio* news sg; **journalisme** m journalism; **journaliste** m/f journalist

journée f day

jovial jovial

joyeux, -euse joyful; ~ **Noël!** Merry Christmas!

jubilation f jubilation; **jubiler** be jubilant; *péj* gloat

jucher perch

judiciaire legal

judicieux, -euse sensible, judicious

judo m judo

juge m judge; ~ **d'instruction** examining magistrate; ~ **de touche** SP linesman; **jugement** m judg(e)ment; **en matière criminelle** sentence; **porter un** ~ **sur** pass judg(e)-

ment on; **juger 1** v/t JUR try; (*évaluer*) judge; **~ qch/s.o. intéressant** consider sth/s.o. interesting; **~ que** think that; **~ de qn/qc** judge s.o./sth **2** v/i judge

juif, -ive adj Jewish; **Juif, -ive** m/f Jew

juillet m July

juin m June

jumeau, jumelle m/f & adj twin; **jumeler** villes twin; **jumelles** fpl binoculars

jument f mare

jungle f jungle

jupe f skirt

juré m JUR juror; **jurer** swear (**de qch** to sth)

juridiction f jurisdiction

juridique legal

juron m curse

jury m JUR jury; **d'un concours** panel, judges pl; ÉDU board of examiners

jus m juice

jusque 1 prép: **jusqu'à** lieu as far as, up to; temps until; **jusqu'où vous allez?** how far are you going? **2** adv even, including **3** conj: **jusqu'à ce qu'il s'endorme** (subj) until he falls asleep

juste 1 adj fair, just; salaire, récompense fair; (précis) right, correct; vêtement tight **2** adv just; viser, tirer accurately; **chanter ~** sing in tune; **justesse** f accuracy; **de ~** only just; **justice** f fairness, justice; JUR justice; **la ~** the law; **faire ~ à qn** do s.o. justice

justification f justification

justifier justify; **~ de qc** prove sth

juteux, -euse juicy

juvénile youthful; **délinquance ~** juvenile delinquency

juxtaposer juxtapose

K

kaki khaki

kamikaze m/f suicide bomber

kangourou m kangaroo

kébab m kabob, Br kebab

kermesse f fair

kérosène m kerosene

ketchup m ketchup

kg (= **kilogramme**) kg (= kilogram)

kidnapping m kidnapping;

kidnapper kidnap

kilo(gramme) m kilo(gram); **kilométrage** m mileage; **kilomètre** m kilometer, Br kilometre; **kilo-octet** m kilobyte, k

kinésithérapeute m/f physiotherapist

kiosque m pavilion; COMM kiosk; **~ à journaux** newsstand

kit m: **en ~** kit

klaxon *m* AUTO horn; **klaxonner** sound one's horn, hoot
km (= *kilomètre*) km (= kilometer)

knock-out *m* knockout
K-O *m* (= *knock-out*) KO
Ko *m* (= *kilo-octet* *m*) k (= kilobyte)

L

la[1] → **le**

la[2] *pron personnel* her; *chose* it

là here; *dans un autre lieu qu'ici* there; *causal* hence; *par~* that way; **là-bas** (over) there

laboratoire *m* laboratory, lab
laborieux, -euse laborious; *personne* hardworking
labourer plow
labyrinthe *m* labyrinth, maze
lac *m* lake
lacer tie
lacérer lacerate
lacet *m de chaussures* lace; *de la route* sharp turn
lâche 1 *adj* loose; *personne* cowardly **2** *m* coward
lâcher 1 *v/t* let go of; (*laisser tomber*) drop; (*libérer*) release; *ceinture* loosen; *juron, vérité* let sl; SP leave behind **2** *v/i de freins* fail; *d'une corde* break
lâcheté *f* cowardice
lacrymogène *gaz* tear atr; *grenade* tear-gas atr
lacune *f* gap
là-dedans inside; **là-dessous** underneath; *derrière* behind it; **là-dessus** on it,

on top; *à ce moment* at that instant; *sur ce point* about it; **là-haut** up there

laid ugly; **laideur** *f* ugliness; (*bassesse*) meanness
lainage *m étoffe* woolen *ou* Br woollen fabric; *vêtement* woolen, Br woollen; **laine** *f* wool; **laineux, -euse** fleecy
laïque 1 *adj* REL secular; (*sans confession*) State atr **2** *m/f* lay person
laisse *f* leash
laisser leave; (*permettre*) let; **se ~ aller** let o.s. go
laisser-aller *m* casualness
laissez-passer *m* pass
lait *m* milk; **laitage** *m* dairy product; **laitier, -ère** dairy atr
laiton *m* brass
laitue *f* BOT lettuce
lambin, ~e *m/f* F slowpoke F, Br slowcoach F
lambris *m* paneling, Br panelling
lame *f* blade; (*plaque*) strip; (*vague*) wave
lamentable deplorable; **lamenter: se ~** complain
lampadaire *m* floor lamp; *dans la rue* street light

lampe f lamp; **~ de poche** flashlight, Br torch

lancé established; **lancement** m launch; **lancer** throw; **avec force** hurl; **lancer** throw; hurl (**à** at); **cri** give; **fusée**, COMM launch; INFORM **programme** run; **moteur** start; **se ~ sur** marché enter; **piste de danse** step out onto; **se ~ dans** des activités take up; des explications launch into; des discussions get involved in

langage m language

langouste f spiny lobster

langue f tongue; LING language; **mauvaise ~** gossip; **~ maternelle** mother tongue

languette f d'une chaussure tongue

languir languish; d'une conversation flag

lanière f strap

laper lap up

lapider stone

lapin m rabbit

laps m: **~ de temps** period of time

laque f lacquer

larcin m petty theft

lard m bacon

lardon m lardon, diced bacon

large 1 adj wide; épaules, hanches broad; mesure, rôle large; (généreux) generous **2** adv: **voir ~** think big **3** m MAR open sea; **prendre le ~** fig take off; **largesse** f generosity; **largeur** f width; **~ d'es-**

prit broad-mindedness

larme f tear; **une ~ de** a drop of; **larmoyer** des yeux water; (se plaindre) complain

laryngite f laryngitis

las, ~se weary

laser m laser

lasser weary, tire; **se ~ de** tire ou weary of

latent latent

latéral lateral, side atr

latitude f latitude

latte f lath; de plancher board

lauréat, ~e m/f prizewinner

laurier m laurel; **feuille f de ~** CUIS bayleaf

lavabo m (wash)basin; **~s** toilets

lavage m washing

lavande f lavender

laver wash; tâche wash away; **laverie** f: **~ automatique** laundromat, Br laundrette; **lavette** f dishcloth; fig péj spineless individual

lave-vaisselle m dishwasher

laxatif, -ive adj & m laxative

laxisme m laxness

le complément d'objet direct him; chose it; **oui, je ~ sais** yes, I know

le, f la, pl les article défini the; **le garçon m les garçons** the boy/the boys; **je me suis cassé la jambe** I broke my leg; **j'aime le vin** I like wine; **les dinosaures avaient ...** dinosaurs had ...; **le premier mai** May first, Br the first of May; **ouvert le samedi**

open (on) Saturdays; **10 euros les 5** 10 euros for 5; **tu connais la France?** do you know France; **le printemps est là** spring is here; **je ne parle pas l'italien** I don't speak Italian

leader *m* POL leader

lécher lick

leçon *f* lesson

lecteur, -trice 1 *m/f* reader; **à l'université** foreign language assistant **2** *m* INFORM drive; **~ de CDs** CD player; **lecture** *f* reading

ledit, ladite the said

légal legal; **légaliser** *signature* authenticate; (*rendre légal*) legalize; **légalité** *f* legality

légende *f* legend; *sous image* caption; *d'une carte* key

léger, -ère light; *erreur, retard* slight; *mœurs* loose; (*frivole, irréfléchi*) thoughtless; **à la légère** lightly; **légèrement** lightly; (*un peu*) slightly; **légèreté** *f* lightness; (*frivolité, irréflexion*) thoughtlessness

légion *f* legion; **~ étrangère** Foreign Legion; **légionnaire** *m* legionnaire

législation *f* legislation

légitime legitimate

legs *m* legacy

léguer bequeath

légume *m* vegetable

lendemain *m*: **le ~** the next *ou* following day; **le ~ de son**

élection the day after he was elected

lent slow; **lentement** slowly; **lenteur** *f* slowness

lentille *f* TECH lens; *légume sec* lentil

léopard *m* leopard

lequel, laquelle (*pl* lesquels, lesquelles) *interrogatif* which (one); *relatif, avec personne* who, *avec chose* which

les[1] → **le**

les[2] *pron personnel* them

lesbien, ~ne *adj & f* lesbian

léser injure; *intérêts* damage; *droits* infringe

lésiner skimp (**sur** on)

lésion *f* MÉD lesion

lessive *f* *produit* laundry detergent, *Br* washing powder; *liquide* detergent; *linge* laundry; **faire la ~** do the laundry

leste agile; *propos* crude

léthargie *f* lethargy

lettre *f* letter; **à la ~, au pied de la ~** literally; **en toutes ~s** in full; *fig* in black and white; **~s** literature; *études* arts; **lettré** well-read

leucémie *f* MÉD leukemia, *Br* leukaemia

leur 1 *adj possessif* their **2** *pron personnel*: **le/la ~, les ~s** theirs **3** *complément d'objet indirect* (to) them

leurrer *fig* deceive

levé: *m*, **levée** *f* lifting; *d'une séance* adjournment; *du courrier* collection; *aux cartes* trick; *lever 1 v/t* raise, lift; *poids, interdiction* lift; *impôts* collect **2** *v/i de la pâte* rise; *se ~* get up; *du soleil* rise; *du jour* break **3** *m:* **~ du jour** daybreak; **~ du soleil** sunrise

levier *m* lever; **~ de vitesse** gear shift, *surtout Br* gear lever

lèvre *f* lip

levure *f* yeast; **~ chimique** baking powder

lézard *m* lizard

lézarde *f* crack

liaison *f* connection; *amoureuse* affair; *de train* link; LING liaison

liant sociable

libellule *f* dragonfly

libéral liberal; *profession f ~e* profession; **libéralisme** *m* liberalism

libérateur, -trice 1 *adj* liberating **2** *m/f* liberator; **libération** *f* liberation; *d'un prisonnier* release; **~ conditionnelle** parole; **libérer** liberate; *prisonnier* release, free (*de* from); *gaz, d'un engagement* release

liberté *f* freedom, liberty; *mettre en ~* set free, release

librairie *f* bookstore, *Br* bookshop

libre free (*de faire* to do); **libre-service** *m* self-service; *magasin* self-service shop

Libye *f* Libya; **libyen**, **~ne** Libyan; **Libyen**; **~ne** *m/f* Libyan

licence *f* license, *Br* licence; *diplôme* degree

licenciement *m* layoff; (*renvoi*) dismissal; **licencier** lay off; (*renvoyer*) dismiss

lié: *être ~ par* be bound by; *être très ~ avec qn* be very close to s.o.

lien *m* tie, bond; (*rapport*) connection; *avoir un ~ de parenté* be related

lier tie (up); *d'un contrat* be binding on; CUIS thicken; *pensées, personnes* connect; **~ amitié avec qn** make friends with s.o.

lierre *m* BOT ivy

lieu *m* place; **~x** premises; JUR scene; *au ~ de (faire) qch* instead of (doing) sth; *avoir ~* take place; *donner ~ à* give rise to; *en premier ~* in the first place; *s'il y a ~* if necessary

lièvre *m* hare

ligne *f* line; *d'autobus* number; *garder la ~* keep one's figure; *entrer en ~ de compte* be taken into consideration; *pêcher à la ~* go angling; *en ~* INFORM on line; *achats en ~* on-line shopping

liguer: *se ~* join forces (*pour faire* to do)

lilas *m* & *adj inv* lilac

limace *f* slug

lime *f* file; **~ à ongles** nail file; **limer** file

limitation *f* limitation; **~ de**

vitesse speed limit; **limite** *f* limit; (*frontière*) boundary; **à la** ~ if absolutely necessary; **date** *f* ~ deadline; **vitesse** ~ speed limit; **limiter** limit (*à* to)

limoger POL dismiss

limonade *f* lemonade

limousine *f* limousine

lin *m* BOT flax; *toile* linen

linéaire linear

linge *m* linen; (*lessive*) washing

lingerie *f* lingerie

linguiste *m/f* linguist

lion *m* lion; ASTROL **Lion** Leo; **lionne** *f* lioness

liposuccion *f* liposuction

liqueur *f* liqueur

liquidation *f* liquidation; *vente au rabais* sale

liquide 1 *adj* liquid; **argent** *m* ~ cash **2** *m* liquid; ~ **de freins** brake fluid; **liquider** liquidate; *stock* sell off; *problème* dispose of

lire read

lis *m* BOT lily

lisible legible

lisse smooth; **lisser** smooth

liste *f* list; ~ **d'attente** waiting list; ~ **de commissions** shopping list; **lister** list; **listing** *m* printout

lit *m* bed; **aller au** ~ go to bed; ~ **de camp** cot, *Br* camp bed; **literie** *f* bedding

litige *m* dispute

litre *m* liter, *Br* litre

littéraire literary; **littérature** *f* literature

littoral 1 *adj* coastal **2** *m* coastline

livraison *f* delivery

livre[1] *m* book; ~ **de poche** paperback

livre[2] *f poids, monnaie* pound

livrer *marchandises* deliver; *prisonnier* hand over; *secret* divulge; **se** ~ (*se confier*) open up; (*se soumettre*) give o.s. up; **se** ~ **à** (*se confier*) confide in; *activité* indulge in; *l'abattement* give way to

livret *m* booklet; *d'opéra* libretto

livreur *m/f* delivery man; ~ **de journaux** paper boy

lobby *m* lobby

lobe *m*: ~ **de l'oreille** earlobe

local 1 *adj* local **2** *m* (*salle*) premises *pl*; **locaux** premises; **localisation** *f* location; *de software etc* localization; **localiser** locate; (*limiter*), *de software* localize

locataire *m/f* tenant; **location** *f par propriétaire* renting out; *par locataire* renting; (*loyer*) rent; *au théâtre* reservation

logement *m* accommodations, *Br* accommodation, *pl*; (*appartement*) apartment, *Br aussi* flat; **loger 1** *v/t* accommodate **2** *v/i* live; **logeur** *m* landlord; **logeuse** *f* landlady

logiciel *m* INFORM software

logique 1 *adj* logical **2** *f* logic

loi f law

loin far (**de** from); *dans le passé* long ago; *dans l'avenir* a long way off; *au ~* in the distance

lointain 1 adj distant **2** m distance

loisir m leisure; *~s* leisure activities

Londres London

long, longue 1 adj long; *à ~ terme* in the long term; *à la longue* in time; *être ~ (à faire qch)* take a long time (doing sth) **2** adv: *en dire ~* speak volumes **3** m: *de deux mètres de ~* two meters long; *le ~ de* along

longer follow

longitude f longitude

longtemps a long time

longueur f for a long time; *parler at length*

longueur f length; *sur la même ~ d'onde* on the same wavelength

loquace talkative

loque f rag

loquet m latch

lorgner eye; *héritage, poste* have one's eye on

lors: *dès ~* from now on; *~ de* during

lorsque when

lot m (*destin*) fate; *à la loterie* prize; (*portion*) share; COMM batch

loterie f lottery

loti: *bien/mal ~* well/badly off

lotion f lotion

lotissement m (*parcelle*) plot; *terrain loti* housing development

louable praiseworthy; **louange** f praise

louche[1] adj sleazy

louche[2] f ladle

loucher squint

louer[1] rent

louer[2] f (*vanter*) praise (**de**, **pour** for)

loup m wolf

loupe f magnifying glass

louper F *travail* botch; *bus* miss

lourd heavy; *plaisanterie* clumsy; *temps* oppressive; **lourdaud, ~e 1** adj clumsy **2** m/f oaf; **lourdement** heavily

loyal honest; *adversaire* fairminded; *ami* loyal

loyer m rent

lubie f whim

lubrifiant m lubricant; **lubrifier** lubricate

lucarne f skylight

lucide lucid; (*conscient*) conscious; **lucidité** f lucidity

lucratif, -ive lucrative

lueur f faint light; *une ~ d'espoir* a glimmer of hope

luge f toboggan; *faire de la ~* go tobogganing

lugubre gloomy, lugubrious

lui *complément d'objet indirect, masculin* (to) him; *féminin* (to) her; *chose, animal* (to) it; *après prép, masculin* him; *animal* it

lui-même himself; *de chose* itself

luire glint, glisten

lumière f light; *à la ~ de* in the light of

lumineux, -euse luminous; *ciel, couleur* bright; *affiche* illuminated; *idée* brilliant

lunaire lunar

lunatique lunatic

lundi m Monday

lune f moon; *~ de miel* honeymoon

lunette f: *~s* glasses; *~s de soleil* sunglasses; *~s de ski* ski goggles

lustre m (*lampe*) chandelier; *fig* luster, *Br* lustre; **lustrer** polish

lutte f fight, struggle; SP wrestling; **lutter** fight, struggle; SP wrestle

luxe m luxury; *de ~* luxury *atr*

Luxembourg: *le ~* Luxembourg; **luxembourgeois, ~e** of/from Luxemburg, Luxemburg *atr*; **Luxembourgeois, ~e** m/f Luxemburger

luxer: *se ~ l'épaule* dislocate one's shoulder

luxueux, -euse luxurious

luxuriant luxuriant

lycée m senior high, *Br* grammar school; **lycéen, ~ne** m/f student (at a lycéa)

lyophilisé freeze-dried

lyrique lyric; *qui a du lyrisme* lyrical; *artiste ~* opera singer

M

M. (= *monsieur*) Mr

ma → *mon*

macabre macabre

macédoine f: *~ de légumes* mixed vegetables pl; *~ de fruits* fruit salad

macérer CUIS: *faire ~* marinate

mâcher chew

machin m F thing

machinal mechanical

machine f machine; NAUT engine; *fig* machinery; *~ à laver* washing machine; *~ à sous* slot machine

machisme m machismo; **macho 1** *adj* male chauvinist **2**

m macho type

mâchoire f jaw; **mâchonner** chew (on); (*marmonner*) mutter

maçon m bricklayer; *avec des pierres* mason; **maçonnerie** f masonry

maculer spatter

madame f: *Madame Durand* Mrs Durand; *mesdames et messieurs* ladies and gentlemen

mademoiselle f: *Mademoiselle Durand* Miss Durand

madone f Madonna

magasin m (*boutique*) store, *surtout Br* shop; (*dépôt*) store room; **grand** ~ department store; **magasinier** *m* storeman

magazine *m* magazine

mage *m*: **les Rois** ~**s** the Three Wise Men, the Magi

magicien, ~**ne** *m/f* magician

magie *f* magic; **magique** *f* magic, magical

magistral *ton* magisterial; *fig* masterly; **cours** *m* ~ lecture

magistrat *m* JUR magistrate

magnanime magnanimous

magner: **se** ~ F move it F

magnétique magnetic

magnétophone *m* tape recorder

magnétoscope *m* video (recorder)

magnifique magnificent

magouille *f* F scheming; ~**s électorales** election shenanigans F

mai *m* May

maigre thin; *résultat, salaire* meager, *Br* meagre; **maigrir** get thin, lose weight

mailing *m* mailshot

maille *f* stitch

maillet *m* mallet

maillot *m* SP shirt, jersey; *de coureur* vest; ~ **(de bain)** swimsuit

main *f* hand; **fait à la** ~ handmade; **prendre qc en** ~ *fig* take sth in hand; **perdre la** ~ *fig* lose one's touch; **sous la** ~ to hand, within reach

main-d'œuvre *f inv* manpower, labor, *Br* labour

maint *fml* many; **à** ~**es reprises** time and again

maintenance *f* maintenance

maintenant now; ~ **que** now that

maintenir keep; *tradition* uphold; *(tenir fermement)* hold; *d'une poutre* hold up; *(soutenir)* maintain; **se** ~ *d'un prix* hold steady; *d'une tradition, de la paix* last; **se** ~ **au pouvoir** stay in power; **maintien** *m* maintenance; ~ **de la paix** peace keeping

maire *m* mayor; **mairie** *f* town hall

mais 1 *conj* but **2** *adv*: ~ **bien sûr!** of course!; ~ **non!** no!

maïs *m* BOT corn, *Br aussi* maize; *en boîte* sweet corn

maison *f* house; *(chez-soi)* home; COMM company; **à la** ~ at home; **pâté** *m* ~ homemade pâté; ~ **de campagne** country house

maître *m* master; *(professeur)* school teacher; *(peintre, écrivain)* maestro; ~ **chanteur** blackmailer; ~ **d'hôtel** maître d', *Br* head waiter; ~ **nageur** swimming instructor

maîtresse 1 *f* mistress *(aussi amante)*; *(professeur)* schoolteacher **2** *adj*: **idée** *f* ~ main idea

maîtrise *f* mastery; *diplôme* MA, master's (degree); ~ **de soi** self-control; **maîtri-**

ser master; *cheval* gain control of; *incendie* bring under control

majestueux, -euse majestic

majeur 1 *adj* major; *être ~* JUR be of age **2** *m* middle finger; **majorité** *f* majority

majuscule *f & adj*: (*lettre f*) ~ capital (letter)

mal 1 *m* evil; (*maladie*) illness; (*difficulté*) difficulty; *faire ~* hurt; *avoir ~ aux dents* have toothache; *se donner du ~* go to a lot of trouble; *faire du ~ à qn* hurt s.o.; *~ de mer* seasickness **2** *adv* badly; *pas ~* not bad; *se sentir ~* feel ill **3** *adj*: *faire/dire qc de ~* do/say sth bad

malade ill, sick; *tomber ~* fall ill; *~ mental* mentally ill; **maladie** *f* illness

maladresse *f* clumsiness; **maladroit** clumsy

malaise *m* discomfort; POL malaise; *faire un ~* faint

malavisé ill-advised

malchance *f* bad luck

mâle *m & adj* male

malédiction *f* curse

malencontreux, -euse unfortunate

malentendant hard of hearing

malfaiteur *m* malefactor

malgré in spite of

malheur *m* misfortune; (*malchance*) bad luck; *par ~* unfortunately; **malheureusement** unfortunately;

malheureux, -euse unfortunate; (*triste*) unhappy; (*insignifiant*) silly little

malhonnête dishonest; **malhonnêteté** *f* dishonesty

malice *f* malice; (*espièglerie*) mischief; **malicieux, -euse** malicious; (*coquin*) mischievous

malin, -igne (*rusé*) crafty, cunning; (*méchant*) malicious; MÉD malignant

malle *f* trunk; **mallette** *f* little bag

malodorant foul-smelling

malpoli impolite

malpropre dirty

malsain unhealthy

malt *m* malt

Malte *f* Malta; **maltais, ~e** Maltese; **Maltais, ~e** *m/f* Maltese

maltraiter mistreat, maltreat

malveillant malevolent

malvoyant, ~e 1 *adj* visually impaired **2** *m/f* visually impaired person

maman *f* Mom, *Br* Mum

mamelle *f de vache* udder; *de chienne* teat

mamie *f F* granny

mammifère *m* mammal

manager *m* manager

manche¹ *m d'outils* handle; *d'un violon* neck

manche² *f* sleeve; SP round; **la Manche** the English Channel

manchette *f* cuff; *d'un journal* headline

mandarine *f* mandarin (orange)

mandat *m* POL term of office, mandate; (*procuration*) proxy; *de la poste* postal order; *~ d'arrêt* arrest warrant; **mandataire** *m/f* *à une réunion* proxy

manège *m* riding school; (*carrousel*) carousel, *Br* roundabout; *fig* game

mangeable edible, eatable

mangeoire *f* manger

manger eat; *argent, temps* eat up; *mots* swallow

maniable *voiture* easy to handle

maniaque fussy; **manie** *f* mania

manier handle

manière *f* way, manner; *~s* manners; *affectées* airs and graces; *à la ~ de* in the style of; *de cette ~* (in) that way; *de toute ~* anyway; *d'une ~ générale* generally speaking; *de ~ à faire qch* so as to do sth; **maniéré** affected

manifestant, -e *m/f* demonstrator; **manifestation** *f de joie etc* expression; POL demonstration; *culturelle, sportive* event

manifeste 1 *adj* obvious **2** *m* POL manifesto; **manifester 1** *v/t* show; *se ~ de maladie, problèmes* manifest itself/themselves **2** *v/i* demonstrate

manipulateur, -trice manipu-

lative; **manipulation** *f d'un appareil* handling; *d'une personne* manipulation; *~ génétique* genetic engineering; **manipuler** handle; *personne* manipulate

mannequin *m dans magasin* dummy; *personne* model

manœuvre 1 *f* maneuver, *Br* manœuvre; *d'un outil, une machine etc* operation **2** *m* unskilled laborer *ou Br* labourer; **manœuvrer** maneuver, *Br* manœuvre

manoir *m* manor (house)

manque *m* lack; *par ~ de* for lack of; **manqué** unsuccessful; *rendez-vous* missed; **manquer 1** *v/i* (*être absent*) be missing; (*faire défaut*) be lacking; (*échouer*) fail; *tu me manques* I miss you; *~ à promesse* fail to keep; *devoir* fail in **2** *v/t* (*être absent à*) miss; *examen* fail; *elle a manqué* (*de*) *se faire écraser* she was almost run over **3** *impersonnel il manque des preuves* there's a lack of evidence

manteau *m* coat; *de neige* blanket; *~ de cheminée* mantelpiece

manucure *f* manicure

manuel, -le *adj & m* manual; *~ d'utilisation* instruction manual

manufacturé: *produits mpl ~s* manufactured goods

manuscrit 1 *adj* handwritten

2 *m* manuscript

maquereau *m* zo mackerel; F (*souteneur*) pimp

maquette *f* model

maquillage *m* make-up; **maquiller** make up; *crime, vérité* conceal; **se ~** put one's make-up on

marais *m* swamp

marathon *m* marathon

marbre *m* marble

marc *m*: **~ de café** coffee grounds *pl*

marchand, ~e 1 *adj valeur* market *atr*; *rue* shopping *atr*; *marine* merchant *atr* **2** *m/f* merchant, storekeeper, *Br* shopkeeper; **marchander** haggle, bargain; **marchandise** *f*: **~s** merchandise; *train m de ~s* freight train

marche *f* walking; *d'escalier* step; MUS, MIL march; *des événements* course; (*démarche*) walk; **~ arrière** AUTO reverse; **mettre en ~** start (up)

marché *m* market; (*accord*) deal; (*à*) **bon ~** cheap; **par-dessus le ~** into the bargain; **~ boursier** stock market; **le Marché Commun** POL the Common Market; **~ noir** black market

marcher walk; MIL march; *d'une machine* run, work; F (*réussir*) work; *d'un bus, train* run; **faire ~ qn** pull s.o.'s leg

mardi *m* Tuesday; **Mardi gras**

Mardi Gras, *Br* Shrove Tuesday

mare *f* pond; **~ de sang** pool of blood

marécage *m* swamp; **marécageux, -euse** swampy

marée *f* tide; **~ basse/haute** low/high tide; **~ noire** oil slick

margarine *f* margarine

marge *f* margin; **en ~ de** on the fringes of

marguerite *f* daisy

mari *m* husband

mariage *m fête* wedding; *état* marriage

marié 1 *adj* married **2** *m* (bride)groom; **mariée** *f* bride; **marier** marry; **se ~** get married; **se ~ avec** marry, get married to

marijuana *f* marijuana

marin 1 *adj air* sea *atr*; *animaux* marine **2** *m* sailor

marine *f* MIL navy; (**bleu**) **~** navy (blue)

marionnette *f* puppet; *avec des ficelles aussi* marionnette

marmelade *f* marmalade

marmite *f* (large) pot

marmonner mutter

maroquinerie *f* leather goods shop; *articles* leather goods *pl*

marquant remarkable

marque *f* mark; COMM brand; *de voiture* make; COMM (*signe*) trademark; **~ déposée** registered trademark; **de ~**

matinée

COMM branded; *fig: personne* distinguished; **marquer** mark; (*noter*) write down; *personnalité* leave its mark on; *d'un baromètre etc* show; (*accentuer*) *taille* emphasize; **~ un but** score (a goal); **marqueur** *m* marker pen

marraine *f* godmother

marrant F funny

marre F: *j'en ai* ~ I've had enough

marrer F: *se* ~ have a good laugh

marron 1 *m* chestnut **2** *adj inv* brown; **marronnier** *m* chestnut tree

mars *m* March

marteau *m* hammer; **~ piqueur** pneumatic drill; **marteler** hammer

martyr, **~e1** *m/f* martyr; **martyre2** *m* martyrdom; **martyriser** abuse; *petit frère, camarade de classe* bully

masculin male; GRAM masculine

masque *m* mask; **masquer** mask

massacre *m* massacre; **massacrer** massacre

massage *m* massage

masse *f* mass; ÉL ground, *Br* earth,; *en* ~ in large numbers, en masse; *manifestation* massive; *une* ~ *de choses à faire* masses *pl* (of things) to do

massif, **-ive 1** *adj* massif; *or, chêne* solid **2** *m* massif; ~

de fleurs flowerbed

massue *f* club

mastiquer *nourriture* chew

mat1 matt; *son* dull

mat2 *inv aux échecs* checkmated

mât *m* mast

match *m* game, *Br aussi* match; **~ nul** tied game, *Br* draw

matelas *m* mattress; **~ pneumatique** air bed

matelot *m* sailor

matérialiser: *se* ~ materialize; **matériau** *m* material; **matériel**, **~le 1** *adj* material **2** *m de camping*, SP equipment; INFORM hardware

maternel, **~le 1** *adj* maternal; *langue f* **~le** mother tongue **2** *f* nursery school; **maternité** *f* motherhood; *établissement* maternity hospital; (*enfantement*) pregnancy

mathématicien, **~ne** *m/f* mathematician; **mathématique 1** *adj* mathematical **2** *fpl*: **~s** mathematics

matière *f* material; PHYS, PHIL matter; (*sujet*) subject; **entrée en** ~ introduction; **en** ~ **de** when it comes to; **~ première** raw material

matin *m* morning; *le* ~ in the morning; *tous les lundis* **~s** every Monday morning; **matinal** morning *atr*; *être* ~ be an early riser; **matinée** *f* morning; (*spectacle*) matinée; *faire la grasse* ~ sleep late

matou *m* tom cat

matricule *m* number

matrimonial matrimonial

maturité *f* maturity

maudire curse; **maudit** F damn F

mauvais 1 *adj* bad; (*erroné*) wrong **2** *adv* bad; **il fait ~** the weather is bad

mauve mauve

maximum *adj* & *m* maximum; **au ~** at most, at the maximum

mayonnaise *f* mayonnaise, mayo F

me me; *complément d'objet indirect* (to) me; **je ~ suis coupé** I've cut myself; **je ~ lève à …** I get up at …

mec *m* guy F

mécanicien *m* mechanic; **mécanique 1** *adj* mechanical **2** *f* mechanics; **mécanisme** *m* mechanism

méchanceté *f* nastiness; *action, parole* nasty thing to do/say; **méchant, ~e 1** *adj* nasty; *enfant* naughty **2** *m/f* F: **les gentils et les ~s** the goodies and the baddies

mèche *f de bougie* wick; *d'explosif* fuse; *de perceuse* bit; *de cheveux* strand

méconnaissable unrecognizable

mécontent unhappy, displeased (*de* with); **mécontenter** displease

médaille *f* medal; **médaillon**

m medallion

médecin *m* doctor

médecine *f* medicine; **les ~s douces** alternative medicines

média *m* media *pl*

médiateur, -trice *m/f* mediator

médiatique media *atr*

médical medical

médicament *m* medicine, drug

médiéval medieval, Br mediaeval

médiocre mediocre; **~ en** EDU poor at

médire: **~ de qn** run s.o. down

méditation *f* meditation; **méditer 1** *v/t* think about, reflect on **2** *v/i* meditate (**sur** on)

Méditerranée: **la ~** the Mediterranean; **méditerranéen, ~ne** Mediterranean; **Méditerranéen, ~ne** *m/f* Mediterranean *atr*

méduse *f* zo jellyfish

meeting *m* meeting

méfait *m* JUR misdemeanor, Br misdemeanour; **~s de la drogue** harmful effects

méfiance *f* mistrust, suspicion; **méfiant** suspicious; **méfier:** **se ~ de** mistrust, be suspicious of; (*se tenir en garde*) be wary of

mégaoctet *m* INFORM megabyte

mégarde *f*: **par ~** inadvertently

mention

mégot m cigarette butt

meilleur 1 adj better; **le ~ ...** the best ... **2** m: **le ~** the best

mél m email

mélancolie f gloom, melancholy

mélange f mixture; de thés blend; action mixing; de thés blending; **mélanger** mix; thés blend; (brouiller) jumble up, mix up

mêlée f fray, melee; en rugby scrum; **mêler** mix; (réunir) combine; (brouiller) jumble up, mix up; **~ qn à qc** fig involve s.o. in sth; **se ~ à qc** get involved with sth; **se ~ de qc** interfere in sth

mélodie f tune, melody; **mélodieux, -euse** tuneful, melodious; voix melodious

mélodramatique melodramatic; **mélodrame** m melodrama

melon m BOT melon

membre m ANAT limb; fig member

même 1 adj: le/la **~**, les **~**s the same; la **bonté ~** kindness itself **2** pron: le/la **~** the same one; les **~**s the same ones; **cela revient au ~** it comes to the same thing **3** adv even; **~ pas** not even; **faire de ~** do the same; **de ~!** likewise!; **être à ~ de faire** be able to do; **tout de ~** all the same; **quand ~** all the same; **moi de ~** me too

mémoire 1 f memory; **à la ~**

de in memory of **2** m (exposé) report; (dissertation) thesis; **~s** memoirs; **mémorable** memorable; **mémoriser** memorize

menace f threat; **menacer** threaten (**de** with; **de faire** to do)

ménage m (famille) household; (couple) (married) couple; **faire le ~** clean house, Br do the housework; **ménagement** m consideration; **ménager**[1] v/t treat with consideration; temps, argent use sparingly; (arranger) arrange; **ménager**[2], **-ère 1** adj household atr **2** f home-maker, housewife

mendiant, ~e m/f beggar; **mendier 1** v/i beg **2** v/t beg for

mener 1 v/t lead; (amener, transporter) take **2** v/i: **~ d'un chemin** lead to; **ne ~ à rien** des efforts come to nothing; **meneur** m leader; péj ringleader

mensonge m lie; **mensonger, -ère** false

mensualité f somme à payer monthly payment; **mensuel, ~le** the monthly

mental mental; **calcul** m **~** mental arithmetic; **mentalité** f mentality

menteur, -euse m/f liar

menthe f BOT mint

mention f mention; à un examen grade, Br aussi mark;

mentionner mention

mentir lie (**à** to)

menton *m* chin

menu 1 *adj* slight; *morceaux* small 2 *adv* finely, fine 3 *m* menu (*aussi* INFORM); (*repas*) set meal; **par le ~** in minute detail

menuisier *m* carpenter

méprendre: **se ~** be mistaken (**sur** about)

mépris *m* (*indifférence*) disdain; (*dégoût*) scorn; **méprisable** despicable; **méprisant** scornful; **mépriser** *argent, ennemi* despise; *conseil, danger* scorn

mer *f* sea; **en ~** at sea; **la Mer du Nord** the North Sea

mercenaire *m* mercenary

mercerie *f magasin* notions store, *Br* haberdashery; *articles* notions, *Br* haberdashery *pl*

merci 1 *int* thanks, thank you (**de, pour** for); **~ bien** thanks a lot, thank you very much 2 *f* mercy

mercredi *m* Wednesday

merde *f* P shit P; **merder** P screw up P

mère *f* mother

méridional southern

mérite *m* merit; **mériter** deserve; **~ le détour** be worth a visit

merle *m* blackbird

merveille *f* wonder, marvel; **à ~** wonderfully well; **merveilleux, -euse** wonderful

mes → **mon**

mésaventure *f* mishap

mesquin mean

message *m* message; **messager, -ère** *m/f* messenger, courier; **messagerie** *f* parcels service; **électronique** electronic mail; **~ vocale** voicemail

messe *f* REL mass

mesure *f* measurement; *disposition* measure, step; MUS (*rythme*) time; **à ~ que** as; **être en ~ de faire qch** be in a position to do sth; **outre ~** excessive; **sur ~** *fig* tailor-made; **mesurer** measure; *risque, importance* gauge; *paroles* weigh; **se ~ avec qn** pit o.s. against s.o.

métal *m* metal; **métallique** metallic

métamorphoser: **se ~** metamorphose

météo *f* weather forecast

météore *m* meteor

météorologie *f* meteorology; *service* weather office

méthode *f* method

méticuleux, -euse meticulous

métier *m* profession; *manuel* trade; (*expérience*) experience; *machine* loom

métrage *m d'un film* footage; **court ~** short

mètre *m* meter, *Br* metre; (*règle*) tape measure

métrique metric

métro *m* subway, *Br* under-

ground; *à Paris* metro
métropole *f* metropolis; *de colonie* mother country
mettre put; *vêtements, lunettes, chauffage* put on; *réveil* set; *argent dans entreprise* put in; *~ deux heures à faire qc* take two hours to do sth; *se ~ à faire* start to do
meuble *m* piece of furniture; *~s* furniture; **meubler** furnish
meurtre *m* murder; **meurtrier, -ère 1** *adj* deadly **2** *m/f* murderer
meurtrir bruise; **meurtrissure** *f* bruise
meute *f* pack; *fig* mob
mexicain, ~e *m* Mexican; **Mexicain, ~e** *m/f* Mexican; **Mexique:** *le ~* Mexico
mi-... half; *à mi-chemin* half-way; *(à la) mi-janvier* mid-January
mi-bas *mpl* knee-highs, pop socks
miche *f* large round loaf
micro *m* mike; INFORM computer, PC; *d'espionnage* bug
microbe *m* microbe
microfilm *m* microfilm
micro-ondes *m* microwave
microphone *m* microphone
microscope *m* microscope
midi *m* noon, twelve o'clock; *(sud)* south; **le Midi** the South of France
mie *f de pain* crumb
miel *m* honey
mien: *le mien, la mienne, les*

miens, les miennes mine
miette *f* crumb
mieux 1 *adv comparatif de bien* better; *superlatif de bien* best; *le ~* best; *de ~ en ~* better and better; *tant ~* so much the better; *vous feriez ~ de ...* you would ou should do best to ... **2** *m:* *(progrès)* progress; *j'ai fait de mon ~* I did my best; *le ~, c'est de ...* the best thing is to ...
mièvre insipid
mignon, ~ne *(charmant)* cute; *(gentil)* nice
migraine *f* migraine
migration *f* migration; **migrer** migrate
mijoter CUIS simmer; *fig* hatch
milieu *m (centre)* middle; *biologique, social* environment; *au ~ de* in the middle of; *le ~* the underworld
militaire 1 *adj* military **2** *m* soldier; *les ~s* the military *sg ou pl*
militant active
militer: *~ dans* be an active member of; *~ pour/contre* *fig* militate for/against
mille 1 (a) thousand **2** *m mesure* mile; *~ marin* nautical mile
millénaire 1 *adj* thousand-year old **2** *m* millennium
milliard *m* billion; **milliardaire** *m/f* billionaire
millième thousandth

millier *m* thousand

milligramme *m* milligram

millimètre millimeter, *Br* millimetre

million *m* million; **millionnaire** *m/f* millionaire

minable mean, shabby; *un salaire* ~ a pittance

mince thin, *personne* slim; *espoir* slight; *somme, profit* small; *argument* flimsy

mine¹ *f* appearance, look; *avoir bonne/mauvaise* ~ look/not look well

mine² *f* mine (*aussi* MIL); *de crayon* lead; **miner** undermine; MIL mine

minéral *adj & m* mineral

minéralogique AUTO: *plaque f* ~ license plate, *Br* number plate

mineur¹ *adj* JUR, MUS minor

mineur² *m* (*ouvrier*) miner

miniature *f* miniature

minimal minimum; **minime** minimal; *salaire* tiny; **minimiser** minimize; **minimum** *adj & m* minimum; *au* ~ at the very least; *un* ~ *de* the least little bit of

ministère *m* department; (*gouvernement*) government; REL ministry; **ministre** *m* minister; ~ *des Affaires étrangères* Secretary of State, *Br* Foreign Secretary; ~ *de l'Intérieur* Secretary of the Interior, *Br* Home Secretary

minitel *m* small home terminal connected to a number of data banks

minorité *f* JUR, POL minority

minuit *m* midnight

minuscule 1 *adj* tiny, minuscule; *lettre* small, lower case **2** *f* small *ou* lower-case letter

minute *f* minute

minuterie *f* time switch

minutie *f* meticulousness; **minutieux, -euse** meticulous

miracle *m* miracle; **miraculeux, -euse** miraculous

mirage *m* mirage; *fig* illusion

miroir *m* mirror

miroiter sparkle

mise *f au jeu* stake; *de* ~ acceptable; ~ *en bouteilles* bottling; ~ *en marche ou route* start-up; **miser** stake (*sur* on)

misérable wretched; **misère** *f* destitution; (*chose pénible*) misfortune

miséricordieux, -euse merciful

misogyne *m* misogynist

missile *m* MIL missile

mission *f* mission; (*tâche*) task

mite *f* ZO (clothes) moth

mi-temps 1 *f* SP half-time **2** *m* part-time job; *à* ~ *travail* part-time

mitigé moderate; *sentiments* mixed

mi-voix: *à* ~ under one's breath

mixer, mixeur *m* CUIS blender; **mixte** mixed; **mixture** *f* *péj* vile concoction

MM (= *Messieurs*) Messrs.

Mme (= *Madame*) Mrs

Mo *m* (= *mégaoctet*) Mb (= megabyte)

mobile 1 *adj* mobile; (*amovible*) movable; *feuilles* loose; *ombres* moving **2** *m* motive; ART mobile

mobilier, -ère 1 *adj* JUR movable, personal **2** *m* furniture

mobilisation *f* mobilization; **mobilité** *f* mobility

mobylette® *f* moped

moche F ugly; (*méprisable*) mean

mode[1] *m* method; ~ *d'emploi* instructions (for use); ~ *de vie* life-style

mode[2] *f* fashion; *être à la* ~ be fashionable, be in fashion

modèle *m* model; *tricot* pattern; **modeler** modeler

modem *m* INFORM modem

modération *f* moderation; **modéré** moderate; **modérer** moderate; *se* ~ control o.s.

moderne modern; **modernisation** *f* modernization; **moderniser** modernize

modeste modest; **modestie** *f* modesty

modification *f* modification; **modifier** modify

modique modest

module *m* TECH module; **moduler** modulate

moelle *f* marrow; ~ *épinière* spinal cord; **moelleux, -euse** *lit* soft; *chocolat, vin* smooth

mœurs *fpl* morals; (*coutumes*) customs

moi me; *avec* ~ with me

moi-même myself

moindre lesser; *prix* lower; *quantité* smaller; *le/la* ~ the least

moine *m* monk

moineau *m* sparrow

moins *adv* less; *au* ~ *du* ~ at least; *à* ~ *que ... ne* (+ *subj*) unless; *de ... en* ~ less and less; *20 euros de* ~ 20 euros less **2** *m*: *le* ~ the least **3** *prép* MATH minus; *dix heures* ~ *cinq* it's five of ten , *Br* it's five to ten; *il fait* ~ *deux* it's 2 below zero

mois *m* month

moisi 1 *adj* moldy, *Br* mouldy **2** *m* BOT mold, *Br* mould; **moisir** go moldy *ou* Br mouldy; **moisissure** *f* BOT mold, *Br* mould

moisson *f* harvest; **moissonner** harvest

moite damp, moist

moitié *f* half; *à* ~ *vide/endormi* half-empty/-asleep; ~ ~ fifty-fifty

molaire *f* molar

molécule *f* molecule

molester rough up

molette *f de réglage* knob

mollesse *f* softness; *d'une personne, d'actions* lethargy

mollet[1], **-te** *adj* soft; *œuf* soft-boiled

mollet[2] *m* calf

môme *m/f* F kid F

moment *m* moment; *d'un ~ à l'autre* at any moment; *par ~s* at times, sometimes; *pour le ~* for the moment

momentané temporary; **momentanément** for a short while

mon *m*, **ma** *f*, **mes** *pl* my

monarchie *f* monarchy; **monarque** *m* monarch

monastère *m* monastery

monceau *m* mound

mondain society *atr*; **mondanités** *fpl* social niceties

monde *m* world; *gens* people *pl*; *tout le ~* everybody, everyone; *mettre au ~* bring into the world

mondial world *atr*, global; **mondialisation** *f* globalization

monétaire monetary; *marché money* after

moniteur, -trice 1 *m/f* instructor **2** *m* INFORM monitor

monnaie *f* money; *(pièces)* change; *(unité monétaire)* currency

monologue *m* monolog, *Br* monologue

monopole *m* monopoly; **monopoliser** monopolize

monospace *m* people carrier, MPV

monotone monotonous; **monotonie** *f* monotony

monsieur *m* (*pl* **messieurs**) *dans lettre* Dear Sir; **Mon-**

sieur Durand Mr Durand; **bonjour ~** good morning

monstre 1 *m* monster **2** *adj* colossal

mont *m* mountain

montage *m* TECH assembly; *d'un film* editing; *d'une photographie* montage; ÉL connecting

montagnard, ~e 1 *adj* mountain *atr* **2** *m/f* mountain dweller; **montagne** *f* mountain; *à la ~* in the mountains; *~s russes* roller coaster; **montagneux, -euse** mountainous

montant 1 *adj* robe highnecked; *mouvement* upward **2** *m somme* amount

montée *f sur montagne* ascent; *(pente)* slope; *de prix, de température* rise; **monter 1** *v/t* climb, go up; *valise* take/bring up; *machine* assemble; *tente* put up; THÉÂT put on; *film* edit; *entreprise* set up; *cheval* ride **2** *v/i* come/go upstairs; *d'avion, de route* climb; *des prix* rise, go up; *de baromètre, fleuve* rise; *~ dans* avion, train get on; *voiture* get in(to) **3**: *se ~ à de frais* amount to

montre *f* (wrist)watch

montrer show; *~ qn/qc du doigt* point at s.o./sth

monture *f* (*cheval*) mount; *de lunettes* frame; *d'un diamant* setting

monument *m* monument; **monumental** monumental

moquer: se ~ de (*railler*) make fun of; (*dédaigner*) not care about; (*tromper*) fool; **moquerie** *f* mockery

moquette *f* wall-to-wall carpet

moqueur, -euse 1 *adj* mocking **2** *m/f* mocker

moral, ~e 1 *adj* moral; *souffrance, santé* spiritual **2** *m* morale **3** *f* morality, morals *pl*; *d'une histoire* moral

morbide morbid

morceau *m* piece; *d'un livre* passage

morceler divide up

mordant biting; **mordre** bite; *d'un acide* eat into

morfondre: se ~ mope; (*s'ennuyer*) be bored

morgue *f lieu* mortuary, morgue

moribond dying

morne gloomy

morose morose

mors *m* bit

morsure *f* bite

mort¹ *f* death

mort², ~e 1 *adj* dead; *eau* stagnant; *yeux* lifeless; *membre* numb; **ivre ~** dead drunk; **être ~ de rire** F die laughing **2** *m/f* dead man; dead woman; **les ~s** the dead *pl*

mortalité *f* mortality; **taux** *m* **de ~** death rate, mortality; **mortel, ~le** mortal; *blessure,* *dose, maladie* fatal; *péché* deadly

morue *f* cod

morveux, -euse *m/f* F squirt F

mosaïque *f* mosaic

Moscou Moscow

mosquée *f* mosque

mot *m* word; (*court message*) note; **bon ~** witticism; **~ clé** key word; **~ de passe** password; **gros ~** rude word, swearword; **~ à ~** word for word

motard *m* motorcyclist, biker; *de la gendarmerie* motorcycle policeman

moteur, -trice 1 *m* engine, motor; *fig: personne* driving force (**de** behind) **2** *adj* arbre drive; *force* driving

motif *m* motive, reason; (*forme*) pattern; MUS theme, motif; *en peinture* motif

motion *f* POL motion

motivation *f* motivation; **motiver** motivate; (*expliquer*) be the reason for, prompt; (*justifier par des motifs*) give a reason for

moto *f* motorbike, motorcycle; **faire de la ~** ride one's motorbike; **motocycliste** *m/f* motorcyclist

motoriser mechanize; **je suis motorisé** F I have a car

mou, molle soft; *caractère, résistance* weak

mouche *f* fly

moucher: se ~ blow one's nose

moucheron *m* gnat

mouchoir *m* handkerchief

moudre grind

moue *f* pout; **faire la ~** pout

mouette *f* seagull

moufle *f* mitten

mouillé wet; **mouiller 1** *v/t* wet; (*humecter*) dampen; *liquide* water down **2** *v/i* MAR anchor

moule 1 *m* mold, *Br* mould; CUIS tin **2** *f* ZO mussel

mouler mold, *Br* mould

moulin *m* mill; **~ à vent** windmill; **~ à café** coffee grinder

mourir die (**de** of); **~ de froid** freeze to death

mousse *f* foam; BOT moss; CUIS mousse; **mousser** lather; **mousseux, -euse 1** *adj* foamy **2** *m* sparkling wine

moustache *f* mustache, *Br* moustache

moustique *m* mosquito

moutarde *f* mustard

mouton *m* sheep; *viande* mutton; *fourrure* sheepskin

mouvement *m* movement; *trafic* traffic; **en ~** moving; **mouvementé** eventful; *débat* lively

mouvoir: **se ~** move

moyen, ~ne 1 *adj* average; *classe* middle; **Moyen Âge** *m* Middle Ages *pl*; **Moyen-Orient** *m* Middle East **2** *m* (*façon, méthode*) means *sg*; **~s** (*argent*) means *pl*; *intellectuelles* faculties; **au ~ de,**

par le ~ de by means of **3** *f* average; *statistique* mean; **en ~ne** on average; **moyenâgeux, -euse** medieval

moyennant for

Mt (= *Mont*) Mt (= Mount)

muer *d'oiseau* molt, *Br* moult; *de voix* break

muet, ~te dumb; *fig* silent

mufle *m* muzzle; *fig* F boor

mugir moo; *du vent* moan

muguet *m* BOT lily of the valley

mule *f* mule

multicolore multicolored, *Br* multicoloured

multimédia *m* & *adj* multimedia

multinational, ~e 1 *adj* multinational **2** *f*: **multinationale** multinational

multiplication *f* multiplication; **la ~ de** (*augmentation*) the increase in the number of; **multiplier** multiply; **se ~** *d'une espèce* multiply

multitude *f*: **une ~ de** a host of; **la ~** *péj* the masses *pl*

multiusages versatile

municipal town *atr*, municipal; **municipalité** *f* (*commune*) municipality; **conseil** town council

munir: **~ de** fit with; *personne* provide with; **se ~ de qc** *d'un parapluie, de son passeport* take sth

mur *m* wall

mûr ripe

muraille *f* wall

mûre f BOT mulberry; *des ronces* blackberry

murer *enclos* wall in; *porte* wall up

mûrier m mulberry (tree)

mûrir ripen

murmure m murmur; **murmurer** murmur; (*médire*) talk

muscle m muscle; **musclé** muscular; **musculation** f body-building

museau m muzzle

musée m museum

museler muzzle (*aussi fig*); **muselière** f muzzle

musical musical; **musicien, ~ne 1** *adj* musical **2** *m/f* musician; **musique** f music; **~ de fond** piped music

must m must

musulman, ~e *m/f & adj* Muslim

mutation f change; BIOL mutation; *de fonctionnaire* transfer

mutiler mutilate

mutuel, ~le mutual

myope shortsighted

myrtille f bilberry

mystère m mystery; **mystérieux, -euse** mysterious

mystifier fool, take in

mystique 1 *adj* mystical **2** *m/f* mystic **3** f mystique

mythe m myth; **mythologie** f mythology

mythomane *m/f* pathological liar

N

nabot m péj midget

nacre f mother-of-pearl

nage f swimming; *style* stroke; *être en ~ fig* be dripping with sweat

nageoire f fin

nager 1 v/i swim **2** v/t: **~ la brasse** do the breaststroke

naïf, naïve naive

nain, ~e *m/f & adj* dwarf

naissance f birth (*aussi fig*)

naître be born (*aussi fig*); **faire ~** *sentiment* give rise to

naïveté f naivety

nana f F chick F, girl

nantir provide (*de* with)

nappe f tablecloth; *de gaz, pétrole* layer

narcotique m & adj narcotic

narguer taunt

narine f nostril

narquois taunting

narrateur, -trice *m/f* narrator; **narration** f narration

nasal nasal

natal *pays etc* of one's birth, native; **natalité** f: (*taux m de*) **~** birth rate

natation f swimming

natif, -ive native

nation f nation; **national, ~e 1** *adj* national **2** *mpl*: **natio-**

naux nationals **3** *f* highway;
nationaliser nationalize;
nationaliste 1 *adj* nationalist; *péj* nationalistic **2** *m/f*
nationalist; **nationalité** *f* nationality

natte *f* (*tapis*) mat; *de cheveux* braid, plait

naturalisation *f* naturaliza-
tion

nature 1 *adj yaourt* plain; *thé,
café* without milk or sugar;
personne natural **2** *f* nature;
~ **morte** ART still life; natu-
rel, ~le **1** *adj* natural **2** *m* (*caractère*) nature; (*spontanéi-
té*) naturalness; **naturellement** naturally

naufrage *m* shipwreck; **faire
~** be shipwrecked

nausée *f* nausea; *j'ai la* ~ I'm
nauseous, *Br* I feel sick;
nauséeux, -euse nauseous

nautique nautical; *ski* water
atr

nautisme *m* water sports and
sailing

naval naval; *construction* ship
atr

navet *m* rutabaga, *Br* swede;
fig turkey F, *Br* flop

navette *f* shuttle; **faire la ~**
shuttle

navigable navigable; **navigation** *f* sailing; (*pilotage*) navigation; ~ **aérienne** air travel; ~ **spatiale** space travel;
naviguer *d'un navire, marin*
sail; *d'un avion* fly; (*conduire*), INFORM navigate; ~ **sur**

Internet surf the Net

navire *m* ship

navrant upsetting; **navré:** *je
suis* ~ I am so sorry

ne: *je* ~ *comprends pas* I
don't understand, I do not
understand; *ne ... guère*
hardly; *ne ... jamais* never;
ne ... personne nobody; *ne
... plus* no longer; not any
more; *ne ... que* only; *ne
... rien* nothing, not anything; → *aussi* **guère, jamais**
etc

né born; ~**e** *Lepic* nee Lepic

néanmoins nevertheless

néant *m* nothingness

nécessaire 1 *adj* necessary **2**
m necessity; *le strict* ~ the
bare minimum; ~ **de toilette**
toiletries *pl*; **nécessité** *f* necessity; **nécessiter** require,
necessitate

néerlandais, ~e 1 *adj* Dutch
2 *m langue* Dutch; **Néerlandais, ~e** *m/f* Dutchman;
Dutchwoman

néfaste harmful

négatif, -ive *adj & m* negative; **négation** *f* negation;
GRAM negative

négligé 1 *adj travail* careless;
tenue untidy; *épouse, enfant*
neglected **2** *m* negligee; **négligence** *f* negligence, care-
lessness; *d'une épouse, d'un
enfant* neglect; (*nonchalan-
ce*) casualness; **négligent**
careless, negligent; *parent*
negligent; *geste* casual; **né-**

gliger neglect; *occasion* miss; *avis* disregard; **~ de faire** fail to do

négoce *m* trade; **négociant** *m* merchant; **négociateur, -trice** *m/f* negotiator; **négociation** *f* negotiation; **négocier** negotiate

neige *f* snow; **neiger** snow

néon *m* neon

nerf *m* nerve; (*vigueur*) energy; **être à bout de ~s** be at the end of one's tether

nerveux, -euse nervous; (*vigoureux*) full of energy; AUTO responsive; **nervosité** *f* nervousness

n'est-ce pas: il fait beau, ~? it's a fine day, isn't it?; **tu la connais, ~?** you know her, don't you?

net, ~te **1** *adj* (*propre*) clean; (*clair*) clear; *différence* distinct; COMM net **2** *adv* (*aussi* **nettement**) *tué* outright; *refuser* flatly; *parler* plainly; **netteté** *f* cleanliness; (*clarté*) clarity

nettoyage *m* cleaning; **~ ethnique** ethnic cleansing; **~ à sec** dry cleaning; **nettoyer** clean; F (*ruiner*) clean out F; **~ à sec** dryclean

neuf[1] nine

neuf[2]**, neuve** *adj* new; **refaire à ~** *maison etc* renovate; *moteur* recondition

neutraliser neutralize; **neutralité** *f* neutrality; **neutre** neutral

neuvième ninth

neveu *m* nephew

névralgie *f* MÉD neuralgia

névrosé, ~e *m/f* neurotic

nez *m* nose

ni neither, nor; **je n'ai ~ intérêt ~ désir** I have neither interest nor inclination; **sans sucre ~ lait** without sugar or milk, with neither sugar nor milk; **~ moi non plus** neither *ou* nor do I, me neither

niais stupid; **niaiserie** *f* stupidity

niche *f dans un mur* niche; *d'un chien* kennel; **nicher** nest; *fig* F live

nicotine *f* nicotine

nid *m* nest; **~ de poule** *fig* pothole

nièce *f* niece

nier: ~ (*avoir fait*) deny (doing)

nigaud 1 *adj* silly **2** *m* idiot, fool

niveau *m* level; ÉDU standard; *outil* spirit level; **~ de vie** standard of living; **niveler** *terrain* level; *fig: différences* even out

noble noble; **noblesse** *f* nobility

noce *f* wedding; **faire la ~** F paint the town red

nocif, -ive harmful, noxious

nocturne 1 *adj* night *atr*; ZO nocturnal **2** *f*: **un match joué en ~** an evening match

Noël *m* Christmas; **joyeux ~!**

Merry Christmas!; *le père* ~ Santa Claus, *Br aussi* Father Christmas

nœud *m* knot (*aussi* NAUT); *fig: d'un problème* nub; ~ *papillon* bow tie

noir 1 *adj* black; (*sombre*) dark; *il fait* ~ it's dark **2** *m* black; (*obscurité*) dark; *travail au* ~ moonlighting

Noir *m* black man

noircir blacken

Noire *f* black woman

noisetier *m* hazel; **noisette** *f* & *adj inv* hazelnut

noix *f* walnut

nom *m* name; GRAM noun; *au* ~ *de qn* in *ou Br* on behalf of s.o.; ~ *de famille* surname, family name; ~ *de jeune fille* maiden name

nombre *m* number; *sans* ~ countless; **nombreux, -euse** numerous, many; *famille* large

nombril *m* navel

nomination *f* appointment; *à un prix* nomination

nommer name, call; *à une fonction* appoint; *se* ~ be called

non no; *j'espère que* ~ I hope not; *moi* ~ *plus* me neither; *c'est normal,* ~? that's normal, isn't it?

non-alcoolique non-alcoholic

nonchalant nonchalant, casual

nonobstant notwithstanding

non-polluant environ-

mentally friendly, non-polluting

nord 1 *m* north; *au* ~ *de* (to the) north of **2** *adj* north; *hémisphère* northern

nord-américain, ~**e** North-American; **Nord-Américain,** ~**e** *m/f* North-American

nord-est *m* north-east

nord-ouest *m* north-west

normal, ~**e 1** *adj* normal **2** *f: inférieur/supérieur à la* ~ *e* above/below average; **normalement** normally; **normalisation** *f* normalization; TECH standardization; **normalité** *f* normality

norme *f* norm; TECH standard

Norvège *f: la* ~ Norway; **norvégien,** ~**ne 1** *adj* Norwegian **2** *m langue* Norwegian; **Norvégien,** ~**ne** *m/f* Norwegian

nos → **notre**

nostalgie *f* nostalgia; *avoir la* ~ *de son pays* be homesick

notaire *m* notary

notamment particularly

note *f* note; *à l'école* grade, *Br* mark; (*facture*) check, *Br* bill; ~ *de frais* expense account; ~ *de service* memo; **noter** (*écrire*) write down; (*remarquer*) note

notice *f* note; (*mode d'emploi*) instructions *pl*

notifier *v/t:* ~ *qch à qn* notify s.o. of sth

notion *f* (*idée*) notion, con-

nylon

cept; ~s basics pl
notre, pl **nos** our
nôtre: **le/la ~, les ~s** ours
nouer tie; relations establish
nougat m nougat
nouilles fpl noodles
nounou f F nanny
nounours m teddy bear
nourrice f child minder
nourrir feed; fig: espoir nurture
nourrisson m infant
nourriture f food
nous sujet we; complément d'objet direct us; complément d'objet indirect (to) us; ~ **sommes levés tôt** we got up early; ~ **aimons** we love each other
nouveau, nouvelle (m **nouvel** before a vowel or silent h; mpl **nouveaux**) **1** adj new; **de** ou **à** ~ again; **Nouvel An** m New Year('s) **2** m/f new person
nouveau-né 1 adj newborn **2** m newborn baby
nouveauté f novelty
nouvelle f (récit) short story; **une** ~ **dans les médias** a piece of news; **nouvelles** fpl news sg; **Nouvelle Zélande** f New Zealand
novembre m November
novice 1 m/f novice **2** adj inexperienced
noyade f drowning
noyau m pit, Br stone; PHYS nucleus; fig (small) group
noyer¹ v/t drown; AUTO flood;

se ~ drown; **se suicider** drown o.s.
noyer² m arbre, bois walnut
nu 1 adj naked; arbre, bras, tête etc bare **2** m ART nude
nuage m cloud; **nuageux, -euse** cloudy
nuance f shade; fig slight difference; (subtilité) nuance; **nuancé** subtle; **nuancer** qualify
nucléaire 1 adj nuclear **2** m: **le** ~ nuclear power
nudiste m/f & adj nudist; **nudité** f nudity
nuée f d'insectes cloud; de journalistes horde
nuire: ~ **à** hurt, harm
nuit f night; **il fait** ~ it's dark
nul, ~le 1 adj no; (non valable) invalid; (sans valeur) hopeless; (inexistant) nonexistent; **~le part** nowhere **2** pron no-one; **nullement** not in the least; **nullité** f JUR invalidity; fig hopelessness; personne loser
numérique numerical; INFORM digital
numéro m number; ~ **vert** toll-free number, Br Freefone number; **numéroter 1** v/t number **2** v/i TÉL dial
nuque f nape of the neck
nurse f nanny
nutritif, -ive nutritional; aliment nutritious; **nutrition** f nutrition
nylon m nylon

O

obéir obey; **~ à** obey; **obéissance** *f* obedience; **obéissant** obedient

obèse obese; **obésité** *f* obesity

objecter: **~ qch pour ne pas faire qch** give sth as a reason; **~ que** object that; **objectif, -ive 1** *adj* objective **2** *m* objective; PHOT lens; **objection** *f* objection; **objectivité** *f* objectivity

objet *m* object; *de réflexions, d'une lettre* subject

obligation *f* obligation; COMM bond; **obligatoire** compulsory, obligatory

obligeant obliging; **obliger** oblige; (*forcer*) force; **être obligé de faire qc** be obliged to do

oblique oblique

oblitérer *timbre* cancel

obscène obscene

obscur obscure; *nuit, rue* dark; **obscurcir** darken; **s'~** grow dark; **obscurité** *f* obscurity; *de la nuit, d'une rue* darkness

obséder obsess

obsèques *fpl* funeral

observateur, -trice *m/f* observer; **observation** *f* observation; *d'une règle* observance; **observatoire** *m* observatory; **observer** ob-

serve; *changement* notice; **faire ~ qc à qn** point out sth to s.o.

obsession *f* obsession

obstacle *m* obstacle; SP hurdle; *pour cheval* jump; **faire ~ à qc** stand in the way of sth

obstination *f* obstinacy; **obstiné** obstinate; **s'~ à faire qc** persist in doing sth

obstruction *f* obstruction; *dans tuyau* blockage; **obstruer** obstruct, block

obtenir get, obtain

obturer seal; *dent* fill

obtus MATH, *fig* obtuse

obus *m* MIL shell

occasion *f* opportunity; *marché* bargain; **d'~** second-hand; **à l'~** when the opportunity arises; **occasionner** cause

Occident *m*: **l'~** the West; **occidental, ~e** western; **Occidental, ~e** *m/f* Westerner

occulte occult

occupant 1 *adj* occupying **2** *m* occupant; **occupation** *f* occupation; **occupé** busy; *pays, appartement* occupied; *chaise* taken; TÉL busy; **occuper** occupy; *personnel* employ; **s'~ de** take an interest in; *malade, organisation* look after

occurrence *f*: **en l'~** as it hap-

pens
océan m ocean
octet m INFORM byte
octobre m October
oculaire eye atr
oculiste m/f eye specialist
odeur f smell; **~ corporelle** BO
odieux, -euse hateful, odious
odorant scented
odorat m sense of smell
œil m (pl yeux) eye; **à vue d'~** visibly
œillet m BOT carnation
œuf m egg; **~s brouillés** scrambled eggs; **~ à la coque** soft-boiled egg; **~ sur le plat** fried egg
œuvre 1 f work; **~ d'art** work of art; **mettre en ~** (employer) use; (exécuter) carry out **2** m ART, littérature works pl
offense f (insulte) insult; (péché) sin; **offenser** offend; **s'~ de** take offense ou Br offence at
office m office; REL service; **d'~** automatically; **faire ~ de** act as
officiel, ~le official
officier m officer
officieux, -euse semi-official
officinal plante medicinal
offre f offer; **~ d'emploi** job offer; **offrir** offer; cadeau give; **s'~ qc** treat o.s. to sth
offusquer offend
oie f goose
oignon m onion; BOT bulb

oiseau m bird; **à vol d'~** as the crow flies
oiseux, -euse idle
oisif, -ive idle; **oisiveté** f idleness
olive f olive; **olivier** m olive (tree)
olympique Olympic
ombrage m shade; **ombragé** shady; **ombrageux, -euse** cheval skittish; personne touchy; **ombre** f shade; (silhouette) shadow; fig (anonymat) obscurity; **de regret** hint
ombrelle f sunshade
omelette f omelet, Br omelette
omettre leave out, omit; **~ de faire** fail ou omit to do; **omission** f omission
omnibus m: (**train** m) **~** slow train
on (après que, et, où, qui, si souvent l'on) (nous) we; (tu, vous, indéterminé) you; (quelqu'un) someone; (eux, les gens) they, people; autorités they; **m'a dit que...** I was told that ...; **~ ne sait jamais** you never know, one never knows fml
oncle m uncle
onction f REL unction; **onctueux, -euse** smooth; fig smarmy F, unctuous
onde f wave; **sur les ~s** RAD on the air; **grandes ~s** long wave
ondée f downpour

on-dit *m* rumor, *Br* rumour
ondoyer *du blés* sway
ondulation *f de terrain* undulation; *de coiffure* wave; **onduler** *d'ondes* undulate; *de cheveux* be wavy
onéreux, -euse expensive
ongle *m* nail; *zo* claw
onguent *m* cream, salve
onze eleven; **le ~** the eleventh; **onzième** eleventh
opaque opaque
opéra *m* opera; *bâtiment* opera house
opérable MÉD operable; **opérateur, -trice** *m/f* operator; *en cinéma* cameraman; FIN trader; **opération** *f* operation; *action* working; FIN transaction; **opérer** 1 *v/t* MÉD operate on; (*produire*) make; (*exécuter*) implement 2 *v/i* MÉD operate; (*avoir effet*) work; (*procéder*) proceed; **se faire ~** have an operation
opiner: ~ *de la tête* nod in agreement
opiniâtre stubborn; **opiniâtreté** *f* stubbornness
opinion *f* opinion
opium *m* opium
opportun *ou* opportune; *moment* right; **opportuniste** *m/f* opportunist; **opportunité** *f* timeliness; (*occasion*) opportunity
opposant, ~e 1 *adj* opposing 2 *m/f* opponent; **les ~s** the opposition; **opposé** 1 *adj*

pôles opposite; *opinions* conflicting; **être ~ à qc** be opposed to sth 2 *m* opposite; **à l'~ de qn** unlike s.o.; **opposer** bring into conflict; *argument* put forward; **s'~ à qn/à qc** oppose s.o./sth; **opposition** *f* opposition; (*contraste*) contrast
oppresser oppress, weigh down; **oppression** *f* oppression
opprimer oppress
opter **~ pour** opt for
opticien, ~ne *m/f* optician
optimisme *m* optimism; **optimiste** 1 *adj* optimistic 2 *m/f* optimist
option *f* option
optique 1 *adj* nerf optic; *verre* optical 2 *f* science optics; *fig* viewpoint
opulent wealthy; *poitrine* ample
or[1] *m* gold
or[2] *conj* now
orage *m* storm; **orageux, -euse** stormy
oraison *f* REL prayer
oral *adj* & *m* oral
orange *f* & *adj inv* orange; **oranger** *m* orange tree
orateur, -trice *m/f* orator
orbital orbital
orbite *f* ANAT eyesocket; ASTR orbit (*aussi fig*)
orchestre *m* orchestra; *de théâtre* orchestra, *Br* stalls *pl*
orchidée *f* orchid
ordinaire 1 *adj* ordinary 2 *m*

essence regular; **d'~** ordinarily

ordinateur m computer

ordonnance f arrangement, layout; (ordre) order (aussi JUR); MÉD prescription; **ordonné** tidy; **ordonner** organize; (commander) order; MÉD prescribe

ordre m order; **~ du jour** agenda; **de premier ~** first-rate; **mettre en ~** tidy

ordures fpl (détritus) garbage, Br rubbish; fig filth

oreille f ear; **d'un bol** handle; **dur d'~** hard of hearing

oreiller m pillow

oreillons mpl MÉD mumps sg

orfèvre m goldsmith

organe m organ; (voix, porte-parole) voice; **d'un mécanisme** part

organisation f organization; **organiser** organize; **s'~ d'une personne** get organized; **organiseur** m INFORM personal organizer

organisme m organism; ANAT system; (organisation) organization, body

orgue m organ

orgueil m pride; **orgueilleux, -euse** proud

Orient m: **l'~** the East; **Asie** the East, the Orient; **oriental, ~e** east, eastern; **d'Asie** eastern, Oriental; **Oriental, ~e** m/f Oriental

orientation f direction; **d'une maison** exposure; **orienter**

orient, Br orientate; (diriger) direct; **s'~** get one's bearings; **s'~ vers** fig go in for

orifice m opening

originaire original; **être ~ de** come from; **original 1** adj original, péj eccentric **2** m ouvrage original; personne eccentric; **origine** f origin; **à l'~** originally; **originel, ~le** original

orme m BOT elm

ornement m ornament; **ornementer** ornament

orner decorate (**de** with)

orphelin, ~e m/f orphan; **orphelinat** m orphanage

orteil m toe

orthographe f spelling

ortie f BOT nettle

os m bone

osciller PHYS oscillate; **d'un pendule** swing; **~ entre** fig waver between

osé daring; **oser: ~ faire** dare to do

osier m BOT osier; **en ~** wicker

ossements mpl bones; **osseux, -euse** ANAT bone atr; visage, mains bony

ostensible evident

otage m hostage

ôter remove; MATH take away

ou or; **~ bien** or (else); **~ ... ~** either ... or

où where; **d'~ vient-il?** where does he come from?; **d'~ l'on peut déduire que ...** from which it can be deduced that

...; **le jour ~** ... the day when ...

ouate f absorbent cotton, Br cotton wool; **ouater** pad, quilt

oubli m forgetting; (omission) oversight; **tomber dans l'~** sink into oblivion; **oublier** forget; **~ de faire** forget to do

ouest 1 m west; **à l'~ de** (to the) west of 2 adj west, western

oui yes

ouï-dire: par ~ by hearsay

ouïe f hearing; **~s** zo gills

ouragan m hurricane

ourler hem; **ourlet** m hem

ours m bear; **ourse** f she-bear; **la Grande Ourse** ASTR the Great Bear

oursin m zo sea urchin

outil m tool; **outillage** m tools pl

outrage m insult; **outrager** insult

outrance f excessiveness; **à ~** excessively

outre 1 prép in addition to 2 adv: **en ~** besides; **passer ~** ignore

outré: être ~ de ou **par** be outraged by

outre-Atlantique on the other side of the Atlantic

outre-Manche on the other side of the Channel

outre-mer: d'~ overseas atr

ouvert open; **ouverture** f opening; MUS overture

ouvrable working; **jour m ~** workday; **ouvrage** m work; **ouvragé** ornate

ouvre-boîtes m can opener, Br aussi tin opener; **ouvre-bouteilles** m bottle opener

ouvrier, -ère 1 adj working-class 2 m/f worker

ouvrir 1 v/t open; radio, gaz turn on 2 v/i d'un magasin open; **s'~** open; fig open up

ovale m & adj oval

ovni m (= **objet volant non identifié**) UFO (= unidentified flying object)

oxygène m oxygen

P

pacifier pacify; **pacifique** 1 adj personne peace-loving; coexistence peaceful 2 m **le Pacifique** the Pacific; **pacifiste** m/f & adj pacifist

pacte m pact; **pactiser: ~ avec** come to terms with

pagaie f paddle

pagaïe, pagaille f F mess

page f page; **~ d'accueil** INFORM home page

paie, paye f pay; **paiement** m payment

païen, -ne m/f & adj pagan

paillasson m doormat

paille f straw

pape

pain m bread; **~ au chocolat** chocolate croissant; **~ complet** whole wheat ou Br wholemeal bread; **~ d'épice** gingerbread; **petit ~** roll

pair 1 adj nombre even **2** m: **hors ~** unrivalled; **fille f au ~** au pair

paire f: **une ~ de** a pair of

paisible peaceful; personne quiet

paître graze

paix f peace; (calme) peace and quiet

Pakistan: le ~ Pakistan; **pakistanais, ~e** Pakistani; **Pakistanais, ~e** m/f Pakistani

palais m **1** palace; **~ de justice** law courts pl **2** ANAT palate

pale f blade

pâle pale; fig: style colorless, Br colourless; imitation pale

Palestine: la ~ Palestine; palestinien, **~ne** Palestinian; **Palestinien, ~ne** m/f Palestinian

palette f de peinture palette

pâleur f paleness, pallor

palier m d'un escalier landing; TECH bearing; (phase) stage

pâlir go pale; de couleurs fade

palissade f fence

pallier alleviate; manque make up for

palme f BOT palm; de natation flipper; **palmier** m BOT palm tree

pâlot, ~te pale

palper feel; MÉD palpate

palpitant fig exciting, thrilling; **palpitations** fpl palpitations; **palpiter** du cœur pound

pamplemousse m grapefruit

pan m de vêtement tail; de mur section

panache m plume; **avoir du ~** have panache; **panaché** m shandy-gaff, Br shandy

pancarte f sign; de manifestation placard

pané breaded

panier m basket

panique f panic; **paniquer** panic

panne f breakdown; **~ en panne** have a breakdown; **tomber en ~ sèche** run out of gas ou Br petrol; **~ d'électricité** power outage, Br power failure

panneau m board; TECH panel; **~ de signalisation** roadsign

panorama m panorama

pansement m dressing; **panser** blessure dress; cheval groom

pantalon m pants pl, Br trousers pl; **un ~** a pair of pants

pantelant panting

pantois inv: **rester ~** be speechless

pantoufle f slipper

paon m peacock

papa m dad

papal REL papal; **pape** m REL pope

paperasse f (souvent au pl ~s) péj papers pl

papeterie f magasin stationery store, Br stationer's

papi, papy m F grandpa

papier m paper; ~ (d')**aluminium** kitchen foil; ~ **hygiénique** toilet tissue; ~**s d'identité** identification, ID

papillon m butterfly; TECH wing nut; F (contravention) (parking) ticket

paquebot m liner

pâquerette f BOT daisy

Pâques msg ou fpl Easter; **joyeuses ~!** happy Easter

paquet m packet; de sucre, café bag; de la poste parcel

par prép through; passif, moyen by; ~ **terre** on the ground; ~ **beau temps** in fine weather; ~ **curiosité** out of curiosity; ~ **hasard** by chance; **diviser ~ quatre** divide by four; ~ **an** a year; **finir ~ faire** finish by doing

parabolique: antenne f ~ satellite dish

paracétamol m paracetamol

parachute m parachute; **parachutiste** m/f parachutist; MIL para(trooper)

parade f parade; en escrime parry; à un argument counter

paradis m paradise

paradoxe m paradox

parages mpl: ; **dans les ~** around; **dans les ~ de** in the vicinity of

paragraphe m paragraph

paraître appear; d'un livre come out, be published; **il paraît que** it seems that, it would appear that; **laisser ~** show

parallèle 1 adj parallel (à to) **2** f MATH parallel (line) **3** m GÉOGR parallel (aussi fig)

paralyser paralyse; **paralysie** f paralysis

paramètre m parameter

paranoïaque m/f & adj paranoid

parapharmacie f (non-dispensing) pharmacy; **produits** toiletries pl

paraplégique m/f & adj paraplegic

parapluie m umbrella

parasite 1 adj parasitic **2** m parasite; ~**s** radio interference

parasol m parasol; de plage beach umbrella

paratonnerre m lightning rod, Br lightning conductor

paravent m windbreak

parc m park; **pour enfant** playpen

parcelle f de terrain parcel

parce que because

par-ci adv: ~, **par-là** espace here and there; temps now and then

parcimonie f: **avec ~** parcimoniously

parcourir région travel through; distance cover; texte read quickly

partager

parcours *m* route; *course d'automobiles* circuit

par-derrière from behind

par-dessous underneath

pardessus *m* overcoat

par-dessus over

par-devant from the front

pardon *m* forgiveness; *~!* sorry!; *~?* excuse me?; **pardonner:** *~ qc à qn* forgive s.o. sth

pare-brise *m* windshield, *Br* windscreen

pare-chocs *m* bumper

pareil, *~le* **1** *adj* similar (*à* to); (*tel*) such; *c'est toujours ~* it's always the same **2** *adv:* *habillés ~* similarly dressed, dressed the same way

parent, *~e* **1** *adj* related **2** *m/f* relative; *~s* (*mère et père*) parents; **parenté** *f* relationship

parenthèse *f* parenthesis, *Br* (round) bracket; *entre ~s* *fig* by the way

parer *attaque* ward off; *en escrime* parry

paresse *f* laziness; **paresseux, -euse** lazy

parfait 1 *adj* perfect; *avant le substantif* complete **2** *m* GRAM perfect (tense)

parfois sometimes

parfum *m* perfume; *d'une glace* flavor, *Br* flavour

pari *m* bet; **parier** bet

parisien, *~ne* Parisian, of/from Paris; **Parisien,** *~ne* *m/f* Parisian

parité *f* ÉCON parity

parking *m* parking lot, *Br* car park; *édifice* parking garage, *Br* car park

parlant *comparaison* striking; *preuves* decisive

Parlement *m* Parliament; **parlementaire 2** *m/f* Parliamentarian

parler 1 *v/i* speak, talk; *sans ~ de* not to mention **2** *v/t:* *~ affaires* talk business; *~ anglais* speak English

parmi among

parodie *f* parody

paroi *f* partition

paroisse *f* REL parish

parole *f* word; *faculté* speech; *donner la ~ à qn* give s.o. the floor

parquer *bétail* pen; *réfugiés* dump

parquet *m* (parquet) floor; JUR public prosecutor's office

parrain *m* godfather; *dans un club* sponsor

parsemer sprinkle (*de* with)

part *f* share; (*fraction*) part; *faire ~ de qc à qn* inform s.o. of sth; *de la ~ de qn* in *ou Br* on behalf of s.o.; *d'une ~ ... d'autre ~* on the one hand ... on the other hand; *autre ~* elsewhere; *nulle ~* nowhere; *quelque ~* somewhere; *à ~ traiter etc* separately; *à ~ cela* apart from that

partage *m* division; **partager**

share; (*couper, diviser*) divide (up)

partenaire *m/f* partner

parterre *m* de fleurs bed; *au théâtre* rear orchestra, Br rear stalls *pl*

parti[1] *m* side; POL party; **prendre ~ pour** side with; **tirer ~ de qc** turn sth to good use; **~ pris** preconceived idea

parti[2] *adj* F: **être ~** (*ivre*) be tight

partial biassed

participant, ~e *m/f* participant; **participer: ~ à** participate in, take part in; *bénéfices* share; *frais* contribute to; *douleur, succès* share in

particularité *f* special feature; **particulier, ~ère 1** *adj* particular, special; *privé* private; **~ à** peculiar to **2** *m* (*privé*) individual; **particulièrement** particularly

partie *f* part; *d'un jeu* game; JUR party; *lutte* struggle; **en ~** partly; **faire ~ de qch** be part of sth

partiel, ~le partial

partir leave (**à, pour** for); SP start; *de la saleté* come out; **~ de qc** (*provenir de*) come from sth; **à ~ de** (*starting*) from

partisan *m/f* supporter; MIL *m* partisan

partition *f* MUS score; POL partition

partout everywhere

parure *f* finery; *de bijoux* set

parvenir arrive; **faire ~ qc à qn** forward sth to s.o.; **~ à faire** manage to do

parvenu, ~e *m/f* upstart

pas[1] *m* step, pace; **faux ~** stumble; *fig* blunder, faux pas

pas[2] *adv* not; **ne ... ~** not; **il ne pleut ~** it's not raining; **il n'a ~ plu** it didn't rain

passable acceptable

passage *m* passage; *fig* (*changement*) changeover; **~ à niveau** grade crossing, Br level crossing; **de ~** passing

passager, ~ère 1 *adj* passing **2** *m/f* passenger

passant, ~e *m/f* passerby

passe *f* SP pass

passé 1 *adj* past **2** *prép*: **~ dix heures** after ten o'clock **3** *m* past; **~ composé** GRAM perfect

passe-partout *m* skeleton key

passe-passe *m*: **tour m de ~** conjuring trick

passeport *m* passport

passer 1 *v/i* pass, go past; *d'un film* show; **~ chez qn** drop by at s.o.'s place; **de mode** go out of fashion; **~ en seconde** AUTO shift into second; **~ pour qc** pass as sth; **faire ~** *personne* let past; *plat, journal* pass; **laisser ~** *personne* let past; *lumière* let in; *chance* let slip **2** *v/t*

pauvre

frontière cross; (*omettre*) miss (out); *temps* spend; *examen* take; *film* show; *contrat* enter into; **~ qc à qn** pass s.o. sth, pass sth to s.o. **3**: *se~* (*se produire*) happen; **se~ de qc** do without sth

passerelle *f* footbridge; MAR gangway; AVIAT slip on;

passe-temps *m* hobby, pastime

passif, -ive 1 *adj* passive **2** *m* GRAM passive; COMM liabilities *pl*

passion *f* passion; **passionnant** exciting; **passionné, ~e 1** *adj* passionate **2** *m/f* enthusiast; **passionner** excite; **se~ pour** have a passion for

passivité *f* passiveness, passivity

passoire *f* sieve

pastel *m* pastel

pastèque *f* BOT watermelon

pasteur *m* REL pastor

pasteuriser pasteurize

pastille *f* pastille

patate *f* F potato, spud F

patauger flounder

pâte *f* paste; CUIS: *à pain* dough; *à tarte* pastry; **~s** pasta *sg*

pâté *m* paté; **~ de maisons** block of houses

patère *f* coat peg

paternaliste paternalistic

paternel, ~le paternal

pâteux, -euse doughy; *bouche* dry

pathétique touching; F (*mauvais*) pathetic

pathologique pathological

patience *f* patience; **patient, ~e** *m/f & adj* patient; **patienter** wait

patin *m*: **faire du~** go skating; **~ à roulettes** roller skate; **patinage** *m* skating; **patiner** skate; AUTO skid; *de~* peg spin; **patineur, -euse** *m/f* skater; **patinoire** *f* skating rink

pâtisserie *f* cake shop; *gâteaux* cakes; **pâtissier, -ère** *m/f* pastrycook

patois *m* dialect

patrie *f* homeland

patrimoine *m* heritage

patriote 1 *adj* patriotic **2** *m/f* patriot

patron *m* boss; (*propriétaire*) owner; *d'une auberge* landlord; REL patron saint; *de couture* pattern

patronne *f* boss; (*propriétaire*) owner; *d'une auberge* landlady; REL patron saint

patronner sponsor

patrouille *f* patrol

patte *f* paw; *d'un oiseau* foot; *d'un insecte* leg; F hand, paw péj

paume *f* palm

paumer F lose

paupière *f* eyelid

pause *f* (*silence*) pause; (*interruption*) break; **~ café** coffee break

pauvre 1 *adj* poor **2** *m/f* poor

person; **les ~s** the poor *pl*;
pauvreté *f* poverty

pavé *m* paving; *(chaussée)*
pavement, *Br* road surface;
pierres rondes cobbles *pl*;
un ~ a paving stone; **rond**
a cobblestone; **paver** pave

pavillon *m* *(maisonnette)*
small house; MAR flag

pavot *m* BOT poppy

payable payable

payant *spectateur* paying;
parking which charges; *fig*
profitable

payer 1 *v/t* pay; **~ qc dix eu-**
ros pay ten euros for sth **2**
v/i pay **3**: **se ~ qc** treat o.s.
to sth

pays *m* country; **mal m du ~**
homesickness

paysage *m* landscape

paysan, ~ne 1 *m/f* small farmer; HIST peasant **2** *adj mœurs*
country *atr*

Pays-Bas *mpl*: **les ~** the
Netherlands

PC *m* (= *personal computer*)
PC

PDG *m* (= *président-direc-*
teur général) President,
CEO (= Chief Executive
Officer)

péage *m d'une autoroute* toll-
booth; *autoroute à ~* turnpike, toll road

peau *f* skin; *cuir* leather

pêche¹ *f* BOT peach

pêche² *f* fishing; *poissons*
catch

péché *m* sin; **pécher** sin

pêcher¹ *m* BOT peach tree

pêcher² **1** *v/t* fish for; *(attra-*
per) catch **2** *v/i* fish; **~ à la li-**
gne go angling

pécheur, -eresse *m/f* sinner

pêcheur *m* fisherman; **~ à la**
ligne angler

pédagogie *f* education,
teaching; **pédagogique** educational; *méthode* teaching

pédale *f* pedal; **pédaler** *à vélo*
pedal

pédéraste *m* homosexual

pédestre: *sentier* **~** footpath; *randonnée f* **~** hike

pédiatre *m/f* MÉD pediatrician

pédicure *m/f* podiatrist, *Br*
chiropodist

pègre *f* underworld

peigne *m* comb; **peigner**
comb; **se ~** comb one's hair

peignoir *m* robe, *Br* dressing
gown

peindre paint; *(décrire)* depict

peine *f* *(punition)* punishment; *(effort)* trouble; *(diffi-*
culté) difficulty; *(chagrin)*
sorrow; *ce n'est pas la ~*
there's no point, it's not
worth it; *valoir la ~ de faire*
qc be worth doing sth; *à ~*
scarcely, hardly

peiner 1 *v/t* upset **2** *v/i* labor,
Br labour

peintre *m* painter

peinture *f* paint; *action, ta-*
bleau painting; *description*
depiction

perception

péjoratif, -ive pejorative
pelage m coat
peler peel
pèlerin m pilgrim
pelle f spade
pellicule f film; **~s** dandruff
pelote f de fil ball
peloter F grope, feel up
peloton m ball; MIL platoon; SP pack; **pelotonner** wind into a ball; **se ~ contre qn** snuggle up to s.o.
pelouse f lawn
peluche f jouet soft toy; **ours** m **en ~** teddy bear
pelure f de fruit peel
pénaliser penalize; **pénalité** f penalty
penchant m (inclination) liking, penchant
pencher 1 v/t pot tilt; **penché** écriture sloping; **la tête en avant** head ou **~** lean forward **2** v/i tuck; d'un plateau tilt; d'un bateau list; **se ~ sur un problème** fig examine a problem
pendant[1] **1** prép during; avec chiffre for **2** conj: **~ que** while
pendant[2] adj oreilles pendulous; (en instance) pending
penderie f armoire, Br wardrobe
pendre hang; **se ~** hang o.s.
pendule 1 m pendulum **2** f (horloge) clock
pénétrer 1 v/t penetrate; pensées, personne fathom out **2** v/i: **~ dans** penetrate; mai-

son, bureaux get into
pénible travail, vie hard; nouvelle painful; caractère difficult
pénicilline f penicillin
péninsule f peninsula
pénis m penis
pénitence f REL penitence; (punition) punishment; **pénitencier** m penitentiary, Br prison
pénombre f semi-darkness
pense-bête m reminder
pensée f thought; BOT pansy; **penser** think; **~ à** (réfléchir à) think about; **faire ~ à qn à faire qch** remind s.o. to do sth; **~ faire qch** (avoir l'intention) be thinking of doing sth; **penseur** m thinker; **pensif, -ive** thoughtful
pension f (allocation) allowance; logement rooming house, Br boarding house; école boarding school; **~ complète** American plan, Br full board; **pensionnaire** m/f d'un hôtel guest; écolier boarder; **pensionnat** m boarding school
pente f slope; **en ~** sloping
Pentecôte: **la ~** Pentecost
pénurie f shortage
pépin m de fruit seed
perçant regard, froid piercing
percée f breakthrough
percepteur m tax collector
perception f perception; des impôts collection; bureau tax office

percer 1 v/t make a hole in; *porte* make; (*transpercer*) pierce **2** v/i *du soleil* break through; **perceuse** f drill

percevoir perceive; *impôts* collect

perche f ZO perch; *en bois, métal* pole

percher: (*se*) ~ *d'un oiseau* perch; **F** live; **perchoir** m perch

percolateur m percolator

percussion f MUS percussion

percuter crash into

perdant, ~e 1 adj losing **2** m/f loser

perdre 1 v/t lose; *occasion* miss; *son temps* waste; **se** ~ *disparaître* disappear; *d'une personne* get lost **2** v/i: ~ *au change* lose out

perdrix f partridge

père m father (*aussi* REL)

perfection f perfection; **perfectionnement** m perfecting; **perfectionner** perfect; **se** ~ **en anglais** improve one's English

perfide treacherous

perforer perforate; *cuir* punch

performance f performance; **performant** high-performance

péril m peril; **périlleux, -euse** perilous

périmé out of date

périmètre m MATH perimeter

période f period; **en** ~ **de** in times of; **périodique 1** adj

periodic **2** m periodical

périphérie f *d'une ville* outskirts pl; **périphérique** m beltway, *Br* ringroad

périr perish; **périssable** *nourriture* perishable

péritel: prise f ~ **SCART**

perle f pearl; (*boule percée*) bead; *fig: personne* gem; *de sang* drop; perler: **la sueur perlait sur son front** he had beads of sweat on his forehead

permanence f permanence; **être de** ~ be on duty; **en** ~ constantly; **permanent, ~e 1** adj permanent **2** f coiffure perm

perméable permeable

permettre allow, permit; ~ **à qn de faire qch** allow s.o. to do sth; **se** ~ **qc** allow o.s. sth

permis m permit; **passer son** ~ sit one's driving test; ~ **de conduire** driver's license, *Br* driving licence; ~ **de séjour** residence permit

permission f permission; MIL leave

perpendiculaire perpendicular (**à** to)

perpétrer JUR perpetrate

perpétuel, ~le adj perpetual; **perpétuer** perpetuate; **perpétuité: à** ~ in perpetuity; JUR *condamné* to life imprisonment

perplexe perplexed, puzzled

perron m steps pl

perroquet *m* parrot

perruque *f* wig

persécuter persecute

persévérance *f* perseverance; **persévérer** persevere (**dans** in)

persienne *f* shutter

persil *m* BOT parsley

persistance *f* persistence; **persister** persist (**à faire** in doing); **~ dans sa décision** stick to one's decision

personnage *m* character; (*dignitaire*) important person

personnalité *f* personality

personne[1] *f* person; **deux ~s** two people; **par ~** per person, each; **les ~s âgées** the old *pl*, old people *pl*

personne[2] *pron* no-one, nobody; **il n'y avait ~** no-one was there, there wasn't anyone there; **je ne vois jamais ~** I never see anyone; *qui que ce soit*, anybody

personnel, ~le 1 *adj* personal; *conversation, courrier* private **2** *m* personnel *pl*, staff *pl*

perspective *f* perspective; *fig:* **pour l'avenir** prospect

perspicace shrewd; **perspicacité** *f* shrewdness

persuader persuade (**de faire** to do); **se ~** convince o.s.

perte *f* loss; *fig (destruction)* ruin; **à ~ de vue** as far as the eye can see; **une ~ de temps** a waste of time

pertinent relevant

perturbateur, -trice disruptive; **perturber** *personne* upset; *trafic* disrupt

pervers perverse; **pervertir** pervert

pesant heavy; **pesanteur** *f* PHYS gravity

pèse-personne *f* scales *pl*

peser weigh; *fig* weigh up; *mots* weigh

pessimisme *m* pessimism; **pessimiste 1** *adj* pessimistic **2** *m/f* pessimist

pétale *f* petal

pétard *m* firecracker; F (*bruit*) racket

péter F fart *fig*

pétillant sparkling; **pétiller** *du feu* crackle; *d'une boisson, d'yeux* sparkle

petit, ~e 1 *adj* small, little; **~ à ~** gradually, little by little; **~ ami** *m* boyfriend; **~e amie** *f* girlfriend **2** *m/f* child; **une chatte et ses ~s** a cat and her young; **attendre des ~s** be pregnant

petite-fille *f* granddaughter

petit-fils *m* grandson

pétition *f* petition

pétrifier turn to stone; *fig* petrify

pétrin *m* fig F mess

pétrir knead

pétrole *m* oil, petroleum; **~ brut** crude (oil); **pétrolier, -ère 1** *adj* oil **2** *m* tanker

peu 1 *adv:* **~ gentil** not very nice; **~ après** a little after;

j'ai ~ *dormi* I didn't sleep much; ~ *de pain* not much bread; ~ *de choses à faire* not many things to do; ~ *de gens* few people; *dans* ~ *de temps* in a little while; *un* ~ *a bit*, a bit; *un tout petit* ~ just a very little, just a little bit; *un* ~ *de chocolat* a little chocolate, a bit of chocolate; *un* ~ *plus long* a bit *ou* little longer; *de* ~ *rater le bus etc* only just; ~ *à* ~ little by little; *à* ~ *près* (*plus ou moins*) more or less; (*presque*) almost

peuple *m* people; **peupler** *région* populate; *maison* live in

peuplier *m* BOT poplar

peur *f* fear (*de* of); *avoir* ~ be frightened, be afraid (*de* of); *faire* ~ *à qn* frighten s.o.; *de* ~ *que* (+*subj*) in case; *peureux, -euse* fearful, timid

peut-être perhaps, maybe

phare *m* MAR lighthouse; AVIAT beacon; AUTO headlight; *se mettre en* (*pleins*) ~*s* switch to full beam

pharmacie *f* pharmacy, *Br aussi* chemist's; *science* pharmacy; *médicaments* pharmaceuticals *pl*; **pharmacien, -ne** *m/f* pharmacist

phénomène *m* phenomenon

philosophe *m* philosopher; **philosophie** *f* philosophy; **philosophique** philosophical

phobie *f* phobia

photo *f* photo; *l'art* photography; *prendre qn en* ~ take a photo of s.o.

photocopie *f* photocopy; **photocopier** photocopy; **photocopieur** *m*, **photocopieuse** *f* photocopier

photographe *m/f* photographer; **photographie** *f* photograph; *l'art* photography; **photographier** photograph

phrase *f* GRAM sentence; MUS phrase; *sans* ~*s* straight out

physicien, -ne *m/f* physicist

physique 1 *adj* physical **2** *m* physique **3** *f* physics

piailler *d'un oiseau* chirp; F *d'un enfant* scream

pianiste *m/f* pianist; **piano** *m* piano; ~ *à queue* grand piano

pic *m* pick; *d'une montagne* peak; *à* ~ *tomber* steeply

pichet *m* pitcher, *Br* jug

pickpocket *m* pickpocket

pick-up *m* pick-up (truck)

pie *f* ZO magpie

pièce *f* piece; *de machine* part; (*chambre*) room; (*document*) document; *de monnaie* coin; *de théâtre* play; *cinq euros* (*la*) ~ five euros each; *mettre en* ~*s* smash to smithereens; ~ *jointe* enclosure

pied *m* foot; *d'un meuble* leg; *d'un champignon* stalk; *à* ~ on foot; ~*s nus* barefoot; *au* ~ *de* at the foot of; *mettre*

sur ~ set up

piège m trap; **piégé: voiture** f **~e** car bomb; **piéger** trap; *voiture* booby-trap

piercing m body piercing

pierre f stone; **~ tombale** gravestone; **pierreux, -euse** *sol* stony

piétiner 1 v/t trample; *fig* trample underfoot **2** v/i *fig* (*ne pas avancer*) mark time

piéton, ~ne 1 m/f pedestrian **2** adj: *zone* f **~ne** pedestrianized zone, *Br* pedestrian precinct

pieu m stake; F pit F

pieuvre f octopus

pieux, -euse pious

pigeon m pigeon

piger F understand, get F

pigment m pigment

pile¹ f (*tas*) pile; ÉL battery; *monnaie* tails

pile² adv: **s'arrêter ~** stop dead; **à deux heures ~** at two o'clock on the dot

piler *ail* crush; *amandes* grind

pilier m pillar (*aussi fig*)

pillage m pillage, plunder; **piller** pillage

pilote 1 m pilot; AUTO driver **2** adj: *usine* f **~** pilot plant; **piloter** pilot; AUTO drive

pilule f pill

piment m pimento; *fig* spice

pimenter spice up

pin m BOT pine

pinard m F wine

pince f pliers pl; *d'un crabe* pincer; **~ à épiler** tweezers

pl; **~ à linge** clothespin, *Br* clothespeg

pinceau m brush

pincer pinch; MUS pluck

ping-pong m ping-pong

pinson m chaffinch

pintade f guinea fowl

pioche f pickax, *Br* pickaxe; **piocher** dig

pioncer F sleep, *Br* kip F

pipe f pipe

pipi m F pee F

pique m *aux cartes* spades

pique-nique m picnic

piquer *d'une abeille, des orties* sting; *d'un moustique, serpent* bite; *d'épine* prick; *fig: curiosité* excite; *fig* F (*voler*) pinch F; **se ~** prick o.s.; *se faire une piqûre* inject o.s.

piquet m stake; **~ de tente** tent peg; **~ de grève** picket line

piquette f cheap wine

piqûre f *d'abeille* sting; *de moustique* bite; MÉD injection

pirate m pirate; **~ informatique** hacker; **~ de l'air** hijacker; **pirater** pirate

pire worse; *le/la* **~** the worst

piscine f (swimming) pool; **~ couverte/en plein air** indoor/outdoor pool

pisser F pee F, piss F

piste f track; AVIAT runway; *ski alpin* piste; *ski de fond* trail; **~ cyclable** cycle path

pistolet m pistol

piston *m* piston; **pistonner** F pull strings for

pitié *f* pity; *avoir ~ de qn* take pity on s.o.

pitoyable pitiful

pittoresque picturesque

pivot *m* pivot

pIzza *f* pizza

PJ (= *pièce(s) jointe(s)*) enclosure(s)

placard *m* (*armoire*) cabinet, Br cupboard; (*affiche*) poster; **placarder** *avis* stick up

place *f de ville* square; (*siège*) seat; (*espace libre*) room, space; (*emploi*) position; *sur ~* on the spot; *à la ~ de* instead of; *~ de place* change places with

placement *m* (*emploi*) placement; FIN investment; *agence f de ~* employment agency; **placer** put, place; (*procurer emploi à*) find a job for; *argent* invest; *dans une famille* find a place for; *se ~* take one's place

plafond *m* ceiling

plage *f* beach; *lieu* seaside resort

plagiat *m* plagiarism

plaider 1 *v/i* JUR plead 2 *v/t*: *~ la cause de qn* defend s.o.; *fig* plead s.o.'s cause

plaidoyer *m* JUR speech for the defense *ou* Br defence; *fig* plea

plaie *f* cut; *fig* wound

plaignant, *~e m/f* JUR plaintiff

plaindre pity; *se ~* complain (*de* about; *à* to)

plaine *f* plain

plainte *f* complaint; (*lamentation*) moan

plaire: *s'il vous plaît, s'il te plaît* please; *Paris me plaît* I like Paris; *ça me plairait d'aller ...* I would like to go ...; *se ~ de personnes* be attracted to each other

plaisance *f*: *port m de ~* marina

plaisanter joke; **plaisanterie** *f* joke

plaisir *m* pleasure; *par ~, pour le ~* for pleasure; *faire ~ à* please

plan 1 *adj* flat, level 2 *m* (*surface*) surface; (*projet, relevé*) plan; *premier ~* foreground; *sur ce ~* in that respect; *sur le ~ économique* in economic terms

planche *f* plank; *~ à voile* sailboard

plancher *m* floor

planer hover; *fig* live in another world

planète *f* planet

planeur *m* glider

planifier plan

planning *m*: *~ familial* family planning

planquer F hide; *se ~* hide

plant *m* AGR seedling; (*plantation*) plantation

plante¹ *f* plant

plante² *f*: *~ du pied* sole of the foot

planter plant; *jardin* plant up;

plus

poteau hammer in; *tente* put up

plaque *f* plate; (*inscription*) plaque; **~ électrique** hotplate; **~ tournante** turntable; *fig* hub

plaquer *argent, or* plate; *meuble* veneer; *fig* pin (**contre** to, against); F (*abandonner*) dump F; *au rugby* tackle

plastique *adj & m* plastic

plat 1 *adj* flat; *eau* still **2** *m* dish

plateau *m* tray; *de théâtre* stage; TV, *d'un film* set; GÉOGR plateau; **~ de fromages** cheeseboard

plate-bande *f* flower bed

plate-forme *f* platform; **~ de lancement** launch pad

platine 1 *m* CHIM platinum **2** *f*: **~ laser** *ou* **CD** CD player

platitude *f* dullness; (*lieu commun*) platitude

plâtre *m* plaster; **plâtrer** plaster

plausible plausible

plein 1 *adj* full (**de** of); **en ~ air** in the open (air); **en ~ Paris** in the middle of Paris; **en ~ jour** in broad daylight **2** *adv*: **~ de** F lots of, a whole bunch of F **3** *m*: **faire le ~** AUTO fill up

pleurer 1 *v/i* cry; **~ sur** complain about **2** *v/t* (*regretter*) mourn

pleurnicher F snivel

pleuvoir rain; *il pleut* it's raining

pli *m* fold; *d'une jupe* pleat; *d'un pantalon* crease; (*enveloppe*) envelope; (*lettre*) letter; **plier 1** *v/t* (*rabattre*) fold; (*courber, ployer*) bend **2** *v/i* bend; *fig* (*céder*) give in; **se ~ à** (*se soumettre*) submit to

plomb *m* lead; **sans ~** *essence* unleaded

plombage *m* filling

plomberie *f* plumbing; **plombier** *m* plumber

plongée *f* diving; **plonger 1** *v/i* dive **2** *v/t* plunge; **se ~ dans** bury o.s. in; **plongeur, -euse** *m/f* diver

pluie *f* rain; *fig* shower

plumage *m* plumage; **plume** *f* feather; **plumer** pluck; *fig* fleece

plupart: *la ~ d'entre nous* most of us; *pour la ~* mostly; *la ~ du temps* most of the time

pluriel, ~le *adj & m* plural

plus 1 *adv* more (**que**, **de** than); **~ grand** bigger; **~ efficace** more efficient; **le ~ grand** the biggest; **le ~ efficace** the most efficient; *il vieillit ~ il dort* the older he gets the more he sleeps; *le ~* the most; *tu en veux ~?* do you want some more?; *20 euros de ~* 20 euros more; *nous n'avons ~ d'argent* we have no more money, we don't have any more money; *elle n'y habite ~*

she doesn't live there any more, she no longer lives there; **je ne le reverrai ~ jamais** I won't see him ever again; **moi non ~** me neither

2 *prép* MATH plus

plusieurs several

plutôt rather

pluvieux, -euse rainy

pneu *m* tire, *Br* tyre

pneumonie *f* pneumonia

poche *f* pocket; zo pouch; **livre** *m* **de ~** paperback; **argent de ~** pocket money

pocher *œufs* poach

pochette *f* pour photos etc folder; *d'un disque*, CD sleeve; (*sac*) bag

poêle 1 *m* stove **2** *f* frypan, *Br* frying pan

poème *m* poem

poésie *f* poetry; (*poème*) poem

poète *m* poet; **poétique** poetic; *atmosphère* romantic

poids *m* weight; *fig* (*charge, fardeau*) burden; (*importance*) weight; **perdre/prendre du ~** lose/gain weight

poignard *m* dagger; **poignarder** stab

poignée *f petit nombre* handful; *d'une valise etc* handle; **~ de main** handshake

poignet *m* wrist

poil *m* hair; **à ~** naked; **poilu** hairy

poinçonner *argent* hallmark; *billet* punch

poing *m* fist; **coup m de ~**

punch

point¹ *m* point; *de couture* stitch; **deux ~s** colon; **être sur le ~ de faire** be on the point of doing; **à ~** *viande* medium; **à ce ~** so much; **~ du jour** dawn; **~ de vue** point of view

point² *adv litt*: **il ne le fera ~** he will not do it

pointe *f* point; *d'asperge* tip; **en ~** pointed; **de ~** *technologie* leading-edge; *secteur* high-tech; **une ~ de** a touch of

pointer 1 *v/t sur liste* check, *Br* tick off **2** *v/i d'un employé* clock in

pointillé *m*: **les ~s** the dotted line

pointilleux, -euse fussy

pointu pointed; *voix* high-pitched

pointure *f* (shoe) size

point-virgule *m* GRAM semi-colon

poire *f* pear

poireau *m* BOT leek

poirier *m* BOT pear (tree)

pois *m* BOT pea; **petits ~** garden peas

poison 1 *m* poison **2** *m/f fig* F nuisance, pest

poisson *m* fish; **Poissons** *mpl* ASTROL Pisces

poissonnerie *f* fish shop, *Br* fishmonger's

poitrine *f* chest; (*seins*) bosom

poivre *m* pepper; **poivrer**

pepper

poivron *m* bell pepper, *Br* pepper

polaire polar; **pôle** *m* pole; *fig* center, *Br* centre, focus; **~ Nord** North Pole; **~ Sud** South Pole

poli (*courtois*) polite; *métal, caillou* polished

police *f* police; **~ d'assurance** insurance policy

policier, **-ère 1** *adj* police *atr*; *film, roman* detective *atr* **2** *m* police officer

polir polish

politesse *f* politeness

politicien, **~ne** *m/f* politician

politique 1 *adj* political; **homme ~** politician **2** *f d'un parti etc* policy; (*affaires publiques*) politics *sg*

pollen *m* pollen

polluer pollute; **pollution** *f* pollution; **~ atmosphérique** air pollution

Pologne: **la ~** Poland; **polonais**, **~e 1** *adj* Polish **2** *m langue* Polish; **Polonais**, **~e** *m/f* Pole

poltron, **~ne** *m/f* coward

polyclinique *f* (general) hospital

polycopié *m* (photocopied) handout

polystyrène *m* polystyrene

polyvalence *f* versatility; **polyvalent** multipurpose; *personne* versatile

pommade *f* MÉD ointment

pomme *f* apple; **~ de terre** po-

tato

pommette *f* ANAT cheekbone

pommier *m* BOT apple tree

pompe[1] *f faste* pomp; **~s funèbres** funeral director

pompe[2] *f* TECH pump; **~ à essence** gas pump, *Br* petrol pump; **pomper** pump; *fig* (*épuiser*) knock out

pompeux, **-euse** pompous

pompier *m* firefighter; **~s** fire department, *Br* fire brigade

pomponner F: **se ~** get dolled up F

poncer sand

ponctualité *f* punctuality; **ponctuel**, **~le** *personne* punctual; *fig*: *action* one-off

ponctuer punctuate

pondération *f d'une personne* level-headedness; *de forces* balance; ÉCON weighting; **pondéré** *personne* level-headed; *forces* balanced; ÉCON weighted

pondre *œufs* lay; *fig* F come up with; *roman* churn out

poney *m* pony

pont *m* bridge; MAR deck; **faire le ~** make a long weekend of it

pontage *m*: **~ coronarien** (heart) bypass

pop *f* MUS pop

populaire popular; **populariser** popularize; **popularité** *f* popularity

population *f* population

porc *m* hog, pig; *fig* pig; *viande* pork

porcelaine f porcelain

porcherie f hog ou pig farm

pore m pore; **poreux, -euse** porous

pornographique pornographic

port[1] m port; ~ **de pêche** fishing port

port[2] m d'armes carrying; courrier postage

portable 1 adj portable **2** m ordinateur laptop; téléphone cellphone, cell, Br mobile

portail m ARCH portal; d'un parc gate

portant mur load-bearing; **à bout** ~ at point-blank range; **bien** ~ well; **mal** ~ not well

portatif, -ive portable

porte f door; d'une ville gate; **mettre qn à la** ~ show s.o. the door

porte-bagages m AUTO roof rack; filet luggage rack; **porte-bonheur** m lucky charm; **porte-clés** m keyring; **porte-documents** m briefcase

portée f ZO litter; d'une arme range; (importance) significance; **être à la** ~ **de qn** fig be accessible to s.o.

portefeuille m portfolio (aussi POL, FIN); (porte-monnaie) billfold, Br wallet

portemanteau m coat rack; sur pied coatstand

porte-monnaie m coin purse, Br purse

porte-parole m spokesperson

porter 1 v/t carry; un vêtement, des lunettes etc wear; (apporter) take; bring; yeux, attention turn (**sur** to); toast drink; fruits, nom bear; ~ **plainte** make a complaint **2** v/i d'une voix carry; ~ **sur** (appuyer sur) rest on; (concerner) be about **3**: **il se porte bien/mal** he's well/not well; **se** ~ **candidat** be a candidate, run

porteur m d'un message bearer

portier m doorman

portière f de train, voiture door

portion f portion

portrait m portrait

portugais, ~e 1 adj Portuguese **2** m langue Portuguese; **Portugais, ~e** m/f Portuguese; **Portugal: le** ~ Portugal

pose f d'un radiateur installation; de moquette fitting; de papier peint, rideaux hanging; (attitude) pose; **posé** poised, composed; **poser 1** v/t (mettre) put (down); compteur, radiateur install, Br instal; moquette fit; papier peint, rideaux hang; problème pose; question ask; **se** ~ **en** set o.s. up as **2** v/i pose

positif, -ive positive

position f position

possédé possessed (**de** by); **posséder** own, possess;

possesseur *m* owner; **possession** *f* possession, ownership

possibilité *f* possibility; **possible 1** *adj* possible; *le plus souvent* ~ as often as possible; *autant que* ~ as far as possible **2** *m*: *faire tout son* ~ do everything one can

poste¹ *f* mail, *Br aussi* post; (*bureau m de*) ~ post office; *mettre à la* ~ mail, *Br aussi* post

poste² *m* post; (*profession*) position; *RAD, TV set*; *TÉL* extension; ~ *de secours* first-aid post; ~ *de travail* INFORM work station

poster *soldat* post; *lettre* mail, *Br aussi* post

postérieur 1 *adj dans l'espace* back *atr*, rear *atr*; *dans le temps* later; ~ *à qch* after sth **2** *m* F posterior F

postérité *f* posterity

posthume posthumous

postier, -ère *m/f* post office employee

postillonner splutter

postuler apply for

posture *f* position, posture; *fig* position

pot *m* pot; ~ *à eau* water jug; *prendre un* ~ F have a drink; *avoir du* ~ F be lucky

potable fit to drink; *eau* ~ drinking water

potage *m* soup; **potager, -ère**: *jardin m* ~ kitchen garden

pot-au-feu *m* boiled beef dinner

pot-de-vin *m* F kickback F, bribe

poteau *m* post; ~ *indicateur* signpost

poterie *f* pottery; *objet* piece of pottery

potion *f* potion

potiron *m* BOT pumpkin

pou *m* louse

poubelle *f* trash can, *Br* dustbin

pouce *m* thumb

poudre *f* powder; *chocolat m en* ~ chocolate powder; **poudrier** *m* powder compact

pouffer: ~ *de rire* burst out laughing

poulailler *m* henhouse; *au théâtre* gallery, *Br* gods *pl*

poulain *m* ZO foal

poule *f* hen; **poulet** *m* chicken

poulpe *m* octopus

pouls *m* pulse

poumon *m* lung

poupée *f* doll (*aussi fig*)

poupon *m* little baby

pour 1 *prép* for; ~ *20 euros de courses* 20 euros' worth of shopping; *je l'ai dit* ~ *te prévenir* I said that to warn you **2** *conj*: ~ *que* (+ *subj*) so that; *il parle trop vite* ~ *que je le comprenne* he speaks too fast for me to understand **3** *m*: *le* ~ *et le contre* the pros and the cons *pl*

pourboire *m* tip

pourcentage *m* percentage
pourparlers *mpl* talks
pourpre purple
pourquoi why
pourri rotten (*aussi fig*);
  pourrir 1 *v/i* rot; *fig*: *d'une
  situation* deteriorate **2** *v/t*
  rot; *fig* (*corrompre*) corrupt;
  (*gâter*) spoil; **pourriture** *f* rot
  (*aussi fig*)
poursuite *f* chase, pursuit; *fig*
  pursuit; **~s** JUR proceedings;
  poursuivre pursue, chase;
  fig: *bonheur* pursue; *de pensées* haunt; JUR sue; *malfaiteur* prosecute; (*continuer*)
  carry on with
pourtant yet
pourvoir 1 *v/t emploi* fill; **~** *de
  voiture, maison* equip with **2**
  v/i: **~** **à besoins** provide for;
  se ~ de provide o.s.
pourvu: **~ que** (+ *subj*) provided that; *exprimant désir*
  hopefully
pousse *f* AGR shoot; **poussée**
  f thrust; MÉD outbreak; *de
  fièvre* rise; *fig*: *de racisme
  etc* upsurge; **pousser 1** *v/t*
  push; *du vent* drive; *cri*, *soupir* give; *fig*: *recherches* pursue; **se ~** *d'une foule* push
  forward; *pour faire de la place* move over **2** *v/i* push; *de
  cheveux*, *plantes* grow;
  poussette *f pour enfants*
  stroller, *Br* pushchair
poussière *f* dust; *particule*
  speck of dust
poussin *m* chick

poutre *f* beam
pouvoir 1 *v/aux* be able to,
  can; *je ne peux pas aider*
  I can't *ou* cannot help; *je
  ne pouvais pas accepter* I
  couldn't *ou* cannot accept, I
  wasn't able to accept; *il se peut
  que* (+ *subj*) it's possible
  that; *tu aurais pu me prévenir!* you could have *ou* might
  have warned me! **2** *m* power;
  procuration power of attorney; *les ~s publics* the
  authorities
prairie *f* meadow; *plaine* prairie
praline *f* praline
praticable *projet* feasible;
  route passable
pratique 1 *adj* practical **2** *f*
  practice; *expérience* practical experience; **pratiquement** (*presque*) practically;
  dans la pratique in practice;
  pratiquer practice, *Br* practise; *sports* play; *technique*
  use; TECH *trou*, *passage*
  make
pré *m* meadow
préado *m/f* pre-teen
préalable 1 *adj* (*antérieur*)
  prior; (*préliminaire*) preliminary **2** *m* condition; *au ~* beforehand
préavis *m* notice
précaire precarious
précaution *f* caution; *mesure*
  precaution; *par ~* as a precaution
précédent 1 *adj* previous **2** *m*

precedent; **précéder** precede

prêcher preach

précieux, -euse precious

précipice m precipice

précipitamment hastily, in a rush; **précipitation** f haste; **~s** temps precipitation; **précipiter** (faire tomber) plunge (dans into); (pousser) hurl; (brusquer) precipitate; pas hasten; **se ~** (se jeter) throw o.s.; (se dépêcher) rush

précis 1 adj precise **2** m precis, summary; **préciser** specify; **~ que** (souligner) make it clear that; **précision** f accuracy; **pour plus de ~s** for further details

précoce early; enfant precocious; **précocité** f earliness; d'un enfant precociousness

préconçu preconceived

précurseur 1 m precursor **2** adj: **signe** m **~** warning sign

prédateur, -trice 1 adj predatory **2** m/f predator

prédécesseur m predecessor

prédestiner predestine (à qc for sth; à faire to do)

prédiction f prediction

prédilection f predilection; **de ~** favorite, Br favourite

prédire predict

prédominer predominate

préfabriqué prefabricated

préface f preface

préférable preferable (à to);

préféré favorite, Br favourite; **préférence** f preference; **de ~** preferably; **préférer** prefer (à to); **~ faire qc** prefer to do sth; **je préfère que tu viennes** (subj) **demain** I would ou I'd prefer you to come tomorrow, I'd rather you came tomorrow

préfet m prefect; **~ de police** chief of police

préfixe m prefix

préjudice m harm; **porter ~ à** harm

préjugé m prejudice

prélever échantillon take; montant deduct (**sur** from)

préliminaire preliminary

préluder fig: **~ à** be the prelude to

prématuré premature

préméditer premeditate

premier, -ère 1 adj first; rang front; objectif, cause primary; nombre prime; **au ~ étage** on the second floor, Br on the first floor; **Premier ministre** Prime Minister; **le ~ août** August first, Br the first of August **2** m/f: **partir le ~** leave first **3** m second floor, Br first floor; **en ~** first **4** f THÉÂT first night; AUTO first (gear); **en train** first (class)

prémisse f premise

prémonition f premonition; **prémonitoire** rêve prophetic

prendre **1** v/t take; (enlever) take away; froid catch; poids put on; **~ qch à qn** take sth (away) from s.o. **2** *v/i* (*durcir*) set; *de mode* catch on; *d'un feu* take hold; **~ à droite** turn right **3**: **se ~** (*se laisser attraper*) get caught; **se ~ d'amitié pour qn** take a liking to s.o.

prénom *m* first name; **deuxième ~** middle name

préoccuper preoccupy; (*inquiéter*) worry; **se ~ de** worry about

préparatifs *mpl* preparations; **préparation** *f* preparation; **préparer** prepare; (*organiser*) arrange; **~ qn à qch** prepare s.o. for sth; **~ un examen** prepare for an exam; **se ~** get ready; *de dispute, d'orage* be brewing

prépondérant predominant

préposé *m* (*facteur*) mailman, *Br* postman; *au vestiaire* attendant; *des douanes* official; **préposée** *f* (*factrice*) mailwoman, *Br* postwoman

préretraite *f* early retirement

près 1 *adv* close, near; **de ~** closely **2** *prép*: **~ de** close to, near; **~ de 500** nearly 500

présage *m* omen

presbyte farsighted, *Br* long-sighted

prescription *f* rule; MÉD prescription; **prescrire** stipulate; MÉD prescribe

présence *f* presence; **en ~ de**

in the presence of; **présent 1** *adj* present **2** *m* present (*aussi* GRAM); **les ~s** those present; **à ~** at present; **à ~ que** now that; **jusqu'à ~** till now

présentateur, -trice *m/f* TV presenter; **~ météo** weatherman; **présentation** *f* presentation; **présenter** present; *chaise* offer; *personne* introduce; *pour un concours* put forward; *billet* show, present; *condoléances, félicitations* offer; *difficultés, dangers* involve; **se ~** introduce o.s.; *pour un poste, un emploi* apply; *aux élections* run; *de difficultés* come up

préservatif *m* condom

préserver protect (**de** from); *bois, patrimoine* preserve

présidence *f* chairmanship; POL presidency; **président, ~e** *m/f* *d'une réunion* chair; POL president; **présidentiel, ~le** presidential; **présider** *réunion* chair

présomption *f* presumption; **présomptueux, -euse** presumptuous

presque almost, nearly

presqu'île *f* peninsula

pressant *besoin* pressing, urgent; *personne* insistent

presse *f* press; **mise ~ sous ~** going to press

pressé *lettre, requête* urgent; *citron* fresh; **je suis ~** I'm in a hurry

pressentiment *m* foreboding, presentiment; **pressentir:** ~ *qch* have a premonition that sth is going to happen; ~ *qn pour un poste* approach s.o., sound s.o. out

presser 1 *v/t bouton* push, press; *fruit* squeeze; (*harceler*) press; (*quicken*) *étape* speed up; (*étreindre*) press, squeeze; **se** ~ **contre** press (o.s.) against **2** *v/i* be urgent; **se** ~ hurry up

pressing *m magasin* dry cleaner

pression *f* pressure; *bouton* snap fastener, *Br aussi* press-stud fastener; (*bière f*) ~ draft beer, *Br* draught beer; **faire** ~ **sur** pressure, put pressure on

prestance *f* presence

prestation *f* (*allocation*) allowance; **~s familiales** child benefit

prestige *m* prestige

présumer 1 *v/t:* ~ *que* presume *ou* assume that **2** *v/i:* ~ *de* overrate

prêt[1] *adj* ready (*à* for; *à faire* to do)

prêt[2] *m* loan; ~ *immobilier* mortgage

prêt-à-porter *m* ready-to--wear clothes *pl*

prétendre 1 *v/t* maintain; ~ *faire qch* claim to do sth **2** *v/i:* ~ *à* lay claim to sth; **prétendu** so-called

prétentieux, -euse pretentious

prêter 1 *v/t* lend **2** *v/i:* ~ *à* give rise to; **se** ~ *à d'une chose* lend itself to; *d'une personne* be a party to

prétexte *m* pretext; **sous** ~ *de faire* on the pretext of doing

prêtre *m* priest; **prêtresse** *f* woman priest

preuve *f* proof, evidence; MATH proof; **faire** ~ *de courage* show courage

prévenance *f* consideration

prévenir (*avertir*) warn (*de* of); (*informer*) inform (*de* of); *besoin, question* anticipate; *crise, maladie* avert

préventif, -ive preventive; **prévention** *f* prevention; ~ *routière* road safety

prévision *f* forecast; **~s météorologiques** weather forecast

prévoir (*pressentir*) foresee; (*planifier*) plan; **comme prévu** as expected; **prévoyance** *f* foresight; **prévoyant** farsighted

prier 1 *v/i* REL pray **2** *v/t* (*supplier*) beg; REL pray to; ~ *qn de faire qc* ask s.o. to do sth; *je vous en prie* don't mention it

prière *f* REL prayer; (*demande*) entreaty; *faire sa* ~ say one's prayers

primaire primary; *péj* narrow-minded

prime[1]: *de* ~ *abord* at first sight

prime² *f d'assurance* premium; *de fin d'année* bonus; *(cadeau)* free gift

primer 1 *v/i* take precedence **2** *v/t* take precedence over

primeur *f*: **avoir la ~ de** *nouvelle* be the first to hear *objet* have first use of; **~s** early fruit and vegetables

primitif, -ive primitive; *couleur, sens* original

primordial essential

prince *m* prince; **princesse** princess

principal, ~e 1 *adj* main, principal **2** *m*: **le ~** the main thing **3** *m/f* principal, *Br* head teacher

principe *m* principle; **par ~** on principle; **en ~** in principle

printemps *m* spring

priorité *f* priority (**sur** over); *sur la route* right of way

pris *place* taken; *personne* busy

prise *f* hold; *d'un pion, une ville etc* capture, taking; *de poissons* catch; ÉL outlet, *Br* socket; *d'un film* take; **être aux ~s avec** be struggling with; **~ de conscience** awareness; **~ de courant** outlet, *Br* socket

prison *f* prison; **prisonnier, -ère** *m/f* prisoner

privation *f* deprivation

privatisation *f* privatization; **privatiser** privatize

privé 1 *adj* private **2** *m*: **en ~** in private; **priver**: **~ qn de** deprive s.o. of; **se ~ de** go without

privilège *m* privilege; **privilégier** favor, *Br* favour

prix *m* price; *(valeur)* value; *(récompense)* prize; **à tout ~** at all costs; **hors de ~** prohibitive; **au ~ de** at the cost of; **~ fort** full price; **~ de revient** cost price

probabilité *f* probability; **probable** probable

probant convincing

problème *m* problem

procédé *m* (*méthode*) method; TECH process; **~s** (*comportement*) behavior, *Br* behaviour

procéder proceed; **~ à qc** carry out sth

procès *m* JUR trial

processus *m* process

procès-verbal *m* minutes *pl*; *(contravention)* ticket

prochain, ~e 1 *adj* next **2** *m/f*: **son ~** one's neighbor *ou Br* neighbour

proche 1 *adj* close (**de** to), near; *ami* close; *événement* recent; **~ de** *fig* close to **2** *mpl*: **~s** family and friends

proclamer *roi, république* proclaim; *résultats, innocence* declare

procréer procreate

procuration *f* proxy, power of attorney; **procurer** get, procure *fml*

prodigieux, -euse enormous,

tremendous

prodigue extravagant; **prodiguer** lavish

producteur, -trice 1 *adj* producing **2** *m/f* producer; **productif, -ive** productive; **production** *f* production; **produire** produce; *se* **~** happen; **produit** *m* product; *d'un investissement* yield; **~ d'entretien** cleaning product; **~ fini** end product

profane 1 *adj* art, musique secular **2** *m/f* fig lay person; **profaner** desecrate, profane

proférer menaces utter

professeur *m* teacher; *d'université* professor

profession *f* profession; **professionnel, ~le** *m/f & adj* professional

profil *m* profile

profit *m* COMM profit; *(avantage)* benefit; **profitable** beneficial; COMM profitable; **profiter: ~ de qc** take advantage of sth; **~ à qn** to be to s.o.'s advantage

profond deep; *personne, pensées* deep, profound; *influence* profound; **profondément** deeply, profoundly; **profondeur** *f* depth

programme *m* program, Br programme; INFORM program; **~ télé** TV program; **programmer** TV schedule; INFORM program; **programmeur, -euse** *m/f* programmer

progrès *m* progress; *d'un incendie, d'une épidémie* spread; **progresser** progress; *d'une incendie, d'une épidémie* spread; **progressif, -ive** progressive; **progression** *f* progress

prohiber ban, prohibit; **prohibition** *f* ban; *la Prohibition* HIST Prohibition

proie *f* prey (*aussi fig*); *en* **~ à** prey to

projecteur *m* (*spot*) spotlight; *au cinéma* projector

projection *f* projection

projet *m* project; *personnel* plan; *(ébauche)* draft; **~ de loi** bill; **projeter** (*jeter*) throw; *film* screen; *travail, voyage* plan

proliférer proliferate

prologue *m* prologue

prolongation *f* extension; **~** SP overtime, Br extra time; **prolonger** prolong; *mur, route* extend; *se* **~** continue

promenade *f* walk; *en voiture* drive; **promener** take for a walk; *se* **~** go for a walk; *en voiture* go for a drive; **promeneur, -euse** *m/f* stroller, walker

promesse *f* promise; **prometteur, -euse** promising; **promettre** promise (*qc à qn* s.o. sth, sth to s.o., *de faire* to do); *se* **~ de faire qc** make up one's mind to do sth

promiscuité *f* overcrowding;

sexuelle promiscuity

promontoire *m* promontory

promoteur, -trice 1 *m/f* (*instigateur*) instigator **2** *m*: ~ **immobilier** property developer; **promotion** *f* promotion; *sociale* advancement; ÉDU class, Br year; **en** ~ on special offer; **promouvoir** promote

prompt swift

pronom *m* GRAM pronoun

prononcé *fig* marked, pronounced; *accent, traits* strong; **prononcer** (*dire*) say, utter; (*articuler*) pronounce; *discours* give; JUR *sentence* pass, pronounce; **se** ~ *d'un mot* be pronounced; (*se déterminer*) express an opinion; **se** ~ **pour/contre qch** come out in favor *ou* Br favour of /against sth; **prononciation** *f* pronunciation; JUR passing

propager *idée, nouvelle* spread; BIOL propagate; **se** ~ spread; BIOL reproduce

propension *f* propensity (*à* for)

propice favorable, Br favourable; *moment* right

proportion *f* proportion; **toutes ~s gardées** on balance; **proportionnel, ~le** proportional (*à* to)

propos 1 *mpl* (*paroles*) words **2** *m* (*intention*) intention; **à** ~ at the right moment; **mal à** ~, **hors de** ~ at the wrong

moment; **à** ~**!** by the way; **à** ~ **de** (*au sujet de*) about

proposer suggest, propose; (*offrir*) offer; **se** ~ **de faire** propose doing; **se** ~ offer one's services; **proposition** *f* (*suggestion*) proposal, suggestion; (*offre*) offer; GRAM clause

propre 1 *adj* own; (*net*) clean; (*approprié*) suitable; ~ **à** (*particulier à*) characteristic of **2** *m*: **mettre au** ~ make a clean copy of; **propreté** *f* cleanliness

propriétaire *m/f* owner; *qui loue* landlord; *femme* landlady; **propriété** *f* ownership; (*caractéristique*) property

propulser propel; **propulsion** *f* propulsion

proscrire (*interdire*) ban; (*bannir*) banish

prospectus *m* brochure; FIN prospectus

prospère prosperous; **prospérer** prosper; **prospérité** *f* prosperity

prosterner: se ~ prostrate o.s.

prostituée *f* prostitute; **prostitution** *f* prostitution

protecteur, -trice 1 *adj* protective; *péj: ton* patronizing **2** *m/f* protector; (*mécène*) sponsor, patron; **protection** *f* protection; **protéger** protect (*contre, de* from); *arts, artistes* be a patron of

protéine *f* protein

protestant, **~e** REL *m/f* & *adj* Protestant

protestation *f* (*plainte*) protest; (*déclaration*) protestation; **protester** protest

prothèse *f* prosthesis

protocole *m* protocol

prototype *m* prototype

prouesse *f* prowess

prouver prove

provenance *f* origin; **en ~ de** avion, train from

provenir: **~ de** come from

proverbe *m* proverb

providence *f* providence

province *f* province

proviseur *m* principal, *Br* head (teacher)

provision *f* supply; **~s** (*vivres*) provisions; (*achats*) shopping; *d'un chèque* funds *pl*; **chèque m sans ~** bad check *ou Br* cheque

provisoire provisional

provocant, provocateur, -trice provocative; **provoquer** provoke; *accident* cause

proximité *f* proximity; **à ~ de** near, in the vicinity of

prude prudish

prudence *f* caution, prudence; **prudent** cautious, prudent; *conducteur* careful

prune *f* BOT plum

pruneau *m* prune

prunier *m* plum (tree)

PS *m* (= *Parti socialiste*) Socialist Party; (= *Post Scriptum*) PS (= postscript)

psaume *m* psalm

pseudonyme *m* pseudonym

psychanalyser psychoanalyze; **psychanalyste** *m/f* psychoanalyst

psychiatre *m/f* psychiatrist

psychologie *f* psychology; **psychologique** psychological; **psychologue** *m/f* psychologist

psychopathe *m/f* psychopath

puant stinking; *fig* arrogant; **puanteur** *f* stink

pub *f*: **une ~** an ad; **faire de la ~** do some advertising

public, publique 1 *adj* public **2** *m* public; *d'un spectacle* audience

publication *f* publication

publicitaire advertising *atr*; **publicité** *f* publicity; COMM advertising; (*affiche*) ad

publier publish

publipostage *m* mailshot

puce *f* ZO flea; INFORM chip

pudeur *f* modesty; **pudique** modest; *discret* discreet

puer 1 *v/i* stink; **~ des pieds** have smelly feet **2** *v/t* stink of

puéril childish

puis then

puiser draw (*dans* from)

puisque since

puissance *f* power; *d'une armée* strength; **puissant** powerful; *musculature, médicament* strong

puits *m* well; *d'une mine* shaft; **~ de pétrole** oil well

pull(-over) *m* sweater, *Br*

aussi pullover
pulluler swarm
pulsation *f* beat, beating
pulsion *f* drive; **~s** *fpl* **de mort** death wish
pulvériser *solide* pulverize (*aussi fig*); *liquide* spray
punaise *f* zo bug; (*clou*) thumbtack, *Br* drawing pin
punir punish; **punition** *f* punishment
pupille 1 *m/f* JUR ward **2** *f* ANAT pupil
pur pure; *whisky* straight
purée *f* puree; **~ (de pommes de terre)** mashed potatoes *pl*
pureté *f* purity

purge *f* purge; **purger** TECH bleed; POL purge; JUR *peine* serve
purification *f* purification; **purifier** purify
pur-sang *m* thoroughbred
pus *m* pus
pute *f* F slut
puzzle *m* jigsaw (puzzle)
P.-V. *m* (= *procès-verbal*) ticket
pyjama *m* pajamas *pl*, *Br* pyjamas *pl*
pyramide *f* pyramid
Pyrénées *fpl* Pyrenees
pyromane *m* pyromaniac; JUR arsonist

Q

quadragénaire *m/f* & *adj* forty-year old
quadrillé *papier* squared; **quadriller** *fig*: *région* put under surveillance
quadruple quadruple
quai *m* *d'un port* quay; *d'une gare* platform
qualification *f* qualification; (*appellation*) name; **qualifier** qualify; **~ qn d'idiot** describe s.o. as an idiot; **se~** SP qualify
qualité *f* quality; **de ~** quality *atr*; **en ~ d'ambassadeur** as ambassador, in his capacity as ambassador
quand when; **~ je serai de retour** when I'm back

quant à as for
quantifier quantify
quantité *f* quantity; **une ~ de grand nombre** a great many; *abondance* a great deal of
quarantaine *f* MÉD quarantine; **une ~ de** about forty, forty or so; **avoir la ~** be in one's forties; **quarante** forty
quart *m* quarter; *de vin* quarter liter, *Br* quarter litre; **~ d'heure** quarter of an hour; **~ de finale** quarter-final
quartier *m* (*quart*) quarter; *d'orange* segment; *d'une ville* area; **~ général** MIL headquarters *pl*
quasiment virtually
quatorze fourteen

quatre four; **quatre-vingt(s)** eighty; **quatre-vingt-dix** ninety; **quatrième** fourth

quatuor *m* MUS quartet

que 1 *pron relatif personne* who, that; *chose, animal* which, that; *les étudiants ~ j'ai rencontrés* the students (who *ou* that) I met **2** *pron interrogatif* what; *qu'y a-t-il?* what's the matter?; *qu'est-ce que c'est?* what's that? **3** *dans exclamations:* ~ *c'est beau!* it's so beautiful!; ~ *de fleurs!* what a lot of flowers! **4** *conj* that; *je croyais ~ ...* I thought (that) ...; *plus grand ~ moi* bigger than me; *aussi petit ~ cela* as small as that; *ne ... ~* only

quel, **~le** what, which; **~le femme!** what a woman!

quelconque (*médiocre*) mediocre; *un travail ~* some sort of job

quelque some, a few; **~s** some, a few; **~ ... que** (+ *subj*) whatever, whichever

quelque chose something; *avec interrogatif, conditionnel aussi* anything

quelquefois sometimes

quelques-uns, **quelques-unes** a few, some

quelqu'un someone, somebody; *avec interrogatif, conditionnel aussi* anyone, anybody

querelle *f* quarrel; **quereller:** *se ~* quarrel; **querelleur, -euse** quarrelsome

question *f* question; **questionnaire** *m* questionnaire; **questionner** question (*sur* about)

quête *f* search; (*collecte*) collection

queue *f d'un animal* tail; *d'un fruit* stalk; *d'une casserole* handle; *d'un train* rear; *d'une classe* bottom; *d'une file* line, Br queue; *faire la ~* stand in line, Br queue (up); *à la ~*, *en ~* at the rear

qui *interrogatif* who; *relatif, personne* who, that; *relatif, chose, animal* which, that

quiconque whoever; (*n'importe qui*) anyone, anybody

quincaillerie *f* hardware; *magasin* hardware store

quinquagénaire *m/f* & *adj* fifty-year old

quintal *m* hundred kilos *pl*

quinte *f:* ~ (*de toux*) coughing fit

quinzaine *f de jours* two weeks *pl*, Br aussi fortnight; *une ~ de personnes* about fifteen people *pl*; **quinze** fifteen; ~ *jours* two weeks, Br aussi fortnight

quitte: *être ~ envers qn* be quits with s.o.

quitter leave; *vêtement* take off; *se ~* part; **ne quittez pas** TÉL hold the line please

quoi what; *après ~*, *il ...* after which he ...; *à ~ bon?* what's

the point?; **il n'y a pas de ~!**
don't mention it; **~ que** (+
subj) whatever
quoique (+ *subj*) although,

though

quotidien, ~ne 1 *adj* daily; *de
tous les jours* everyday **2** *m*
daily

R

rabâcher keep on repeating
rabais *m* discount, reduction;
rabaisser *prix* reduce; *mérites* belittle
rabattre 1 *v/t siège* pull down;
couvercle shut; *col* turn
down **2** *v/i fig:* **se ~ sur** fall
back on; *d'une voiture* pull
back into
râblé stocky
rabot *m* plane
rabougri stunted
rabrouer snub
racaille *f* rabble
raccommoder mend; *chaussettes* darn
**raccompagner: je vais vous
~ chez vous** à pied I'll take
you home
raccord *m* join; *d'un film*
splice; **raccorder** join
raccourci *m* shortcut; **en ~**
briefly; **raccourcir 1** *v/t*
shorten **2** *v/i* get shorter
raccrocher 1 *v/t* put back up;
~ le téléphone hang up; **se ~
à** cling to **2** *v/i* TÉL hang up
race *f* race; (*ascendance*) descent; zo breed
rachat *m d'un otage* ransoming; *d'une société* buyout;
racheter buy back; *otage*

ransom; *fig:* *faute* make up
for; **se ~** make amends
racine *f* root
racisme *m* racism; **raciste**
m/f & adj racist
racler scrape; **se ~ la gorge**
clear one's throat
raconter tell
radar *m* radar
radeau *m* raft
radiateur *m* radiator
radiation *f* radiation; *d'une
liste* deletion
radical *adj & m* radical
radier strike out
radieux, -euse radiant; *temps*
glorious
radin F mean, tight
radio *f* radio; (*radiographie*)
X-ray
radioactif, -ive radioactive
radiocassette *f* radio cassette player
radiographie *f procédé* radiography; *photo* X-ray
radioréveil radio alarm
radis *m* BOT radish
radoter ramble
radoucir make milder; **se ~
du temps** get milder
rafale *f de vent* gust; MIL burst
raffermir *chair* firm up; *auto-*

rité re-assert

raffinage *m* refining; **raffiné** refined; **raffiner** refine; **raffinerie** *f* refinery

raffoler: ~ *de* adore

rafraîchir 1 *v/t* cool down; *mémoire* refresh 2 *v/i du vin* chill; **se** ~ *de la température* get cooler; *d'une personne* have a drink (in order to cool down); **rafraîchissant** refreshing (*aussi fig*); **rafraîchissement** *m de la température* cooling; ~**s** (*boissons*) refreshments

rage *f* rage; *MÉD* rabies *sg*; **rageur, -euse** furious

ragoût *m* CUIS stew

raide *personne, membres* stiff; *pente* steep; *cheveux* straight; (*ivre, drogué*) stoned; **raideur** *f* stiffness; *d'une pente* steepness; **raidir**: **se** ~ *de membres* stiffen up

raie *f* (*rayure*) stripe; *des cheveux* part, *Br* parting; *zo* skate

rail *m* rail; ~ *de sécurité* crash barrier

railler mock; **raillerie** *f* mockery

raisin *m* grape; ~ *sec* raisin

raison *f* reason; *avoir* ~ be right; *avoir* ~ *de* get the better of; *à* ~ *de* at a rate of; *à plus forte* ~ all the more so; *en* ~ *de* (*à cause de*) because of; ~ *sociale* company name; **raisonnable** reasona-

ble; **raisonnement** *m* reasoning; **raisonner** 1 *v/i* reason 2 *v/t*: ~ *qn* make s.o. see reason

rajeunir 1 *v/t thème* modernize; ~ *qn* make s.o. look (years) younger 2 *v/i* look younger

rajouter add

rajuster adjust; *coiffure* put straight

ralenti *m* AUTO idle; *dans un film* slow motion; *au* ~ *fig* at a snail's pace; **ralentir** slow down; **ralentissement** *m* slowing down; **ralentisseur** *m de circulation* speedbump

râler moan; F beef F; **râleur, -euse** F 1 *adj* grumbling 2 *m/f* grumbler

rallier rally; (*s'unir à*) join; **se** ~ *à* rally to

rallonger 1 *v/t* lengthen 2 *v/i* get longer

rallumer *télé, lumière* switch on again; *fig* revive

ramassage *m* collection; *de fruits* picking; **ramasser** collect; *ce qui est par terre* pick up; *fruits* pick; F *coup* get

rame *f* oar; ~ *de métro* train

rameau *m* branch

ramener bring back (*rapporter*) bring back; *l'ordre* restore; **se** ~ *à* (*se réduire à*) come down to

ramer row; **rameur, -euse** *m/f* rower

ramification *f* ramification

ramollir soften; **se ~** soften; *fig* go soft

rampant crawling; BOT creeping; *fig: inflation* rampant

rampe *f* ramp; *d'escalier* bannisters *pl*; *au théâtre* footlights *pl*

ramper crawl; BOT creep

rance rancid

rancœur *f* resentment (**contre** toward)

rançon *f* ransom; **la ~ de** *fig* the price of

rancune *f* resentment; **rancunier, -ère** resentful

randonnée *f* walk; *en montagne* hill walk; **randonneur** *m* walker; *en montagne* hillwalker

rang *m* row; (*niveau*) rank; **être au premier ~** be in the forefront

rangée *f* row

ranger put away; *chambre* tidy up; *voiture* park; (*classer*) arrange; **se ~** (*s'écarter*) move aside; AUTO pull over; *fig* (*assagir*) settle down; **se ~ à une opinion** come around to a point of view

ranimer *personne* bring around; *fig: force* revive

rap *m* MUS rap

rapace 1 *adj animal* predatory; *personne* greedy **2** *m* bird of prey

rapatrier repatriate

râpe *f* grater; TECH rasp; **râper** CUIS grate; *bois* file; **râpé** CUIS grated; *manteau* threadbare

rapide 1 *adj* fast, rapid; *coup d'œil, décision* quick **2** *m dans l'eau* rapid; *train* fast train; **rapidité** *f* speed, rapidity

rapiécer patch

rappel *m* reminder; *d'un ambassadeur, produit* recall; THÉÂT curtain call; MÉD booster; **rappeler** call back; *ambassadeur* recall; **~ qc/qn à qn** remind s.o. of sth/s.o.; **se ~ qc** remember sth

rapport *m écrit, oral* report; (*lien*) connection; (*proportion*) proportion; COMM return; MIL briefing; **~s (sexuels)** sexual relations; **par ~ à** compared with; **être en ~ avec** be in touch with; **rapporter** return, bring/take back; *d'un chien* fetch; COMM bring in; (*relater*) report; **se ~ à** be connected with; **rapporteur** *m* reporter; *enfant* sneak

rapprochement *m fig* reconciliation; POL rapprochement; *analogie* connection; **rapprocher** bring closer (**de** to); *établir un lien* connect; **se ~** come closer

rapt *m* abduction

raquette *f* racket

rare rare; *marchandises* scarce; (*peu dense*) sparse; **raréfier: se ~** become rare; *de l'air* become rarefied; **rarement** rarely; **rareté** *f* rarity

ras short; *rempli à ~ bord* full to the brim; *faire table ~e* make a clean sweep

raser shave; *barbe* shave off; (*démolir*) raze to the ground; *murs* hug; F (*ennuyer*) bore

rasoir *m* razor; **~ électrique** electric shaver

rassasier satisfy

rassembler collect, assemble; **se ~** gather

rasseoir replace; **se ~** sit down again

rassis stale; *fig* sedate

rassurer reassure; *rassurez-vous* don't be concerned

rat *m* rat

ratatiner: *se ~* shrivel up

rate *f* ANAT spleen

raté, ~e 1 *adj* unsuccessful; *occasion* missed **2** *m/f per-sonne* failure

râteau *m* rake

rater 1 *v/t* miss; *examen* fail **2** *v/i d'une arme* misfire; *d'un projet* fail

ration *f* ration; *fig* (fair) share

rationaliser rationalize; *ra-tionnel, ~le* rational; *ration-ner* ration

ratisser rake; (*fouiller*) search

rattacher *chien* tie up again; *cheveux* put up again; *lacets* do up again; *conduites d'eau* connect; *idées* connect; *se ~ à* be linked to

rattraper recapture; *objet qui tombe* catch; (*rejoindre*)

catch up (with); *retard* make up; *imprudence* make up for; **se ~** make up for it; (*se raccrocher*) get caught

rature *f* deletion

rauque hoarse

ravages *mpl* devastation; *les ~ du temps* the ravages of time; *ravager* devastate

ravaler swallow; *façade* clean up

rave *f: céleri ~* celeriac

rave *f* rave

ravi delighted (*de* with; *de faire* to do)

ravir (*enchanter*) delight

raviser: *se ~* change one's mind

ravissant delightful

ravisseur, -euse *m/f* abductor

ravitaillement *m* supplying; *en carburant* refueling, *Br* refuelling; *ravitailler* sup-ply; *en carburant* refuel

raviver revive

rayé striped; *papier* lined; *verre, carrosserie* scratched; *rayer* scratch; *mot* score *ou* scratch out

rayon *m* ray; MATH radius; *d'une roue* spoke; (*étagère*) shelf; *de magasin* depart-ment; **~ laser** laser beam; *rayonner de chaleur* radi-ate; *d'un visage* shine; **~ de** *fig* radiate

rayure *f* stripe; *sur un meu-ble, du verre* scratch

raz *m:* **~ de marée** tidal wave

réacteur *m* reactor; AVIAT jet engine; réaction *f* reaction; **avion réaction à** ~ jet (aircraft); réactionnaire *m/f & adj* reactionary

réagir react (**à** to; **contre** against)

réalisable feasible; réalisateur, -trice *m/f* director; réalisation *f d'un projet* execution, realization; *création*, *œuvre* creation; *d'un film* direction; réaliser *projet* carry out; *rêve* fulfill, *Br* fulfil; *vente* make; *film* direct; *bien, capital* realize; (*se rendre compte*) realize; **se** ~ *d'un rêve* come true; *d'un projet* be carried out

réalisme *m* realism; réaliste **1** *adj* realistic **2** *m/f* realist; réalité *f* reality

réanimer resuscitate

rébarbatif, -ive off-putting, daunting

rebelle **1** *adj* rebellious **2** *m/f* rebel; rebeller: **se** ~ rebel; rébellion *f* rebellion

rebondir bounce; (*faire un ricochet*) rebound; **faire** ~ *qch* fig get sth going again; rebondissement *m* fig unexpected development

rebord *m* edge; *d'une fenêtre* sill

rebours *m*: **compte à** ~ countdown

rebrousser: ~ **chemin** retrace one's footsteps

rebut *m* dregs *pl*; **mettre au** ~ get rid of

rebuter (*décourager*) dishearten; (*choquer*) offend

récapituler recap

récemment recently

recenser *population* take a census of

récent recent

récépissé *m* receipt

récepteur *m* receiver

réception *f* reception; *d'une lettre, de marchandises* receipt; réceptionniste *m/f* receptionist, desk clerk

récession *f* ÉCON recession

recette *f* COMM takings *pl*; CUIS, fig recipe

recevoir receive; **être reçu à un examen** pass an exam

rechange *m*: **de** ~ spare *atr*

rechargeable *pile* rechargeable; recharger *camion, arme* reload; *accumulateur* recharge; *briquet* refill

réchaud *m* stove

réchauffement *m* warming; ~ **de la planète** global warming; réchauffer warm up

recherche *f* search (**de** for); *scientifique* research; ~**s** *de la police* search; rechercher look for, search for; (*prendre*) fetch

rechute *f* MÉD relapse

récif *m* reef

récipient *m* container

réciproque reciprocal

récit *m* account; (*histoire*) story; réciter recite

réclamation *f* claim; (*protes-*

tation) complaint

réclame *f* advertisement

réclamer *secours, aumône* ask for; *son dû* claim; *(nécessiter)* call for

réclusion *f* imprisonment

récolte *f* harvesting; *de produits* harvest, crop; *fig* crop; **récolter** harvest

recommander recommend; *lettre* register

recommencer start again

récompense *f* reward; **récompenser** reward *(de* for)

réconcilier reconcile

reconduire: ~ *qn chez lui* take s.o. home; *à la porte* see s.o. out

réconforter console, comfort

reconnaissance *f* recognition; *d'une faute* acknowledg(e)ment; *(gratitude)* gratitude; MIL reconnaissance; **reconnaissant** grateful *(de* for); **reconnaître** recognize; *faute* acknowledge; **se** ~ *de deux personnes* recognize each other; **se** ~ *à* be recognizable by; **reconnu** known

reconstituer reconstitute; *ville, maison* restore; *événement* reconstruct

reconstruire rebuild

reconvertir ~ retrain

recopier *notes* copy out

record *m* record; **recordman** *m* record holder; **recordwoman** *f* record holder

recourbé bent

recours *m* recourse, resort;

avoir ~ *à* resort to

recouvrer recover; *santé* regain

recouvrir recover; *enfant* cover up again; *(couvrir entièrement)* cover *(de* with); *(cacher, embrasser)* cover

récréation *f* relaxation; ÉDU recess; *Br* recreation

récriminations *fpl* recriminations

recrudescence *f* new outbreak

recrue *f* recruit; **recruter** recruit

rectangle *m* rectangle; **rectangulaire** rectangular

rectifier rectify; *(ajuster)* adjust; *(corriger)* correct

recto *m d'une feuille* front

reçu *m* receipt

recueil *m* collection; **recueillir** collect; *personne* take in; **se** ~ meditate

recul *m d'un fusil* recoil; *d'une armée* retreat; *de la production* drop; *fig* detachment; **reculer 1** *v/t* push back; *décision* postpone **2** *v/i* back away, recoil; MIL retreat; *d'une voiture* back, reverse; ~ *devant fig* back away from; **reculons:** *à* ~ backward, *Br* backwards

récupérer 1 *v/t* recover, retrieve; *ses forces* regain; *vieux matériel* salvage; *temps* make up **2** *v/i* recover

recyclable recyclable; **recyclage** *m du personnel* retraining; TECH recycling; **recycler** retrain; TECH recycle

rédacteur, -trice m/f editor; (*auteur*) writer; **~ en chef** editor-in-chief; **rédaction** f editing; (*rédacteurs*) editorial team

redescendre 1 v/i come/go down again; **~ d'une voiture** get out of a car again **2** v/t bring/take down again; *montagne* come down again

redevable: être ~ de qc à qn owe s.o. sth; **redevance** f *d'un auteur* royalty; TV licence fee

rédiger write

redire repeat, say again; (*rapporter*) repeat; **trouver à ~ à** find fault with

redoubler 1 v/t double **2** v/i ÉDU repeat a class; *d'une tempête* intensify; **~ d'efforts** redouble one's efforts

redoutable formidable; *hiver* harsh; **redouter** dread (**de faire** doing)

redresser *ce qui est courbe* straighten; *ce qui est tombé* set upright; **se ~ d'un pays** recover

réduction f reduction; MÉD setting; **réduire** reduce; *personnel* cut back; **se ~ à** amount to; **réduit 1** adj reduced; *possibilités* limited **2** m small room

rééducation f MÉD rehabilitation

réel, ~le real

refaire do again; *examen* retake; *erreur* repeat; **remettre en état: maison** do up

réfectoire m refectory

référence f reference; **~s** (*recommandation*) reference

référendum m referendum

référer: en ~ à consult; **se ~ à** refer to

réfléchir 1 v/t reflect **2** v/i think (**à, sur** about)

reflet m *de lumière* glint; *dans miroir* reflection (*aussi fig*)

réflexe m reflex

réflexion f reflection; (*remarque*) remark

réforme f reform; **la Réforme** REL the Reformation; **réformer** reform; MIL discharge

refouler push back; PSYCH repress

refrain m refrain, chorus

réfréner control

réfrigérateur m refrigerator

refroidir cool down; *fig* cool; **se ~ du temps** get colder; MÉD catch a chill; **refroidissement** m cooling; MÉD chill

refuge m refuge, shelter; *pour piétons* traffic island; *en montagne* (mountain) hut; **réfugié, ~e** m/f refugee; **réfugier: se ~** take shelter

refus m refusal; **refuse-fuse; ~ de ou se ~ à faire** refuse to do

réfuter refute

regagner win back, regain; *endroit* get back to

régal m treat; **régaler** regale

(*de* with)

regard *m* look; **regardant avec argent** careful with one's money; **ne pas être ~ sur** not be too worried about; **regarder 1** *v/t* look at; *télé* watch; (*concerner*) regard, concern; **~ qn faire qch** watch s.o. doing sth **2** *v/i* look; **se ~** look at o.s.; *de plusieurs personnes* look at each other

régate *f* regatta

régime *m* POL government, régime; MÉD diet; *fiscal* system

région *f* region; **~ sinistrée** disaster area; **régional** regional

régir govern

régisseur *m* THÉÂT stage manager; *dans le film* assistant director

réglage *m* adjustment

règle *f* rule; *instrument* ruler; **en ~ générale** as a rule; **~s** (*menstruation*) period

réglé *organisé* settled; *vie* well-ordered; *papier* ruled

règlement *m* settlement; (*règles*) regulations *pl*; **réglementaire** in accordance with the rules; *tenue* regulation *atr*; **réglementer** control, regulate

régler *affaire* settle; TECH adjust; COMM pay, settle; *épicier etc* pay, settle up with

règne *m* reign; **régner** reign

régression *f* regression

regret *m* regret (*de* about); **à ~** with regret, reluctantly; **être au ~ de faire** regret to do; **regrettable** regrettable; **regretter** regret; *absente* miss; **~ d'avoir fait qc** regret doing sth, regret having done sth; **je ne regrette rien** I have no regrets; **je regrette mais …** I'm sorry (but) …

régulariser put in order; *situation* regularize; TECH regulate; **régularité** *f* regularity; *d'élections* legality; **régulier, -ère** regular; *allure, progrès* steady; *écriture* even; (*réglementaire*) lawful; (*correct*) honest; **régulièrement** regularly

réhabiliter rehabilitate; *quartier* renovate, redevelop

rehausser raise; *fig* (*accentuer*) emphasize

rein *m* ANAT kidney; **~s** lower back

reine *f* queen

réitérer reiterate

rejaillir spurt

rejeter reject; (*relancer*) throw back; (*vomir*) bring up; *responsabilité, faute* lay (*sur* on)

rejoindre *personne* join, meet; (*rattraper*) catch up with; MIL rejoin; *autoroute* get back onto; **se ~** meet

réjouir make happy, delight; **se ~ de** be delighted about; **réjouissance** *f* rejoicing

212

relâche f: sans ~ without a break, nonstop

relâcher corde, emprise loosen; prisonnier release; se ~ d'un élève, la discipline become slack

relais m SP, ÉL relay; prendre le ~ de take over from

relancer balle throw back; moteur restart; fig: économie kickstart; personne contact again

relater relate

relatif, -ive relative; ~ à relating to; relation f relationship; (connaissance) acquaintance; être en ~ avec qn be in touch with s.o.; ~s relations; (connaissances) contacts; relativement relatively; ~ à compared with; (en ce qui concerne) relating to; relativiser look at in context

relaxer: se ~ relax

relayer take over from; TV, radio relay; se ~ take turns

reléguer relegate

relève f relief; prendre la ~ take over

relevé 1 adj manche turned up; style elevated; CUIS spicy 2 m de compteur reading; ~ de compte bank statement; relever 1 v/t raise; (remettre debout) pick up; chauffage turn up; manches roll up; siège put up; économie improve; (ramasser) collect; défi take up; faute find;

adresse, date copy; (relayer) take over from; se ~ get up; fig recover 2 v/i: ~ de (dépendre de) be answerable to; (ressortir de) be the responsibility of

relief m relief; mettre en ~ fig highlight

relier connect (à to); livre bind

religieux, -euse 1 adj religious 2 m monk 3 f nun; religion f religion

reliure f binding

reluire shine

remanier texte re-work; POL reshuffle

remarquable remarkable

remarque f remark; remarquer notice; (dire) remark; faire ~ qc à qn point sth out to s.o.; se faire ~ d'un acteur etc get o.s. noticed; d'un écolier get into trouble; se différencier be conspicuous

rembourrer stuff

remboursement m refund; de dettes repayment; rembourser frais refund, reimburse; dettes, emprunt pay back

remède m remedy; remédier: ~ à remedy

remerciement m: ~s thanks; remercier thank (de, pour for); (congédier) dismiss

remettre put back; vêtement put on again; peine remit; décision postpone; (ajouter) add; ~ qc à qn give sth to s.o.; **se ~ à qc** take sth up again; **se ~ à faire qc** start doing sth again; **se ~ de qc** recover from sth; **s'en ~ à qn** rely on s.o.

remise f (*hangar*) shed; *d'une lettre* delivery; *de peine* remission; COMM discount; *d'une décision* postponement; **~ en question** questioning

rémission f MÉD remission

remonte-pente m ski lift

remonter 1 v/i come/go up again; *dans une voiture* get back in; *de prix, température* go up again; *d'un avion, chemin* climb, rise **2** v/t *choses* bring/take back up; *rue, escalier* come/go back up; *montre* wind; TECH reassemble; *col* turn up; *stores* raise

remords mpl remorse

remorque f *véhicule* trailer; *câble* towrope; **remorquer** *voiture* tow

remplaçant, ~e m/f replacement; **remplacement** m replacement; **remplacer** replace (*par* with)

remplir fill (*de* with); *formulaire* fill out; *conditions* fulfill, Br fulfil; *tâche* carry out; **remplissage** m filling

remporter take away; *prix* win

remue-ménage m (*agitation*) commotion

remuer 1 v/t move (*aussi fig*);

sauce stir; *salade* toss; *terre* turn over **2** v/i move; **se ~** move; *fig* F get a move on F

rémunération f pay, remuneration; **rémunérer** pay

renaître REL be born again; *fig* be reborn

renard m fox

renchérir go up; **~ sur** outdo

rencontre f meeting; **aller à la ~ de** go and meet; **rencontrer** meet; *accueil* meet with; *difficulté* encounter; *amour* find; (*heurter*) hit; **se ~** meet

rendement m AGR yield; *d'un employé, d'une machine* output; *d'un placement* return

rendez-vous m appointment; *amoureux* date; *lieu* meeting place; **prendre ~** make an appointment

rendre 1 v/t give back; *salut, invitation* return; (*donner*) give; (*traduire*) render; (*vomir*) bring up; MIL surrender; **~ visite à** visit **2** v/i *de terre, d'un arbre* yield; **se ~ à un endroit** go; MIL surrender; **se ~ malade** make o.s. sick

rêne f rein

renfermer (*contenir*) contain; **se ~ dans le silence** withdraw into silence

renforcer reinforce

renfort m reinforcements pl; **à grand ~ de** with copious amounts of

renier qn disown

renifler sniff

renne m reindeer

renom m (célébrité) fame, renown; (réputation) reputation; **renommée** f fame

renoncement m renunciation (**à** of); **renoncer**: ~ **à qc** give sth up; ~ **à faire** give up doing

renouer 1 v/t amitié etc renew **2** v/i: ~ **avec** get in touch with; après brouille get back together with

renouveler renew; demande, promesse repeat; **se ~** (se reproduire) happen again; **renouvellement** m renewal

rénovation f renovation; fig (modernisation) updating

renseignement m piece of information (**sur** about); ~s information; MIL intelligence; **prendre des ~s** find out about; **renseigner**: ~ **qn sur qc** tell ou inform s.o. about sth; **se ~** find out

rentabilité f profitability; **rentable** cost-effective; entreprise profitable; **ce n'est pas ~** there's no money in it

rente f revenu d'un bien privé income; (pension) annuity; **versée à sa femme** etc allowance

rentrée f return; ~ **des classes** beginning of the new school year; ~**s** COMM takings

rentrer 1 v/i go/come in; de nouveau go/come back in; chez soi go/come home; dans un récipient go in, fit; de l'argent come in; ~ **dans** (heurter) collide with; serrure, sac go into; responsabilités be part of **2** v/t bring/take in; voiture put away; ventre pull in

renversement m d'un régime overthrow; **renverser** image reverse; (mettre à l'envers) upturn; (faire tomber) knock over; liquide spill; gouvernement overthrow

renvoi m de personnel dismissal; d'un élève expulsion; d'une lettre return; dans un texte cross-reference (**à** to); **renvoyer** (faire retourner) send back; ballon return; personnel dismiss; élève expel; rencontre, décision postpone

repaire m den

répandre spread; (renverser) spill; **se ~** spread; (être renversé) spill; **répandu** widespread

réparation f repair; (compensation) reparation; **en ~** being repaired; **réparer** repair; fig make up for

repartie f retort; **avoir de la ~** have a gift for repartee

repartir start again; ~ **à zéro** start again from scratch

répartir share out; chargement distribute; en catégories divide; **répartition** f dis-

repriser

tribution; *en catégories* division

repas *m* meal

repassage *m* ironing; **repasser 1** *v/i* come/go back again **2** *v/t linge* iron; *examen* take again

repentir 1: *se* ~ REL repent; *se* ~ **de** be sorry for **2** *m* pénitence

répercussions *fpl* repercussions

repère *m* mark; (**point** *m* **de**) ~ landmark; **repérer** (*situer*) pinpoint; (*trouver*) find; (*marquer*) mark

répertoire *m* directory; THÉÂT repertoire

répéter repeat; THÉÂT rehearse; **répétition** *f* repetition; THÉÂT rehearsal

répit *m* respite

replacer put back, replace

repli *m* fold; *d'une rivière* bend; **replier** fold; *jambes* draw up; *journal* fold up; *manches* roll up; *se* ~ *sur* *soi-même* retreat into one's shell

répliquer retort; *d'un enfant* answer back

répondeur *m*: ~ **automatique** answering machine; **répondre 1** *v/t* answer, reply **2** *v/i* answer; (*réagir*) respond; ~ **à** answer, reply to; (*réagir à*) respond to; *besoin* meet; *attente* come up to; *signalement* match; **réponse** *f* answer; (*réaction*) response

reportage *m* report; **reporter** *m/f* reporter

repos *m* rest; **reposer 1** *v/t* (*remettre*) put back; *question* ask again; (*détendre*) rest; *se* ~ rest **2** *v/i*: ~ *sur* rest on

repoussant ~e *m/f* repulsive; **repousser 1** *v/t* (*dégoûter*) repel; (*différer*) postpone; *pousser en arrière*, MIL push back; (*rejeter*) reject **2** *v/i* grow back again

reprendre 1 *v/t* take back; (*prendre davantage de*) take more; *ville* recapture; (*recommencer*) start again; (*corriger*) correct; *entreprise* take over (**à** from) **2** *v/i* (*recommencer*) start again; *se* ~ (*se corriger*) correct o.s.; (*se maîtriser*) pull o.s. together

représailles *fpl* reprisals

représentant, ~**e** *m/f* representative; **représentation** *f* representation; *au théâtre* performance; **représenter** represent; THÉÂT perform; *se* ~ *qc* imagine sth

répression *f* repression; *mesures fpl de* ~ crackdown (**contre** on)

réprimander reprimand

réprimer suppress

reprise *f* *de ville* recapture; *de marchandise* taking back; *de travail, de lutte* resumption; *à plusieurs* ~**s** on several occasions

repriser darn, mend

reproche m reproach; **reprocher** reproach; ~ **qch à qn** reproach s.o. for sth

reproduction f reproduction; **reproduire** reproduce; **se ~** happen again; BIOL reproduce

républicain, ~e m/f & adj republican, **république** f republic

répugnant repugnant; **répugner**: ~ **à** be repelled by; ~ **à faire** be reluctant to do

répulsion f repulsion

réputation f reputation

requérir require

requête f request

requin m shark

requis necessary

réseau m network

réservation f booking, reservation

réserve f reserve; (entrepôt) storeroom; **sans ~** unreservedly; **sous ~ de** subject to

réserver reserve; dans hôtel, restaurant book, reserve; (mettre de côté) put aside; ~ **qc à qn** keep ou save sth for s.o.

réservoir m tank; lac etc reservoir

résidence f residence; ~ **universitaire** dormitory, Br hall of residence; **résider** live; ~ **dans** fig lie in

résidu m residue; MATH remainder

résigner resign; **se ~** resign o.s. (**à** to)

résilier contrat cancel

résistance f resistance; (endurance) stamina; d'un matériau strength; **la Résistance** HIST the Resistance; **résister** resist; ~ **à** tentation, personne resist; sécheresse withstand

résolu determined (**à faire** to do); **résolution** f (décision) resolution; (fermeté) determination; d'un problème solving

résonner echo, resound

résoudre 1 v/t problème solve **2** v/i: ~ **de faire**, **se ~ à faire** decide to do

respect m respect; **respecter** respect; ~ **le(s) délai(s)** meet the deadline; **se ~** have some self-respect; mutuellement respect each other; **se faire ~** command respect; **respectif**, -ive respective; **respectueux**, -euse respectful

respiration f breathing; **retenir sa ~** hold one's breath; ~ **artificielle** MÉD artificial respiration; **respirer** breathe

resplendir glitter

responsabilité f responsibility (**de** for); JUR liability; **responsable** responsible (**de** for)

ressaisir: **se ~** pull o.s. together

ressemblance f resemblance; **ressembler**: ~ **à** resemble, be like; **se ~** resemble each other, be like each other

ressemeler resole

ressentiment m resentment

ressentir feel; **se ~ de** still feel the effects of

resserrer tighten; fig: amitié strengthen

ressort m TECH spring; fig motive; (énergie) energy; (compétence) province; JUR jurisdiction

ressortir 1 come/go out again 2 (se détacher) stand out; **faire ~** bring out; **~ à** JUR fall within the jurisdiction of

ressource f resource

restant 1 adj remaining 2 m remainder

restaurant m restaurant

restauration f catering; ART restoration; **~ rapide** fast food; **restaurer** restore

reste m rest, remainder; **~s** CUIS leftovers; **du ~, au ~** moreover; **rester** (subsister) be left, remain; (demeurer) stay, remain; **on en reste là** we'll stop there; **il reste du vin** there's some wine left

restituer (rendre) return; (reconstituer) restore; **restitution** f restitution

restreindre restrict

restriction f restriction; **sans ~** unreservedly

résultat m result; **résulter** resulter (de) from)

résumé m summary

rétablir restore; **se ~** recover

retard m lateness; dans travail, paiement delay; **avoir deux heures de ~** be two hours late; **avoir du ~ sur qn** be behind s.o.; **être en ~** be late; **retarder** 1 v/t delay, hold up; montre put back 2 v/i d'une montre be slow; **~ de cinq minutes** be five minutes slow; **~ sur son temps** fig be behind the times

retenir personne keep; argent withhold; (rappeler) remember; proposition accept; (réserver) reserve; **se ~** restrain o.s.

retentir sound; du tonnerre boom; **~ sur** impact on; **retentissant** resounding (aussi fig)

retenu (réservé) reserved; (empêché) delayed

retenue f sur salaire deduction; fig (modération) restraint

réticence f (omission) omission; (hésitation) hesitation

retirer withdraw; vêtement take off; promesse take back; profit derive; **~ qch de** remove sth from; **se ~** withdraw; (prendre sa retraite) retire

retombées fpl fallout; **retomber** fall again; (tomber) land; de cheveux, d'un rideau fall; **~ dans qc** sink back into sth

rétorsion POL: *mesure f de ~* retaliatory measure

retoucher *texte, vêtement* alter; *photographie* retouch

retour *m* return; *être de ~* be back; *bon ~!* have a good trip home!; **retourner 1** *v/i* return, go back; *~ sur ses pas* backtrack 2 *v/t matelas, tête* turn; *lettre* return, *vêtement* turn inside out; *se ~ au lit* turn over (*aussi* AUTO); (*tourner la tête*) turn (around)

retrait *m* withdrawal; *en ~* set back

retraite *f* retirement; (*pension*) retirement pension; MIL retreat; *prendre sa ~* retire; **retraité**, *~e m/f* pensioner, retired person

retrancher (*enlever*) remove, cut (*de* from); (*déduire*) deduct

rétrécir 1 *v/t* shrink; *fig* narrow 2 *v/i de tissu* shrink; *se ~* narrow

rétrograder 1 *v/t* demote 2 *v/i* retreat; AUTO downshift

rétrospectif, -ive 1 *adj* retrospective 2 *f: rétrospective* retrospective

retrousser *manches* roll up

retrouver (*trouver*) find; *de nouveau* find again; (*rejoindre*) meet; *santé* regain; *se ~* meet; *se ~ seul* find o.s. alone

rétroviseur *m* AUTO rear-view mirror

réunion *f* meeting; POL reunion; **réunir** bring together; *pays* reunite; *documents* collect; *se ~* meet

réussi successful; **réussir 1** *v/i* succeed; *~ à faire* manage to do, succeed in doing 2 *v/t vie, projet* make a success of; *examen* be successful in; **réussite** *f* success; *aux cartes* solitaire, *Br aussi* patience

revanche *f* revenge; *en ~* on the other hand

rêve *m* dream

réveil *m* awakening; (*pendule*) alarm (clock); **réveiller** wake up; *fig* revive; *se ~* wake up

révélation *f* revelation; **révéler** reveal; *se ~ faux* prove to be false

revenant *m* ghost

revendeur, -euse *m/f* retailer

revendication *f* claim, demand; **revendiquer** claim

revendre resell

revenir come back, return (*à* to); *~ sur* thème go back to; *décision* go back on; *~ à qn d'une part* be due to s.o.; *~ de* évanouissement come around from; *étonnement* get over; *illusion* lose

revenu *m* income; *~s* revenue

rêver dream (*de, à* about)

réverbère *m* street lamp

rêverie *f* daydream

revers *m* back; *d'un pantalon* cuff, *Br* turn-up; *fig* (*échec*) reversal

revêtir *vêtement* put on; *forme, caractère* assume; *importance* take on

rêveur, -euse 1 *adj* dreamy **2** *m/f* dreamer

revirement *m*: **~ d'opinion** sudden change in the public's attitude

réviser *texte* revise; *machine* service; **révision** *f* revision; AUTO service

révocation *f* revocation; *d'un dirigeant etc* dismissal

revoir 1 *v/t* see again; *texte* review; *m*: **au ~!** goodbye!

révolte *f* revolt; **révolter** revolt; **se ~** rebel, revolt

révolution *f* revolution; **révolutionner** revolutionize

revolver *m* revolver

révoquer *fonctionnaire* dismiss; *contrat* revoke

revue *f* review; *passer en ~* fig review

rez-de-chaussée *m* first floor, Br ground floor

rhubarbe *f* rhubarb

rhum *m* rum

rhumatismes *mpl* rheumatism

rhume *m* cold; **~ des foins** hay fever

ricaner sneer; *bêtement* snigger

riche rich; *sol* fertile; *décoration* elaborate; **richesse** *f* wealth; *du sol* fertility

rictus *m* grimace

ride *f* wrinkle, line

rideau *m* drape, Br curtain

rider *peau* wrinkle; **se ~** become wrinkled

ridicule 1 *adj* ridiculous **2** *m* ridicule; *(absurdité)* ridiculousness; **ridiculiser** ridicule; **se ~** make a fool of o.s.

rien 1 *pron* nothing; *quelque chose* anything; **de ~** *comme réponse* you're welcome; **ne ... ~** nothing, not anything **2** *m* trifle; **en un ~ de temps** in no time

rigide rigid

rigole *f* *(conduit)* channel

rigoler F *(plaisanter)* joke; *(rire)* laugh

rigolo, -te F *(amusant)* funny

rigoureux, -euse rigorous; **rigueur** *f* rigor, Br rigour; **à la ~** if absolutely necessary; **de ~** compulsory

rincer rinse

riposte *f* riposte, response; *avec armes* return of fire; **riposter** reply, response; *avec armes* return fire

rire 1 *v/i* laugh *(de* about, at); *(s'amuser)* have fun; **~ aux éclats** roar with laughter; **~ de qn** laugh at s.o. **2** *m* laugh; **~s** laughter

risque *m* risk; **à tes ~s et périls** at your own risk; **risqué** risky; *plaisanterie* risqué; **risquer** risk; **~ de faire** risk doing; **se ~ dans** venture into to

rituel, ~le *adj* & *m* ritual

rivage *m* shore

rival, ~e m/f & adj rival; **rivaliser** compete, vie; **rivalité** f rivalry

rive f d'un fleuve bank; d'une mer, d'un lac shore

riverain, ~e m/f resident

rivet m TECH rivet

rivière f river

riz m BOT rice

robe f dress; d'un juge robe; ~ **de chambre** robe, Br dressing gown

robinet m faucet, Br tap

robuste robust

roche f rock

rocher m rock; **rocheux, -euse** rocky

rôder prowl

rogne f: **être en ~** F be in a bad mood

rogner cut, trim

rognon m CUIS kidney

roi m king

rôle m role; (registre) roll; **à tour de ~** turn and turn about

roman m novel

romancier, -ère m/f novelist

romantique m/f & adj romantic; **romantisme** m romanticism

romarin m BOT rosemary

rompre 1 v/i break; **avec petit ami** break it off with; tradition break with; habitude break 2 v/t break; négociations, fiançailles break off

ronce f BOT: **~s** brambles

rond, ~e 1 adj round; joues, personne plump; F (ivre)

drunk 2 adv: **tourner ~** run smoothly 3 m figure circle m 4 f: **faire sa ronde** do one's rounds; de soldat, policier be on patrol; **à la ronde** around

rondelle f disk, Br disc; de saucisson slice; TECH washer

rondement (promptement) briskly; (carrément) frankly

rond-point m traffic circle, Br roundabout

ronflement m snoring; d'un moteur purr; **ronfler** snore; d'un moteur purr

ronger gnaw at; fig torment; **se ~ les ongles** bite one's nails; **rongeur** m ZO rodent

ronronner purr

rosbif m CUIS roast beef

rose 1 f BOT rose 2 m couleur pink 3 adj pink

rosé 1 m rosé 2 adj pinkish

roseau m BOT reed

rosée f dew

rosier m rose bush

rossignol m ZO nightingale

rot m F belch; **roter** F belch

rôti m roast; rôtir roast; **rôtisserie** f grill-room

rouage m cogwheel; **~s** d'une montre works; fig machinery

roue f wheel; **deux ~s** m two-wheeler; **quatre ~s motrices** all-wheel drive

roué crafty

rouer: **~ qn de coups** beat s.o. black and blue

rouge 1 adj red 2 adv fig: **voir ~** see red 3 m red; **~ à lèvres** lipstick

rouge-gorge *m* robin (red-breast)

rougeole *f* MÉD measles *sg*

rougir go red; *d'une personne aussi* blush (**de** with); *de colère* flush (**de** with)

rouille *f* rust; **rouillé** rusty; **rouiller** rust; **se ~** rust; *fig* go rusty

rouleau *m* roller; *de pellicule etc* CUIS rolling pin

rouler 1 *v/i* roll; *d'une voiture* travel; **~ sur qc** *d'une conversation* be about sth **2** *v/t* roll; **~ qn** F cheat s.o.

roulette *f de meubles* caster; *jeu* roulette

roumain, ~e 1 *adj* Romanian **2** *m langue* Romanian; **Roumain, ~e** *m/f* Romanian; **Roumanie: la ~** Romania

rouspéter F complain

rousseur *f*: **taches** *fpl* **de ~** freckles

route *f* road; *(parcours)* route; *fig (chemin)* path; **en ~** on the way; **se mettre en ~** set off; *fig* get under way; **faire ~ vers** be heading for

routier, -ère 1 *adj* road *atr* **2** *m (conducteur)* truck driver, Br long-distance lorry driver; *restaurant* truck stop, Br *aussi* transport café

routine *f* routine; **de ~** routine *atr*

roux, rousse *personne* red-haired; *cheveux* red

royal royal; *fig: pourboire, accueil* superb, right royal

royaume *m* kingdom; **le Royaume-Uni** the United Kingdom

R.-U. (= **Royaume-Uni**) UK (= United Kingdom)

ruban *m* ribbon; **~ adhésif** adhesive tape

rubéole *f* MÉD German measles *sg*

rubrique *f* heading

ruche *f* hive

rude *manières* uncouth; *(sévère)* harsh; *travail, lutte* hard

rudimentaire rudimentary; **rudiments** *mpl* rudiments

rue *f* street; **dans la ~** on the street

ruée *f* rush

ruelle *f* alley

rugby *m* rugby

rugir roar; *du vent* howl

rugueux, -euse rough

ruine *f* ruin; **ruiner** ruin

ruisseau *m* stream; *(caniveau)* gutter

ruisseler run

rumeur *f* hum; *de personnes* murmuring; *(nouvelle)* rumor, Br rumour

ruminer 1 *v/i* chew the cud, ruminate **2** *v/t fig*: **~ qch** mull sth over

rupture *f* breaking; *fig* split; *de négociations* breakdown; *de relations* breaking off; *de contrat* breach

ruse *f* ruse; **la ~** cunning; **rusé** crafty, cunning

russe 1 adj Russian **2** m langue Russian; **Russe** m/f Russian; **Russie:** la ~ Russia
rustique rustic

rustre péj **1** adj uncouth **2** m oaf
rythme m rhythm; (vitesse) pace; **rythmique** rhythmical

S

sa → **son**[1]
S.A. f (= **société anonyme**) Inc, Br plc
sable m sand; **sabler** sand; ~ **le champagne** break open the champagne
sablier m CUIS eggtimer
sabot m clog; zo hoof
sabotage m sabotage; **saboter** sabotage; F travail make a mess of
sac m bag; de pommes de terre sack; ~ **de couchage** sleeping bag; ~ **à dos** backpack; ~ **à main** purse, Br handbag
saccadé mouvements jerky; voix breathless
saccager (piller) sack; (détruire) destroy
saccharine f saccharine
sachet m sachet; ~ **de thé** teabag
sacoche f bag; de vélo saddlebag
sacré sacred; F damn F
sacrement m REL sacrament
sacrifice m sacrifice; **sacrifier** sacrifice; **se** ~ sacrifice o.s.
sacrilège 1 adj sacrilegious **2** m sacrilege

sadique 1 adj sadistic **2** m/f sadist
safran m saffron
sagace shrewd; **sagacité** f shrewdness
sage 1 adj wise; enfant good **2** m sage, wise man; **sage-femme** f midwife; **sagesse** f wisdom; d'un enfant goodness
Sagittaire m ASTROL Sagittarius
saignant bleeding; CUIS rare; **saigner** v/i bleed **2** v/t fig bleed dry
saillant pommettes prominent; fig salient; **saillie** f ARCH projection; fig quip; **saillir** ARCH project
sain healthy; gestion sound; ~ **d'esprit** sane
saint, ~**e 1** adj holy **2** m/f saint; **sainteté** f holiness; **Saint-Sylvestre:** la ~ New Year's Eve
saisie f seizure; ~ **de données** INFORM data capture; **saisir** seize; sens, intention grasp; INFORM capture; **saisissant** striking; froid penetrating
saison f season; **saisonnier,**

-ère 1 *adj* seasonal **2** *m ouvrier* seasonal worker

salade *f* salad; **saladier** *m* salad bowl

salaire *m d'un ouvrier* wages *pl*; *d'un employé* salary; **~ net** take-home pay

salarié, ~e 1 *adj travail* paid **2** *m/f ouvrier* wage-earner; *employé* salaried employee

salaud *m* P bastard P

sale *après le substantif* dirty; *devant le substantif* nasty

salé *eau* salt; CUIS salted; *histoire* daring; *prix* steep; **saler** salt

saleté *f* dirtiness; **~s** *fig* (*grossièretés*) filthy remarks; F *choses sans valeur, mauvaise nourriture* junk

salière *f* salt cellar

salir: ~ qch get sth dirty

salive *f* saliva

salle *f* room; **~ d'attente** waiting room; **~ d'eau** shower room; **~ à manger** dining room

salon *m* living room; *d'un hôtel* lounge; (*foire*) show; **~ de l'automobile** auto show, *Br* motor show; **~ de thé** tea room

salope *f* P bitch; **saloperie** *f* F *chose sans valeur* piece of junk; (*bassesse*) dirty trick

salopette *f* dungarees *pl*

salubre healthy

saluer *qn* salute; **~ qn (de la main)** wave to s.o.

salut *m* greeting; MIL salute;

(*sauvegarde*) safety; REL salvation; **~!** F hi!; (*au revoir*) bye!

salutaire salutary

samedi *m* Saturday

sanction *f* sanction

sanctuaire *m* sanctuary

sandale *f* sandal

sandwich *m* sandwich

sang *m* blood; **sang-froid** *m* composure; **garder son ~** keep one's cool; **tuer qn de ~** kill s.o. in cold blood; **sanglant** bloodstained; *combat, mort* bloody

sanglot *m* sob; **sangloter** sob

sanguin blood *atr*; *tempérament* sanguine; **groupe** *m* **~** blood group

sanitaire sanitary

sans without; **~ manger** without eating; **~ balcon** without a balcony

sans-abri *m/f*: **les ~** the homeless *pl*

sans-emploi *m*: **les ~** the unemployed *pl*

santé *f* health; **à votre ~!** cheers!, your very good health!

saper undermine

sapeur-pompier *m* firefighter

saphir *m* sapphire

sapin *m* BOT fir

sarcasme *m* sarcasm; **sarcastique** sarcastic

sardine *f* sardine

sardonique sardonic

S.A.R.L. *f* (= **société à res-**

***ponsabilité limitée*) Inc, *Br* Ltd

satellite *m* satellite

satin *m* satin

satirique satirical

satisfaction *f* satisfaction; **satisfaire** 1 *v/i*: **~ à 2** *v/t* satisfy; *attente* come up to; **satisfaisant** satisfactory; **satisfait** satisfied (*de* with)

saturer saturate

sauce *f* sauce

saucisse *f* sausage

saucisson *m* (dried) sausage

sauf[1] *prép* except; **~ avis contraire** unless you/I / *etc* hear to the contrary

sauf[2], **sauve** *adj* safe

sauf-conduit *m* safe-conduct

saugrenu ridiculous

saule *m* BOT willow; **~ pleureur** weeping willow

saumon *m* salmon

sauna *m* sauna

saupoudrer sprinkle (*de* with)

saut *m* jump; **faire un ~ chez qn** *fig* drop in briefly on s.o.; **~ à l'élastique** bungee jumping; **~ en longueur** broad jump, *Br* long jump; **~ à la perche** pole vault

sauter 1 *v/i* jump; (*exploser*) blow up; *d'un fusible* blow; *d'un bouton* come off; **~ sur** *personne* pounce on; *occasion, offre* jump at; *cela saute aux yeux* it's obvious 2 *v/t fossé* jump (over); *mot, repas* skip

sauterelle *f* grasshopper

sautiller hop

sauvage 1 *adj* wild; (*insociable*) unsociable; (*primitif, barbare*) savage; *pas autorisé* unauthorized 2 *m/f* savage; (*solitaire*) unsociable person

sauvegarde *f* safeguard; INFORM back-up

sauver save; *personne en danger* rescue; *navire* salvage; *se ~* run away; F (*partir*) be off; (*déborder*) boil over

sauvetage *m* rescue; *de navire* salvaging; **sauveteur** *m* rescuer

sauveur *m* savior, *Br* saviour

savant 1 *adj* (*érudit*) learned; (*habile*) skillful, *Br* skilful 2 *m* scientist

saveur *f* taste

savoir 1 *v/t & v/i* know; **sais-tu nager?** can you swim?, do you know how to swim? 2 *m* knowledge

savoir-faire *m* expertise, knowhow

savoir-vivre *m* good manners *pl*

savon *m* soap

savourer savor, *Br* savour; **savoureux, -euse** tasty; *fig: récit* spicy

saxophone *m* saxophone, sax

scandale *m* scandal; **faire ~** cause a scandal; **faire tout un ~** make a scene; **scanda-**

liser scandalize; **se ~ de** be shocked by

scanner 1 v/t scan **2** m scanner

scaphandrier m diver

scarlatine f scarlet fever

sceau m seal; fig (marque, signe) stamp

scellé m official seal; **sceller** seal

scénario m scenario; (script) screenplay; **~ catastrophe** worst-case scenario

scène f scene (aussi fig); (plateau) stage; **mettre en ~ pièce, film** direct; **présenter** stage; **~ de ménage** domestic argument

sceptique 1 adj skeptical, Br sceptical **2** m skeptic, Br sceptic

schéma m diagram; **schématiser** oversimplify

sciatique f sciatica

scie f saw; fig F bore

sciemment knowingly

science f science; (connaissance) knowledge; **scientifique 1** adj scientific **2** m/f scientist

scier saw; branche etc saw off

scinder fig split; **se ~** split up

scintiller sparkle

scission f split

scolaire school atr; succès, échec academic; **scolarité** f education, schooling

scooter m (motor) scooter

score m SP score; POL share of the vote

scorpion m ZO scorpion; ASTROL Scorpio

scotch® m Scotch tape®, Br sellotape®

scrupule m scruple; **scrupuleux, -euse** scrupulous

scruter scrutinize

scrutin m ballot; **~ majoritaire** majority vote system; **~ proportionnel** proportional representation

sculpter sculpt; pierre carve; **sculpteur** m sculptor; **sculpture** f sculpture

SDF m/f (= sans domicile fixe) homeless person

se réfléchi masculin himself; féminin herself; chose, animal itself; pluriel themselves; avec 'one' oneself; réciproque each other; **cela ne ~ fait pas** that isn't done; **ils ~ lèvent à ...** they get up at ...

séance f session; de cinéma show, performance; **~ tenante** fig immediately

seau m bucket

sec, sèche 1 adj dry; fruits, légumes dried; (maigre) thin; réponse, ton curt **2** m: **tenir au ~** keep in a dry place **3** adv boire neat, straight

sèche-cheveux m hair dryer; **sèche-linge** m clothes dryer; **sécher** dry; d'un lac dry up; **sécheresse** f dryness; manque de pluie drought; de réponse, ton curtness

second, **~e 1** *adj* second **2** *m*
étage third floor; *Br* second
floor; (*adjoint*) second in
command **3** *f* second; **en**
train second class; **secon-**
daire secondary; **seconder**
personne assist

secouer shake; *poussière*
shake off

secouriste *m/f* first-aider;
secours *m* help; *matériel*
aid; **au ~!** help!; **sortie** *f* **de**
~ emergency exit; **premiers**
~s first aid

secousse *f* jolt; *électrique*
shock; *tellurique* tremor

secret, **-ète 1** *adj* secret **2** *m*
secret; (*discrétion*) secrecy;
en ~ in secret

secrétaire 1 *m/f* secretary **2**
m writing desk

secrétariat *m* secretariat;
profession secretarial work

secte *f* REL sect

secteur *m* sector; (*zone*) area, district; **~ mains** *pl*

section *f* section; **sectionner**
(*couper*) sever; *région etc* divide up

séculaire a hundred years
old; *très ancien* centuries-
-old

séculier, **-ère** secular

sécurité *f* security; (*manque*
de danger) safety; **Sécurité**
sociale welfare, *Br* social
security; **être en ~** be safe

sédatif *m* sedative

sédentaire sedentary; *popu-*
lation settled

séduction *f* seduction; *fig*
(*charme*) attraction; **séduire**
seduce; *fig* (*charmer*) appeal
to; *d'une personne* charm;
séduisant appealing; *per-*
sonne attractive

ségrégation *f* segregation

seigle *m* AGR rye

seigneur *m* HIST the lord of
the manor; REL: **le Seigneur**
the LORD

sein *m* breast; *fig* bosom; **au ~**
de within

seize sixteen; **seizième** sixteenth

séjour *m* stay; (**salle** *f* **de**)
~ living room; **séjourner** stay

sel *m* salt

sélection *f* selection; **sélec-**
tionner select

selle *f* saddle; MÉD stool

selon according to; **~ moi** in
my opinion; **c'est ~** it all de-
pends

semaine *f* week; **à la ~** by the
week; **en ~** during the week,
on weekdays

semblable 1 *adj* similar; *tel*
such; **~ à** like, similar to **2**
m (*être humain*) fellow human being

semblant *m* semblance; **faire**
~ de faire pretend to do

sembler seem

semelle *f* sole; *pièce inté-*
rieure insole

semence *f* AGR seed

semer sow; *fig* (*répandre*)
spread; **~ qn** F shake s.o. off

semestre *m* half-year

séminaire *m* seminar; REL seminary

semi-remorque *m* semi, Br articulated lorry

semonce *f* reproach

semoule *f* CUIS semolina

Sénat *m* POL Senate; **sénateur** *m* senator

sénile senile

sens *m* sense; (*direction*) direction; **~ interdit** no entry; **~ dessus dessous** upside down; **~ de l'humour** sense of humor *ou* Br humour; (*rue f à*) **~ unique** one-way street

sensation *f* feeling, sensation; *effet de surprise* sensation; **faire ~** cause a sensation; **sensationnel, ~le** sensational

sensé sensible

sensibilité *f* sensitivity; **sensible** sensitive; (*notable*) appreciable; **sensiblement** appreciably; **plus ou moins** more or less

sensualité *f* sensuality; **sensuel, ~le** sensual

sentence *f* JUR sentence

sentier *m* path

sentiment *m* feeling; **sentimental** *vie* love *atr*; *péj* sentimental

sentinelle *f* MIL guard

sentir 1 *v/t* feel; (*humer*) smell; (*dégager une odeur de*) smell of; **se ~ bien** feel well **2** *v/i:* **~ bon** smell good

séparable separable; **séparation** *f* separation; (*cloison*) partition; **séparatisme** *m* POL separatism; **séparé** separate; *époux* separated; **séparément** separately; **séparer** separate; **se ~** separate

sept seven

septembre *m* September

septennat *m* term of office (of French President)

septentrional northern

septième seventh

septique septic

séquelles *fpl* MÉD after-effects; *fig* aftermath

séquence *f* sequence

serein calm

sérénité *f* serenity

série *f* series *sg; de casseroles, timbres* set; SP (*épreuve*) heat; **hors ~** *numéro* special; **fabriquer en ~** mass-produce

sérieux, -euse 1 *adj* serious; *entreprise, employé* professional; (*consciencieux*) conscientious **2** *m* seriousness; **prendre au ~** take seriously

seringue *f* MÉD syringe

serment *m* oath; **prêter ~** take the oath

sermon *m* sermon

séropositif, -ive HIV-positive

serpent *m* snake; **serpenter** wind, meander

serpillière *f* floor cloth

serre *f* greenhouse; **~s** ZO talons

serré tight; *pluie* heavy; *per-*

sonnes closely packed; *café* strong

serrer 1 v/t (*tenir*) clasp; *ceinture* tighten; *d'un vêtement* be too tight for **2** v/i: **se ~** (*s'entasser*) squeeze up; **se ~ contre qn** press against s.o.

serrure f lock; **serrurier** m locksmith

serveur m *dans un café* bartender; *Br* barman; *dans un restaurant* waiter; INFORM server

serveuse f *dans un café* bartender; *Br* barmaid; *dans un restaurant* server, waitress

serviable helpful

service m service; (*faveur*) favor, *Br* favour; *au tennis* service, serve; *d'une entreprise, d'un hôpital* department; **être de ~** be on duty; **rendre~ à qn** do s.o. a favor; **mettre en ~** put into service; **hors ~** out of order

serviette f serviette; *de toilette* towel; *pour documents* briefcase; **~ hygiénique** sanitary napkin

servile servile

servir serve; (*être utile*) be useful; **~ à qn** be of use to s.o.; **~ à qch/à faire qch** be used for sth/for doing sth; **~ de qc** act as sth; **se ~ à table** help o.s. (*en* to); **se ~ de** (*utiliser*) use

ses → son¹

seuil m doorstep; *fig* thresh-

old

seul 1 *adj* alone; (*solitaire*) lonely; *devant le subst* only, sole **2** *adv* alone; **faire qch tout ~** do sth all by o.s. *ou* all on one's own

seulement only; **non ~ ... mais encore** *ou* **mais aussi** not only ... but also

sévère severe; **sévérité** f severity

sévices *mpl* abuse

sévir *d'une épidémie* rage; **~ contre qn** come down hard on s.o.; **~ contre qc** clamp down on sth

sexagénaire *m/f & adj* sixty-year old

sexe m sex; *organes* genitals *pl*; **sexiste** *m/f & adj* sexist; **sexualité** f sexuality; **sexuel, ~le** sexual

shampo(o)ing m shampoo

short m shorts *pl*

si 1 *conj* (*s'il, s'ils*) if; **~ bien que** with the result that **2** *adv* (*tellement*) so; *après négation* yes; **de ~ bonnes vacances** such a good vacation; **~ riche qu'il soit** (*subj*) however rich he may be; **tu ne veux pas? - mais ~!** you don't want to? - oh yes, I do

sida m MÉD Aids

sidéré F thunderstruck

siècle m century; *fig* (*époque*) age

siège m seat; *d'une entreprise* headquarters *pl*; MIL siege; **~**

social COMM head office; **siéger** sit; **~ à d'une entreprise** be headquartered in

sien: *le sien, la sienne, les siens, les siennes* d'homme his; *de femme* hers; *de chose, d'animal* its; *avec 'one'* one's

sieste f siesta, nap

sifflement m whistle; **siffler** whistle; *d'un serpent* hiss; **sifflet** m whistle; **coup m de ~** blow on the whistle

signal m signal; **~ d'alarme** alarm (signal); **signalement** m description; **signaler** *par un signal* signal; *(faire remarquer)* point out; *(dénoncer)* report; **se ~ par** distinguish o.s. by

signature f signature

signe m sign; **faire ~ à** gesture *ou* signal to s; *(contacter)* get in touch with; **~ de ponctuation** punctuation mark; **signer** sign

signet m bookmark

signification f meaning; **signifier** mean; **~ qch à qn** *(faire savoir)* notify s.o. of sth

silence m silence; **silencieux, -euse 1** adj silent **2** m d'une arme muffler; *Br* silencer

silhouette f outline, silhouette; *(figure)* figure

sillage m wake *(aussi fig)*

sillon m dans un champ furrow; d'un disque groove; **sil-**

lonner *(parcourir)* criss-cross

similaire similar; **similitude** f similarity

simple 1 adj simple **2** m au tennis singles pl; **simplicité** f simplicity

simplifier simplify

simulateur, -trice m/f: **c'est un ~** he's pretending **2** m TECH simulator; **simulation** f simulation; **simuler** simulate

simultané simultaneous

sincère sincere; **sincérité** f sincerity

singe m monkey; **singer** ape; **singerie** f imitation; **~s** F antics

singulier, -ère 1 adj odd, strange **2** m GRAM singular

sinistre 1 adj sinister; *(triste)* gloomy **2** m disaster; **sinistré 1** adj stricken **2** m/f disaster victim

sinon *(autrement)* or else, otherwise; *(sauf)* except; *(si ce n'est)* if not

sinueux, -euse *route* winding; *ligne* squiggly; *explication* complicated

sinus m sinus; **sinusite** f sinusitis

sirène f siren

sirop m syrup

siroter sip

sismique seismic

sitcom m ou f sitcom

site m site; *(paysage)* area; **~ Web** website

sitôt 1 *adv*: ~ *parti, il ...* as soon as he had left he ... **2** *conj*: ~ *que* as soon as

situation *f* situation; (*emplacement, profession*) position; **situé** situated

six *m*; **sixième** sixth

skateboard *m* skateboard; *activité* skateboarding

sketch *m* sketch

ski *m* ski; *activité* skiing; ~ *alpin* downhill (skiing); ~ *de fond* cross-country (skiing); ~ *nautique* water-skiing; **skier** ski; **skieur, -euse** *m/f* skier

slip *m de femme* panties *pl*; *d'homme* briefs; ~ *de bain* swimming trunks *pl*

slogan *m* slogan

slovaque *adj* Slovak(ian); **Slovaque** *m/f* Slovak(ian)

slovène Slovene, Slovenian; **Slovène** *m/f* Slovene, Slovenian

smoking *m* tuxedo, *Br* dinner jacket

SMS *m* text (message)

S.N.C.F. *f* (= *Société nationale des chemins de fer français*) French national railroad company

sobre sober; *style* restrained

sociable sociable

social social; COMM company *atr*; **socialiser** socialize

socialisme *m* socialism; **socialiste** *m/f* & *adj* socialist

société *f* society; *firme* company; ~ *anonyme* corpora-

tion, *Br* public limited company, plc

sociologie *f* sociology

socquette *f* anklet, *Br* ankle sock

soda *m* soda, *Br* fizzy drink; *un whisky* ~ a whiskey and soda

sœur *f* sister; REL nun

sofa *m* sofa

soi oneself; *avec* ~ with one; *ça va de* ~ that goes without saying

soi-disant *inv* so-called

soie *f* silk

soif *f* thirst; *avoir* ~ be thirsty

soigné *personne* well-groomed; *travail* careful; **soigner** look after, take care of; *d'un médecin* treat; *se* ~ take care of o.s.; **soigneux, -euse** careful (*de* about)

soi-même oneself

soin *m* care; ~*s* care; MÉD care, treatment; *prendre* ~ *de* look after, take care of; *être sans* ~ be untidy

soir *m* evening; *le* ~ in the evening; **soirée** *f* evening; (*fête*) party

soit¹ *adv* very well, so be it

soit² *conj* ~ ..., ~ ... either ..., or ...; (*à savoir*) that is, ie

soixantaine *f* about sixty; **soixante** sixty; **soixante-dix** seventy

soja *m* BOT soy bean, *Br* soya

sol *m* ground; (*plancher*) floor; (*patrie*), GÉOL soil

solaire solar

soldat *m* soldier

solde¹ *f* MIL pay

solde² *m* COMM balance; **~s** *marchandises* sale goods; *vente au rabais* sale; **solder** *compte* close, balance; *marchandises* sell off

sole *f* ZO sole

soleil *m* sun; *il y a du* **~** it's sunny; *coup m de* **~** sunburn

solennel, **~le** solemn

solidaire: *être* **~** suport s.o.; **solidarité** *f* solidarity

solide 1 *adj* solid; *tissu* strong; *argument* sound; *personne* sturdy **2** *m* PHYS solid; **solidité** *f* solidity; *d'un matériau* strength; *d'un argument* soundness

solitaire 1 *adj* solitary **2** *m/f* loner **3** *m diamant* solitaire; **solitude** *f* solitude

sollicitation *f* plea; **solliciter** request; *attention* attract; *curiosité* arouse; **~** *un emploi* apply for a job; **sollicitude** *f* solicitude

solstice *m* ASTR solstice

soluble soluble; *café m* **~** instant coffee

solution *f* solution

solvable solvent; *digne de crédit* creditworthy

sombre *couleur*, *salle* dark; *temps* overcast; *avenir*, *regard* somber, *Br* sombre

sommaire 1 *adj* brief; *exécution* summary **2** *m* summary

somme¹ *f* sum; *(quantité)* amount; *en* **~**, **~** *toute* in

short

somme² *m* nap, snooze

sommeil *m* sleep; *avoir* **~** be sleepy; **sommeiller** doze

sommelier *m* wine waiter

sommer: **~** *qn de faire qc* order s.o. to do sth

sommet *m* *d'une montagne* summit, top; *d'un arbre*, *d'une tour* top; *fig* pinnacle; POL summit

sommier *m* mattress

somnambule *m/f* sleepwalker

somnifère *m* sleeping tablet

somnolence *f* drowsiness, sleepiness; **somnoler** doze

somptueux, **-euse** sumptuous; **somptuosité** *f* sumptuousness

son¹ *m*, *sa f*, *ses pl d'homme* his; *de femme* her; *de chose*, *d'animal* its; *avec 'one'* one's

son² *m* sound

sondage *m* probe; TECH drilling; **~** *(d'opinion)* opinion poll, survey

sonde *f* probe; **sonder** MÉD probe; *personne*, *atmosphère* sound out

songe *m* *litt* dream; **songer**: **~** *à* **(faire)** *qc* think about (doing) sth; **songeur**, **-euse** thoughtful

sonner 1 *v/i de cloches*, *sonnette* ring; *d'un réveil* go off; *d'un instrument*, *d'une voix* sound; *d'une horloge* strike; *midi a sonné* it has struck noon; **~** *creux/faux* *fig* ring hollow/false **2** *v/t cloches* ring; **sonnerie** *f de cloches* ringing; *(sonnette)* bell; **sonnette** *f* bell

sonore *voix* loud; *rire* resounding; *cuivres* sonorous; *onde, film* sound *atr*; **sonorité** *f* sound, tone; *d'une salle* acoustics *pl*

sophistiqué sophisticated

soporifique sleep-inducing, soporific

soprano 1 *f* soprano **2** *m* treble

sorcellerie *f* sorcery, witchcraft

sorcier *m* sorcerer; **sorcière** *f* witch

sordide filthy; *fig* sordid

sort *m* fate; *(condition)* lot; **tirer au ~** draw lots; **jeter un ~ à** *fig* cast a spell on

sorte *f* *(manière)* way; *(espèce)* sort, kind; **en quelque ~** in a way; **de (telle) ~ que** and so

sortie *f* exit; *(promenade, excursion)* outing; *d'un livre* publication; *d'un disque* release; *d'une voiture* launch; TECH outlet; MIL sortie; **~ (sur) imprimante** printout

sortir 1 *v/i* come/go out; *pour se distraire* go out (**avec** with); *d'un livre, un disque* come out; **~ de** *endroit* leave; *accident, entretien* emerge from; *(provenir de)* come from **2** *v/t chose* bring/take out;

chien, personne take out; COMM bring out; F **bêtises** come out with **3**: **s'en ~** *d'un malade* pull through

sot *m* fate **1** *adj* silly, foolish **2** *m/f* fool; **sottise** *f* foolishness; *action/remarque* foolish thing to do/say

sou *m* *fig* penny; **être sans le ~** be penniless

souche *f* *d'un arbre* stump; *d'un carnet* stub

souci *m* worry, care; **sans ~** carefree; **soucier**: **se ~ de** worry about; **soucieux, -euse** anxious, concerned (**de** about)

soucoupe *f* saucer

soudain 1 *adj* sudden **2** *adv* suddenly

souder TECH weld; *fig* bring closer together

souffle *m* breath; *d'une explosion* blast; **à bout de ~** breathless, out of breath; **souffler 1** *v/i du vent* blow; *(haleter)* puff; *(respirer)* breathe; *(reprendre son souffle)* get one's breath back **2** *v/t chandelle* blow out; ÉDU, *au théâtre* prompt; **~ qc à qn** F *(dire)* whisper sth to s.o.; *(enlever)* steal sth from s.o.

souffrance *f* suffering; **souffrant** unwell; **souffrir 1** *v/i* suffer; **~ de** suffer from **2** *v/t* suffer

soufre *m* CHIM sulfur, *Br* sul-

phur
souhait *m* wish; **à vos ~s!**
bless you!; **souhaitable** desirable; **souhaiter** wish for;
~ que (+ *subj*) hope that

souiller dirty, soil; *fig: réputation* tarnish

soûl drunk

soulagement *m* relief; **soulager** relieve; **~ qn au travail**
help s.o. out

soûler F: **~ qn** get s.o. drunk;
se ~ get drunk

soulèvement *m* uprising;
soulever raise; *enthousiasme* arouse; *protestations*
generate; **(se révolter)** raise o.s.;
(se révolter) rise up

souligner underline

soumettre *pays, peuple* subdue; *à un examen* subject
(**à** to); **(présenter)** submit;
se ~ à submit to; **soumis**
peuple subject; *(obéissant)*
submissive; **soumission** *f*
submission; COMM tender

soupçon *m* suspicion; **un ~
de** a hint of; **soupçonner**
suspect; **soupçonneux, -eu-
se** suspicious

soupe *f* CUIS (thick) soup

souper 1 *v/i* have dinner *ou*
supper **2** *m* dinner, supper

soupir *m* sigh; **soupirer** sigh

souple flexible; **souplesse** *f*
flexibility

source *f* spring; *fig* source

sourcil *m* eyebrow

sourd deaf; *voix* low; *douleur, bruit* dull; *colère* re-

pressed; **~-muet** deaf-and-
-dumb

souriant smiling

souricière *f* mousetrap; *fig*
trap

sourire *v/i & m* smile

souris *f* mouse

sournois, ~e 1 *adj* under-
handed **2** *m/f* underhanded
person

sous under; **~ peu** soon; **~ la
pluie** in the rain

souscription *f* subscription;
souscrire: ~ à subscribe to
(*aussi fig*); *emprunt* approve

sous-entendre imply; **sous-
-entendu 1** *adj* implied **2** *m*
implication

sous-estimer underestimate

sous-jacent underlying

sous-louer sublet

sous-marin 1 *adj* underwater
2 *m* submarine

sous-sol *m* *d'une maison*
basement

sous-titre *m* subtitle

soustraire MATH subtract (**de**
from); *fig: au regard de* remove; *à un danger* protect
(**à** from)

sous-traitance *f* sub-con-
tracting

sous-vêtements *mpl* underwear

soutane *f* REL cassock

soute *f* MAR, AVIAT hold

soutenir support; *pression*
withstand; *conversation*
keep going; *opinion* maintain; **~ que** maintain that;

se ~ support each other;
soutenu *effort* sustained;
style elevated

souterrain 1 *adj* underground, subterranean **2** *m* underground passage

soutien *m* support

soutien-gorge *m* brassiere, bra

souvenir 1: *se* ~ *de qn/qch* remember s.o./sth; *se* ~ *que* remember that **2** *m* memory; *objet* souvenir

souvent often; *le plus* ~ most of the time

souverain, ~**e** *m/f* sovereign

soyeux, -euse silky

spacieux, -euse spacious

spaghetti *mpl* spaghetti *sg*

sparadrap *m* Band-Aid®, *Br* Elastoplast®

spasme *m* MÉD spasm; **spasmodique** spasmodic

spatial spatial; ASTR space *atr*

spécial special; **spécialiser**: *se* ~ specialize; **spécialiste** *m/f* specialist; **spécialité** *f* speciality

spécifier specify

spécifique specific

spécimen *m* specimen

spectacle *m* spectacle; *théâtre, cinéma* show, performance; **spectaculaire** spectacular

spectateur, -trice *m/f* (*témoin*) onlooker; SP spectator; *au théâtre* member of the audience

spectre *m* ghost; PHYS spectrum

spéculer speculate

spéléologie *f* caving

spermatozoïde *m* BIOL sperm

sperme *m* BIOL sperm

sphère *f* MATH sphere (*aussi fig*)

spirale *f* spiral

spirituel, ~**le** spiritual; (*amusant*) witty

spiritueux *mpl* spirits

splendeur *f* splendor, *Br* splendour, magnificence; **splendide** splendid

sponsor *m* sponsor; **sponsoriser** sponsor

spontané spontaneous

sport 1 *m* sport; *faire du* ~ do sport **2** *adj vêtements* casual *atr*

sportif, -ive **1** *adj résultats, association* sports *atr*; *allure* sporty; (*fair-play*) sporting **2** *m* sportsman **3** *f* sportswoman

square *m* public garden

squash *m* SP squash

squatter squat; **squatteur**, -euse *m/f* squatter

squelette *m* skeleton

stabilisateur, -trice **1** *adj* stabilizing **2** *m* stabilizer; **stabiliser** stabilize; **stabilité** *f* stability; **stable** stable

stade *m* SP stadium; *d'un processus* stage

stage *m* training period; (*cours*) training course; *pour professeur* teaching practice; (*expérience professionnelle*) work placement; **stagiaire** *m/f* trainee

stagnant *eau* stagnant

stalle *f d'un cheval* box; **~s** REL stalls

stand *m de foire* booth, *Br* stand; *de kermesse* stall

standard *m* standard; TÉL switchboard

standardiser standardize

standardiste *m/f* TÉL (switchboard) operator

starter *m* AUTO choke

station *f* station; *de bus* stop; *de vacances* resort; **~ de taxis** cab stand, *Br* taxi rank; **~ thermale** spa

stationnement *m* parking; **stationner** park

station-service *f* gas station, *Br* petrol station

statistique 1 *adj* statistical **2** *f* statistic; *science* statistics *sg*

statue *f* statue

stature *f* stature

statut *m* status; **~s d'une société** statutes

stéréo *f* stereo

stéréotype *m* stereotype; **stéréotypé** stereotype

stérile sterile; **stériliser** sterilize; **stérilité** *f* sterility

steward *m* flight attendant, steward

stigmate *m* mark; **~s** REL stigmata

stimuler stimulate

stipulation *f* stipulation; **stipuler** stipulate

stock *m* stock; **stocker** stock; INFORM store

stoïque stoical

stop *m* stop; *écriteau* stop sign; (*feu m*) **~** AUTO brake light; **faire du ~** F hitchhike; **stopper** stop

store *m d'une fenêtre* shade, *Br* blind; *d'un magasin, d'une terrasse* awning

strapontin *m* tip-up seat

stratagème *m* stratagem

stratégie *f* strategy

stress *m* stress; **stressant** stressful; **stressé** stressed-out

strict strict; **le ~ nécessaire** the bare minimum

strident strident

strip-tease *m* strip(tease)

structure *f* structure

studieux, -euse studious

stupéfait stupefied; **stupéfiant 1** *adj* stupefying **2** *m* drug; **stupéfier** stupefy

stupeur *f* stupor

stupide stupid

style *m* style; **styliste** *m de mode, d'industrie* stylist

stylo *m* pen; **~ plume** fountain pen

suave *voix, goût* sweet

subalterne 1 *adj* junior **2** *m/f* junior, subordinate

subir (*endurer*) suffer; (*se soumettre volontairement à*) undergo

subit sudden

subjectif, -ive subjective

subjuguer *fig* captivate

sublime sublime

submerger submerge; *être submergé de* fig be buried in

subordonné, ~e adj & m/f subordinate; **subordonner** subordinate (*à* to)

subrepticement surreptitiously

subsidiaire subsidiary

subsistance f subsistence; **subsister** survive; *d'une personne aussi* live

substance f substance; **substantiel**, ~le substantial

substituer: ~ *X à Y* substitute X for Y

subterfuge m subterfuge

subtil subtle; **subtilité** f subtlety

subvenir: ~ *à* provide for

subvention f grant, subsidy; **subventionner** subsidize

subversif, -ive subversive

suc m: ~*s gastriques* gastric juices

succéder: ~ *à* follow; *personne* succeed; *se* ~ follow each other

succès m success

successeur m successor; **succession** f succession; JUR (*biens dévolus*) inheritance

succomber (*mourir*) die, succumb; ~ *à* succumb to

succulent succulent

succursale f COMM branch

sucer suck; **sucette** f *bonbon* lollipop; *de bébé* pacifier, Br

dummy

sucre m sugar; **sucré** sweet; *au sucre* sugared; *péj* sugary; **sucrer** sweeten; *avec sucre* sugar; **sucreries** fpl sweet things

sud 1 m south; *au* ~ *de* (to the) south of **2** adj south; *hémisphère* southern

sud-américain, ~e South American, **Sud-Américain**, ~e m/f South American

sud-est m south-east

sud-ouest m south-west

Suède: *la* ~ Sweden; **suédois**, ~e **1** adj Swedish **2** m *langue* Swedish; **Suédois**, ~e m/f Swede

suer 1 v/i sweat **2** v/t sweat; fig (*dégager*) ooze; **sueur** f sweat

suffire be enough; *il suffit que tu le lui dises* (*subj*) all you have to do is tell her; *ça suffit!* that's enough!

suffisamment sufficiently, enough; ~ *intelligent* sufficiently intelligent, intelligent enough; ~ *de* ... enough ..., sufficient ...; **suffisance** f arrogance; **suffisant** sufficient, enough; (*arrogant*) arrogant

suffocant suffocating; fig breath-taking; **suffocation** f suffocation; **suffoquer** suffocate

suffrage m vote; ~ *universel* universal suffrage

suggérer suggest (**à** to); **suggestion** *f* suggestion

suicide *m* suicide; **suicider**: **se ~** commit suicide

suinter *d'un mur* ooze

suisse Swiss; **Suisse 1** *m/f* Swiss **2 la Suisse** Switzerland

suite *f* pursuit; (*série*) series *sg*; (*continuation*) continuation; *d'un film, un livre* sequel; MUS, *appartement* suite; **la ~ de l'histoire** the rest of the story; **~s** (*conséquences*) consequences; *d'un choc, d'une maladie* after-effects; **trois fois de ~** three times in a row; **et ainsi de ~** and so on; **par ~ de** as a result of; **tout de ~** immediately

suivant ~e 1 *adj* next, following **2** *m/f* next person; **au ~!** next! **3** *prép* (*selon*) according to **4** *conj*: **~ que** depending on whether

suivi *effort* sustained; *relations* continuous; *argumentation* coherent

suivre 1 *v/t* follow; *cours* take **2** *v/i* follow; *à l'école* keep up; **faire ~** *lettre* please forward; **à ~** to be continued

sujet ~te 1 *adj*: **~ à** subject to **2** *m* subject; **au ~ de** on the subject of

sulfureux, -euse sultry

super 1 *adj* F great F, neat F **2** *m essence* premium

superbe superb

supercherie *f* hoax

superficie *f fig* surface; (*surface, étendue*) (surface) area; **superficiel, ~le** superficial

superflu 1 *adj* superfluous **2** *m* surplus

supérieur, ~e 1 *adj* higher; *étages, mâchoire* upper; (*meilleur, dans une hiérarchie*) superior (*aussi péj*) **2** *m/f* superior; **supériorité** *f* superiority

supermarché *m* supermarket

superposer stack; *couches* superimpose; **lits** *mpl* **superposés** bunk beds

superstitieux, -euse superstitious; **superstition** *f* superstition

superviser supervise

supplanter supplant

suppléant, ~e 1 *adj* acting **2** *m/f* stand-in, replacement; **suppléer**: **~ à** make up for

supplément *m* supplement; **un ~ de** ... additional *ou* extra ...; **supplémentaire** additional

supplication *f* plea

supplice *m* torture; *fig* agony; **supplicier** torture

supplier: **~ qn de faire** beg s.o. to do

support *m* support; **supportable** bearable; **supporter**[1] *v/t* TECH, ARCH support, hold up; *conséquences* take; *frais, douleur, personne* bear; *chaleur, alcool* tolerate; **sup-**

porter² *m* SP supporter, fan
supposer suppose; (*impliquer*) presuppose; **supposition** *f* supposition
suppression *f* suppression; **supprimer** *institution, impôt* abolish; *emplois* cut; *mot* delete; *concert* cancel
suprême supreme
sur *on*; *prendre qch ~ l'étagère* take sth off the shelf; *une fenêtre ~ la rue* a window looking onto the street; *tirer ~ qn* shoot at s.o.; *un film ~ ...* a movie on *ou* about ...; *un ~ dix* one out of ten
sûr sure; (*non dangereux*) safe; (*fiable*) reliable; *bien ~* of course; *à coup ~ il sera ...* he's bound to be ...
surcharge *f* overloading; (*poids excédentaire*) excess weight
surchauffer overheat
surclasser outclass
surcroît *m*: *un ~ de travail* extra work; *de ~, par ~* moreover
surdité *f* deafness
surdoué extremely gifted
surélever raise
sûrement surely
surenchère *f dans vente aux enchères* higher bid
surestimer overestimate
sûreté *f* safety; MIL security; *de jugement* soundness
surexciter overexcite
surexposer overexpose

surface *f* surface; *grande ~* COMM supermarket
surfait overrated
surfer surf; *~ sur Internet* surf the Net
surgelé 1 *adj* deep-frozen **2** *mpl*: *~s* frozen food
surgir suddenly appear; *d'un problème* crop up
sur-le-champ at once, straightaway
surlendemain *m* day after tomorrow
surligner highlight
surmener overwork; *se ~* overwork, overdo it F
surmonter dominate; *fig* overcome, surmount
surnaturel, ~le supernatural
surnom *m* nickname; **surnommer** nickname
surpasser surpass
surpeuplé *pays* overpopulated; *endroit* overcrowded
surplomber overhang
surplus *m* surplus; *au ~* moreover
surprenant surprising; **surprendre** surprise; *voleur* catch (in the act); *se~ à faire qch* catch o.s. doing sth; **surpris** surprised; **surprise** *f* surprise
sursaut *m* jump, start; **sursauter** jump
sursis *m fig* reprieve, stay of execution; *peine avec ~* JUR suspended sentence
surtaxe *f* surcharge
surtout especially; (*avant*

tout above all; ~ *que* F especially since

surveillance f supervision; *par la police etc* surveillance; **surveillant**, ~*e* m/f supervisor; *de prison* guard; **surveiller** watch; *élèves, employés* supervise; *se* ~ *comportement* watch one's step; *poids* watch one's figure

survenir *d'une personne* arrive unexpectedly; *d'un événement* happen; *d'un problème* come up, arise

survêtement m sweats *pl, Br* tracksuit

survie f survival; REL afterlife; **survivant**, ~**e 1** *adj* surviving **2** m/f survivor; **survivre**: ~ *à* survive

susceptible sensitive, touchy; ~ *de faire qch* likely to do sth

susciter arouse

suspect (*équivoque*) suspicious; (*d'une qualité douteuse*) suspect; ~ *de qc* suspected of sth; **suspecter** suspect

suspendre suspend; (*accrocher*) hang up; **suspendu** suspended

suspens: *en* ~ *personne* in suspense; *affaire* outstand-

ing

suspense m suspense

suspension f suspension

suspicion f suspicion

svelte trim, slender

sweat(-shirt) m sweatshirt

syllabe f syllable

symbole m symbol; **symboliser** symbolize

symétrie f symmetry

sympathie f sympathy; (*amitié, inclination*) liking; **sympathique** nice, friendly; **sympathiser** get on

symphonie f symphony

symptôme m symptom

synagogue f synagogue

synchroniser synchronize

syndical labor *atr, Br* (trade) union *atr*

syndicat m (labor) union, *Br* (trade) union; ~ *d'initiative* tourist information office

syndiqué unionized

synonyme 1 *adj* synonymous (*de* with) **2** m synonym

synthèse f synthesis; **synthétiseur** m MUS synthesizer

systématique systematic; **système** m system; ~ *antidémarrage* immobilizer; ~ *d'exploitation* INFORM operating system

T

ta → ton²

tabac m tobacco; *bureau m de~* tobacco store; *Br* tobacconist's

table f table; *se mettre à ~* sit down to eat

tableau m *à l'école* board; *(peinture)* painting; *fig* picture; *(liste)* list; *(schéma)* table; *~ de bord* AVIAT instrument panel

tablette f shelf; *~ de chocolat* chocolate bar

tablier m apron

tabouret m stool

tache f stain

tâche f task

tacher stain

tâcher *~ de faire* try to do

tacheté stained

tacite tacit

taciturne taciturn

tact m tact; *avoir du ~* be tactful

tactique 1 adj tactical **2** f tactics pl

taie f: *~ (d'oreiller)* pillowslip

taille¹ f BOT pruning; *de la pierre* cutting

taille² f *(hauteur)* height; *(dimension)* size; ANAT waist

taille-crayon(s) m pencil sharpener

tailler BOT prune; *vêtement* cut out; *crayon* sharpen; *pierre* cut; **tailleur** m *(couturier)* tailor; *vêtement* (woman's) suit

taire: se ~ keep quiet *(sur* about); *s'arrêter de parler* stop talking; *tais-toi!* be quiet!, shut up!

talc m talc

talent m talent; **talentueux, -euse** talented

talon m heel; *d'un chèque* stub; **talonner** *(serrer de près)* follow close behind; *(harceler)* harass

talus m bank

tambour m MUS, TECH drum; **tambouriner** drum

Tamise: *la ~* the Thames

tamiser sieve; *lumière* filter

tampon m *d'ouate* pad; *hygiène féminine* tampon; *(amortisseur)* buffer; *(cachet)* stamp; **tamponnement** m AUTO collision; **tamponner** *plaie* clean; *(cacheter)* stamp; AUTO collide with

tandis que while

tangente f MATH tangent

tangible tangible

tango m tango

tanière f lair, den *(aussi fig)*

tanné tanned; *peau* weatherbeaten; **tanner** tan; *fig* F pester

tant 1 adv so much; *~ de vin* so much wine; *~ d'erreurs* so many errors; *~ mieux* so much the better; **~ pis** too bad, tough **2** *conj*: **~ que temps** as long as; **en ~ que Français** as a Frenchman; **~ ... que ...** both ... and ...

tante *f* aunt

tantôt this afternoon; **à ~** see you soon; **~ ... ~ ...** now ... now ...

taon *m* horsefly

tapage *m* racket; *fig* fuss; **tapageur, -euse** (*voyant*) flashy, loud; (*bruyant*) noisy

tape *f* pat

taper 1 *v/t personne* hit; *table* bang on; **~ (à l'ordinateur)** F key, type **2** *v/i* hit; *à l'ordinateur* key; **~ sur les nerfs de qn** F get on s.o.'s nerves

tapir: **se ~** crouch

tapis *m* carpet; SP mat; **~ roulant** TECH conveyor belt; *pour personnes* traveling *ou Br* travelling walkway; **~ de souris** mouse mat

tapisser *avec du papier peint* (wall)paper; **tapisserie** *f* tapestry; (*papier peint*) wallpaper

tapoter tap; *personne* pat

taquiner tease; **taquinerie** *f* teasing

tard 1 *adv* late; **plus ~** later (on); **au plus ~** at the latest **2** *m*: **sur le ~** late in life

tarder delay; **~ à faire** take a long time doing; **il me tarde de te revoir** I'm longing to see you again

tardif, -ive late

targuer: **se ~ de qc** *litt* pride o.s. on sth

tarif *m* rate; **~ unique** flat rate

tarir dry up (*aussi fig*); **se ~** dry up

tartan *m* tartan

tarte *f* tart; **tartelette** *f* tartlet

tartine *f* slice of bread; **~ de confiture** slice of bread and jam

tas *m* heap, pile; **un ~ de choses** heaps *pl ou* piles *pl* of things

tasse *f* cup; **une ~ de café** a cup of coffee; **une ~ à café** a coffee cup

tasser (*bourrer*) cram; **se ~** settle

tâter 1 *v/t* feel **2** *v/i* F: **~ de qc** try sth

tatillon, ~ne fussy

tâtons: **avancer à ~** feel one's way forward

tatouage *m action* tattooing; *signe* tattoo

taudis *m* slum

taupe *f* zo mole

taureau *m* bull; ASTROL **Taureau** Taurus

taux *m* rate; **~ d'alcoolémie** blood alcohol level; **~ de change** exchange rate; **~ d'intérêt** interest rate

taxe *f* duty; (*impôt*) tax; **~ sur ou à la valeur ajoutée** sales tax, *Br* value added tax, VAT; **taxer**; tax; **~ qn de qc** *fig* (*accuser*) tax s.o. with sth

taxi *m* taxi, cab

tchèque 1 *adj* Czech **2** *m* lan-

gue Czech; **Tchèque** *m/f* Czech

te you; *complément d'objet indirect* (to) you; *tu t'es coupé* you've cut yourself; *si tu lèves à ...* if you get up at ...

technicien, **ne** *m/f* technician

technique 1 *adj* technical **2** *f* technique

technologie *f* technology; **~ informatique** computer technology; **~ de pointe** high-tech; **technologique** technological

tee-shirt *m* T-shirt

teindre dye

teint, **~e 1** *adj* dyed **2** *m* complexion; *fond m de ~* foundation (cream) **3** *f* tint; *fig* tinge; **teinter** tint; *bois* stain; **teinture** *f action* dyeing; *produit* dye; **pharm** tincture

tel, **~le** such; *une ~le surprise* such a surprise; *de ce genre* a surprise like that; **~(s)** *ou* **~le(s) que** such as, like

télé *f* F TV, tube F, *Br* telly F

télécharger inform download

télécommande *f* remote control

télécommunications *f pl* telecommunications

téléconférence *f* teleconference

téléguidage *m* remote control

téléobjectif *m* telephoto lens

télépathie *f* telepathy

téléphone *m* phone, telephone; **~ portable** cellphone, *Br* mobile (phone); *coup m de ~* (phone) call; **~ avec appareil photo intégré** camera phone; **téléphoner 1** *v/i* phone, telephone; **~ à qn** call s.o., *Br aussi* phone s.o. **2** *v/t* phone, telephone; **téléphonique** phone *atr*, telephone *atr*; *appel m ~* phone

téléréalité *f* reality TV

télescope *m* telescope; **télescoper** crash into; *se ~* crash

télésiège *m* chair lift

téléski *m* ski lift

téléspectateur, **-trice** *m/f* (TV) viewer

télévision *f* television; **~ câblée** cable (TV)

tellement so; *avec verbe* so much; *pas ~* not really; **~ de chance** so much good luck; **~ de filles** so many girls

téméraire reckless; **témérité** *f* recklessness

témoignage *m jur* testimony, evidence; *(rapport)* account; *fig: d'estime* token; **témoigner jur** testify, give evidence; **~ de** (*être le témoignage de*) show; **témoin** *m* witness; *être (le) ~ de qch* witness sth

tempe *f* anat temple

tempérament *m* temperament; *à ~* in installments *ou Br* instalments

température *f* temperature; *avoir de la ~* have a fever, *Br aussi* have a temperature

tempérer moderate

tempête *f* storm

temple *m* temple; *protestant* church

temporaire temporary

temporel, ~le temporal

temporiser stall, play for time

temps *m* time; (*atmosphérique*) weather; *TECH* stroke; *à ~* in time; *de ~ en ~* from time to time; *il est ~ de partir* it's time to go; *il est ~ que tu t'en ailles* (*subj*) it's time you left; *en même ~* at the same time; *par beau ~* in good weather; *quel ~ fait-il?* what's the weather like?

tenace tenacious

tenailles *fpl* pincers

tendance *f* trend; (*disposition*) tendency; *avoir ~ à faire* have a tendency to do, tend to do

tendon *m* ANAT tendon

tendre[1] *v/t* filet, ailes spread; *piège* set; *bras, main* hold out; *muscles* tense; *corde* tighten; *~ qch à qn* hold sth out to s.o.; *se ~ de rapports* become strained **2** *v/i*: *~ à qc* strive for sth; *~ à faire qch* tend to do sth

tendre[2] *adj* tender; *couleur* soft

tendresse *f* tenderness

tendu *corde* tight; *fig* tense;

relations strained

ténèbres *fpl* darkness; **ténébreux, -euse** dark

teneur *f d'une lettre* contents *pl*; (*concentration*) content

tenir 1 *v/t* hold; (*maintenir*) keep; *registre, promesse* keep; *caisse* be in charge of; *restaurant* run; *place* take up; *~ à qc/qn* (*donner de l'importance à*) value sth/s.o.; *à qn objet* be attached to sth; *~ à faire qc* want to do sth; *cela ne tient qu'à toi* (*dépend de*) it's entirely up to you **2** *v/i* hold; *~ dans* fit into 3: *se ~ d'un spectacle* be held; (*être, se trouver*) stand; *se ~ à qch* hold on to sth; *s'en ~ à* confine o.s. to

tennis *m* tennis; *terrain* tennis court; *~ pl* sneakers, *Br* trainers; *SP* tennis shoes

ténor *m* MUS tenor

tension *f* tension; MÉD blood pressure; *faire de la ~ F* have high blood pressure

tentacule *m* tentacle

tentant tempting; **tentation** *f* temptation

tentative *f* attempt

tente *f* tent

tenter tempt; (*essayer*) attempt, try (*de faire* to do)

tenture *f* wallhanging

tenu: *être ~ de faire qc* be obliged to do sth; *bien ~* well looked after; *mal ~* badly kept; *enfant* neglected ténu 244

ténu fine; *espoir* slim

tenue *f de comptes* keeping; *de ménage* running; (*conduite*) behavior, Br behaviour; *du corps* posture; (*vêtements*) clothes *pl*; **~ de soirée** evening wear

tergiverser hum and haw

terme *m* (*fin*) end; (*échéance*) time limit; (*expression*) term; **à court/long ~** in the short/long term; *emprunt, projet* short-/long-term

terminaison *f* GRAM ending; **terminer** finish; **se ~** end; **se ~ par** end with; **d'un mot** end in

terminus *m* terminus

ternir tarnish

terrain *m* ground; GÉOL, MIL terrain; SP field; **un ~** a piece of land; **sur le ~** *essai* field *atr*; *essayer* in the field; **~ d'aviation** airfield; **~ à bâtir** building lot; **~ de jeu** play park; **véhicule** *m* **tout ~** 4x4, off-road vehicle

terrasse *f* terrace; **terrasser** *adversaire* fell

terre *f* (*sol, surface*) ground; *matière* earth, soil; *opposé à mer, propriété* land; (*monde*) earth, world; *pays, région* land, country; ÉL ground, Br earth; **à ~ personne** down to earth; **à ou par ~** down to the ground; **tomber par ~** fall down; **sur ~** on earth; **sur la ~** on the ground

terre-plein *m*: **~ central** median strip, Br central reservation

terrestre *animaux* land *atr*; REL earthly; TV terrestrial

terreur *f* terror

terrible terrible; F (*extraordinaire*) terrific; **c'est pas ~** it's not that good

terrien, ~ne 1 *adj*: **propriétaire** *m* **~** landowner **2** *m/f* (*habitant de la Terre*) earthling

terrier *m de renard* earth; ZO terrier

terrifier terrify

territoire *m* territory

terroir *m viticulture* soil; **du ~** (*régional*) local

terroriser terrorize; **terrorisme** *m* terrorism; **terroriste** *m/f & adj* terrorist

tertre *m* mound

tes → **ton²**

test *m* test; **~ de résistance** endurance test

testament *m* JUR will; **Ancien/Nouveau Testament** REL Old/New Testament

tester test

testicule *m* testicle

tête *f* head; (*cheveux*) hair; (*visage*) face; SP header; **de ~ calculer** in one's head; **répondre** without looking anything up; **avoir la ~ dure** be stubborn; **se casser la ~** fig rack one's brains; **n'en faire qu'à sa ~** do exactly as one likes; **tenir ~ à qn** stand up to s.o.; *péj* defy s.o.; **faire la ~** sulk; **il se paie ta ~** fig he's making a fool of you; **en ~** in the lead

tête-à-queue *m* AUTO spin; **tête-à-tête** *m* tête-à-tête; **en ~** in private

têtu obstinate

texte *m* text; **~s choisis** selected passages

textile *m* textile; **le ~ industrie** the textile industry, textiles *pl*

texto *m* text (message); **envoyer un ~ à qn** send s.o. a text, text s.o.

texture *f* texture

T.G.V. *m* (= *train à grande vitesse*) high-speed train

thé *m* tea

théâtre *m* theater, *Br* theatre; *fig:* cadre scene

théière *f* teapot

thème *m* theme; ÉDU translation (into a foreign language)

théorie *f* theory; **théorique** theoretical

thérapeute *m/f* therapist; **thérapeutique 1** *f* (*thérapie*) therapy **2** *adj* therapeutic; **thérapie** *f* therapy

thermal thermal

thermomètre *m* thermometer

thermos *f ou m* thermos®

thèse *f* thesis

thon *m* tuna

thym *m* BOT thyme

tic *m* tic, twitch; *fig* habit

ticket *m* ticket; **~ de caisse** receipt

tiède warm; *péj* tepid, lukewarm (*aussi fig*); **tiédir** cool down; *devenir plus chaud* warm up

tien, ~ne: le tien, la tienne, les tiens, les tiennes yours

tiers, tierce 1 *adj* third; **le ~ monde** the Third World **2** *m* MATH third; JUR third party

tige *f* BOT stalk; TECH stem

tigre *m* tiger; **tigresse** *f* tigress

tilleul *m* BOT lime (tree); *boisson* lime-blossom tea

timbre *m* stamp; (*sonnette*) bell; (*son*) timbre; (*tampon*) stamp; **timbre-poste** *m* postage stamp

timide timid; **en société** shy

timoré timid

tintement *m* tinkle; *de clochettes* ringing; **tinter** *de verres* clink; *de clochettes* ring

tir *m* fire; *action,* SP shooting; **~ à l'arc** archery

tirage *m* **à la loterie** draw; PHOT print; TYP printing; (*exemplaires de journal*) circulation; *d'un livre* print run; COMM *d'un chèque* drawing; F (*difficultés*) trouble; **par un ~ au sort** by drawing lots

tirailler pull; **tiraillé entre** *fig* torn between

tire *f* P AUTO car, jeep F; **vol** *m* **à la ~** pickpocketing

tiré traits drawn

tire-bouchon *m* corkscrew

tirelire *f* piggy bank

tirer 1 v/t pull; *chèque, ligne, conclusions* draw; *coup de fusil* fire; *oiseau, cible* shoot at; PHOT, TYP print; *plaisir, satisfaction* derive **2** v/i pull (**sur** on); *avec arme* shoot (**sur** at); **~ à sa fin** draw to a close **3: se ~ de situation difficile** get out nf; **se ~** F take off

tiret m dash; (*trait d'union*) hyphen

tiroir m drawer

tisane f herbal tea

tisser weave; *d'une araignée* spin; *fig* hatch

tissu m fabric, material; BIOL tissue

titre m title; *d'un journal* headline; FIN security; **à ce ~** therefore; **à juste ~** rightly; **à ~ d'essai** on a trial basis; **au même ~** on the same basis

tituber stagger

titulaire m/f *d'un document, d'une charge* holder

toast m (*pain grillé*) piece of toast; *de bienvenue* toast

toboggan m slide; *rue* flyover

tocsin m alarm bell

toi you

toile f *de lin* linen; (*peinture*) canvas; **~ d'araignée** spiderweb, *Br* spider's web; **~ cirée** oilcloth; **~ de fond** backcloth; *fig* backdrop

toilette f (*lavage*) washing; (*mise*) outfit; (*vêtements*) clothes pl; **~s** toilet; **aller**

aux~s go to the toilet; **faire sa ~** get washed

toi-même yourself

toiser *fig*: **~ qn** look s.o. up and down

toison f *de laine* fleece; (*cheveux*) mane of hair

toit m roof; **~ ouvrant** AUTO sun roof; **toiture** f roof

tôle f sheet metal; **~ ondulée** corrugated iron

tolérance f *aussi* TECH tolerance; **tolérant** tolerant; **tolérer** tolerate

tomate f tomato

tombe f grave

tombeau m tomb

tombée f: **à la ~ de la nuit** at nightfall

tomber fall; *de cheveux* fall out; *d'une colère* die down; *d'une fièvre, d'un prix, d'une demande* drop, fall; **~ malade** fall sick; **laisser ~** drop (*aussi fig*); **~ sur** MIL attack; (*rencontrer*) bump into; **~ d'accord** reach agreement

tome m volume

ton[1] m tone; MUS key; **il est de bon ~** it's the done thing

ton[2] m, **ta** f, **tes** pl your

tondeuse f lawnmower; *de coiffeur* clippers pl; AGR shears pl; **tondre** *mouton* shear; *haie* clip; *herbe* mow, cut; *cheveux* shave off

tonifier tone up

tonique 1 m tonic **2** adj *climat* bracing

tonitruant thunderous

tonne f (metric) ton

tonneau m barrel; MAR ton

tonner thunder; fig rage

tonnerre m thunder

tonton m F uncle

tonus m d'un muscle tone; (dynamisme) dynamism

toqué F mad (de about)

torche f flashlight, Br torch

torchon m dishtowel

tordre twist; linge wring; se ~ twist; se ~ le pied twist one's ankle

tornade f tornado

torpille f torpedo; **torpiller** torpedo (aussi fig)

torrent m torrent; fig: de larmes flood; d'injures torrent

torse m torso

tort m fault; (préjudice) harm; à ~ wrongly; à ~ et à travers wildly; avoir ~ be wrong (de faire to do); donner ~ à qn prove s.o. wrong; (désapprouver) blame s.o.; faire du ~ à hurt, harm

torticolis m MÉD stiff neck

tortiller twist; se ~ wriggle

tortue f tortoise; ~ de mer turtle

tortueux, -euse winding; fig tortuous; esprit, manœuvres devious

torture f torture; **torturer** torture

tôt early; (bientôt) soon; le plus ~ possible as soon as possible; au plus ~ at the soonest ou earliest; ~ ou tard sooner or later

total 1 adj total **2** m total; au ~ in all; fig on the whole; **totalement** totally; **totaliser** total; **totalité** f: la ~ de all of; en ~ in full; **totalitaire** POL totalitarian

touchant touching

touche f touch; de clavier key; SP touchline; (remise en jeu) throw-in; pêche bite; être mis sur la ~ fig F be sidelined

toucher¹ v/t touch; but hit; (émouvoir) touch, move; (concerner) concern; (contacter) contact, get in touch with; argent get; réserves break into; d'une maison adjoin; ~ au but near one's goal; se ~ touch; de maisons, terrains adjoin

toucher² m touch

touffu dense, thick

toujours always; (encore) still; **pour ~** for ever

toupet m F nerve

tour¹ f tower; (immeuble) high-rise

tour² m turn; (circonférence) circumference; (circuit) lap; (promenade) stroll, walk; (excursion, voyage) tour; (ruse) trick; TECH lathe; de potier wheel; à mon ~, c'est mon ~ it's my turn; en un ~ de main in no time at all

tourbe f matière peat

tourbillon m de vent whirlwind; *d'eau* whirlpool

tourelle *f* turret

tourisme *m* tourism; ~ *écolo-gique* ecotourism; **touriste** *m/f* tourist

tourment *m litt* torture, torment

tourmente *f litt* storm

tourmenter torment; **se ~** worry, torment o.s.

tournant 1 *adj* revolving **2** *m* turn; *fig* turning point

tournée *f* round; *d'un artiste* tour

tourner 1 *v/t* turn; *sauce* stir; *salade* toss; *difficulté* get around; *film* shoot; **bien tourné(e)** well-put **2** *v/i* turn; *du lait* turn; **j'ai la tête qui tourne** my head is spinning; *faire* ~ *clé* turn; *entreprise* run **3**: *se* ~ turn; *se* ~ *vers fig* turn to

tournesol *m* BOT sunflower

tournevis *m* screwdriver

tournoyer *d'oiseaux* wheel; *de feuilles* swirl

tournure *f* (*expression*) turn of phrase; *des événements* turn

tourterelle *f* turtledove

tous → **tout**

Toussaint *m*: *la* ~ All Saints' Day

tousser cough

toussoter have a slight cough

tout *m*, **toute** *f*, **tous** *mpl*, **toutes** *fpl* **1** *adj* all; (*n'importe lequel*) any; ~ *Français* every Frenchman, all French-

men; *tous les deux jours* every two days; *tous les ans* every year **2** *pron sg* **tout** everything; *pl* **tous**, **toutes** all of us/them; *après* ~ after all; *facile comme* ~ F as easy as anything; *nous tous* all of us; **3** *adv* **tout** very, quite; *c'est* ~ *comme un* ,.. it's just like a ...; ~ *nu* completely naked; *c'est* ~ *près d'ici* it's just nearby; *je suis* ~*e seule* I'm all alone; ~ *à fait* altogether; *oui*, ~ *à fait* yes, absolutely; ~ *de suite* straight away; ~ *pauvres qu'ils sont* (*ou soient* (*subj*)) however poor they are **4** *m* **tout** the whole lot, everything; *pas du* ~ not at all

toutefois however

toux *f* cough *m*

toxique 1 *adj* toxic **2** *m* poison

trac *m* nervousness; *pour un acteur* stage fright

traçabilité *f* traceability

tracas *m*: *des* ~ worries; **tra-casser**: ~ *qn d'une chose* worry s.o.; *d'une personne* pester s.o.; *se* ~ worry

trace *f* (*piste*) track, trail; (*marque*) mark; *fig* impression; ~*s de sang*, *poison* traces; *des* ~*s de pas* footprints; **tracer** *plan* draw

trachée *f* windpipe, trachea

tractation *f péj*: ~*s* horse-trading

tracteur *m* tractor

tradition f tradition; **traditionaliste** m/f & adj traditionalist; **traditionnel, -elle** adj traditional

traducteur, -trice m/f translator; **traduction** f translation; **traduire** translate (**en** into); fig be indicative of; **se ~ par** result in

trafic m traffic; **trafiquant** m trafficker; **~ de drogue(s)** drug trafficker; **trafiquer** traffic in; **moteur** tinker with

tragédie f tragedy; **tragique 1** adj tragic **2** m tragedy; crime treason

trahir betray; **trahison** f betrayal; crime treason

train m train; fig: de lois, décrets etc series sg; **être en ~ de faire qc** be doing sth; **mettre en ~** set in motion; **au ~ où vont les choses** at the rate things are going; **~ d'atterrissage** undercarriage, landing gear; **~ de vie** lifestyle

traîner 1 v/t drag; d'une voiture pull, tow **2** v/i de vêtements, livres lie around; d'une discussion drag on; **~ dans les rues** hang around street corners **3**: **se ~** drag o.s. along

train-train m F: **le ~ quotidien** the daily routine

traire milk

trait m (ligne) line; du visage feature; de caractère trait; d'une œuvre, époque feature, characteristic; **avoir ~**

à be about; **~ d'esprit** witticism; **~ d'union** hyphen

traite f COMM draft, bill of exchange; d'une vache milking; **d'une seule ~** in one go

traité m treaty

traitement m treatment; (salaire) pay; TECH, INFORM processing; **traiter 1** v/t treat; TECH, INFORM process; **~ qn de menteur** call s.o. a liar **2** v/i (négocier) negotiate; **~ de qc** deal with sth

traître, ~sse 1 m/f traitor **2** adj treacherous

trajet m (voyage) journey; (chemin) way

trame f fig: d'une histoire background; de la vie fabric

tramway m streetcar, Br tram

tranchant 1 adj cutting **2** m d'un couteau cutting edge

tranche f (morceau) slice; (bord) edge; **~ d'âge** age bracket

tranché fig clear-cut; couleur definite

tranchée f trench

trancher 1 v/t cut; fig settle **2** v/i: **~ sur** stand out against

tranquille quiet; (sans inquiétude) easy in one's mind; **laisse-moi ~!** leave me alone!; **tranquillisant** m tranquilizer, Br tranquillizer; **tranquilliser: ~ qn** set s.o.'s mind at rest; **tranquillité** f quietness, tranquillity; du sommeil peacefulness; (stabilité morale) peace of mind

transaction f JUR compromise; COMM transaction

transatlantique 1 adj transatlantic **2** m bateau transatlantic liner; chaise deck chair

transcription f transcription; **transcrire** transcribe

transférer transfer; **transfert** m transfer; PSYCH transference

transformation f transformation; TECH processing; en rugby conversion; **transformer** transform; TECH process; appartement, en rugby convert

transfuge m defector

transfusion f: ~ (**sanguine**) (blood) transfusion

transgénique genetically modified

transgresser loi break, transgress

transi: ~ (**de froid**) frozen

transiger come to a compromise

transistor m transistor

transit m: **en ~** in transit

transition f transition

transmettre transmit; message, talen, maladie pass on; tradition, titre hand down; **transmissible**: **sexuellement**~ sexually transmitted; **transmission** f transmission; d'un message passing on; d'une tradition, d'un titre handing down; RAD, TV broadcast

transparence f transparency; **transparent** transparent

transpercer pierce; de l'eau, de la pluie go right through

transpiration f perspiration; **transpirer** perspire

transplant m transplant; **transplantation** f transplanting; MÉD transplant; **transplanter** transplant

transport m transport; ~**s publics** mass transit, Br public transport; **transporter** transport, carry

transposer transpose

transversal cross atr

trapèze m trapeze

trappe f (ouverture) trapdoor

trapu stocky

traquer hunt

traumatiser PSYCH traumatize; **traumatisme** m MÉD, PSYCH trauma

travail m work; **être sans**~ be out of work; **travaux** (construction) construction work; **travailler 1** v/i work **2** v/t work on; d'une pensée trouble; **travailleur, -euse 1** adj hard-working **2** m/f worker

travers 1 adv: **de** ~ crooked; marcher not straight; **en** ~ across **2** prép: **à** ~ **qc, au** ~ **de qc** through sth **3** m shortcoming

traversée f crossing; **traverser** rue, mer cross; forêt, crise go through; (percer) go right through travesti **1** adj pour fête fancy-dress **2** m (déguisement) fancy dress; (homosexuel) transvestite; **travestir** vérité distort; **se ~** dress up (**en** as a)

trébucher trip (**sur** over)

trèfle m BOT clover; aux cartes clubs pl

treize thirteen; **treizième** thirteenth

tremblant trembling, quivering; **tremblement** m trembling; **~ de terre** earthquake; **trembler** tremble, shake (**de** with); de la terre shake

trémousser: **se ~** wriggle

trempe f fig caliber, Br calibre

trempé soaked; sol saturated; **tremper** soak; pain dans café etc dunk; pied dans l'eau dip; acier harden; **~ dans** fig be involved in

tremplin m springboard; pour ski ski jump; fig stepping stone

trentaine f: **une ~ de personnes** about thirty people pl; **trente** thirty; **trentième** thirtieth

trépied m tripod

trépigner stamp (one's feet)

très very; **~ lu/visité** much read/visited

trésor m treasure; **Trésor** Treasury; **trésorier, -ère** m/f treasurer

tressaillir jump

tresse f de cheveux braid, Br

plait

trêve f truce; **~ de ...** that's enough ...; **sans ~** without respite

tri m sort; **faire un ~ dans qc** sort sth out

triangle m triangle

tribord m MAR starboard

tribu f tribe

tribulations fpl tribulations

tribunal m court

tribune f platform; (débat) discussion; **~s dans stade** bleachers, Br stands

tributaire: **être ~ de** be dependent on

tricher cheat; **tricheur, -euse** m/f cheat

tricolore: **drapeau** m **~** tricolor or ou Br tricolour

tricot m knitting; vêtement sweater; **tricoter** knit

trier (choisir) pick through; (classer) sort

trimballer F hump F, lug

trimer F work like a dog F

trimestre m quarter; ÉDU trimester, Br term

trinquer (porter un toast) clink glasses; **~ à** fig F toast, drink to

triomphe m triumph; **triompher** triumph (**de** over)

tripes fpl guts; CUIS tripe

triple triple; **triplés, -ées** mpl, fpl triplets

tripoter F objet play around with; femme feel up

triste sad; temps, paysage dreary; **tristesse** f sadness

trivial vulgar; *litt* (*banal*) trite
troc *m* barter
trognon *m d'un fruit* core; *d'un chou* stump
trois 1 *adj* three; **le ~ mai** May third, *Br* the third of May **2** *m* three; **troisième** *m* three
trombe *f*: **des ~s d'eau** sheets of water, **en ~** *fig* at top speed
trombone *m* MUS trombone; *pour papiers* paper clip
trompe *f* MUS horn; *d'un éléphant* trunk
tromper deceive; *époux* be unfaithful to; *confiance* abuse; **se ~** be mistaken; **se ~ de numéro** get the wrong number; **tromperie** *f* deception
trompette 1 *f* trumpet **2** *m* trumpet player
trompeur, -euse deceptive; (*traître*) deceitful
tronc *m* BOT, ANAT trunk; *à l'église* collection box
tronçon *m* section
trône *m* throne
trop too; *avec verbe* too much; **~ de lait/gens** too much milk/too many people
tropical tropical; **tropique** *m* tropic
trot *m* trot; **aller au ~** trot; **trotter** *d'un cheval* trot; *d'une personne* run around
trottiner scamper
trottinette *f* scooter
trottoir *m* sidewalk, *Br* pavement

trou *m* hole; **~ de mémoire** lapse of memory
trouble 1 *adj eau, liquide* cloudy; *explication* unclear; *situation* murky **2** *m* (*désarroi*) trouble; (*émoi*) excitement; MÉD disorder; **~s** POL unrest; **trouble-fête** *m* party-pooper F
troubler *liquide* make cloudy; *silence, sommeil* disturb; *réunion* disrupt; (*inquiéter*) bother; **se ~** get flustered *d'un liquide* go cloudy
trouée *f* gap; **trouer** make a hole in
troupe *f* troop; *de comédiens* troupe
troupeau *m de vaches* herd; *de moutons* flock
trousse *f* kit; **être aux ~s de** *qn fig* be on s.o.'s heels; **~ de toilette** toilet bag
trousseau *m d'une mariée* trousseau; **~ de clés** bunch of keys
trouver find; *plan* come up with; (*rencontrer*) meet; **~ que** think that; **se ~** (*être*) be; **il se trouve que** it turns out that
truc *m* F (*chose*) thing, thingamajig F; (*astuce*) trick
truffe *f* BOT truffle; *d'un chien* nose; **truffé** with truffles; **~ de** *fig*: *citations* peppered with
truie *f* sow
truite *f* trout
truquage *m dans film* special

effect; *d'une photo* faking;
truquer *élections, cartes* rig
tu you
tuba *m* snorkel; MUS tuba
tube *m* tube; F (*chanson*) hit
tuberculose *f* MÉD tuberculosis, TB
tuer kill; *fig* (*épuiser*) exhaust;
(*peiner*) bother; **se ~** (*se suicider*) kill o.s.; (*trouver la
mort*) be killed; **tue-tête: à
~** at the top of one's voice;
tueur *m* killer
tulipe *f* tulip
tumeur *f* MÉD tumor, *Br* tumour
tumulte *m* uproar; *fig* (*activité*) hustle and bustle; **tumultueux, -euse** noisy; *passion*
tumultuous, stormy
tunique *f* tunic
Tunisie: la ~ Tunisia; **tuni-
sien, ~ne** Tunisian; **Tuni-
sien, ~ne** *m/f* Tunisian
tunnel *m* tunnel
turbo-réacteur *m* AVIAT tur-
bojet
turbulence *f* turbulence;
d'un élève unruliness; **turbu-**

lent turbulent; *élève* unruly
turc, turque 1 *adj* Turkish **2** *m
langue* Turkish; **Turc, Tur-
que** *m/f* Turk
turf *m* SP horseracing; *terrain*
racecourse
Turquie: la ~ Turkey
tutelle *f* JUR guardianship;
d'un état, d'une société supervision, control; *fig* protection
tuteur, -trice 1 *m/f* JUR guardian **2** *m* BOT stake
tutoyer address as 'tu'
tuyau *m* pipe; *flexible* hose; F
(*information*) tip; **~ d'arro-
sage** garden hose; **tuyauter**
F: **~ qn** tip s.o. off
T.V.A. *f* (= **taxe sur ou à la valeur ajoutée**) sales tax, *Br*
VAT (= value added tax)
type *m* type; F (*gars*) guy F;
contrat **~** standard contract
typhon *m* typhoon
typique typical (**de** of)
tyran *m* tyrant; **tyrannie** *f* tyranny; **tyranniser** tyrannize;
petit frère etc bully

U

U.E. *f* (= **Union européenne**)
EU (= European Union)
ulcère *m* MÉD ulcer; **ulcérer**
fig aggrieve
ultérieur later, subsequent
ultimatum *m* ultimatum
ultime last

ultrason *m* PHYS ultrasound
ultraviolet, ~te *adj & m* ultraviolet
un, une 1 *article* a; *devant
voyelle* an **2** *pron* one; **à la
une** on the front page; **l'un
des touristes** one of the

tourists; *les uns avaient ...* some (of them) had ...; *elles s'aident les unes les autres* they help each other; *l'un et l'autre* both of them **3** *chiffre* one

unanime unanimous; **unanimité** *f* unanimity; *à l'~* unanimously

uni *pays* united; *surface* smooth; *tissu* solid(-colored), *Br* self-coloured; *famille* close-knit

unification *f* unification; **unifier** unite, unify

uniforme 1 *adj* uniform; *existence* unchanging **2** *m* uniform; **uniformité** *f* uniformity

unilatéral unilateral

union *f* union; (*cohésion*) unity; **Union européenne** European Union

unique (*seul*) single; *fils* only; (*extraordinaire*) unique; **uniquement** only

unir POL unite; *par moyen de communication* link; *couple* marry; *s'~* unite; (*se marier*) marry

unité *f* unit

univers *m* universe; *fig* world; **universel, ~le** universal

universitaire 1 *adj* university *atr* **2** *m/f* academic; **université** *f* university

uranium *m* CHIM uranium

urbain urban; **urbaniser** ur-

banize; **urbanisme** *m* town planning

urgence *f* urgency; *une ~* an emergency; *d'~* emergency *atr*; *urgent* urgent

urine *f* urine; **uriner** urinate

urne *f*: *aller aux ~s* go to the polls

usage *m* use; (*coutume*) custom; *linguistique* usage; *hors d'~* out of use; *à l'~ de qn* for the use by s.o.; *d'~* customary; **usager** *m* user

usé worn; *vêtement, personne* worn-out; **user** *du gaz, de l'eau* use, consume; *vêtement* wear out; *yeux* ruin; *s'~* wear out; *personne* wear o.s. out; *~ de qc* use sth

usine *f* plant, factory; **usiner** machine

usité *mot* common

ustensile *m* tool; *~ de cuisine* kitchen utensil

usuel, ~le usual; *expression* common

usure *f* (*détérioration*) wear; *du sol* erosion

utérus *m* ANAT womb, uterus

utile useful; *en temps ~* in due course

utilisateur, -trice *m/f* user; *~ final* end user; **utilisation** *f* use; **utiliser** use

utilitaire utilitarian

utilité *f* usefulness, utility; *ça n'a aucune ~* it's no use whatever

V

vacance f poste opening, Br vacancy; **~s** vacation, Br holiday(s); **vacancier, -ère** m/f vacationer, Br holiday-maker

vacarme m din, racket

vaccin m vaccine; **vaccination** f vaccination; **vacciner** vaccinate

vache 1 f cow **2** adj F mean

vachement F bon, content damn F, Br bloody F; changer, vieillir one helluva lot F

vaciller sur ses jambes sway; d'une flamme flicker; (hésiter) vacillate

vagabond -e 1 adj wandering **2** m/f hobo, Br tramp

vagin m vagina

vague [1] f wave (aussi fig); **~ de froid** cold snap

vague [2] **1** adj vague; regard faraway; terrain m **~** waste ground **2** m vagueness; regarder dans le **~** stare into the middle distance

vaillant brave, valiant

vain adj vain; mots empty; **en~** in vain

vaincre conquer; SP defeat; fig: angoisse overcome, conquer; obstacle overcome; **vaincu 1** adj conquered; SP defeated **2** m loser; **vainqueur** m winner, victor

vaisseau m ANAT, litt (bateau)

vessel; **~ spatial** spaceship

vaisselle f dishes pl; **laver** ou **faire la ~** do ou wash the dishes

valable valid

valeur f value, worth; d'une personne worth; **~s** COMM securities; **sans ~** worthless; **mettre en ~** emphasize, highlight

valide (sain) fit; passeport, ticket valid; **valider** validate; ticket stamp; **validité** f validity

valise f bag, suitcase

vallée f valley

valoir be worth; (coûter) cost; **~ mieux** be better (**que** than); **faire ~** droits assert; capital make work; (mettre en valeur) emphasize

valoriser enhance the value of; personne enhance the image of

valse f waltz

vandale m/f vandal; **vandaliser** vandalize

vanille f vanilla

vanité f (fatuité) vanity; (inutilité) futility; **vaniteux, -euse** vain

vanne f sluice gate; F dig F

vantard, ~e 1 adj boastful **2** m/f boaster; **vanter** praise; **se ~ de qch** pride o.s. on sth

vapeur f vapor, Br vapour; **~**

(*d'eau*) steam; *cuire à la ~* steam

vaporeux, -euse *paysage* misty; *tissu* filmy

vaporisateur *m* spray; **vaporiser** spray

varappe *f* rock-climbing

variable variable; *temps, humeur* changeable; **variante** *f* variant; **variation** *f* (*changement*) change; (*écart*) variation

varice *f* ANAT varicose vein

varicelle *f* MÉD chickenpox

varié varied; **varier** vary; **variété** *f* variety; **~s** *spectacle* vaudeville, *Br* variety show

variole *f* MÉD smallpox

vase[1] *m* vase

vase[2] *f* mud; **vaseux, -euse** muddy; *F* (*nauséeux*) off-color, *Br* off-colour; *F explication* muddled

vasistas *m* fanlight

vaurien, ~ne *m/f* good-for-nothing

vautour *m* vulture

veau *m* calf; *viande* veal

vedette *f* star; (*bateau*) launch; *mettre en ~* highlight

végétal 1 *adj* plant atr; *huile vegetable* **2** *m* plant; **végétalien, ~ne** *m/f & adj* vegan

végétarien, ~ne *m/f & adj* vegetarian

végétation *f* vegetation; **végéter** vegetate

véhémence *f* vehemence; **véhément** vehement

véhicule *m* vehicle (*aussi fig*)

veille *f* previous day; *absence de sommeil* wakefulness; *à la ~ de* on the eve of; **veiller** stay up late; *~ à faire qch* see to it that sth is done; *~ sur qn* watch over s.o.

veinard, ~e *m/f* F lucky devil F; **veine** *f* vein; *F* luck

vélo *m* bike; *faire du ~* go cycling; **vélomoteur** *m* moped

velours *m* velvet; *~ côtelé* corduroy

velouté velvety; (*soupe*) creamy

velu hairy

venaison *f* venison

vendable saleable

vendange *f* grape harvest

vendeur *m* sales clerk, *Br* shop assistant; **vendeuse** *f* sales clerk, *Br* shop assistant; **vendre** sell; *fig* betray; *à ~* for sale

vendredi *m* Friday; **Vendredi saint** Good Friday

vendu, ~e 1 *adj* sold **2** *m/f péj* traitor

vénéneux, -euse poisonous

vénérable venerable; **vénération** *f* veneration; **vénérer** revere

vénérien, ~ne: maladie f ~ne venereal disease

vengeance *f* vengeance; **venger** avenge (*qn de qc* s.o. for sth); *se ~ de qn* get one's revenge on s.o.; *se ~ de qc sur qn* get one's revenge for sth on s.o.

venimeux, -euse poisonous; **venin** *m* venom (*aussi fig*)

venir come; **à ~** to come; **où veut-il en ~?** what's he getting at?; **~ de** come from; **je viens de faire la vaisselle** I have just washed the dishes; **faire ~ médecin** send for

vent *m* wind; **coup m de ~** gust of wind; **il y a du ~** it's windy

vente *f* sale; *activité* selling; **~ à crédit** installment plan, *Br* hire purchase

venteux, -euse windy

ventilateur *m* ventilator; *électrique* fan; **ventilation** *f* ventilation; **ventiler** *pièce* air; *montant* break down

ventre *m* stomach; **~ à bière** beer belly

ventriloque *m* ventriloquist

venu *m* arrival

venu,~e 1 *adj*: **bien/mal ~** appropriate/inappropriate **2** *m/f*: **le premier ~, la première ~e** the first to arrive; (*n'importe qui*) anybody; **venue** *f* arrival

ver *m* worm; **~ de terre** earthworm; **~ à soie** silkworm

verbal verbal; **verbe** *m* verb

verdâtre greenish

verdict *m* verdict

verdir turn green

verdure *f* (*feuillages*) greenery; (*salade*) greens *pl*

verge *f* ANAT penis; (*baguette*) rod

verger *m* orchard

verglas *m* black ice

vergogne *f*: **sans ~** shameless; **avec verbe** shamelessly

véridique truthful

vérification *f* check; **vérifier** check; **se ~** turn out to be true

véritable real; *amour* true

vérité *f* truth; **en ~** actually; **à la ~** to tell the truth

vermeil, ~le bright red, vermillion

vermine *f* vermin

verni varnished; F lucky; **vernir** varnish; *céramique* glaze; **vernis** *m* varnish; *de céramique* glaze; **~ à ongle** nail polish, *Br aussi* nail varnish

verre *m* glass; **prendre un ~** have a drink; **~s de contact** contact lenses

verrerie *f* glassmaking; *fabrique* glassworks *sg*; *objets* glassware

verrière *f* (*vitrail*) stained-glass window; *toit* glass roof

verrou *m* bolt; **verrouillage** *m*: **~ central** AUTO central locking; **verrouiller** bolt; F lock up

verrue *f* wart

vers[1] *m* verse

vers[2] *prép* toward, *Br* towards; (*environ*) around

versant *m* slope

verser 1 *v/t* pour (out); *sang,*

larmes shed; *argent à un compte* pay in; *intérêts, pension* pay **2** *v/i* (*basculer*) overturn

version *f* version; (*traduction*) translation

verso *m d'une feuille* back

vert 1 *adj* green; *fruit* unripe; *vin* too young; *fig: personne âgée* spry; *propos risqué* **2** *m* green; *les ~s* POL *mpl* the Greens

vertébral vertebral; *colonne f ~e* spine, spinal column; **vertèbre** *f* vertebra

vertical, ~e 1 *adj* vertical **2** *f* vertical (line)

vertige *m* vertigo, dizziness; *fig* giddiness; *un ~* a dizzy spell; *j'ai le ~* I feel dizzy

vertu *f* virtue; (*pouvoir*) property; *en ~ de* in accordance with; **vertueux, -euse** virtuous

verve *f* wit

vésicule *f* ANAT: *~ biliaire* gall bladder

vessie *f* ANAT bladder

veste *f* jacket

vestiaire *m de théâtre* checkroom, *Br* cloakroom; *d'un stade* locker room

vestibule *m* hall

vestiges *mpl* traces

veston *m* jacket, coat

vêtement *m* item of clothing, garment; *~s* clothes; (*industrie f du*) *~* clothing industry

vétérinaire 1 *adj* veterinary **2** *m/f* veterinarian, vet

vêtu dressed

vétuste *bâtiment* dilapidated, ramshackle

veuf 1 *adj* widowed **2** *m* widower

veuve 1 *adj* widowed **2** *f* widow

vexant humiliating; **vexation** *f* humiliation; **vexer:** *~ qn* hurt s.o.'s feelings; *se ~* get upset

viable *projet*, BIOL viable

viaduc *m* viaduct

viager, -ère: *rente f viagère* life annuity

viande *f* meat

vibration *f* vibration; **vibrer** vibrate

vice *m* (*défaut*) defect; (*péché*) vice

vice-président *m* COMM, POL vice-president; *Br* COMM vice-chairman

vicié *air* stale

vicieux, -euse lecherous; *cercle* vicious

victime *f* victim

victoire *f* victory; SP win, victory; **victorieux, -euse** victorious

vidange *f* emptying, draining; AUTO oil change

vide 1 *adj* empty **2** *m* (*néant*) emptiness; *physique* vacuum; (*espace non occupé*) (empty) space; *avoir peur du ~* be afraid of heights

vidéo *adj & f* video *~ amateur* home movie; **vidéocassette** *f* video cassette

vide-ordures *m* rubbish chute

vider empty (out); F *personne* throw out; *cuis volaille* draw; *salle* vacate, leave; *se ~* empty; **videur** *m* F bouncer

vie *f* life; *moyens matériels* living; *à ~* for life; *être en ~* be alive; *coût de la ~* cost of living; *gagner sa ~* earn one's living

vieil → **vieux**

vieillard *m* old man; *les ~s* old people *pl*, the elderly *pl*

vieille → **vieux**

vieillesse *f* old age

vieillir 1 *v/t*: *~ qn* age s.o. **2** *v/i* *d'une personne* get old, age; *d'un visage* age; *d'une théorie, d'un livre* become dated; *d'un vin* age, mature

viennoiseries *fpl croissants and similar types of bread*

vierge 1 *f* virgin; *Vierge* ASTROL Virgo **2** *adj* virgin; *feuille* blank

Viêt-nam: *le ~* Vietnam; **vietnamien, ~ne 1** *adj* Vietnamese **2** *m langue* Vietnamese; **Vietnamien, ~ne** *m/f* Vietnamese

vieux, *vieil before a vowel or silent h*, **vieille** (*f*) **1** *adj* old **2** *m/f* old man/old woman; *an; les ~* old people *pl*, the aged *pl*

vif, vive 1 *adj* lively; (*en vie*) alive; *plaisir, satisfaction* great; *critique, douleur*

sharp; *air* bracing; *froid* biting; *couleur* bright **2** *m* **à ~** *plaie* open; **piqué au ~** cut to the quick; **le ~ du sujet** the heart of the matter; **avoir les nerfs à ~** be on edge

vigilance *f* vigilance; **vigilant** vigilant

vigile *m* (*gardien*) security man, guard

vigne *f.* (*arbrisseau*) vine; (*plantation*) vineyard

vigneron, ~ne *m/f* wine grower

vignoble *m* plantation vineyard; *région* wine-growing area

vigoureux, -euse robust, vigorous; **vigueur** *f* vigor, *Br* vigour, robustness; **entrer en ~** come into force

V.I.H. *m* (= **V**irus de l'**I**mmunodéficience **H**umaine) HIV (= human immunodeficiency virus)

vilain nasty; *enfant* naughty; (*laid*) ugly

villa *f* villa

village *m* village; **villageois, ~e 1** *adj* village *atr* **2** *m/f* villager

ville *f* town; *grande city*; *aller en ~* go into town

vin *m* wine; *~ d'honneur* reception; *~ de pays* regional wine

vinaigre *m* vinegar

vinaigrette *f* salad dressing

vingt twenty; **vingtaine:** *une*

~ de personnes about twenty people *pl*; **vingtième** twentieth

viol *m* rape; *d'un lieu saint* violation; **violation** *f d'un traité* violation; *d'une église* desecration

violemment violently; *fig* intensely; **violence** *f* violence; *fig* intensity; **violent** violent; *fig* intense

violer *loi* break, *sexuellement* rape; *(profaner)* desecrate

violet, ~te violet

violette *f* BOT violet

violon *m* violin; *musicien* violinist

violoncelle *m* cello

virage *m de la route* curve, corner; *d'un véhicule* turn; *fig* change of direction; **virement** *m* COMM transfer; **virer 1** *v/i (changer de couleur)* change color *ou Br* colour; *d'un véhicule* corner **2** *v/t argent* transfer; **~ qn** F kick s.o. out

virginité *f* virginity

virgule *f* comma

viril male; *(courageux)* manly; **virilité** *f* manhood; *(vigueur sexuelle)* virility

virtuel, ~le virtual; *(possible)* potential

virulent virulent

virus *m* MÉD, INFORM virus

vis *f* screw; **escalier** *m à ~** spiral staircase

visa *m* visa

visage *m* face

vis-à-vis 1 *prép*: **~ de** opposite; *(envers)* toward, *Br* towards; *(en comparaison de)* compared with **2** *m* person sitting opposite; *(rencontre)* face-to-face meeting

viser 1 *v/t* aim at; *(s'adresser à)* be aimed at **2** *v/i* aim (**à** at); **~ à faire** aim to do

viseur *m d'une arme* sights *pl*; PHOT viewfinder

visibilité *f* visibility; **visible** visible; *(évident)* clear

vision *f* sight; *(conception, apparition)* vision; **visionnaire** *m/f & adj* visionary

visite *f* visit; *d'une ville* tour; **rendre~à qn** visit s.o.; **avoir droit de~** *d'un parent divorcé* have access; **~ de douane** customs inspection; **~ médicale** medical (examination); **visiter** visit; *(faire le tour de)* tour; *bagages* inspect; **visiteur, -euse** *m/f* visitor

vison *m* mink

visqueux, -euse viscous; *péj* slimy

visser screw

visuel, ~le visual; **champ** *m* **~** field of vision

vital vital; **vitalité** *f* vitality

vitamine *f* vitamin

vite fast, quickly; *(sous peu, bientôt)* soon; **~!** quick!; **vitesse** *f* speed; AUTO gear; **à toute ~** at top speed

viticulture *f* wine-growing

vitrage *m cloison* glass partition; *action* glazing; *ensem-*

ble de vitres windows *pl*

vitrail *m* stained-glass window

vitre *f* window (pane); *de voiture* window; **vitrer** glaze; **vitrier** *m* glazier

vitrine *f* (*étalage*) (store) window; *meuble* display cabinet

vivace hardy; *haine, amour* lasting; **vivacité** *f* liveliness, vivacity

vivant *1 adj* alive; (*plein de vie*) lively; (*doué de vie*) living; *langue* modern *2 m* living person; **en ~** in his lifetime

vivement (*d'un ton vif*) sharply; (*vite*) briskly; *ému, touché* deeply

vivoter just get by

vivre *1 v/i* live *2 v/t* experience *3 mpl*: **~s** supplies

vocabulaire *m* vocabulary

vociférer shout

vodka *f* vodka

vœu *m* REL vow; (*souhait*) wish; **tous mes ~x!** best wishes!

voici here is *sg*, here are *pl*; **me ~!** here I am!; **le livre que ~** this book

voie *f* way; *de chemin de fer* track; *d'autoroute* lane; **en ~ de développement** developing; **être en ~ de guérison** be on the mend; **par ~ aérienne** by air; **par la ~ hiérarchique** through channels; **~ d'eau** leak; **~ express** expressway

voilà there is *sg*, there are *pl*; (*et*) **~!** there you are!; **en ~ assez!** that's enough!; **~ tout** that's all

voile 1 *m* veil **2** *f* MAR sail; SP sailing

voiler[1] *v/t* veil; **se ~** *d'une femme* wear the veil; *du ciel* cloud over

voiler[2]: **se ~** *du bois* warp; *d'une roue* buckle

voir see; *faire* **~** show; **se ~** see each other; *cela se voit* that's obvious; **je ne peux pas le ~** I can't stand him

voisin, ~e 1 *adj* neighboring, *Br* neighbouring; (*similaire*) similar **2** *m/f* neighbor, *Br* neighbour; **voisinage** *m* neighborhood, *Br* neighbourhood; (*proximité*) vicinity

voiture *f* car; *d'un train* car, *Br* carriage; **en ~** by car; **~ de fonction** company car

voix *f* voice (*aussi* GRAM); POL vote; **à haute ~** in a loud voice, aloud; **à ~ basse** in a low voice, quietly

vol[1] *m* theft; **~ à main armée** armed robbery

vol[2] *m* flight; **à ~ d'oiseau** as the crow flies; **au ~** in flight; **~ à voile** gliding

volaille *f* poultry; (*poulet etc*) bird

volant *m* AUTO (steering) wheel; SP shuttlecock; *d'un vêtement* flounce

volcan *m* volcano

volée f d'oiseaux flock; en tennis, de coups de feu volley; **à la ~** in mid-air

voler[1] v/t steal; **~ qch à qn** steal sth from s.o.

voler[2] v/i fly

volet m de fenêtre shutter; fig part; **trier sur le ~** fig handpick

voleur, -euse 1 adj thieving **2** m/f thief; **~ à l'étalage** shoplifter

volontaire 1 adj voluntary; (délibéré) deliberate; (décidé) headstrong **2** m/f volunteer

volonté f will; (souhait) wish; (fermeté) willpower; **de l'eau à ~** as much water as you like; **faire preuve de bonne ~** show willing

volontiers willingly, with pleasure

volt m ÉL volt; **voltage** m ÉL voltage

volte-face f about-turn (aussi fig)

volubilité f volubility

volume m volume; **volumineux, -euse** bulky

voluptueux, -euse voluptuous

vomir v/i vomit, throw up **2** v/t bring up; fig spew out; **vomissement** m vomiting

vorace voracious

vos → votre

vote m vote; action voting; **voter 1** v/i vote **2** v/t loi pass

votre, pl vos your

vôtre: le/la ~, les ~s yours

vouer dedicate (**à** to); **se ~ à** fig dedicate o.s. to

vouloir want; **il veut que tu partes** (subj) he wants you to leave; **je voudrais** I would like, I'd like; **je veux bien** I'd like to; **veuillez ne pas fumer** please do not smoke; **~ dire** mean; **en ~ à qn** have something against s.o.; **veux-tu te taire!** will you shut up!

voulu requisite; délibéré deliberate

vous sg et pl you; complément d'objet indirect, sg et pl (to) you; avec verbe pronominal yourself; pl yourselves; **~ ~ êtes coupé** you've cut yourself; **si ~ ~ levez à ...** if you get up at ...

vous-même, pl vous-mêmes yourself; pl yourselves

voûte f ARCH vault; **voûté** personne hunched; dos bent; ARCH vaulted

vouvoyer adress as 'vous'

voyage m trip, journey; en paquebot voyage; **~ d'affaires** business trip; **~ de noces** honeymoon; **~ organisé** package holiday; **voyager** travel; **voyageur, -euse** m/f traveler, Br traveller; par train, avion passenger; **~ de commerce** traveling ou Br travelling salesman

voyant, ~e 1 adj couleur garish **2** m (signal) light **3** m/f *(devin)* clairvoyant

voyelle *f* GRAM vowel

voyou *m* jeune lout

vrac *m*: **en ~** COMM loose; *fig* jumbled together

vrai 1 *adj (après le subst)* true; *(devant le subst)* real, genuine; *ami* true **2** *m*: **à ~ dire, à dire ~** to tell the truth; **vraiment** really

vraisemblable likely, probable; **vraisemblance** *f* likelihood, probability

vrombir throb

VTT *m* (= *vélo tout terrain*) mountain bike

vu in view of

vue *f* view; *sens, faculté* sight; **à première ~** at first sight; **connaître qn de ~** know s.o. by sight; **avoir la ~ basse** be shortsighted; **point** *m* **de ~** viewpoint, point of view; **en ~ de faire** with a view to doing

vulgaire *(banal)* common; *(grossier)* common, vulgar

vulnérable vulnerable

W

wagon *m* car, *Br* carriage; *de marchandises* car, *Br* wagon; **wagon-lit** *m* sleeping car; **wagon-restaurant** *m* dining car

walkman *m* Walkman®

watt *m* ÉL watt

W.-C. *mpl* WC *sg*

week-end *m* weekend; **ce ~** on the weekend

whisky *m* whiskey, *Br* whisky

X, Y

xénophobe xenophobic; **xénophobie** *f* xenophobia

xérès *m* sherry

y there; **on ~ va!** let's go!; **ça ~ est!** that's it!; **j'~ suis** *(je comprends)* now I get it; **~**

compris including; **j'~ travaille** I'm working on it

yacht *m* yacht; **yachting** *m* yachting

yaourt *m* yoghurt

yeux *pl* → **œil**

Z

zapper channel-hop, *Br aussi* zap

zèbre *m* zebra

zèle *m* zeal; **faire du ~** be overzealous, **zélé** zealous

zéro 1 *m* zero, *Br aussi* nought; *SP Br* nil; *fig* nonentity **2** *adj:* **~ faute** no mistakes; **partir de ~** start from nothing

zeste *m* peel, zest

zézayer lisp

zigouiller F bump off F

zigzag *m* zigzag; **zigzaguer** zigzag

zinc *m* zinc

zona *m* shingles *sg*

zone *f* area, zone; *péj* slums *pl*; **~ euro** euro zone; **~ industrielle** industrial park, *Br* industrial estate; **~ interdite** prohibited area

zoo *m* zoo

zoologie *f* zoology; **zoologiste** *m/f* zoologist

zut! F blast!

English – French
Anglais – Français

A

a [ə] un(e)

abandon [əˈbændən] abandonner

abbreviate [əˈbriːvɪeɪt] abréger; **abbreviation** abréviation f

abduct [əbˈdʌkt] enlever

ability [əˈbɪlətɪ] capacité f; *skill* faculté f

able [ˈeɪbl] (*skillful*) compétent; **be ~ to do** pouvoir faire

abnormal [æbˈnɔːrml] anormal

aboard [əˈbɔːrd] à bord

abolish [əˈbɑːlɪʃ] abolir; **abolition** abolition f

abort [əˈbɔːrt] suspendre; **abortion** MED avortement m; **have an ~** se faire avorter; **abortive** avorté

about [əˈbaʊt] **1** *prep* (*concerning*) à propos de; *a book* **~** un livre qui parle de; **what's it ~?** *of book, movie* de quoi ça parle? **2** *adv* (*roughly*) à peu près; **~ noon** aux alentours de midi; **be ~ to do** (*be going to*) être sur le point de faire

above [əˈbʌv] au-dessus de; **on the floor ~** à l'étage du dessus

abrasive [əˈbreɪsɪv] *personality* abrupt

abreast [əˈbrest]: **three ~** les trois l'un à côté de l'autre; **keep ~ of** se tenir au courant de

abridge [əˈbrɪdʒ] abréger

abroad [əˈbrɔːd] à l'étranger

abrupt [əˈbrʌpt] brusque

abscess [ˈæbsɪs] abcès m

absence [ˈæbsəns] absence f; **absent** absent; **absentee** absent(e) m(f); **absenteeism** absentéisme m; **absent-minded** distrait

absolute [ˈæbsəluːt] absolu; **absolution** REL absolution f; **absolve** absoudre

absorb [əbˈsɔːrb] absorber; **absorbent** absorbant; **absorbent cotton** coton m hydrophile; **absorbing** absorbant

abstain [əbˈsteɪn] *in vote* s'abstenir; **abstention** *in vote* abstention f

abstract [ˈæbstrækt] abstrait

absurd [əbˈsɜːrd] absurde; **absurdity** absurdité f

abundance [əˈbʌndəns] abondance f; **abundant** abondant

abuse[1] [ə'bjuːs] *n verbal insults fpl; physical violences fpl physiques; sexual sévices mpl sexuels; of power etc* abus *m*

abuse[2] [ə'bjuːz] *v/t verbally* insulter; *physically* maltraiter; *sexually* faire subir des sévices sexuels à; *power etc* abuser de

abysmal [ə'bɪzml] *(very bad)* lamentable

academic [ækə'demɪk] **1** *n* universitaire *m/f* **2** *adj year: at school* scolaire; *at university* universitaire; *interests* intellectuel; **academy** académie *f*

accelerate [ək'seləreɪt] accélérer; **acceleration** accélération *f*; **accelerator** accélérateur *m*

accent ['æksənt] accent *m*; **accentuate** accentuer

accept [ək'sept] accepter; **acceptable** acceptable; **acceptance** acceptation *f*

access ['ækses] **1** *n* accès *m* **2** *v/t also* COMPUT accéder à; **accessible** accessible

accessory [ək'sesərɪ] *n for wearing* accessoire *m*; LAW complice *m/f*

accident ['æksɪdənt] accident *m*; **by** ~ par hasard; **accidental** accidentel; **accidentally** accidentellement

acclimate, **acclimatize** [ə'klaɪmət, ə'klaɪmətaɪz] s'acclimater

accommodate [ə'kɑːmədeɪt] loger; *needs* s'adapter à; **accommodations** logement *m*

accompaniment [ə'kʌmpənɪmənt] MUS accompagnement *m*; **accompany** *also* MUS accompagner

accomplice [ə'kʌmplɪs] complice *m/f*

accomplished [ə'kʌmplɪʃt] accompli; **accomplishment** *of task* accomplissement *m*; *(achievement)* réussite *f*; *(talent)* talent *m*

accord [ə'kɔːrd] accord *m*; *of one's own* ~ de son plein gré

accordance [ə'kɔːrdəns]: *in* ~ *with* conformément à

according [ə'kɔːrdɪŋ]: ~ *to* selon; **accordingly** *(consequently)* par conséquent; *(appropriately)* en conséquence

account [ə'kaunt] *financial* compte *m*; *(report)* récit *m*; **give an** ~ **of** faire le récit de; **on no** ~ en aucun cas; **on** ~ **of** en raison de; **take ... into** ~ tenir compte de; **accountable**: **be held** ~ être tenu responsable; **accountant** comptable *m/f*; **accounts** comptabilité *f*

accumulate [ə'kjuːmjuleɪt] **1** *v/t* accumuler **2** *v/i* s'accumuler; **accumulation** accumulation *f*

accuracy ['ækjurəsɪ] justesse *f*; **accurate** juste; **accurately** avec justesse

accusation [əkjuː'zeɪʃn] accusation *f*; **accuse**: *~ s.o. of doing sth* accuser qn de faire qch; **accused** LAW accusé(e) *m(f)*; **accusing** accusateur

accustom [ə'kʌstəm]: *get ~ed to* s'accoutumer à

ace [eɪs] *in cards* as *m*; *tennis* shot ace *m*

ache [eɪk] **1** *n* douleur *f* **2** *v/i*: *my arm ~s* j'ai mal au bras

achieve [ə'tʃiːv] accomplir; **achievement** (*thing achieved*) accomplissement *m*; *of ambition* réalisation *f*

acid ['æsɪd] acide *m*

acknowledge [ək'nɒlɪdʒ] reconnaître; *~ receipt of* accuser réception de; **acknowledg(e)ment** reconnaissance *f*; *of a letter* accusé *m* de réception

acoustics [ə'kuːstɪks] acoustique *f*

acquaint [ə'kweɪnt]: *be ~ed with* connaître; **acquaintance** *person* connaissance *f*

acquire [ə'kwaɪr] acquérir; **acquisition** acquisition *f*

acquit [ə'kwɪt] LAW acquitter; **acquittal** LAW acquittement *m*

acre ['eɪkər] acre *m* (4.047m²)

across [ə'krɒs] **1** *prep* de l'autre côté de; *walk ~ the street* traverser la rue; *~ Europe* all over dans toute l'Europe; *~ from* en face de **2** *adv*: *swim ~* traverser à la na-

ge; *10m ~* 10 m de large

act [ækt] **1** *v/i* (*take action*) agir; THEA faire du théâtre **2** *n* (*deed*) fait *m*; *of play* acte *m*; *in vaudeville* numéro *m*; (*law*) loi *f*

action ['ækʃn] action *f*; *take ~* prendre des mesures

active ['æktɪv] actif *m*; **activist** POL activiste *m/f*; **activity** activité *f*

actor ['æktər] acteur *m*

actress ['æktrɪs] actrice *f*

actual ['æktʃʊəl] véritable; **actually** ['æktʃʊəlɪ] en fait; *in expressing surprise* vraiment

acute [ə'kjuːt] *pain* intense; *sense* très développé

AD [eɪ'diː] (= *anno domini*) apr. J.-C. (= après Jésus Christ)

ad [æd] → *advertisement*

adamant ['ædəmənt]: *be ~ that ...* soutenir catégoriquement que ...

adapt [ə'dæpt] **1** *v/t* adapter **2** *v/i of person* s'adapter; **adaptability** faculté *f* d'adaptation; **adaptable** adaptable; **adaptation** *of play etc* adaptation *f*; **adapter** ELEC adaptateur *m*

add [æd] **1** *v/t* ajouter; MATH additionner **2** *v/i of person* faire des additions

◆ **add on** 1% *etc* ajouter

◆ **add up 1** *v/t* additionner **2** *v/i* avoir du sens

addict ['ædɪkt] (*drug ~*) drogué(e) *m(f)*; *of TV program* *etc* accro *m*/*f*; **addicted to drugs** drogué; *to TV program etc* accro F; **addiction to drugs** dépendance *f* (**to** de); **additive: be ~** entraîner une dépendance

addition ['ədɪʃn] MATH addition *f*; *to list* ajout *m*; *to company* recrue *f*; **in ~ to** en plus de; **additional** supplémentaire; **additive** additif *m*; **add-on** accessoire *m*

address [ə'dres] **1** *n* adresse *f* **2** *v*/*t letter* adresser; *audience* s'adresser à; **addressee** destinataire *m*/*f*

adequate ['ædɪkwət] (*sufficient*) suffisant; (*satisfactory*) satisfaisant; **adequately** suffisamment

◆ **adhere to** [əd'hɪr] adhérer à

adhesive [əd'hiːsɪv] adhésif *m*

adjacent [ə'dʒeɪsnt] adjacent

adjective ['ædʒɪktɪv] adjectif *m*

adjoining [ə'dʒɔɪnɪŋ] attenant

adjourn [ə'dʒɜːrn] ajourner; **adjournment** ajournement *m*

adjust [ə'dʒʌst] ajuster; **adjustable** ajustable; **adjustment** ajustement *m*

ad lib [æd'lɪb] **1** *adj* improvisé **2** *v*/*i* improviser

administer [əd'mɪnɪstər] *country* administrer; **administration** administration *f*;

(*administrative work*) tâches *fpl* administratives; **administrative** administratif; **administrator** administrateur(-trice) *m*(*f*)

admirable ['ædmərəbl] admirable; **admiration** admiration *f*; **admire** admirer; **admirer** admirateur(-trice) *m*(*f*); **admiring** admiratif; **admiringly** admirativement

admissible [əd'mɪsəbl] admis; **admission** (*confession*) aveu *m*; **~ free** entrée *f* gratuite; (*access*) admettre; (*confess*) avouer; **admittance: no ~** entrée *f* interdite

adolescence [ædə'lesns] adolescence *f*; **adolescent 1** *adj* adolescent **2** *n* adolescent(e) *m*(*f*)

adopt [ə'dɑːpt] adopter; **adoption** adoption *f*

adorable [ə'dɔːrəbl] adorable; **adoration** adoration *f*; **adore** adorer

adrenalin [ə'drenəlɪn] adrénaline *f*

adult [ædʌlt] **1** *adj* adulte **2** *n* adulte *m*/*f*; **adultery** adultère *m*

advance [əd'væns] **1** *n money* avance *f*; *in science etc* avancée *f*; MIL progression *f*; **in ~** à l'avance; **payment in ~** paiement *m* anticipé; **make ~s** (*progress*) faire des progrès; *sexually* faire des avances **2** *v*/*i* MIL, (*make progress*) avancer **3** v/t theory, sum of money avancer; human knowledge, cause faire avancer; **advanced** avancé

advantage [əd'væntɪdʒ] avantage m; **take ~ of** opportunity profiter de; **advantageous** [ædvən'teɪdʒəs] avantageux

adventure [əd'ventʃər] aventure f; **adventurous** aventureux

adverb ['ædvɜːrb] adverbe m

adversary ['ædvərsərɪ] adversaire m/f

adverse ['ædvɜːrs] adverse

advertise ['ædvərtaɪz] product faire de la publicité pour; job mettre une annonce pour; **advertisement** for product publicité f, pub f; for job annonce f; **advertiser** annonceur(-euse) m(f); **advertising** publicité f

advice [əd'vaɪs] conseils mpl; **a bit of ~** un conseil; **advisable** conseillé; **advise** conseiller

advocate ['ædvəkeɪt] recommander

aerial ['erɪəl] Br antenne f; **aerial photograph** photographie f aérienne

aerobics [e'roʊbɪks] aérobic m

aerodynamic [eroʊdaɪ'næmɪk] aérodynamique

aeroplane ['eroʊpleɪn] avion m

aerosol ['erəsɒl] aérosol m

aesthetic etc → **esthetic** etc

affair [ə'fer] (matter) affaire f; (love ~) liaison f

affection [ə'fekʃn] affection f; **affectionate** affectueux; **affectionately** affectueusement

affirmative [ə'fɜːrmətɪv] affirmatif

affluence ['æfluəns] richesse f; **affluent** riche

afford [ə'fɔːrd]: **be able to ~ sth** financially pouvoir se permettre d'acheter qch

afloat [ə'floʊt] boat sur l'eau

afraid [ə'freɪd]: **be ~** avoir peur (of de); **I'm ~** expressing regret je crains

afresh [ə'freʃ]: **start ~** recommencer

Africa ['æfrɪkə] Afrique f

African ['æfrɪkən] **1** adj africain **2** n Africain(e) m(f); **African-American 1** adj afro-américain(e) **2** n Afro-Américain(e) m(f)

after ['æftər] **1** prep après; **it's ten ~ two** il est deux heures dix **2** adv (afterward) après; **the day ~** le lendemain

afternoon [æftər'nuːn] après-midi m; **in the ~** l'après-midi; **this ~** cet après-midi; **good ~** bonjour

'after sales service service m après-vente; **aftershave** lotion f après-rasage; **afterward** ensuite

again [ə'geɪn] encore; **I never saw him ~** je ne l'ai jamais revu

against [ə'genst] contre

age [eɪdʒ] âge m; **she's five years of ~** elle a cinq ans; **aged:** ~ **16** âgé de 16 ans; **age group** catégorie f d'âge; **age limit** limite f d'âge

agency ['eɪdʒənsɪ] agence f

agenda [ə'dʒendə] ordre m du jour

agent ['eɪdʒənt] COM agent m

aggravate ['æɡrəveɪt] faire empirer; (annoy) agacer

aggression [ə'greʃn] agression f; **aggressive** agressif; **aggressively** agressivement

aghast [ə'ɡæst] horrifié

agile ['ædʒəl] agile; **agility** agilité f

agitated ['ædʒɪteɪtɪd] agité; **agitation** agitation f; **agitator** agitateur(-trice) m(f)

agnostic [æɡ'nɒstɪk] agnostique m/f

ago [ə'ɡoʊ]: **two days ~** il y a deux jours; **long ~** il y a longtemps

agonize ['æɡənaɪz] se tourmenter (**over** sur); **agonizing** (terrible); **agony** ['æɡənɪ] mental tourment m; physical grande douleur f

agree [ə'ɡriː] **1** v/i être d'accord; (of figures) s'accorder; (reach agreement) s'entendre **2** v/t price s'entendre sur; **agreeable** (pleasant) agréable; **agreement** accord m

agricultural [æɡrɪ'kʌltʃərəl] agricole; **agriculture** agri-

culture f

ahead [ə'hed] devant; **plan/ think ~** prévoir/penser à l'avance

aid [eɪd] **1** n aide f **2** v/t aider

aide [eɪd] aide m/f

Aids [eɪdz] sida m

ailing ['eɪlɪŋ] economy mal en point

ailment ['eɪlmənt] mal m

aim [eɪm] **1** n (objective) but m **2** v/i in shooting viser; **~ to do sth** essayer de faire qch **3** v/t: **be ~ed at** of remark viser; of gun être pointé sur; **aimless** ['eɪmlɪs] sans but

air [er] **1** n air m; **by ~** par avion; **in the open ~** en plein air **2** v/t room aérer; views exprimer; **airbag** airbag m; **air-conditioned** climatisé; **air-conditioning** climatisation f; **aircraft** avion m; **aircraft carrier** porte-avions m inv; **air force** armée f de l'air; **air hostess** hôtesse f de l'air; **airline** compagnie f aérienne; **airliner** avion m de ligne; **airmail: by ~** par avion; **airplane** avion m; **airport** aéroport m; **air terminal** aérogare f; **air-traffic controller** contrôleur(-euse) aérien(ne) m(f)

aisle [aɪl] in airplane couloir m; in theater allée f

ajar [ə'dʒɑːr]: **be ~** être entrouvert

alarm [ə'lɑːrm] **1** n (fear) inquiétude f; device alarme f;

(~ *clock*) réveil *m* 2 *v/t* alarmer; **alarming** alarmant; **alarmingly** de manière alarmante

album ['ælbəm] album *m*

alcohol ['ælkəhɒl] alcool *m*; **alcoholic** [ælkə'hɒlɪk] 1 *adj drink* alcoolisé 2 *n* alcoolique *m/f*

alert [ə'lɜːrt] 1 *adj* vigilant 2 *n* signal alerte *f* 3 *v/t* alerter

alibi ['ælɪbaɪ] alibi *m*

alien ['eɪliən] 1 *adj* étranger (**to** à) 2 *n* étranger-(ère) *m(f)*; *from space* extra-terrestre *m/f*; **alienate** s'aliéner

align [ə'laɪn] aligner

alike [ə'laɪk] 1 *adj*: **be** ~ se ressembler 2 *adv*: **old and young** ~ les vieux comme les jeunes

alimony ['ælɪmənɪ] pension alimentaire

alive [ə'laɪv]: **be** ~ être en vie

all [ɒːl] 1 *adj* tout 2 *pron* tout; ~ **of us/them** nous/eux tous; **he ate** ~ **of it** il l'a mangé en entier; **for** ~ **I know** pour autant que je sache; ~ **but him** (*except*) tous sauf lui 3 *adv*: ~ **at once** (*suddenly*) tout d'un coup; (*at the same time*) tous ensemble; ~ **but** (*nearly*) presque; ~ **the better** encore mieux; **they're not** ~ **alike** ils ne se ressemblent pas du tout; **not at** ~! pas du tout!; **two** ~ SP deux à deux

allegation [ælɪ'geɪʃn] allégation *f*; **allege** alléguer; **alleged** supposé; **allegedly**

he ~ **killed two women** il aurait assassiné deux femmes

allegiance [ə'liːdʒəns] loyauté *f* (**to** à)

allergic [ə'lɜːrdʒɪk] allergique (**to** à)

alleviate [ə'liːvɪeɪt] soulager

alley ['ælɪ] ruelle *f*

alliance [ə'laɪəns] alliance *f*

allocate ['æləkeɪt] assigner; **allocation** [ælə'keɪʃn] *action* assignation *f*; *amount allocated* part *f*

allot [ə'lɒt] assigner

allow [ə'laʊ] (*permit*) permettre; (*calculate for*) compter

◆ **allow for** prendre en compte

allowance [ə'laʊəns] *money* allocation *f*; (*pocket money*) argent *m* de poche

alloy ['ælɔɪ] alliage *m*

'all-purpose universel; *vehicle* tous usages; **all-round** général; *athlete* complet;

◆ **allude to** [ə'luːd] faire allusion à

alluring [ə'lʊrɪŋ] alléchant

all-wheel 'drive quatre roues motrices *fpl*; *vehicle* 4x4 *m*

ally ['ælaɪ] allié(e) *m(f)*

almond ['ɑːmənd] amande *f*

almost ['ɒːlmoʊst] presque

alone [ə'loʊn] seul

along [ə'lɒːŋ] 1 *prep* le long de; **walk** ~ **this path** prenez ce chemin 2 *adv*: **bring** ~ amener; ~ **with** in addition to ainsi que

alongside [əlɒːŋ'saɪd] paral-

lel to à côté de; *in coopera-*
tion with aux côtés de

aloof [ə'luːf] distant

aloud [ə'laud] à haute voix

alphabet ['ælfəbet] alphabet
m; **alphabetical** alphabéti-
que

already [ɔːl'redɪ] déjà

alright [ʊ,l'raɪt] (*permitted*)
permis; (*acceptable*) convenable; **be ~** (*in working or-*
der) fonctionner; **she's ~**
not hurt elle n'est pas blessée; **everything is ~** tout va
bien

altar ['ɔːltər] autel *m*

alter ['ɔːltər] changer; **alteration** modification *f*

alternate 1 ['ɔːltərneɪt] *v/i* alterner **2** ['ɔːltərnət] *adj*: **on ~**
Mondays un lundi sur deux

alternative [ɔːl'tɜːrnətɪv] **1**
adj alternatif **2** *n* alternative
f; **alternatively** sinon; *or ~* ou
bien

although [ɔːl'ðou] bien que
(*+subj*), quoique (*+subj*)

altitude ['æltɪtuːd] altitude *f*

altogether [ɔːltə'geðər]
(*completely*) totalement; (*in*
all) en tout

altruism ['æltruːɪzm] altruisme *m*; **altruistic** altruiste

aluminum [ə'luːmənəm] aluminium (*Br* **aluminium**
[æljʊ'mɪnɪəm] alu-
minium *m*

always ['ɔːlweɪz] toujours

a.m. ['eɪem] (= *ante meri-*
diem) du matin

amass [ə'mæs] amasser

amateur ['æməʃʊr] *sp* amateur *m/f*; **amateurish** *at-*
tempt d'amateur; *painter*
sans talent

amaze [ə'meɪz] étonner;
amazed étonné; **amaze-**
ment étonnement *m*;
amazing étonnant; (*very*
good) impressionnant;
amazingly étonnamment

ambassador [æm'bæsədər]
ambassadeur(-drice) *m(f)*

amber ['æmbər]: *at ~* à l'orange

ambience ['æmbɪəns] ambiance *f*

ambiguity [æmbɪ'gjuːətɪ]
ambiguïté *f*; **ambiguous**
ambigu

ambition [æm'bɪʃn] ambition
f; **ambitious** ambitieux

ambivalent [æm'bɪvələnt]
ambivalent

amble ['æmbl] déambuler

ambulance ['æmbjʊləns] ambulance *f*

ambush ['æmbʊʃ] **1** *n* embus-
cade *f* **2** *v/t* tendre une em-
buscade à

amend [ə'mend] modifier;
amendment modification *f*;
amends: *make ~* se racheter

amenities [ə'miːnɪtɪz] facili-
tés *fpl*

America [ə'merɪkə] (*United*
States) États-Unis *mpl*; *conti-*
nent Amérique *f*; **American**
1 *adj* américain **2** *n* Améri-
cain(e) *m(f)*

amicable ['æmɪkəbl] à l'amiable; **amicably** à l'amiable

ammunition [æmjʊ'nɪʃn] munitions *fpl*

amnesia [æm'niːzɪə] amnésie *f*

amnesty ['æmnəstɪ] amnistie *f*

among(st) [ə'mʌŋ(st)] parmi

amoral [eɪ'mɒrəl] amoral

amount [ə'maʊnt] quantité *f*; (*sum of money*) somme *f*

◆ **amount to** s'élever à; (*be equivalent to*) revenir à

amphibian [æm'fɪbɪən] amphibien *m*

ample ['æmpl] beaucoup de

amplifier ['æmplɪfaɪər] amplificateur *m*; **amplify** amplifier

amputate ['æmpjʊteɪt] amputer; **amputation** amputation *f*

amuse [ə'mjuːz] (*make laugh*) amuser; (*entertain*) distraire; **amusement** (*merriment*) amusement *m*; (*entertainment*) divertissement *m*; **amusement park** parc *m* d'attractions; **amusing** amusant

an [æn] → **a**

anaemia *etc* → **anemia** *etc*

anaesthetic *etc* → **anesthetic** *etc*

analog ['ænəlɒg] analogique; **analogy** analogie *f*

analysis [ə'næləsɪs] PSYCH analyse *f*; **analyst** PSYCH analyste *m/f*; **analytical** analytique; **analyze** *also* PSYCH analyser

lyser

anarchy ['ænərkɪ] anarchie *f*

ancestor ['ænsestər] ancêtre *m/f*

anchor ['æŋkər] **1** *n* NAUT ancre *f*; TV présentateur(-trice) principal(e) *m(f)* **2** *v/i* NAUT ancrer

ancient ['eɪnʃənt] ancien; *Rome etc* antique

and [ænd] et

anemia [ə'niːmɪə] anémie *f*; **anemic** anémique

anesthetic [ænəs'θetɪk] anesthésiant *m*

angel ['eɪndʒl] ange *m*

anger ['æŋgər] **1** *n* colère *f* **2** *v/t* mettre en colère

angle ['æŋgl] angle *m*

angry ['æŋgrɪ] *person* en colère; *mood, look* fâché

animal ['ænɪml] animal *m*

animated ['ænɪmeɪtɪd] animé; **animated cartoon** dessin *m* animé; **animation** animation *f*

animosity [ænɪ'mɒsətɪ] animosité *f*

ankle ['æŋkl] cheville *f*

annex ['æneks] **1** *n* annexe *f* **2** *v/t state* annexer

annihilate [ə'naɪəleɪt] anéantir; **annihilation** anéantissement *m*

anniversary [ænɪ'vɜːrsərɪ] anniversaire *m*

announce [ə'naʊns] annoncer; **announcement** annonce *f*; **announcer** [ə'naʊnsər] TV, RAD speaker *m*, speakrine

f

annoy [ə'nɔɪ] agacer; **annoyance** (*anger*) agacement *m*; (*nuisance*) désagrément *m*; **annoying** agaçant

annual ['ænjʊəl] annuel

annul [ə'nʌl] annuler; **annulment** annulation *f*

anonymous [ə'nɒ:nɪməs] anonyme

anorexia [ænə'reksɪə] anorexie *f*

another [ə'nʌðər] **1** *adj* autre **2** *pron* un(e) autre; **they know one** ~ ils se connaissent

answer ['ænsər] **1** *n* réponse *f*; (*solution*) solution *f* (**to** à) **2** *v/t* répondre à **3** *v/i* répondre; **answerphone** répondeur *m*

ant [ænt] fourmi *f*

antagonism [æn'tægənɪzm] antagonisme *m*; **antagonistic** hostile; **antagonize** provoquer

Antarctic [ænt'ɑ:rktɪk]: **the** ~ l'Antarctique *m*

antenatal [æntɪ'neɪtl] prénatal

antenna [æn'tenə] antenne *f*

antibiotic [æntɪbaɪ'ɒ:tɪk] antibiotique *m*

anticipate [æn'tɪsɪpeɪt] prévoir; **anticipation** prévision *f*

antics ['æntɪks] singeries *fpl*

antidote ['æntɪdoʊt] antidote *m*

antifreeze ['æntɪfri:z] antigel *m*

antipathy [æn'tɪpəθɪ] antipathie *f*

antiquated ['æntɪkweɪtɪd] antique

antique [æn'ti:k] antiquité *f*; **antiseptic** [æntaɪ'septɪk] **1** *adj* antiseptique **2** *n* antiseptique *m*

antisocial [æntaɪ'soʊʃl] asocial, antisocial

antivirus program [æntaɪ'vaɪrəs] COMPUT programme *m* antivirus

anxiety [æŋ'zaɪətɪ] inquiétude *f*; **anxious** inquiet; (*eager*) soucieux

any ['enɪ] **1** *adj*: **are there** ~ **glasses?** est-ce qu'il y a des verres?; **is there** ~ **bread/improvement?** est-ce qu'il y a du pain/une amélioration?; **there isn't/aren't** ~ ... il n'y a pas de ...; **have you** ~ **idea at all?** est-ce que vous avez une idée? **2** *pron*: ~? est-ce que vous en avez?; **there aren't/isn't** ~ **left** il n'y en a plus; ~ **of them could be guilty** ils pourraient tous être coupables

anybody ['enɪbɑ:dɪ] quelqu'un; *with negatives* personne; *no matter who* n'importe qui; **there wasn't** ~ **there** il n'y avait personne

anyhow ['enɪhaʊ] (*anyway*) enfin; (*in any way*) de quelque façon que ce soit

anyone ['enɪwʌn] → **anybody**

anything ['enɪθɪŋ] quelque chose; *with negatives* rien; *I didn't hear* ~ je n'ai rien entendu ~ *but* ... tout sauf ...

anyway ['enɪweɪ] → *anyhow*

anywhere ['enɪweər] quelque part; *with negatives* nulle part; *I can't find it* ~ je ne le trouve nulle part

apart [ə'pɑːrt] séparé; ~ *from* (*except*) à l'exception de; (*in addition to*) en plus de

apartment [ə'pɑːrtmənt] appartement *m*; **apartment block** immeuble *m*

ape [eɪp] singe *m*

aperitif [ə'perɪtiːf] apéritif *m*

apologize [ə'pɑːlədʒaɪz] s'excuser (*to s.o.* auprès de qn)

apology excuses *fpl*

appalling [ə'pɔːlɪŋ] scandaleux

apparatus [æpə'reɪtəs] appareils *mpl*

apparent [ə'pærənt] (*obvious*) évident; (*seeming*) apparent; **apparently** apparemment

appeal [ə'piːl] (*charm*) charme *m*; *for funds etc*, LAW appel *m*

♦ **appeal for** *calm etc* appeler à; *funds* demander

♦ **appeal to** (*be attractive to*) plaire à

appealing [ə'piːlɪŋ] séduisant

appear [ə'pɪr] apparaître; *in court* comparaître; (*seem*) paraître; ~ *to be* ... avoir l'air d'être ...; **appearance**

apparition *f*; *in court* comparution *f*; (*look*) apparence *f*

appendicitis [əpendɪ'saɪtɪs] appendicite *f*

appendix [ə'pendɪks] MED, *of book etc* appendice *m*

appetite ['æpɪtaɪt] appétit *m*; **appetizer** *to drink* apéritif *m*; *to eat* amuse-gueule *m*; **appetizing** appétissant

applaud [ə'plɔːd] applaudir; **applause** applaudissements *mpl*

apple ['æpl] pomme *f*

appliance [ə'plaɪəns] appareil *m*

applicable [ə'plɪkəbl] applicable; **applicant** *for job* candidat(e) *m(f)*; **application** *for job* candidature *f*; *for passport etc* demande *f*; **apply 1** *v/t* appliquer **2** *v/i* of *rule, law* s'appliquer

♦ **apply for** *job* poser sa candidature pour; *passport etc* faire une demande de

♦ **apply to** (*contact*) s'adresser à; *of rules etc* s'appliquer à

appoint [ə'pɔɪnt] *to position* nommer; **appointment** *to position* nomination *f*; (*meeting*) rendez-vous *m*

appraisal [ə'preɪzl] évaluation *f*

appreciable [ə'priːʃəbl] considérable; **appreciate 1** *v/t* apprécier; (*acknowledge*) reconnaître **2** *v/i* FIN s'apprécier; **appreciative** *grateful* reconnaissant; *understanding* approbateur; *audience* réceptif

apprehensive [æprɪ'hensɪv] appréhensif

approach [ə'prəʊtʃ] **1** *n* approche *f*; *(proposal)* proposition *f* **2** *v/t (get near to)* approcher; *(contact)* faire des propositions à; *problem* aborder; **approachable** *person* d'un abord facile

appropriate [ə'prəʊprɪət] approprié

approval [ə'pruːvl] approbation *f*; **approve** **1** *v/i* être d'accord **2** *v/t plan* approuver

approximate [ə'prɒksɪmət] approximatif; **approximately** approximativement

apricot ['eɪprɪkɑːt] abricot *m*

April ['eɪprəl] avril *m*

apt [æpt] *remark* pertinent; *aptitude* aptitude *f*

aquarium [ə'kweərɪəm] aquarium *m*

Arab ['ærəb] **1** *adj* arabe **2** *n* Arabe *m/f*; **Arabic 1** *adj* arabe **2** *n* arabe *m*

arbitrary ['ɑːrbɪtrəri] arbitraire

arbitrate ['ɑːrbɪtreɪt] arbitrer; **arbitration** arbitrage *m*

arch [ɑːrtʃ] voûte *f*

archaeology *etc* → **archeology** *etc*

archaic [ɑːr'keɪɪk] archaïque

archeological [ɑːrkɪə'lɑːdʒ-ɪkl] archéologique; **archeologist** archéologue *m/f*; **ar-**

cheology archéologie *f*

architect ['ɑːrkɪtekt] architecte *m/f*; **architectural** architectural; **architecture** architecture *f*

archives ['ɑːrkaɪvz] archives *fpl*

Arctic ['ɑːrktɪk]: **the ~** l'Arctique *m*

ardent ['ɔːrdənt] fervent

arduous ['ɑːrdʒʊəs] ardu

area ['erɪə] *of city* quartier *m*; *of country* région *f*; *of research* domaine *m*; *of room* surface *f*; GEOM, *of land* superficie *f*; **area code** TELEC indicatif *m* régional

arena [ə'riːnə] SP arène *f*

Argentina [ɑːrdʒən'tiːnə] Argentine *f*

Argentinian [ɑːrdʒən'tɪnɪən] **1** *adj* argentin **2** *n* Argentin(e) *m(f)*

arguably ['ɑːrgjʊəblɪ]: **it was ~** ... on peut dire que ...; **argue** *(quarrel)* se disputer; *(reason)* argumenter; **argument** *(quarrel)* dispute *f*; *(discussion)* discussion *f*; *(reasoning)* argument *m*

arid ['ærɪd] *land* aride

arise [ə'raɪz] *of situation* survenir

arithmetic [ə'rɪθmətɪk] arithmétique *f*

arm¹ [ɑːrm] *n* bras *m*

arm² [ɑːrm] *v/t* armer

armaments ['ɑːrməmənts] armes *fpl*

'armchair fauteuil *m*

armed [ɑːrmd] armé; **armed forces** forces fpl armées; **armed robbery** vol m à main armée

'armpit aisselle f

arms [ɑːrmz] (*weapons*) armes fpl

army ['ɑːrmi] armée f

around [ə'raʊnd] **1** prep (*encircling*) autour de; **it's ~ the corner** c'est juste à côté **2** adv (*in the area*) dans les parages; (*encircling*) autour; (*roughly*) à peu près; **with expressions of time** à environ

arouse [ə'raʊz] susciter; *sexually* exciter

arrange [ə'reɪndʒ] arranger; *furniture* disposer; *meeting etc* organiser; *time* fixer; *appointment* prendre; **I've ~d to meet her** j'ai prévu de la voir; **arrangement** (*agreement*), *music* arrangement m; *of furniture* disposition f; *flowers* composition f

arrears [ə'rɪərz] arriéré m

arrest [ə'rest] **1** n arrestation f; **be under ~** être en état d'arrestation **2** v/t arrêter

arrival [ə'raɪvl] arrivée f; **arrive** arriver

♦ **arrive at** arriver à

arrogance ['erəgəns] arrogance f; **arrogant** arrogant

arrow ['erəʊ] flèche f

arson ['ɑːrsn] incendie m criminel

art [ɑːrt] art m

artery ['ɑːrtəri] artère f

'art gallery galerie f d'art

arthritis [ɑːr'θraɪtɪs] arthrite f

artichoke ['ɑːrtɪtʃoʊk] artichaut m

article ['ɑːrtɪkl] article m

articulate [ɑːr'tɪkjʊlət] *person* qui s'exprime bien

artificial [ɑːrtɪ'fɪʃl] artificiel

artillery [ɑːr'tɪləri] artillerie f

artist ['ɑːrtɪst] artiste m/f; **artistic** artistique

'arts degree licence f de lettres

as [æz] **1** conj (*while, when*) alors que; (*because*) comme; (*like*) comme; **~ if** comme si; **~ usual** comme d'habitude **2** adv: **~ high ...** aussi haut que ...; **~ much ~ that?** autant que ça?; **~ soon ~ possible** aussi vite que possible **3** prep comme; **work ~ a teacher** travailler comme professeur; **~ for** quant à; **~ from** or **of Monday** à partir de lundi

ash [æʃ] cendres fpl

ashamed [ə'ʃeɪmd] honteux; **be ~ of** avoir honte de

'ash can poubelle f

ashore [ə'ʃɔːr] à terre; **go ~** débarquer

ashtray ['æʃtreɪ] cendrier m

Asia ['eɪʃə] Asie f; **Asian 1** adj asiatique **2** n Asiatique m/f; **Asian-American 1** adj; Asian **2** n Américain(e) m(f) d'origine asiatique que **2** n Américain(e) m(f) d'origine asiatique

aside [ə'saɪd] de côté; **move ~**

please poussez-vous, s'il vous plaît; **take s.o.** ~ prendre qn à part; ~ **from s.o.** demander qch à qn

ask [æsk] demander; *question* poser; (*invite*) inviter; ~ **s.o. for sth** demander qch à qn

♦ **ask after** *person* demander des nouvelles de

♦ **ask for** demander; *person* demander à parler à

♦ **ask out**: **he's asked me out** il m'a demandé de sortir avec lui

asleep [ə'sliːp]: **be (fast)** ~ être (bien) endormi; **fall** ~ s'endormir

asparagus [ə'spærəgəs] asperges *fpl*

aspect ['æspekt] aspect *m*

aspirations [æspə'reɪʃnz] aspirations *fpl*

aspirin ['æsprɪn] aspirine *f*

ass¹ [æs] (*idiot*) idiot(e) *m(f)*

ass² [æs] (*butt*) cul *m*

assassin [ə'sæsɪn] assassin *m*; **assassinate** assassiner

assassination assassinat *m*

assault [ə'sɔːlt] **1** *n* agression *f*; MIL attaque *f* (**on** contre) **2** *v/t* agresser

assemble [ə'sembl] **1** *v/t parts* assembler **2** *v/i of people* se rassembler; **assembly** POL assemblée *f*; *of parts* assemblage *m*; **assembly line** chaîne *f* de montage

assent [ə'sent] consentir

assertive [ə'sɜːrtɪv] *person* assuré

assess [ə'ses] *situation* éva-

luer; *value* estimer; **assessment** *of situation* évaluation *f*; *of value* estimation *f*

asset ['æset] FIN actif *m*; atout *m*

assign [ə'saɪn] assigner; **assignment** mission *f*; EDU devoir *m*

assimilate [ə'sɪmɪleɪt] assimiler

assist [ə'sɪst] aider; **assistance** aide *f*; **assistant** assistant(e) *m(f)*; **assistant manager** sous-directeur *m*, sous-directrice *f*; **assistant** *of department* assistant(e) *m(f)* du/de la responsable

associate **1** *v/t* [ə'souʃɪeɪt] associer **2** *n* [ə'souʃɪət] (*colleague*) collègue *m/f*; **association** association *f*

assortment [ə'sɔːrtmənt] assortiment *m*

assume [ə'suːm] (*suppose*) supposer; **assumption** supposition *f*

assurance [ə'ʃuːrəns] (*reassurance, confidence*) assurance *f*; **assure** (*reassure*) assurer

asthma ['æsmə] asthme *m*

astonish [ə'stɑːnɪʃ] étonner; **astonishing** étonnant; **astonishment** étonnement *m*

astound [ə'staund] stupéfier

astride [ə'straɪd] à califourchon sur

astrology [ə'strɑːlədʒɪ] astrologie *f*

astronaut ['æstrənɔːt] astronaute *m/f*

astronomer [ə'strɑːnəmər] astronome *m/f*; **astronomical** *price etc* astronomique; **astronomy** astronomie *f*

astute [ə'stuːt] fin

asylum [ə'saɪləm] *political,* *(mental* ~*)* asile *m*

at [æt] *with places* à; ~ *Joe's* chez Joe; ~ *10 dollars* au prix de 10 dollars; ~ *the age of 18* à l'âge de 18 ans; ~ *5 o'clock* à 5 heures; *be good/bad* ~ *...* être bon/mauvais en ...

atheist ['eɪθɪɪst] athée *m/f*

athlete ['æθliːt] athlète *m/f*; **athletic** d'athlétisme; *(strong,* *sporting)* sportif; **athletics** athlétisme *m*

Atlantic [ət'læntɪk]: *the* ~ l'Atlantique *m*

atlas ['ætləs] atlas *m*

ATM [eɪtiː'em](= *automatic teller machine*) distributeur *m* automatique (de billets)

atmosphere ['ætməsfɪr] atmosphère *f*

atom ['ætəm] atome *m*; **atomic** atomique

◆ **atone for** [ə'toun] racheter

atrocious [ə'trouʃəs] atroce; **atrocity** atrocité *f*

at-'seat TV *télévision que l'on regarde à sa place, par exemple en avion*

attach [ə'tæʧ] attacher; **attachment** *to e-mail* fichier *m* joint

attack [ə'tæk] **1** *n* attaque *f* **2** *v/t* attaquer

attempt [ə'tempt] **1** *n* tentative *f* **2** *v/t* essayer

attend [ə'tend] assister à; *school* aller à

◆ **attend to** s'occuper de

attendance [ə'tendəns] présence *f*; **attendant** *in museum etc* gardien(ne) *m(f)*

attention [ə'tenʃn] attention *f*; *pay* ~ faire attention; **attentive** attentif

attic ['ætɪk] grenier *m*

attitude ['ætɪtuːd] attitude *f*

attorney [ə'tɜːrnɪ] avocat *m*

attract [ə'trækt] attirer; **attraction** *of job, doing sth* attrait *m*; *romantic* attirance *f*; *touristic* attraction *f*; **attractive** *person* attirant; *idea, city* attrayant

auction ['ɔːkʃn] vente *f* aux enchères

audacity [ɔː'dæsətɪ] audace *f*

audible ['ɔːdəbl] audible

audience ['ɔːdɪəns] public *m*

audio ['ɔːdɪoʊ] audio; **audio-visual** audiovisuel

audit ['ɔːdɪt] **1** *n* audit *m* **2** *v/t* contrôler; *course* suivre en auditeur libre

audition [ɔː'dɪʃn] **1** *n* audition *f* **2** *v/i* passer une audition

auditor ['ɔːdɪtər] FIN auditeur(-trice) *m(f)*

auditorium [ɔːdɪ'tɔːrɪəm] *of theater etc* auditorium *m*

August ['ɔːgəst] août *m*

aunt [ænt] tante *f*

au pair [oʊ'per] jeune fille *f* au pair

aura ['ɔːrə] aura f

auspicious [ɔː'spɪʃəs] favorable

austere [ɔː'stɪər] austère; **austerity** austérité f

Australia [ɒ'streɪljə] Australie f; **Australian 1** adj australien **2** n Australien(ne) m(f)

Austria ['ɒstrɪə] Autriche f; **Austrian 1** adj autrichien **2** n Autrichien(ne) m(f)

authentic [ɔː'θentɪk] authentique; **authenticity** authenticité f

author ['ɔːθər] auteur m

authoritarian [əθɔːrɪ'terɪən] autoritaire; **authoritative** source qui fait autorité; person, manner autoritaire; **authority** [ɔː'θɒrətɪ] autorité f; (permission) autorisation f; **authorization** autorisation f; **authorize** autoriser

autistic [ɔː'tɪstɪk] autiste

autobiography [ɔːtəbaɪ'ɒɡrəfɪ] autobiographie f

autocratic [ɒtə'krætɪk] autocratique

autograph ['ɔːtəɡræf] autographe m

automate ['ɔːtəmeɪt] automatiser; **automatic 1** adj automatique **2** n car automatique f; gun automatique m; **automatically** automatiquement; **automation** automatisation f

automobile ['ɔːtəmbiːl] automobile f; **automobile**

industry industrie f automobile

autonomous [ɔː'tɒnəməs] autonome

autopilot ['ɔːtoupaɪlət] pilotage m automatique

autopsy ['ɔːtɑːpsɪ] autopsie f

autumn ['ɔːtəm] Br automne m

auxiliary [ɔːɡ'zɪljərɪ] auxiliaire

available [ə'veɪləbl] disponible

avalanche ['ævəlænʃ] avalanche f

avenue ['ævənuː] avenue f; **explore all ~s** explorer toutes les possibilités

average ['ævərɪdʒ] **1** adj moyen **2** n moyenne f; **on ~** en moyenne

◆ **average out at** faire une moyenne de

averse [ə'vɜːrs]: **not be ~ to** ne rien avoir contre; **aversion** aversion f (**to** pour)

avid ['ævɪd] avide

avocado [ɑːvə'kɑːdou] avocat m

avoid [ə'vɔɪd] éviter

await [ə'weɪt] attendre

awake [ə'weɪk] éveillé; **it's keeping me ~** ça m'empêche de dormir

award [ə'wɔːrd] **1** n (prize) prix m **2** v/t décerner; damages attribuer; **awards ceremony** cérémonie f de remise des prix; EDU cérémonie f de remise des diplômes

aware [ə'wer]: **be ~ of sth**
avoir conscience de qch; **become ~ of sth** prendre conscience de qch; **awareness**
conscience *f*

away [ə'weɪ]: **be ~** être absent,
ne pas être là; **walk ~** s'en aller; **look ~** tourner la tête;
it's 2 miles ~ c'est à 2 miles
d'ici; **take sth ~ from s.o.**
enlever qch à qn; **away
game** SP match *m* à l'extérieur

awesome ['ɔːsəm] F (*terrific*)
super *inv*

awful ['ɔːfəl] affreux

awkward ['ɔːkwərd] (*clumsy*)
maladroit; (*difficult*) difficile; (*embarrassing*) gênant;
feel ~ se sentir mal à l'aise

ax, *Br* axe [æks] **1** *n* hache *f* **2**
v/t *project* abandonner;
budget faire des coupures
dans; *job* supprimer

axle ['æksl] essieu *m*

B

baby ['beɪbɪ] bébé *m*; **baby-
-sit** faire du baby-sitting

bachelor ['bætʃələr] célibataire *m*

'back [bæk] **1** *n of person,
clothes* dos *m*; *of chair* dossier *m*; *of drawer* fond *m*;
of house arrière *m*; SP arrière
m; **in ~ (of the car)** à l'arrière
(de la voiture); **at the ~ of the
book** à la fin du livre; **~ to
front** à l'envers **2** *adj* dos
de derrière; *wheels, legs* arrière *inv* **3** *adv*: **move ~** reculer; **give sth ~ to s.o.** rendre qch à qn; **she'll be ~ tomorrow** elle sera de retour
demain **4** *v/t* (*support*) soutenir; *car* faire reculer; *horse*
miser sur

◆ **back down** faire marche
arrière

◆ **back out** *of commitment* se

dégager

◆ **back up** *v/t* (*support*) soutenir; *file* sauvegarder **2** *v/i in
car* reculer

'backache mal *m* de dos;
backbone colonne *f* vertébrale; **backdate** antidater;
backdoor porte *f* arrière;
backer bailleur *m* de fonds;
for artist, show producteur
(-trice) *m(f)*; **background**
of picture arrière-plan *m*; *social* milieu *m*; *of crime* contexte *m*; **his work ~** son expérience professionnelle;
backhand *in tennis* revers
m; **backing** (*support*) soutien
m; MUS accompagnement *m*;
backing group groupe *m*
d'accompagnement; **back-
lash** répercussion *f* *(pl)*;
backlog retard *m* (*of* dans);
backpack sac *m* à dos; **back-**

packer randonneur(-euse) *m(f)*; **back seat** siège *m* arrière; **back streets** petites rues *fpl*; *poor area* quartiers *mpl* pauvres; **backstroke** sp dos *m* crawlé; **backtrack** retourner sur ses pas; **backup** *(support)* renfort *m*; COMPUT copie *f* de sauvegarde; **back-yard** arrière-cour *f*

bacon ['beɪkn] bacon *m*

bacteria [bæk'tɪrɪə] bactéries *fpl*

bad [bæd] mauvais; *person* méchant; *(rotten)* avarié; **go ~** s'avarier; **it's not ~** c'est pas mal; **that's really too ~** *(shame)* c'est vraiment dommage

badge [bædʒ] insigne *f*

bad language grossièretés *fpl*; **badly** mal; *injured* grièvement; *damaged* sérieusement; **he ~ needs ...** il a grand besoin de ...

badminton ['bædmɪntən] badminton *m*

bad-tempered [bæd'tempərd] de mauvaise humeur

baffle ['bæfl] déconcerter; **be ~d** être perplexe

bag [bæg] sac *m*; *(piece of baggage)* bagage *m*

baggage ['bægɪdʒ] bagages *mpl*; **baggage check** contrôle *m* des bagages

baggy ['bægɪ] flottant; *fashionably* large

bail [beɪl] LAW caution *f*; **be**

out on ~ être en liberté provisoire sous caution

bait [beɪt] appât *m*

bake [beɪk] cuire au four; **baked potato** pomme *f* de terre au four; **baker** boulanger(-ère) *m(f)*; **bakery** boulangerie *f*

balance ['bæləns] **1** *n* équilibre *m*; *(remainder)* reste *m*; *of bank account* solde *m* **2** *v/t* mettre en équilibre **3** *v/i* rester en équilibre; *of accounts* s'équilibrer; **balanced** *(fair)* objectif; *diet, personality* équilibré; **balance sheet** bilan *m*

balcony ['bælkənɪ] balcon *m*

bald [bɔːld] chauve; **balding** qui commence à devenir chauve

ball [bɔːl] *for soccer etc* ballon *m*; *for tennis, golf* balle *f*

ballad ['bæləd] ballade *f*

ballet ['bæleɪ] ballet *m*; **ballet dancer** danceur(-euse) *m(f)* de ballet

'ball game match *m* de baseball

ballistic missile [bə'lɪstɪk] missile *m* balistique

balloon [bə'luːn] *child's* ballon *m*; *for flight* montgolfière *f*

ballot ['bælət] **1** *n* vote *m* **2** *v/t members* faire voter; **ballot box** urne *f*

'ballpark terrain *m* de baseball; **ballpark figure** chiffre *m* en gros; **ballpoint (pen)**

barrel

stylo *m* bille
balls [bɔːlz] V couilles *fpl*
bamboo [bæm'buː] bambou *m*
ban [bæn] **1** *n* interdiction *f* **2** *v/t* interdire
banal [bə'næl] banal
banana [bə'nɑːnə] banane *f*
band [bænd] MUS orchestre *m*; *pop* groupe *m*; *of material* bande *f*
bandage ['bændɪdʒ] **1** *n* bandage *m* **2** *v/t* faire un bandage à
'Band-Aid® sparadrap *m*
bandit ['bændɪt] bandit *m*
bandy ['bændɪ] *legs* arqué
bang [bæŋ] **1** *n noise* boum *m*; (*blow*) coup *m* **2** *v/t door* claquer; (*hit*) taper
bangle ['bæŋgl] bracelet *m*
bangs [bæŋz] frange *f*
banisters ['bænɪstərz] rampe *f*
banjo ['bændʒou] banjo *m*
bank[1] [bæŋk] *of river* bord *m*, rive *f*
bank[2] [bæŋk] FIN banque *f*
♦ **bank on** compter sur
'bank account compte *m* en banque; **banker** banquier (-ière) *m(f)*; **banker's card** carte *f* d'identité bancaire; **banking** banque *f*; **bank loan** emprunt *m* bancaire; **bank manager**2 directeur (-trice) *m(f)* de banque; **bank rate** taux *m* bancaire; **bankroll** financer; **bankrupt: go ~** faire faillite;

bankruptcy faillite *f*
banner ['bænər] bannière *f*
banquet ['bæŋkwɪt] banquet *m*
baptism ['bæptɪzm] baptême *m*; **baptize** baptiser
bar[1] [bɑːr] *of iron, chocolate* barre *f*; *for drinks, counter* bar *m*
bar[2] [bɑːr] *v/t* exclure
barbaric [bɑːr'bærɪk] barbare
barbecue ['bɑːrbɪkjuː] **1** *n* barbecue *m* **2** *v/t* cuire au barbecue
barbed 'wire [bɑːrbd] fil *m* barbelé
barber ['bɑːrbər] coiffeur *m*
'bar code code *m* barre
bare [ber] *room, shelves* vide; *barefoot:* **be ~** être pieds nus; **bare-headed** tête nue; **barely** à peine
bargain ['bɑːrgɪn] **1** *n* (*deal*) marché *m* (*good buy*) bonne affaire *f* **2** *v/i* marchander
barge [bɑːrdʒ] NAUT péniche *f*
♦ **barge into** se heurter contre; (*enter noisily*) faire irruption dans
baritone ['bærɪtoun] baryton *m*
bark[1] [bɑːrk] **1** *n of dog* aboiement *m* **2** *v/i* aboyer
bark[2] [bɑːrk] *of tree* écorce *f*
barn [bɑːrn] grange *f*
barometer [bə'rɑːmɪtər] *also fig* baromètre *m*
barracks ['bærəks] MIL caserne *f*
barrel ['bærəl] tonneau *m*

barren ['bærən] *land* stérile

barrette [bə'ret] barrette *f*

barricade [bærı'keıd] barricade *f*

barrier ['bærıər] barrière *f*

'bar tender barman *m*, barmaid *f*

barter ['bɑːrtər] **1** *n* troc *m* **2** *v/t* troquer (*for* contre)

base [beıs] **1** *n* base *f* **2** *v/t* baser (*on* sur); **baseball** baseball *m*; *ball* ballon *m* de baseball; **baseball cap** casquette *f* de baseball; **baseboard** plinthe *f*; **basement** sous-sol *m*

basic ['beısık] (*rudimentary*) rudimentaire; (*fundamental*), *salary* de base; **basically** au fond

basin ['beısn] *for washing dishes* bassine *f*; *in bathroom* lavabo *m*

basis ['beısıs] base *f*; *of argument* fondement *m*

bask [bæsk] se dorer

basket ['bæskıt] panier *m*; **basketball** *game* basket (-ball) *m*; *ball* ballon *m* de basket

bass [beıs] base *f*; **double ~**, contrebasse *f*; **~ guitar** basse *f*

bastard ['bæstərd] salaud(e) *m(f)*

bat¹ [bæt] **1** *n for baseball* batte *f*; *for table tennis* raquette *f* **2** *v/i in baseball* batter

bat² [bæt] *animal* chauve-souris *f*

batch [bætʃ] *of students, data* lot *m*; *of bread* fournée *f*

bath [bæθ] (*~tub*) baignoire *f*

bathe [beıð] (*have a bath*) se baigner

bathrobe peignoir *m*; **bathroom** salle *f* de bains, *toilet* toilettes *fpl*; **bath towel** serviette *f* de bain; **bathtub** baignoire *f*

batter ['bætər] *for cakes, pancakes etc* pâte *f* lisse; *in baseball* batteur *m*; **battered** *wife, children* battu

battery ['bætərı] pile *f*; MOT batterie *f*

battle ['bætl] **1** *n* bataille *f*; *fig* lutte *f* **2** *v/i against illness etc* se battre, lutter; **battleship** cuirassé *m*

bawl [bɔːl] (*shout, weep*) brailler

bay [beı] (*inlet*) baie *f*

BC [biː'siː] (= *before Christ*) av. J.-C.

be [biː] ◇ être; **~ 15** avoir 15 ans; *it's me* c'est moi; *how much is...?* combien coûte ...?; *there is/are* il y a; *how are you?* comment ça va?
◇ *has the mailman been?* est-ce que le facteur est passé?; *I've never been to Japan* je ne suis jamais allé au Japon
◇ *tags: that's right, isn't it?* c'est juste, n'est-ce pas?; *she's American, isn't she?* elle est américaine, n'est-ce pas?

◇ *passive*: **he was killed** il a été tué; **it hasn't been decided** on n'a encore rien décidé
beach [biːtʃ] plage *f*; **beachwear** vêtements *mpl* de plage
beads [biːdz] collier *m* de perles
beak [biːk] bec *m*
beam [biːm] **1** *n* in ceiling etc poutre *f* **2** *v/i* (smile) rayonner
bean [biːn] haricot *m*; of coffee grain *m*
bear[1] [ber] *n* animal ours *m*
bear[2] [ber] **1** *v/t* weight porter; costs prendre en charge; (tolerate) supporter; **bearable** supportable
beard [bɪrd] barbe *f*
beat [biːt] **1** *n* of heart battement *m*; of music mesure *f* **2** *v/i* of heart battre; of rain s'abattre **3** *v/t* in competition, (hit) battre; (pound) frapper
◆ **beat up** tabasser
beaten [ˈbiːtən]: **off the ~ track** à l'écart; **beating** *physical* raclée *f*; **beat-up** déglingué
beautiful [ˈbjuːtəful] beau; **beautifully** admirablement; **beauty** beauté *f*
beaver [ˈbiːvər] castor *m*
because [bɪˈkɑːz] parce que; **~ of** à cause de
become [bɪˈkʌm] devenir; **what's ~ of her?** qu'est-elle devenue?; **becoming** seyant
bed [bed] *also of sea* lit *m*; of

flowers parterre *m*; **go to ~** aller se coucher; **bedding** literie *f*; **bedridden** cloué au lit; **bedroom** chambre *f* (à coucher); **bedtime** heure *f* du coucher
bee [biː] abeille *f*
beech [biːtʃ] hêtre *m*
beef [biːf] bœuf *m*; **beefburger** steak *m* haché
beep [biːp] **1** *n* bip *m* **2** *v/i* faire bip
beer [bɪr] bière *f*
beet [biːt] betterave *f*
beetle [ˈbiːtl] coléoptère *m*, cafard *m*
before [bɪˈfɔːr] **1** *prep* avant; **~ signing it** avant de le signer; **~ a vowel** devant une voyelle **2** *adv* auparavant; (already) déjà; **the week/day ~** la semaine/le jour d'avant **3** *conj* avant que (+*subj*); **I had a coffee ~ I left** j'ai pris un café avant de partir; **beforehand** à l'avance
befriend [bɪˈfrend] se lier d'amitié avec
beg [beg] **1** *v/i* mendier **2** *v/t*: **~ s.o. to do sth** prier qn de faire qch; **beggar** mendiant (e) *m (f)*
begin [bɪˈgɪn] **1** *v/i* commencer; **beginner** débutant(e) *m(f)*; **beginning** début *m*
behalf [bɪˈhɑːf]: **in or on ~ of** de la part de
behave [bɪˈheɪv] se comporter; **~ (yourself)!** sois sage!; **behavior**, *Br* **behaviour**

comportement m

behind [bɪ'haɪnd] **1** prep derrière; **be ~ ...** (responsible for, support) être derrière ... **2** adv (at the back) à l'arrière; leave, stay derrière; **be ~** in match être derrière

beige [beɪʒ] beige

being ['biːɪŋ] (creature) être m; (existence) existence f

belated [bɪ'leɪtɪd] tardif

belch [beltʃ] **1** n éructation f, rot m **2** v/i éructer, roter

Belgian ['beldʒən] **1** adj belge **2** n Belge m/f; **Belgium** Belgique f

belief [bɪ'liːf] conviction f; REL also croyance f; in person foi f (in en); **believe** croire
◆ **believe in** God, person croire en; sth croire; cacher la vérité aux gens

believer [bɪ'liːvər] in God croyant(e) m(f); in sth partisan(e) m(f) (in de)

bell [bel] on bike, door sonnette f; in church cloche f; in school: electric sonnerie f; **bellhop** groom m

belligerent [bɪ'lɪdʒərənt] belligérant

bellow ['beloʊ] brailler; of bull beugler

belly ['belɪ] of person ventre m; fat bedaine f; of animal panse f
◆ **belong to** of object appartenir à; club, organization faire partie de

belongings [bɪ'lɔːŋɪŋz] affai-

res fpl

beloved [bɪ'lʌvɪd] bien-aimé

below [bɪ'loʊ] **1** prep au-dessous de **2** adv en bas, au-dessous; in text en bas; **10 degrees ~** moins dix

belt [belt] ceinture f

benchmark référence f

bend [bend] **1** n tournant m **2** v/t head baisser; arm, knees plier; metal, plastic tordre **3** v/i of road tourner; of person se pencher
◆ **bend down** se pencher

beneath [bɪ'niːθ] **1** prep sous **2** adv (au-)dessous

benefactor ['benɪfæktər] bienfaiteur(-trice) m(f)

beneficial [benɪ'fɪʃl] bénéfique

benefit ['benɪfɪt] **1** n bénéfice m **2** v/t bénéficier à **3** v/i bénéficier (**from** de)

benevolent [bɪ'nevələnt] bienveillant

benign [bɪ'naɪn] doux; MED bénin

bequeath [bɪ'kwiːð] léguer; **bequest** legs m

beret ['bereɪ] béret m

berry ['berɪ] baie f

berth [bɜːrθ] couchette f; for ship mouillage m

beside [bɪ'saɪd] à côté de; **be ~ o.s.** être hors de soi; **that's ~ the point** c'est hors de propos

besides [bɪ'saɪdz] **1** adv d'ailleurs **2** prep (apart from) à part

best [best] **1** *adj* meilleur **2**
   adv le mieux; **I like her ~**
   c'est elle que j'aime le plus
   3 *n*: **do one's ~** faire de son
   mieux; **the ~** le mien, mien-
   (ne) *m(f)*; **the ~** *(outstanding thing or person)* le (la) meilleur(e)
   m(f); **all the ~!** meilleurs
   vœux!; **best before date** date *f* limite de consommation;
   best man *at wedding* garçon
   m d'honneur

bet [bet] **1** *n* pari *m* **2** *v/t & v/i*
   parier; **you ~!** évidemment!

betray [bɪ'treɪ] trahir; **betrayal** trahison *f*

better ['betər] **1** *adj* meilleur;
   get ~ s'améliorer; **he's ~ in**
   health il va mieux **2** *adv*
   mieux; **I'd really ~not** je ne
   devrais vraiment pas; **I like**
   her ~ je l'aime plus; **better-
   -off** *(richer)* plus aisé

between [bɪ'twiːn] entre

beware [bɪ'wer]: **~ of** attention à

bewilder [bɪ'wɪldər] confondre; **bewilderment** confusion *f*

beyond [bɪ'jɑːnd] au-delà de

bias ['baɪəs] parti *m* pris, préjugé *m*; **bias(s)ed** partial,
   subjectif

Bible ['baɪbl] Bible *f*; **biblical**
   biblique

bicentennial [baɪsen'teniəl]
   bicentenaire *m*

bicker ['bɪkər] se chamailler

bicycle ['baɪsɪkl] bicyclette *f*

bid [bɪd] **1** *n* *at auction* enchè-

re *m*; *(attempt)* tentative *f*; *in*
   takeover offre *f* **2** *v/i at auc-*
   tion faire une enchère; **bid-**
   der enchérisseur(-euse) *m(f)*

biennial [baɪ'enɪəl] biennal

big [bɪg] **1** *adj* grand; *sum of*
   money, mistake gros; **my ~**
   brother/sister mon grand
   frère/ma grande sœur **2**
   adv: **~ talk** se vanter

bigamist ['bɪɡəmɪst] bigame
   m(f)

'bighead crâneur(-euse) *m(f)*

bigot ['bɪɡət] fanatique *m/f*,
   sectaire *m/f*

bike [baɪk] vélo *m*; *(motor-*
   bike) moto *f*; **biker** ['baɪkər]
   motard(e) *m(f)*

bikini [bɪ'kiːnɪ] bikini *m*

bilingual [baɪ'lɪŋgwəl] bilingue

bill [bɪl] facture *f*; *money* billet
   m (de banque); POL projet *m*
   de loi; *(poster)* affiche *f*; **bill-
   board** panneau *m* d'affichage; **billfold** portefeuille *m*

billion ['bɪljən] milliard *m*

bin [bɪn] *for storage* boîte *f*

bind [baɪnd] *(connect)* unir;
   (tie) attacher; LAW *(oblige)*
   obliger; **binding** *agreement*
   obligatoire

binoculars [bɪ'nɑːkjʊlərz] jumelles *fpl*

biodegradable [baɪoʊdɪ-
   'greɪdəbl] biodégradable

biographer [baɪ'ɑːɡrəfər]
   biographe *m/f*; **biography**
   biographie *f*

biological [baɪoʊ'lɑːdʒɪkl]

biologique; **biology** biologie f

bird [bɜːrd] oiseau m

biro® ['baɪrəʊ] *Br* stylo m bille

birth [bɜːrθ] naissance f; (*labor*) accouchement m; **give ~ to** child donner naissance à; **date of ~** date f de naissance; **birth certificate** acte m de naissance; **birth control** contrôle m des naissances; **birthday** anniversaire m **happy ~!** bon anniversaire!

biscuit ['bɪskɪt] biscuit m

bisexual ['baɪseksjʊəl] **1** *adj* bisexuel **2** n bisexuel(le) m(f)

bishop ['bɪʃəp] évêque m

bit [bɪt] (*piece*) morceau m; (*part: of book*) passage m; (*part: of garden, road*) partie f; COMPUT bit m; **a ~ of** (*a little*) un peu de

bitch [bɪtʃ] **1** n dog chienne f; F: woman garce f **2** v/i F (*complain*) rouspéter

bite [baɪt] **1** n of dog, snake morsure f; of flea, mosquito piqûre f; of food morceau m **2** v/t & v/i of dog, snake, person mordre; of flea, mosquito piquer

bitter ['bɪtər] taste, person amer

black [blæk] **1** *adj* noir; tea nature; future sombre **2** n color noir m; person Noir(e) m(f)

♦ **black out** (*faint*) s'évanouir

'**blackboard** tableau m noir;

black **coffee** café m noir; black **economy** économie f souterraine; black **eye** œil m poché; **blacklist** liste f noire; **blackmail** n chantage m **2** v/t faire chanter; black **market** marché m noir; **blackness** noirceur f; black**out** ELEC panne f d'électricité; MED évanouissement m

bladder ['blædər] vessie f

blade [bleɪd] of knife lame f; of propeller ailette f; of grass brin m

blame [bleɪm] **1** n responsabilité f v/t: **~ s.o. for sth** reprocher qch à qn

bland [blænd] fade

blank [blæŋk] **1** *adj* paper, tape vierge; look vide **2** n (*empty space*) espace m vide; blank **check**, *Br* blank **cheque** chèque m en blanc

blanket ['blæŋkɪt] couverture f

blast [blæst] **1** n (*explosion*) explosion f; (*gust*) rafale f **2** v/t tunnel etc percer (à l'aide d'explosifs); **~!** mince!; blast**-off** lancement m

blatant ['bleɪtənt] flagrant; person éhonté

blaze [bleɪz] **1** n (*fire*) incendie m **2** v/i of fire flamber

blazer ['bleɪzər] blazer m

bleach [bliːtʃ] n for clothes eau f de Javel; for hair décolorant m **2** v/t for hair décolorer

bleak [bliːk] countryside désolé; weather morne; future

sombre

bleary-eyed ['blɪrɪaɪd] aux yeux troubles

bleat [bliːt] *of sheep* bêler

bleed [bliːd] saigner; **bleeding** saignement *m*

bleep [bliːp] **1** *n* bip *m* **2** *v/i* faire bip

blemish ['blemɪʃ] tache *f*

blend [blend] **1** *n* mélange *m* **2** *v/t* mélanger; **blender** *machine* mixeur *m*

bless [bles] bénir; **~** *you!* *in response to sneeze* à vos souhaits!; **blessing** bénédiction *f*

blind [blaɪnd] **1** *adj* aveugle; **~ corner** virage *m* masqué **2** *v/t of sun* aveugler; **blind alley** impasse *f*; **blind date** rendez-vous *m* arrangé; **blindfold 1** *n* bandeau *m* sur les yeux **2** *v/t* bander les yeux à; **blinding** *light* aveuglant; *headache* terrible; **blindly** sans rien voir; *fig* aveuglément; **blind spot** *in road* angle *m* mort

blink [blɪŋk] *of person* cligner des yeux; *of light* clignoter

blizzard ['blɪzərd] tempête *f* de neige

bloc [blɑːk] POL bloc *m*

block [blɑːk] **1** *n* bloc *m*; *buildings* pâté *m* de maisons; *(blockage)* obstruction *f m*; *it's three ~s away* c'est à trois rues d'ici **2** *v/t* bloquer; **blockage** obstruction *f*; **blockbuster** *movie* film *m*

à grand succès; *novel* roman *m* à succès; **block letters** capitales *fpl*

blond [blɑːnd] blond; **blonde** *woman* blonde *f*

blood [blʌd] sang *m*; **blood donor** donneur(-euse) *m(f)* de sang; **blood group** groupe *m* sanguin

'blood poisoning empoisonnement *m* du sang; **blood pressure** tension *f* (artérielle); **blood sample** prélèvement *m* sanguin; **bloodshed** carnage *m*; **without ~** sans effusion de sang; **bloodshot** injecté de sang; **bloodstained** taché de sang; **blood test** *m* sanguin; **bloodthirsty** sanguinaire

bloom [bluːm] *also fig* fleurir

blossom ['blɑːsəm] **1** *n* fleur *f* **2** *v/i* fleurir; *fig* s'épanouir

blot [blɑːt] tache *f*

◆ **blot out** effacer

blouse [blauz] chemisier *m*

blow[1] [bloʊ] *n also fig* coup *m*

blow[2] [bloʊ] **1** *v/t* souffler; **~ one's whistle** donner un coup de sifflet **2** *v/i of wind, person* souffler; *of whistle* retentir; *of fuse* sauter; *of tire* éclater

◆ **blow out 1** *v/t candle* souffler **2** *v/i of candle* s'éteindre

◆ **blow over 1** *v/t* renverser **2** *v/i* se renverser; *(pass)* passer

◆ **blow up 1** *v/t with explosives* faire sauter; *balloon* gonfler; *photograph* agrandir **2** *v/i* of boiler etc sauter, exploser

'**blow-dry** sécher (au sèche-cheveux); **blow-out** of tire éclatement *m*; **blue** [bluː] bleu; *movie* porno; **blueberry** myrtille *f*; **blue chip** de premier ordre; **blues** MUS blues *m*; **have the ~** avoir le cafard

bluff [blʌf] **1** *n* (deception) bluff *m* **2** *v/i* bluffer

blunder ['blʌndər] **1** *n* gaffe *f* **2** *v/i* faire une gaffe

blunt [blʌnt] émoussé; person franc; **bluntly** franchement

blur [blɜːr] **1** *n* masse *f* confuse **2** *v/t* brouiller

◆ **blurt out** [blɜːrt] *v/t* lâcher

blush [blʌʃ] **1** *n* rougissement *m* **2** *v/i* rougir; **blusher** cosmetic rouge *m*

blustery ['blʌstəri] à bourrasques

BO [biː'ou] (= *body odor*) odeur *f* corporelle

board [bɔːrd] **1** *n* of wood planche *f*; cardboard carton *m*; for game plateau *m* de jeu; for notices panneau *m*; **~ (of directors)** conseil *m* d'administration; **on ~** à bord **2** *v/t* plane, ship monter à bord de; train, bus monter dans **3** *v/i* of passengers embarquer; on train, bus monter (à bord)

◆ **board up** windows condamner

boarder ['bɔːrdər] pension-naire *m/f*; EDU interne *m/f*; **board game** jeu *m* de société; **boarding card** carte *f* d'embarquement; **boarding school** internat *m*, pensionnat *m*; **board meeting** réunion *f* du conseil d'administration; **board room** salle *f* du conseil

boast [boust] se vanter (**about** de)

boat [bout] bateau *m*; small, for leisure canot *m*

bodily ['bɑːdɪlɪ] **1** *adj* corporel **2** *adv*: **they ~ ejected him** ils l'ont saisi à bras-le-corps et l'ont mis dehors **body** corps *m*; dead cadavre *m*; **bodyguard** garde *m* du corps; **bodywork** MOT carrosserie *f*

bogus ['bougəs] faux

boil¹ [bɔɪl] *n* (swelling) furoncle *m*

boil² [bɔɪl] **1** *v/t* faire bouillir **2** *v/i* bouillir

◆ **boil down to** se ramener à

boiler ['bɔɪlər] chaudière *f*

boisterous ['bɔɪstərəs] bruyant

bold [bould] **1** *adj* courageux; text en caractères gras **2** *n* print caractères *mpl* gras

bolster ['boulstər] confidence soutenir

bolt [boult] **1** *n* (metal pin) boulon *m*; on door verrou *m* **2** *adv*: **~ upright** tout droit **3** *v/t* (fix with bolts) boulonner; close verrouiller **4** *v/i* (run off) décamper; of horse s'emballer

bomb [bɑːm] **1** *n* bombe *f* **2** *v/t*
MIL bombarder; *of terrorist*
faire sauter; **bombard**
[bɑːmˈbɑːrd] *also fig* bombarder; **bomb attack** attaque
f à la bombe; **bomber** *airplane* bombardier *m*; *terrorist* poseur *m(f)* de bombes;
bomb scare alerte *f* à la
bombe; **bombshell:** *come
as a* ~ faire l'effet d'une
bombe

bond [bɑːnd] **1** *n* (*tie*) lien *m*;
FIN obligation *f* **2** *v/i of glue*
se coller

bone [boʊn] os *m*; *in fish* arête
f

bonnet [ˈbɑːnɪt] *Br of car* capot *m*

bonus [ˈboʊnəs] *money* prime *f*; (*something extra*) plus
m

boob [buːb] P (*breast*) nichon
m

booboo [ˈbuːbuː] F bêtise *f*

book [buk] **1** *n* livre *m* **2** *v/t
seat* réserver; *ticket* prendre;
of policeman donner un P.V.
à; **bookcase** bibliothèque *f*;
booked up complet; *perso*
complètement pris; **bookie**
F bookmaker *m*; **booking** réservation *f*; **bookkeeper**
comptable *m*

'bookkeeping comptabilité *f*;
booklet livret *m*; **bookmaker** bookmaker *m*; **books** (*accounts*) comptes *mpl*; **bookseller** libraire *m/f*; **book-**

store librairie *f*

boom¹ [buːm] **1** *n* boum *m* **2**
v/i of business aller très fort

boom² [buːm] *n noise* boum
m

boost [buːst] **1** *n:* *give sth a* ~
stimuler qc **2** *v/t* stimuler

boot [buːt] botte *f*; *for climbing, football* chaussure *f*

◆ **boot up** COMPUT **1** *v/i* démarrer **2** *v/t* faire démarrer

booth [buːð] *at market* tente *f*
(de marché); *at fair* baraque
f; *at trade fair* stand *m*; *in restaurant* alcôve *f*

booze [buːz] boisson *f* (alcoolique)

border [ˈbɔːrdər] **1** *n* frontière
f; (*edge*) bordure *f* **2** *v/t country* avoir une frontière avec

◆ **border on** avoir une frontière avec; (*be almost*) friser

bore¹ [bɔːr] *v/t hole* percer

bore² [bɔːr] **1** *n person* raseur(-euse) *m(f)* **2** *v/t* ennuyer

bored [bɔːrd] ennuyé; *be* ~
s'ennuyer; **boredom** ennui
m; *boring* ennuyeux, chiant
m

born [bɔːrn]: *be* ~ être né

borrow [ˈbɑːroʊ] emprunter

bosom [ˈbuzm] poitrine *f*

boss [bɑːs] patron(-onne)
m(f)

◆ **boss around** donner des
ordres à

bossy [ˈbɑːsɪ] autoritaire

botanical [bəˈtænɪkl] botanique

botch [bɑːtʃ] bâcler

both 292

both [bəʊθ] **1** *adj & pron* les deux; ~ **of them** tous(-tes) m(f) les deux **2** *adv*: ~ ... **and** ... à la fois ... et ...

bother ['bɑːðər] **1** problemes *mpl* **2** *v/t* (*disturb*) déranger; (*worry*) ennuyer **3** *v/i* s'inquiéter (**with** de)

bottle ['bɑːtl] bouteille *f*; *for medicines* flacon *m*; *for baby* biberon *m*

◆ **bottle up** *feelings* réprimer

'bottle bank conteneur *m* à verre; **bottled water** eau *f* en bouteille; **bottleneck** rétrécissement *m*; *in production* goulet *m* d'étranglement; **bottle-opener** ouvre-bouteilles *m inv*

bottom ['bɑːtəm] **1** *adj* du bas **2** *n of drawer, pan, garden* fond *m*; (*underside*) dessous *m*; (*lowest part*) bas *m*; *of street* bout *m*; (*buttocks*) derrière *m*

◆ **bottom out** se stabiliser

bottom 'line *financial* résultat *m*; (*real issue*) la question principale

boulder ['bəʊldər] rocher *m*

bounce [baʊns] **1** *v/t ball* faire rebondir **2** *v/i of ball* rebondir; *on sofa etc* sauter; *of check* être refusé; **bouncer** videur *m*

bound[^1] [baʊnd] *adj*: **be ~ to do sth** (*sure to*) aller forcément faire qch

bound[^2] [baʊnd] *adj*: **be ~ for** *of ship* être à destination de

bound[^3] [baʊnd] *n* (*jump*) bond *m*

boundary ['baʊndərɪ] frontière *f*

bouquet [buˈkeɪ] bouquet *m*

bourbon ['bɜːrbən] bourbon *m*

bout [baʊt] MED accès *m*; *in boxing* match *m*

bow[^1] [baʊ] **1** *n as greeting* révérence *f* **2** *v/i* faire une révérence **3** *v/t head* baisser

bow[^2] [bəʊ] (*knot*) nœud *m*; MUS archet *m*; *for archery* arc *m*

bow[^3] [baʊ] *of ship* avant *m*

bowels ['baʊəlz] intestins *mpl*

bowl[^1] [bəʊl] *n* bol *m*; *for soup etc* assiette *f* creuse; *for serving salad etc* saladier *m*; *for washing dishes* cuvette *f*

bowl[^2] [bəʊl] *v/i* jouer au bowling

bowling ['bəʊlɪŋ] bowling *m*; **bowling alley** bowling *m*

bow 'tie [bəʊ] (nœud *m*) papillon *m*

box[^1] [bɑːks] *n container* boîte *f*; *on form* case *f*

box[^2] [bɑːks] *v/i* boxer

boxer ['bɑːksər] boxeur *m*; **boxing** boxe *f*; **boxing glove** gant *m* de boxe; **boxing match** match *m* de boxe

'box number boîte *f* postale; **box office** bureau *m* de location

boy [bɔɪ] garçon *m*; (*son*) fils *m*

boycott ['bɔɪkɑːt] **1** *n* boycott

breakdown

m **2** *v/t* boycotter

'**boyfriend** petit ami *m*; *younger* copain *m*

bra [brɑː] soutien-gorge *m*

bracelet ['breɪslɪt] bracelet *m*

bracket ['brækɪt] *for shelf* support *m* (d'étagère)

brag [bræg] se vanter (*about* de)

braid [breɪd] *in hair* tresse *f*; *trimming* galon *m*

braille [breɪl] braille *m*

brain [breɪn] ANAT cerveau *m*; **brainless** écervelé; **brains** cerveau *m*; **brain surgeon** neurochirurgien(ne) *m(f)*; **brain tumor**, *Br* **brain tumour** tumeur *f* au cerveau; **brainwash** conditionner

brake [breɪk] **1** *n* frein *m* **2** *v/i* freiner

branch [brɑːntʃ] *of tree, company* branche *f*

brand [brænd] **1** *n* marque *f* **2** *v/t*: **be ..ed a liar** être étiqueté comme voleur; **brand image** image *f* de marque

brand 'leader marque *f* dominante; **brand name** nom *m* de marque; **brand-new** flambant neuf

brandy ['brændɪ] brandy *m*

brassière [brə'zɪr] soutien-gorge *m*

brat [bræt] garnement *m*

brave [breɪv] courageux; **bravery** courage *m*

brawl [brɔːl] **1** *n* bagarre *f* **2** *v/i* se bagarrer

Brazil [brə'zɪl] Brésil *m*; **Brazilian 1** *adj* brésilien **2** *n* Brésilien(ne) *m(f)*

breach [briːtʃ] (*violation*) violation *f*; *in party* désaccord *m*; **breach of contract** rupture *f* de contrat

bread [bred] pain *m*

breadth [bredθ] largeur *f*; *of knowledge* étendue *f*

'**breadwinner** soutien *m* de famille

break [breɪk] **1** *n* fracture *f*; (*rest*) repos *m*; *in relationship* séparation *f* **2** *v/t* casser; *rules, law, promise* violer; *news* annoncer; *record* battre **3** *v/i* se casser; *of news, storm* éclater

◆ **break down 1** *v/i of vehicle, machine* tomber en panne; *of talks* échouer; *in tears* s'effondrer; *mentally* faire une dépression **2** *v/t door* défoncer; *figures* détailler

◆ **break even** rentrer dans ses frais

◆ **break in** (*interrupt*) interrompre qn; *of burglar* s'introduire par effraction

◆ **break up 1** *v/t into parts* décomposer; *fight* interrompre **2** *v/i of ice* se briser; *of couple, band* se séparer; *of meeting* se dissoudre

breakable ['breɪkəbl] cassable; **breakage** casse *f*; **breakdown** *of talks* échec *m*; (*nervous ~*) dépression *f* (nerveuse); *of figures* détail

m

breakfast ['brekfəst] petit déjeuner *m*; **have ~** prendre son petit déjeuner; **break-in** cambriolage *m*; **breakthrough** percée *f*; **breakup** *of partnership* échec *m*

breast [brest] *of woman* sein *m*; **breastfeed** allaiter; **breaststroke** brasse *f*

breath [breθ] souffle *m*; **out of ~** à bout de souffle

breathe [briːð] respirer

◆ **breathe in** inspirer

◆ **breathe out** expirer

breathing ['briːðɪŋ] respiration *f*

breathtaking ['breθteɪkɪŋ] à vous couper le souffle

breed [briːd] **1** *n* race *f* **2** *v/t animals* élever; *plants, also fig* cultiver **3** *v/i of animals* se reproduire; **breeding** *of animals* élevage *m*; *of person* éducation *f*

breeze [briːz] brise *f*; **breezy** venteux

brew [bruː] **1** *v/t beer* brasser **2** *v/i* couver; **brewery** brasserie *f*

bribe [braɪb] **1** *n* pot-de-vin *m* **2** *v/t* soudoyer; **bribery** corruption *f*

brick [brɪk] brique *m*

bride [braɪd] *about to be married* (future) mariée *f*; *married* jeune mariée *f*; **bridegroom** *about to be married* (futur) marié *m*; *married* jeune marié *m*; **bridesmaid** de-

moiselle *f* d'honneur

bridge [brɪdʒ] **1** *n* pont *m*; *of ship* passerelle *f* **2** *v/t gap* combler

bridle ['braɪdl] bride *f*

brief¹ [briːf] *adj* bref, court

brief² [briːf] **1** *n* (*mission*) instructions *fpl* **2** *v/t* **~ s.o. on sth** (*give information*) informer qn de qch

'briefcase serviette *f*; **briefing** session séance *f* d'information; *instructions* instructions *fpl*; **briefly** brièvement; (*to sum up*) en bref; **briefs** slip *m*

bright [braɪt] *color* vif; *smile* radieux; *future* brillant; (*sunny*) clair; (*intelligent*) intelligent; **brightly** *smile* d'un air radieux; *colored* vivement; **shine ~** resplendir

brilliance ['brɪljəns] *of person* esprit *m* lumineux; *of color* vivacité *f*; *of sunshine etc* resplendissant; (*very good*) génial; (*very intelligent*) brillant

brim [brɪm] *of container, hat* bord *m*

bring [brɪŋ] *object* apporter; *person, peace* amener; *hope, happiness* donner

◆ **bring back** (*return*) ramener; (*re-introduce*) réintroduire; *it brought back memories of … childhood* ça m'a rappelé …

◆ **bring down** *also fig: government* faire tomber; *air-*

plane abattre; *price* faire baisser

◆ **bring on** *illness* donner

◆ **bring out** (*produce*) sortir

◆ **bring up** *child* élever; *subject* soulever; (*vomit*) vomir

brink [brɪŋk] bord *m*

brisk [brɪsk] vif; (*businesslike*) énergique; *trade* florissant

bristles ['brɪslz] *on chin* poils *mpl* raides; *of brush* poils *mpl*

Britain ['brɪtn] Grande-Bretagne; **British 1** *adj* britannique **2** *npl*: **the** ~ les Britanniques

brittle ['brɪtl] fragile

broad [brɔːd] **1** *adj* large; *smile* grand; (*general*) général; **in** ~ **daylight** en plein jour **2** *n* F gonzesse *f*; **broadcast 1** *n* émission *f* **2** *v/t* transmettre; **broadcaster** présentateur(-trice) *m(f)* (radio/télé); **broad jump** saut *m* en longueur; **broadly**: ~ **speaking** en gros; **broadminded** large d'esprit

broccoli ['brɑːkəlɪ] brocoli(s) *m(pl)*

brochure ['brəʊʃər] brochure *f*

broil [brɔɪl] griller; **broiler** *on stove* grill *m*; *chicken* poulet *m* à rôtir

broke [brəʊk] fauché; **broken** cassé; *home* brisé; **broker** courtier *m*

bronchitis [brɑːŋ'kaɪtɪs] bronchite *f*

bronze [brɑːnz] bronze *m*

brooch [brəʊtʃ] broche *f*

brothel ['brɑːθl] bordel *m*

brother ['brʌðər] frère *m*; **brother-in-law** beau-frère *m*; **brotherly** fraternel

brow [braʊ] (*forehead*) front *m*; *of hill* sommet *m*

brown [braʊn] **1** *adj* marron *inv*; (*tanned*) bronzé **2** *n* marron *m*; **brownie** brownie *m*; **brown paper 'bag** sac *m* en papier kraft

browse [braʊz] *in store* flâner; COMPUT surfer; ~ **through a book** feuilleter un livre; **browser** COMPUT navigateur *m*

bruise [bruːz] bleu *m*; *on fruit* meurtrissure *f*

brunette [bruːˈnet] brune *f*

brush [brʌʃ] **1** *n* brosse *f*; (*conflict*) accrochage *m* **2** *v/t* brosser; (*touch lightly*) effleurer

◆ **brush aside** *person* mépriser; *remark, criticism* écarter

◆ **brush up** réviser

brusque [brusk] brusque

brutal ['bruːtl] brutal; **brutality** brutalité *f*; **brutally** brutalement; **brute** brute *f*

bubble ['bʌbl] bulle *f*

buck[1] [bʌk] *n* F (*dollar*) dollar *m*

buck[2] [bʌk] *v/i of horse* ruer

bucket ['bʌkɪt] seau *m*

buckle[1] ['bʌkl] **1** *n* boucle *f* **2** *v/t belt* boucler

buckle[2] ['bʌkl] *v/i of metal* déformer

bud [bʌd] BOT bourgeon m

buddy ['bʌdɪ] copain m, copine f; form of address mec

budge [bʌdʒ] **1** v/t (move) déplacer **2** v/i (move) bouger

budget ['bʌdʒɪt] budget m

buff [bʌf] passionné(e) m(f)

buffalo ['bʌfələʊ] buffle m

buffer ['bʌfər] RAIL, COMPUT, fig tampon m

buffet ['bʊfeɪ] meal buffet m

bug [bʌg] **1** n (insect) insecte m; (virus) virus m; COMPUT bogue f; (spying device) micro m **2** v/t room, telephone mettre sur écoute; F (annoy) énerver

buggy ['bʌgɪ] for baby poussette f

build [bɪld] **1** n of person carrure f **2** v/t construire

◆ **build up 1** v/t strength développer; relationship construire **2** v/i s'accumuler; fig s'intensifier

builder ['bɪldər] constructeur(-trice) m(f); **building** bâtiment m; activity construction f

'building site chantier m; **building society** Br caisse f d'épargne-logement; **building trade** (industrie f du) bâtiment m; **build-up** accumulation f; **give s.o./sth a big ~** faire beaucoup de battage autour de qn/qch; **built-in** encastré; flash incorporé

bulb [bʌlb] BOT bulbe m; (light

~) ampoule f

bulge [bʌldʒ] **1** n gonflement m, saillie f **2** v/i être gonflé, faire saillie

'bulky ['bʌlkɪ] encombrant; sweater gros

bull [bʊl] animal taureau m; **bulldozer** ['bʊldəʊzər] bulldozer m

bullet ['bʊlɪt] balle f

bulletin ['bʊlɪtɪn] bulletin m

'bulletin board tableau m d'affichage; COMPUT serveur m télématique

'bullet-proof protégé contre les balles; vest pare-balles

'bull's-eye mille m; **hit the ~** also fig mettre dans le mille; **bullshit** merde f V, conneries fpl P

bully ['bʊlɪ] **1** n brute f **2** v/t brimer; **bullying** brimades fpl

bum [bʌm] **1** n F (worthless person) bon à rien m; (tramp) clochard m **2** v/t: **can I ~ a cigarette?** est-ce que je peux vous taper une cigarette?

bump [bʌmp] **1** n bosse f **2** v/t se cogner; **bumper** MOT pare-chocs mpl; **bumpy** road cahoteux; **we had a ~ flight** nous avons été secoués pendant le vol

bunch [bʌntʃ] of people groupe m; of keys trousseau m; of grapes grappe f; of flowers bouquet m; **thanks a ~** merci beaucoup

bungle ['bʌŋgl] bousiller

bunk [bʌŋk] couchette f

buoy [bɔɪ] NAUT bouée f; **buoyant** mood jovial; economy prospère

burden ['bɜːrdn] **1** n fardeau m **2** v/t: **~ s.o. with sth** accabler qn de qch

bureau ['bjʊroʊ] bureau m; **bureaucrat** bureaucrate m/f; **bureaucratic** bureaucratique

burger ['bɜːrgər] steak m haché; in roll hamburger m

burglar ['bɜːrglər] cambrioleur(-euse) m(f); **burglar alarm** alarme f antivol; **burglarize** cambrioler; **burglary** cambriolage m

burial ['beriəl] enterrement m

burn [bɜːrn] **1** n brûlure f **2** v/t & v/i brûler

♦ **burn down 1** v/t incendier **2** v/i être réduit en cendres

burp [bɜːrp] **1** n rot m **2** v/i roter

burst [bɜːrst] **1** n in pipe trou m **2** adj tire creuvé **3** v/t & v/i crever; of pipe éclater; **~ into tears** fondre en larmes; **~ out laughing** éclater de rire

bus [bʌs] (auto)bus m; long distance (auto)car m

bush [bʊʃ] plant buisson m

bushy ['bʊʃɪ] beard touffu

business ['bɪznɪs] commerce m; (company) entreprise f; (work) travail m; (sector) secteur m; (matter) affaire f; **on ~** en déplacement (profes-

sionnel); **mind your own ~!** occupe-toi de tes affaires!; **business card** carte f de visite; **business class** classe f affaires; **businesslike** sérieux; **businessman** homme m d'affaires; **business meeting** réunion f d'affaires; **business school** école f de commerce; **business studies course** études fpl de commerce; **business trip** voyage m d'affaires; **businesswoman** femme f d'affaires

'**bus station** gare f routière; '**bus stop** arrêt m d'autobus

bust¹ [bʌst] n of woman poitrine f

bust² [bʌst] F (broken) cassé

'**bust-up** F brouille f; **busty** à la poitrine plantureuse

busy ['bɪzɪ] person, TELEC occupé; day, life bien rempli; street, shop plein de monde; **busybody** curieux(-se) m(f)

but [bʌt] **1** conj mais **2** prep: **all ~ him** tous sauf lui; **the last ~ one** l'avant-dernier; **~ for you** si tu n'avais pas été là; **nothing ~ the best** rien que le meilleur

butcher ['bʊtʃər] boucher (-ère) m(f)

butt [bʌt] **1** n of cigarette mégot m; F (backside) cul m **2** v/t donner un coup de tête à

butter ['bʌtər] beurre m; **butterfly** also swimming papillon m

buttocks ['bʌtəks] fesses fpl

button ['bʌtn] bouton *m*; (*badge*) badge *m*

buy [baɪ] acheter

◆ **buy out** COM racheter la part de

buyer ['baɪr] acheteur(-euse) *m* (*f*)

buzz [bʌz] **1** *n* bourdonnement *m* **2** *v/i* of *insect* bourdonner; **buzzer** sonnerie *f*

by [baɪ] *to show agent* par; (*near, next to*) près de; (*no*

later than) pour; *mode of transport* en; ~ **bus** en bus; ~ **day** le jour; ~ *my watch* selon ma montre; ~ **o.s.** tout seul

bye(-bye) [baɪ] au revoir

'bypass *road* déviation *f*; MED pontage *m* (*coronarien*); **by-product** sous-produit *m*; **bystander** spectateur(-trice) *m* (*f*)

C

cab [kæb] taxi *m*; of *truck* cabine *f*; **cab driver** chauffeur *m* de taxi

cabin ['kæbɪn] of *plane, ship* cabine *f*; **cabin attendant** *male* steward *m*; *female* hôtesse *f* (de l'air); **cabin crew** équipage *m*

cabinet ['kæbɪnɪt] *furniture* meuble *m* (de rangement); POL cabinet *m*; *display* ~ vitrine *f*

cable ['keɪbl] câble *m*; **cable car** téléphérique *m*; *on rail* funiculaire *m*; **cable television** (télévision *f* par) câble *m*

'cab stand station *f* de taxis

cactus ['kæktəs] cactus *m*

cadaver [kə'dævər] cadavre *m*

caddie ['kædɪ] *in golf* caddie *m*

Caesarean *Br* → **Cesarean**

café ['kæfeɪ] café *m*; **cafeteria** cafétéria *f*

caffeine ['kæfiːn] caféine *f*

cage [keɪdʒ] cage *f*; **cagey** évasif

cake [keɪk] gâteau *m*

calculate ['kælkjuleɪt] (*work out*) évaluer; *in arithmetic* calculer; **calculating** calculateur; **calculation** calculation *m*; **calculator** calculatrice *f*

calendar ['kælɪndər] calendrier *m*

calf [kæf] (*young cow*) veau *m*

calf [kæf] of *leg* mollet *m*

caliber, *Br* **calibre** ['kælɪbər] of *gun* calibre *m*

call [kɔːl] **1** *n* appel *m*; (*phone ~ also*) coup *m* de téléphone **2** *v/t on phone* appeler; *be* ~**ed** ... s'appeler ... **3** *v/i on phone* appeler; (*visit*) passer

◆ **call back 1** *v/t* rappeler **2** *v/i*

on phone rappeler; *(make another visit)* repasser

♦ **call for** *(collect)* venir chercher; *(demand)* demander

♦ **call off** annuler

caller ['kɔːlər] *on phone* personne *f* qui appelle; *(visitor)* visiteur *m*

callous ['kæləs] dur

calm [kɑːm] **1** *adj* calme, tranquille **2** *n* calme *m*

♦ **calm down 1** *v/t* calmer **2** *v/i* se calmer

calmly ['kɑːmlɪ] calmement

calorie ['kælərɪ] calorie *f*

camcorder ['kæmkɔːrdər] caméscope *m*

camera ['kæmərə] appareil *m* photo; **tv** caméra *f*; **cameraman** cadreur *m*, caméraman *m*; **camera phone** téléphone *m* avec appareil photo intégré

camouflage ['kæmʊflɑːʒ] **1** *n* camouflage *m* **2** *v/t* camoufler

camp [kæmp] **1** *n* camp *m* **2** *v/i* camper

campaign [kæm'peɪn] **1** *n* campagne *f* **2** *v/i* faire campagne

camper ['kæmpər] *person* campeur *m*; *vehicle* camping-car *m*; **camping ground** camping *m*; **campsite** (terrain *m* de) camping *m*

campus ['kæmpəs] campus *m*

can¹ [kæn] *v/aux expr* **∼ you hear me?** tu m'entends?; **∼ she swim?** sait-elle

nager?; **∼ I help you?** est-ce que je peux t'aider?

can² [kæn] *n for food* boîte *f*; *for drinks* canette *f*; *of paint* bidon *m*

Canada ['kænədə] Canada *m*; **Canadian 1** *adj* canadien **2** *n* Canadien *m*

canal [kə'næl] canal *m*

cancel ['kænsl] annuler; **cancellation** annulation *f*

cancer ['kænsər] cancer *m*

candid ['kændɪd] franc

candidacy ['kændɪdəsɪ] candidature *f*; **candidate** candidat *m*

candle ['kændl] bougie *f*; *in church* cierge *m*

candor, *Br* **candour** ['kændər] franchise *f*

candy ['kændɪ] *(sweet)* bonbon *m*; *(sweets)* bonbons *mpl*

cane [keɪn] canne *f*

canister ['kænɪstər] boîte *f* (métallique); *for gas, spray* bombe *f*

canned [kænd] en conserve, en boîte; *(recorded)* enregistré

cannot ['kænɑːt] = **can not**

canny ['kænɪ] *(astute)* rusé

canoe [kə'nuː] canoë *m*

'can opener ouvre-boîte *m*

can't [kænt] = **can not**

canteen [kæn'tiːn] *in factory* cantine *f*

canvas ['kænvəs] toile *f*

canyon ['kænjən] canyon *m*

cap [kæp] *hat* bonnet *m*; *with peak* casquette *f*; *of soldier,* *policeman* képi *m*

capability [keɪpə'bɪlətɪ] capacité *f*; **capable** capable

capacity [kə'pæsətɪ] capacité *f*

capital ['kæpɪtl] *of country* capitale *f*; *letter* majuscule *f*; *money* capital *m*; **capitalism** capitalisme *m*; **capitalist 1** *adj* capitaliste **2** *n* capitaliste *m/f*; **capital punishment** peine *f* capitale

capsize [kæp'saɪz] chavirer

capsule ['kæpsʊl] *of medicine* gélule *f*; *(space ~)* capsule *f* spatiale

captain ['kæptɪn] capitaine *m*; *of aircraft* commandant *m* de bord

caption ['kæpʃn] légende *f*

captivate ['kæptɪveɪt] captiver, fasciner; **captive** captif *m*; **captivity** captivité *f*; **capture 1** *n of city* prise *f*; *of person, animal* capture *f* **2** *v/t person, animal* capturer; *city, building* prendre; *market share* conquérir

car [kɑːr] voiture *f*, automobile *f*; *of train* wagon *m*, voiture *f*; **by ~** en voiture

carbon monoxide [kɑːrbən-mən'ɑːksaɪd] monoxyde *m* de carbone

carbureter, carburetor [kɑːrbʊ'retər] carburateur *m*

carcass ['kɑːrkəs] carcasse *f*

card [kɑːrd] carte *f*; **cardboard box** carton *m*

cardiac ['kɑːrdɪæk] cardiaque

cardinal ['kɑːrdɪnl] REL cardinal *m*

care [ker] **1** *n of baby, pet* garde *f*; *of the elderly, sick* soins *mpl*; *(medical ~)* soins *mpl* médicaux; *(worry)* souci *m*; **care of → c/o; take ~** *(be cautious)* faire attention; **take ~ of** s'occuper de **2** *v/i* se soucier; **I don't ~!** ça m'est égal!
◆ **care about** s'intéresser à
◆ **care for** *(look after)* s'occuper de

career [kə'rɪr] carrière *f*

careful ['kerfl] *(cautious)* prudent; *(thorough)* méticuleux; **(be) ~!** (fais) attention!; **carefully** *(with caution)* prudemment; *worded etc* soigneusement; **careless** négligent; *work* négligé; **carelessly** négligemment

caress [kə'res] caresser

car ferry (car-)ferry *m*, transbordeur *m*

cargo ['kɑːrgoʊ] cargaison *f*

caricature ['kærɪkətʃər] caricature *f*

carnival ['kɑːrnɪvl] fête *f* foraine; *with processions etc* carnaval *m*

carpenter ['kɑːrpɪntər] charpentier *m*; *for smaller objects* menuisier *m*

carpet ['kɑːrpɪt] tapis *m*; *fitted* moquette *f*

car phone téléphone *m* de voiture; **carpool** faire du co-voiturage; **car rental** location *f* de voitures

carrier ['kærɪər] *company* entreprise *f* de transport; *of disease* porteur(-euse) *m(f)*

carrot ['kærət] carotte *f*

carry ['kærɪ] **1** *v/t* porter; *of ship, bus etc* transporter **2** *v/i of sound* porter

◆ **carry on 1** *v/i (continue)* continuer (**with sth** qch) **2** *v/t business* exercer

◆ **carry out** *survey etc* faire; *orders etc* exécuter

cart [kɑːrt] charrette *f*

carton ['kɑːrtn] carton *m; of cigarettes* cartouche *f*

cartoon [kɑːrˈtuːn] dessin *m* humoristique; *on TV* dessin *m* animé; *(strip ~)* BD *f*, bande *f* dessinée

carve [kɑːrv] *meat* découper; *wood* sculpter

case¹ [keɪs] *for eyeglasses, camera* étui *m; for gadget* pochette *f; of wine etc* caisse *f; Br (suitcase)* valise *f*

case² [keɪs] *(instance)*, MED cas *m; for police* affaire *f;* LAW procès *m;* **in ~.** au cas où ...; **in any ~.** en tout cas

cash [kæʃ] **1** *n (money)* argent *m; (coins and notes)* argent *m)* liquide **m 2** *v/t check* toucher; **cash desk** caisse *f;* **cash flow** trésorerie *f;* **I've got ~ problems** j'ai des problèmes de trésorerie; **cashier** *in store etc* caissier(-ère) *m(f)*; **cashpoint** *Br* distributeur *m* automatique (de billets); **cash register** caisse *f*

enregistreuse

casino [kəˈsiːnou] casino *m*

casket ['kæskɪt] *(coffin)* cercueil *m*

casserole ['kæsəroul] *meal* ragoût *m; container* cocotte *f*

cassette [kəˈset] cassette *f;* **cassette player** lecteur *m* de cassettes

cast [kæst] **1** *n of play* distribution *f; (mold)* moule *m* **2** *v/t doubt* jeter; *metal* couler

cast ˈiron fonte *f*

castle ['kæsl] château *m*

casual ['kæʒuəl] *(chance)* fait au hasard; *(offhand)* désinvolte; *(not formal)* décontracté; **casually** *dressed* de manière décontractée; *say* de manière désinvolte; **casualty** victime *f*

cat [kæt] chat(te) *m(f)*

catalog, *Br* **catalogue** ['kætəlɔːg] catalogue *m*

catalyst ['kætəlɪst] catalyseur *m*

catastrophe [kəˈtæstrəfɪ] catastrophe *f;* **catastrophic** catastrophique

catch [kætʃ] **1** *n* prise *f* (au vol); *of fish* pêche *f; (lock: on door)* loquet *m; (problem)* entourloupette *f* **2** *v/t ball, prisoner, illness* attraper; *(get on: bus, train)* prendre; *(hear)* entendre; **catching** *also fig* contagieux; **catchy** facile à retenir

categoric [kætəˈgɑːrɪk] catégorique; **category** catégorie

f
caterer ['keɪtərər] traiteur m
cathedral [kə'θiːdrl] cathédrale f
Catholic ['kæθəlɪk] **1** adj catholique **2** n catholique m/f; **Catholicism** catholicisme m
catty ['kætɪ] méchant
cause [kɔːz] **1** n cause f; (grounds) raison f **2** v/t causer
caution ['kɔːʃn] **1** n (carefulness) prudence f **2** v/t (warn) avertir; **cautious** prudent; **cautiously** prudemment
cave [keɪv] caverne f, grotte f
cavity ['kævətɪ] cavité f
CD [siː'diː] (= compact disc) CD m (= compact-disc m, disque m compact)
C'D player lecteur m de CD; **CD-ROM** CD-ROM m
cease [siːs] cesser
'cease-fire cessez-le-feu m
ceiling ['siːlɪŋ] plafond m
celebrate ['selɪbreɪt] **1** v/i faire la fête **2** v/t fêter; Christmas, event célébrer; **celebrated** célèbre; **celebration** fête f, of event, wedding célébration f; **celebrity** célébrité f
cell [sel] for prisoner, of spreadsheet, BIO cellule f
cellar ['selər] cave f
cello ['tʃelou] violoncelle m
cell phone, cellular phone ['seljulər] (téléphone m) portable m
cement [sɪ'ment] ciment m

cemetery ['semətrɪ] cimetière m
censor ['sensər] censurer
census ['sensəs] recensement m
cent [sent] cent m
centenary [sen'tiːnərɪ] centenaire m
center ['sentər] **1** n centre m **2** v/t centrer
centigrade ['sentɪgreɪd] centigrade
centimeter, Br **centimetre** ['sentɪmiːtər] centimètre m
central ['sentrəl]
central 'heating chauffage m central; **centralize** centraliser; **central locking** MOT verrouillage m central; **centrally** centralisé
centre Br → **center**
century ['sentʃərɪ] siècle m
CEO [siːiː'oʊ] (= Chief Executive Officer) directeur m général
ceramic [sɪ'ræmɪk] en céramique
cereal ['sɪrɪəl] céréale f; (breakfast ~) céréales fpl
ceremonial [serɪ'moʊnɪəl] **1** adj de cérémonie **2** n cérémonial m; **ceremony** cérémonie f
certain ['sɜːrtn] (sure) certain, sûr; (particular) certain; **certainly** certainement; **certainty** certitude f
certificate [sər'tɪfɪkət] certificat m
certified public accountant ['sɜːrtɪfaɪd] expert m comp-

table; **certify** certifier

Cesarean [sɪˈzeərɪən] césarienne f

CFO [siːefˈou] (= *chief financial officer*) directeur m financier

chain [tʃeɪn] **1** n *also of stores etc* chaîne f **2** v/t: ~ *sth. to sth* enchaîner qch à qch

chair [tʃer] **1** n chaise f; (*arm*~) fauteuil m; *at university* chaire f **2** v/t *meeting* présider; **chair lift** télésiège m; **chairman** président m; **chairmanship** présidence f; **chairperson** président(e) m(f)

chalk [tʃɔːk] craie f

challenge [ˈtʃælɪndʒ] **1** n défi m, challenge m **2** v/t (*defy*) défier; (*call into question*) mettre en doute; ~ *s.o. to a game* proposer à qn de faire une partie; **challenger** challenger m; **challenging** *job, undertaking* stimulant

Chamber of 'Commerce Chambre f de commerce

champagne [ʃæmˈpeɪn] champagne m

champion [ˈtʃæmpɪən] **1** n SP, *of cause* champion(ne) m(f) **2** v/t *cause* être le (la) champion(ne) m(f) de; **championship** *event* championnat m; *title* titre m de champion(ne)

chance [tʃæns] (*possibility*) chances fpl; (*opportunity*) occasion f; (*luck*) hasard m; **by** ~ par hasard; **take a** ~

prendre un risque

change [tʃeɪndʒ] **1** n changement m; (*money*) monnaie f; **for a** ~ pour changer un peu **2** v/t changer; *bankbill* faire la monnaie de **3** v/i changer; (*put on different clothes*) se changer; **change-over** changement m; **changing room** SP vestiaire m; *in shop* cabine f d'essayage

channel [ˈtʃænl] *on TV, radio* chaîne f; (*waterway*) chenal m

chant [tʃænt] **1** n *slogans* mpl scandés; REL chant m **2** v/i *of crowds* scander des slogans; REL psalmodier

chaos [ˈkeɪɑːs] chaos m; **chaotic** chaotique

chapel [ˈtʃæpl] chapelle f

chapter [ˈtʃæptər] chapitre m

character [ˈkærɪktər] caractère m; (*person*) personne f; *in book* personnage m; **characteristic 1** n caractéristique f **2** adj caractéristique; **characterize** caractériser

charge [tʃɑːrdʒ] **1** n (*fee*) frais mpl; LAW accusation f; **free of** ~ gratuit; **be in** ~ être responsable **2** v/t *sum of money* faire payer; LAW inculper (**with**); *battery* charger; **can you** ~ **it?** (*put on account*) pouvez-vous le mettre sur mon compte? **3** v/i (*attack*) charger; **charge account** compte m; **charge card** carte f de paiement

charitable ['tʃærɪtəbl] charitable; **charity** charité f; (organization) organisation f caritative

charm [tʃɑːrm] **1** n also on bracelet charme m **2** v/t (delight) charmer; **charming** charmant

charred [tʃɑːd] carbonisé

chart [tʃɑːrt] diagramme m; (map) carte f

'**charter flight** (vol m) charter m

chase [tʃeɪs] **1** n poursuite f **2** v/t poursuivre

◆ **chase away** v/t chasser

chassis ['ʃæsɪ] of car châssis m

chat [tʃæt] **1** n causette f **2** v/i causer; **chatline** chat m téléphonique; **chat room** chat m

chatter ['tʃætər] **1** n bavardage m **2** v/i (talk) bavarder; **my teeth were ~ing** je claquais des dents

chauffeur ['ʃoʊfər] chauffeur m

chauvinist ['ʃoʊvɪnɪst] (male ~) machiste m

cheap [tʃiːp] bon marché, pas cher; (nasty) méchant; (mean) pingre

cheat [tʃiːt] **1** n person tricheur(-euse) m(f) **2** v/t tromper **3** v/i tricher

check¹ [tʃek] **1** adj shirt à carreaux **2** n carreaux m

check² [tʃek] n FIN chèque m; in restaurant etc addition f

check³ [tʃek] **1** n to verify sth contrôle m, vérification f **2** v/t vérifier; with a ~mark cocher; coat etc mettre au vestiaire **3** v/i vérifier

◆ **check in** v/i at airport se faire enregistrer; at hotel s'inscrire

◆ **check out 1** v/i of hotel régler sa note **2** v/t (look into) enquêter sur; club etc essayer

◆ **check up on** se renseigner sur

'**checkbook** carnet m de chèques; **checked** material à carreaux

checkered ['tʃekərd] pattern à carreaux; career varié

'**check-in** (counter) enregistrement m; **checking account** compte m courant; **checklist** liste f (de contrôle); **check mark**: put a ~ against sth cocher qch; **check-out** caisse f; **check-point** contrôle m; **check-room** for coats vestiaire m; for baggage consigne f; **checkup** medical examen m médical; dental examen m dentaire

cheek [tʃiːk] on face joue f

cheer [tʃɪr] **1** n hourra m **2** v/t acclamer **3** v/i pousser des hourras

◆ **cheer up 1** v/i reprendre courage; cheer up! **2** v/t remonter le moral à

cheerful ['tʃɪrfl] gai, joyeux; **cheering** acclamations fpl; **cheerleader** meneuse f de ban

cheese [tʃiːz] fromage *m*

chef [ʃef] chef *m* (de cuisine)

chemical ['kemɪkl] **1** *adj* chimique **2** *n* produit *m* chimique; **chemist** *in laboratory* chimiste *m/f*; *Br* pharmacien(ne) *m(f)*; **chemistry** chimie *f*

chemotherapy [kiːmou'θerəpɪ] chimiothérapie *f*

cheque [tʃek] *Br* → **check²**

chess [tʃes] (jeu *m* d'échecs *mpl*; **play** ~ jouer aux échecs

chest [tʃest] poitrine *f*; (*box*) coffre *m*, caisse *f*

chew [tʃuː] mâcher; *of rat* ronger; **chewing gum** chewing-gum *m*

chick [tʃɪk] poussin *m*; F *girl* nana

chicken ['tʃɪkɪn] poulet *m*

chief [tʃiːf] **1** *n* chef *m* **2** *adj* principal; **chiefly** principalement

child [tʃaɪld] enfant *m/f*; **childhood** enfance *f*; **childish** puéril; **childlike** enfantin

children ['tʃɪldrən] *pl* → **child**

Chile ['tʃɪlɪ] Chili *m*; **Chilean 1** *adj* chilien *m* **2** *n* Chilien(ne) *m(f)*

♦ **chill out** se relaxer

chilly ['tʃɪlɪ] *also fig* froid

chimney ['tʃɪmnɪ] cheminée *f*

chin [tʃɪn] menton *m*

China ['tʃaɪnə] Chine *f*

china ['tʃaɪnə] **1** *n* porcelaine *f* **2** *adj* en porcelaine

Chinese [tʃaɪ'niːz] **1** *adj* chi-

nois **2** *n* *language* chinois *m*; *person* Chinois(e) *m(f)*

chip [tʃɪp] **1** *n* *damage* brèche *f*; *in gambling* jeton *m*; COMPUT puce *f*; ~**s** (*potato* ~s) chips *mpl*; *Br* pommes frites *fpl* **2** *v/t damage* ébrécher

chipmunk tamia *m* rayé

chisel ['tʃɪzl] ciseau *m*, burin *m*

chlorine ['klɔːriːn] chlore *m*

chocolate ['tʃɑːkələt] chocolat *m*

choice [tʃɔɪs] **1** *n* choix *m*; **I had no** ~ je n'avais pas le choix **2** *adj* (*top quality*) de choix

choir ['kwaɪr] chœur *m*

choke [tʃouk] **1** *v/i* s'étrangler **2** *v/t* (*strangle*) étrangler

cholesterol [kə'lestəroul] cholestérol *m*

choose [tʃuːz] choisir; **choosey** difficile

chop [tʃɑːp] **1** *n* *of meat* côtelette *f* **2** *v/t* couper

♦ **chop down** *tree* abattre

chore [tʃɔːr] ~**s** travaux *mpl* domestiques

choreography [kɔːriˈɑːgrəfi] chorégraphie *f*

chorus ['kɔːrəs] *singers* chœur *m*; *of song* refrain *m*

Christ [kraɪst] Christ *m*; ~! mon Dieu!

christen ['krɪsn] baptiser

Christian ['krɪstʃən] **1** *n* chrétien(ne) *m(f)* **2** *adj* chrétien; **Christianity** christianisme *m*

Christmas ['krɪsməs] Noël *m*;
Merry ~! Joyeux Noël!;
Christmas card carte *f* de
Noël; Christmas Day jour
m de Noël; Christmas Eve
veille *f* de Noël; Christmas
present cadeau *m* de
Noël; Christmas tree arbre *m* de
Noël

chronic ['krɒnɪk] chronique
chubby ['tʃʌbɪ] potelé
chuck [tʃʌk] lancer
chuckle ['tʃʌkl] **1** *n* petit rire
m **2** *v/i* rire tout bas
chunk [tʃʌŋk] gros morceau *m*
church [tʃɜːrtʃ] église *f*;
church service office *m*;
churchyard cimetière *m* (autour d'une église)
chute [ʃuːt] *for garbage* vide-ordures *m*; *for escape* toboggan *m*
cigar [sɪ'gɑːr] cigare *m*
cigarette [sɪgə'ret] cigarette
f; cigarette lighter briquet *m*
cinema ['sɪnɪmə] *Br* cinéma
m
circle ['sɜːrkl] **1** *n* cercle *m* **2**
v/i of plane tournoyer
circuit ['sɜːrkɪt] circuit *m*;
(*lap*) tour *m* (de circuit); circuit board COMPUT plaquette
f; circular ['sɜːrkjələr] **1** *n*
circulaire *f* **2** *adj* circulaire;
circulate ['sɜːrkjəleɪt] **1** *v/i*
circuler **2** *v/t memo* faire circuler; circulation circulation
f; *of newspaper* tirage *m*
circumstances ['sɜːrkəmstænsɪs] circonstances *fpl*;

financial situation *f* financière
circus ['sɜːrkəs] cirque *m*
cistern ['sɪstərn] réservoir *m*;
of WC réservoir *m* de chasse
d'eau
citizen ['sɪtɪzn] citoyen(ne)
m(f); citizenship citoyenneté *f*
city ['sɪtɪ] (grande) ville *f*
city 'center, *Br* city 'centre
centre-ville *m*; city hall hôtel
m de ville
civic ['sɪvɪk] municipal; *pride,
responsibilities* civique
civil ['sɪvl] civil; (*polite*) poli;
civil ceremony mariage *m*
civil; civil engineer ingénieur *m* des travaux publics
civilian [sɪ'vɪljən] civil(e)
m(f); civilization civilisation
f; civilize civiliser; civil
rights droits *mpl* civils; civil
servant fonctionnaire *m/f*;
civil service fonction *f* publique, administration *f*; civil
war guerre *f* civile
claim [kleɪm] **1** *n* (*request*) demande *f*; (*assertion*) affirmation *f* **2** *v/t* (*ask for as a right*)
demander, réclamer; (*assert*)
affirmer; *lost property* réclamer; claimant ['kleɪmənt]
demandeur(-euse) *m(f)*
clam [klæm] palourde *f*, clam
m
clammy ['klæmɪ] moite
clamp [klæmp] *fastener* pince
f, crampon *m*
◆ clamp down on sévir con-

tre
clandestine [klæn'destɪn] clandestin

clap [klæp] (*applaud*) applaudir

clarification [klærɪfɪ'keɪʃn] clarification *f*; **clarify** clarifier; **clarity** clarté *f*

clash [klæʃ] **1** *n between people* affrontement *m* **2** *v/i* s'affronter; *of colors* détonner; *of events* tomber en même temps

clasp [klæsp] **1** *n* agrafe *f* **2** *v/t in hand* serrer

class [klæs] **1** *n* (*lesson*) cours *m*; (*group of people, category*) classe *f*; **the ∼ of 2002** la promo(tion) 2002 **2** *v/t* classer

classic ['klæsɪk] **1** *adj* classique **2** *n* classique *m*; **classical** *music* classique; **classification** classification *f*; **classified** *information* secret; **classified** ad(**vertisement**) petite annonce *f*; **classify** classifier; **classroom** salle *f* de classe; **classy** F *restaurant etc* chic *inv*; *person* classe

clause [klɔːz] *in agreement* clause *f*; GRAM proposition *f*

claustrophobia [klɔːstrə-'fəʊbɪə] claustrophobie *f*

claw [klɔː] *of cat* griffe *f*; *of lobster* pince *f*

clay [kleɪ] argile *f*, glaise *f*

clean [kliːn] **1** *adj* propre **2** *adv* (*completely*) complètement **3** *v/t* nettoyer; **cleaner**

male agent m de propreté; *female* femme *f de ménage*; (*dry∼*) teinturier(-ère) *m(f)*

cleanse [klenz] *skin* nettoyer; **cleanser** *for skin* démaquillant *m*

clear [klɪr] **1** *adj voice, photo* net; *to understand, sky, water* clair; *conscience* tranquille **2** *v/t roads etc* dégager; *place* (faire) évacuer; *table* débarrasser; *ball* dégager; (*acquit*) innocenter; (*authorize*) autoriser **3** *v/i of sky* se dégager; *of mist* se dissiper; *of face* s'éclaircir

◆ **clear out** *v/t closet* vider **2** *v/i* ficher le camp

◆ **clear up 1** *v/i in room etc* ranger; *of weather* s'éclaircir; *of illness* disparaître **2** *v/t* (*tidy*) ranger; *problem* résoudre

clearance ['klɪrəns] (*space*) espace *m* (libre); (*authorization*) autorisation *f*; **clearance sale** liquidation *f*; **clearing** clairière *f*; **clearly** *speak, see* clairement; *hear* distinctement; (*evidently*) manifestement

cleavage ['kliːvɪdʒ] décolleté *m*

clench [klentʃ] serrer

clergy ['klɜːrdʒɪ] clergé *m*; **clergyman** ecclésiastique *m*; *Protestant* pasteur *m*

clerk [klɜːrk] *administrative* employé(e) *m(f)* de bureau; *in store* vendeur(-euse) *m(f)*

clever ['klevər] intelligent; *gadget* ingénieux; *(skillful)* habile

click [klɪk] **1** *n* COMPUT clic *m* **2** *v/i* cliqueter

◆ **click on** COMPUT cliquer sur

client ['klaɪənt] client(e) *m(f)*; **clientele** clientèle *f*

climate ['klaɪmət] *also fig* climat *m*

climax ['klaɪmæks] point *m* culminant

climb [klaɪm] **1** *n up mountain* ascension *f f* **2** *v/i* monter sur; *mountain* escalader **3** *v/i* monter; **climber** alpiniste *m/f*

clinch [klɪntʃ] *deal* conclure

cling [klɪŋ] *of clothes* coller

◆ **cling to** s'accrocher à

clingy ['klɪŋɪ] *person* collant

clinic ['klɪnɪk] clinique *f*; **clinical** clinique

clip[1] [klɪp] **1** *n fastener* pince *f*; *for hair* barrette *f* **2** *v/t*: **~ sth to sth** attacher qch à qch

clip[2] [klɪp] **1** *n (extract)* extrait *m* **2** *v/t hair, grass* couper; **clipping** *from press* coupure *f* (de presse)

clock [klɑːk] horloge *f*; **clock radio** radio-réveil *m*; **clockwise** dans le sens des aiguilles d'une montre

clone [kloʊn] **1** *n* clone *m* **2** *v/t* cloner; **cloning** clonage *m*

close[1] [kloʊs] **1** *adj family, friend* proche **2** *adv* près; **~ at hand, ~ by** tout près; **~ to** près de

close[2] [kloʊz] *v/t* fermer

closed-circuit 'television télévision *f* en circuit fermé; **close-knit** très uni; **closely** *listen* attentivement; *watch* de près; *cooperate* étroitement

closet ['klɑːzɪt] armoire *f*, placard *m*

close-up ['kloʊsʌp] gros plan *m*

closing date ['kloʊzɪŋ] date *f* limite

closure ['kloʊʒər] fermeture *f*

clot [klɑːt] **1** *n of blood* caillot *m* **2** *v/i of blood* coaguler

cloth [klɑːθ] tissu *m*; *for drying* torchon *m*; *for washing* lavette *f*

clothes [kloʊðz] vêtements *mpl*; **clothing** vêtements *mpl*

cloud [klaʊd] nuage *m*; **cloudless** sans nuages; **cloudy** nuageux

clout [klaʊt] *fig (influence)* influence *f*

clove of 'garlic [kloʊv] gousse *f* d'ail

clown [klaʊn] *also pej* clown *m*

club [klʌb] *n* club *m*; *weapon* massue *f*

clue [kluː] indice *m*

clumsiness ['klʌmzɪnɪs] maladresse *f*; **clumsy** maladroit

cluster ['klʌstər] groupe *m*

clutch [klʌtʃ] **1** *n* MOT embrayage *m* **2** *v/t* étreindre

◆ **clutch at** s'agripper à

c/o(= *care of*) chez

collar

Co. (= **Company**) Cie (= Compagnie)

coach [kəʊtʃ] **1** n (trainer) entraîneur(-euse) m(f); Br (bus) (auto)car m **2** v/t SP entraîner; **coaching** entraînement m

coagulate [kəʊˈægjʊleɪt] of blood coaguler

coal [kəʊl] charbon m

coalition [kəʊəˈlɪʃn] coalition f

'coalmine mine f de charbon

coarse [kɔːrs] fabric rugueux; hair épais; (vulgar) grossier; **coarsely** (vulgarly), ground grossièrement

coast [kəʊst] côte f; **coastal** côtier; **coastguard** gendarmerie f maritime; person gendarme m maritime; **coastline** littoral m

coat [kəʊt] **1** n veston m; (over~) pardessus m; of animal pelage m; of paint etc couche f **2** v/t (cover) couvrir (**with** de); **coathanger** cintre m; **coating** couche f

coax [kəʊks] cajoler

cocaine [kəˈkeɪn] cocaïne f

cock [kɑːk] chicken coq m; any male bird (oiseau m) mâle m; of plane cockpit m de pilotage; **cockpit** cockpit m; **cockroach** cafard m; **cocktail** cocktail m

cocoa [ˈkəʊkəʊ] cacao m

coconut [ˈkəʊkənʌt] noix m de coco; **coconut palm** cocotier m

code [kəʊd] code m; **in ~** codé

coeducational [kəʊedu-ˈkeɪʃnl] mixte

coerce [kəʊˈɜːrs] forcer

coexist [kəʊɪgˈzɪst] coexister; **coexistence** coexistence f

coffee [ˈkɑːfɪ] café m; **coffee maker** machine f à café; **coffee pot** cafetière f; **coffee shop** café m

cohabit [kəʊˈhæbɪt] cohabiter

coherent [kəʊˈhɪrənt] cohérent

coil [kɔɪl] of rope rouleau m; of snake anneau m

coin [kɔɪn] pièce f (de monnaie)

coincide [kəʊɪnˈsaɪd] coïncider; **coincidence** coïncidence f

Coke® [kəʊk] coca® m

cold [kəʊld] **1** adj froid; **I'm ~** j'ai froid; **it's ~ of weather** il fait froid **2** n froid m; MED rhume m; **cold-blooded** à sang froid: murder commis de sang-froid; **coldly** froidement; **coldness** froideur f; **cold sore** bouton m de fièvre

collaborate [kəˈlæbəreɪt] collaborer; **collaboration** collaboration f; **collaborator** collaborateur(-trice) m(f)

collapse [kəˈlæps] s'effondrer; of building s'écrouler; **collapsible** pliant

collar [ˈkɑːlər] col m; for dog collier m

colleague ['kɒliːg] collègue *m/f*

collect [kə'lekt] **1** *v/t person, cleaning etc* aller/venir chercher; *as hobby* collectionner; *(gather together)* recueillir **2** *v/i (gather together)* s'assembler; **collect call** communication *f* en PCV; **collection** [kə'lekʃn] collection *f*; *in church* collecte *f*; **collective** collectif; **collector** collectionneur(-euse) *m(f)*

college ['kɒlɪdʒ] université *f*

collide [kə'laɪd] se heurter; **collision** collision *f*

colon ['koʊlən] *punctuation* deux-points *mpl*

colonel ['kɜːrnl] colonel *m*

colonial [kə'loʊnɪəl] colonial; **colonize** coloniser; **colony** colonie *f*

color ['kʌlər] couleur *f*; **color-blind** daltonien; **colored** *person* de couleur; **colorful** *also fig* coloré

colossal [kə'lɑːsl] colossal

colour *Br* → **color**

colt [koʊlt] poulain *m*

column ['kɒləm] *architectural, of text* colonne *f*; **columnist** chroniqueur(-euse) *m(f)*

coma ['koʊmə] coma *m*

comb [koʊm] **1** *n* peigne *m* **2** *v/t* peigner; *area* passer au peigne fin

combat ['kɒmbæt] **1** *n* combat *m* **2** *v/t* combattre

combination [kɒmbɪ'neɪʃn]

also of safe combinaison *f*; **combine 1** *v/t* combiner; *ingredients* mélanger **2** *v/i* se combiner

come [kʌm] venir; *of train, bus* arriver

◆ **come across** *(find)* tomber sur

◆ **come along** *(come too)* venir (aussi); *(turn up)* arriver; *(progress)* avancer

◆ **come back** revenir

◆ **come down** descendre; *in price etc* baisser; *of rain, snow* tomber

◆ **come for** *(attack)* attaquer; *(to collect)* venir chercher

◆ **come forward** se présenter

◆ **come from** venir de

◆ **come in** entrer; *of train, in race* arriver; *of tide* monter

◆ **come in for** *criticism* recevoir

◆ **come off** *of handle etc* se détacher

◆ **come out** sortir; *of results* être communiqué; *of sun, product* apparaître; *of stain* partir

◆ **come to 1** *v/t (reach)* arriver à; *that comes to $70* ça fait 70 $ **2** *v/i (regain consciousness)* revenir à soi

◆ **come up** monter; *of sun* se lever

'**comeback** retour *m*, come-back *m*

comedian [kə'miːdɪən] *(comic)* comique *m/f*; *pej* pitre *m/f*; **comedy** comédie *f*

comfort ['kʌmfərt] **1** n confort m; (consolation) réconfort m **2** v/t réconforter; **comfortable** confortable; **be ~** of person être à l'aise

comic ['kɑːmɪk] **1** n to read bande f dessinée; (comedian) comique m/f **2** adj comique; **comical** comique; **comic book** bande f dessinée, BD f; **comics** bandes fpl dessinées; **comic strip** bande f dessinée

comma ['kɑːmə] virgule f

command [kə'mænd] **1** n (order) ordre m; MIL commandement m **2** v/t commander

commandeer [kɑːmən'dɪr] réquisitionner

commander [kə'mændər] commandant(e) m(f); **commander-in-chief** commandant(e) m(f) en chef

commemorate [kə'meməreɪt] commémorer

commence [kə'mens] commencer

commendable [kə'mendəbl] louable; **commendation** for bravery éloge m

comment ['kɑːment] **1** n commentaire m **2** v/i: **~ on** commenter; **commentary** commentaire m; **commentator** commentateur(-trice) m(f)

commerce ['kɑːmɜːrs] commerce m; **commercial 1** adj commercial **2** n (ad) publicité f; **commercial break** page f de publicité; **commercial-**

ize commercialiser

commission [kə'mɪʃn] (payment, committee) commission f; (job) commande f

commit [kə'mɪt] crime commettre; money engager; **commitment** in relationship engagement m; (responsibility) responsabilité f; **committee** comité m

commodity [kə'mɑːdətɪ] marchandise f

common ['kɑːmən] courant; species etc commun; (shared) commun; **have sth in ~ with s.o.** avoir qch en commun; **commonly** communément; **common sense** bon sens m

commotion [kə'moʊʃn] agitation f

communal [kəm'juːnl] en commun

communicate [kə'mjuːnɪkeɪt] communiquer; **communication** communication f; **communicative** communicatif

Communion [kə'mjuːnjən] REL communion f

Communism ['kɑːmjʊnɪzəm] communisme m; **Communist 1** adj communiste **2** n communiste m/f

community [kə'mjuːnətɪ] communauté f

commute [kə'mjuːt] **1** v/i faire la navette (pour aller travailler) **2** v/t LAW commuer

compact [kəm'pækt] **1** adj compact **2** n ['kɑːmpækt]

MOT petite voiture f
companion [kəm'pænjən] compagnon m
company ['kʌmpəni] COM société f; (companionship) compagnie f; (guests) invités mpl
comparable ['kɑːmpərəbl] comparable; comparatimentcomparative; **compare** comparer; **comparison** comparaison f
compartment [kəm'pɑːrtmənt] compartiment m
compass ['kʌmpəs] compas m
compassion [kəm'pæʃn] compassion f; **compassionate** compatissant
compatibility [kəmpætə'biliti] compatibilité f; **compatible** compatible
compel [kəm'pel] obliger
compensate ['kɑːmpənseit] 1 v/t dédommager 2 v/i: ~ **for** compenser; **compensation** (money) dédommagement m; (reward) compensation f; (comfort) consolation f
compete [kəm'piːt] être en compétition; (take part) participer (**in** à)
competence ['kɑːmpitəns] compétence f; **competent** person compétent, capable; piece of work (très) satisfaisant
competition [kɑːmpə'tiʃn] (contest) concours m; SP

competition f; (competing, competitors) concurrence f; **competitive** compétitif; price, offer concurrentiel; **competitiveness** COM compétitivité f; of person esprit m de compétition; **competitor** concurrent m
complacent [kəm'pleisənt] complaisant, suffisant
complain [kəm'plein] se plaindre; **complaint** plainte f; IN SHOP réclamation f; MED maladie f
complementary [kɑːmpli'mentəri] complémentaire
complete [kəm'pliːt] 1 adj complet; (finished) terminé 2 v/t task, building etc terminer, achever; form remplir; **completely** complètement; **completion** achèvement m
complex ['kɑːmpleks] 1 adj complexe 2 n building, PSYCH complexe m; **complexion** facial teint m; **complexity** complexité f
compliance [kəm'plaiəns] conformité f
complicate ['kɑːmplikeit] compliquer; **complicated** compliqué; **complication** complication f
complimentary [kɑːmpli'mentəri] élogieux, flatteur; (free) gratuit
comply [kəm'plai] obéir; ~ **with** ... se conformer à
component [kəm'pounənt] composant m

condescend

compose [kəm'pəʊz] composer; **composed** calme; **composer** MUS compositeur *m*; **composition** composition *f*; **composure** calme *m*

compound ['kɑːmpaʊnd] CHEM composé *m*

comprehend [kɑːmprɪ'hend] comprendre; **comprehension** compréhension *f*; **comprehensive** complet

compress [kəm'pres] comprimer; *information* condenser

comprise [kəm'praɪz] comprendre; *(make up)* constituer; **be ~d of** se composer de

compromise ['kɑːmprəmaɪz] **1** *n* compromis *m* **2** *v/i* trouver un compromis **3** *v/t* compromettre

compulsion [kəm'pʌlʃn] PSYCH compulsion *f*; **compulsive** *behavior* compulsif; *reading* captivant; **compulsory** obligatoire

computer [kəm'pjuːtər] ordinateur *m*; **computer game** jeu *m* informatique; **computerize** informatiser; **computer science** informatique *f*; **computing** informatique *f*

comrade ['kɑːmreɪd] camarade *m/f*; **comradeship** camaraderie *f*

conceal [kən'siːl] cacher; **concealment** dissimulation *f*

conceit [kən'siːt] vanité *f*; **conceited** vaniteux

conceivable [kən'siːvəbl] concevable; **conceive** *of woman* concevoir

concentrate ['kɑːnsəntreɪt] **1** *v/i* se concentrer **2** *v/t energies* concentrer; **concentration** concentration *f*

concept ['kɑːnsept] concept *m*; **conception** *of child* conception *f*

concern [kən'sɜːrn] **1** *n (anxiety, care)* inquiétude *f*, souci *m*; *(business)* affaire *f*; *(company)* entreprise *f* **2** *v/t (involve)* concerner; *(worry)* préoccuper; **concerned** *(anxious)* inquiet; *(caring, involved)* concerné; **concerning** concernant, au sujet de

concert ['kɑːnsərt] concert *m*; **concerted** concerté

concession [kən'seʃn] concession *f*

concise [kən'saɪs] concis

conclude [kən'kluːd] conclure; **~ sth from sth** déduire qch de qch; **conclusion** conclusion *f*; **conclusive** concluant

concrete ['kɑːnkriːt] **1** *n* béton *m* **2** *adj* concret

concussion [kən'kʌʃn] commotion *f* cérébrale

condemn [kən'dem] condamner; **condemnation** condamnation *f*

condescend [kɑːndɪ'send]

daigner (**to do** faire); **condescending** condescendant

condition [kənˈdɪʃn] **1** n (*state, requirement*) condition f; MED maladie f **2** v/t PSYCH conditionner; **conditioning** PSYCH conditionnement m

condo [ˈkɑːndoʊ] *building* immeuble m (en copropriété); *apartment* appart m

condolences [kənˈdoʊlənsɪz] condoléances fpl

condom [ˈkɑːndəm] préservatif m

condominium [kɑːndəˈmɪnɪəm] → **condo**

condone [kənˈdoʊn] excuser

conduct [ˈkɑːndʌkt] **1** n (*behavior*) conduite f **2** v/t [kənˈdʌkt] (*carry out*) mener; ELEC conduire; MUS diriger; **conducted tour** visite f guidée; **conductor** *of car* m d'orchestre; *on train* chef m de train

cone [koʊn] cône m; *for ice cream* cornet m; *of pine tree* pomme f de pin

conference [ˈkɑːnfərəns] conférence f; *discussion* réunion f; **conference room** salle f de conférences

confess [kənˈfes] **1** v/t avouer, confesser **2** v/i *also to police* avouer; REL se confesser; **confession** confession f

confide [kənˈfaɪd] **1** v/t confier **2** v/i: ~ **in s.o.** (*trust*) faire confiance à qn; **confidence**

confiance f; (*in self*) assurance f; **confident** (*self-assured*) sûr de soi; (*convinced*) confiant; **confidential** confidentiel; **confidently** avec assurance

confine [kənˈfaɪn] (*imprison*) enfermer; (*restrict*) limiter; **confined** *space* restreint

confirm [kənˈfɜːrm] confirmer; **confirmation** confirmation f

confiscate [ˈkɑːnfɪskeɪt] confisquer

conflict [ˈkɑːnflɪkt] **1** n conflit m **2** v/i [kənˈflɪkt] être en conflit; *of dates* coïncider

confront [kənˈfrʌnt] (*face*) affronter; (*tackle*) confronter; **confrontation** confrontation f; (*clash, dispute*) affrontement m

confuse [kənˈfjuːz] (*muddle*) compliquer; *person* embrouiller; ~ **s.o. with s.o.** confondre qn avec qn; **confused** *person* désorienté; *ideas, situation* confus; **confusing** déroutant; **confusion** confusion f

congestion [kənˈdʒestʃn] *on roads* encombrement m

congratulate [kənˈgrætʊleɪt] féliciter (**on** pour); **congratulations** félicitations fpl

congregate [ˈkɑːngrɪgeɪt] se rassembler; **congregation** REL assemblée f

Congress [ˈkɑːngres] le Congrès; **Congressional** du

Congrès; **Congressman** membre *m* du Congrès; **Congresswoman** membre *m* du Congrès

conjecture [kən'dʒektʃər] conjecture *f*

con man ['kɑːmæn] escroc *m*, arnaqueur *m*

connect [kə'nekt] raccorder, relier; TELEC passer; (*link*) associer; *to power supply* brancher; **connected**: *be well-~* avoir des relations; *be ~ with* être lié à; **connection** *in wiring* branchement *m*, connexion *f*; *causal etc* rapport *m*; *when traveling* correspondance *f*; (*personal contact*) relation *f*

connoisseur [kɑːnə'sɜːr] connaisseur *m*, connaisseuse *f*

conquer ['kɑːŋkər] conquérir; *fear etc* vaincre; **conqueror** conquérant *m*; **conquest** conquête *f*

conscience ['kɑːnʃəns] conscience *f*; **conscientious** consciencieux; **conscientiousness** conscience *f*

conscious ['kɑːnʃəs] conscient; (*deliberate*) délibéré; **consciously** (*knowingly*) consciemment; (*deliberately*) délibérément; **consciousness** conscience *f*; (*factor*) facteur *m*; (*thoughtfulness, concern*) attention *f*; *take sth into ~* prendre qch en considération

consensus [kən'sensəs] consensus *m*

consent [kən'sent] **1** *n* consentement *m* **2** *v/i* consentir (*to* à)

consequence ['kɑːnsıkwəns] conséquence *f*; **consequently** par conséquent

conservation [kɑːnsər'veıʃn] protection *f*; **conservationist** écologiste *m/f*; **conservative** conservateur; *clothes* classique; *estimate* prudent; **conserve** **1** *n* (*jam*) confiture *f* **2** *v/t energy* économiser

consider [kən'sıdər] considérer; (*show regard for*) prendre en compte; **considerable** considérable; **considerably** considérablement; **considerate** attentionné; **considerately** gentiment; **consideration** (*thought*) réflexion *f*; (*factor*) facteur *m*; (*thoughtfulness, concern*) attention *f*; *take sth into ~* prendre qch en considération

◆ **consist of** [kən'sıst] consister en

consistency [kən'sıstənsı] (*texture*) consistance *f*; (*unchangingness*) constance *f*; (*logic*) cohérence *f*; **consistent** (*unchanging*) constant; *logically etc* cohérent

consolidate [kən'sɑːlıdeıt] consolider

conspicuous [kən'spıkjuəs]

conscious ['kɑːnʃəs] conscient; (*deliberate*) délibéré; **consciously** (*knowingly*) consciemment; (*deliberately*) délibérément; **consciousness** conscience *f*; *lose/regain ~* perdre/reprendre connaissance

consecutive [kən'sekjʊtɪv] consécutif

voyant; **look~** se faire remarquer

conspiracy [kən'spɪrəsɪ] conspiration *f*; **conspirator** conspirateur(-trice) *m(f)*; **conspire** conspirer

constant ['kɑːnstənt] constant; **constantly** constamment

constipated ['kɑːnstɪpeɪtɪd] constipé; **constipation** constipation *f*

constitute ['kɑːnstɪtuːt] constituer; **constitution** constitution *f*; **constitutional** POL constitutionnel

constraint [kən'streɪnt] *(restriction)* contrainte *f*

construct [kən'strʌkt] construire; **construction** construction *f*; *(trade)* bâtiment *m*; **constructive** constructif

consul ['kɑːnsl] consul *m*; **consulate** consulat *m*

consult [kən'sʌlt] consulter; **consultancy** *company* cabinet-conseil *m*; *(advice)* conseil *m*; **consultant** consultant *m*; **consultation** consultation *f*

consume [kən'suːm] consommer; **consumer** consommateur *m*; **consumption** consommation *f*

contact ['kɑːntækt] **1** *n* contact *m* **2** *v/t* contacter; **contact lens** lentille *f* de contact

contagious [kən'teɪdʒəs] contagieux

contain [kən'teɪn] contenir;

container récipient *m*; COM conteneur *m*, container *m*

contaminate [kən'tæmɪneɪt] contaminer; **contamination** contamination *f*

contemporary [kən'tempəreɪrɪ] **1** *adj* contemporain **2** *n* contemporain *m*

contempt [kən'tempt] mépris *m*; **contemptible** méprisable; **contemptuous** méprisant

contender [kən'tendər] *in sport* prétendant *m*; *in competition* concurrent *m*; POL candidat *m*

content[1] ['kɑːntent] *n* contenu *m*

content[2] [kən'tent] **1** *adj* content **2** *v/t*: **~ o.s. with** se contenter de

contented [kən'tentɪd] satisfait; **contentment** contentement *m*

contents ['kɑːntents] contenu *m*

contest[1] ['kɑːntest] *n* *(competition)* concours *m*; *in sport* compétition *f*; *(struggle for power)* lutte *f*

contest[2] [kən'test] *leadership etc* disputer; *(oppose)* contester; **~ an election** se présenter à une élection

contestant [kən'testənt] concurrent *m*

context ['kɑːntekst] contexte *m*

continent ['kɑːntɪnənt] continent *m*; **continental** continental

continual [kən'tınuəl] continuel; **continually** continuellement; **continuation** continuation *f*; *of story* suite *f*; **continue** continuer; **continuous** continu; **continuously** continuellement

contort [kən'tɔːrt] *face* tordre; **~ one's body** se contorsionner

contraception [kɑːntrə-'sepʃn] contraception *f*; **contraceptive** contraceptif *m*

contract[1] ['kɑːntrækt] *n* contrat *m*

contract[2] [kən'trækt] **1** *v/i* (*shrink*) se contracter **2** *v/t illness* contracter

contractor [kən'træktər] entrepreneur *m*

contractual [kən'træktʃuəl] contractuel

contradict [kɑːntrə'dıkt] contredire; **contradiction** contradiction *f*; **contradictory** contradictoire

contrary[1] ['kɑːntrəri] **1** *adj* contraire; **~ to** ... contrairement à ... **2** *n*: **on the ~** au contraire

contrary[2] [kən'treri] *adj* (*perverse*) contrariant

contrast ['kɑːntræst] **1** *n* contraste *m* **2** *v/t* mettre en contraste **3** *v/i* contraster; **contrasting** contrastant; *views* opposé

contravene [kɑːntrə'viːn] enfreindre

contribute [kən'trıbjuːt] **1** contribuer (**to** à); *to magazine* collaborer (**to** à) **2** *v/t money*, *suggestion* donner, apporter; **contribution** contribution *f*; *to political party*, *church* don *m*; **contributor** *of money* donateur *m*; *to magazine* collaborateur(-trice) *m(f)*

control [kən'troul] **1** *n* contrôle *m*; **be in ~ of** contrôler **2** *v/t* contrôler; *company* diriger

controversial [kɑːntrə'vɜːrʃl] controversé; **controversy** controverse *f*

convenience [kən'viːnıəns] commodité *f*; **at your ~** à votre convenance; **convenience store** magasin *m* de proximité; **convenient** commode, pratique

convent ['kɑːnvənt] couvent *m*

convention [kən'venʃn] (*tradition*) conventions *fpl*; (*conference*) convention *f*; **conventional** conventionnel; *person* conformiste

conversation [kɑːnvər'seıʃn] conversation *f*; **conversational** de conversation

conversion [kən'vɜːrʃn] conversion *f*; *of building* aménagement *m*; **convert 1** *n* converti *m* **2** *v/t* convertir; *building* aménager; **convertible** *car* (voiture *f*) décapotable *f*

convey [kən'veı] (*transmit*) transmettre; (*carry*) transporter; **conveyor belt** convoyeur *m*, tapis *m* roulant

convict 1 ['kɑːnvɪkt] *n* détenu *m* **2** [kənˈvɪkt] *v/t* LAW déclarer coupable; **conviction** LAW condamnation *f*; (belief) conviction *f*

convince [kənˈvɪns] convaincre

convoy ['kɑːnvɔɪ] convoi *m*

cook [kuk] **1** *n* cuisinier(-ière) *m(f)*; **2** *v/t meal* préparer; *food* faire cuire **3** *v/i* faire la cuisine; *of food* cuire; **cookbook** livre *m* de cuisine; **cookery** cuisine *f*; **cookie** cookie *m*; **cooking** cuisine *f*

cool [kuːl] **1** *n*: *keep one's ~* garder son sang-froid **2** *adj* frais; *dress* léger; (calm) calme; (unfriendly) froid; P (great) génial **3** *v/i* refroidir; *of tempers* se calmer; *of interest* diminuer **4** *v/t*: *~ it* on se calme

◆ **cool down 1** *v/i* refroidir; *of weather* se rafraîchir; *of tempers* se calmer **2** *v/t food* (faire) refroidir; *fig* calmer

cooperate [kouˈɑːpəreɪt] coopérer; **cooperation** coopération *f*; **cooperative 1** *n* COM coopérative *f* **2** *adj* coopératif

coordinate [kouˈɔːrdɪneɪt] coordonner; **coordination** coordination *f*

cop [kɑːp] F flic *m* F

cope [koup] se débrouiller; *~*

with ... faire face à ...

copier ['kɑːpɪər] *machine* photocopieuse *f*

copper ['kɑːpər] cuivre *m*

copy ['kɑːpɪ] **1** *n* copie *f*; *of book* exemplaire *m* **2** *v/t* copier; (photocopy) photocopier

cord [kɔːrd] (string) corde *f*; (cable) fil *m*, cordon *m*

cordon ['kɔːrdn] cordon *m*

cords [kɔːrdz] *pants* pantalon *m* en velours (côtelé)

core [kɔːr] **1** *n of fruit, problem* cœur *m*; *of party* noyau *m* **2** *adj issue* fondamental

cork [kɔːrk] *in bottle* bouchon *m*; *material* liège *m*; **corkscrew** tire-bouchon *m*

corn [kɔːrn] *grain* maïs *m*

corner ['kɔːrnər] **1** *n* coin *m*; *in road* virage *m*, tournant *m*; *in soccer* corner *m*; *on the ~ of street* au coin **2** *v/t person* coincer; *~ the market* accaparer le marché **3** *v/i of driver, car* prendre le/les virage(s)

coronary ['kɑːrənerɪ] **1** *adj* coronaire **2** *n* infarctus *m* (du myocarde)

coroner ['kɑːrənər] coroner *m*

corporal ['kɔːrpərəl] caporal *m*; **corporal punishment** châtiment *m* corporel

corporate ['kɔːrpərət] COM d'entreprise; **corporation** (business) société *f*, entreprise *f*

corpse [kɔːrps] cadavre *m*, corps *m*

corral [kəˈræl] corral *m*

correct [kəˈrekt] **1** *adj* correct; *the ~ answer* la bonne réponse; *that's ~* c'est ça **2** *v/t* corriger; **correction** correction *f*; **correctly** correctement

correspond [kɑːrɪˈspɑːnd] correspondre (*to* à); **correspondence** correspondance *f*; **correspondent** correspondant(e) *m(f)*

corridor [ˈkɔːrɪdər] couloir *m*

corroborate [kəˈrɑːbəreɪt] corroborer

corrosion [kəˈrouʒn] corrosion *f*

corrupt [kəˈrʌpt] **1** *adj also* COMPUT corrompu; MORALS, YOUTH dépravé **2** *v/t* corrompre; **corruption** corruption *f*

cosmetic [kɑːzˈmetɪk] cosmétique; *fig* esthétique; **cosmetics** cosmétiques *mpl*; **cosmetic surgery** chirurgie *f* esthétique

cosmopolitan [kɑːzməˈpɑːlɪtən] cosmopolite

cost [kɑːst] **1** *n also fig* coût *m* **2** *v/t* coûter; *how much does it ~?* combien ça coûte?

'cost-effective rentable; **cost of living** coût *m* de la vie

costume [ˈkɑːstuːm] *for actor* costume *m*

cosy *Br* → **cozy**

cot [kɑːt] (*camp-bed*) lit *m* de camp; *Br for child* lit *m* d'en-fant

cottage [ˈkɑːtɪdʒ] cottage *m*

cotton [ˈkɑːtn] **1** *n* coton *m* **2** *adj* en coton; **cotton candy** barbe *f* à papa; **cotton wool** *Br* coton *m* hydrophile, ouate *f*

couch [kautʃ] canapé *m*; **couch potato** téléphage *m/f*

cough [kɑːf] **1** *n* toux *f* **2** *v/i* tousser; **cough medicine**, **cough syrup** sirop *m* contre la toux

could [kʊd]: *I have my key?* pourrais-je avoir ma clef?; *~ you help me?* pourrais-tu m'aider?; *you ~ be right* vous avez peut-être raison; *you ~ have warned me!* tu aurais pu me prévenir!

council [ˈkaunsl] (*assembly*) conseil *m*, assemblée *f*; **councilor**, *Br* **councillor** conseiller *m*

counsel [ˈkaunsl] **1** *n* (*advice*) conseil *m*; (*lawyer*) avocat *m* **2** *v/t* conseiller; **counseling**, *Br* **counselling** aide *f* (psychologique); **counselor**, *Br* **counsellor** (*adviser*) conseiller *m*; LAW maître *m*

count [kaunt] **1** *n* compte *m* **2** *v/t* & *v/i* compter

◆ **count on** compter sur

'countdown compte *m* à rebours

counter [ˈkauntər] *in shop*, *café* comptoir *m*; *in game* pion *m*

'counteract neutraliser, contrecarrer; **counter-attack 1**

n contre-attaque *f* **2** *v/i* contre-attaquer; **counterclockwise** dans le sens inverse des aiguilles d'une montre; **counterespionage** contre-espionnage *m*; **counterfeit 1** *v/t* contrefaire **2** *adj* faux; **counterpart** *person* homologue *m/f*; **counterproductive** contre-productif

countless ['kaʊntlɪs] innombrable

country ['kʌntrɪ] pays *m*; *as opposed to town* campagne *f*

county ['kaʊntɪ] comté *m*

coup [kuː] POL coup d'État, *fig* beau coup *m*

couple ['kʌpl] (*two people*) couple *m*; **a ~ of** (*a pair*) deux; (*a few*) quelques

courage ['kʌrɪdʒ] courage *m*; **courageous** courageux

courier ['kʊrɪər] (*messenger*) coursier *m*; *with tourist party* guide *m/f*

course [kɔːrs] *of lessons* cours *m(pl)*; *of meal* plat *m*; *of ship, plane* route *f*; *for sports* piste *f*; *for golf* terrain *m*; **of ~** bien sûr; **of ~ not** bien sûr que non

court [kɔːrt] LAW tribunal *m*, cour *f*; FOR TENNIS cour *f*; *for basketball* terrain *m*; **take s.o. to ~** faire un procès à qn; **court case** affaire *f*, procès *m*

courtesy ['kɜːrtəsɪ] courtoisie *f*

'**courthouse** palais *m* de justi-

ce, tribunal *m*; **courtroom** salle *f* d'audience; **courtyard** cour *f*

cousin ['kʌzn] cousin(e) *m(f)*

cover ['kʌvər] **1** *n protective* housse *f*; *of book, magazine* couverture *f*; (*shelter*) abri *m*; (*insurance*) couverture *f*, assurance *f* **2** *v/t* couvrir

◆ **cover up 1** *v/t* couvrir; *scandal* dissimuler **2** *v/i* cacher la vérité

coverage ['kʌvərɪdʒ] *by media* couverture *f* (médiatique)

covert ['koʊvɜːrt] secret, clandestin

'**cover-up** black-out *m inv*

cow [kaʊ] vache *f*

coward ['kaʊərd] lâche *m/f*; **cowardice** lâcheté *f*

'**cowboy** cow-boy *m*

co-worker ['koʊwɜːrkər] collègue *m/f*

cozy ['koʊzɪ] confortable, douillet

crab [kræb] crabe *m*

crack [kræk] **1** *n* fissure *f*; *in cup, glass* fêlure *f*; (*joke*) vanne *f* **2** *v/t cup, glass* fêler; *nut* casser; (*solve*) résoudre; *code* décrypter **3** *v/i* se fêler; **crack** (*cocaine*) crack *m*; **cracked cup** fêlé *m*; **cracker** *to eat* cracker *m*

cradle ['kreɪdl] berceau *m*

craft[1] [kræft] NAUT embarcation *f*

craft[2] (*trade*) métier *m*; *weaving, pottery etc* artisanat *m*

(*craftsmanship*) art m;
craftsman (*artisan*) artisan m; **crafty** malin, rusé

crag [kræg] (*rock*) rocher m escarpé

cram [kræm] fourrer; *food* enfourner; *people* entasser

cramps [kræmps] crampe f

crane [kreɪn] **1** n (*machine*) grue f **2** v/t: **~ one's neck** tendre le cou

crank [kræŋk] *person* allumé m; **cranky** (*bad-tempered*) grognon

crash [kræʃ] **1** n *noise* fracas m; *accident* accident m; COM faillite f; *of stock exchange* krach m; COMPUT plantage m **2** v/i s'écraser; *of car* avoir un accident; *of market* s'effondrer; COMPUT se planter **3** v/t *car* avoir un accident avec; **crash course** cours m intensif; **crash diet** régime m intensif; **crash helmet** casque m; **crash-land** atterrir en catastrophe

crate [kreɪt] caisse f

crater ['kreɪtər] cratère m

crave [kreɪv] avoir très envie de; **craving** envie f (irrépressible)

crawl [krɔːl] **1** n *in swimming* crawl m **2** v/i *on belly* ramper; *on hands and knees* marcher à quatre pattes; (*move slowly*) se traîner

crayon ['kreɪɑːn] crayon m de couleur

craze [kreɪz] engouement m;

the latest ~ la dernière mode; **crazy** fou

creak [kriːk] craquer, grincer; **creaky** qui craque, grinçant

cream [kriːm] **1** n crème f; *color* crème m **2** *adj* crème *inv*

crease [kriːs] **1** n pli m **2** v/t *accidentally* froisser

create [kriːˈeɪt] créer; **creation** création f; **creative** créatif; **creator** créateur(-trice) m(f)

creature ['kriːtʃər] animal m; (*person*) créature f

credibility [kredəˈbɪlətɪ] crédibilité f; **credible** crédible

credit ['kredɪt] crédit m; (*honor*) honneur m, mérite m; **creditable** honorable; **credit card** carte f de crédit; **credit limit** limite f de crédit; **creditor** créancier m; **creditworthy** solvable

creep [kriːp] **1** n *pej* sale type m **2** v/i se glisser (en silence); (*move slowly*) avancer lentement; **creepy** F flippant F

cremate [krɪˈmeɪt] incinérer; **cremation** incinération f, crémation f

crest [krest] crête f

crevice ['krevɪs] fissure f

crew [kruː] *of ship, airplane* équipage m; **crew cut** cheveux mpl en brosse

crib [krɪb] *for baby* lit m d'enfant

crime [kraɪm] crime m; **criminal 1** n criminel m **2** *adj* criminel; (*shameful*) honteux

crimson ['krɪmzn] cramoisi

cripple ['krɪpl] **1** n handicapé(e) m(f) **2** v/t person estropier; fig paralyser

crisis ['kraɪsɪs] crise f

crisp [krɪsp] weather vivifiant; lettuce, apple croquant; bacon, toast croustillant; **crisps** Br chips fpl

criterion [kraɪ'tɪrɪən] critère m

critic ['krɪtɪk] critique m; **critical** critique; **criticism** critique f; **criticize** critiquer

crocodile ['krɑːkədaɪl] crocodile m

crony ['krəʊnɪ] pote m, copain m

crook [krʊk] escroc m; **crooked** de travers; streets tortueux; (*dishonest*) malhonnête

crop [krɑːp] **1** n culture f; (*harvest*) récolte f **2** v/t hair, photo couper

◆ **crop up** surgir

cross [krɑːs] **1** adj (*angry*) fâché **2** n croix f **3** v/t (go across) traverser; ~ **o.s.** REL se signer **4** v/i (go across) traverser; of lines se croiser

◆ **cross off, cross out** rayer

'crosscheck 1 n recoupement m **2** v/t vérifier par recoupement; **cross-examine** LAW faire subir un contre-interrogatoire à; **cross-eyed** qui louche; **crossing** NAUT traversée f; **crossroads** also

fig carrefour m; **crosswalk** passage m (pour) piétons; **crossword (puzzle)** mots mpl croisés

crotch [krɑːtʃ] entrejambe m

crouch [kraʊtʃ] s'accroupir

crowd [kraʊd] foule f; at sports event public m; **crowded** bondé, plein (de monde)

crown [kraʊn] also on tooth couronne f

crucial ['kruːʃl] crucial

crucifix ['kruːsɪfɪks] crucifix m; **crucifixion** of Christ crucifixion f; **crucify** REL crucifier; fig assassiner

crude [kruːd] **1** adj (*vulgar*) grossier; (*unsophisticated*) rudimentaire **2** n: ~ **(oil)** pétrole m brut

cruel ['kruːəl] cruel; **cruelty** cruauté f

cruise [kruːz] **1** n croisière f **2** v/i of people faire une croisière; of car rouler (à une vitesse de croisière); of plane voler (à une vitesse de croisière)

crumb [krʌm] miette f

crumble ['krʌmbl] of bread s'émietter; of stonework s'effriter; fig: of opposition etc s'effondrer

crumple ['krʌmpl] **1** v/t (*crease*) froisser **2** v/i (*collapse*) s'écrouler

crush [krʌʃ] **1** n (*crowd*) foule f **2** v/t écraser; (*crease*) froisser

crust [krʌst] *on bread* croûte f
crutch [krʌtʃ] *for injured person* béquille f
cry [kraɪ] **1** *n (call)* cri m **2** *v/i (weep)* pleurer
◆ **cry out** crier
cryptic ['krɪptɪk] énigmatique
crystal ['krɪstl] cristal m
cube [kjuːb] cube m; **cubic** cubique; **~ meter** mètre cube
cubicle ['kjuːbɪkl] *(changing room)* cabine f
cuddle ['kʌdl] câliner
cue [kjuː] *for actor etc* signal m; *for pool* queue f
cuff [kʌf] *of shirt* poignet m; *of pants* revers m; *(blow)* gifle f
culminate ['kʌlmɪneɪt]: **~ in** se terminer par; **culmination** apogée f
culprit ['kʌlprɪt] coupable m/f
cult [kʌlt] *(sect)* secte f
cultivate ['kʌltɪveɪt] *land, person* cultiver; **cultivated** *person* cultivé; **cultivation** *of land* culture f
cultural ['kʌltʃərəl] culturel; **culture** culture f; **cultured** cultivé
cumulative ['kjuːmjʊlətɪv] cumulatif
cunning ['kʌnɪŋ] **1** n ruse f **2** adj rusé
cup [kʌp] tasse f; *(trophy)* coupe f
cupboard ['kʌbərd] placard m
curb [kɜːrb] **1** n *of street* bord m du trottoir; *on powers etc* frein m **2** v/t réfréner

cure [kjʊr] **1** n MED remède m **2** v/t MED guérir; *meat* saurer
curiosity [kjʊrɪ'ɑːsətɪ] curiosité f; **curious** curieux
curl [kɜːrl] **1** n *in hair* boucle f; *of smoke* volute f **2** v/t *hair* boucler; *(wind)* enrouler **3** v/i *of hair* boucler; *of leaf, paper etc* se gondoler
◆ **curl up** se pelotonner
curly ['kɜːrlɪ] *hair* bouclé; *tail* en tire-bouchon
currency ['kʌrənsɪ] monnaie f; **foreign ~** devise f étrangère; **current 1** n *in sea*, ELEC courant m **2** adj actuel; **current affairs** actualité f
curse [kɜːrs] **1** n *(spell)* malédiction f; *(swearword)* juron m **2** v/t maudire **3** v/i *(swear)* jurer
cursor ['kɜːrsər] COMPUT curseur m
cursory ['kɜːrsərɪ] superficiel
curt [kɜːrt] abrupt
curtain ['kɜːrtn] *also* THEA rideau m
curve [kɜːrv] **1** n courbe f **2** v/i *(bend)* s'incurver; *of road* faire une courbe
cushion ['kʊʃn] **1** n coussin m **2** v/t *blow, fall* amortir
custody ['kʌstədɪ] *of children* garde f; **in ~** LAW en détention
custom ['kʌstəm] coutume f; COM clientèle f; **customer** client m; **customer service** service m clientèle
customs ['kʌstəmz] douane

f; **customs officer** douanier m

cut [kʌt] **1** n with knife, scissors entaille f; (injury) coupure f; of garment, hair coupe f; (reduction) réduction f **2** v/t couper; (reduce) réduire; **get one's hair ~** se faire couper les cheveux
◆ **cut down 1** tree abattre **2** v/i on smoking etc réduire
◆ **cut off** couper; (isolate) isoler
◆ **cut up** meat etc découper
cutback réduction f
cute [kju:t] in appearance mignon; (clever) malin
'cutoff date date f limite; **cut--price** à prix m réduit; **cut--throat** competition acharné; **cutting 1** n from newspaper coupure f **2** adj remark blessant

cyber ... ['saɪbər] cyber...
cycle ['saɪkl] **1** n vélo m; of events cycle m **2** v/i aller en vélo; **cycling** cyclisme m; **cyclist** cycliste m/f
cylinder ['sɪlɪndər] in engine cylindre m; **cylindrical** cylindrique
cynic ['sɪnɪk] cynique m/f; **cynical** cynique; **cynicism** cynisme m
Czech [tʃek] **1** adj tchèque; **the ~ Republic** la République tchèque **2** n person Tchèque m/f; language tchèque m

D

DA [di:'eɪ] (= **district attorney**) procureur m
◆ **dabble in** toucher à
dad [dæd] papa m
daily ['deɪlɪ] **1** n paper quotidien m **2** adj quotidien
'dairy products produits mpl laitiers
dam [dæm] for water barrage m
damage ['dæmɪdʒ] **1** n dommage(s) m(pl); to reputation préjudice m **2** v/t endommager; fig: reputation nuire à; **damages** LAW dommages--intérêts mpl; **damaging** préjudiciable

damn [dæm] F **1** interj zut **2** adj sacré **3** adv (very) vachement F; **damning** evidence, report accablant
damp [dæmp] humide
dance [dɑ:ns] **1** n danse f; social event bal m **2** v/i danser; **dancer** danseur(-euse) m(f); **dancing** danse f
Dane [deɪn] Danois(e) m(f)
danger ['deɪndʒər] danger m; **dangerous** dangereux
dangle ['dæŋgl] **1** v/t balancer **2** v/i pendre
Danish ['deɪnɪʃ] **1** adj danois **2** n language danois m
Danish (pastry) feuilleté m

(sucré)

dare [der] **1** *v/i* oser; **~ to do sth** oser faire qch **2** *v/t*: **~ s.o. to do sth** défier qn de faire qch; **daring** audacieux

dark [dɑːrk] **1** *n* noir *m* **2** *adj room* sombre, noir; *hair* brun; *eyes, color, clothes* foncé; **dark glasses** lunettes *fpl* noires; **darkness** obscurité *f*

darling ['dɑːrlɪŋ] chéri(e) *m(f)*

dart [dɑːrt] **1** *n for game* fléchette *f* **2** *v/i* se précipiter

dash [dæʃ] **1** *n punctuation* tiret *m*; **a ~ of** un peu de **2** *v/i* se précipiter **3** *v/t hopes* anéantir; **dashboard** tableau *m* de bord

data ['deɪtə] données *fpl*; **database** base *f* de données

date[1] [deɪt] *fruit* datte *f*

date[2] [deɪt] date *f*; *meeting, person* rendez-vous *m*; **out of ~** *clothes* démodé; *passport* périmé; **up to ~** *information* à jour; *style* à la mode; **dated** démodé

daughter ['dɔːtər] fille *f*; **daughter-in-law** belle-fille *f*

dawn [dɔːn] *also fig* aube *f*

day [deɪ] jour *m*; *stressing duration* journée *f*; **the ~ after** le lendemain; **the ~ after tomorrow** après-demain; **the ~ before** la veille; **the ~ before yesterday** avant-hier; **in those ~s** en ce temps-là, à l'époque; **the other ~** (*recently*) l'autre jour; **day-**

break aube *f*, point *m* du jour; **daydream 1** *n* rêverie *f* **2** *v/i* rêvasser; **daylight** jour *m*; **day spa** spa *m* urbain

dazzle ['dæzl] éblouir

dazed [deɪzd] *by news* hébété; *by blow* étourdi

dead [ded] **1** *adj* mort; *battery* à plat; **the phone's ~** il n'y a pas de tonalité **2** *adv* F (*very*) très; **~ beat, ~ tired** crevé **3** *npl*: **the ~** les morts *mpl*; **dead end** *street* impasse *f*; **dead heat** arrivée *f* ex æquo; **deadline** date *f* limite; heure *f* limite, délai *m*; *for newspaper* heure *f* de clôture; **meet the ~** respecter le(s) délai(s); **deadlock** *in talks* impasse *f*; **deadly** mortel

deaf [def] sourd; **deafening** assourdissant; **deafness** surdité *f*

deal [diːl] **1** *n* accord *m*, marché *m*; **a great ~ of** beaucoup de **2** *v/t cards* distribuer

◆ **deal in** com être dans le commerce de; *drugs* dealer

◆ **deal with** (*handle*) s'occuper de; (*do business with*) traiter avec; (*be about*) traiter de

dealer ['diːlər] marchand *m*; (*drug ~*) dealer *m*, dealeuse *f*; *large-scale* trafiquant *m* de drogue; **dealing** (*drug ~*) trafic *m* de drogue; **dealings** (*business*) relations *fpl*

dear [dɪr] cher; **Dear Sir** Monsieur

death [deθ] mort f; **death toll** nombre m de morts

debatable [dɪ'beɪtəbl] discutable; **debate 1** n débat m **2** v/i débattre **3** v/it débattre de

debit ['debɪt] **1** n débit m **2** v/it *account* débiter; *amount* porter au débit; **debit card** carte f bancaire

debris [də'briː] débris mpl

debt [det] dette f; **be in ~** être endetté; **debtor** débiteur m

debug [diː'bʌg] COMPUT déboguer

decade ['dekeɪd] décennie f

decadent ['dekədənt] décadent

decaffeinated [diː'kæfɪneɪtɪd] décaféiné

decay [dɪ'keɪ] **1** n détérioration f; *in wood, plant* pourriture f; *in teeth* carie f **2** v/i *of wood, plant* pourrir; *of civilization* tomber en décadence; *of teeth* se carier

deceased [dɪ'siːst]: **the ~** le défunt/la défunte

deceit [dɪ'siːt] duplicité f; **deceitful** fourbe; **deceive** tromper

December [dɪ'sembər] décembre m

decency ['diːsənsɪ] décence f; **decent** *person* correct, honnête; *salary* correct, décent; *meal, sleep* bon

deception [dɪ'sepʃn] tromperie f; **deceptive** trompeur

decide [dɪ'saɪd] décider; de-cided (*definite*) décidé; *views* arrêté; *improvement* net

decimal ['desɪml] décimale f

decipher [dɪ'saɪfər] déchiffrer

decision [dɪ'sɪʒn] décision f; **decisive** décidé; (*crucial*) décisif

deck [dek] *of ship* pont m; *of cards* jeu m (de cartes)

declaration [deklə'reɪʃn] déclaration f; **declare** déclarer

decline [dɪ'klaɪn] **1** n baisse f; *of civilization, health* déclin m **2** v/it *invitation* décliner; **~ to comment** refuser de commenter **3** v/i (*refuse*) refuser; (*decrease*) baisser; *of health* décliner

decode [diː'koʊd] décoder

décor ['deɪkɔːr] décor m

decorate ['dekəreɪt] *room* refaire; *with paint* peindre; *with paper* tapisser; (*adorn*), *soldier* décorer; **decoration** décoration f; **decorator** (*interior ~*) décorateur m (d'intérieur)

decoy ['diːkɔɪ] appât m, leurre m

decrease [diː'kriːs] **1** n baisse f, diminution f; *in size* réduction f **2** v/it & v/i diminuer

dedicate ['dedɪkeɪt] *book etc* dédicacer; **dedicated** dévoué; **dedication** *in book* dédicace f; *to cause, work* dévouement m

deduce [dɪ'duːs] déduire

deduct [dɪ'dʌkt] déduire

(*from* de); **deduction** *from salary* prélèvement *m*; (*conclusion*) déduction *f*

deed [diːd] (*act*) acte *m*; LAW acte *m* (notarié)

deep [diːp] profond; *voice* grave; *color* intense; **deepen 1** *v/t* creuser **2** *v/i* devenir plus profond; *of mystery* s'épaissir; **deep freeze** congélateur *m*

deer [dɪr] cerf *m*; *female* biche *f*

deface [dɪˈfeɪs] abîmer

defamation [defəˈmeɪʃn] diffamation *f*; **defamatory** diffamatoire

defeat [dɪˈfiːt] **1** *n* défaite *f* **2** *v/t* battre

defect [ˈdiːfekt] défaut *m*; **defective** défectueux

defence *Br* → **defense**

defend [dɪˈfend] défendre; *decision* justifier; **defendant** défendeur *m*, défenderesse *f*; *in criminal case* accusé(e) *m(f)*; **defense** défense *f*; **defenseless** sans défense; **Defense Secretary** POL ministre de la Défense; **defensive 1** *n*: **go on (to) the ~** se mettre sur la défensive **2** *adj* défensif

deference [ˈdefərəns] déférence *f*

defiance [dɪˈfaɪəns] défi *m*; **defiant** [dɪˈfaɪənt] provocant; *look* de défi

deficiency [dɪˈfɪʃənsɪ] manque *m*; MED carence *f*

deficit [ˈdefɪsɪt] déficit *m*

define [dɪˈfaɪn] définir

definite [ˈdefɪnɪt] définitif; *improvement* net; (*certain*) catégorique; **definitely** sans aucun doute; **~ not** certainement pas!

definition [defɪˈnɪʃn] définition *f*

deformity [dɪˈfɔːrmətɪ] difformité *f*

defrost [diːˈfrɒst] *food* décongeler; *fridge* dégivrer

defuse [diːˈfjuːz] *bomb, situation* désamorcer

defy [dɪˈfaɪ] défier; *superiors* braver

degrading [dɪˈgreɪdɪŋ] dégradant

degree [dɪˈgriː] degré *m*; *from university* diplôme *m*

dehydrated [diːhaɪˈdreɪtɪd] déshydraté

deign [deɪn]: **~ to** daigner

dejected [dɪˈdʒektɪd] déprimé

delay [dɪˈleɪ] **1** *n* retard *m* **2** *v/t* retarder; **be ~ed** être en retard **3** *v/i* tarder

delegate [ˈdelɪgət] **1** *n* délégué(e) *m(f)* **2** *v/t* déléguer; **delegation** délégation *f*

delete [dɪˈliːt] effacer; (*cross out*) rayer; **deletion** *act* effacement *m*; *that deleted* rature *f*

deliberate 1 [dɪˈlɪbərət] *adj* délibéré **2** [dɪˈlɪbəreɪt] *v/i* délibérer; (*reflect*) réfléchir; **deliberately** délibérément, exprès

delicate ['delɪkət] délicat
delicatessen [delɪkə'tesn]
traiteur m, épicerie f fine
delicious [dɪ'lɪʃəs] délicieux
delight [dɪ'laɪt] joie f, plaisir
m; **delighted** ravi; **delightful**
charmant
deliver [dɪ'lɪvər] lIvIєr; *letters*
distribuer; *parcel etc* remettre; *message* transmettre; *baby* mettre au monde; *speech*
faire; **delivery** *of goods* livraison f; *of mail* distribution f; *of baby* accouchement
m; *of speech* débit m; **delivery date** date f de livraison
de luxe [də'lʌks] de luxe;
model haut de gamme *inv*
demand [dɪ'mænd] **1** *n also*
COM demande f; *of terrorist,
unions etc* revendication f;
in ~ demandé **2** *v/t* exiger;
pay rise etc réclamer; **demanding** *job* éprouvant;
person exigeant
demo ['deməʊ] (*protest*) ma-
nif f; *of video etc* démo f
democracy [dɪ'mɑːkrəsɪ] démocratie f; **democrat** démocrate m/f; **democratic** dé-
mocratique
demolish [dɪ'mɑːlɪʃ] *building,
argument* démolir; **dem-
olition** démolition f
demonstrate ['demənstreɪt]
1 *v/t* (*prove*) démontrer; *machine etc* faire une démonstration de **2** *v/i politically* manifester; **demonstration** dé-

monstration f; (*protest*) manifestation f; **demonstrator**
(*protester*) manifestant(e)
m(f)
demoralized [dɪ'mɔːrəlaɪzd]
démoralisé; **demoralizing**
démoralisant
demote [diː'məʊt] rétrograder
den [den] *room* antre f
denial [dɪ'naɪəl] *of accusation*
démenti m, dénégation f; *of
request* refus m
denim ['denɪm] jean m
Denmark ['denmɑːrk] le Danemark
denomination [dɪnɑːmɪ-
'neɪʃn] *of money* coupure f;
religious confession f
dense [dens] (*thick*) dense;
density ['densɪtɪ] densité f
dent [dent] **1** *n* bosse f **2** *v/t*
bosseler
dental ['dentl] dentaire
dented ['dentɪd] bosselé
dentist ['dentɪst] dentiste
m/f; **dentures** dentier m
Denver boot ['denvər] sabot
m de Denver
deny [dɪ'naɪ] *charge* nier;
right, request refuser
deodorant [diː'əʊdərənt]
déodorant m
department [dɪ'pɑːrtmənt] *of
company* service m; *of university* département m; *of
government* ministère m; *of
store* rayon m; **Department
of State** ministère m des Affaires étrangères; **depart-**

design

ment store grand magasin *m*

departure [dɪ'pɑːrtʃər] départ *m*; *from standard etc* entorse *f* (**from** à); **departure lounge** salle *f* d'embarquement; **departure time** heure *f* de départ

depend [dɪ'pend] dépendre; *that* **~s** cela dépend; **dependence, dependency** dépendance *f*

depict [dɪ'pɪkt] représenter

deplorable [dɪ'plɔːrəbl] déplorable; **deplore** déplorer

deploy [dɪ'plɔɪ] (*use*) faire usage de; (*position*) déployer

deport [dɪ'pɔːrt] expulser; **deportation** expulsion *f*

deposit [dɪ'pɑːzɪt] **1** *n in bank* dépôt *m*; *on purchase* acompte *m*; *security* caution *f*; *of mineral* gisement *m* **2** *v/t money, object* déposer; **deposition** LAW déposition *f*

depot ['depoʊ] *for storage* dépôt *m*, entrepôt *m*

depreciation [dɪpriːʃɪ'eɪʃn] FIN dépréciation *f*

depress [dɪ'pres] *person* déprimer; **depressed** déprimé; **depressing** déprimant; **depression** MED, *meteorological* dépression *f*; *economic* crise *f*, récession *f*

deprivation [deprɪ'veɪʃn] privation(s) *f(pl)*; **deprive**: **~ s.o. of sth** priver qn de qch; **deprived** déprimé

depth [depθ] profondeur *f*; *of color* intensité *f*; *in* **~** en pro-

fondeur

deputy ['depjuti] adjoint(e) *m(f)*; *of sheriff* shérif *m* adjoint

derail [dɪ'reɪl]: *be* **~ed** *of train* dérailler

derelict ['derəlɪkt] délabré

deride [dɪ'raɪd] se moquer de; **derision** dérision *f*; **derisory** dérisoire

derivative [dɪ'rɪvətɪv] (*not original*) dérivé

derive [dɪ'raɪv] tirer (**from** de); *be* **~d from** dériver de

dermatologist [dɜːrmə'tɑːlədʒɪst] dermatologue *m/f*

derogatory [dɪ'rɑːgətɔːri] désobligeant; *term* péjoratif

descendant [dɪ'sendənt] descendant(e) *m(f)*; **descent** descente *f*; (*ancestry*) descendance *f*

describe [dɪ'skraɪb] décrire; **description** description *f*; *of criminal* signalement *m*

desegregate [diː'segreɪt] supprimer la ségrégation dans

desert[1] ['dezərt] *n* désert *m*

desert[2] [dɪ'zɜːrt] **1** *v/t* abandonner **2** *v/i of soldier* déserter; **deserted** désert; **deserter** MIL déserteur *m*; **desertion** abandon *m*; MIL désertion *f*

deserve [dɪ'zɜːrv] mériter

design [dɪ'zaɪn] **1** *n* (*subject*) design *m*; (*style*) style *m*; (*drawing, pattern*) dessin *m*

2 v/t (draw) dessiner; building, car concevoir

designate ['dezigneit] person désigner

designer [di'zainər] designer m/f; of car, ship concepteur(-trice) m/f; of clothes styliste m/f; **designer clothes** vêtements mpl de marque

desirable [di'zairəbl] souhaitable; sexually, change désirable; house beau; **desire** désir m

desk [desk] bureau m; in hotel réception f; **desk clerk** réceptionniste m/f; **desktop publishing** publication f assistée par ordinateur

desolate ['desələt] place désolé

despair [di'sper] **1** n désespoir m; **in ~** désespéré **2** v/i désespérer (**of** de); **desperate** désespéré; **be ~ for sth** avoir très envie de qch; **desperation** désespoir m; **in ~** en désespoir de cause

despicable [dis'pikəbl] méprisable; **despise** mépriser

despite [di'spait] malgré, en dépit de

dessert [di'zɜːrt] dessert m

destination [desti'neiʃn] destination f

destroy [di'stroi] détruire; **destroyer** NAUT destroyer m; **destruction** destruction f; **destructive** power destructeur; **a ~ child** un enfant

qui casse tout

detach [di'tætʃ] détacher; **detached** (objective) neutre; **detachment** (objectivity) neutralité f

detail ['diːteil] détail m; **detailed** détaillé

detain [di'tein] (hold back) retenir; as prisoner détenir; **detainee** détenu(e) m/f; **political ~** prisonnier m politique

detect [di'tekt] déceler; of device détecter; **detection** of criminal découverte f; of smoke etc détection f; **detective** inspecteur m de police; **detector** détecteur m

détente ['deitaːnt] POL détente f

deter [di'tɜːr] dissuader

detergent [di'tɜːrdʒənt] détergent m

deteriorate [di'tiriəreit] se détériorer

determination [ditɜːrmɪ'neiʃn] (resolution) détermination f; **determine** (establish) déterminer; **determined** déterminé, résolu; effort délibéré

detest [di'test] détester; **detestable** détestable

detour ['diːtur] détour m; (diversion) déviation f

devaluation [diːvæljuˈeiʃn] dévaluation f; **devalue** dévaluer

devastate ['devəsteit] dévaster; fig: person anéantir

develop [dɪˈveləp] **1** *v/t film, business* développer; *site* aménager; *technique, vaccine* mettre au point; *illness* attraper **2** *v/i* (*grow*) se développer; **developing country** pays *m* en voie de développement; **development** *of film, business* développement *m*; *of site* aménagement *m*; (*event*) événement *m*; *of technique, vaccine* mise *f* au point

device [dɪˈvaɪs] (*tool*) appareil *m*

devil [ˈdevl] diable *m*; **a little ~** un petit monstre

devise [dɪˈvaɪz] concevoir

devote [dɪˈvoʊt] consacrer; **devoted** *son etc* dévoué (**to** à); **devotion** dévouement *m*

devour [dɪˈvaʊr] dévorer

devout [dɪˈvaʊt] pieux

diabetes [daɪəˈbiːtiːz] diabète *m*; **diabetic** diabétique *m/f*

diagnose [ˈdaɪəgnoʊz] diagnostiquer; **diagnosis** diagnostic *m*

diagonal [daɪˈægənl] diagonal; **diagonally** en diagonale

diagram [ˈdaɪəgræm] diagramme *m*

dial [ˈdaɪl] **1** *n* cadran *m* **2** *v/i* TELEC faire le numéro **3** *v/t* TELEC *number* composer

dialog, *Br* **dialogue** [ˈdaɪəlɑːg] dialogue *m*

'dial tone tonalité *f*

diameter [daɪˈæmɪtər] diamètre *m*

diamond [ˈdaɪmənd] diamant *m*; *shape* losange *m*

diaper [ˈdaɪpər] couche *f*

diaphragm [ˈdaɪəfræm] diaphragme *m*

diarrhea, *Br* **diarrhoea** [daɪəˈriːə] diarrhée *f*

diary [ˈdaɪrɪ] journal *m*; *for appointments* agenda *m*

dice [daɪs] dé *m*; *pl* dés *mpl*

dictate [dɪkˈteɪt] dicter; **dictator** POL dictateur *m*; **dictatorship** dictature *f*

dictionary [ˈdɪkʃənrɪ] dictionnaire *m*

die [daɪ] mourir
◆ **die down** *of storm* se calmer; *of excitement* s'apaiser
◆ **die out** disparaître

diet [ˈdaɪət] **1** *n* (*regular food*) alimentation *f*; *to lose weight, for health* régime *m* **2** *v/i* faire un régime

differ [ˈdɪfər] différer; (*disagree*) différer; **difference** différence *f*; **different** différent; **differently** différemment

difficult [ˈdɪfɪkəlt] difficile; **difficulty** difficulté *f*

dig [dɪg] creuser

digest [daɪˈdʒest] digérer; *information* assimiler; **digestion** digestion *f*

digit [ˈdɪdʒɪt] chiffre *m*; **digital** numérique; **digital camera** appareil *m* photo numérique; **digital photo** photo *f* numérique

dignified [ˈdɪgnɪfaɪd] digne; **dignity** dignité *f*

dilapidated [dɪˈlæpɪdeɪtɪd] délabré

dilemma [dɪˈlemə] dilemme m

dilute [daɪˈluːt] diluer

dim [dɪm] **1** adj room, prospects sombre; light faible; outline vague; (stupid) bête **2** v/i of lights baisser

dime [daɪm] (pièce f de) dix cents mpl

dimension [daɪˈmenʃn] dimension f

diminish [dɪˈmɪnɪʃ] diminuer

din [dɪn] brouhaha m

dine [daɪn] dîner

dinghy [ˈdɪŋgɪ] small yacht dériveur m; rubber boat canot m pneumatique

dining car [ˈdaɪnɪŋ] RAIL wagon-restaurant m; **dining room** salle f à manger; in hotel salle f de restaurant

dinner [ˈdɪnər] dîner m; at midday déjeuner f; gathering repas m; **dinner party** dîner m, repas m

dip [dɪp] **1** n for food sauce f (dans laquelle on trempe des aliments); in road inclinaison f **2** v/i of road s'incliner

diploma [dɪˈpləʊmə] diplôme m

diplomacy [dɪˈpləʊməsɪ] also (tact) diplomatie f; **diplomat** diplomate m/f; **diplomatic** diplomatique; (tactful) diplomate

direct [daɪˈrekt] **1** adj direct **2** v/t to a place indiquer (**to sth** qch); play mettre en scène; movie réaliser; attention diriger

direction [daɪˈrekʃn] direction f; of movie réalisation f; **~s** (instructions) indications fpl; for use mode m d'emploi; for medicine instructions fpl; **ask for ~s** to a place demander son chemin; **directly** (straight) directement; (soon) dans très peu de temps; (immediately) immédiatement; **director** of company directeur(-trice) m(f); of movie réalisateur(-trice) m(f); of play metteur(-euse) m(f) en scène; **directory** répertoire m (d'adresses); TELEC annuaire m (des téléphones)

dirt [dɜːrt] saleté f; **dirty 1** adj sale; (pornographic) cochon **2** v/t salir

disability [dɪsəˈbɪlətɪ] infirmité f; **disabled** handicapé f; **disabled** handicapé

disadvantage [dɪsədˈvæntɪdʒ] désavantage m; **disadvantaged** défavorisé

disagree [dɪsəˈgriː] of person ne pas être d'accord; **disagreeable** désagréable

disagreement désaccord m; (argument) dispute f

disappear [dɪsəˈpɪr] disparaître; **disappearance** disparition f

disappoint [dɪsəˈpɔɪnt] décevoir; **disappointing** décevant; **disappointment** dé-

disgusting

ception f

disapproval [dɪsə'pruːvl] désapprobation f; **disapprove** désapprouver; **~ of actions** désapprouver; **s.o.** ne pas aimer; **disapproving** désapprobateur

disarm [dɪs'ɑːrm] désarmer; **disarmament** désarmement m

disaster [dɪ'zæstər] désastre m; **disastrous** désastreux

disband [dɪs'bænd] **1** v/t disperser **2** v/i se disperser

disbelief [dɪsbə'liːf] incrédulité f

disc [dɪsk] disque m; **CD CD** m

discard [dɪ'skɑːrd] old clothes etc se débarrasser de; boyfriend abandonner

disciplinary [dɪsɪ'plɪnərɪ] disciplinaire; **discipline** discipline f

'disc jockey disc-jockey m

disclaim [dɪs'kleɪm] nier

disclose [dɪs'kləʊz] révéler; **disclosure** [dɪs'kləʊʒər] révélation f

disco ['dɪskəʊ] discothèque f; type of dance, music disco m

discomfort [dɪs'kʌmfərt] gêne f; **be in ~** être incommodé

disconcert [dɪskən'sɜːrt] déconcerter

disconnect [dɪskə'nekt] hose détacher; electrical appliance débrancher; supply, phones couper

discontent [dɪskən'tent] mécontentement m

discontinue [dɪskən'tɪnuː]

product arrêter; bus service supprimer

discotheque ['dɪskətek] discothèque f

discount ['dɪskaʊnt] remise f

discourage [dɪs'kʌrɪdʒ] décourager

discover [dɪs'kʌvər] découvrir; **discovery** découverte f

discredit [dɪs'kredɪt] discréditer

discreet [dɪs'kriːt] discret

discrepancy [dɪs'krepənsɪ] divergence f

discretion [dɪs'kreʃn] discrétion f

discriminate [dɪ'skrɪmɪneɪt]: **~ against** pratiquer une discrimination contre; **discriminating** avisé; **discrimination sexual etc** discrimination f

discuss [dɪ'skʌs] discuter de; of article traiter de; **discussion** discussion f

disease [dɪ'ziːz] maladie f

disembark [dɪsəm'bɑːrk] débarquer

disentangle [dɪsən'tæŋgl] démêler

disfigure [dɪs'fɪgər] défigurer

disgrace [dɪs'greɪs] **1** n honte f **2** v/t faire honte à; **disgraceful** honteux

disguise [dɪs'gaɪz] **1** n déguisement m **2** v/t déguiser; fear, anxiety dissimuler

disgust [dɪs'gʌst] **1** n dégoût m **2** v/t dégoûter; **disgusting** dégoûtant

dish [dɪʃ] plat m; **~es** vaisselle f

disheartening [dɪs'hɑːrtnɪŋ] décourageant

dishonest [dɪs'ɑːnɪst] malhonnête; **dishonesty** malhonnêteté f

dishonor [dɪs'ɑːnər] déshonneur m; **dishonorable** dishonorant

dishonour etc Br → **dishonor** etc

disillusion [dɪsɪ'luːʒn] désillusionner; **disillusionment** désillusion f

disinfect [dɪsɪn'fekt] désinfecter; **disinfectant** désinfectant m

disinherit [dɪsɪn'herɪt] déshériter

disintegrate [dɪs'ɪntəɡreɪt] se désintégrer; of marriage se désagréger

disjointed [dɪs'dʒɔɪntɪd] décousu

disk [dɪsk] also COMPUT disque m; floppy disquette f; **disk drive** COMPUT lecteur m de disque/disquette; **diskette** disquette f

dislike [dɪs'laɪk] **1** n aversion f **2** v/t ne pas aimer

dislocate ['dɪsləkeɪt] disloquer

disloyalty [dɪs'lɔɪəltɪ] déloyauté f

dismal ['dɪzməl] weather morne; prospect sombre; person (sad) triste; person (negative) lugubre; failure lamentable

dismantle [dɪs'mæntl] object démonter; organization démanteler

dismay [dɪs'meɪ] consternation f

dismiss [dɪs'mɪs] employee renvoyer; suggestion rejeter; idea écarter; **dismissal** of employee renvoi m

disobedience [dɪsə'biːdɪəns] désobéissance f; **disobedient** désobéissant; **disobey** désobéir à

disorganized [dɪs'ɔːrɡənaɪzd] désorganisé

disoriented [dɪs'ɔːrɪəntɪd] désorienté

disparaging [dɪ'spærɪdʒɪŋ] désobligeant

disparity [dɪ'spærətɪ] disparité f

dispassionate [dɪ'spæʃənət] impartial, objectif

dispatch [dɪ'spætʃ] (send) envoyer

disperse [dɪ'spɜːrs] se disperser

display [dɪ'spleɪ] **1** n of paintings etc exposition f; of emotion, in store window étalage m; COMPUT affichage m **2** v/t emotion montrer; at exhibition, for sale exposer; COMPUT afficher

displease [dɪs'pliːz] déplaire à; **displeasure** mécontentement m

disposable [dɪ'spouzəbl] jetable; **disposal** of waste élimination f; (sale) cession f;

put sth at s.o.'s~ mettre qch à la disposition de qn

◆ **dispose of** *[dɪs'spəuz]* *(get rid of)* se débarrasser de

disprove *[dɪs'pruːv]* réfuter

dispute *[dɪs'pjuːt]* **1** *n* contestation *f*; *between two countries* conflit *m*; ***industrial ~*** conflit *m* social **2** *v/t* contester; *(fight over)* se disputer

disqualification *[dɪskwɒlɪfɪ'keɪʃn]* disqualification *f*; **disqualify** disqualifier

disregard *[dɪsrə'gɑːrd]* **1** *n* indifférence *f* (**for** à l'égard de) **2** *v/t* ne tenir aucun compte de

disreputable *[dɪs'repjʊtəbl]* peu recommandable

disrespect *[dɪsrə'spekt]* manque *m* de respect, irrespect *m*; **disrespectful** irrespectueux

disrupt *[dɪs'rʌpt]* perturber; **disruption** perturbation *f*

dissatisfaction *[dɪssætɪs'fækʃn]* mécontentement *m*; **dissatisfied** mécontent

dissident *[ˈdɪsɪdənt]* dissident(e) *m(f)*

dissolve *[dɪ'zɒlv]* **1** *v/t* dissoudre **2** *v/i* se dissoudre

distance *[ˈdɪstəns]* distance *f*; ***in the ~*** au loin; **distant** éloigné, *fig (aloof)* distant

distaste *[dɪs'teɪst]* dégoût *m*; **distasteful** désagréable

distinct *[dɪ'stɪŋkt]* *(clear)* net; *(different)* distinct; **distinctive** distinctif; **distinctly** dis-

tinctement; *(decidedly)* vraiment

distinguish *[dɪ'stɪŋgwɪʃ]* distinguer; ***~ between X and Y*** distinguer X de Y; **distinguished** distingué

distort *[dɪ'stɔːrt]* déformer

distract *[dɪ'strækt]* *person* distraire; *attention* détourner; **distraught** *[dɪ'strɔːt]* angoissé

distress *[dɪ'stres]* **1** *n* douleur *f* **2** *v/t (upset)* affliger; **distressing** pénible

distribute *[dɪ'strɪbjuːt]* *also* COM distribuer; **distribution** *also* COM distribution *f*; *of wealth* répartition *f*; **distributor** COM distributeur *m*

district *[ˈdɪstrɪkt]* *of town* quartier *m*; *of country* région *f*; **district attorney** procureur *m*

distrust *[dɪs'trʌst]* méfiance *f*

disturb *[dɪ'stɜːrb]* *(interrupt)* déranger; *(upset)* inquiéter; **disturbance** *(interruption)* dérangement *m*; ***~s*** *(civil unrest)* troubles *mpl*; **disturbed** perturbé; *mentally* dérangé; **disturbing** perturbant

disused *[dɪs'juːzd]* désaffecté

ditch *[dɪtʃ]* **1** *n* fossé *m* **2** *v/t* F *(get rid of)* se débarrasser de; *boyfriend, plan* laisser tomber

dive *[daɪv]* **1** *n* plongeon *m*; *underwater* plongée *f*; *of* *plane* (vol *m*) piqué *m*; F *bar etc* bouge *m* **2** *v/i* plonger; *underwater* faire de la plongée sous-marine; *of plane* descendre en piqué; *diver* plongeur(-euse) *m(f)*

diverge [daɪ'vɜːdʒ] diverger

diversification [daɪvɜːsɪfɪ-'keɪʃn] COM diversification *f*; **diversify** COM se diversifier

diversion [daɪ'vɜːʃn] *for traffic* déviation *f*; *to distract attention* diversion *f*; **divert** *traffic* dévier; *attention* détourner

divide [dɪ'vaɪd] (*share*) partager; MATH, *country, family* diviser

dividend ['dɪvɪdend] FIN dividende *m*

diving ['daɪvɪŋ] *from board* plongeon *m*; *underwater* plongée *f* (sous-marine); **diving board** plongeoir *m*

division [dɪ'vɪʒn] division *f*

divorce [dɪ'vɔːs] **1** *n* divorce *m* **2** *v/t* divorcer de **3** *v/i* divorcer; **divorced** divorcé; **divorcee** divorcé(e) *m(f)*

divulge [daɪ'vʌldʒ] divulguer

DIY [diːaɪ'waɪ] = **do-it-yourself** bricolage *m*

dizziness ['dɪzɪnɪs] vertige *m*; **dizzy**: **feel ~** avoir un vertige des vertiges

DJ [diːdʒeɪ] (= **disc jockey**) D.J. *m/f* (= disc-jockey)

DNA [diːen'eɪ] (= **deoxyribonucleic acid**) AND *m* (= acide *m* désoxyribonucléique)

do [duː] **1** *v/t* faire; **~ one's hair** se coiffer **2** *v/i* (*be suitable, enough*) aller; *that will ~!* ça va!; **~ well** in health, *of business* aller bien; (*be successful*) réussir; **well done!** (*congratulations!*) bien!; **how ~ you ~?** enchanté
◆ **do away with** supprimer
◆ **do up** *building* rénover; *street* refaire; (*fasten*), *coat etc* fermer; *laces* lacer
◆ **do with**: *I could do with ...* j'aurais bien besoin de ...
◆ **do without 1** *v/i* s'en passer **2** *v/t* se passer de

docile ['dəʊsaɪl] docile

dock[1] [dɒk] **1** *n* NAUT bassin *m* **2** *v/i of ship* entrer au bassin; *of spaceship* s'arrimer

dock[2] [dɒk] *n* LAW banc *m* des accusés

doctor ['dɒktər] MED docteur *m*, médecin *m*; *form of address* docteur; **doctorate** doctorat *m*

doctrine ['dɒktrɪn] doctrine *f*

document ['dɒkjəmənt] document *m*; **documentary** documentaire *m*; **documentation** documentation *f*

dodge [dɒdʒ] *blow, person* éviter; *question* éluder

dog [dɒg] **1** *n* chien *m* **2** *v/t of bad luck* poursuivre

dogma ['dɒgmə] dogme *m*; **dogmatic** dogmatique

dog tag MIL plaque *f* d'identification; **dog-tired** F crevé

do-it-yourself [duːɪtjər'self]

bricolage *m*

doldrums ['dɒuldrəmz]: *be in the~ of economy* être dans le marasme; *of person* avoir le cafard

doll [dɑ:l] *also* F *woman* poupée *f*

dollar ['dɑ:lər] dollar *m*

dolphin ['dɒlfin] dauphin *m*

dome [dɒum] *of building* dôme *m*

domestic [də'mestik] *chores* domestique; *news* national; *policy* intérieur; **domestic flight** vol *m* intérieur

dominant ['dɑ:minənt] dominant; **dominate** dominer; **domination** domination *f*; **domineering** dominateur

donate [dɒu'neit] faire don de; **donation** don *m*

donkey ['dɑ:ŋki] âne *m*

donor ['dɒunər] *of money* donateur(-trice) *m(f)*; MED donneur(-euse) *m(f)*

donut ['dɒunʌt] beignet *m*

doom [du:m] *(fate)* destin *m*; *(ruin)* ruine *f*; **doomed** *project* voué à l'échec

door [dɔ:r] porte *f*; *of car* portière *f*; **doorbell** sonnette *f*; **doorman** portier *m*; **doorway** embrasure *f* de porte

dope [dɒup] **1** *n* *(drugs)* drogue *f*; *(idiot)* idiot(e) *m(f)*

dormant ['dɔ:rmənt]: *~ volcano* volcan en repos

dormitory ['dɔ:rmitɔ:ri] résidence *f* universitaire; *Br* dortoir *m*

dose [dɒus] dose *f*

dot [dɑ:t] point *m*

double ['dʌbl] **1** *n* double *m*; *of film star* doublure *f* **2** *adj* ~ *the size* deux fois plus grand **4** *v/t & v/i* doubler; **double bed** grand lit *m*; **doublecheck** revérifier; **double-click** double-cliquer; **doublecross** trahir; **doublepark** stationner en double file; **double room** chambre *f* pour deux personnes; **doubles** *in tennis* double *m*

doubt [daut] **1** *n* doute *m*; *be in ~* être incertain; *no ~ (probably)* sans doute **2** *v/t* douter de; **doubtful** *look* douteux; *be~ of person* avoir des doutes; **doubtless** sans aucun doute

dough [dɒu] pâte *f*

dove [dʌv] colombe *f*

down [daun] **1** *adv* *(downward)* en bas, vers le bas; *~ there* là-bas; *$200 ~ (as deposit)* 200 dollars d'acompte; *~ south* le sud; *be ~ of price, numbers* être en baisse; *(not working)* être en panne; F *(depressed)* être déprimé **2** *prep* *(along)* le long de; *run ~ the stairs* descendre les escaliers en courant; *it's just ~ the street* c'est à deux pas; **down-and-out** clochard(e) *m(f)*; **download** COMPUT *v/t* télécharger **2** *n* fichier *m* téléchargé;

downmarket Br bas de gamme; **down payment** paiement m au comptant; **downplay** minimiser; **downpour** averse f; **downscale** bas de gamme; **downside** (disadvantage) inconvénient m; **downsize** car etc réduire la taille de; company réduire les effectifs de; **downstairs 1** adj neighbors etc d'en bas **2** adv en bas; **down-town 1** adj du centre-ville **2** adv en ville

doze [douz] sommeiller

dozen ['dʌzn] douzaine f

draft [dræft] **1** n of air courant m d'air; of document brouillon m; MIL conscription f; ~ **beer** bière f à la pression **2** v/t document faire le brouillon de; MIL appeler; **draft dodger** réfractaire m; **draftsman** dessinateur(-trice) m(f)

drag [dræg] **1** n/t traîner, tirer; (search) draguer **2** v/i of time se traîner; of show, movie traîner en longueur

drain [dreɪn] **1** n pipe tuyau m d'écoulement; under street égout m **2** v/t oil vidanger; vegetables égoutter; land drainer; glass, tank vider; (exhaust: person) épuiser; **drainage** (drains) système m d'écoulement; of water from soil drainage m; of water from soil drainage m; **drainpipe** tuyau m d'écoulement

drama ['drɑːmə] drame m; **dramatic** dramatique; scenery spectaculaire; **dramatist** dramaturge m/f; **dramatize** story adapter (**for** pour); fig dramatiser

drapes [dreɪps] rideaux mpl

drastic ['dræstɪk] radical; measures also drastique

draught [dræft] Br → **draft**

draw [drɔː] **1** n in competition match m nul; in lottery tirage m (au sort); (attraction) attraction f **2** v/t picture dessiner; (pull), gun tirer; (attract) attirer; (lead) emmener; from bank account retirer **3** v/i of artist dessiner; in competition faire match nul

◆ **draw back** v/i (recoil) reculer **2** v/t (pull back) retirer; drapes ouvrir

◆ **draw out** wallet, from bank retirer

◆ **draw up** v/t document rédiger; chair approcher **2** v/i of vehicle s'arrêter

'drawback désavantage m, inconvénient m

drawer [drɔːr] of desk tiroir m

drawing ['drɔːɪŋ] dessin m

drawl [drɔːl] voix f traînante

dread [dred]: ~ **doing** redouter de faire; **dreadful** épouvantable

dream [driːm] **1** n rêve m **2** v/i rêver (**about, of** de)

◆ **dream up** inventer

dreary ['drɪrɪ] morne

dress [dres] **1** *n for woman* robe *f*; (*clothing*) tenue *f* **2** *v/t person* habiller; *wound* panser; **get ~ed** s'habiller **3** *v/i* s'habiller

◆ **dress up** s'habiller chic; (*wear a disguise*) se déguiser (*as* en)

'**dress circle** premier balcon *m*; **dresser** (*dressing table*) coiffeuse *f*; *in kitchen* buffet *m*; **dressing** *for salad* assaisonnement *m*; *for wound* pansement *m*; **dress rehearsal** (répétition *f*) générale *f*

dribble ['drɪbl] *of person* baver; *of water* dégouliner; SP dribbler

dried [draɪd] *fruit etc* sec

drier ['draɪr] → **dryer**

drift [drɪft] *of snow* s'amonceler; *of ship* être à la dérive; (*go off course*) dériver; *of person* aller à la dérive; **drifter** personne qui vit au jour le jour

drill [drɪl] **1** *n tool* perceuse *f*; *exercise*, MIL exercice *m* **2** *v/t hole* percer **3** *v/i for oil* forer; MIL faire l'exercice

drily ['draɪlɪ] *say* d'un ton pince-sans-rire

drink [drɪŋk] **1** *n* boisson *f*; **can I have a ~ of water** est-ce que je peux avoir de l'eau? **2** *v/t & v/i* boire; **I don't ~** je ne bois pas; **drinkable** buvable; *water* potable

drinker ['drɪŋkər] buveur(-eu-

se) *m(f)*; **drinking water** eau *f* potable

drip [drɪp] **1** *n liquid* goutte *f*; MED goutte-à-goutte *m*, perfusion *f* **2** *v/i* goutter

drive [draɪv] **1** *n outing* promenade *f* (en voiture); (*energy*) dynamisme *m*; COMPUT unité *f*, lecteur *m*; (*campaign*) campagne *f* **2** *v/t vehicle* conduire; (*be the owner of*) avoir; (*take in car*) amener; TECH actionner **3** *v/i* conduire; **~ to work** aller au travail en voiture; **drive-in** *movie theater* drive-in *m*

drivel ['drɪvl] bêtises *fpl*

driver ['draɪvər] conducteur (-trice) *m(f)*; *of truck* camionneur(-euse) *m(f)*; COMPUT pilote *m*; **driver's license** permis *m* de conduire

'driveway allée *f*; **drive-thru** drive-in *m inv*

drizzle ['drɪzl] **1** *n* bruine *f* **2** *v/i* bruiner

drop [drɑːp] **1** *n* goutte *f*; *in price, temperature* chute *f* **2** *v/t object* faire tomber; *bomb* lancer; *person from car* déposer; *person from team* écarter; (*stop seeing*), *charges, subject* laisser tomber; (*give up*) arrêter **3** *v/i* tomber

◆ **drop in** (*visit*) passer

◆ **drop off 1** *v/t person, goods* déposer **2** *v/i* (*fall asleep*) s'endormir; (*decline*) diminuer

◆ **drop out** (*withdraw*) se retirer (**of** de); *of school* abandonner (**of sth** qch)

drought [draʊt] sécheresse *f*

drown [draʊn] se noyer

drug [drʌg] **1** *n* MED médicament *m*; *illegal* drogue *f* **2** *v/t* droguer; **drug addict** toxicomane *m/f*; **drug dealer** dealer *m*, dealeuse *f*; *large-scale* trafiquant(e) *m(f)* de drogue; **druggist** pharmacien(ne) *m(f)*; **drugstore** drugstore *m*; **drug trafficking** trafic *m* de drogue

drum [drʌm] MUS tambour *m*; *container* tonneau *m*; **~s** batterie *f*; **drumstick** MUS baguette *f* de tambour

drunk [drʌŋk] **1** *n* ivrogne *m/f*; *habitually* alcoolique *m/f* **2** *adj* ivre, soûl; **get~** se soûler; **drunk driving** conduite *f* en état d'ivresse

dry [draɪ] **1** *adj* sec **2** *v/t clothes* faire sécher; *dishes, eyes* essuyer **3** *v/i* sécher; **dryclean** nettoyer à sec; **dry cleaner** pressing *m*; **dry cleaner's** nettoyage *m* à sec; **dryer** *machine* sèche-linge *m*

dual ['duːəl] double

dub [dʌb] *movie* doubler

dubious ['duːbɪəs] douteux; *I'm still ~ about ...* j'ai encore des doutes quant à ...

duck [dʌk] **1** *n* canard *m*; *female* cane *f* **2** *v/i* se baisser

dud [dʌd] F (*false bill*) faux *m*

due [duː] (*owed*) dû; *the rent is ~ tomorrow* il faut payer le loyer demain

dull [dʌl] *weather* sombre; *sound, pain* sourd; (*boring*) ennuyeux

duly ['duːlɪ] (*as expected*) comme prévu; (*properly*) dûment, comme il se doit

dumb [dʌm] (*mute*) muet; F (*stupid*) bête

dump [dʌmp] **1** *n for garbage* décharge *f*; (*unpleasant place*) trou *m*; *house, hotel* taudis *m* **2** *v/t* (*deposit*) déposer; (*throw away*) jeter; (*leave*) laisser; *waste* déverser

dune [duːn] dune *f*

duplex (**apartment**) ['duːpleks] duplex *m*

duplicate ['duːplɪkət] double *m*

durable ['dʊrəbl] *material* résistant

during ['dʊrɪŋ] pendant

dusk [dʌsk] crépuscule *m*

dust [dʌst] **1** *n* poussière *f* **2** *v/t* épousseter; **duster** chiffon *m* (à poussière); **dustpan** pelle *f* à poussière; **dusty** poussiéreux

duty ['duːtɪ] devoir *m*; (*task*) fonction *f*; *on goods* droit(s) *m(pl)*; **be on ~** être de service; **dutyfree** hors taxes

DVD [diːviːˈdiː] (= *digital versatile disk*) DVD *m*; **DVD-ROM** DVD-ROM *m*

dwarf [dwɔːrf] **1** *n* nain(e) *m(f)* **2** *v/t* rapetisser

dwindle ['dwɪndl] diminuer

dye [daɪ] **1** *n* teinture *f* **2** *v/t*

teindre

dying ['daɪɪŋ] *person* mourant; *industry* moribond; *tradition* qui se perd

dynamic [daɪ'næmɪk] dynamique; **dynamism** dynamis-me. *m*

dynasty ['dɪnəstɪ] dynastie *f*

dyslexic [dɪs'leksɪk] **1** *adj* dyslexique **2** *n* dyslexique *m/f*

E

each [iːtʃ] **1** *adj* chaque **2** *adv* chacun; **they're $1.50 ~** ils coûtent $1.50 chacun, ils sont 1,50 $ pièce **3** *pron* chacun(e) *m(f)*; **~ of them** chacun(e) d'entre eux(elles) *m(f)*; **we know ~ other** nous nous connaissons

eager ['iːgər] désireux; *look* avide; **be ~ to do sth** désirer vivement faire qch; **eagerly** avec empressement; *wait* impatiemment; **eagerness** empressement *m*

eagle ['iːgl] aigle *m*; **eagle-eyed**: **be ~** avoir des yeux d'aigle

ear¹ [ɪr] oreille *f*

ear² [ɪr] *of corn* épi *m*

'earache mal *m* d'oreilles

early ['ɜːrlɪ] **1** *adv* (*not late*) tôt; (*ahead of time*) en avance **2** *adj* stages, Romans premier; *arrival* en avance; *retirement* anticipé; *music* ancien; (*in the near future*) prochain; (*in*) **~ October** début octobre; **have an ~ supper** dîner tôt *or* de bonne heure; **early bird**: **be an ~** (*early ris-*

er) être matinal

earmark ['ɪrmɑːrk] réserver

earn [ɜːrn] gagner; *interest* rapporter

earnest ['ɜːrnɪst] sérieux

earnings ['ɜːrnɪŋz] salaire *m*; *of company* profits *mpl*

'earphones écouteurs *mpl*; **earring** boucle *f* d'oreille

earth [ɜːrθ] terre *f*; **earthenware** poterie *f*; **earthly** terrestre; **it's no ~ use doing that** F ça ne sert strictement à rien de faire cela; **earthquake** tremblement *m* de terre; **earth-shattering** stupéfiant

ease [iːz] **1** *n* facilité *f*; **feel at ~** se sentir à l'aise **2** *v/t* pain, mind soulager; *suffering*, *shortage* diminuer **3** *v/i* *of pain* diminuer

easel ['iːzl] chevalet *m*

easily ['iːzəlɪ] facilement; (*by far*) de loin

east [iːst] **1** *n* est *m* **2** *adj* est *inv*; *wind* d'est **3** *adv* *travel* vers l'est

Easter ['iːstər] Pâques *fpl*; **Easter Day** (jour *m* de) Pâques *m*; **Easter egg** œuf *m* de Pâques

easterly ['i:stərlɪ] *wind* de l'est; *direction* vers l'est

Easter Monday lundi *m* de Pâques

eastern ['i:stərn] de l'est; *(oriental)* oriental; **easterner** habitant(e) *m(f)* de l'Est des États-Unis

Easter Sunday (jour *m* de) Pâques *m*

eastward ['i:stwərd] vers l'est

easy ['i:zɪ] facile; *(relaxed)* tranquille; **easy chair** fauteuil *m*; **easy-going** accommodant

eat [i:t] manger

◆ **eat out** manger au restaurant

eatable ['i:təbl] mangeable

eavesdrop ['i:vzdrɒp] écouter de façon indiscrète (**on s.o.** qn)

ebb [eb] *of tide* descendre

e-book ['i:bʊk] livre *m* électronique; **e-business** commerce *m* électronique

eccentric [ɪk'sentrɪk] **1** *adj* excentrique **2** *n* original(e) *m(f)*; **eccentricity** excentricité *f*

echo ['ekəʊ] **1** *n* écho *m* **2** *v/i* faire écho **3** *v/t words* répéter; *views* se faire l'écho de

eclipse [ɪ'klɪps] **1** *n* éclipse *f* **2** *v/t fig* éclipser

ecological [i:kə'lɒdʒɪkl] écologique; **ecologically** écologiquement; **ecologically**

friendly écologique; **ecologist** écologiste *m/f*; **ecology** écologie *f*

economic [i:kə'nɒːmɪk] économique; **economical** *(cheap)* économique; *(thrifty)* économe; **economics** économie *f*; *financial aspects* aspects *mpl* économiques; **economist** économiste *m/f*; **economize** économiser

◆ **economize on** économiser

economy [ɪ'kɑːnəmɪ] économie *f*; **economy class** classe *f* économique

ecosystem ['i:kəʊsɪstm] écosystème *m*; **ecotourism** tourisme *m* écologique

ecstasy ['ekstəsɪ] extase *f*; **ecstatic** extatique

eczema ['eksmə] eczéma *m*

edge [edʒ] **1** *n* bord *m*; *of knife* tranchant *m*; **on ~** énervé *f* **2** *v/i (move slowly)* se faufiler; **edgewise**: *I couldn't get a word in ~* je n'ai pas pu en placer une *F*; **edgy** énervé

edible ['edɪbl] comestible

edit ['edɪt] *text* mettre au point; *book* préparer pour la publication; *newspaper* diriger; *TV program* réaliser; *film* monter; **edition** édition *f*; **editor** *of text, book* rédacteur(-trice) *m(f)*; *of newspaper* rédacteur(-trice) *m(f)* en chef; *of TV program* réalisateur(-trice) *m(f)*; *of film* monteur(-euse) *m(f)*; **edito-**

rial 1 *adj* de la rédaction **2** *n* éditorial *m*

educate ['edʒəkeɪt] instruire (*about* sur); *she was ~d in France* elle a fait sa scolarité en France; **educated** instruit; **education** éducation f; *as subject* pédagogie f; **educational** scolaire; (*informative*) instructif

eerie ['ɪrɪ] inquiétant

effect [ɪ'fekt] effet *m*; **effective** (*efficient*) efficace; (*striking*) frappant

effeminate [ɪ'femɪnət] efféminé

efficiency [ɪ'fɪʃənsɪ] efficacité f; *in motel* chambre f avec coin-cuisine; **efficient** efficace; **efficiently** efficacement

effort ['efərt] effort *m*; **effortless** aisé, facile

e.g. [iː'dʒiː] ex; *spoken par* example

egg [eg] œuf *m*; **eggcup** coquetier *m*; **egghead** F intello *m/f* F; **eggplant** aubergine f

ego ['iːgoʊ] PSYCH ego *m*; **egocentric** égocentrique; **egoism** égoïsme *m*; **egoist** égoïste *m/f*

eiderdown ['aɪdərdaʊn] (*quilt*) édredon *m*

eight [eɪt] huit; **eighteen** dix-huit; **eighteenth** dix-huitième; **eighth** huitième; **eightieth** quatre-vingtième; **eighty** quatre-vingts; **~-two/four** *etc* quatre-vingt-deux/-quatre *etc*

either ['iːðər] **1** *adj* l'un ou l'autre; (*both*) chaque 2 *pron* l'un(e) ou l'autre **3** *adv*: *I won't go ~* je n'irai pas non plus **4** *conj*: *~ ... or* soit ...; *with negative* ni ... ni ...

eject [ɪ'dʒekt] **1** *v/t* éjecter **2** *v/i from plane* s'éjecter

◆ **eke out** [iːk] suppléer à l'insuffisance de; *eke out a living* vivoter

el [el] métro *m* aérien

elaborate [ɪ'læbərət] **1** *adj* compliqué **2** *v/i* [ɪ'læbəreɪt] donner des détails (*on* sur)

elapse [ɪ'læps] (s)e passer

elastic [ɪ'læstɪk] **1** *adj* élastique **2** *n* élastique *m*; **elasticated** élastique

elated [ɪ'leɪtɪd] transporté (de joie); **elation** exaltation f

elbow ['elboʊ] coude *m*

elder ['eldər] **1** *adj* aîné **2** *n* aîné(e) *m(f)*; **elderly 1** *adj* âgé **2** *npl*: *the ~* les personnes *fpl* âgées; **eldest 1** *adj* aîné(e); **eldest** ... **2** *n*: *the ~* l'aîné(e) *m(f)*

elect [ɪ'lekt] élire; **elected** élu; **election** élection f; **election campaign** campagne f électorale; **election day** jour *m* des élections; **electorate** électorat *m*

electric [ɪ'lektrɪk] *also fig* électrique; **electrical** électrique; **electric chair** chaise f électrique; **electrician** électricien(ne) *m(f)*; **electricity** électricité f; **electrify** électriser; *fig* électriser

electrocute [ɪ'lektrəkjuːt] électrocuter

electron [ɪ'lektrɒn] électron *m*; **electronic** électronique *f*; **electronics** électronique *f*

elegance ['elɪgəns] élégance *f*; **elegant** élégant

element ['elɪmənt] élément *m*; **elementary** élémentaire *f*; **elementary schoo** école *f* primaire

elephant ['elɪfənt] éléphant *m*

elevate ['elɪveɪt] élever; **elevated railroad** métro *m* aérien; **elevation** (*altitude*) altitude *f*; **elevator** ascenseur *m*

eleven [ɪ'levn] onze *m*; **eleventh** onzième

eligible ['elɪdʒəbl]: **be ~ to do sth** avoir le droit de faire qch

eliminate [ɪ'lɪmɪneɪt] éliminer; **elimination** élimination *f*

elite [er'liːt] **1** *n* élite *f* **2** *adj* d'élite

eloquence ['eləkwəns] éloquence *f*; **eloquent** éloquent

else [els]: **anything ~?** autre chose?; **nothing ~** rien d'autre; **no one ~** personne d'autre; **everyone~ is going** tous les autres y vont; **someone~** quelqu'un d'autre; **something ~** autre chose; **let's go somewhere ~** allons autre part; **or ~** sinon; **elsewhere** ailleurs

elude [ɪ'luːd] (*escape from*) échapper à; (*avoid*) éviter

elusive insaisissable

emaciated [ɪ'meɪsɪeɪtɪd] émacié

e-mail ['iːmeɪl] **1** *n* e-mail *m*, courrier *m* électronique **2** *v/t person* envoyer un e-mail à; **e-mail address** adresse *f* e-mail, adresse *f* électronique

emancipation [ɪmænsɪ'peɪʃn] émancipation *f*

embalm [ɪm'baːm] embaumer

embankment [ɪm'bæŋkmənt] *of river* berge *f*; RAIL remblai *m*

embargo [em'baːrgoʊ] embargo *m*

embark [ɪm'baːrk] (s')embarquer

embarrass [ɪm'bærəs] gêner, embarrasser; **embarrassed** gêné, embarrassé; **embarrassing** gênant, embarrassant; **embarrassment** gêne *f*, embarras *m*

embassy ['embəsɪ] ambassade *f*

embezzle [ɪm'bezl] détourner; **embezzlement** détournement *m* de fonds

emblem ['embləm] emblème *m*

embodiment [ɪm'baːdɪmənt] personnification *f*; **embody** personnifier

embrace [ɪm'breɪs] **1** *n* étreinte *f* **2** *v/t* (*hug*) serrer dans ses bras, étreindre; (*take in*) embrasser **3** *v/i of two people* se serrer dans les bras, s'étreindre

embroider [ɪmˈbrɔɪdər] broder; *fig* enjoliver

embryo [ˈembrɪəʊ] embryon *m*; **embryonic** *fig* embryonnaire

emerald [ˈemərəld] émeraude *f*

emerge [ɪˈmɜːdʒ] sortir; *from mist, of truth* émerger

emergency [ɪˈmɜːdʒənsɪ] urgence *f*; **emergency exit** sortie *f* de secours; **emergency landing** atterrissage *m* forcé; **emergency services** services *mpl* d'urgence

emigrate [ˈemɪɡreɪt] émigrer; **emigration** émigration *f*

Eminence [ˈemɪnəns] REL: **His ~** son Éminence; **eminent** éminent

emission [ɪˈmɪʃn] *of gases* émission *f*; **emit** émettre

emotion [ɪˈməʊʃn] émotion *f*; **emotional** *problems* émotionnel, affectif; *(full of emotion)* ému; *reunion* émouvant

emphasis [ˈemfəsɪs] accent *m*; **emphasize** *syllable* accentuer; *fig* souligner; **emphatic** catégorique

empire [ˈempaɪr] *also fig* empire *m*

employ [ɪmˈplɔɪ] employer; **employee** employé(e) *m(f)*; **employer** employeur(-euse) *m(f)*; **employment** *(jobs)* emplois *mpl*; *(work)* emploi *m*

emptiness [ˈemptɪnɪs] vide *m*; **empty 1** *adj* vide; *promises* vain **2** *v/t* vider **3** *v/i of room, street* se vider

emulate [ˈemjʊleɪt] imiter

enable [ɪˈneɪbl] permettre

enchanting [ɪnˈtʃɑːntɪŋ] ravissant

encircle [ɪnˈsɜːrkl] encercler

enclose [ɪnˈkləʊz] *in letter* joindre; *area* entourer; **enclosure** *with letter* pièce *f* jointe

encore [ˈɑːŋkɔːr] bis *m*

encounter [ɪnˈkaʊntər] **1** *n* rencontre *f* **2** *v/t person* rencontrer; *problem, resistance* affronter

encourage [ɪnˈkʌrɪdʒ] encourager; **encouragement** encouragement *m*; **encouraging** encourageant

encyclopedia [ɪnsaɪkləˈpiːdɪə] encyclopédie *f*

end [end] **1** *n (conclusion, purpose)* fin *f*; *(extremity)* bout *m*; **in the ~** à la fin **2** *v/t* terminer, finir **3** *v/i* se terminer, finir

◆ **end up** finir

endanger [ɪnˈdeɪndʒər] mettre en danger; **endangered species** espèce *f* en voie de disparition

endeavor, *Br* **endeavour** [ɪnˈdevər] **1** *n* effort *m* **2** *v/t* essayer *(to do sth* de faire qch)

endemic [ɪnˈdemɪk] endémique

ending ['endɪŋ] fin f; GRAM terminaison f; **endless** sans fin

endorse [ɪn'dɔːrs] candidacy appuyer; product associer son image à; **endorsement** of candidacy appui m; of product association f de son image à

end 'product produit m fini

endurance [ɪn'dʊrəns] of person endurance f; of car résistance f; **endure 1** v/t endurer **2** v/i (last) durer; **enduring** durable

enemy ['enəmɪ] ennemi(e) m(f)

energetic [enərdʒetɪk] also fig énergique; **energy** énergie f; **energy supply** alimentation f en énergie

enforce [ɪn'fɔːrs] mettre en vigueur

engage [ɪn'geɪdʒ] **1** v/t (hire) engager **2** v/i of machine part s'engrener; **engaged** to be married fiancé; Br TELEC occupé; **get** ~ se fiancer; **engagement** to be married fiançailles fpl; MIL engagement m; **engagement ring** bague f de fiançailles

engine ['endʒɪn] moteur m; **engineer** ingénieur m/f; NAUT, RAIL mécanicien(ne) m(f); **engineering** ingénierie f

England ['ɪŋglənd] Angleterre f; **English 1** adj anglais **2** n language anglais m; **the** ~ les Anglais mpl; **English-man** Anglais m; **English-woman** Anglaise f

engrave [ɪn'greɪv] graver; **engraving** gravure f

engrossed [ɪn'groʊst]: ~ **in** absorbé dans

engulf [ɪn'gʌlf] engloutir

enhance [ɪn'hæns] flavor rehausser; reputation accroître; performance améliorer; enjoyment augmenter

enigma [ɪ'nɪgmə] énigme f

enjoy [ɪn'dʒɔɪ] aimer; ~ **o.s.** s'amuser; ~! said to s.o. eating bon appétit!; **enjoyable** agréable; **enjoyment** plaisir m

enlarge [ɪn'lɑːrdʒ] agrandir; **enlargement** agrandissement m

enlighten [ɪn'laɪtn] éclairer

enlist [ɪn'lɪst] MIL enrôler

enmity ['enmɪtɪ] inimitié f

enormous [ɪ'nɔːrməs] énorme

enough [ɪ'nʌf] **1** adj assez de **2** pron assez; **will $50 be** ~? est-ce que $50 suffiront?; **that's** ~ ça suffit **3** adv assez; **big** ~ assez grand

enquire etc [ɪn'kwaɪr] → **inquire** etc

enroll, Br **enrol** [ɪn'roʊl] s'inscrire

en suite (bathroom) ['ɑːnswiːt] salle f de bains attenante

ensure [ɪn'ʃʊər] assurer; ~ **that ...** s'assurer que ...

entail [ɪn'teɪl] entraîner

entangle [ɪn'tæŋgl] *in rope* empêtrer

enter ['entər] **1** *v/t room, house* entrer dans; *competition* entrer en; COMPUT entrer **2** *v/i* entrer; *in competition* s'inscrire **3** *n* COMPUT touche *f* entrée

enterprise ['entərpraɪz] (*initiative*) (esprit *m* d')initiative *f*; (*venture*) entreprise *f*; **enterprising** entreprenant

entertain [entər'teɪn] (*amuse*) amuser; (*consider: idea*) envisager; **entertainer** artiste *m/f* de variété; **entertaining** amusant, divertissant; **entertainment** divertissement *m*

enthusiasm [ɪn'θuːzɪæzəm] enthousiasme *m*; **enthusiast** enthousiaste *m/f*; **enthusiastic** enthousiaste; **enthusiastically** avec enthousiasme

entire [ɪn'taɪr] entier; **entirely** entièrement

entitle [ɪn'taɪtl]: **~ s.o. to sth** donner à qn droit à qch; **be ~d to** avoir droit à

entrance ['entrəns] entrée *f*

entranced [ɪn'trænst] enchanté

'entrance exam(ination) examen *m* d'entrée

entrant ['entrənt] inscrit(e) *m(f)*

entrepreneur [ɑːntrəprə'nɜːr] entrepreneur(-euse) *m(f)*; **entrepre-**

neurial *skills* d'entrepreneur

entrust [ɪn'trʌst] confier

entry ['entrɪ] entrée *f*; *for competition: person* participant(e) *m(f)*; **entryphone** interphone *m*

envelop [ɪn'veləp] envelopper

envelope ['envəloup] enveloppe *f*

enviable ['envɪəbl] enviable; **envious** ['envɪəs] envieux; **be ~ of s.o.** envier qn

environment [ɪn'vaɪrənmənt] environnement *m*; **environmental** écologique; **environmentalist** écologiste *m/f*; **environmentally friendly** écologique; **environs** environs *mpl*

envisage [ɪn'vɪzɪdʒ] envisager

envoy ['envɔɪ] envoyé(e) *m(f)*

envy ['envɪ] **1** *n* envie *f* **2** *v/t*: **~ s.o. sth** envier qch à qn

epic ['epɪk] **1** *n* épopée *f*; *movie* film *m* à grand spectacle **2** *adj journey* épique

epicenter, *Br* epicentre ['epɪsentər] épicentre *m*

epidemic [epɪ'demɪk] *also fig* épidémie *f*

episode ['epɪsoud] épisode *m*

epitaph ['epɪtæf] épitaphe *f*

equal ['iːkwl] **1** *adj* égal; **be ~ to task** être à la hauteur de **2** *n* égal *m* **3** *v/t* égaler; **equality** égalité *f*; **equalize 1** *v/t* égaliser **2** *v/i Br* SP égaliser; **equalizer** *Br* SP but *m* égali-

sateur; **equally** *divide* de manière égale; *qualified, intelligent* tout aussi; **equal rights** égalité *f* des droits
equation [ɪ'kweɪʒn] MATH équation *f*
equator [ɪ'kweɪtər] équateur *m*
equip [ɪ'kwɪp] équiper; **equipment** équipement *m*
equity ['ekwətɪ] FIN capitaux *mpl* propres
equivalent [ɪ'kwɪvələnt] **1** *adj* équivalent **2** *n* équivalent *m*
era ['ɪrə] ère *f*
eradicate [ɪ'rædɪkeɪt] éradiquer
erase [ɪ'reɪz] effacer
erect [ɪ'rekt] **1** *adj* droit **2** *v/t* ériger, élever; **erection** *of building, penis* érection *f*
ergonomic [ɜːrgoʊ'nɑːmɪk] ergonomique
erode [ɪ'roʊd] éroder; *fig: power* miner; *rights* supprimer progressivement; **erosion** érosion *f*; *fig: of rights* suppression *f* progressive
errand ['erənd] commission *f*
erratic [ɪ'rætɪk] *performance, course* irrégulier; *driving* capricieux; *behavior* changeant
error ['erər] erreur *f*
erupt [ɪ'rʌpt] *of volcano* entrer en éruption; *of violence* éclater; *of person* exploser F; **eruption** *of volcano* éruption *f*; *of violence* explosion *f*
escalate ['eskəleɪt] s'intensifier; **escalation** intensifica-

tion *f*; **escalator** escalier *m* mécanique, escalator *m*
escape [ɪ'skeɪp] **1** *n* *of prisoner* évasion *f*; *of animal, gas* fuite *f* **2** *v/i* s'échapper
escort ['eskɔːrt] **1** *n* cavalier (-ière) *m(f)*; *(guard)* escorte *f* **2** *v/t* [ɪ'skɔːrt] *socially* accompagner; *(act as guard to)* escorter
especially [ɪ'speʃlɪ] particulièrement
espionage ['espɪənɑːʒ] espionnage *m*
espresso (coffee) [es'presoʊ] expresso *m*
essay ['eseɪ] *at school* rédaction *f*; *at university* dissertation *f*; *by writer* essai *m*
essential [ɪ'senʃl] essentiel
establish [ɪ'stæblɪʃ] *company* fonder; *(create, determine)* établir; **establishment** *firm, shop etc* établissement *m*
estate [ɪ'steɪt] *land* propriété *f*; *of dead person* biens *mpl*
esthetic [ɪs'θetɪk] esthétique
estimate ['estɪmət] **1** *n* estimation *f*; *from builder etc* devis *m* **2** *v/t* estimer
estuary ['estʃəwerɪ] estuaire *m*
etc [et'setrə] (= *et cetera*) etc.
eternal [ɪ'tɜːrnl] éternel; **eternity** éternité *f*
ethical ['eθɪkl] *problem* éthique; *(morally right)* moral; **ethics** éthique *f*
ethnic ['eθnɪk] ethnique
EU [iː'juː] (= *European Un-*

ion) U.E. *f* (= Union *f* euro-péenne)

euphemism ['ju:fəmɪzm] eu-phémisme *m*

euro ['jʊərəʊ] FIN euro *m*

Europe ['jʊərəp] Europe *f*; **European 1** *adj* européen **2** *n* Européen(ne) *m(f)*

euthanasia [ju:θə'neɪzɪə] eu-thanasie *f*

evacuate [ɪ'vækjʊeɪt] (*clear people from*) faire évacuer; (*leave*) évacuer

evade [ɪ'veɪd] éviter; *question* éluder

evaluate [ɪ'væljʊeɪt] évaluer; **evaluation** évaluation *f*

evaporate [ɪ'væpəreɪt] *also fig* s'évaporer; **evaporation** évaporation *f*

evasion [ɪ'veɪʒn] fuite *f*; **eva-sive** évasif

eve [i:v] veille *f*

even ['i:vn] **1** *adj breathing* ré-gulier; *distribution* égal; (*lev-el*) plat; *surface* plan; *num-ber* pair; **get ~ with ...** pren-dre sa revanche sur ... **2** *adv* même; **~ bigger** encore plus grand; **not ~** pas même; **~ so** quand même; **~ if** même si **3** *v/t*: **~ the score** égaliser

evening ['i:vnɪŋ] soir *m*; **in the ~** le soir; **this ~** ce soir; **good ~** bonsoir; **evening class** cours *m* du soir; **eve-ning dress** *for woman* robe *f* du soir; *for man* tenue *f* de soirée

evenly ['i:vnlɪ] (*regularly*) de

manière égale; *breathe* régu-lièrement

event [ɪ'vent] événement *m*; SP épreuve *f*; **eventful** mouve-menté

eventually [ɪ'ventʃʊəlɪ] fina-lement

ever ['evər] jamais; **have you been to Japan?** est-ce que tu es déjà allé au Japon?; **for ~** pour toujours; **~ since** de-puis lors; **~ since we ...** de-puis le jour où nous ...; **~-lasting** éternel

every ['evrɪ]: **~ day** tous les jours, chaque jour; **~ one of ...** chacun de ...; **every-body → everyone**; **every-day** de tous les jours; **every-one** tout le monde; **~ who ...** tous ceux qui ...; **everything** tout; **everywhere** partout; (*wherever*) partout où

evict [ɪ'vɪkt] expulser

evidence ['evɪdəns] preuve(s) *f(pl)*; LAW témoignage *m*; **give ~** témoigner; **evident** évident; **evidently** (*clearly*) à l'évidence; (*apparently*) de toute évidence

evil ['i:vl] **1** *adj* mauvais **2** *n* mal *m*

evolution [i:və'lu:ʃn] évolu-tion *f*; **evolve** évoluer

ex [eks] *wife, husband* ex *m/f* F

exact [ɪg'zækt] exact; **exact-ing** exigeant; **exactly** exacte-ment

exaggerate [ɪg'zædʒəreɪt]

exagérer; **exaggeration** exagération f

exam [ɪgˈzæm] examen m; **examination** examen m; **examine** examiner

example [ɪgˈzæmpl] exemple m; **for ~** par exemple

excavate [ˈekskəveɪt] (dig) excaver; of archeologist fouiller; **excavation** excavation f; archeological fouille(s) f(pl)

exceed [ɪkˈsiːd] dépasser; authority outrepasser; **exceedingly** extrêmement

excel [ɪkˈsel] **1** v/i exceller (**at** en) **2** v/t: ~ **o.s.** se surpasser; **excellence** excellence f; **excellent** excellent

except [ɪkˈsept] sauf; ~ **for** à l'exception de; **exception** exception f; **exceptional** exceptionnel

excerpt [ˈeksɜːrpt] extrait m

excess [ɪkˈses] **1** n excès m **2** adj: ~ **water** excédent m d'eau; **excessive** excessif

exchange [ɪksˈtʃeɪndʒ] **1** n échange m **2** v/t échanger; **exchange rate** FIN cours m du change

excite [ɪkˈsaɪt] (make enthusiastic) enthousiasmer; **excited** excité; **get ~** s'exciter; **excitement** excitation f; **exciting** passionnant

exclaim [ɪkˈskleɪm] s'exclamer; **exclamation** exclamation f; **exclamation point** point m d'exclamation

exclude [ɪkˈskluːd] exclure; **excluding** sauf; **exclusive** hotel huppé; rights, interview exclusif

excuse [ɪkˈskjuːs] **1** n excuse f **2** v/t [ɪkˈskjuːz] excuser; (forgive) pardonner; ~ **me** excusez-moi

ex-directory Br: **be~** être sur liste rouge

execute [ˈeksɪkjuːt] criminal, plan exécuter; **execution** of criminal, plan exécution f; **executive** cadre m

exempt [ɪgˈzempt] exempt

exercise [ˈeksərsaɪz] **1** n exercice m **2** v/t muscle exercer; dog promener; caution, restraint user de **3** v/i prendre de l'exercice

exhale [eksˈheɪl] exhaler

exhaust [ɪgˈzɔːst] **1** n fumes gaz m d'échappement; pipe tuyau m d'échappement **2** v/t (tire, use up) épuiser; **exhausted** (tired) épuisé; **exhausting** épuisant; **exhaustion** épuisement m; **exhaustive** exhaustif

exhibit [ɪgˈzɪbɪt] **1** n in exhibition objet m exposé **2** v/t of artist exposer; (give evidence of) montrer; **exhibition** exposition f; of bad behavior étalage m; of skill démonstration f

exhilarating [ɪgˈzɪləreɪtɪŋ] weather vivifiant; sensation grisant

exile [ˈeksaɪl] **1** n exil m; per-

son exilé(e) *m(f)* **2** *v/t* exiler

exist [ɪg'zɪst] exister; **~ on** subsister avec; **existing** existence *f*; **be in ~** exister; **existing** existant

exit ['eksɪt] **1** *n* sortie *f* **2** *v/i* COMPUT sortir

exonerate [ɪg'zɑːnəreɪt] (*clear*) disculper

exotic [ɪg'zɑːtɪk] exotique

expand [ɪk'spænd] **1** *v/t* étendre **2** *v/i* of population s'accroître; of business, city se développer; of metal, gas se dilater; **expanse** étendue *f*; **expansion** of population accroissement *m*; of business, city développement *m*; of metal, gas dilatation *f*

expect [ɪk'spekt] **1** *v/t* also baby attendre; (*suppose*) penser; (*demand*) exiger **2** *v/i*: **be ~ing** attendre un bébé; **I ~ so** je pense que oui; **expectant mother** future maman *f*; **expectation** attente *f*, espérance *f*

expedition [ekspɪ'dɪʃn] expédition *f*

expel [ɪk'spel] expulser

expendable [ɪk'spendəbl] person pas indispensable

expenditure [ɪk'spendɪtʃər] dépenses *fpl* (on de)

expense [ɪk'spens] dépense *f*; **expenses** frais *mpl*; **at the ~ of** aux dépens de; **expense account** note *f* de frais; **expensive** cher

experience [ɪk'spɪrɪəns] **1** *n* expérience *f* **2** *v/t* pain, pleasure éprouver; difficulty con-

naître; **experienced** expérimenté

experiment [ɪk'sperɪmənt] **1** *n* expérience *f* **2** *v/i* faire des expériences; **experimental** expérimental

expert ['ekspɜːrt] **1** *adj* expert **2** *n* expert(e) *m(f)*; **expertise** savoir-faire *m*

expiration date ['ekspɪreɪʃn] date *f* d'expiration; **expire** expirer; **expiry** expiration *f*; **expiry date** Br date *f* d'expiration

explain [ɪk'spleɪn] expliquer; **explanation** explication *f*; **explanatory** explicatif

explicit [ɪk'splɪsɪt] instructions explicite

explode [ɪk'sploʊd] **1** *v/i* of bomb, fig exploser **2** *v/t* bomb faire exploser

exploit[1] ['eksplɔɪt] *n* exploit *m*

exploit[2] [ɪk'splɔɪt] *v/t* person, resources exploiter

exploitation [eksplɔɪ'teɪʃn] of person exploitation *f*

exploration [eksplə'reɪʃn] exploration *f*; **explore** country, possibility explorer; **explorer** explorateur(-trice) *m(f)*

explosion [ɪk'sploʊʒn] also in population explosion *f*; **explosive** explosif *m*

export ['eksport] **1** *n* exportation *f* **2** *v/t* also COMPUT exporter; **exporter** exportateur(-trice) *m(f)*

expose [ɪk'spoʊz] (*uncover*)

mettre à nu; *scandal* dévoiler; *person* démasquer; **~ X to Y** exposer X à Y; **exposure** exposition *f*; MED effets *mpl* du froid; *of dishonest behavior* dénonciation *f*; PHOT pose *f*; *in media* couverture *f*

express [ɪk'spres] **1** *adj (fast)* express; *(explicit)* explicite **2** *n train* express *m* **3** *v/t* exprimer; **expression** expression *f*; **expressive** expressif; **expressly** *(explicitly)* expressément; *(deliberately)* exprès; **expressway** voie *f* express

expulsion [ɪk'spʌlʃn] expulsion *f*

extend [ɪk'stend] **1** *v/t house, garden* agrandir; *search* étendre **(to** à); *runway, contract, visa* prolonger **2** *v/i of garden* s'étendre; **extension** *to house* agrandissement *m*; *of contract, visa* prolongation *f*; TELEC poste *m*; **extensive** *search, knowledge* vaste, étendu; *damage* considérable; **extent** étendue *f*, ampleur *f*; **to a certain ~** jusqu'à un certain point

exterior [ɪk'stɪrɪər] **1** *adj* extérieur **2** *n of building* extérieur *m*; *of person* dehors *mpl*

exterminate [ɪk'stɜːrmɪneɪt] exterminer

external [ɪk'stɜːrnl] extérieur

extinct [ɪk'stɪŋkt] *species* disparu; **extinction** *of species* extinction *f*; **extinguish** *fire,*

cigarette éteindre; **extinguisher** extincteur *m*

extortion [ɪk'stɔːrʃn] extortion *f*

extra ['ekstrə] **1** *n* extra *m* **2** *adj (spare)* de rechange; *(additional)* en plus; **be ~** *(cost more)* être en supplément **3** *adv* ultra-

extract[1] ['ekstrækt] *n* extrait *m*

extract[2] [ɪk'strækt] extraire; *tooth also* arracher; *information* arracher; **extraction** extraction *f*

extradite ['ekstrədaɪt] extrader; **extradition** extradition *f*

extramarital [ekstrə'mærɪtl] extraconjugal

extraordinary [ɪkstrə'ɔːrdɪnerɪ] extraordinaire

extra 'time Br SP prolongation(s) *f(pl)*

extravagance [ɪk'strævəgəns] dépenses *fpl* extravagantes; *single act* dépense *f* extravagante; **extravagant** *person* dépensier; *price* exorbitant; *claim* excessif

extreme [ɪk'striːm] **1** *n* extrême *m* **2** *adj* extrême; **extremely** extrêmement; **extremist** extrémiste *m/f*

extrovert ['ekstrəvɜːrt] **1** *n* extraverti(e) *m(f)* **2** *adj* extraverti

exuberant [ɪg'zuːbərənt] exubérant

eye [aɪ] **1** n œil m **2** v/t regarder; **eye-catching** accrocheur; **eyeglasses** lunettes fpl; **eyeliner** eye-liner m;

eyeshadow ombre f à paupières; **eyesight** vue f; **eyewitness** témoin m oculaire

F

fabric ['fæbrɪk] tissu m
fabulous ['fæbjələs] fabuleux
façade [fə'sɑːd] façade f
face [feɪs] **1** n visage m, figure f **2** v/t person, sea faire face à
◆ **face up to** bully affronter; responsibilities faire face à
'facecloth gant m de toilette; **facelift** lifting m
facial ['feɪʃl] soin m du visage
facilitate [fə'sɪlɪteɪt] faciliter;
facilities of school, town etc installations fpl; (equipment) équipements mpl
fact [fækt] fait m; **in ~, as a matter of ~** en fait
faction ['fækʃn] faction f
factor ['fæktər] facteur m
faculty ['fækəltɪ] faculté f
fad [fæd] lubie f
fade [feɪd] v/i of colors passer; **faded** color passé
fag [fæg] pej F (homosexual) pédé m F
fail [feɪl] **1** v/i échouer **2** v/t exam être refusé à; **failing** défaut m, faiblesse f; **failure** échec m
faint [feɪnt] **1** adj faible, léger **2** v/i s'évanouir; **faintly** légèrement
fair¹ [fer] (fun~), COM foire f

fair² [fer] hair blond; complexion blanc
fairly ['ferlɪ] treat équitablement; (quite) assez; **fairness** of treatment équité f
faith [feɪθ] also REL foi f; **faithful** fidèle; **faithfully** fidèlement
fake [feɪk] **1** n (article m) faux m **2** adj faux; suicide attempt simulé **3** v/t (forge) falsifier; (feign) feindre; suicide, kidnap simuler
fall¹ [fɔːl] n season automne m
fall² [fɔːl] **1** v/i tomber; of prices baisser **2** n chute f; in price, temperature baisse f
◆ **fall behind** prendre du retard
◆ **fall for** person tomber amoureux de; (be deceived by) se laisser prendre à
◆ **fall through** of plans tomber à l'eau
fallible ['fæləbl] faillible
false [fɔːls] faux; **false start** in race faux départ m; **false teeth** fausses dents fpl; **falsify** falsifier
fame [feɪm] célébrité f
familiar [fə'mɪljər] familier; **be ~ with sth** bien connaître

qch; **familiarity** *with subject etc* (bonne) connaissance *f* (**with** de); **familiarize:** ~ **o.s. with** se familiariser avec

family ['fæməlɪ] famille *f*; **family doctor** médecin *m* de famille; **family planning clinic** centre *m* de planning familial; **family tree** arbre *m* généalogique

famine ['fæmɪn] famine *f*

famous ['feɪməs] célèbre

fan¹ [fæn] *n in sport* fana *m/f* F; *of singer, band* fan *m/f*

fan² [fæn] **1** *n electric* ventilateur *m*; *handheld* éventail *m* **2** *v/t:* ~ **o.s.** s'éventer

fanatical [fə'nætɪkl] fanatique; **fanaticism** fanatisme *m*

fantasize ['fæntəsaɪz] fantasmer (**about** sur); **fantastic** fantastique; **fantasy** *hopeful* rêve *m*; *unrealistic, sexual* fantasme *m*

fanzine ['fænziːn] fanzine *m*

far [fɑːr] loin; (*much*) bien; ~ **away** très loin; **as** ~ **as the corner** jusqu'au coin

farce [fɑːrs] farce *f*

fare [fer] *for ticket* prix *m* du billet; *for taxi* prix *m*

Far East Extrême-Orient *m*

farewell [fer'wel] adieu *m*

farfetched [fɑːr'fetʃt] tiré par les cheveux

farm [fɑːrm] ferme *f*; **farmer** fermier(-ière) *m(f)*; **farming** agriculture *f*; **farmworker** ouvrier(-ière) *m(f)* agricole; **farmyard** cour *f* de ferme

far-'off lointain, éloigné; **far-sighted** prévoyant; *visually* hypermétrope; **farther** plus loin; **farthest** le plus loin

fascinate ['fæsɪneɪt] fasciner; **fascinating** fascinant; **fascination** fascination *f*

fascism ['fæʃɪzm] fascisme *m*; **fascist 1** *n* fasciste *m/f* **2** *adj* fasciste

fashion ['fæʃn] mode *f*; (*manner*) manière *f*, façon *f*; **in** ~ à la mode; **out of** ~ démodé; **fashionable** à la mode; **fashionably** à la mode; **fashion-conscious** au courant de la mode; **fashion designer** créateur(-trice) *m(f)* de mode; **fashion show** défilé *m* de mode

fast¹ [fæst] **1** *adj* rapide; **be** ~ *of clock* avancer **2** *adv* vite; **be** ~ **asleep** dormir à poings fermés

fast² [fæst] *n* (*not eating*) jeûne *m*

fasten ['fæsn] **1** *v/t* attacher; *lid, window* fermer **2** *v/i* of *dress etc* s'attacher; **fastener** ['fæsnər] *for dress* agrafe *f*; *for lid* fermeture *f*

fast 'food fast-food *m*; **fast lane** voie *f* rapide; **fast train** train *m* rapide

fat [fæt] **1** *adj* gros **2** *n on meat* gras *m*; *for baking* graisse *f*

fatal ['feɪtl] *also error* fatal; **fatality** *accident m* mortel; **fatally** fatalement; ~ **injured** mortellement blessé

fermentation

fate [feɪt] destin *m*

'fat free sans matières grasses; yoghurt sans 0%

father ['fɑːðər] père *m*; fatherhood paternité *f*; father-in-law beau-père *m*; fatherly paternel

fatigue [fə'tiːg] fatigue *f*

fatten ['fætn] *animal* engraisser; fatty 1 *adj* adipeux 2 *n* F *person* gros(se) *m(f)*

faucet ['fɔːsɪt] robinet *m*

fault [fɔːlt] (*defect*) défaut *m*; **it's your/my ~** c'est de ta/ma faute; faultless impeccable; faulty défectueux

favor ['feɪvər] 1 *n* faveur *f*; **do s.o. a ~** rendre (un) service à qn 2 *v/t* (*prefer*) préférer; favorable favorable; favorite 1 *n person* préféré(e) *m(f)*; *food* plat *m* préféré; *in race* favori *m* 2 *adj* préféré; favoritism favoritisme *m*

favour Br → **favor**

fax [fæks] 1 *n* fax *m* 2 *v/t* faxer

fear [fɪr] 1 *n* peur *f* 2 *v/t* avoir peur de; fearless sans peur; fearlessly sans peur

feasibility study [fiːzə'bɪlətɪ] étude *f* de faisabilité; feasible faisable

feast [fiːst] festin *m*

feat [fiːt] exploit *m*

feather ['feðər] plume *f*

feature ['fiːtʃər] *n on face* trait *m*; *of city, building, style* caractéristique *f*; *article in paper* chronique *f*; feature film long métrage *m*

February ['februərɪ] février *m*

federal ['fedərəl] fédéral; federation fédération *f*

fed 'up F: **be ~ with** en avoir ras-le-bol de F

fee [fiː] *of lawyer, doctor etc* honoraires *mpl*; *for membership* frais *mpl*

feeble ['fiːbl] faible

feed [fiːd] nourrir; feedback réactions *fpl*

feel [fiːl] 1 *v/t* (*touch*) toucher; (*sense*) sentir; *pain, pleasure* ressentir; (*think*) penser 2 *v/i*: **it ~s like silk** on dirait de la soie; **do you ~ like a drink?** est-ce que tu as envie de boire quelque chose?

◆ feel up to se sentir capable de

feeler ['fiːlər] *of insect* antenne *f*; feeling sentiment *m*; (*sensation*) sensation *f*

fellow 'citizen concitoyen(ne) *m(f)*

felony ['felənɪ] crime *m*

felt [felt] feutre *m*; felt tip stylo *m* feutre

female ['fiːmeɪl] 1 *adj* femelle; *relating to people* féminin 2 *n* femelle *f*; *person* femme *f*

feminine ['femɪnɪn] 1 *adj* féminin 2 *n* GRAM féminin *m*; feminism féminisme *m*; feminist 1 *n* féministe *m/f* 2 *adj* féministe

fence [fens] barrière *f*, clôture *f*

fender ['fendər] MOT aile *f*

fermentation [fɜːrmen'teɪʃn]

fermentation f
ferocious [fə'rouʃəs] féroce
ferry ['ferɪ] ferry m
fertile ['fɜːrtl] fertile; **fertility**
fertilité f; **fertilize** féconder;
fertilizer for soil engrais m
fervent ['fɜːrvənt] fervent
fester ['festər] of wound suppurer
festival ['festɪvl] festival m;
festive de fête; **festivities**
festivités fpl
fetal ['fiːtl] fœtal
fetch [fetʃ] (go and ~) aller
chercher (**from** à); (come
and ~) venir chercher (**from**
à); price atteindre
fetus ['fiːtəs] fœtus m
feud [fjuːd] querelle f
fever ['fiːvər] fièvre f; **feverish** also fig fiévreux
few [fjuː] 1 adj (not many) peu
de; **a ~ ...** quelques; **quite a
~**, **a good ~** (a lot) beaucoup
de 2 pron (not many) peu; **a ~**
quelques-un(e)s m(f); **quite
a ~**, **a good ~** beaucoup; **few-
er** moins de
fiancé [fɪ'ɑːnseɪ] fiancé m; **fiancée** fiancée f
fiber ['faɪbər] fibre f; **fiber-
glass** n fibre f de verre; **fiber
optics** fibres fpl optiques
fibre Br → **fiber**
fickle ['fɪkl] inconstant
fiction ['fɪkʃn] romans mpl;
(made-up story) fiction f; **fic-
tional** de roman; **fictitious**
fictif
fiddle ['fɪdl] 1 n (violin) violon

m 2 v/i: ~ **around with** tripoter 3 v/t accounts, results truquer
fidgety ['fɪdʒɪtɪ] remuant
field [fiːld] champ m; for sport
terrain m; (competitors in
race) concurrent(e)s m(f)pl;
fielder in baseball joueur m
de champ
fierce [fɪrs] animal féroce;
wind, storm violent; **fiercely**
avec férocité
fiery ['faɪrɪ] ardent, fougueux
fifteen [fɪf'tiːn] quinze; **fif-
teenth** quinzième; **fifth** cinquième; **fiftieth** cinquantième; **fifty** cinquante; **fifty-fifty**
moitié-moitié
fight [faɪt] 1 n combat m; (argument) dispute f; for survival etc lutte f 2 v/t enemy, person combattre; in boxing se
battre contre; injustice lutter
contre 3 v/i se battre; (argue)
se disputer; **fighter** combat-
tant(e) m(f); airplane avion
m de chasse; (boxer) boxeur
m; **fighting** physical combat
m; verbal dispute f
figure ['fɪgjər] 1 n (digit) chiffre m; of person ligne f;
(form, shape) figure f 2 v/t
F (think) penser:
◆ **figure on** F (plan) compter
◆ **figure out** comprendre;
calculation calculer
file¹ [faɪl] 1 n of documents
dossier m; COMPUT fichier m
2 v/t documents classer
file² [faɪl] for wood etc lime f

'**file cabinet** classeur *m*

fill [fɪl] remplir; *tooth* plomber; *prescription* préparer

◆ **fill in** *form* remplir; *hole* boucher

◆ **fill out 1** *v/t form* remplir **2** *v/i (get fatter)* grossir

fillet ['fɪlɪt] filet *m*

filling ['fɪlɪŋ] **1** *n in sandwich* garniture *f; in tooth* plombage *m* **2** *adj food* nourrissant; **filling station** station-service *f*

film [fɪlm] **1** *n* pellicule *f; (movie)* film *m* **2** *v/t* filmer; **film-maker** réalisateur(-trice) *m(f)* de films; **film star** star *f* de cinéma

filter ['fɪltər] **1** *n* filtre *m* **2** *v/t* filtrer

filth [fɪlθ] saleté; **filthy** sale; *language etc* obscène

final ['faɪnl] **1** *adj* dernier; *decision* définitif, irrévocable **2** *n* sp finale *f;* **finale** apothéose *f;* **finalist** finaliste *m/f;* **finalize** finaliser, mettre au point; **finally** finalement, enfin

finance ['faɪnæns] **1** *n* finance *f; (funds)* financement *m* **2** *v/t* financer; **financial** financier; **financially** financièrement; **financier** financier (-ière) *m(f)*

find [faɪnd] trouver

◆ **find out** découvrir; *(enquire about)* se renseigner sur

findings ['faɪndɪŋz] *of report* constatations *fpl*

fine[1] [faɪn] *day* beau; *(good)* bon, excellent; *distinction* subtil; *line* fin; **how's that? – that's ~** que dites-vous de ça? – c'est bien

fine[2] [faɪn] **1** *n* amende *f* **2** *v/t* condamner à une amende de $5.000

finger ['fɪŋgər] **1** *n* doigt *m* **2** *v/t* toucher; **fingerprint** empreinte *f* digitale

finicky ['fɪnɪkɪ] *person* tatillon; *design* alambiqué

finish ['fɪnɪʃ] **1** *v/t* finir, terminer **2** *v/i* finir **3** *n of product* finition *f; of race* arrivée *f*

◆ **finish with** *boyfriend etc* en finir avec

fire ['faɪr] **1** *n* feu *m; (blaze)* incendie *m; (electric, gas)* radiateur *m;* **be on ~** être en feu; **set ~ to sth** mettre le feu à qch **2** *v/i (shoot)* tirer **3** *v/t* F *(dismiss)* virer F; **fire alarm** signal *m* d'incendie; **firearm** arme *f* à feu; **firecracker** pétard *m;* **fire department** sapeurs-pompiers *mpl;* **fire engine** *esp Br* voiture *f* de pompiers; **fire escape** *ladder* échelle *f* de secours; *stairs* escalier *m* de secours; **fire extinguisher** extincteur *m* (d'incendie); **fire fighter** pompier *m;* **fireplace** cheminée *f;* **fire station** caserne *f* de pompiers; **fire truck** voiture *f* de pompiers; **firework** pièce *f* d'artifice; **~s**

(*display*) feu m d'artifice

firm[1] [fɜːrm] *adj* ferme

firm[2] [fɜːrm] *n* COM firme *f*

first [fɜːrst] **1** *adj* premier **2** *n* premier(-ière) *m(f)* **3** *adv* arrive, finish le/la premier(-ière) (*beforehand*) d'abord; **at ~** au début; **first aid** premiers secours *mpl*; **first class 1** *adj* ticket de première classe; (*very good*) de première qualité **2** *adv* travel en première classe; **first floor** *Am* premier étage *m*; *Br* premier étage m; **First Lady** première dame *f*; **firstly** premièrement; **first name** prénom *m*; **first night** première *f*; **first-rate** de premier ordre

fiscal ['fɪskl] fiscal; **fiscal year** année *f* fiscale

fish [fɪʃ] **1** *n* poisson *m* **2** *v/i* pêcher; **fisherman** pêcheur *m*; **fishing** pêche *f*; **fishing boat** bateau *m* de pêche; **fish stick** bâtonnet *m* de poisson; **fishy** F (*suspicious*) louche

fist [fɪst] *n* poing *m*

fit[1] [fɪt] *n* MED crise *f*, attaque *f*

fit[2] [fɪt] *adj* physically en forme; *morally* digne

fit[3] [fɪt] **1** *v/t* of clothes aller à; (*install, attach*) poser; *it doesn't ~ me any more* je ne rentre plus dedans **2** *v/i* of clothes aller

fitness ['fɪtnɪs] *physical* (bonne) forme *f*; **fitting** approprié; **fittings** installations *fpl*

five [faɪv] cinq

fix [fɪks] **1** *n* (*solution*) solution *f* **2** *v/t* (*attach*) attacher; (*repair*) réparer; *meeting etc* arranger; *lunch* préparer; *dishonestly: match etc* truquer; **fixed** *time*; **fixings** garniture *f*

flab [flæb] *on body* graisse *f*; **flabby** *muscles etc* mou

flag[1] [flæg] *n* drapeau *m*; NAUT pavillon *m*

flag[2] [flæg] *v/i* (*tire*) faiblir

'flagpole mât *m* (de drapeau)

flagrant ['fleɪɡrənt] flagrant

flair [fler] (*talent*) flair *m*; *have a natural ~ for* avoir un don pour

flake [fleɪk] *of snow* flocon *m*; *of plaster* écaille *f*

flamboyant [flæm'bɔɪənt] extravagant; **flamboyantly** avec extravagance

flame [fleɪm] flamme *f*

flammable ['flæməbl] inflammable

flank [flæŋk] **1** *n* flanc *m* **2** *v/t*: *be ~ed by* être flanqué de

flap [flæp] **1** *n* of envelope, pocket rabat *m* **2** *v/t wings* battre **3** *v/i of flag etc* battre

◆ **flare up** [fler] of violence, rash éclater; of fire s'enflammer; (*get very angry*) s'emporter

flash [flæʃ] **1** *n* of light éclair *m*; PHOT flash *m*; *in a ~* F en un rien de temps; *~ of lightning* éclair *m* **2** *v/i of light* clignoter; **flashback** *in movie* flash-back *m*; **flashlight** lam-

pe *f* de poche; PHOT flash *m*;
flashy *pej* voyant

flask [flɑːsk] (*hip* ~) fiole *f*

flat¹ [flæt] **1** *adj* plat; *beer*
éventé; *battery*, *tire* à plat;
bémol **2** *adv* MUS trop bas **3**
n pneu *m* crevé

flat² [flæt] *n Br* (*apartment*)
appartement *m*

flatly ['flætlɪ] *deny* catégoriquement; **flat rate** tarif *m*
unique; **flatten** *land*, *road*
aplanir; *by bombing*, *demoli-*
tion raser

flatter ['flætər] flatter; **flatter-**
er flatteur(-euse) *m(f)*; **flat-**
tering *comments*, *color*, *clothes* avantageux;
flattery flatterie *f*

flavor ['fleɪvər] **1** *n* goût *m*; *of*
ice cream parfum *m* **2** *v/t*
food assaisonner; **flavoring**
arôme *m*

flavour *Br* → **flavor**

flaw [flɔː] défaut *m*; **flawless**
parfait

flea [fliː] puce *f*

fleck [flek] petite tache *f*

fled [fled] *pret & pp* → **flee**

flee [fliː] *v/i & v/t* s'enfuir

fleece [fliːs] **1** *n of sheep* toison
f **2** *v/t F* (*cheat*) plumer F

fleet [fliːt] NAUT flotte *f*; *of ve-*
hicles parc *m*

fleeting ['fliːtɪŋ] *visit etc* très
court

flesh [fleʃ] *also of fruit* chair *f*

flex [fleks] *muscles* fléchir;
flexibility flexibilité *f*; **flexi-**
ble flexible; **flextime** horaire
m à la carte

flicker ['flɪkər] vaciller

flier ['flaɪr] (*circular*) prospectus *m*

flight [flaɪt] *in airplane* vol *m*;

(*fleeing*) fuite *f*; ~ (**of stairs**)
escalier *m*; **flight attendant**
male steward *m*; *female* hôtesse *f* de l'air; **flight path**
trajectoire *f* de vol; **flight re-**
corder enregistreur *m* de vol;
flight time *departure* heure *f*
de vol; *duration* durée *f* de
vol; **flighty** frivole

flimsy ['flɪmzɪ] *furniture* fragile; *dress*, *material* léger; *ex-*
cuse faible

flinch [flɪntʃ] tressaillir

flipper ['flɪpər] nageoire *f*

flirt [flɜːrt] **1** *v/i* flirter **2** *n* flir-
teur(-euse) *m(f)*; **flirtatious**
flirteur

float [floʊt] *also* FIN flotter

flock [flɑːk] **1** *n of sheep* troupeau *m* **2** *v/i* venir en masse

flood [flʌd] **1** *n* inondation *f* **2**
v/t of river inonder; **flooding**
inondation(s) *f(pl)*

'**floodlight** projecteur *m*;
flood waters inondations *fpl*

floor [flɔːr] sol *m*; *wooden*
plancher *m*; (*story*) étage *m*

flop [flɑːp] **1** *v/i* s'écrouler; F
(*fail*) faire un bide F **2** *n* F
(*failure*) bide *m* F; **floppy**
(*disk*) disquette *f*

florist ['flɔːrɪst] fleuriste *m/f*

flour ['flaʊr] farine *f*

flourish ['flʌrɪʃ] *of plants*
fleurir; *fig* prospérer; **flour-**
ishing *business* fleurissant,
prospère

flow [floʊ] *v/i of river* couler; *of*
electric current passer; *of*
traffic circuler; *of work* se

dérouler **2** *n of river* cours *m*;
of information circulation *f*;
flowchart organigramme *m*
flower ['flaur] **1** *n* fleur *f* **2** *v/i*
fleurir
flu [fluː] grippe *f*
fluctuate ['flʌktʃueit] fluctuer; **fluctuation** fluctuation *f*
fluency ['fluːənsi] *in a language* maîtrise *f* (**in** de); **fluent** *person* qui s'exprime avec aisance; **he speaks ~ Spanish** il parle couramment l'espagnol; **fluently** couramment; *in own language* avec aisance
fluid ['fluːid] fluide *m*
flunk [flʌŋk] F *subject* rater
flush [flʌʃ] **1** *v/t*: **~ the toilet** tirer la chasse d'eau **2** *v/i* (*go red*) rougir
flutter ['flʌtər] *of bird* voleter; *of wings* battre; *of flag* s'agiter; *of heart* palpiter
fly[1] [flai] *n* (*insect*) mouche *f*
fly[2] [flai] *n on pants* braguette *f*
fly[3] [flai] **1** *v/i* voler; *in airplane* prendre l'avion; *of flag* flotter **2** *v/t airplane* piloter, voler; *airline* voyager par; (*transport by air*) envoyer par avion
◆ **fly past** *of time* filer
flying ['flaiiŋ]: **I hate ~** je déteste prendre l'avion
foam [foum] *on sea* écume *f*; *on drink* mousse *f*; **foam rubber** caoutchouc *m* mous-

se
focus ['foukəs] *of attention* centre *m*; PHOT mise *f* au point
◆ **focus on** se concentrer sur; PHOT mettre au point sur
fodder ['fɒdər] fourrage *m*
fog [fɒg] brouillard *m*; **foggy** brumeux
foil[1] [fɔil] *n silver* feuille *f* d'aluminium
foil[2] [fɔil] *v/t* (*thwart*) faire échouer
fold [fould] **1** *v/t paper etc* plier; **~ one's arms** croiser les bras **2** *v/i of business* fermer (ses portes) **3** *n in cloth etc* pli *m*
◆ **fold up 1** *v/t chair, table se (re)plier
folder ['fouldər] *for documents* chemise *f*; COMPUT dossier *m*; **folding** pliant
foliage ['foulɪdʒ] feuillage *m*
folk [fouk] (*people*) gens *mpl*; **folk music** folk *m*; **folk singer** chanteur(-euse) *m(f)* de folk
follow ['fɒlou] **1** *v/t also* (*understand*) suivre **2** *v/i logically* s'ensuivre
◆ **follow up** *inquiry* donner suite à
follower ['fɒlouər] *of politician etc* partisan(e) *m(f)*; *of football team* supporteur (-trice) *m(f)*; **following 1** *adj* suivant **2** *n people* partisans *mpl*
fond [fɒnd] (*loving*) aimant;

memory agréable; **be ~ of** beaucoup aimer

fondle ['fɒndl] caresser

fondness ['fɒndnɪs] *for s.o.* tendresse *f*; *for sth* penchant *m*

font [fɒnt] *for printing* police *f*; *in church* fonts *mpl* baptismaux

food [fuːd] nourriture *f*; **French ~** la cuisine française; **food poisoning** intoxication *f* alimentaire

fool [fuːl] **1** *n* idiot(e) *m(f)* **2** *v/t* berner; **foolhardy** téméraire; **foolish** idiot, bête; **foolproof** à toute épreuve

foot [fut] *also measurement* pied *m*; *of animal* patte *f*; **put one's ~ in it** F mettre les pieds dans le plat F; **footage** séquences *fpl*; **football** football *m* américain; (*soccer*) football *m* F; (*ball*) ballon *m* de football; **football player** joueur(-euse) *m(f)* de football américain; *soccer* joueur(-euse) *m(f)* de football; **foothills** contreforts *mpl*; **footnote** note *f* (de bas de page); **footpath** sentier *m*; **footprint** trace *f* de pas; **footstep** pas *m*

for [fɔːr] *destination; a train ~ ...* un train à destination de ...; *what is this ~?* pour quoi est-ce que c'est fait?; *what ~?* pourquoi?; *~ three days* pendant trois jours; *it lasted ~ three days* ça a duré trois

jours; *I've been waiting ~ an hour* j'attends depuis une heure

forbid [fər'bɪd] interdire; **forbidden** interdit; **forbidding** menaçant

force [fɔːrs] **1** *n* force *f*; **come into ~** *of law etc* entrer en vigueur **2** *v/t* door, lock forcer; **~ s.o. to do sth** forcer qn à faire qch; **forced** forcé; **forced landing** atterrissage *m* forcé; **forceful** *argument*, *speaker* puissant; *character* énergique

forceps ['fɔːrseps] MED forceps *m*

forcibly ['fɔːrsəblɪ] *restrain* par force

foreboding [fər'boʊdɪŋ] pressentiment *m*; **forecast 1** *n of results* pronostic *m*; *of weather* prévisions *fpl* **2** *v/t result* pronostiquer; *future, weather* prévoir; **forefathers** ancêtres *mpl*; **forefinger** index *m*; **foreground** premier plan *m*; **forehead** front *m*

foreign ['fɒrən] étranger; **foreign affairs** affaires *fpl* étrangères; **foreign body** corps *m* étranger; **foreign currency** devises *fpl* étrangères; **foreigner** étranger (-ère) *m(f)*; **foreign exchange** devises *fpl* étrangères

'foreman chef *m* d'équipe; **foremost 1** *adv* (*uppermost*) le plus important **2** *adj* (*lead-*

ing) premier

forensic 'medicine [fə'ren-
sɪk] médecine f légale; forensic scientist expert m lé-
giste

'forerunner person prédécesseur m; thing ancêtre m/f;
foresee prévoir; foresight
prévoyance f

forest [forɪst] forêt f; forest-
ry sylviculture f

fore'tell prédire

forever [fə'revər] toujours

'foreword avant-propos m

forfeit ['fɔːfɪt] (lose) perdre;
(give up) renoncer à

forge [fɔːdʒ] contrefaire; forgery bank bill faux billet m;
document faux m; signature
contrefaçon f

forget [fər'get] oublier; for-
getful: you're so ~ tu as vraiment mauvaise mémoire

forgive [fər'gɪv] 1 v/t ~ s.o.
sth pardonner qch à qn 2
v/i pardonner; forgiveness
pardon m

fork [fɔːrk] fourchette f; for
gardening fourche f; in road
embranchement m

form [fɔːrm] 1 n (shape) forme
f; document formulaire m 2
v/t former; friendship développer; opinion se faire 3
v/i (take shape, develop) se
former; formal language
soutenu; dress de soirée;
manner, reception cérémo-
nieux; recognition etc officiel; formality of language

caractère m soutenu; of occasion cérémonie f; it's just
a ~ c'est juste une formalité;
formally speak cérémonieu-
sement; recognized officiellement

format [fɔːrmæt] 1 v/t formater 2 n format m

formation [fɔːr'meɪʃn] formation f

former ['fɔːrmər] ancien; the
~ le premier, la première;
formerly autrefois

formidable ['fɔːrmɪdəbl] redoutable

formula ['fɔːrmjulə] MATH,
CHEM formule f; fig recette f

fort [fɔːrt] MIL fort m

forthcoming ['fɔːrθkʌmɪŋ]
(future) futur; personality
ouvert

'forthright franc

fortieth ['fɔːrtɪɪθ] quarantiè-
me

fortnight ['fɔːrtnaɪt] Br quinze jours mpl, quinzaine f

fortress ['fɔːrtrɪs] MIL forte-
resse f

fortunate ['fɔːrtʃnət] decision
heureux; be ~ avoir de la
chance; fortunately heureusement; fortune (fate) destin
m; (luck) chance f; (lot of
money) fortune f

forty ['fɔːrtɪ] quarante

forward ['fɔːrwərd] 1 adv en
avant 2 adj pej: person effronté 3 n SP avant m 4 v/t letter faire suivre; forward-
-looking moderne

fossil ['fɒːsl] fossile m

foster ['fɒːstər] child servir de famille d'accueil à; attitude, belief encourager

foul [faʊl] **1** n SP faute f **2** adj smell infect; weather sale **3** v/t SP commettre une faute contre

found [faʊnd] school etc fonder; **foundation** of theory etc fondement m; (organization) fondation f; **foundations** of building fondations fpl; **founder** fondateur(-trice) m(f)

fountain ['faʊntɪn] fontaine f; with vertical spout jet m d'eau

four [fɔːr] quatre; **four-star** quatre étoiles; **fourteen** quatorze; **fourteenth** quatorzième; **fourth** quatrième; **four-wheel drive** MOT quatre-quatre m

fox [fɒːks] **1** n renard m **2** v/t (puzzle) mystifier

foyer ['fɔɪər] hall m d'entrée

fraction ['frækʃn] fraction f; **fractionally** très légèrement

fracture ['fræktʃər] **1** n fracture f **2** v/t fracturer

fragile ['frædʒəl] fragile

fragment ['frægmənt] fragment m

fragrance ['freɪgrəns] parfum m; **fragrant** parfumé

frail [freɪl] frêle

frame [freɪm] **1** n of picture, bicycle cadre m; of window châssis m; of eyeglasses mon-

ture f **2** v/t picture encadrer; F person monter un coup contre; **framework** structure f; **within the ~ of** dans le cadre de

France [fræns] France f

franchise ['fræntʃaɪz] for business franchise f

frank [fræŋk] franc; **frankly** franchement; **frankness** franchise f

frantic ['fræntɪk] frénétique

fraternal [frə'tɜːrnl] fraternel

fraud [frɔːd] fraude f; person imposteur m; **fraudulent** frauduleux

frayed [freɪd] cuffs usé

freak [friːk] **1** n (unusual event) phénomène m étrange; (two-headed animal etc) monstre m; F (strange person) taré(e) m(f) F **2** adj storm etc anormalement violent

free [friː] **1** adj libre; no cost gratuit **2** v/t prisoners libérer; **freedom** liberté f; **free enterprise** libre entreprise f; **free kick** in soccer coup m franc; **freelance** indépendant, free-lance inv; **freely** admit volontiers; **free speech** libre parole f; **freeway** autoroute f

freeze [friːz] **1** v/t congeler; bank account bloquer; **~ a video** faire un arrêt sur image **2** v/i of water geler; **freeze-dried** lyophilisé; **freezer** congélateur m;

freezing 1 *adj* glacial **2** *n*: **10 below** ~ 10 degrés au-dessous de zéro

freight [freɪt] fret *m*; **freighter** ship cargo *m*; *airplane* avion-cargo *m*

French [frentʃ] **1** *adj* français **2** *n language* français *m*; **the** ~ les Français *mpl*; **French fries** frites *fpl*; **Frenchman** Français *m*; **Frenchwoman** Française *f*

frenzied ['frenzɪd] *attack, activity* forcené; *mob* déchaîné; **frenzy** frénésie *f*

frequency ['fri:kwənsɪ] *also of radio* fréquence *f*

frequent¹ *adj* fréquent

frequent² [frɪ'kwent] *v/t bar etc* fréquenter

frequently ['fri:kwəntlɪ] fréquemment

fresh [freʃ] frais; *start* nouveau; *sheets* propre; *(impertinent)* insolent; **fresh air** air *m*
♦ **freshen up 1** *v/i* se rafraîchir **2** *v/t paintwork* rafraîchir

freshly ['freʃlɪ] fraîchement; **freshman** étudiant(e) *m(f)* de première année; **freshwater** d'eau douce

fret [fret] s'inquiéter

friction ['frɪkʃn] friction *f*

Friday ['fraɪdeɪ] vendredi *m*

fridge [frɪdʒ] frigo *m* F

friend [frend] ami(e) *m(f)*; **friendliness** amabilité *f*; **friendly** amical; *hotel, city* sympathique; *argument* entre amis; **friendship** amitié *f*

fries [fraɪz] frites *fpl*

fright [fraɪt] peur *f*; **frighten** faire peur à; **be ~ed** avoir peur (**of** de); **frightening** effrayant

frill [frɪl] *on dress etc*, *(extra)* falbala *m*

fringe [frɪndʒ] frange *f*; *of city* périphérie *f*; *of society* marge *f*; **fringe benefits** avantages *mpl* sociaux

frisk [frɪsk] fouiller
♦ **fritter away** ['frɪtər] *time, fortune* gaspiller

frivolity [frɪ'vɑːlətɪ] frivolité *f*; **frivolous** frivole

frizzy ['frɪzɪ] *hair* crépu

frog [frɑːg] grenouille *f*; **frogman** homme-grenouille *m*

from [frɑːm] de; ~ **9 to 5 (o'clock)** de 9 heures à 5 heures; ~ **the 18th century** à partir du XVIIIe siècle; ~ **today on** à partir d'aujourd'hui; ~ **here to there** d'ici à là(-bas); **I am** ~ **New Jersey** je viens du New Jersey; **tired** ~ **the journey** fatigué par le voyage; **it's** ~ **overeating** c'est d'avoir trop mangé

front [frʌnt] **1** *n of building* façade *f*, devant *m*; *of book* devant *m*; *(cover organization)* façade *f*; MIL, *of weather* front *m*; **in** ~ devant; **in** ~ **in** race en tête; **in** ~ **of** devant **2** *adj wheel, seat* avant **3** *v/t* TV program présenter; **front door** porte *f* d'entrée

frontier ['frʌntɪr] *also fig*

frontière f

'front line MIL front m; **front page** of newspaper une f; **front-wheel drive** traction f avant

frost [frɒst] gel m; **frostbite** gelure f; **frosted** on cake glaçage m; **frosty** also fig glacial

froth [frɒθ] écume f, mousse f

frown [fraʊn] froncer les sourcils

frozen ['frəʊzn] gelé; food surgelé

fruit [fruːt] fruit m; collective fruits mpl; **fruitful** discussions etc fructueux; **fruit juice** jus m de fruit; **fruit salad** salade f de fruits

frustrate ['frʌstreɪt] person frustrer; plans contrarier; **frustrating** frustrant; **frustration** frustration f

fry [fraɪ] (faire) frire; **frypan** poêle f (à frire)

fuck [fʌk] V baiser V; ~ **putain!** V

fuel ['fjuːəl] **1** n carburant m **2** v/t fig entretenir

fugitive ['fjuːdʒətɪv] fugitif (-ive) m(f)

fulfill, Br **fulfil** [fʊl'fɪl] dreams réaliser; task accomplir; contract remplir; **fulfillment**, Br **fulfilment** of contract etc exécution f; moral, spiritual accomplissement m

full [fʊl] plein (**of** de); hotel, account complet; **pay in** ~ tout payer; **full moon** pleine

lune f; **full stop** Br point m; **full-time** à plein temps; fully complètement; describe en détail

fumble ['fʌmbl] catch mal attraper

fumes [fjuːmz] s fumée f.

fun [fʌn] **1** n amusement m; **it was great** ~ on s'est bien amusé; **have** ~! amuse-toi bien! **2** adj F marrant F

function ['fʌŋkʃn] **1** n fonction f; (reception etc) réception f **2** v/i fonctionner; ~ **as** faire fonction de; **functional** fonctionnel

fund [fʌnd] **1** n fonds m **2** v/t project etc financer

fundamental [fʌndə'mentl] fondamental; **fundamentalist** fondamentaliste m/f; **fundamentally** fondamentalement

funding ['fʌndɪŋ] (money) financement m

funeral ['fjuːnərəl] enterrement m; **funeral home** établissement m de pompes funèbres

fungus ['fʌŋgəs] champignon m; mold moisissure f

funnies ['fʌnɪz] F pages fpl drôles; **funnily** (oddly) bizarrement; (comically) comiquement; ~ **enough** chose curieuse; **funny** (comical) drôle; (odd) bizarre, curieux

fur [fɜːr] fourrure f

furious ['fjʊrɪəs] furieux

furnace ['fɜːrnɪs] four(neau)

m

furnish ['fɜːrnɪʃ] *room* meubler; (*supply*) fournir; **furniture** meubles *mpl*; *a piece
of* ~ un meuble

further ['fɜːrðər] **1** *adj* supplémentaire; (*more distant*) plus
éloigné **2** *adv* walk, drive
plus loin **3** *v/t cause etc* faire
avancer, promouvoir; **fur-
thermore** de plus, en outre

furtive ['fɜːrtɪv] furtif

fury ['fjʊrɪ] fureur *f*

fuse [fjuːz] **1** *n* ELEC fusible *m*,
plomb *m* F **2** *v/i* ELEC: *the*

lights have ~*d* les plombs
ont sauté **3** *v/t* ELEC faire sauter; **fusebox** boîte *f* à fusi-
bles

fusion ['fjuːʒn] fusion *f*

fuss [fʌs] agitation *f*; **fussy**
person difficile; *design etc*
trop compliqué

futile ['fjuːtl] futile; **futility** fu-
tilité *f*

future ['fjuːtʃər] **1** *n* avenir *f*;
GRAM futur *m* **2** *adj* futur; **fu-
turistic** *design* futuriste

fuzzy ['fʌzɪ] *hair* crépu; (*out
of focus*) flou

G

gadget ['gædʒɪt] gadget *m*

gag [gæg] **1** *n* bâillon *m*;
(*joke*) gag *m* **2** *v/t also fig*
bâillonner

gain [geɪn] acquérir; *victory*
remporter; *advantage, sympathy* gagner

gala ['gɑːlə] gala *m*

galaxy ['gæləksɪ] galaxie *f*

gale [geɪl] tempête *f*

gallery ['gælərɪ] *for art, in theater* galerie *f*

gallon ['gælən] gallon *m*
(0,785l, *en* GB 0,546l)

gallop ['gæləp] galoper

gamble ['gæmbl] jouer; **gambler** joueur(-euse) *m(f)*;
gambling jeu *m*

game [geɪm] *also in tennis* jeu
m; *have a* ~ *of tennis* faire
une partie de tennis

gang [gæŋ] gang *m*; *of friends*
bande *f*; **gangster** gangster
m; **gangway** passerelle *f*

gap [gæp] trou *m*; *in time* intervalle *m*; *between personal-
ities* fossé *m*

gape [geɪp] rester bouche
bée; **gaping** *hole* béant

garage [gəˈrɑːʒ] garage *m*

garbage ['gɑːrbɪdʒ] ordures
fpl; (*fig : nonsense*) bêtises
fpl; **garbage can** poubelle
f; **garbage truck** benne *f* à
ordures

garbled ['gɑːrbld] *message*
confus

garden ['gɑːrdn] jardin *m*;
gardening jardinage *m*

garish ['gerɪʃ] criard

garlic ['gɑːrlɪk] ail *m*

garment ['gɑːrmənt] vêtement *m*

garnish ['gɑːrnɪʃ] garnir (**with** de)

gas [gæs] gaz *m*; (*gasoline*) essence *f*

gash [gæʃ] entaille *f*

gasket ['gæskɪt] joint *m* d'étanchéité

gasoline ['gæsəliːn] essence *f*

gasp [gæsp] **1** *n* in surprise hoquet *m*; with exhaustion halètement *m* **2** *v/i* with exhaustion haleter; **with surprise** pousser une exclamation de surprise

'gas pedal accélérateur *m*; **gas pump** pompe *f* (à essence); **gas station** station-service *f*

gate [geɪt] also at airport porte *f*; **gateway** entrée *f*; also fig porte *f*

gather ['gæðər] **1** *v/t* facts recueillir; ~ **speed** prendre de la vitesse **2** *v/i* of crowd s'assembler; **gathering** (*group of people*) assemblée *f*

gaudy ['gɔːdɪ] voyant

gauge [geɪdʒ] **1** *n* jauge *f* **2** *v/t* pressure jauger; opinion mesurer

gaunt [gɔːnt] émacié

gawky ['gɔːkɪ] gauche

gawp [gɔːp] F rester bouche bée (**at** devant)

gay [geɪ] gay

gaze [geɪz] **1** *n* regard *m* (fixe) **2** *v/i* regarder fixement

gear [gɪr] (*equipment*) équipement *m*; in vehicles vitesse *f*;

gearbox MOT boîte *f* de vitesses; **gear shift** MOT levier *m* de vitesse

gel [dʒel] for hair, shower gel *m*

gem [dʒem] pierre *f* précieuse; fig perle *f*

gender ['dʒendər] genre *m*

gene [dʒiːn] gène *m*

general ['dʒenrəl] **1** *n* MIL général(e) *m(f)* **2** *adj* général; **generalization** généralisation *f*; **generalize** généraliser; **generally** généralement; ~ **speaking** de manière générale

generate ['dʒenəreɪt] produire; **generation** génération *f*; **generator** générateur *m*

generosity [dʒenə'rɑːsətɪ] générosité *f*; **generous** généreux

genetic [dʒɪ'netɪk] génétique; **genetically** génétiquement; **genetically engineered** transgénique; **genetically modified** génétiquement modifié; **genetic engineering** génie *m* génétique; **genetic fingerprint** empreinte *f* génétique; **genetics** génétique *f*

genial ['dʒiːnjəl] agréable

genitals ['dʒenɪtlz] organes *mpl* génitaux

genius ['dʒiːnjəs] génie *m*

genocide ['dʒenəsaɪd] génocide *m*

gentle ['dʒentl] doux; breeze léger; **gentleman** monsieur *m*; **he's a real ~** c'est un vrai gentleman; **gentleness** douceur *f*; **gently** doucement; *blow* légèrement

genuine ['dʒenʊɪn] authentique; **genuinely** vraiment, sincèrement

geographical [dʒɪə' græfɪkl] géographique; **geography** géographie *f*

geological [dʒɪə'lɒːdʒɪkl] géologique; **geologist** géologue *m/f*; **geology** géologie *f*

geometric, geometrical [dʒɪə'metrɪk(l)] géométrique; **geometry** géométrie *f*

geriatric [dʒerɪ'ætrɪk] **1** *adj* gériatrique **2** *n* patient(e) *m(f)* gériatrique

germ [dʒɜːrm] *also of idea etc* germe *m*

German ['dʒɜːrmən] **1** *adj* allemand **2** *n person* Allemand(e) *m(f)*; *language* allemand *m*; **German shepherd** berger *m* allemand; **Germany** Allemagne *f*

gesture ['dʒestʃər] *also fig* geste *m*

get [get] (*obtain*) obtenir; (*buy*) acheter; (*fetch*) aller chercher; (*receive: letter*) recevoir; (*receive: knowledge, respect etc*) acquérir; (*catch: bus, train etc*) prendre; (*understand*) comprendre; (*become*) devenir; **when we ~ home** quand nous arrivons chez nous; **~ old/tired** vieil-

lir/se fatiguer; **~ sth done** (*by s.o. else*) faire faire qch; **~ s.o. to do sth** faire faire qch à qn; **~ one's hair cut** se faire couper les cheveux; **~ sth ready** préparer qch; *have got* avoir; **have got to** devoir; **I have got to study** je dois étudier, il faut que j'étudie (subj); **~ to know** commencer à bien connaître

◆ **get at** (*criticize*) s'en prendre à; (*imply, mean*) vouloir dire

◆ **get by** (*pass*) passer; *financially* s'en sortir

◆ **get down 1** *v/i from ladder etc* descendre; (*duck*) se baisser **2** *v/t* (*depress*) déprimer

◆ **get in 1** *v/i* (*of train, plane*) arriver; (*come home*) rentrer; *to car* entrer **2** *v/t to suitcase etc* rentrer

◆ **get into** *house* entrar dans; *car* monter dans

◆ **get off 1** *v/i from bus etc* descendre; (*finish work*) finir; (*not be punished*) s'en tirer **2** *v/t* (*remove*) enlever

◆ **get on 1** *v/i to bike, bus* monter; (*be friendly*) s'entendre; (*advance: of time*) se faire tard; (*become old*) prendre de l'âge; (*progress: of book*) avancer **2** *v/t*: **get on the bus** monter dans le bus

◆ **get out 1** *v/i of car, prison*

etc sortir; **get out!** va-t-en! **2** *v/t* nail, stain enlever; *gun, pen* sortir

♦ **get through** *on telephone* obtenir la communication

♦ **get up 1** *v/i* se lever **2** *v/t* (*climb: hill*) monter

ghastly ['gɑːstlɪ] horrible

ghetto ['getəu] ghetto *m*

ghost [gəust] fantôme *m*, spectre *m*; **ghostly** spectral

ghoul [guːl] personne *f* morbide

giant ['dʒaɪənt] **1** *n* géant(e) *m(f)* **2** *adj* géant

gibberish ['dʒɪbərɪʃ] F charabia *m*

gibe [dʒaɪb] moquerie *f*

giddiness ['gɪdɪnɪs] vertige *m*; **giddy: feel ~** avoir le vertige

gift [gɪft] cadeau *m*; *talent* don *m*; **gift card** carte *f* cadeau; **gifted** doué; **giftwrap: ~ sth** faire un paquet-cadeau

gig [gɪg] F concert *m*

gigabyte ['gɪgəbaɪt] COMPUT gigaoctet *m*

gigantic [dʒaɪ'gæntɪk] gigantesque

giggle ['gɪgl] **1** *v/i* glousser **2** *n* gloussement *m*

gimmick ['gɪmɪk] truc F

gin [dʒɪn] gin *m*; **~ and tonic** gin *m* tonic

gipsy ['dʒɪpsɪ] gitan(e) *m(f)*

girder ['gɜːrdər] poutre *f*

girl [gɜːrl] (*jeune*) fille *f*; **girl-friend** *of boy* petite amie *f*; *younger also* copine *f*; *of girl* amie *f*, *younger also* copine *f*; **girlish** de jeune fille

gist [dʒɪst] essence *f*

give [gɪv] donner; *present* offrir; (*supply: electricity etc*) fournir; *talk, lecture* faire; *cry, groan* pousser

♦ **give away** *as present* donner; (*betray*) trahir

♦ **give back** rendre

♦ **give in 1** (*surrender*) se rendre **2** *v/t* (*hand in*) remettre

♦ **give onto** (*open onto*) donner sur

♦ **give out 1** *v/t leaflets etc* distribuer **2** *v/i of supplies, strength* s'épuiser

♦ **give up 1** *v/t smoking etc* arrêter de **2** *v/i* (*stop making effort*) abandonner

♦ **give way** *of bridge etc* s'écrouler

give-and-take concessions *fpl* mutuelles

gizmo ['gɪzməu] F truc *m*

glad [glæd] heureux; **gladly** volontiers, avec plaisir

glamor ['glæmər] éclat *m*, fascination *f*; **glamorize** donner un aspect séduisant à; **glamorous** séduisant, fascinant; *job* prestigieux; **glamour** *Br* → **glamor**

glance [glæns] **1** *n* regard *m* **2** *v/i* jeter un regard, lancer un coup d'œil

gland [glænd] glande *f*

glare [gler] **1** *n of sun, lights* éclat *m* (éblouissant) **2** *v/i of sun, lights* briller d'un éclat éblouissant

♦ **glare at** lancer un regard furieux à

glaring ['gleriŋ] *mistake* flagrant

glass [glæs] *material, for drink* verre *m*; **glasses** lunettes *fpl*

glazed [gleizd] *expression* vitreux

gleam [gli:m] **1** *n* lueur *f* **2** *v/i* luire

glee [gli:] joie *f*; **gleeful** joyeux

glib [glib] désinvolte; **glibly** avec désinvolture

glide [glaid] glisser; *of bird, plane* planer; **glider** plane *m*; **gliding** *sport* vol *m* à voile

glimpse [glimps] **1** *n*: **catch a ~ of ...** entrevoir **2** *v/t* entrevoir

glint [glint] **1** *n* lueur *f* **2** *v/i of light, eyes* luire

glisten ['glisn] *of light* luire; *of water* miroiter; *of silk* chatoyer

glitter ['glitr] *of light, jewels* briller, scintiller

gloat [glout] jubiler

♦ **gloat over** se réjouir de

global ['gloubl] *(worldwide)* mondial; *(without exceptions)* global; **globalization** mondialisation *f*; **global warming** réchauffement *m* de la planète; **globe** globe *m*

gloom [glu:m] *(darkness)* obscurité *f*; *mood* tristesse *f*; **gloomy** sombre

glorious ['glɔ:riəs] *weather* magnifique; *victory* glorieux; **glory** gloire *f*

gloss [glɑ:s] *(shine)* brillant *m*; *(general explanation)* glose *f*; **glossary** glossaire *m*; **glossy 1** *adj paper* glacé **2** *n magazine* magazine *m* de luxe

glove [glʌv] gant *m*; **glove compartment** boîte *f* à gants

glow [glou] **1** *n of light* lueur *f*; *of fire* rougeoiement *m*; *in cheeks* couleurs *fpl* **2** *v/i of light* luire; *of fire* rougeoyer; *of cheeks* être rouge; **glowing** *description* élogieux

glucose ['glu:kous] glucose *m*

glue [glu:] **1** *n* colle *f* **2** *v/t* coller

glum [glʌm] morose

glut [glʌt] surplus *m*

glutton ['glʌtən] glouton(ne) *m(f)*

gnaw [nɔ:] *bone* ronger

go [gou] aller; *(leave)* partir; *(work, function)* marcher, fonctionner; *(come out: of stain etc)* s'en aller; *(cease: of pain etc)* partir, disparaître; *(match: of colors etc)* aller ensemble: *hamburger to ~* hamburger à emporter

♦ **go away** *of person* s'en aller, partir; *of rain* cesser; *of*

goose bumps

pain, clouds partir
◆ **go back** (*return*) retourner; (*date back*) remonter (**to** à)
◆ **go by** *of car, time* passer
◆ **go down** descendre; *of sun* se coucher
◆ **go in** *to room, house* entrer; *of sun* se cacher; (*fit: of part etc*) s'insérer
◆ **go off** (*leave*) partir; *of bomb* exploser; *of gun* partir; *of alarm* se déclencher
◆ **go on** (*continue*) continuer; (*happen*) se passer
◆ **go out** *of person* sortir; *of light, fire* s'éteindre
◆ **go over** (*check*) revoir
◆ **go through** *hard times* traverser; *illness* subir; (*check*) revoir; (*read through*) lire en entier
◆ **go under** (*sink*) couler; *of company* faire faillite
◆ **go up** (*climb*) monter; *of prices* augmenter
◆ **go without 1** *v/t food etc* se passer de **2** *v/i* s'en passer
'go-ahead 1 *n* feu vert *m* **2** *adj* (*enterprising, dynamic*) entreprenant, dynamique
goal [gəul] *in sport,* (*objective*) but *m*; **goalkeeper** gardien *m* de but; **goal kick** remise *f* en jeu; **goalpost** poteau *m* de but
goat [gəut] chèvre *m*
gobble ['gɑːbl] dévorer
gobbledygook ['gɑːbldɪguːk] F charabia *m* F
'go-between intermédiaire

m/f
god [gɑːd] dieu *m*; **thank God!** Dieu merci!
'godchild filleul(e) *m(f)*; **godfather** *also in mafia* parrain *m*; **godmother** marraine *m*
gofer ['gəufər] F coursier(-ière) *m(f)*
goggles ['gɑːglz] lunettes *fpl*
goings-on [gəuɪŋz'ɑːn] activités *fpl*
gold [gəuld] **1** *n* or *m* **2** *adj* en or; **ingot** d'or; **golden** *sky* doré; *hair also* d'or; **golden wedding** noces *fpl* d'or; **gold medal** médaille *f* d'or; **gold mine** *fig* mine *f* d'or
golf [gɑːlf] golf *m*; **golf ball** balle *f* de golf; **golf club** *organization,* stick club *m* de golf; **golf course** terrain *m* de golf; **golfer** golfeur(-euse) *m(f)*
good [gud] bon; *weather* beau; *child* sage; **goodbye** au revoir; **good-for-nothing** *n* bon(ne) *m(f)* à rien; **Good Friday** Vendredi *m* saint; **good-humored**, *Br* **good-humoured** jovial; **good-looking** beau; **good-natured** bon, au bon naturel; **goodness** *moral* bonté *f*; *of fruit etc* bonnes choses *fpl*; **goods** COM marchandises *fpl*; **goodwill** bonne volonté *f*
goof [guːf] F gaffer F
goose [guːs] oie *f*; **goose bumps** chair *f* de poule

gorgeous ['gɔːrdʒəs] magnifique, superbe

gospel ['gɑːspl] évangile *m*

gossip ['gɑːsɪp] **1** *n* potins *mpl*; *malicious* commérages *mpl*; *person* commère *f* **2** *v/i* bavarder; *maliciously* faire des commérages; **gossip column** échos *mpl*

gourmet ['gʊrmeɪ] gourmet *m*

govern ['gʌvərn] gouverner; **government** gouvernement *m*; **governor** gouverneur *m*

gown [gaʊn] robe *f*; *wedding dress* robe *f* de mariée; *of academic, judge* toge *f*; *of surgeon* blouse *f*

grab [græb] saisir; *food* avaler

grace [greɪs] *of dancer etc* grâce *f*; *before meals* bénédicité *m*; **graceful** gracieux; **gracious** *person* bienveillant; *style* élégant

grade [greɪd] **1** *n* (*quality*) qualité *f*; EDU classe *f*; (*mark*) note *f* **2** *v/t* classer; *school work* noter; **grade crossing** passage *m* à niveau; **grade school** école *f* primaire

gradient ['greɪdɪənt] pente *f*

gradual ['grædʒʊəl] graduel; **gradually** peu à peu, progressivement

graduate 1 ['grædʒʊət] *n* diplômé(e) *m(f)* **2** ['grædʒʊeɪt] *v/i* obtenir son diplôme (*from* de); **graduation** obtention *f* du diplôme

graffiti [grə'fiːtiː] graffitis *mpl*; *single* graffiti *m*

graft [græft] **1** *n* BOT, MED greffe *f*; F (*corruption*) corruption *f* **2** *v/t* BOT, MED greffer

grain [greɪn] blé *m*; *of rice etc*, *in wood* grain *m*

gram [græm] gramme *m*

grammar ['græmər] grammaire *f*; **grammatical** grammatical

grand [grænd] **1** *adj* grandiose; F (*very good*) génial **2** *n* F (*$1000*) mille dollars *mpl*; **grandchild** petit-fils *m*, petite-fille *f*; **granddaughter** petite-fille *f*; **grandeur** grandeur *f*; **grandfather** grand-père *m*; **grand jury** jury grand jury; **grandmother** grand-mère *f*; **grandparents** grands-parents *mpl*; **grand piano** piano *m* à queue; **grandson** petit-fils *m*

granite ['grænɪt] granit *m*

grant [grænt] **1** *n money* subvention *f* **2** *v/t wish, visa* accorder

granule ['grænuːl] grain *m*

grape [greɪp] (grain *m* de) raisin *m*; *some ~s* du raisin; **grapefruit juice** jus *m* de pamplemousse

graph [græf] graphique *m*, courbe *f*; **graphic 1** *adj* (*vivid*) très réaliste **2** *n* COMPUT graphique *m*

◆ **grapple** with ['græpl] *attacker* en venir aux prises avec; *problem etc* s'attaquer à

grasp [grɑːsp] **1** *n physical* prise *f*; *mental* compréhension *f* **2** *v/t physically* saisir; *(understand)* comprendre

grass [grɑːs] herbe *f*; **grasshopper** sauterelle *f*; **grass roots** *people* base *f*; **grassy** ['grɑːsɪ] herbeux, herbu

grate[1] [greɪt] *n metal* grille *f*

grate[2] [greɪt] **1** *v/t in cooking* râper **2** *v/i*: **~ on the ear** faire mal aux oreilles

grateful ['greɪtfʊl] reconnaissant; **gratefully** avec reconnaissance

gratify ['grætɪfaɪ] satisfaire

grating ['greɪtɪŋ] **1** *n* grille *f* **2** *adj sound, voice* grinçant

gratitude ['grætɪtuːd] gratitude *f*, reconnaissance *f*

grave[1] [greɪv] *n* tombe *f*

grave[2] [greɪv] *adj* grave

gravel ['grævl] gravier *m*

'gravestone pierre *f* tombale; **graveyard** cimetière *m*

gravity ['grævɪtɪ] PHYS, *of situation* gravité *f*

gray [greɪ] gris; **gray-haired** aux cheveux gris

graze[1] [greɪz] *v/i of cow etc* paître

graze[2] [greɪz] **1** *v/t arm etc* écorcher **2** *n* écorchure *f*

grease [griːs] *for cooking* graisse *f*; *for car* lubrifiant *m*; **greasy** gras; *(covered in grease)* graisseux

great [greɪt] grand; *mistake, sum* gros; F *(very good)* super *F*; **Great Britain** Grande-Bretagne *f*; **greatly** beaucoup; **not ~ different** pas très différent; **greatness** grandeur *f*

Greece [griːs] Grèce *f*

greed [griːd] *for money* avidité *f*; *for food also* gourmandise *f*; **greedily** avec avidité; *for food also* gourmand

Greek [griːk] **1** *n* Grec(que) *m(f)*; *language* grec *m* **2** *adj* grec

green [griːn] vert; **green beans** haricots *mpl* verts; **green belt** ceinture *f* verte; **green card** *(work permit)* permis *m* de travail; **greenhouse effect** effet *m* de serre; **greens** légumes *mpl* verts

greet [griːt] saluer; *(welcome)* accueillir; **greeting** salut *m*

grenade [grɪ'neɪd] grenade *f*

grey [greɪ] *Br* → **gray**

grid [grɪd] grille *f*; **gridiron** SP terrain *m* de football; **gridlock** *in traffic* embouteillage *m*

grief [griːf] chagrin *m*, douleur *f*; **grief-stricken** affligé; **grievance** grief *m*; **grieve** être affligé; **~ for s.o.** pleurer qn

grill [grɪl] **1** *n on window* grille *f* **2** *v/t (interrogate)* mettre sur la sellette

grille [grɪl] grille *f*

grim [grɪm] sinistre, sombre

grimace ['grɪməs] grimace f
grime [graɪm] crasse f; grimy
crasseux
grin [grɪn] 1 n (large) sourire
m 2 v/i sourire
grind [graɪnd] coffee moudre;
meat hacher
grip [grɪp] saisir, serrer; gripping prenant, captivant
gristle ['grɪsl] cartilage m
grit [grɪt] 1 n for roads gravillon m 2 v/t: ~ one's teeth
grincer des dents; gritty F
réaliste
groan [groun] 1 n gémissement m 2 v/i gémir
groceries ['grousəriz] provisions fpl; grocery store épicerie f l'épicerie
groggy ['gragi] F groggy F
groin [grɔɪn] ANAT aine f
groom [gru:m] 1 n for bride
marié m; for horse palefre-
nier(-ère) m(f) 2 v/t horse
panser; (train, prepare) préparer
groove [gru:v] rainure f; on
record sillon m
grope [group] 1 v/i in the dark
tâtonner 2 v/t sexually peloter F
gross [grous] (coarse, vulgar)
grossier; exaggeration gros;
FIN brut
ground [graund] 1 n sol m,
terre f; for football etc, fig
terrain; (reason) motif m;
ELEC terre f 2 v/t ELEC mettre
une prise de terre à; ground-
ing in subject bases fpl;

groundless sans fonde-
ment; ground meat viande
f hachée; groundwork tra-
vail m préparatoire
group [gru:p] 1 n groupe m 2
v/t grouper
groupie ['gru:pɪ] F groupie f F
grouse [graus] 1 n F rouspéter
F 2 v/i F plainte f
grovel ['gra:vl] fig ramper (to
devant)
grow [grou] 1 v/i grandir; of
plants, hair pousser; of number augmenter; of business
se développer; (become) devenir 2 v/t flowers faire pousser
♦ grow up of person devenir
adulte; of city se développer
growl [graul] 1 n grognement
m 2 v/i grogner
'grown-up 1 n adulte m/f 2 adj
adulte
growth [grouθ] of person,
company croissance f; (increase) augmentation f; MED
tumeur f
grudge [grʌdʒ] rancune f;
grudging accordé à contre-
cœur; person plein de ressentiment; grudgingly à contre-
cœur
grueling, Br gruelling
['gru:əlɪŋ] épuisant
gruff [grʌf] bourru, revêche
grumble ['grʌmbl] ronchon-
ner; grumbler grognon(ne)
m(f)
grunt [grʌnt] 1 n grognement
m 2 v/i grogner

guarantee [gærən'tiː] **1** n garantie f **2** v/t garantir; **guarantor** garant(e) m(f)

guard [gɑːrd] **1** n gardien(ne) m(f); MIL garde f **2** v/t garder; **guard dog** chien m de garde; **guarded** reply prudent; **guardian** LAW tuteur(-trice) m(f)

guerrilla [gə'rɪlə] guérillero m; **guerrilla warfare** guérilla f

guess [ges] **1** n conjecture f **2** v/t answer deviner **2** v/i deviner; **I ~ so** je crois; **guesswork** conjecture(s) f(pl)

guest [gest] invité(e) m(f); in hotel hôte m/f; **guestroom** chambre f d'amis

guidance ['gaɪdəns] conseils mpl; **guide 1** n person guide m/f; book guide m **2** v/t guider; **guidebook** guide m; **guided missile** missile m téléguidé; **guided tour** visite f guidée; **guidelines** directives fpl

guilt [gɪlt] culpabilité f; **guilty** also LAW coupable

guinea pig ['gɪnɪpɪg] also fig cobaye m

guitar [gɪ'tɑːr] guitare f; **guitarist** guitariste m/f

gulf [gʌlf] golfe m; fig gouffre m

gull [gʌl] mouette f; bigger goéland m

gullet ['gʌlɪt] ANAT gosier m

gullible ['gʌlɪbl] crédule

gulp [gʌlp] **1** n of drink gorgée

f **2** v/i in surprise dire en s'étranglant

♦ **gulp down** drink avaler à grosses gorgées; food avaler à grosses bouchées

gum[1] [gʌm] in mouth gencive f

gum[2] [gʌm] (glue) colle f; (chewing gum) chewing--gum m

gun [gʌn] arme f à feu; pistol pistolet m; revolver revolver m; rifle fusil m; cannon canon m

♦ **gun down** abattre

'gunfire coups mpl de feu; **gunman** homme m armé; **gunshot** coup m de feu; **gunshot wound** blessure f par balle

gurgle ['gɜːrgl] of baby gazouiller; of drain gargouiller

guru ['guːruː] fig gourou m

gush [gʌʃ] of liquid jaillir

gust [gʌst] rafale f, coup m de vent

gusto ['gʌstoʊ]: **with ~** avec enthousiasme

gusty ['gʌstɪ] weather très venteux

gut [gʌt] **1** n intestin m; F (stomach) bide m F **2** v/t (destroy) ravager; **guts** F (courage) cran m F; **gutsy** ['gʌtsɪ] F (brave) qui a du cran

gutter ['gʌtər] on sidewalk caniveau m; on roof gouttière f

guy [gaɪ] F type m F

guzzle ['gʌzl] food engloutir; drink avaler

gym [dʒɪm] *sports club* club m
de gym; *in school* gymnase
m; *activity* gym(nastique) f;
gymnast gymnaste m/f;
gymnastics gymnastique f

gynecology, Br **gynaecology** [gaɪnɪˈkɑːlədʒɪ] gynécologie

gypsy [ˈdʒɪpsɪ] gitan(e) m(f)

H

habit [ˈhæbɪt] habitude f
habitable [ˈhæbɪtəbl] habitable; *habitat* habitat m
habitual [həˈbɪtʃʊəl] habituel; *smoker, drinker* invétéré
hacker [ˈhækər] COMPUT pirate m informatique
hackneyed [ˈhæknɪd] rebattu
haemorrhage Br → **hemorrhage**
haggard [ˈhægərd] hagard, égaré
haggle [ˈhægl] chipoter
hail [heɪl] grêle f
hair [her] cheveux mpl; *single* cheveu m; *on body* poils mpl; *single* poil m; **hairbrush** brosse f à cheveux; **haircut** coupe f de cheveux; **have a ~** se faire couper les cheveux
'hairdo coiffure f; **hairdresser** coiffeur(-euse) m(f); **hairdryer** sèche-cheveux m; **hairpin** épingle f à cheveux; **hairpin curve** virage m en épingle à cheveux; **hair-raising** horrifique; **hair remover** crème f épilatoire; **hair-splitting** ergotage m; **hairstyle** coiffure f; **hairstylist** coiffeur(-euse) m(f); **hairy** arm,

animal poilu; F *(frightening)* effrayant
half [hæf] **1** n moitié f; ~ **past ten** dix heures et demie; ~ **an hour** une demi-heure **2** adj demi; **at ~ price** à moitié prix **3** adv à moitié; **half-hearted** tiède; **half time** SP mi-temps f; **halfway 1** adj: **reach the ~ point** être à la moitié **2** adv in space, distance à mi-chemin
hall [hɔːl] *(large room)* salle f; *(hallway in house)* vestibule m
Hallowe'en [hæloʊˈwiːn] halloween f
halo [ˈheɪloʊ] auréole f
halt [hɔːlt] **1** v/i faire halte, s'arrêter **2** v/t arrêter
halve [hæv] couper en deux; *input, costs* réduire de moitié
ham [hæm] jambon m; **hamburger** hamburger m
hammer [ˈhæmər] **1** n marteau m **2** v/i marteler; ~ **at the door** frapper à la porte à coups redoublés
hammock [ˈhæmək] hamac m
hamper[1] [ˈhæmpər] n *for food* pannier m
hamper[2] [ˈhæmpər] v/t *(ob-*

struct) entraver, gêner

hand [hænd] **1** *n* main *f; of clock* aiguille *f; (worker)* ouvrier(-ère) *m(f); at ~, to ~ thing* sous la main; *at ~ person* à disposition; **on the one ~ ..., on the other ~** d'une part ..., d'autre part; **on your right ~** sur votre droite; **give s.o. a ~** donner un coup de main à qn

◆ **hand down** transmettre

◆ **hand out** distribuer

◆ **hand over** donner; *to authorities* livrer

'**handbag** *Br* sac *m* à main; **hand baggage** bagages *mpl* à main; **handcuff** menotter; **handcuffs** menottes *fpl*

handicap ['hændɪkæp] handicap *m;* **handicapped** handicapé; **handiwork** *object* ouvrage *m*

handkerchief ['hæŋkərtʃif] mouchoir *m*

handle ['hændl] **1** *n of door, suitcase* poignée *f; of knife, pan* manche *m* **2** *v/t goods* manier, manipuler; *case, deal* s'occuper de; **handlebars** guidon *m*

'**hand luggage** bagages *m* à main; **handmade** fait (à la) main; **hands-free** mains libres; **handshake** poignée *f* de main

handsome ['hænsəm] beau

'**handwriting** écriture *f;* **handwritten** écrit à la main;

handy *device* pratique

hang ['hæŋ] **1** *v/t person* pendre **2** *v/i of dress, hair* tomber

◆ **hang on** *(wait)* attendre

◆ **hang up** TELEC raccrocher

hangar ['hæŋər] hangar *m*

hanger ['hæŋər] *for clothes* cintre *m*

'**hang glider** *person* libériste *m/f; device* deltaplane *m;* **hang gliding** deltaplane *m;* **hangover** gueule *f* de bois

hankie, hanky ['hæŋkɪ] F mouchoir *m*

haphazard [hæp'hæzərd] au hasard

happen ['hæpn] se passer, arriver

happily ['hæpɪlɪ] gaiement; *spend* volontiers; *(luckily)* heureusement; **happiness** bonheur *m;* **happy** heureux; **happy-go-lucky** insouciant

harass [hə'ræs] harceler; **harassed** surmené; **harassment** harcèlement *m*

harbor, *Br* **harbour** ['hɑːrbər] **1** *n* port *m* **2** *v/t criminal* héberger; *grudge* entretenir

hard [hɑːrd] **1** *adj* dur; *facts* brut; *evidence* concret **2** *adv* dur; *rain, pull, push* fort; **try ~** faire tout son possible; **hardback** livre *m* cartonné; **hard-boiled** *egg* dur; **hard copy** copie *f* sur papier; **hard core** *pornography* (pornographie *f*) hard *m;* **hard currency** monnaie *f* forte; **hard disk** disque *m* dur; **harden 1** v/t durcir **2** v/i *of glue, attitude* se durcir; **hard hat** casque m; *(construction worker)* ouvrier m du bâtiment; **hardheaded** réaliste; **hardhearted** au cœur dur; **hard line** ligne f dure; **hardliner** dur(e) m(f)

hardly ['hɑːrdlɪ] à peine; *see s.o.* presque pas

hardness ['hɑːrdnɪs] dureté f; *(difficulty)* difficulté f; **hardship** privation f; **hardware** COMPUT hardware m, matériel m; **hardware store** quincaillerie f; **hard-working** travailleur; harpe robuste

harm [hɑːrm] **1** n mal m **2** v/t faire du mal à; *non-physically* nuire à; **harmful** *substance* nocif; *influence* nuisible; **harmless** inoffensif

harmonious [hɑːr'moʊnɪəs] harmonieux; **harmonize** s'harmoniser; **harmony** harmonie f

harsh [hɑːrʃ] *words* dur; *color* criard; *light* cru; **harshly** durement

harvest ['hɑːrvɪst] moisson f

hash browns [hæʃ] pommes de terre fpl sautées; **hash mark** caractère m #, dièse f

haste [heɪst] hâte f; **hastily** à la hâte; **hasty** hâtif, précipité

hat [hæt] chapeau m

hatch [hætʃ] *for serving* guichet m; *on ship* écoutille f

◆ **hatch out** éclore

hatchet ['hætʃɪt] hachette f;

bury the ~ enterrer la hache de guerre

hate [heɪt] **1** n haine f **2** v/t détester, haïr; **hatred** haine f

haul [hɔːl] **1** n *of fish* coup m de filet **2** v/t *(pull)* tirer, traîner; **haulage** transports mpl (routiers)

haunch [hɔːntʃ] *of person* hanche f; *of animal* arrière-train m

haunt [hɔːnt] hanter; **this place is ~ed** ce lieu est hanté

have [hæv] **1** v/t *(own)* avoir; *breakfast, lunch* prendre; ~ *(got) to* devoir; **you don't ~ to do it** tu n'es pas obligé de le faire; **do I ~ to pay?** est-ce qu'il faut payer?; **I'll ~ it sent to you** je vous le ferai envoyer; **I had my hair cut** je me suis fait couper les cheveux **2** v/aux *(past tense)*: ~ **you seen her?** l'as-tu vue?; **they ~ arrived** ils sont arrivés

◆ **have on** *(wear)* porter

haven ['heɪvn] fig havre m

hawk [hɔːk] also fig faucon m

hay [heɪ] foin m; **hay fever** rhume m des foins

hazard ['hæzərd] danger m; **hazard lights** MOT feux mpl de détresse; **hazardous** dangereux

haze [heɪz] brume f; **hazy** *view* brumeux; *image* flou; *memories* vague

he [hiː] il; **there ~ is** le voilà

head [hed] **1** n tête f; *(boss,*

leader) chef *m/f*; Br : of *school* directeur(-trice) *m(f)*; *on beer* mousse *f* **2** *v/t* (*lead*) être à la tête de; *ball* jouer de la tête

◆ **head for** se diriger vers
'**headache** mal *m* de tête; **headband** bandeau *m*; **header** *in soccer* (coup *m* de) tête *f*; *in document* en-tête *m*; **headhunter** COM chasseur *m* de têtes; **heading** *in list* titre *m*; **headlamp** phare *m*; **headline** *in newspaper* (gros) titre *m*; **head office** *of company* bureau *m* central; **head-on 1** *adv crash* de front **2** *adj* frontal; **headphones** écouteurs *mpl*; **headquarters** quartier *m* général; **headrest** appui-tête *m*; **headroom** *under bridge* hauteur *f* limite; *in car* hauteur *f* au plafond; **headscarf** foulard *m*; **headstrong** entêté; **head waiter** maître *m* d'hôtel; **heady** *wine etc* capiteux

heal [hi:l] guérir
health [helθ] santé *f*; **health food store** magasin *m* d'aliments diététiques; **health insurance** assurance *f* maladie; **healthy** *person* en bonne santé; *food, lifestyle, economy* sain
heap [hi:p] tas *m*
hear [hɪr] entendre

◆ **hear from** (*have news from*) avoir des nouvelles de

hearing ['hɪrɪŋ] ouïe *f*; LAW audience *f*; **hearing aid** appareil *m* acoustique, audiophone *m*

hearse [hɜ:rs] corbillard *m*
heart [hɑ:rt] *also fig* cœur *m*; ***know sth by ~*** connaître qch par cœur; **heart attack** crise *f* cardiaque; **heartbreaking** navrant; **heartbroken**: ***be ~*** avoir le cœur brisé; **heartburn** brûlures *fpl* d'estomac
hearth [hɑ:rθ] foyer *m*, âtre *f*
heartless ['hɑ:rtlɪs] insensible, cruel; **hearty** *appetite* gros; *meal* copieux; *person* jovial

heat [hi:t] chaleur *f*

◆ **heat up** réchauffer
heated ['hi:tɪd] *pool* chauffé; *discussion* passionné; **heater** radiateur *m*; *in car* chauffage *m*; **heating** chauffage *m*; **heatproof**, **heat-resistant** résistant à la chaleur; **heatwave** vague *f* de chaleur
heave [hi:v] (*lift*) soulever
heaven ['hevn] ciel *m*; **heavenly** F divin
heavy ['hevɪ] *also food, loss* lourd; *cold* grand; *rain, accent* fort; *traffic, smoker, bleeding* gros; **heavy-duty** très résistant; **heavyweight** SP poids lourd
hectic ['hektɪk] agité
hedge [hedʒ] haie *f*
heel [hi:l] talon *m*; **heel bar** talon-minute *m*
hefty ['heftɪ] gros; *person also*

costaud

height [haɪt] *of person* taille *f*; *of building* hauteur *f*; *of airplane* altitude *f*; **heighten** tension accroître

heir [er] héritier *m*; **heiress** héritière *f*

helicopter ['helɪkɔːptər] hélicoptère *m*

hell [hel] enfer *m*; **what the ~ are you doing?** F mais enfin qu'est-ce que tu fais?; **go to ~!** F va te faire foutre! P

hello [hə'ləu] bonjour; TELEC allô

helmet ['helmɪt] casque *m*

help [help] **1** *n* aide *f* **2** *v/t* aider; **~ o.s. to food** se servir; **I can't ~ it** je ne peux pas m'en empêcher; **helper** aide *m/f*, assistant(e) *m(f)*; **helpful** *advice* utile; *person* serviable; **helping** *of food* portion *f*; **helpless** (*unable to cope*) sans défense; (*powerless*) impuissant; **helplessness** impuissance *f*

hem [hem] *of dress etc* ourlet *m*

hemisphere ['hemɪsfɪr] hémisphère *m*

'hemline ourlet *m*

hemorrhage ['hemərɪdʒ] **1** *n* hémorragie *f* **2** *v/i* faire une hémorragie

hen [hen] poule *f*; **hen party** soirée *f* entre femmes

hepatitis [hepə'taɪtɪs] hépatite *f*

her [hɜːr] **1** *adj* son, sa; *pl* ses **2**

pron object la; *before vowel* l'; *indirect object* lui, à elle; *with prep* elle; **I know ~** je la connais; **I gave ~ a dollar** je lui ai donné un dollar; **this is for ~** c'est pour elle; **who? – ~** qui? – elle

herb [ɜːrb] herbe *f*; **herb(al) tea** tisane *f*

herd [hɜːrd] troupeau *m*

here [hɪr] ici; **in ~, over ~** ici; **~'s to you!** as you're à votre santé!; **~ you are** voilà

hereditary [hə'redɪterɪ] héréditaire; **heredity** hérédité *f*;

heritage héritage *m*

hero ['hɪrou] héros *m*; **heroic** héroïque; **heroically** héroïquement

heroin ['herouɪn] héroïne *f*

heroine ['herouɪn] héroïne *f*

heroism ['herouɪzm] héroïsme *f*

herpes ['hɜːrpiːz] herpès *m*

hers [hɜːrz] le sien, la sienne; *pl* les siens, les siennes; **it's ~** c'est à elle

herself [hɜːr'self] elle-même; *reflexive* se; *after prep* elle; **she hurt ~** elle s'est blessée

hesitant ['hezɪtənt] hésitant; **hesitantly** avec hésitation; **hesitate** hésiter; **hesitation** hésitation *f*

heterosexual [hetərou'sekʃuəl] hétérosexuel

hi [haɪ] salut

hibernate ['haɪbərneɪt] hiberner

hiccup ['hɪkʌp] hoquet *m*; (*minor problem*) hic *m* F

hidden ['hɪdn] caché

hide¹ [haɪd] **1** *v/t* cacher **2** *v/i* se cacher

hide² [haɪd] *n of animal* peau *f*; *as product* cuir *m*

hide-and-seek cache-cache *m*; **hideaway** cachette *f*

hideous ['hɪdɪəs] affreux, horrible

hiding ['haɪdɪŋ] (*beating*) rossée *f*; **hiding place** cachette *f*

hierarchy ['haɪrɑːrkɪ] hiérarchie *f*

high [haɪ] **1** *adj* haut; *salary, price, rent, temperature* élevé; *wind* fort; *speed* grand; *on drugs* défoncé F **2** *n* MOT quatrième *f*; cinquième *f*; *in statistics* pointe *f*; EDU collège *m*, lycée *m*; **highbrow** intellectuel; **highchair** chaise *f* haute; **high-class** de première classe; **high-frequency** de haute fréquence; **high-grade** *ore* à haute teneur; ~ **gasoline** supercarburant *m*; **high-handed** arbitraire; **high-heeled** à talons hauts; **high jump** saut *m* en hauteur; **high-level** à haut niveau; **highlight 1** *n* (*main event*) point *m* marquant; *in hair* reflets *mpl*, mèches *fpl* **2** *v/t with pen* surligner; COMPUT mettre en relief; **highlighter** *pen* surligneur *m*; **highly** *desirable, likely* fort, très; **think ~ of s.o.** pen-

ser beaucoup de bien de qn; **high performance** *drill, battery* haute performance; **high-pitched** aigu; **high point** *of career* point *m* culminant; **high-powered** *engine* très puissant; *intellectual* très compétent; **high pressure** *weather* anticyclone *m*; **high-pressure** TECH à haute pression; *salesman* de choc; *job, lifestyle* dynamique; **high school** collège *m*, lycée *m*; **high-strung** nerveux, très sensible; **high tech 1** *n* technologie *f* de pointe, high-tech *m* **2** *adj* de pointe, high-tech; **highway** grande route *f*

hijack ['haɪdʒæk] **1** *v/t* détourner **2** *n* détournement *m*; **hijacker** *of plane* pirate *m* de l'air; *of bus* pirate *m* de la route

hike¹ [haɪk] **1** *n* randonnée *f* à pied **2** *v/i* marcher à pied

hike² [haɪk] *n in prices* hausse *f*

hiker ['haɪkər] randonneur (-euse) *m(f)*; **hiking** randonnée *f* (pédestre)

hilarious [hɪ'lerɪəs] hilarant, désopilant

hill [hɪl] colline *f*; (*slope*) côte *f*; **hilltop** sommet *m* de la colline; **hilly** montagneux; *road* vallonné

hilt [hɪlt] poignée *f*

him [hɪm] *object* le; *before vowel* l'; *indirect object, with* *prep* lui; **I know ~** je le connais; **I gave ~ a dollar** je lui ai donné un dollar; **this is for ~** c'est pour lui; **who? – him** qui? – lui; himself lui-même; *reflexive* se; *after prep* lui; **he hurt ~** il s'est blessé

hinder ['hɪndər] gêner, entraver; **~ s.o. from doing sth** empêcher qn de faire qch; **hindrance** obstacle *m*

hinge [hɪndʒ] charnière *f*

hint [hɪnt] (*clue*) indice *m*; (*piece of advice*) conseil *m*; (*suggestion*) allusion *f*; *of red, sadness etc* soupçon *m*

hip [hɪp] hanche *f*; **hip pocket** poche *f* revolver

hire [haɪr] louer

his [hɪz] **1** *adj* son, sa; *pl* ses **2** *pron* le sien, la sienne; *pl* les siens, les siennes; **it's ~** c'est à lui

Hispanic [hɪ'spænɪk] **1** *n* Hispano-Américain(e) *m(f)* **2** *adj* hispano-américain

hiss [hɪs] siffler

historian [hɪ'stɔːrɪən] historien(ne) *m(f)*; **historic** historique; **historical** historique; **history** histoire *f*

hit [hɪt] **1** *v/t* frapper; (*collide with*) heurter; **he was ~ by a bullet** il a été touché par une balle **2** *n* (*blow*) coup *m*; MUS, (*success*) succès *m*; *on website* visiteur *m*

hitch [hɪtʃ] **1** *n* (*problem*) anicroche *f*, accroc *m* **2** *v/t* atta-

cher; **hitchhike** faire du stop; **hitchhiker** auto-stoppeur (-euse) *m(f)*

hi-'tech 1 *n* technologie *f* de pointe, high-tech *m* **2** *adj* de pointe, high-tech

'hitman tueur *m* à gages; **hit-or-miss** aléatoire

HIV [eɪtʃaɪ'viː] (**~ human immunodeficiency virus**) V.I.H. *m* (= Virus de l'Immunodéficience Humaine); **people with ~** les séropositifs

hive [haɪv] *for bees* ruche *f*

HIV-'positive séropositif

hoard [hɔːrd] **1** *n* réserves *fpl* **2** *v/t money* amasser; *in times of shortage* faire des réserves de

hoarse [hɔːrs] rauque

hoax [hoʊks] canular *m*

hobble ['hɑːbl] boitiller

hobby ['hɑːbɪ] hobby *m*

hobo ['hoʊboʊ] F vagabond *m*

hockey ['hɑːkɪ] (*ice hockey*) hockey *m* (sur glace)

hog [hɑːg] (*pig*) cochon *m*

hoist [hɔɪst] **1** *n* palan *m* **2** *v/t* hisser

hold [hoʊld] **1** *v/t in hand* tenir; (*support, keep in place*) soutenir; (*passport, license, prisoner*) détenir; (*contain*) contenir; *job, post* occuper; **~ the line** TELEC ne quittez pas! **2** *n in ship* cale *f*; *in plane* soute *f*; **take ~ of sth** saisir qch

♦ **hold back** *crowds* contenir; *facts* retenir

◆ **hold out 1** *v/t hand* tendre; *pripse* offrir **2** *v/i of supplies* durer; *(survive)* tenir *(bon)*

◆ **hold up** *hand lever; bank etc* attaquer; *(make late)* retenir

holder ['həʊldər] *(container)* boîtier *m; of passport, ticket, record* détenteur(-trice) *m(f)*; **holding company** holding *m*; **holdup** *(robbery)* hold-up *m; (delay)* retard *m*

hole [həʊl] trou *m*

holiday ['hɒlədeɪ] *jour m de congé; Br: period* vacances *fpl*

hollow ['hɒləʊ] creux; *promise* faux

holocaust ['hɒləkɔ:st] holocauste *m*

hologram ['hɒləɡræm] hologramme *m*

holster ['həʊlstər] holster *m*

holy ['həʊlɪ] saint; **Holy Spirit** Saint-Esprit *m*

home [həʊm] **1** *n* maison *f; (native country, town)* patrie *f; for old people* maison *f* de retraite; **at ~** chez moi/lui *etc; (in own country)* dans mon/son *etc* pays; **at ~** à domicile; **make o.s. at ~** faire comme chez soi **2** *adv* à la maison, chez soi; *(in own country)* dans son pays; *(in own town)* dans sa ville; **go ~** rentrer; **home address** adresse *f* personnelle; **home banking** services *mpl* télématiques (ban-

caires); **homecoming** retour *m* (à la maison); **home computer** ordinateur *m* familial; **home game** match *m* à domicile; **homeless 1** *adj* sans abri **2** *npl*: **the ~** les sans-abri *mpl*, les S.D.F. *mpl* (sans domicile fixe); **homeloving** casanier; **homely** *(homelike)* simple, comme à la maison; *(not good-looking)* sans beauté; **homemade** fait (à la) maison; **home page** COMPUT page *f* d'accueil; **homesick**: **be ~** avoir le mal du pays; **home town** ville *f* natale; **homeward** *to own house* vers la maison; *to own country* vers son pays; **homework** EDU devoirs *mpl*

homicide ['hɑ:mɪsaɪd] homicide *m; department* homicides *mpl*

homophobia [həʊmə'fəʊbɪə] homophobie *f*

homosexual [həʊmə'sekfʊəl] **1** *adj* homosexuel **2** *n* homosexuel(le) *m(f)*

honest ['ɑ:nɪst] honnête; **honestly** honnêtement; **~!** vraiment!; **honesty** honnêteté *f*

honey ['hʌnɪ] miel *m; F (darling)* chéri(e) *m(f)*; **honeymoon** lune *f* de miel

honk [hɑ:ŋk] *horn* klaxonner

honor ['ɑ:nər] **1** *n* honneur *f* **2** *v/t* honorer; **honorable** honorable; **honour** *Br* → **honor**

hood [hʊd] *over head* capuche f; *over cooker* hotte f; MOT capot m; F (*gangster*) truand m

hook [hʊk] *to hang clothes on* patère f; *for fishing* hameçon m; **off the ~** TELEC décroché; **hooked** accro F; **be ~ on sth** être accro de qch; **hooker** F putain f P; *in rugby* talonneur m

hoot [huːt] 1 *v/t horn* donner un coup de 2 *v/i of car* klaxonner; *of owl* huer

hop [hɑːp] sauter, sautiller

hope [hoʊp] 1 n espoir m 2 *v/i* espérer; **I ~ so** je l'espère, j'espère que oui 2 *v/t*: **~ that** espérer que; (*promising*) **hopeful** plein d'espoir; (*promising*) prometteur; **hopefully** *say, wait* avec espoir; (*I/we hope*) avec un peu de chance; **hopeless** *position* sans espoir, désespéré; (*useless: person*) nul

horizon [həˈraɪzn] horizon m; **horizontal** horizontal

hormone [ˈhɔːrmoʊn] hormone f

horn [hɔːrn] *of animal* corne f; MOT klaxon m

hornet [ˈhɔːrnɪt] frelon m

horny [ˈhɔːrnɪ] F *sexually* excité

horrible [ˈhɑːrɪbl] horrible, affreux; **horrify** horrifier; **horrifying** horrifiant; **horror** horreur f

horse [hɔːrs] cheval m; **horse race** course f de chevaux;

horseshoe fer m à cheval

horticulture horticulture f

hose [hoʊz] tuyau m

hospitable [ˈhɑːspɪtəbl] hospitalier

hospital [ˈhɑːspɪtl] hôpital m; **hospitality** hospitalité f

host [hoʊst] *at party* hôte m/f; *of TV program* présentateur(-trice) m(f)

hostage [ˈhɑːstɪdʒ] otage m; **hostage taker** preneur(-euse) m(f) d'otages

hostel [ˈhɑːstl] *for students* foyer m; (*youth ~*) auberge f de jeunesse

hostess [ˈhoʊstɪs] hôtesse f

hostile [ˈhɑːstl] hostile; **hostility** hostilité f; **hostilities** hostilités

hot [hɑːt] chaud; (*spicy*) épicé, fort; **I'm ~** j'ai chaud; **it's ~** *weather* il fait chaud; **hot dog** hot-dog m

hotel [hoʊˈtel] hôtel m

hour [ˈaʊr] heure f

house [haʊs] maison f; **at your ~** chez vous; **housebreaking** cambriolage m; **household** ménage m; **household name** nom m connu de tous; **housekeeper** femme f de ménage; **House of Representatives** Chambre f des Représentants; **housewarming (party)** pendaison f de crémaillère; **housewife** femme f au foyer; **housework** travaux mpl domestiques; **housing**

logement *m*; TECH boîtier *m*

hovel ['hɒvl] taudis *m*

hover ['hɒvər] planer

how [haʊ] comment; **~ are you?** comment allez-vous?; **~ about a drink?** et si on allait prendre un pot?; **~ much?** combien?; **~ much is it?** *cost* combien ça coûte?; **~ many?** combien?; **~ often?** tous les combien?; **~ sad!** comme c'est triste!; however cependant; **~ big they are** qu'ils soient grands ou non

howl [haʊl] hurler

hub [hʌb] *of wheel* moyeu *m*; **hubcap** enjoliveur *m*

♦ **huddle together** ['hʌdl] se blottir les uns contre les autres

hug [hʌg] serrer dans ses bras

huge [hjuːdʒ] énorme

hull [hʌl] coque *f*

hum [hʌm] fredonner

human ['hjuːmən] **1** *n* être *m* humain **2** *adj* humain; **human being** être *m* humain

humane [hjuː'meɪn] humain, plein d'humanité

humanitarian [hjuːmænɪ'terɪən] humanitaire

humanity [hjuː'mænətɪ] humanité *f*; **human race** race *f* humaine; **human resources** ressources *fpl* humaines

humble ['hʌmbl] modeste

humdrum ['hʌmdrʌm] monotone, banal

humid ['hjuːmɪd] humide; **humidifier** humidificateur *m*; **humidity** humidité *f*

humiliate [hjuː'mɪlɪeɪt] humilier; **humiliating** humiliant; **humiliation** humiliation *f*; **humility** humilité *f*

humor ['hjuːmər] humour *m*; *(mood)* humeur *f*; **sense of ~** sens *m* de l'humour; **humorous** drôle; **humour** *Br* → **humor**

hunch [hʌntʃ] *(idea)* intuition *f*, pressentiment *m*

hundred ['hʌndrəd] cent *m*; **hundredth** centième

hung·over: be ~ avoir la gueule de bois

hunger ['hʌŋgər] faim *f*

hung·over: be ~ avoir la gueule de bois

hungry ['hʌŋgrɪ] affamé; **I'm ~** j'ai faim

hunk [hʌŋk] gros morceau *m*; F *man* beau mec F

hunt [hʌnt] **1** *n* chasse *f* *(for* à*)*; *for new leader, missing child etc* recherche *f* *(for* de*)* **2** *v/t* chasser; **hunter** chasseur (-euse) *m(f)*; **hunting** chasse *f*

hurdle ['hɜːrdl] SP haie *f*; *fig* obstacle *m*

hurl [hɜːrl] lancer, jeter

hurray [hʊ'reɪ] hourra

hurricane ['hʌrɪkən] ouragan *m*

hurried ['hʌrɪd] précipité; **hurry 1** *n* hâte *f*; **be in a ~** être pressé **2** *v/i* se dépêcher

♦ **hurry up 1** *v/i* se dépêcher; **hurry up!** dépêchez-vous! **2** *v/t* presser

hurt [hɜːrt] **1** *v/i* faire mal **2** *v/t* faire mal à; *emotionally* blesser

husband ['hʌzbənd] mari *m*

hush [hʌʃ] silence *m*

♦ **hush up** *scandal etc* étouffer

husky ['hʌski] *voice* rauque

hut [hʌt] cabane *f*, hutte *f*

hybrid ['haɪbrɪd] hybride *m*

hydrant ['haɪdrənt] prise *f* d'eau; *(fire ~)* bouche *f* d'incendie

hydraulic [haɪ'drɒlɪk] hydraulique

hydroelectric [haɪdrouɪ'lektrɪk] hydroélectrique

hydrogen ['haɪdrədʒən] hydrogène *m*

hygiene ['haɪdʒiːn] hygiène *f*; **hygienic** hygiénique

hymn [hɪm] hymne *m*

hype [haɪp] battage *m* publicitaire

hyperactive [haɪpər'æktɪv] hyperactif; **hypersensitive** hypersensible; **hypertext** COMPUT hypertexte *m*

hypnosis [hɪp'nousɪs] hypnose *f*; **hypnotize** hypnotiser

hypocrisy [hɪ'pɑːkrəsi] hypocrisie *f*; **hypocrite** hypocrite *m/f*; **hypocritical** hypocrite

hypothesis [haɪ'pɑːθəsɪs] hypothèse *f*; **hypothetical** hypothétique

hysterectomy [hɪstə'rektəmɪ] hystérectomie *f*

hysteria [hɪ'stɪrɪə] hystérie *f*; **hysterical** hystérique; F *(very funny)* à mourir de rire F; **hysterics** crise *f* de nerfs; *laughter* fou rire *m*

I

I [aɪ] je; *before vowel* j'; *here ~ am* me voici

ice [aɪs] glace *f*; *on road* verglas *m*; **icebox** glacière *f*; **ice cream** glace *f*; **ice cube** glaçon *m*; **iced** *drink* glacé; **ice hockey** hockey *m* sur glace; **ice rink** patinoire *f*; **ice skate** patin *m* (à glace); **ice skating** patinage *m* (sur glace)

icon ['aɪkɑːn] symbole *m*; COMPUT icône *f*

icy ['aɪsɪ] gelé; *welcome* glacial

ID [aɪ'diː] (= *identity*) identité *f*

idea [aɪ'diːə] idée *f*; **ideal** idéal; **idealistic** idéaliste

identical [aɪ'dentɪkl] identique; **identification** identification *f*; *(papers etc)* papiers *mpl* d'identité; **identify** identifier; **identity** identité *f*; **~ card** carte *f* d'identité

ideological [aɪdɪə'lɑːdʒɪkl] idéologique; **ideology** idéologie *f*

idiomatic [ɪdɪəˈmætɪk] (*natural*) idiomatique
idiot [ˈɪdɪət] idiot(e) *m(f)*; **idiotic** idiot, bête
idle [ˈaɪdl] **1** *adj* (*not working*) inoccupé; (*lazy*) paresseux; *threat* oiseux; *machinery* non utilisé **2** *v/i of engine* tourner au ralenti
idol [ˈaɪdl] idole *f*; **idolize** idolâtrer
if [ɪf] si
ignite [ɪgˈnaɪt] mettre le feu à; **ignition** *in car* allumage *m*; **~ key** clef *f* de contact
ignorance [ˈɪgnərəns] ignorance *f*; **ignorant** ignorant; (*rude*) grossier; **ignore** ignorer
ill [ɪl] malade; **fall ~, be taken ~** tomber malade
illegal [ɪˈliːgl] illégal
illegible [ɪˈledʒəbl] illisible
illegitimate [ɪlɪˈdʒɪtɪmət] *child* illégitime
illicit [ɪˈlɪsɪt] illicite
illiterate [ɪˈlɪtərət] illettré
illness [ˈɪlnɪs] maladie *f*
illogical [ɪˈlɑːdʒɪkl] illogique
ill-treat maltraiter
illuminating [ɪˈluːmɪneɪtɪŋ] *remarks etc* éclairant
illusion [ɪˈluːʒn] illusion *f*
illustrate [ˈɪləstreɪt] illustrer; **illustration** illustration *f*; **illustrator** illustrateur(-trice) *m(f)*
image [ˈɪmɪdʒ] image *f*
imaginary [ɪˈmædʒɪnərɪ] imaginaire; **imagination** imagi-

nation *f*; **imaginative** imaginatif; **imagine** imaginer; **you're imagining things** tu te fais des idées
IMF [aɪemˈef] (= *International Monetary Fund*) F.M.I. *m* (= Fonds *m* Monétaire International)
imitate [ˈɪmɪteɪt] imiter; **imitation** imitation *f*
immaculate [ɪˈmækjʊlət] impeccable
immature [ɪməˈtʊr] immature
immediate [ɪˈmiːdɪət] immédiat; **immediately** immédiatement
immense [ɪˈmens] immense
immerse [ɪˈmɜːrs] immerger, plonger
immigrant [ˈɪmɪgrənt] immigrant(e) *m(f)*; **immigrate** immigrer; **immigration** immigration *f*
imminent [ˈɪmɪnənt] imminent
immobilize [ɪˈmoʊbɪlaɪz] immobiliser
immoderate [ɪˈmɑːdərət] immodéré
immoral [ɪˈmɔːrəl] immoral; **immorality** immoralité *f*
immortal [ɪˈmɔːrtl] immortel; **immortality** immortalité *f*
immune [ɪˈmjuːn] *to illness* immunisé (**to** contre); *from ruling* exempt (**from** de); **immune system** MED système *m* immunitaire; **immunity** immunité *f*; *from ruling* exemption *f*

impact ['ɪmpækt] impact *m*

impair [ɪm'per] affaiblir

impartial [ɪm'pɑːrʃl] impartial

impassable [ɪm'pæsəbl] *road* impraticable

impassioned [ɪm'pæʃnd] *speech, plea* passionné

impatience [ɪm'peɪʃəns] impatience *f*; **impatient** impatient

impatiently impatiemment

impeccable [ɪm'pekəbl] impeccable

impede [ɪm'piːd] gêner, empêcher; **impediment** *obstacle* obstacle *m*; *speech* ~ défaut *m* d'élocution

impending [ɪm'pendɪŋ] imminent

imperative [ɪm'perətɪv] **1** *adj* impératif **2** *n* GRAM impératif *m*

imperfect [ɪm'pɜːrfekt] **1** *adj* imparfait **2** *n* GRAM imparfait *m*

impersonal [ɪm'pɜːrsənl] impersonnel; **impersonate** *as a joke* imiter; *illegally* se faire passer pour

impertinence [ɪm'pɜːrtɪnəns] impertinence *f*; **impertinent** impertinent

impervious [ɪm'pɜːrvɪəs]: ~ **to** insensible à

impetuous [ɪm'petʃʊəs] impétueux

impetus ['ɪmpətəs] *of campaign etc* force *f*, élan *m*

implement ['ɪmplɪmənt] **1** *n* instrument *m*, outil *m* **2** *v/t* ['ɪmplɪment] appliquer

implicate ['ɪmplɪkeɪt] impliquer; **implication** implication *f*

implore [ɪm'plɔːr] implorer

imply [ɪm'plaɪ] impliquer; (*suggest*) suggérer

impolite [ɪmpə'laɪt] impoli

import [ɪm'pɔːrt] **1** *n* importation *f* **2** *v/t* importer

importance [ɪm'pɔːrtəns] importance *f*; **important** important

importer [ɪm'pɔːrtər] importateur(-trice) *m(f)*

impose [ɪm'pəʊz] *tax* imposer; **imposing** imposant

impossibility [ɪmpɑːsɪ'bɪlɪtɪ] impossibilité *f*; **impossible** impossible

impotence ['ɪmpətəns] impuissance *f*; **impotent** impuissant

impractical [ɪm'præktɪkəl] dénué de sens pratique

impress [ɪm'pres] impressionner; **impression** impression *f*; (*impersonation*) imitation *f*; **impressive** impressionnant

imprint ['ɪmprɪnt] *of credit card* empreinte *f*

imprison [ɪm'prɪzn] emprisonner; **imprisonment** emprisonnement *m*

improbable [ɪm'prɑːbəbl] improbable

improve [ɪm'pruːv] **1** *v/t* améliorer **2** *v/i* s'améliorer; **im-**

provement amélioration f

improvize ['improvaiz] improviser

impudent ['impjudənt] impudent

impulse ['impʌls] impulsion f; impulsive impulsif

in [in] 1 prep dans; with time en; ~ **Rouen** à Rouen; ~ **1999** en 1999; ~ **the morning** le matin; ~ **the summer** l'été; ~ **August** en août, au mois d'août; ~ **two hours** from now dans deux heures; over period of en deux heures; ~ **English** en anglais; ~ **yellow** en jaune; ~ **crossing the road** en traversant la route 2 adv (at home, in the building etc) là; (arrived: train) arrivé; (in its position) dedans; ~ **here** ici 3 adj (fashionable, popular) à la mode

inability [inə'biliti] incapacité f

inaccurate [in'ækjurət] inexact

inadequate [in'ædikwət] insuffisant, inadéquat

inadvisable [inəd'vaizəbl] peu recommandé

inanimate [in'ænimət] inanimé

inappropriate [inə'proupriət] peu approprié

inaudible [in'ɔ:dəbl] inaudible

inaugural [ɪ'nɔ:gjurəl] speech inaugural; inaugurate inaugurer

inborn ['inbɔ:rn] inné

inc. (= incorporated) S.A. f (= Société f Anonyme)

incalculable [in'kælkjuləbl] damage incalculable

incapable [in'keipəbl] incapable

incentive [in'sentiv] encouragement m, stimulation f

incessant [in'sesnt] incessant; incessantly sans arrêt

incest ['insest] inceste m

inch [intʃ] pouce m

incident ['insidənt] incident m; incidental fortuit; ~ **expenses** frais mpl accessoires; incidentally soit dit en passant

incision [in'siʒn] incision f; incisive incisif

incite [in'sait] inciter

inclination [inkli'neiʃn] (liking) penchant m; (tendency) tendance f

inclose, inclosure → enclose, enclosure

include [in'klu:d] inclure, comprendre; including y compris; ~ **service** service compris; inclusive 1 adj price tout compris 2 prep: ~ **of** en incluant 3 adv tout compris; from Monday to Thursday ~ du lundi au jeudi inclus

incoherent [inkou'hirənt] incohérent

income ['inkʌm] revenu m; income tax impôt m sur le revenu

incomparable [ɪnˈkɒmpə-rəbl] incomparable

incompatibility [ɪnkəmpætɪ-ˈbɪlɪtɪ] incompatibilité *f*; **in-compatible** incompatible

incompetence [ɪnˈkɒmpɪ-təns] incompétence *f*; **in-competent** incompétent

incomplete [ɪnkəmˈpliːt] in-complet

incomprehensible [ɪnkɒm-prɪˈhensɪbl] incompréhensi-ble

inconceivable [ɪnkənˈsiːv-əbl] inconcevable

inconsiderate [ɪnkənˈsɪd-ərət] *action* inconsidéré; **be ~ of** *person* manquer d'é-gards

inconsistent [ɪnkənˈsɪstənt] incohérent; *person* incons-tant

inconspicuous [ɪnkənˈspɪk-juəs] discret

inconvenience [ɪnkənˈviːn-ɪəns] inconvénient *m*; **incon-venient** *time* inopportun; *place, arrangement* peu com-mode

incorporate [ɪnˈkɔːrpəreɪt] incorporer

incorrect [ɪnkəˈrekt] incor-rect

increase 1 [ɪnˈkriːs] *v/t & v/i* augmenter **2** [ˈɪnkriːs] *n* aug-mentation *f*; **increasing** croissant; **increasingly** de plus en plus

incredible [ɪnˈkredɪbl] in-croyable

incur [ɪnˈkɜːr] *costs* encourir; *debts* contracter; *s.o.'s anger* s'attirer

incurable [ɪnˈkjʊrəbl] *also fig* incurable

indecent [ɪnˈdiːsnt] indécent

indecisive [ɪndɪˈsaɪsɪv] *argu-ment* peu concluant; *person* indécis; **indecisiveness** in-décision *f*

indeed [ɪnˈdiːd] *(in fact)* vrai-ment; *(yes, agreeing)* en ef-fet; **very much ~** beaucoup

indefinable [ɪndɪˈfaɪnəbl] in-définissable

indefinite [ɪnˈdefɪnɪt] indéfi-ni; **indefinitely** indéfiniment

indelicate [ɪnˈdelɪkət] indéli-cat

independence [ɪndɪˈpend-əns] indépendance *f*; **Inde-pendence Day** fête *f* de l'In-dépendance; **independent** indépendant

indescribable [ɪndɪˈskraɪbə-bl] indescriptible; *(very bad)* inqualifiable

index [ˈɪndeks] *for book* index *m*

India [ˈɪndɪə] Inde *f*; **Indian 1** *adj* indien **2** *n also American* Indien(ne) *m(f)*

indicate [ˈɪndɪkeɪt] **1** *v/t* indi-quer **2** *v/i when driving* met-tre ses clignotants; **indica-tion** indication *f*, signe *m*

indict [ɪnˈdaɪt] accuser

indifference [ɪnˈdɪfrəns] in-différence *f*; **indifferent** in-différent; *(mediocre)* médiocre

indigestion [ɪndɪ'dʒestʃn] indigestion *f*

indignant [ɪn'dɪgnənt] indi-
gné; **indignation** indignation
f

indirect [ɪndɪ'rekt] indirect;
indirectly indirectement

indiscreet [ɪndɪ'skriːt] indiscret

indiscriminate [ɪndɪ'skrim-
ɪnət] aveugle; *accusations* à
tort et à travers

indispensable [ɪndɪ'spen-
səbl] indispensable

indisposed [ɪndɪ'spəʊzd]
(*not well*) indisposé

indisputable [ɪndɪ'spjuːtəbl]
incontestable

indistinct [ɪndɪ'stɪŋkt] indistinct

indistinguishable [ɪndɪ'stɪ-
ŋgwɪʃəbl] indifférenciable

individual [ɪndɪ'vɪdʒʊəl] **1** *n*
individu *m* **2** *adj* (*separate*)
particulier; (*personal*) individuel; **individually** indivi-
duellement

indoctrinate [ɪn'dɑːktrɪneɪt]
endoctriner

Indonesia [ɪndə'niːʒə] Indo-
nésie *f*; **Indonesian 1** *adj* in-
donésien **2** *n person* Indoné-
sien(ne) *m(f)*

indoor ['ɪndɔːr] *activities,
games* d'intérieur; *sport* en
salle; *arena* couvert; **indoors**
à l'intérieur; (*at home*) à la
maison

indorse → **endorse**

indulgent [ɪn'dʌldʒənt] (*not
strict enough*) indulgent

industrial [ɪn'dʌstrɪəl] industriel; **industrial dispute** conflit *m* social; **industrialist** in-
dustriel(le) *m(f)*; **industri-
ous** travailleur; **industry** industrie *f*

ineffective [ɪnɪ'fektɪv] ineffi-
cace

inefficient [ɪnɪ'fɪʃənt] ineffi-
cace

inept [ɪ'nept] inepte

inequality [ɪnɪ'kwɑːlɪtɪ] inégalité *f*

inescapable [ɪnɪ'skeɪpəbl]
inévitable

inevitable [ɪn'evɪtəbl] inévitable; **inevitably** inévitable-
ment

inexcusable [ɪnɪk'skjuːzəbl]
inexcusable

inexhaustible [ɪnɪg'zɔːstəbl]
inépuisable

inexpensive [ɪnɪk'spensɪv]
bon marché, pas cher

inexperienced [ɪnɪk'spɪri-
ənst] inexpérimenté

inexplicable [ɪnɪk'splɪkəbl]
inexplicable

infallible [ɪn'fælɪbl] infaillible

infamous ['ɪnfəməs] infâme

infancy ['ɪnfənsɪ] *of person*
petite enfance *f*; *of state, institution* débuts *mpl*; **infant**
petit(e) *m(f)*; **infantile** *pej* infantile

infantry ['ɪnfəntrɪ] infanterie
f

infect [ɪn'fekt] contaminer;

***become ~ed** of wound s'infecter; **infection** contamination *f*; (*disease*), *of wound* infection *f*; **infectious** *disease* infectieux; *laughter* contagieux

infer [ɪn'fɜːr]: ~ **X from Y** déduire X de Y

inferior [ɪn'fɪrɪər] inférieur; **inferiority** infériorité *f*; **inferiority complex** complexe *m* d'infériorité

infertile [ɪn'fɜːtl] stérile; **infertility** stérilité *f*

infidelity [ɪnfɪ'delɪtɪ] infidélité *f*

infinite ['ɪnfɪnət] infini; **infinitive** infinitif *m*

infinity [ɪn'fɪnɪtɪ] infinité *f*; MATH infini *m*

inflammable [ɪn'flæməbl] inflammable; **inflammation** MED inflammation *f*

inflatable [ɪn'fleɪtəbl] *dinghy* gonflable; **inflate** *tire, dinghy* gonfler; **inflation** inflation *f*; **inflationary** inflationniste

inflexible [ɪn'fleksɪbl] *attitude, person* inflexible

inflict [ɪn'flɪkt] infliger (**on** à)

influence ['ɪnfluəns] **1** *v/t* influence *f* **2** *v/t* influencer; **influential** influent

inform [ɪn'fɔːrm] **1** *v/t* informer **2** *v/i*: ~ **on** dénoncer

informal [ɪn'fɔːrməl] *meeting, agreement* non-officiel; *form of address* familier; *conversation, dress* simple; **informality** *of meeting, agreement*

caractère *m* non officiel; *of form of address* familiarité *f*; *of conversation, dress* simplicité *f*

informant [ɪn'fɔːrmənt] informateur(-trice) *m(f)*; **information** renseignements *mpl*; **information technology** informatique *f*; **informative** instructif; **informer** dénonciateur(-trice) *m(f)*

infra-red [ɪnfrə'red] infrarouge

infrastructure ['ɪnfrəstrʌktʃər] infrastructure *f*

infrequent [ɪn'friːkwənt] rare

infuriate [ɪn'fjʊrɪeɪt] rendre furieux; **infuriating** exaspérant

ingenious [ɪn'dʒiːnɪəs] ingénieux

ingot ['ɪŋgət] lingot *m*

ingratitude [ɪn'grætɪtuːd] ingratitude *f*

ingredient [ɪn'griːdɪənt] *for cooking* ingrédient *m*; *for success* recette *f*

inhabit [ɪn'hæbɪt] habiter; **inhabitant** habitant(e) *m(f)*

inhale [ɪn'heɪl] **1** *v/t* inhaler **2** *v/i when smoking* avaler la fumée

inherit [ɪn'herɪt] hériter; **inheritance** héritage *m*

inhibited [ɪn'hɪbɪtɪd] inhibé; **inhibition** inhibition *f*

inhospitable [ɪnhɑː'spɪtəbl] inhospitalier

inhuman [ɪn'hjuːmən] inhumain

initial [ɪˈnɪʃl] **1** *adj* initial **2** *n* initiale *f* **3** *v/t* (*write initials on*) parapher; **initially** au début; **initiate** *procedure* lancer; *person* initier; **initiation** lancement *m*; *of person* initiation *f*; **initiative** initiative *f*

inject [ɪnˈdʒekt] injecter; **injection** injection *f*

injure [ˈɪndʒər] blesser; **injury** blessure *f*

injustice [ɪnˈdʒʌstɪs] injustice *f*

ink [ɪŋk] encre *f*

inland [ˈɪnlənd] intérieur

in-laws [ˈɪnlɔːz] belle-famille *f*

inmate [ˈɪnmeɪt] *of prison* détenu(e) *m(f)*; *of mental hospital* interné(e) *m(f)*

inn [ɪn] auberge *f*

innate [ɪˈneɪt] inné

inner [ˈɪnər] *courtyard* intérieur; *thoughts* intime; *ear* interne

innocence [ˈɪnəsəns] innocence *f*; **innocent** innocent

innocuous [ɪˈnɑːkjuəs] inoffensif

innovation [ɪnəˈveɪʃn] innovation *f*; **innovative** innovant; **innovator** innovateur(-trice) *m(f)*

inoculate [ɪˈnɑːkjuleɪt] inoculer; **inoculation** inoculation *f*

inoffensive [ɪnəˈfensɪv] inoffensif

in-patient patient(e) hospitalisé(e) *m(f)*

input [ˈɪnput] **1** *n into project etc* apport *m*, contribution *f*; COMPUT entrée *f* **2** *v/t into project* apporter; COMPUT entrer

inquest [ˈɪnkwest] enquête *f* (*into* sur)

inquire [ɪnˈkwaɪr] se renseigner; **inquiry** demande *f* de renseignements; **government** ~ enquête *f* officielle

inquisitive [ɪnˈkwɪzətɪv] curieux

insane [ɪnˈseɪn] fou

insanitary [ɪnˈsænɪterɪ] insalubre

insanity [ɪnˈsænɪtɪ] folie *f*

inscription [ɪnˈskrɪpʃn] inscription *f*

insect [ˈɪnsekt] insecte *m*; **insecticide** insecticide *m*

insecure [ɪnsɪˈkjur] *be* ~ *not safe* ne pas se sentir en sécurité; *not sure of self* manquer d'assurance; **insecurity** *psychological* manque *m* d'assurance

insensitive [ɪnˈsensɪtɪv] insensible (*to* à)

insert 1 [ˈɪnsɜːrt] *n in magazine etc* encart *m* **2** [ɪnˈsɜːrt] *v/t* insérer

inside [ɪnˈsaɪd] **1** *n* intérieur *m*; ~ **out** à l'envers 2 *prep* à l'intérieur de; ~ **of 2 hours** en moins de 2 heures **3** *adv* à l'intérieur **4** *adj*: ~ **information** informations *fpl* internes; ~ **lane** SP couloir *m* intérieur

inside pocket poche f intérieure; **insider** insider initié(e) m(f); **insider trading** FIN délit m d'initié; **insides** (stomach) ventre m

insignificant [ɪnsɪg'nɪfɪkənt] insignifiant

insincere [ɪnsɪn'sɪr] peu sincère; **insincerity** manque f de sincérité

insinuate [ɪn'sɪnjʊeɪt] insinuer

insist [ɪn'sɪst] insister (**on** sur); **insistent** insistant

insolent ['ɪnsələnt] insolent

insolvent [ɪn'sɒlvənt] insolvable

insomnia [ɪn'sɒmnɪə] insomnie f

inspect [ɪn'spekt] work, tickets, baggage contrôler; factory, school inspecter; **inspection** of work, tickets, baggage contrôle m; of factory, school inspection f; **inspector** in factory inspecteur(-trice) m(f)

inspiration [ɪnspə'reɪʃn] inspiration f; **inspire** inspirer

instability [ɪnstə'bɪlɪtɪ] instabilité f

install [ɪn'stɔːl] installer; **installation** installation f; **installment**, Br **instalment** of story etc épisode m; (payment) versement m; **installment plan** vente f à crédit

instance ['ɪnstəns] (example) exemple m; **for ~** par exemple

instant ['ɪnstənt] **1** adj instantané **2** n instant m; **instantaneous** instantané; **instant coffee** café m soluble; **instantly** immédiatement

instead [ɪn'sted] à la place; **~ of me** à ma place; **~ of going home** au lieu de rentrer à la maison

instinct ['ɪnstɪŋkt] instinct m; **instinctive** instinctif

institute ['ɪnstɪtjuːt] **1** n institut m; (special home) établissement m **2** v/t new law, inquiry instituer; **institution** institution f

instruct [ɪn'strʌkt] (order) ordonner; (teach) instruire; **instruction** instruction f; **~s for use** mode m d'emploi; **instructive** instructif; **instructor** moniteur(-trice) m(f)

instrument ['ɪnstrʊmənt] instrument m

insubordinate [ɪnsə'bɔːrdɪneɪt] insubordonné

insufficient [ɪnsə'fɪʃnt] insuffisant

insulate ['ɪnsəleɪt] ELEC, against cold isoler; **insulation** isolation f; material isolement m

insulin ['ɪnsəlɪn] insuline f

insult 1 ['ɪnsʌlt] n insulte f **2** [ɪn'sʌlt] v/t insulter

insurance [ɪn'ʃʊrəns] assurance f; **insurance company** compagnie f d'assurance; **insurance policy** police f d'as-

international

surance; insurance premium prime *f* d'assurance; **insure** assurer

insurmountable [ɪnsər-'maʊntəbl] insurmontable

intact [ɪn'tækt] (*not damaged*) intact

integrate ['ɪntɪɡreɪt] intégrer; **integrity** (*honesty*) intégrité *f*

intellect ['ɪntəlekt] intellect *m*; **intellectual 1** *adj* intellectuel **2** *n* intellectuel(le) *m(f)*

intelligence [ɪn'telɪdʒəns] intelligence *f*; (*information*) renseignements *mpl*; **intelligent** intelligent

intelligible [ɪn'telɪdʒəbl] intelligible

intend [ɪn'tend] *v/i:* ~ **to do sth** avoir l'intention de

intense [ɪn'tens] intense; *personality* passionné; **intensify 1** *v/t* intensifier **2** *v/i of pain, fighting* s'intensifier; **intensity** intensité *f*; **intensive** intensif; **intensive care** MED service *m* de soins intensifs

intention [ɪn'tenʃn] intention *f*; **intentional** intentionnel; **intentionally** délibérément

interaction [ɪntər'ækʃn] interaction *f*; **interactive** interactif

intercept [ɪntər'sept] intercepter

interchange ['ɪntərtʃeɪndʒ] *of highways* échangeur *m*; **interchangeable** interchangeable

intercom ['ɪntərkɑːm] interphone *m*

intercourse ['ɪntərkɔːrs] *sexual* rapports *mpl*

interdependent [ɪntərdɪ-'pendənt] interdépendant

interest ['ɪntrəst] **1** *n* intérêt *m*; *financial* intérêt(s) *m(pl)* **2** *v/t* intéresser; **interested** intéressé; **interesting** intéressant; **interest rate** taux *m* d'intérêt

interface ['ɪntərfeɪs] **1** *n* interface *f* **2** *v/i* avoir une interface (**with** avec)

interfere [ɪntər'fɪr] se mêler (**with** de); **interference** ingérence *f*; *on radio* interférence *f*

interior [ɪn'tɪrɪər] **1** *adj* intérieur **2** *n* intérieur *m*; **interior design** design *m* d'intérieurs; **interior designer** designer *m/f* d'intérieurs

interlude ['ɪntərluːd] intermède *m*

intermediary [ɪntər'miːdɪerɪ] intermédiaire *m/f*; **intermediate** *level* intermédiaire; *course* (de niveau) moyen

intermission [ɪntər'mɪʃn] *in theater* entracte *m*

internal [ɪn'tɜːrnl] interne; *trade* intérieur; **internally** *in organization* en interne; **not to be taken** ~ à usage externe; **Internal Revenue (Service)** direction *f* générale des) impôts *mpl*

international [ɪntər'næʃnl]

international; **internationally** internationalement

Internet ['ɪntənet] Internet *m*; **on the ~** sur Internet

interpret [ɪn'tɜːprɪt] interpréter; **interpretation** interprétation *f*; **interpreter** interprète *m/f*

interrogate [ɪn'terəgeɪt] interroger; **interrogation** interrogatoire *m*; **interrogator** interrogateur(-trice) *m(f)*

interrupt [ɪntə'rʌpt] interrompre; **interruption** interruption *f*

intersect [ɪntər'sekt] **1** *v/t* couper, croiser **2** *v/i* s'entrecouper, s'entrecroiser; **intersection** of roads carrefour *m*

interstate [ɪntər'steɪt] autoroute *f*

interval ['ɪntərvl] intervalle *m*; in theater entracte *m*

intervene [ɪntər'viːn] intervenir; **intervention** intervention *f*

interview ['ɪntərvjuː] **1** *n* interview *f*; for job entretien *m* **2** *v/t* interviewer; for job faire passer un entretien à; **interviewer** interviewer (-euse) *m(f)*; for job personne *f* responsable d'un entretien

intimate ['ɪntɪmət] intime

intimidate [ɪn'tɪmɪdeɪt] intimider; **intimidation** intimidation *f*

into ['ɪntu] dans; **translate ~ English** traduire en anglais;

be ~ sth F (like) aimer qch; politics etc être engagé dans qch

intolerable [ɪn'tɑːlərəbl] intolérable; **intolerant** intolérant

intoxicated [ɪn'tɑːksɪkeɪtɪd] ivre

intravenous [ɪntrə'viːnəs] intraveineux

intricate ['ɪntrɪkət] compliqué, complexe

intrigue 1 ['ɪntriːg] *n* intrigue *f* **2** [ɪn'triːg] *v/t* intriguer; **intriguing** intrigant

introduce [ɪntrə'duːs] new technique etc introduire; **~ s.o. to s.o.** présenter qn à qn; **introduction** to person présentations fpl; in book, of new techniques introduction *f*

intrude [ɪn'truːd] déranger; **intruder** intrus(e) *m(f)*; **intrusion** intrusion *f*

intuition [ɪntuː'ɪʃn] intuition *f*

invade [ɪn'veɪd] envahir

invalid[1] [ɪn'vælɪd] adj non valable

invalid[2] ['ɪnvəlɪd] *n* MED invalide *m/f*

invalidate [ɪn'vælɪdeɪt] claim, theory invalider

invaluable [ɪn'væljubl] inestimable

invariably [ɪn'veɪriəblɪ] (always) invariablement

invasion [ɪn'veɪʒn] invasion *f*

invent [ɪn'vent] inventer; **invention** invention *f*; **inventive** inventif; **inventor** inven-

teur(-trice) *m(f)*
inventory ['ɪnvəntɔːrɪ] inventaire *m*
invert [ɪn'vɜːrt] inverser
invest [ɪn'vest] investir
investigate [ɪn'vestɪgeɪt]
  crime enquêter sur; *scientific phenomenon* étudier; **investigation** *of crime* enquête *f*; *in science* étude *f*
investment [ɪn'vestmənt] investissement *m*; **investor** investisseur *m*
invincible [ɪn'vɪnsəbl] invincible
invisible [ɪn'vɪzɪbl] invisible
invitation [ɪnvɪ'teɪʃn] invitation *f*; **invite** inviter
invoice ['ɪnvɔɪs] **1** *n* facture *f* **2** *v/t customer* facturer
involuntary [ɪn'vɑːləntərɪ] involontaire
involve [ɪn'vɑːlv] *work* nécessiter; *expense* entraîner; (*concern*) concerner; **what does it ~?** qu'est-ce que cela implique?; **involved** (*complex*) compliqué; **involvement** *in project, crime etc* participation *f*; *in politics* engagement *m*
invulnerable [ɪn'vʌlnərəbl] invulnérable
inward ['ɪnwərd] **1** *adj* intérieur **2** *adv* vers l'intérieur; **inwardly** intérieurement
IQ [aɪ'kjuː] (= *intelligence quotient*) Q.I. *m* (= Quotient *m* intellectuel)
Iran [ɪ'rɑːn] Iran *m*; **Iranian 1**

adj iranien **2** *n* Iranien(ne) *m(f)*
Iraq [ɪ'ræk] Iraq *m*; **Iraqi 1** *adj* irakien **2** *n* Irakien(ne) *m(f)*
Ireland ['aɪrlənd] Irlande *f*.
Irish 1 *adj* irlandais **2** *npl*: **the ~** les Irlandais
iron ['aɪərn] **1** *n* fer *m*; *for clothes* fer *m* à repasser **2** *v/t shirts etc* repasser
ironic(al) [aɪ'rɑːnɪk(l)] ironique
'ironing board planche *f* à repasser
irony ['aɪrənɪ] ironie *f*
irrational [ɪ'ræʃənl] irrationnel
irreconcilable [ɪrekən'saɪləbl] *people* irréconciliables; *positions* inconciliables
irregular [ɪ'regjʊlər] irrégulier
irrelevant [ɪ'reləvənt] hors de propos
irreplaceable [ɪrɪ'pleɪsəbl] irremplaçable
irrepressible [ɪrɪ'presəbl] *sense of humor* à toute épreuve; *person* qui ne se laisse pas abattre
irresistible [ɪrɪ'zɪstəbl] irrésistible
irresponsible [ɪrɪ'spɑːnsəbl] irresponsable
irreverent [ɪ'revərənt] irrévérencieux
irrevocable [ɪ'revəkəbl] irrévocable
irrigate ['ɪrɪgeɪt] irriguer; **irrigation** irrigation *f*

irritable ['ırıtəbl] irritable; **irritate** irriter; **irritating** irritant; **irritation** irritation *f*

Islam ['ızla:m] *religion* islam *m*; *peoples, civilization* Islam *m*; **Islamic** islamique

island ['aılənd] île *f*

isolate ['aısəleıt] isoler; **isolated** isolé *m*; **isolation** isolement *m*

ISP [aıes'pi:] (= *Internet service provider*) fournisseur *m* Internet

Israel ['ızreıl] Israël *m*; **Israeli** **1** *adj* israélien **2** *n person* Israélien(ne) *m(f)*

issue ['ıʃu:] **1** *n (matter)* question *f*, problème *m*; *of magazine* numéro *m* **2** *v/t supplies* distribuer; *coins, warning* émettre; *passport* délivrer

IT [aı'ti:] (= *information technology*) informatique *f*

it [ıt] *as subject* il, elle; *as object* le, la; **~'s through there** c'est par là; **give ~ to him**

donne-le lui; **on top of ~** dessus; **let's talk about ~** parlons-en; **~'s raining** il pleut; **~'s me/him** c'est moi/lui; **that's ~!** *(that's right)* c'est ça!; *(finished)* c'est fini!

Italian [ı'tæljən] **1** *adj* italien **2** *n person* Italien(ne) *m(f)*; *language* italien *m*

italics [ı'tælıks] italique *m*

Italy ['ıtəlı] Italie *f*

itch [ıtʃ] **1** *n* démangeaison *f* **2** *v/i*: **it ~es** ça me démange

item ['aıtəm] article *m*; *on agenda* point *m*; **~ of news** nouvelle *f*; **itemize** *invoice* détailler

itinerary [aı'tınərerı] itinéraire *m*

its [ıts] son, sa; *pl* ses

it's [ıts] → **it is, it has**

itself [ıt'self] *reflexive* se; *stressed* lui-même; elle-même; **by ~** *(automatically)* tout(e) seul(e)

J

jab [dʒæb]: **~ a stick into s.o.** donner un coup de bâton à qn

jack [dʒæk] MOT cric *m*; *in cards* valet *m*

jacket ['dʒækıt] veste *f*; *of book* couverture *f*

'jackpot jackpot *m*

jagged ['dʒægıd] découpé

jail [dʒeıl] prison *f*

jam¹ [dʒæm] *n for bread* confiture *f*

jam² [dʒæm] **1** *n* MOT embouteillage *m*; F *(difficulty)* pétrin *m* F **2** *v/t (ram)* fourrer; *(cause to stick)* bloquer; *broadcast* brouiller **3** *v/i (stick)* se bloquer

janitor ['dʒænıtər] concierge *m/f*

January ['dʒænjʊərɪ] janvier *m*

Japan [dʒə'pæn] Japon *m*; **Japanese 1** *adj* japonais **2** *n* personne Japonais(e) *m(f)*; *language* japonais *m*; **the ~** les Japonais *mpl*

jar [dʒɑːr] *container* pot *m*

jargon ['dʒɑːrgən] jargon *m*

jaw [dʒɔː] mâchoire *f*

jaywalker ['dʒeɪwɔːkər] piéton(ne) *m(f)* imprudent(e)

jazz [dʒæz] jazz *m*

jealous ['dʒeləs] jaloux; **jealousy** jalousie *f*

jeans [dʒiːnz] jean *m*

jeep [dʒiːp] jeep *f*

jeer [dʒɪr] **1** *n* raillerie *f*; *of crowd* huée *f* **2** *v/i of crowd* huer

Jello® ['dʒeloʊ] gelée *f*

jelly ['dʒelɪ] jam confiture *f*; **jellyfish** méduse *f*

jeopardize ['dʒepərdaɪz] mettre en danger

jerk¹ [dʒɜːrk] **1** *n* saccade *f* **2** *v/t* tirer d'un coup sec

jerk² [dʒɜːrk] *n* F couillon *m* F

jerky ['dʒɜːrkɪ] *movement* saccadé

Jesus ['dʒiːzəs] Jésus

jet [dʒet] *(airplane)* avion *m* à réaction, jet *m*; *of water* jet *m*; *(nozzle)* bec *m*; **jetlag** (troubles *mpl* du au) décalage *m* horaire

jettison ['dʒetɪsn] jeter par-dessus bord; *fig* abandonner

jetty ['dʒetɪ] jetée *f*

Jew [dʒuː] Juif(-ive) *m(f)*

jewel ['dʒuːəl] bijou *m*; *fig*: *person* perle *f*; **jeweler**, *Br* **jeweller** bijoutier(-ère) *m(f)*; **jewelry**, *Br* **jewellery** bijoux *mpl*

Jewish ['dʒuːɪʃ] juif

jigsaw (puzzle) ['dʒɪgsɔː] puzzle *m*

jilt [dʒɪlt] laisser tomber

jingle ['dʒɪŋgl] **1** *n* song jingle *m* **2** *v/i of keys, coins* cliqueter

jinx [dʒɪŋks] *person* porte-malheur *m/f*; **there's a ~ on this project** ce projet porte malheur

jittery ['dʒɪtərɪ] F nerveux

job [dʒɑːb] travail *m*; **jobless** sans travail

jockey ['dʒɑːkɪ] jockey *m*

jog [dʒɑːg] *as exercise* faire du footing *or* jogging; **jogger** *person* joggeur(-euse) *m(f)*; **jogging** jogging *m*

john [dʒɑːn] F *(toilet)* petit coin *m* F

join [dʒɔɪn] **1** *n* joint *m* **2** *v/i of roads, rivers* se rejoindre; *(become a member)* devenir membre **3** *v/t (connect)* relier; *person, of road* rejoindre; *club* devenir membre de
◆ **join in** participer

joint [dʒɔɪnt] ANAT articulation *f*; *in woodwork* joint *m*; *of meat* rôti *m*; **joint account** compte *m* joint; **joint venture** entreprise *f* commune

joke [dʒoʊk] **1** *n* plaisanterie *f*,

blague f F; (practical ~) tour m **2** v/i plaisanter; **joker** farceur(-euse) m(f), blagueur (-euse) m(f); *in cards* joker m; **jokingly** en plaisantant

journal ['dʒɜːnl] (magazine) revue f; (diary) journal m; **journalism** journalisme m; **journalist** journaliste m/f

journey ['dʒɜːnɪ] voyage m; *across town etc* trajet m

joy [dʒɔɪ] joie f

jubilant ['dʒuːbɪlənt] débordant de joie; **jubilation** jubilation f

judge [dʒʌdʒ] **1** n juge m/f **2** v/t juger; *measurement, age* estimer **3** v/i juger; **judg(e)-ment** jugement m; (opinion) avis m; **Judg(e)ment Day** le Jugement dernier

judicial [dʒuːˈdɪʃl] judiciaire

juggle ['dʒʌgl] also fig jongler avec

juice [dʒuːs] jus m; juicy juteux; gossip croustillant

July [dʒuˈlaɪ] juillet m

jumbo (jet) ['dʒʌmbəʊ] jumbo-jet m; **jumbo-sized** F géant

jump [dʒʌmp] **1** n saut m; (increase) bond m **2** v/i sauter; *in surprise* sursauter; (increase) faire un bond **3** v/t fence etc sauter; F (attack) attaquer; **~ the lights** griller un feu (rouge)

◆ **jump at** opportunity sauter sur

jumper ['dʒʌmpər] dress robe-chasuble f; **jumpy** nerveux

June [dʒuːn] juin m

jungle ['dʒʌŋgl] jungle f

junior ['dʒuːnjər] **1** adj subalterne; (younger) plus jeune **2** n in rank subalterne m/f; **she is ten years my ~** elle est ma cadette de dix ans; **junior high** college m

junk [dʒʌŋk] camelote f F; **junk food** cochonneries fpl; **junkie** F drogué(e) m(f); **junk mail** prospectus mpl

jurisdiction [dʒuːrɪsˈdɪkʃn] LAW juridiction f

juror ['dʒuːrər] juré(e) m(f); **jury** jury m

just [dʒʌst] **1** adj cause juste **2** adv (barely, only) juste; **~ as intelligent** tout aussi intelligent; **I've ~ seen her** je viens de la voir; **~ about** (almost) presque; **I was ~ about to leave when ...** j'étais sur le point de partir quand ...; **~ now** (a few moments ago) tout à l'heure; (at this moment) en ce moment

justice ['dʒʌstɪs] justice f

justifiable [dʒʌstɪˈfaɪəbl] justifiable; **justifiably** à juste titre; **justification** justification f; **justify** also text justifier

justly ['dʒʌstlɪ] (fairly) de manière juste; (rightly) à juste titre

◆ **jut out** [dʒʌt] être en saillie

juvenile ['dʒuːvənəl] crime juvénile; *court* pour enfants; *pej* puéril; **juvenile delin-** **quent** mineur(e) délin- quant(e) *m(f)*

K

k [keɪ] (= *kilobyte*) Ko *m* (= ki- lo-octet *m*); (= ***thousand***) mille

keel [kiːl] NAUT quille *f*

keen [kiːn] (*intense*) vif

keep [kiːp] **1** *v/t* garder; (*de-tain*) retenir; *in specific place* mettre; *family* entretenir; *dog etc* avoir; *bees, cattle* éle- ver; *promise* tenir; **~ sth from s.o.** cacher qch à qn; **~ s.o. from doing sth** empê- cher qn de faire qch; **~ try-ing!** essaie encore! ; **don't ~ interrupting!** arrête de m'in- terrompre tout le temps! **2** *v/i* (*remain*) rester; *of food, milk* se conserver

◆ **keep back** (*hold in check*) retenir; *information* cacher

◆ **keep down** *costs etc* rédui- re; *food* garder

◆ **keep to** *path* rester sur; *rules* s'en tenir à

◆ **keep up 1** *v/i when walk-ing, running etc* suivre; **keep up with** aller au même rythme que **2** *v/t pace, pay-ments* continuer; *bridge, pants* soutenir

'keepsake souvenir *m*

kennel ['kenl] niche *f*; **kennels** chenil *m*

kerosene ['kerəsiːn] AVIA ké- rosène *m*; *for lamps* pétrole *m* (lampant)

ketchup ['ketʃʌp] ketchup *m*

kettle ['ketl] bouilloire *f*

key [kiː] **1** *n* clef *f*, clé *f*; COMPUT, MUS touche *f* **2** *adj* (*vital*) clef *inv*, clé *inv* **3** *v/t* & *v/i* COMPUT taper

◆ **key in** *data* taper

'keyboard COMPUT, MUS cla- vier *m*; **keyboarder** COMPUT claviste *m/f*; **keycard** carte- clef *f*; **keyed up** tendu; **key-ring** porte-clefs *m*

kick [kɪk] **1** *n* coup *m* de pied **2** *v/t* donner un coup de pied dans **3** *v/i of horse* ruer

◆ **kick around** *ball* taper dans; F (*discuss*) débattre

◆ **kick off** donner le coup d'envoi; F (*start*) démarrer

◆ **kick out** mettre à la porte; **be kicked out of the compa-ny** être mis à la porte de la société

'kickback F (*bribe*) dessous- -de-table *m* F

'kickoff SP coup *m* d'envoi

kid [kɪd] **1** *n* F (*child*) gamin(e) *m(f)* F **2** *v/t* F taquiner **3** *v/i* F plaisanter

kidnap ['kɪdnæp] kidnapper; **kidnap(p)er** kidnappeur (-euse) *m(f)*; **kidnap(p)ing**

kidnapping *m*

kidney ['kɪdnɪ] ANAT rein *m*; *in cooking* rognon *m*

kill [kɪl] *also time* tuer; **killer** (*murderer*) tueur(-euse) *m(f)*; **killing** meurtre *m*

kiln [kɪln] four *m*

kilo ['kiːləʊ] kilo *m*; **kilobyte** kilo-octet *m*; **kilogram** kilogramme *m*; **kilometer**, *Br* **kilometre** kilomètre *m*

kind¹ [kaɪnd] *adj* gentil

kind² [kaɪnd] *n* (*sort*) sorte *f*, genre *m*; (*make, brand*) marque *f*; **~ of sad/strange** F plutôt triste/bizarre

kind-hearted [kaɪnd'hɑːrtɪd] bienveillant, bon; **kindly** gentil, bon; **kindness** bonté *f*, gentillesse *f*

king [kɪŋ] roi *m*; **kingdom** royaume *m*

kinky ['kɪŋkɪ] F bizarre

kiosk ['kiːɑːsk] kiosque *m*

kiss [kɪs] **1** *n* baiser *m* **2** *v/t* embrasser **3** *v/i* s'embrasser

kit [kɪt] (*equipment*) trousse *f*; *for assembly* kit *m*

kitchen ['kɪtʃɪn] cuisine *f*

kitten ['kɪtn] chaton(ne) *m(f)*

kitty ['kɪtɪ] *money* cagnotte *f*

klutz [klʌts] F (*clumsy person*) empoté(e) *m(f)*

knack [næk] : **have the ~ of doing** avoir le chic pour faire; **there's a ~ to it** il y a un truc F

knee [niː] genou *m*; **kneecap** rotule *f*

kneel [niːl] s'agenouiller

'knee-length à la hauteur du genou

knife [naɪf] couteau *m*

knit [nɪt] tricoter; **knitwear** tricot *m*

knob [nɑːb] *on door* bouton *m*; *of butter* noix *f*

knock [nɑːk] **1** *n on door*, (*blow*) coup *m* **2** *v/t* (*hit*) frapper; *knee etc* se cogner; F (*criticize*) débiner F **3** *v/i on door* frapper

♦ **knock down** renverser; *wall, building* abattre; F (*reduce the price of*) solder

♦ **knock out** assommer; *boxer* mettre knock-out; *power lines etc* détruire; (*eliminate*) éliminer

♦ **knock over** renverser

'knockout *in boxing* knock-out *m*

knot [nɑːt] **1** *n* nœud *m* **2** *v/t* nouer

know [nəʊ] **1** *v/t* savoir; *person, place, language* connaître; (*recognize*) reconnaître **2** *v/i* savoir; **~ about sth** être au courant de qch; **know-how** F savoir-faire *m*; **knowing** *smile* entendu; **knowingly** (*wittingly*) sciemment; *smile etc* d'un air entendu; **know-it-all** F je-sais-tout *m/f*; **knowledge** savoir *m*; *of a subject* connaissance(s) *f(pl)*; **to the best of my ~** autant que je sache

knuckle ['nʌkl] articulation *f* du doigt

Koran [kəˈræn] Coran *m*

Korea [kəˈriːə] Corée *f*; **Korean 1** *adj* coréen **2** *n* Coréen(ne) *m(f)*; *language* coréen *m*

réen *m*

kosher [ˈkəʊʃər] REL casher *inv*; F réglo *inv* F

kudos [ˈkjuːdɑːs] prestige *m*

L

lab [læb] labo *m*

label [ˈleɪbl] **1** *n* étiquette *f* **2** *v/t also fig* étiqueter

labor [ˈleɪbər] *also in pregnancy* travail *m*

laboratory [ˈlæbrətɔːrɪ] laboratoire *m*

labored [ˈleɪbərd] *style, speech* laborieux; **laborer** travailleur *m* manuel; **laborious** laborieux; **labor union** syndicat *m*

labour Br → **labor**

lace [leɪs] dentelle *f*; *for shoe* lacet *m*

lack [læk] **1** *n* manque *m* **2** *v/t* manquer de **3** *v/i*: **be ~ing** manquer

lacquer [ˈlækər] laque *f*

ladder [ˈlædər] échelle *f*

laden [ˈleɪdn] chargé (**with** de)

ladies room [ˈleɪdiːz] toilettes *fpl* (pour dames)

lady [ˈleɪdɪ] dame *f*; **ladybug** coccinelle *f*; **ladylike** distingué

lager [ˈlɑːgər] Br bière *f* blonde

laidback [leɪdˈbæk] relax F

lake [leɪk] lac *m*

lamb [læm] agneau *m*

lame [leɪm] boîteux; *excuse*

mauvais;

laminated [ˈlæmɪneɪtɪd] *flooring, paper* stratifié; *wood* contreplaqué; *with plastic* plastifié; **~ glass** verre *m* feuilleté

lamp [læmp] lampe *f*; **lamppost** réverbère *m*; **lampshade** abat-jour *m inv*

land [lænd] **1** *n* terre *f*; *(country)* pays *m*; **by ~** (par voie de) terre **2** *v/t airplane* faire atterrir; *job* décrocher **3** *v/i of airplane* atterrir; *of ball* tomber; **landing** *of airplane* atterrissage *m*; *(top of staircase)* palier *m*; **landing strip** piste *f* d'atterrissage; **landlady** propriétaire *f*; *of rented room* logeuse *f*; Br *of bar* patronne *f*; **landlord** propriétaire *m*; *of rented room* logeur *m*; Br *of bar* patron *m*; **landmark** point *m* de repère; **be a ~ in** *fig* faire date dans; **land owner** propriétaire *m* foncier; **landscape 1** *n* paysage *m* **2** *adv print* en format paysage; **landslide** glissement *m* de terrain; **landslide victory** victoire *f* écrasante

lane [leɪn] *in country* petite route *f* (de campagne); *(alley)* ruelle *f*; MOT voie *f*

language ['læŋgwɪdʒ] langue *f*; *(style, code etc)* langage *m*; **language lab** laboratoire *m* de langues

lap[1] [læp] *of track* tour *m*

lap[2] [læp] *of water* clapotis *m*

lap[3] [læp] *of person* genoux *mpl*

lapel [lə'pel] revers *m*

lapse [læps] **1** *n (mistake)* erreur *f*; *in behavior* écart *m* (de conduite); *of time* intervalle *m* **2** *v/i* expirer

laptop ['læptɑːp] COMPUT portable *m*

larceny ['lɑːrsənɪ] vol *m*

larder ['lɑːrdər] garde-manger *m inv*

large [lɑːrdʒ] grand; *sum of money, head* gros; **largely** *(mainly)* en grande partie

laryngitis [lærɪn'dʒaɪtɪs] laryngite *f*

laser ['leɪzər] laser *m*; **laser printer** imprimante *f* laser

lash[1] [læʃ] *v/t with whip* fouetter

lash[2] [læʃ] *n (eyelash)* cil *m*

last[1] [læst] **1** *adj* dernier; ~ **night** hier soir **2** *adv* arrive, leave en dernier; **at** ~ enfin

last[2] [læst] *v/i* durer; **lasting** durable; **lastly** pour finir

late [leɪt] **1** *adj (behind time)* en retard; *in day time*: **it's getting** ~ il se fait tard **2** *adv* arrive, leave tard; **lately**

récemment; **later** plus tard; **latest** dernier

Latin A'merica Amérique *f* latine; **Latin American 1** *n* Latino-Américain *m* **2** *adj* latino-américain

latitude ['lætɪtuːd] *also (freedom)* latitude *f*

latter ['lætər] dernier

laugh [læf] **1** *n* rire *m* **2** *v/i* rire ◆ **laugh at** rire de; *(mock)* se moquer de

laughter ['læftər] rires *mpl*

launch [lɒntʃ] **1** *n boat* vedette *f*; *of rocket, product* lancement *m*; *of ship* mise *f* à l'eau **2** *v/t rocket, product* lancer; *ship* mettre à l'eau

launder ['lɒːndər] *clothes, money* blanchir; **laundromat** laverie *f* automatique; **laundry** *place* blanchisserie *f*; *clothes* lessive *f*

lavatory ['lævətərɪ] W.-C. *mpl*

lavish ['lævɪʃ] somptueux

law [lɒː] loi *f*; *subject* droit *m*; **be against the** ~ être contraire à la loi; **law-abiding** respectueux des lois; **law court** tribunal *m*; **lawful** légal; *wife, child* légitime; **lawless** anarchique

lawn [lɒːn] pelouse *f*; **lawn mower** tondeuse *f* (à gazon)

lawsuit ['lɒːsuːt] procès *m*; **lawyer** avocat *m*

lax [læks] laxiste; *security* relâché

laxative ['læksətɪv] laxatif *m*

lay [leɪ] (*put down*) poser; *eggs* pondre; V *sexually* s'envoyer V

◆ **lay off** *workers* licencier; *temporarily* mettre au chômage technique

◆ **lay out** *objects* disposer; *page* faire la mise en page de

layer ['leɪr] couche *f*

'layman REL laïc *m*; *fig* profane *m*

'lay-out agencement *m*; *of page* mise *f* en page

lazy ['leɪzɪ] *person* paresseux; *day* tranquille

lb (= **pound**) livre *f*

lead¹ [liːd] **1** *v/t* mener; *company* être à la tête de **2** *v/i in race, competition* mener; (*provide leadership*) diriger

lead² [liːd] *of dog* laisse *f*

lead³ [led] *substance* plomb *m*; **leaded** *gas* au plomb

leader ['liːdər] *of state* dirigeant *m*; *in race* leader *m*; *of group* chef *m*; **leadership** *of party etc* direction *f*

lead-free ['ledfriː] *gas* sans plomb

leading ['liːdɪŋ] *runner* en tête (de la course); *company, product* premier; **leading-edge** *company, technology* de pointe

leaf [liːf] feuille *f*

◆ **leaf through** feuilleter

leaflet ['liːflət] dépliant *m*

league [liːg] ligue *f*

leak [liːk] **1** *n also of information* fuite *f* **2** *v/i of pipe* fuir;

of boat faire eau **3** *v/t information* divulguer

lean¹ [liːn] **1** *v/i* (*be at an angle*) pencher; **~ against** *sth* s'appuyer contre qch **2** *v/t* appuyer

lean² [liːn] *adj meat* maigre

leap [liːp] **1** *n* saut *m* **2** *v/i* sauter; **leap year** année *f* bissextile

learn [lɜːrn] apprendre; **learner** apprenant(e) *m(f)*; **learning** (*knowledge*) savoir *m*; *act* apprentissage *m*

lease [liːs] **1** *n for apartment* bail *m*; *for equipment* location *f* **2** *v/t* louer

◆ **lease out** louer

leash [liːʃ] *for dog* laisse *f*

least [liːst] **1** *adj* (*slightest*) (le ou la) moindre; *smallest quantity of* le moins de **2** *adv* (le) moins **3** *n* le moins; **at ~** au moins

leather ['leðər] **1** *n* cuir *m* **2** *adj* de cuir

leave [liːv] **1** *n* (*vacation*) congé *m* **2** *v/t* quitter; *food, scar, memory* laisser; (*forget, leave behind*) oublier; **~ sth alone** ne pas toucher à qch; **~ s.o. alone** laisser qn tranquille; **be left** rester *m* **3** *v/i of person, plane etc* partir

◆ **leave behind** *intentionally* laisser; (*forget*) oublier

◆ **leave out** omettre; (*not put away*) ne pas ranger

leaving party ['liːvɪŋ] soirée *f* d'adieu

lecture ['lektʃər] **1** n conférence f; at university cours m **2** v/i at university donner des cours; **lecturer** conférencier m; at university maître m de conférences

ledge [ledʒ] of window rebord m, on rock face saillie f; **ledger** COM registre m de comptes

left [left] **1** adj gauche **2** n also POL gauche f; **on/to the ~** à gauche **3** adv turn, look à gauche; **left-hand** gauche; **left-handed** gaucher; **left luggage** (office) consigne f; **left-overs** food restes mpl; **left-wing** POL de gauche

leg [leg] jambe f; of animal patte f; of table etc pied m

legacy ['legəsɪ] héritage m, legs m

legal ['liːgl] (allowed) légal; relating to the law juridique; **legal adviser** conseiller (-ère) m(f) juridique; **legality** légalité f; **legalize** légaliser

legend ['ledʒənd] légende f; **legendary** légendaire

legible ['ledʒəbl] lisible

legislate ['ledʒɪsleɪt] légiférer; **legislation** (laws) législation f; **legislative** législatif; **legislature** POL corps m législatif

legitimate [lɪ'dʒɪtɪmət] légitime

'leg room place f pour les jambes

leisure ['liːʒər] loisir m; (free time) temps m libre; **leisurely** tranquille

lemon ['lemən] citron m; **lemonade** citronnade f; carbonated limonade f

lend [lend] prêter

length [leŋθ] longueur f; (piece: of material) pièce f; of piping, road tronçon m; **at ~** describe, explain en détail; (eventually) finalement; **lengthen** sleeve etc allonger; contract prolonger; **lengthy** long

lenient ['liːnɪənt] indulgent

lens [lenz] of microscope etc lentille f; of eyeglasses verre m; of camera objectif m; of eye cristallin m

Lent [lent] REL Carême m

leotard ['liːoutɑːrd] justaucorps m

lesbian ['lezbɪən] **1** n lesbienne f **2** adj lesbien

less [les] **1** adv moins; ~ **than $200** moins de 200 dollars **2** adj money, salt moins de; **lessen 1** v/t réduire **2** v/i diminuer

lesson ['lesn] leçon f; at school cours m

let [let] (allow) laisser; Br house louer; ~**'s stay here** restons ici; ~ **go of sth** lâcher qch

♦ **let down** hair détacher; blinds baisser; (disappoint) décevoir

♦ **let in** to house laisser entrer

life jacket

◆ **let out** *from room, building* laisser sortir; *jacket etc* agrandir; *groan, yell* laisser échapper; *Br (rent)* louer

◆ **let up** *(stop)* s'arrêter

lethal ['liːθl] mortel

lethargic [lɪˈθɑːrdʒɪk] léthargique; **lethargy** léthargie *f*

letter ['letər] *of alphabet, in mail* lettre *f*; **letterbox** *Br* boîte *f* aux lettres; **letterhead** *(heading)* en-tête *m*; *(headed paper)* papier *m* à en-tête

lettuce ['letɪs] laitue *f*

leukemia [luːˈkiːmɪə] leucémie *f*

level ['levl] **1** *adj surface* plat; *in competition* à égalité **2** *n* niveau *m*; *on scale, in hierarchy* échelon *m*; **on the** ~ F *(honest)* régló F; **level-headed** pondéré

lever ['levər] levier *m*; **leverage** effet *m* de levier; *(influence)* poids *m*

levy ['levɪ] *taxes* lever

liability [laɪəˈbɪlətɪ] *(responsibility)* responsabilité *f*; *(likeliness)* disposition *f* (**to** à); **liable** responsable (**for** de); **be ~ to** *(likely)* être susceptible de

◆ **liaise with** [lɪˈeɪz] assurer la liaison avec

liaison [lɪˈeɪzɑːn] *(contacts)* communication *f*

liar [laɪr] menteur(-euse) *m(f)*

libel ['laɪbl] **1** *n* diffamation *f* **2** *v/t* diffamer

liberal ['lɪbərəl] large d'esprit;

portion etc généreux; POL libéral

liberate ['lɪbəreɪt] libérer; **liberated** libéré; **liberation** libération *f*; **liberty** liberté *f*

librarian [laɪˈbreriən] bibliothécaire *m/f*; **library** bibliothèque *f*

Libya ['lɪbɪə] Libye *f*; **Libyan 1** *adj* libyen **2** *n* Libyen(ne) *m(f)*

lice [laɪs] *pl* → **louse**

licence ['laɪsns] *Br* → **license 1** *n*

license ['laɪsns] **1** *n* permis *m* **2** *v/t company* accorder une licence à (**to do** pour faire); **be ~d** *equipment* être autorisé; **license number** numéro *m* d'immatriculation; **license plate** *of car* plaque *f* d'immatriculation

lick [lɪk] lécher

lid [lɪd] couvercle *m*

lie[1] [laɪ] **1** *n (untruth)* mensonge *m* **2** *v/i* mentir

lie[2] [laɪ] *v/i of person (lie down)* s'allonger; *(be lying down)* être allongé; *of object* être; *(be situated)* être, se trouver

◆ **lie down** se coucher

lieutenant [luːˈtenənt] lieutenant *m*

life [laɪf] vie *f*; **life expectancy** espérance *f* de vie; **lifeguard** maître nageur *m*; **life imprisonment** emprisonnement *m* à vie; **life insurance** assurance-vie *f*; **life jacket** gilet *m* de sauvetage; **lifeless** *body* inanimé; *personality* mou; *town* mort; **lifelike** réaliste; **lifelong** de toute une vie; **life-sized** grandeur nature; **life support** (équipement *m* de) maintien *m* artificiel; **life-threatening** *illness* extrêmement grave; **lifetime** vie *f*; *in my* ~ de mon vivant

lift [lɪft] **1** *v/t* soulever **2** *v/i of fog* se lever **3** *n Br* (*elevator*) ascenseur *m*; **give s.o. a ~ in car** emmener qn en voiture; **lift-off** *of rocket* décollage *m*

ligament ['lɪgəmənt] ligament *m*

light¹ [laɪt] **1** *n* lumière *f*; **do you have a ~?** vous avez du feu? **2** *v/t fire, cigarette* allumer; (*illuminate*) éclairer **3** *adj* (*not dark*) clair

light² [laɪt] *adj* (*not heavy*) léger

◆ **light up 1** *v/t* éclairer **2** *v/i* (*start to smoke*) s'allumer une cigarette

'light bulb ampoule *f*

lighten¹ ['laɪtn] *color* éclaircir

lighten² ['laɪtn] *load* alléger

lighter ['laɪtər] *for cigarettes* briquet *m*; **light-headed** étourdi; **lighting** éclairage *m*

lightness *of room, color* clarté *f*; *in weight* légèreté *f*; **lightning** *éclair m*, foudre *f*; **lightweight** *in boxing* poids *m* léger; **light year** année-lumière *f*

like¹ [laɪk] **1** *prep* comme; **be**

~ *s.o./sth* ressembler à qn/qch; **what is she ~?** comment est-elle?; **it's not ~ him** not his character ça ne lui ressemble pas **2** *conj F* (*as*) comme; ~ *I said* comme je l'ai dit

like² [laɪk] *v/t* aimer; *I ~ it* ça me plaît (bien); *I ~ Susie* j'aime bien Susie; *romantically* Susie me plaît (bien); *I would ~ ...* je voudrais, j'aimerais ...; *I would ~ to leave* je voudrais or j'aimerais partir; *would you ~ ...?* voulez-vous...?; *would you ~ to ...?* as-tu envie de ...?; *~ to do sth* aimer faire qch; *if you ~* si vous voulez; **likeable** agréable, plaisant; **likelihood** probabilité *f*; **likely** probable; **likeness** ressemblance *f*; **likewise** de même, aussi; **liking** *for person* affection *f*; *for sth* penchant *m*

limb [lɪm] membre *m*

lime¹ [laɪm] *fruit* citron *m* vert; *tree* limettier *m*

lime² [laɪm] *substance* chaux *f*

limit ['lɪmɪt] **1** *n* limite *f* **2** *v/t* limiter; **limitation** limitation *f*; **limited company** *Br* société *f* à responsabilité limitée

limousine ['lɪməziːn] limousine *f*

limp¹ [lɪmp] *adj* mou

limp² [lɪmp] **1** *n* claudication *f*; **he has a ~** il boite **2** *v/i* boiter

line¹ [laɪn] *n* ligne *f*; RAIL voie

living room

f; of people file *f; of trees* rangée *f; of poem* vers *m;* **stand in ~** faire la queue

line² ['laɪn] *v/t with material* recouvrir, garnir; *clothes* doubler

linear ['lɪnɪər] linéaire

linen ['lɪnɪn] *material* lin *m;* *(sheets etc)* linge *m*

liner ['laɪnər] *ship* paquebot *m* de grande ligne

linesman ['laɪnzmən] SP juge *m* de touche; *tennis* juge *m* de ligne

linger ['lɪŋgər] *of person* s'attarder; *of pain* persister

lingerie ['læŋʒəriː] lingerie *f*

linguist ['lɪŋgwɪst] linguiste *m;* **linguistic** linguistique

lining ['laɪnɪŋ] *of clothes* doublure *f; of brakes, pipes* garniture *f*

link [lɪŋk] **1** *n* lien *m; in chain* maillon *m* **2** *v/t* lier, relier

lion ['laɪən] lion *m*

lip [lɪp] lèvre *f*

liposuction ['lɪpoʊsʌkʃən] liposuccion *f*

'lipread lire sur les lèvres; **lipstick** rouge *m* à lèvres

liqueur [lɪ'kjʊr] liqueur *f*

liquid ['lɪkwɪd] **1** *n* liquide *m* **2** *adj* liquide; **liquidate** liquider; **liquidation** liquidation *f;* **go into ~** entrer en liquidation; **liquidity** FIN liquidité *f;* **liquidize** passer au mixeur; **liquidizer** mixeur *m*

liquor ['lɪkər] alcool *m;* **liquor store** magasin *m* de vins et

spiritueux

lisp [lɪsp] **1** *n* zézaiement *m* **2** *v/i* zézayer

list [lɪst] **1** *n* liste *f* **2** *v/t* faire la liste de; *(enumerate)* énumérer

listen ['lɪsn] écouter

♦ **listen to** écouter

listener ['lɪsnər] *to radio* auditeur(-trice) *m(f)*

listless ['lɪstlɪs] amorphe

liter ['liːtər] litre *m*

literal ['lɪtərəl] littéral; **literally** littéralement

literary ['lɪtəreri] littéraire; **literature** littérature *f; about a product* documentation *f*

litre ['liːtər] Br → **liter**

litter ['lɪtər] détritus *mpl,* ordures *fpl; of animal* portée *f*

little ['lɪtl] **1** *adj* petit **2** *n* peu *m;* **a ~ wine** un peu de vin **3** *adv* peu; **a ~ bigger** un peu plus gros

live¹ [lɪv] *v/i* vivre

live² [laɪv] *adj broadcast* en direct; *bomb* non désamorcé

♦ **live up to** être à la hauteur de

livelihood ['laɪvlɪhʊd] gagne-pain *m inv;* **liveliness** vivacité *f;* **lively** *person, city* plein de vie; *party* animé; *music* entraînant

liver ['lɪvər] foie *m*

livestock ['laɪvstɑːk] bétail *m*

livid ['lɪvɪd] *(angry)* furieux

living ['lɪvɪŋ] **1** *adj* vivant **2** *n* vie *f;* **living room** salle *f* de séjour

lizard ['lɪzərd] lézard *m*

load [loud] **1** *n* charge *f* **2** *v/t* charger

loaf [louf]: *a ~ of bread* un pain

◆ **loaf around** F traîner

loafer ['loufər] *shoe* mocassin *m*

loan [loun] **1** *n* prêt *m* **2** *v/t* ~ *s.o. sth* prêter qch à qn

loathe [louð] détester; **loathing** dégoût *m*

lobby ['lɑːbɪ] *in hotel* hall *m*; *in theater* vestibule *m*; POL lobby *m*

lobe [loub] *of ear* lobe *m*

lobster ['lɑːbstər] homard *m*

local ['loukl] **1** *adj* local **2** *n* habitant *m* de la région/du quartier; **local call** TELEC appel *m* local; **local elections** élections *fpl* locales; **local government** autorités *f* locales; **locality** endroit *m*; **localize** localiser; **locally** *live, work* dans le quartier, dans la région; **local time** heure *f* locale

locate [lou'keit] *new factory etc* établir; *(identify position of)* localiser; **be ~d** se trouver; **location** *(siting)* emplacement *m*; *(identifying position of)* localisation *f*; **on ~** *movie* en extérieur

lock¹ [lɑːk] *n of hair* mèche *f*

lock² [lɑːk] **1** *n on door* serrure *f* **2** *v/t door* fermer à clef

◆ **lock up** *in prison* mettre sous les verrous

locker ['lɑːkər] casier *m*; **locker room** vestiaire *m*

locust ['loukəst] locuste *f*, sauterelle *f*

lodge [lɑːdʒ] **1** *v/t complaint* déposer **2** *v/i of bullet* se loger

lofty ['lɑːftɪ] *heights* haut; *ideals* élevé

log [lɑːg] bûche *f*; *(written record)* journal *m* de bord

◆ **log in** se connecter (*to* à)

◆ **log off** se déconnecter

◆ **log on** se connecter (*to* à)

◆ **log out** se déconnecter

log 'cabin cabane *f* en rondins

logic ['lɑːdʒɪk] logique *f*; **logical** logique; **logically** logiquement

logistics [lə'dʒɪstɪks] logistique *f*

logo ['lougou] logo *m*, sigle *m*

loiter ['lɔɪtər] traîner

lollipop ['lɑːlɪpɑːp] sucette *f*

London ['lʌndən] Londres

loneliness ['lounlɪnɪs] *of person* solitude *f*; *of place* isolement *m*; **lonely** *person* seul, solitaire; *place* isolé; **loner** solitaire *m/f*

long¹ [lɑːŋ] **1** *adj* long; **it's a ~ way** c'est loin **2** *adv* longtemps; **how ~ will it take?** combien de temps cela va-t-il prendre?; **he no ~er works here** il ne travaille plus ici; **so ~ as** *(provided)* pourvu que; **so ~!** à bientôt!

long² [lɑːŋ] *v/i*: ~ **for sth** avoir très envie de qch; **be ~ing to** *do sth* avoir très envie de faire qch

long-'distance *phonecall* longue distance; *race* de fond; *flight* long-courrier; **longevity** longévité *f*; **longing** désir *m*, envie *f*; **longitude** longitude *f*; **long jump** saut *m* en longueur; **long-range** *missile* à longue portée; *forecast* à long terme; **long-sleeved** à manches longues; **long-standing** de longue date; **long-term** à long terme; ~ **unemployment** de longue durée

loo [luː] *Br F* toilettes *fpl*

look [luk] **1** *n* (*appearance*) air *m*; (*glance*) coup *m* d'œil, regard *m*; ~**s** (*beauty*) beauté *f* **2** *v/i* regarder; (*search*) chercher, regarder; (*seem*) avoir l'air

◆ **look after** s'occuper de

◆ **look ahead** *fig* regarder en avant

◆ **look around** jeter un coup d'œil

◆ **look at** regarder; (*examine*) examiner; (*consider*) envisager

◆ **look back** regarder derrière soi

◆ **look down on** mépriser

◆ **look for** chercher

◆ **look into** (*investigate*) examiner

◆ **look onto** *garden etc* donner sur sur

◆ **look out** *of window etc* regarder dehors; (*pay attention*) faire attention

◆ **look over** *house, translation* examiner

◆ **look through** *magazine, notes* parcourir, feuilleter

◆ **look up 1** *v/i from paper etc* lever les yeux; (*improve*) s'améliorer **2** *v/t word, phone number* chercher; (*visit*) passer voir

◆ **look up to** (*respect*) respecter

'lookout *person* sentinelle *f*; **be on the ~** être à l'affût de

loop [luːp] boucle *f*; **loophole** *in law etc* lacune *f*

loose [luːs] *knot* lâche; *connection, screw* desserré; *clothes* ample; *morals* relâché; *wording* vague; ~ **change** petite monnaie *f*; **loosely** *worded* de manière approximative; **loosen** desserrer

loot [luːt] **1** *n* butin *m* **2** *v/i* se livrer au pillage; **looter** pilleur(-euse) *m(f)*

lop-sided [lɑːpˈsaɪdɪd] déséquilibré, disproportionné

Lord [lɔːrd] (*god*) Seigneur *m*

lorry [ˈlɑːrɪ] *Br* camion *m*

lose [luːz] *v/t* perdre **2** *v/i* SP perdre; *of clock* retarder; **loser** perdant(e) *m(f)*

loss [lɑːs] perte *f*

lost [lɑːst] perdu; **lost-and--found**, *Br* **lost property (office)** (bureau *m* des) objets *mpl* trouvés

lot [lɑːt]: **a ~ (of)**, **~s (of)** beaucoup (de)

lotion ['louʃn] lotion *f*

lottery ['lɑːtəri] loterie *f*

loud [laud] *music, voice* fort; *noise* grand; *color* criard; **loudspeaker** haut-parleur *m*

louse [laus] pou *m*; **lousy** F minable F , mauvais

lout [laut] rustre *m*

lovable ['lʌvəbl] sympathique, adorable; **love 1** *n* amour *m*; *in tennis* zéro *m*; **fall in ~** tomber amoureux (**with** de); **make ~** faire l'amour (**to** avec) **2** *v/t* aimer; *wine, music* adorer; **love affair** aventure *f*; **lovely** *beau; house, wife* ravissant; *character* charmant; *meal* délicieux; **lover** *man* amant *m*; *woman* maîtresse *f*; *person in love* amoureux(-euse) *m(f)*; **loving** affectueux; **lovingly** avec amour

low [lou] **1** *adj* bas; *quality* mauvais **2** *n in weather* dépression *f*; *in statistics* niveau *m* bas; **lowbrow** peu intellectuel; **low-calorie** hypocalorique; **low-cut** *dress* décolleté; **lower** baisser; *to the ground* faire descendre; **low-fat** allégé; **lowkey** discret, mesuré

loyal ['lɔɪəl] fidèle, loyal; **loyally** fidèlement; **loyalty** loyauté *f*

lozenge ['lɑːzɪndʒ] *shape* losange *m*; *tablet* pastille *f*

Ltd (= **limited**) **company** à responsabilité limitée

lubricant ['luːbrɪkənt] lubrifiant *m*; **lubricate** lubrifier; **lubrication** lubrification *f*

lucid ['luːsɪd] (*clear*) clair; (*sane*) lucide

luck [lʌk] chance *f*; **good ~!** bonne chance!; **luckily** heureusement; **lucky** *person* chanceux; *number* porte-bonheur *inv*; *coincidence* heureux; **you were ~** tu as eu de la chance

lucrative ['luːkrətɪv] lucratif *m*

ludicrous ['luːdɪkrəs] ridicule

lug [lʌg] F traîner

luggage ['lʌgɪdʒ] bagages *mpl*

lukewarm ['luːkwɔːrm] *also fig* tiède

lull [lʌl] *in storm, fighting* accalmie *f*; *in conversation* pause *f*

lumber ['lʌmbər] (*timber*) bois *m* de construction

luminous ['luːmɪnəs] lumineux

lump [lʌmp] *of sugar* morceau *m*; (*swelling*) grosseur *f*; **lump sum** forfait *m*; **lumpy** *liquid, sauce* grumeleux; *mattress* défoncé

lunacy ['luːnəsɪ] folie *f*

lunar ['luːnər] lunaire

lunatic ['luːnətɪk] fou *m*, folle *f*

lunch [lʌntʃ] déjeuner *m*; **have ~** déjeuner; **lunch box** panier-repas *m*; **lunch**

break pause-déjeuner *f*;
lunchtime heure *f* du déjeuner, midi *m*
lung [lʌŋ] poumon *m*
lurch [lɜːrtʃ] *of person* tituber;
of ship tanguer
lure [lur] **1** *n* appât *m* **2** *v/t* attirer
lurid ['lurɪd] *color* cru; *details*
choquant

lurk [lɜːrk] *of person* se cacher
lush [lʌʃ] *vegetation* luxuriant
lust [lʌst] désir *m*
luxurious [lʌg'ʒurɪəs]
luxueux; **luxuriously** lu-
xueusement; **luxury 1** *n* luxe
m **2** *adj* de luxe
lynch [lɪntʃ] lyncher
lyrics ['lɪrɪks] paroles *fpl*

M

ma'am [mæm] madame
machine [mə'ʃiːn] machine *f*;
  machine gun mitrailleuse *f*;
  machinery machines *fpl*
machismo [mə'kɪzmou] machisme *m*
macho ['mætʃou] macho *inv*;
  ~ type macho *m*
macro ['mækrou] COMPUT macro *f*
mad [mæd] (*insane*) fou; F (*angry*) furieux; **madden** (*infuriate*) exaspérer; **maddening**
exaspérant; **madhouse** *fig*
maison *f* de fous; **madman**
fou *m*; **madness** folie *f*
Madonna [mə'dɑːnə] Madon-
ne *f*
Mafia ['mɑːfɪə]: **the ~** la Mafia
magazine [mægə'ziːn]
printed magazine *m*
Magi ['meɪdʒaɪ] REL: **the ~** les
Rois *mpl* mages
magic ['mædʒɪk] **1** *adj* magique **2** *n* magie *f*; **magical** magique; **magician** *performer*

prestidigitateur(-trice) *m(f)*
magnanimous
  [mæg'nænɪməs] magnanime
magnet ['mægnɪt] aimant *m*;
  magnetic *also fig* magnétique; **magnetism** *also fig* ma-
gnétisme *m*
magnificence [mæg'nɪfɪ-
səns] magnificence *f*; **magnificent** magnifique
magnify ['mægnɪfaɪ] grossir;
  difficulties exagérer; **magnifying glass** loupe *f*
magnitude ['mægnɪtuːd] ampleur *f*
maid [meɪd] *servant* domestique *f*; *in hotel* femme *f* de
chambre
maiden name ['meɪdn] nom
m de jeune fille
mail [meɪl] **1** *n* courrier *m*,
poste *f* **2** *v/t letter* poster;
mailbox boîte *f* aux lettres;
mailing list fichier *m*
d'adresses; **mailman** facteur
m; **mailshot** mailing *m*, pu-

bliepostage *m*

maim [meɪm] estropier, mutiler

main [meɪn] principal; **main course** plat *m* principal; **mainframe** ordinateur *m* central; **mainly** principalement; **main road** route *f* principale; **main street** rue *f* principale

maintain [meɪn'teɪn] *peace, law and order* maintenir; *speed* soutenir; *relationship, machine, building* entretenir; *innocence, guilt* affirmer; **maintenance** *of machine, building* entretien *m*; *Br money* pension *f* alimentaire; *of law and order* maintien *m*

majestic [mə'dʒestɪk] majestueux

major ['meɪdʒər] **1** *adj* (*significant*) important, majeur **2** *n* MIL commandant *m*
♦ **major in** se spécialiser en

majority [mə'dʒɑːrətɪ] *also* POL majorité *f*

make [meɪk] **1** *n* (*brand*) marque *f* **2** *v/t* faire; (*manufacture*) fabriquer; (*earn*) gagner; *decision* prendre; *3 and 3 ~ 6* 3 et 3 font 6; *~ it* (*catch bus, train*) arriver à temps; (*come*) venir; (*succeed*) réussir; (*survive*) s'en sortir; *what time do you ~ it?* quelle heure as-tu?; *~ believe* prétendre; *~ do with* se contenter de, faire avec;

what do you ~ of it? qu'en dis-tu?; *~ s.o. do sth* (*force to*) forcer qn à faire qch; (*cause to*) faire faire qch à qn; *~ s.o. happy/angry* rendre qn heureux/furieux
♦ **make out** *list, check* faire; (*see*) distinguer; (*imply*) prétendre
♦ **make up 1** *v/i of woman, actor* se maquiller; *after quarrel* se réconcilier **2** *v/t story* inventer; *face* maquiller; (*constitute*) constituer
♦ **make up for** compenser
'make-believe: *it's just ~* c'est juste pour faire semblant

maker ['meɪkər] (*manufacturer*) fabricant *m*; **makeshift** de fortune; **make-up** (*cosmetics*) maquillage *m*

maladjusted [mælə'dʒʌstɪd] inadapté

male [meɪl] **1** *adj* masculin; *animal* mâle **2** *n* (*man*) homme *m*; *animal, bird* mâle *m*; **male chauvinism** machisme *m*; **male chauvinist pig** macho *m*

malevolent [mə'levələnt] malveillant

malfunction [mæl'fʌŋkʃn] **1** *n* mauvais fonctionnement *m*, défaillance *f* **2** *v/i* mal fonctionner

malice ['mælɪs] méchanceté *f*, malveillance *f*; **malicious** méchant, malveillant

malignant [mə'lɪgnənt] *tumor* malin

mall [mɔ:l] (*shopping ~*) centre *m* commercial

malnutrition [mælnu:'trɪʃn] malnutrition *f*

maltreat [mæl'tri:t] maltraiter; **maltreatment** mauvais traitement *m*

mammal ['mæml] mammifère *m*

man [mæn] **1** *n* (*pl* **men** [men]) homme *m*; (*humanity*) l'homme *m*; *in checkers* pion *m* **2** *v/t telephones* être de permanence à; *front desk* être de service à

manage ['mænɪdʒ] **1** *v/t business* diriger; *money* gérer; *bags* porter; *~ to ...* réussir à ... **2** *v/i* (*cope*) se débrouiller; **manageable** gérable; *vehicle* maniable; *task* faisable; **management** (*managing*) gestion *f*, direction *f*; (*managers*) direction *f*; **management consultant** conseiller(-ère) *m*(*f*) en gestion; **manager** directeur(-trice) *m*(*f*); *of store, restaurant, hotel* gérant(e) *m*(*f*); *of department* responsable *m*/*f*; *of singer, band, team* manageur(-euse) *m*(*f*); **managerial** de directeur, de gestionnaire; **managing director** directeur(-trice) *m*(*f*) général(e)

mandate ['mændeɪt] mandat *m*; **mandatory** obligatoire

maneuver [mə'nu:vər] **1** *n* manœuvre *f* **2** *v/t* manœuvrer

mangle ['mæŋgl] (*crush*) broyer

manhandle ['mænhændl] *person* malmener; *object* déplacer manuellement

manhood ['mænhʊd] (*maturity*) âge *m* d'homme; (*virility*) virilité *f*; **manhunt** chasse *f* à l'homme

mania ['meɪnɪə] (*craze*) manie *f*; **maniac** F fou *m*, folle *f*

manicure ['mænɪkjʊr] manicure *f*

manifest ['mænɪfest] **1** *adj* manifeste **2** *v/t* manifester

manipulate [mə'nɪpjəleɪt] manipuler; **manipulation** manipulation *f*; **manipulative** manipulateur

mankind humanité *f*; **manly** viril; **man-made** synthétique

manner ['mænər] *of doing sth* manière *f*, façon *f*; (*attitude*) comportement *m*; **manners** manières *fpl*

manoeuvre [mə'nu:vər] *Br →* **maneuver**

'manpower main-d'œuvre *f*

manual ['mænjʊəl] **1** *adj* manuel **2** *n* manuel *m*; **manually** manuellement

manufacture [mænju:'fæktʃər] **1** *n* fabrication *f* **2** *v/t equipment* fabriquer; **manufacturer** fabricant *m*; **manufacturing** *industry* industrie *f*

manure [mə'nʊr] fumier *m*

manuscript ['mænjʊskrɪpt] manuscrit *m*

many ['menɪ] **1** *adj* beaucoup de; ~ **times** bien des fois; **too ~ problems** trop de problèmes; **as ~ as possible** autant que possible **2** *pron* beaucoup; **a great ~, a good ~** un bon nombre; **how ~ do you need?** combien en veux-tu?

map [mæp] carte *f*; *of town* plan *m*

maple ['meɪpl] érable *m*

mar [mɑːr] gâcher

marathon ['mærəθɑːn] *race* marathon *m*

marble ['mɑːbl] *material* marbre *m*

March [mɑːtʃ] mars *m*

march [mɑːtʃ] **1** *n also (demonstration)* marche *f* **2** *v/i* marcher au pas; *in protest* défiler; **marcher** manifestant(e) *m(f)*

Mardi Gras ['mɑːrdɪgrɑː] mardi *m* gras

margin ['mɑːrdʒɪn] *of page,* COM marge *f*; **marginal** *(slight)* léger; **marginally** *(slightly)* légèrement

marihuana, marijuana [mærɪ'hwɑːnə] marijuana *f*

marina [mə'riːnə] port *m* de plaisance

marine [mə'riːn] **1** *adj* marin **2** *n* MIL marine *m*

marital ['mærɪtl] conjugal; **marital status** situation *f* de famille

maritime ['mærɪtaɪm] maritime

mark [mɑːrk] **1** *n* marque *f*; *(stain)* tache *f*; *(sign, token)* signe *m*; *(trace)* trace *f*; *Br* EDU note *f* **2** *v/t* marquer; *(stain)* tacher; *Br* EDU noter **3** *v/i of fabric* se tacher; **marked** *(definite)* marqué; **marker** *(highlighter)* marqueur *m*

market ['mɑːrkɪt] **1** *n* marché *m* **2** *v/t* commercialiser; **marketable** commercialisable; **market economy** économie *f* de marché; **marketing** marketing *m*; **market leader** *product* produit *m* vedette; *company* leader *m* du marché; **market place** *in town* place *f* du marché; *for commodities* marché *m*; **market research** étude *f* de marché; **market share** part *f* du marché

mark-up ['mɑːrkʌp] majoration *f*

marriage ['mærɪdʒ] mariage *m*; **marriage certificate** acte *m* de mariage; **married** marié; **be ~ to** être marié à; **married life** vie *f* conjugale; **marry** épouser, se marier avec; *of priest* marier; **get married** se marier

marsh [mɑːrʃ] *Br* marais *m*

marshal ['mɑːrʃl] *in police* chef *m* de la police; *in security service* membre *m* du service d'ordre

martial 'law loi *f* martiale

martyr ['mɑːrtər] *also fig* martyr(e) *m(f)*

marvel ['mɑːrvl] merveille *f*; **marvelous**, *Br* **marvellous** merveilleux

Marxism ['mɑːrksɪzm] marxisme *m*; **Marxist 1** *adj* marxiste **2** *n* marxiste *m/f*

mascara [mæ'skærə] mascara *m*

mascot ['mæskət] mascotte *f*

masculine ['mæskjʊlɪn] *also* GRAM masculin; **masculinity** masculinité *f*

mash [mæʃ] réduire en purée

mask [mæsk] **1** *n* masque *m* **2** *v/t feelings* masquer

masochism ['mæsəkɪzm] masochisme *m*; **masochist** masochiste *m/f*

mass¹ [mæs] **1** *n* (*great amount*) masse *f*; **~es of** F des tas de F **2** *v/i* se masser

mass² [mæs] *n* REL messe *f*

massacre ['mæsəkər] **1** *n* massacre *m* **2** *v/t also fig* F massacrer

massage ['mæsɑːʒ] **1** *n* massage *m* **2** *v/t* masser; *figures* manipuler

massive ['mæsɪv] énorme; *heart attack* grave

mass 'media médias *mpl*; **mass-produce** fabriquer en série; **mass production** fabrication *f* en série

mast [mæst] *of ship* mât *m*; *for radio signal* pylône *m*

master ['mæstər] **1** *n of dog* maître *m*; *of ship* capitaine *m* **2** *v/t* maîtriser; **master**

bedroom chambre *f* principale; **master key** passe-partout *m inv*; **masterly** magistral; **mastermind 1** *n* cerveau *m* **2** *v/t* organiser; **masterpiece** chef-d'œuvre *m*; **master's (degree)** maîtrise *f*; **mastery** maîtrise *f*

mat [mæt] *for floor* tapis *m*; *for table* napperon *m*

match¹ [mætʃ] *n for cigarette* allumette *f*

match² [mætʃ] **1** *n* (*competition*) match *m*, partie *f* **2** *v/t* (*be the same as*) être assorti à; (*equal*) égaler **3** *v/i of colors, patterns* aller ensemble; **matching** assorti; **match stick** allumette *f*

mate [meɪt] **1** *n of animal* mâle *m*, femelle *f*; NAUT second *m* **2** *v/i* s'accoupler

material [mə'tɪrɪəl] **1** *n* (*fabric*) tissu *m*; (*substance*) matériau *m*, matière *f* **2** *adj* matériel; **materialism** matérialisme *m*; **materialist** matérialiste *m/f*; **materialistic** matérialiste; **materialize** (*appear*) apparaître; (*happen*) se concrétiser

maternal [mə'tɜːrnl] maternel; **maternity** maternité *f*; **maternity leave** congé *m* de maternité

math [mæθ] maths *fpl*; **mathematical** mathématique; **mathematician** mathématicien(ne) *m(f)*; **maths** *Br* → **math**

matinée ['mætɪneɪ] matinée f
matriarch ['meɪtrɪɑːrk] femme f chef de famille
matrimony ['mætrəmoʊnɪ] mariage m
matt [mæt] mat
matter ['mætər] **1** n (affair) affaire f, question f; PHYS matière f; **what's the ~?** qu'est-ce qu'il y a? **2** v/i importer; **it doesn't ~** cela ne fait rien; **matter-of-fact** impassible
mattress ['mætrɪs] matelas m
mature [mə'tjʊr] **1** adj mûr **2** v/i of person mûrir; of insurance policy arriver à échéance; **maturity** maturité f
maximize ['mæksɪmaɪz] maximiser; **maximum 1** adj maximal, maximum **2** n maximum m
May [meɪ] mai m
may [meɪ] ◇ possibility: **it ~ rain** il va peut-être pleuvoir; **it ~ not happen** cela n'arrivera peut-être pas
◇ permission: pouvoir; **~ I help?** puis-je aider?
maybe ['meɪbɪ] peut-être
mayo, mayonnaise ['meɪoʊ, meɪə'neɪz] mayonnaise f
mayor ['meɪr] maire m
maze [meɪz] labyrinthe m
MB (= **megabyte**) Mo (= mégaoctet)
MBA [embiː'eɪ] (= **master of business administration**) MBA m
MD [em'diː] (= **Doctor of Med-**

icine) docteur m en médecine; (= **managing director**) DG m (= directeur général)
me [miː] me; before vowel m'; after prep moi; **he knows ~** il me connaît; **she gave ~ a dollar** elle m'a donné un dollar; **it's for ~** c'est pour moi; **it's ~** c'est moi
meadow ['medoʊ] pré m
meager, Br **meagre** ['miːgər] maigre
meal [miːl] repas m; **enjoy your ~!** bon appétit!
mean¹ [miːn] adj with money avare; (nasty) mesquin
mean² [miːn] v/t (signify) signifier, vouloir dire; **be ~t for** être destiné à; of remark être adressé à; **meaning of word** sens m; **meaningful** (comprehensible) compréhensible; (constructive) significatif; glance éloquent; **meaningless** sentence etc dénué de sens; gesture insignifiant
means [miːnz] financial moyens mpl; (way) moyen m; **by all ~** (certainly) bien sûr; **by ~ of** au moyen de
meantime ['miːntaɪm] entretemps
measles ['miːzlz] rougeole f
measure ['meʒər] **1** n (step) mesure f **2** v/t & v/i mesurer
◆ **measure up to** être à la hauteur de
measurement ['meʒərmənt] action mesure f; (dimension)

dimension *f*; **measuring tape** mètre *m* ruban

meat [miːt] viande *f*; **meatball** boulette *f* de viande

mechanic [mɪˈkænɪk] mécanicien(ne) *m(f)*; **mechanical device** mécanique; *gesture etc also* machinal; **mechanical engineer** ingénieur *m* mécanicien; **mechanically** mécaniquement; *do sth mechanically*: machinalement; **mechanism** mécanisme *m*; **mechanize** mécaniser

medal [ˈmedl] médaille *f*; **medalist**, *Br* **medallist** médaillé *m*

meddle [ˈmedl] se mêler (*in* de)

media [ˈmiːdɪə]: *the ~* les médias *mpl*; **media coverage** couverture *f* médiatique

median strip [miːdɪənˈstrɪp] terre-plein *m* central

'media studies études *fpl* de communication

mediate [ˈmiːdɪeɪt] arbitrer; **mediation** médiation *f*; **mediator** médiateur(-trice) *m(f)*

medical [ˈmedɪkl] **1** *adj* médical **2** *n* visite *f* médicale; **medicated** pharmaceutique, traitant; **medication** médicaments *mpl*; **medicinal** médicinal

medicine *science* médecine *f*; (*medication*) médicament *m*

medieval [medɪˈiːvl] médiéval

mediocre [miːdɪˈoʊkər] médiocre; **mediocrity** *of work etc* médiocrité *f*; *person* médiocre *m/f*

meditate [ˈmedɪteɪt] méditer; **meditation** méditation *f*

Mediterranean [medɪtəˈreɪnɪən] **1** *adj* méditerranéen **2** *n*: *the ~* la Méditerranée

medium [ˈmiːdɪəm] **1** *adj* (*average*) moyen; *steak* à point **2** *n in size* taille *f* moyenne; (*vehicle*) moyen *m*; (*spiritualist*) médium *m*

medley [ˈmedlɪ] (*assortment*) mélange *m*

meet [miːt] **1** *v/t* rencontrer; (*be introduced to*) faire la connaissance de; (*collect*) (aller/venir) chercher; *in competition* affronter; *of eyes* croiser; (*satisfy*) satisfaire **2** *v/i* se rencontrer; *by appointment* se retrouver; *of committee etc* se réunir **3** *n* SP rencontre *f*; **meeting** *by accident* rencontre *f*; *in business, of committee* réunion *f*; *he's in a ~* il est en réunion

megabyte [ˈmegəbaɪt] COMPUT méga-octet *m*

mellow [ˈmeloʊ] **1** *adj* doux **2** *v/i of person* s'adoucir

melodious [mɪˈloʊdɪəs] mélodieux

melodramatic [melədrəˈmætɪk] mélodramatique

melody [ˈmelədɪ] mélodie *f*

melon [ˈmelən] melon *m*

melt [melt] **1** *v/i* fondre **2** *v/t*

faire fondre; **melting pot** fig creuset m

member ['membər] membre m; **Member of Congress** membre m du Congrès; **membership** adhésion f; number of members membres mpl

membrane ['membreɪn] membrane f

memento [me'mentoʊ] souvenir m

memo ['memoʊ] note f (de service)

memoirs ['memwɑːrz] mémoires fpl

memorable ['memərəbl] mémorable

memorial [mɪ'mɔːrɪəl] **1** adj commémoratif **2** n mémorial m; **Memorial Day** jour commémoration des soldats américains morts à la guerre

memorize ['meməraɪz] apprendre par cœur; **memory** mémoire f; sth remembered souvenir m

men [men] pl → **man**

menace ['menɪs] **1** n menace f; person danger m **2** v/t menacer; **menacing** menaçant

mend [mend] réparer; clothes raccommoder

menial ['miːnɪəl] subalterne

menopause ['menoʊpɔːz] ménopause f

'men's room toilettes fpl pour hommes

menstruate ['menstrʊeɪt] avoir ses règles

mental ['mentl] mental; ability, powers intellectuel; health, suffering moral; F (crazy) malade F; **mental hospital** hôpital m psychiatrique; **mental illness** maladie f mentale; **mentality** mentalité f; **mentally** (inwardly) intérieurement; calculate etc mentalement

mention ['menʃn] **1** n mention f **2** v/t mentionner; **don't ~ it** (you're welcome) il n'y a pas de quoi!

mentor ['mentɔːr] mentor m

menu ['menjuː] also COMPUT menu m

mercenary ['mɜːrsɪnerɪ] **1** adj intéressé **2** n MIL mercenaire m

merchandise ['mɜːrtʃəndaɪz] marchandises fpl

merchant ['mɜːrtʃənt] négociant m, commerçant m

merciful ['mɜːrsɪfl] clément; God miséricordieux; **mercifully** (thankfully) heureusement; **merciless** impitoyable; **mercy** clémence f, pitié f

mere [mɪr] simple; **merely** simplement, seulement

merge [mɜːrdʒ] of two lines etc se rejoindre; of companies fusionner; **merger** COM fusion f

merit ['merɪt] **1** n mérite m **2** v/t mériter

mesh [meʃ] of net maille(s) f(pl); of grid grillage m

mess [mes] (*untidiness*) désordre *m*, pagaille *f*; (*trouble*) gâchis *m*

message ['mesɪdʒ] *also of movie* message *m*

messenger ['mesɪndʒər] (*courier*) messager *m*

messy ['mesɪ] *room* en désordre; *person* désordonné; *job* salissant; *divorce* pénible

metabolism [məˈtæbəlɪzm] métabolisme *m*

metal ['metl] **1** *adj* en métal **2** *n* métal *m*; **metallic** métallique; *paint* métallisé

metaphor ['metəfər] métaphore *f*

meteor ['miːtɪər] météore *m*; **meteoric** *fig* fulgurant; **meteorite** météorite *m* or *f*

meteorological [miːtɪərə-ˈlɑːdʒɪkl] météorologique; **meteorologist** météorologiste *m*/*f*; **meteorology** météorologie *f*

meter¹ ['miːtər] *for gas, electricity* compteur *m*; (*parking* ~) parcmètre *m*

meter² ['miːtər] *unit of length* mètre *m*

method ['meθəd] méthode *f*; **methodical** méthodique

meticulous [məˈtɪkjʊləs] méticuleux

metre ['miːtə(r)] *Br* → **meter²**

metropolis [məˈtrɑːpəlɪs] métropole *f*; **metropolitan** citadin; *area* urbain

mew [mjuː] → **miaow**

Mexican ['meksɪkən] **1** *adj*

mexicain **2** *n* Mexicain(e) *m*(*f*); **Mexico** Mexique *m*

miaow [mɪaʊ] **1** *n* miaou *m* **2** *v/i* miauler

mice [maɪs] *pl* → **mouse**

'microchip puce *f*; **microclimate** microclimat *m*; **microcosm** microcosme *m*; **microorganism** micro-organisme *m*; **microphone** microphone *m*; **microprocessor** microprocesseur *m*; **microscope** microscope *m*; **microscopic** microscopique; **microwave oven** micro-ondes *m inv*

midday [mɪdˈdeɪ] midi *m*

middle ['mɪdl] **1** *adj* du milieu **2** *n* milieu *m*; **be in the ~ of doing sth** être en train de faire qch; **middle-aged** entre deux âges; **middle-class** bourgeois; **middle class(es)** classe(s) moyenne(s) *f*(*pl*); **Middle East** Moyen-Orient *m*; **middleman** intermédiaire *m*; **middle name** deuxième prénom *m*; **middleweight** *boxer* poids moyen *m*

midfielder [mɪdˈfiːldər] *in soccer* milieu *m* de terrain

midget ['mɪdʒɪt] miniature

'midnight minuit *m*; **midsummer** milieu *m* de l'été; **midweek** en milieu de semaine; **Midwest** Middle West *m*; **midwife** sage-femme *f*; **midwinter** milieu *m* de l'hiver

might¹ [maɪt] *v/aux*: **I ~ be late** je serai peut-être en retard; **you ~ have told me!**

vous auriez pu m'avertir!

might² [maɪt] *n (power)* puissance *f*

mighty ['maɪtɪ] **1** *adj* puissant **2** *adv* F *(extremely)* vachement F, très

migraine ['miːgreɪn] migraine *f*

migrant worker ['maɪgrənt] travailleur *m* itinérant; **migrate** migrer; **migration** migration *f*

mike [maɪk] F micro *m*

mild [maɪld] doux; *taste* léger; **mildly** doucement; *spicy* légèrement; **mildness** douceur *f; of taste* légèreté *f*

mile [maɪl] mile *m*; **milestone** *fig* événement *m* marquant, jalon *m*

militant ['mɪlɪtənt] **1** *adj* militant **2** *n* militant(e) *m(f)*

military ['mɪlɪterɪ] **1** *adj* militaire **2** *n:* **the** ~ l'armée *f*

militia [mɪ'lɪʃə] milice *f*

milk [mɪlk] **1** *n* lait *m* **2** *v/t* traire; **milk chocolate** chocolat *m* au lait; **milkshake** milk-shake *m*

mill [mɪl] *for grain* moulin *m*; *for textiles* usine *f*

millennium [mɪ'lenɪəm] millénaire *m*

milligram ['mɪlɪgræm] milligramme *m*

millimeter, *Br* **millimetre** ['mɪlɪmiːtər] millimètre *m*

million ['mɪljən] million *m*

millionaire [mɪljə'ner] millionaire *m/f*

mime [maɪm] mimer

mimic ['mɪmɪk] **1** *n* imitateur(-trice) *m(f)* **2** *v/t* imiter

mince [mɪns] hacher

mind [maɪnd] **1** *n* esprit *m*; **bear** *or* **keep sth in** ~ ne pas oublier qch; **change one's** ~ changer d'avis; **make up one's** ~ se décider; **have sth on one's** ~ être préoccupé par qch; **keep one's** ~ **on sth** se concentrer sur qch **2** *v/t (look after)* surveiller; *(heed)* faire attention à; **I don't** ~ **what he thinks** il peut penser ce qu'il veut, cela m'est égal; **do you** ~ **if I smoke?** cela ne vous dérange pas si je fume?; ~ **the step!** attention à la marche! **3** *v/i:* ~**!** *(be careful)* fais attention!; **never** ~**!** peu importe!; **I don't** ~ cela m'est égal; **mind-boggling** ahurissant; **mindless** *violence* gratuit

mine¹ [maɪn] *pron* le mien *m*, la mienne *f; pl* les miens, les miennes; **it's** ~ c'est à moi

mine² [maɪn] *n for coal etc* mine *f*

mine³ [maɪn] **1** *n explosive* mine *f* **2** *v/t* miner; **minefield** MIL champ *m* de mines; *fig* poudrière *f*; **miner** mineur *m*

mineral ['mɪnərəl] minéral *m*; **mineral water** eau *f* minérale

'minesweeper NAUT dragueur *m* de mines

mingle ['mɪŋgl] *of sounds* se

mélanger; *at party* se mêler (aux gens)

mini ['mɪnɪ] *skirt* minijupe *f*

miniature ['mɪnɪtʃər] miniature

minimal ['mɪnɪməl] minime; **minimalism** minimalisme *m*; **minimize** réduire au minimum; (*downplay*) minimiser; **minimum 1** *adj* minimal, minimum **2** *n* minimum *m*

mining ['maɪnɪŋ] exploitation *f* minière

'**miniskirt** minijupe *f*

minister ['mɪnɪstər] POL, REL ministre *m*; **ministerial** ministériel

mink [mɪŋk] vison *m*

minor ['maɪnər] **1** *adj* mineur; *pain* léger **2** *n* LAW mineur(e) *m(f)*; **minority** minorité *f*

mint [mɪnt] *herb* menthe *f*; *chocolate* chocolat *m* à la menthe; *hard candy* bonbon *m* à la menthe

minus ['maɪnəs] **1** *n* (~ *sign*) moins *m* **2** *prep* moins

minuscule ['mɪnəskjuːl] minuscule

minute[1] ['mɪnɪt] *n of time* minute *f*

minute[2] [maɪ'nuːt] *adj* (*tiny*) minuscule; (*detailed*) minutieux

'**minute hand** ['mɪnɪt] grande aiguille *f*

minutely [maɪ'nuːtlɪ] (*in detail*) minutieusement; (*very slightly*) très légèrement

minutes ['mɪnɪts] *of meeting*

procès-verbal *m*

miracle ['mɪrəkl] miracle *m*; **miraculous** miraculeux; **miraculously** par miracle

mirror ['mɪrər] **1** *n* miroir *m*; MOT rétroviseur *m* **2** *v/t* refléter

misanthropist [mɪ'zænθrəpɪst] misanthrope *m/f*

misbehave [mɪsbə'heɪv] se conduire mal

misbehavior, *Br* **misbehaviour** mauvaise conduite *f*

miscalculate [mɪs'kælkjuleɪt] mal calculer; **miscalculation** erreur *f* de calcul; *fig* mauvais calcul *m*

miscarriage ['mɪskærɪdʒ] MED fausse couche *f*

miscellaneous [mɪsə'leɪnɪəs] divers; *collection* varié

mischief ['mɪstʃɪf] (*naughtiness*) bêtises *fpl*; **mischievous** (*naughty*) espiègle; (*malicious*) malveillant

misconception [mɪskən'sepʃn] idée *f* fausse

misconduct [mɪs'kɑːndʌkt] mauvaise conduite *f*

misconstrue [mɪskən'struː] mal interpréter

misdemeanor, *Br* **misdemeanour** [mɪsdə'miːnər] délit *m*

miser ['maɪzər] avare *m/f*

miserable ['mɪzrəbl] (*unhappy*) malheureux; *weather*, *performance* épouvantable

miserly ['maɪzrlɪ] avare; *sum* dérisoire

misery ['mɪzərɪ] (*unhappiness*) tristesse *f*; (*wretchedness*) misère *f*

misfire [mɪs'faɪr] *of scheme* rater; *of joke* tomber à plat

misfit ['mɪsfɪt] *in society* marginal(e) *m(f)*

misfortune [mɪs'fɔ:rtʃən] malheur *m*, malchance *f*

misguided [mɪs'gaɪdɪd] malavisé, imprudent

mishandle [mɪs'hændl] *situation* mal gérer

misinform [mɪsɪn'fɔ:rm] mal informer

misinterpret [mɪsɪn'tɜ:rprɪt] mal interpréter; **misinterpretation** mauvaise interprétation *f*

misjudge [mɪs'dʒʌdʒ] mal juger

mislay [mɪs'leɪ] égarer

mislead [mɪs'li:d] induire en erreur, tromper; **misleading** trompeur

mismanage [mɪs'mænɪdʒ] mal gérer; **mismanagement** mauvaise gestion *f*

misprint ['mɪsprɪnt] faute *f* typographique

mispronounce [mɪsprə'naʊns] mal prononcer; **mispronunciation** mauvaise prononciation *f*

misread [mɪs'ri:d] *word, figures* mal lire; *situation* mal interpréter

misrepresent [mɪsreprɪ'zent] présenter sous un faux jour

miss¹ [mɪs]: **Miss Smith** mademoiselle Smith; **~!** mademoiselle!

miss² [mɪs] **1** *n* sp coup *m* manqué **2** *v/t* manquer, rater; *bus, train etc*, (*not notice*) rater; *I ~ you* tu me manques **3** *v/i* rater son coup

misshapen [mɪs'ʃeɪpən] déformé; *person, limb* difforme

missile ['mɪsəl] *mil* missile *m*; *stone etc* projectile *m*

missing ['mɪsɪŋ]: **be ~** *have disappeared* avoir disparu; *member of school party, one of a set etc* ne pas être là

mission ['mɪʃn] mission *f*

misspell [mɪs'spel] mal orthographier

mist [mɪst] brume *f*

mistake [mɪ'steɪk] **1** *n* erreur *f*, faute *f*; **make a ~** faire une erreur, se tromper **2** *v/t* se tromper de; **~ s.o./sth for s.o./sth** prendre qn/qch pour qn/qch d'autre; **mistaken** erroné, faux; **be ~** faire erreur, se tromper

mister ['mɪstər] → **Mr**

mistress ['mɪstrɪs] maîtresse *f*

mistrust [mɪs'trʌst] **1** *n* méfiance *f* **2** *v/t* se méfier de

misunderstand [mɪsʌndər'stænd] mal comprendre; **misunderstanding** malentendu *m*

misuse **1** [mɪs'ju:s] *n* mauvais usage *m* **2** [mɪs'ju:z] *v/t* faire mauvais usage de; *word* employer à tort

mitigating circumstances ['mɪtɪgeɪtɪŋ] circonstances *fpl* atténuantes

mitt [mɪt] *in baseball* gant *m*; **mitten** moufle *f*

mix [mɪks] **1** *n* mélange *m*; *in cooking*: *ready to use* préparation *f* **2** *v/t* mélanger; *cement* malaxer **3** *v/i socially* être sociable

◆ **mix up** confondre; *get out of order* mélanger; **be mixed up in** être mêlé à; **mixed economy, school, races** mixte; *reactions* mitigé; **mixer** *for food* mixeur *m*; *drink* boisson non-alcoolisée que l'on mélange avec certains alcools; **mixture** mélange *m*; *medicine* mixture *f*; **mix-up** confusion *f*

moan [moʊn] **1** *n of pain* gémissement *m* **2** *v/i in pain* gémir

mob [maːb] **1** *n* foule *f* **2** *v/t* assaillir

mobile ['moʊbəl] **1** *adj* mobile; **be ~** *have car* être motorisé **2** *n for decoration* mobile *m*; *Br phone* portable *m*; **mobile home** mobile home *m*; **mobile phone** *Br* téléphone *m* portable; **mobility** mobilité *f*

mobster ['maːbstər] gangster *m*

mock [maːk] **1** *adj* faux, feint **2** *v/t* se moquer de; **mockery** *(derision)* moquerie *f*; *(travesty)* parodie *f*

mode [moʊd] mode *m*

model ['maːdl] **1** *adj* employee, husband modèle; *boat, plane* modèle réduit *inv* **2** *n (miniature)* maquette *f*; *(pattern)* modèle *m*; *(fashion ~)* mannequin *m* **3** *v/i for designer* être mannequin; *for artist, photographer* poser

modem ['moʊdem] modem *m*

moderate 1 ['maːdərət] *adj also* POL modéré **2** ['maːdərət] *n* POL modéré *m* **3** ['maːdəreɪt] *v/t* modérer; **moderately** modérément; **moderation** *(restraint)* modération *f*

modern ['maːdərn] moderne; **modernization** modernisation *f*; **modernize 1** *v/t* moderniser **2** *v/i* se moderniser

modest ['maːdɪst] modeste; *wage, amount* modique; **modesty** *of apartment* simplicité *f*; *of wage* modicité *f*; *(lack of conceit)* modestie *f*

modification [maːdɪfɪ'keɪʃn] modification *f*; **modify** modifier

module ['maːdʒuːl] module *m*

moist [moɪst] humide; **moisten** humidifier; **moisture** humidité *f*; **moisturizer** *for skin* produit *m* hydratant

molasses [mə'læsɪz] mélasse *f*

mold[1] [moʊld] *on food* moisi *m*, moisissure(s) *f(pl)*

mold[2] [moʊld] **1** *n* moule *m* **2**

v/t clay modeler; *character* façonner

moldy ['məʊldɪ] *food* moisi

molecule ['mɑːlɪkjuːl] molécule *f*

molest [mə'lest] *child, woman* agresser *(sexuellement)*

mollycoddle ['mɑːlɪkɑːdl] F dorloter

molten ['məʊltən] en fusion

mom [mɑːm] F maman *f*

moment ['məʊmənt] instant *m*, moment *m*; **at the ~** en ce moment; **momentarily** *(for a moment)* momentanément; *(in a moment)* dans un instant; **momentary** momentané; **momentous** capital

momentum [mə'mentəm] élan *m*

monarch ['mɑːnərk] monarque *m*

monastery ['mɑːnəstrɪ] monastère *m*; **monastic** monastique

Monday ['mʌndeɪ] lundi *m*

monetary ['mʌnətrɪ] monétaire

money ['mʌnɪ] argent *m*; **money belt** sac *m* banane; **money market** marché *m* monétaire; **money order** mandat *m* postal

mongrel ['mʌŋgrəl] bâtard *m*

monitor ['mɑːnɪtər] **1** *n* COMPUT moniteur *m* **2** *v/t* surveiller, contrôler

monk [mʌŋk] moine *m*

monkey ['mʌŋkɪ] singe *m*; F

child polisson *m*; **monkey wrench** clef *f* anglaise

monolog, Br monologue ['mɑːnəlɑːg] monologue *m*

monopolize [mə'nɑːpəlaɪz] exercer un monopole sur; *fig* monopoliser; **monopoly** monopole *m*

monotonous [mə'nɑːtənəs] monotone; **monotony** monotonie *f*

monster ['mɑːnstər] monstre *m*; **monstrosity** horreur *f*

month [mʌnθ] mois *m*; **monthly 1** *adj* mensuel **2** *adv* mensuellement **3** *n magazine* mensuel *m*

monument ['mɑːnjumənt] monument *m*

mood [muːd] *(frame of mind)* humeur *f*; *(bad ~)* mauvaise humeur *f*; *of meeting, country* état *m* d'esprit; **moody** *changing moods* lunatique; *(bad-tempered)* maussade

moon [muːn] lune *f*; **moonlight** clair *m* de lune; **moonlit** éclairé par la lune

moor [mʊr] *boat* amarrer

moose [muːs] orignal *m*

mop [mɑːp] **1** *n for floor* balai *m* lave-sol; *for dishes* éponge *f* à manche **2** *v/t floor* laver; *eyes, face* éponger, essuyer

◆ **mop up** éponger; MIL balayer

moral ['mɔːrəl] **1** *adj* moral **2** *n of story* morale *f*; **~s** moralité *f*

morale [mə'ræl] moral *m*

morality [mə'rælətɪ] moralité f

morbid ['mɔːrbɪd] morbide

more [mɔːr] **1** *adj* plus de; *some ~ tea?* encore un peu de thé?; *there's no ~ coffee* il n'y a plus de café; *~ and ~ students* de plus en plus d'étudiants **2** *adv* plus; *~ important* plus important; *~ and ~* de plus en plus; *~ or less* plus ou moins; *once ~* une fois de plus; *I don't live there any ~* je n'habite plus là-bas **3** *pron* plus; *do you want some ~?* est-ce que tu en veux encore or davantage?; *a little ~* un peu plus; *moreover* de plus

morgue [mɔːrg] morgue f

morning ['mɔːrnɪŋ] matin m; *in the ~* le matin; *(tomorrow)* demain matin; *tomorrow ~* demain matin; *good ~* bonjour

moron ['mɔːrɑːn] F crétin m

morphine ['mɔːrfiːn] morphine f

mortal ['mɔːrtl] **1** *adj* mortel **2** *n* mortel m; *mortality* condition f mortelle; *(death rate)* mortalité f

mortar ['mɔːrtər] MIL, cement mortier m

mortgage ['mɔːrgɪdʒ] **1** *n* prêt m immobilier; *on own property* hypothèque f **2** *v/t* hypothéquer

mosaic [moʊ'zeɪk] mosaïque f

Moscow ['mɑːskaʊ] Moscou

Moslem ['mʊzlɪm] **1** *adj* musulman **2** *n* Musulman(e) m(f)

mosque [mɒsk] mosquée f

mosquito [mɑːs'kiːtoʊ] moustique m

moss [mɑːs] mousse f

most [moʊst] **1** *adj* la plupart de **2** *adv* (*very*) extrêmement, très; *play, swim, eat etc* le plus; *the ~ beautiful* le plus beau; *~ of all* surtout **3** *pron:* la plupart de; *at (the)* ~ au maximum; *make the ~ of* profiter au maximum de; *mostly* surtout

motel [moʊ'tel] motel m

moth [mɑːθ] papillon m de nuit

mother ['mʌðər] **1** *n* mère f **2** *v/t* materner; *motherhood* maternité f; *Mothering Sunday → Mother's Day;* mother-in-law belle-mère f; *motherly* maternel; *Mother's Day* la fête des Mères; *mother tongue* langue f maternelle

motif [moʊ'tiːf] motif m

motion ['moʊʃn] **1** *n* (*movement*) mouvement m; *(proposal*) motion f; *motionless* immobile

motivate ['moʊtɪveɪt] motiver; *motivation* motivation f; *motive for* crime mobile m

motor ['moʊtər] moteur m; *motorbike* moto f; *motorcycle* moto f; *motorcyclist* motocycliste *m/f*; **motor home** camping-car *m*; **motor mechanic** mécanicien(ne) *m/f*; **motor racing** course *f* automobile; **motor vehicle** véhicule *m* à moteur

motto ['mɒtəʊ] devise *f*

mould *etc Br* → **mold** *etc*

mound [maʊnd] (*hillock*) monticule *m*; (*pile*) tas *m*

mount [maʊnt] **1** *n* (*mountain*) mont *m*; (*horse*) monture *f* **2** *v/t* steps, photo monter; horse, bicycle monter sur; campaign organiser **3** *v/i* monter

◆ **mount up** s'accumuler

mountain ['maʊntɪn] montagne *f*; **mountaineer** alpiniste *m/f*; **mountaineering** alpinisme *m*; **mountainous** montagneux

mourn [mɔːrn] pleurer; **mourner** parent/ami *m* du défunt; **mournful** triste, mélancolique

mouse [maʊs] (*pl* **mice** [maɪs]) *also* COMPUT souris *f*; **mouse mat** tapis *m* de souris

moustache *Br* → **mustache**

mouth [maʊθ] bouche *f*; *of animal* gueule *f*; *of river* embouchure *f*; **mouthful** *of food* bouchée *f*; *of drink* gorgée *f*; **mouthpiece** *of instrument* embouchure *f*; (*spokesperson*) porte-parole *m inv*; **mouthwash** bain *m* de bouche; **mouthwatering** alléchant

move [muːv] **1** *n* mouvement *m*; *in chess etc* coup *m*; (*step, action*) action *f*; (*change of house*) déménagement *m* **2** *v/t* object déplacer; limbs bouger; (*transfer*) transférer; emotionally émouvoir; ~ **house** déménager **3** *v/i* bouger; (*transfer*) être transféré

◆ **move around** bouger, remuer; *from place to place* bouger, déménager

◆ **move in** emménager

movement ['muːvmənt] *also* organization, MUS mouvement *m*; **movers** déménageurs *mpl*

movie ['muːvɪ] film *m*; **go to a/the ~s** aller au cinéma; **moviegoer** amateur *m* de cinéma, cinéphile *m/f*; **movie theater** cinéma *m*

moving ['muːvɪŋ] parts mobile; emotionally émouvant

mow [məʊ] grass tondre; **mower** tondeuse *f* (à gazon)

mph [empi:'eɪtʃ] (= *miles per hour*) miles à l'heure

Mr ['mɪstər] Monsieur, M.

Mrs ['mɪsɪz] Madame, Mme

Ms [mɪz] Madame, Mme

much [mʌtʃ] **1** *adj* beaucoup de; *so* ~ *money* tant d'argent; *as* ~ ... *as* ... autant (de)... que... **2** *adv* beaucoup; *very* ~ beaucoup; *too* ~ trop **3** *pron* beaucoup; *nothing* ~ pas grand-chose; *as* ~ *as* ... autant que...

mud [mʌd] boue f

muddle ['mʌdl] **1** n (mess) désordre m; (confusion) confusion f **2** v/t embrouiller

muddy ['mʌdɪ] boueux

muffin ['mʌfɪn] muffin m

muffle ['mʌfl] étouffer; **muffler** MOT silencieux m

mug[1] [mʌg] n for coffee chope f; F (face) gueule f F

mug[2] v/t (attack) agresser

mugger ['mʌgər] agresseur m; **mugging** agression f; **muggy** lourd, moite

mule [mjuːl] animal mulet m, mule f; slipper mule f

multicultural [mʌltɪ'kʌltʃərəl] multiculturel; **multilateral** POL multilatéral; **multimedia 1** adj multimédia **2** n multimédia m; **multinational 1** adj multinational **2** n COM multinationale f

multiple ['mʌltɪpl] multiple; **multiple sclerosis** sclérose f en plaques

multiplex ['mʌltɪpleks] (cinéma m) multiplex m

multiplication [mʌltɪplɪ-'keɪʃn] multiplication f; **multiply 1** v/t multiplier **2** v/i se multiplier

multitasking [mʌltɪ'tæskɪŋ] multitâche m; for persons multiplicité f des tâches

mumble ['mʌmbl] **1** n marmonnement m **2** v/t & v/i marmonner

munch [mʌntʃ] mâcher

municipal [mjuː'nɪsɪpl] municipal

mural ['mjʊrəl] peinture f murale

murder ['mɜːrdər] **1** n meurtre m **2** v/t person assassiner; song massacrer; **murderer** meurtrier(-ière) m(f)

murky ['mɜːrkɪ] also fig trouble

murmur ['mɜːrmər] **1** n murmure m **2** v/t murmurer

muscle ['mʌsl] muscle m; **muscular** pain musculaire; person musclé

museum [mjuː'zɪəm] musée m

mushroom ['mʌʃrum] **1** n champignon m **2** v/i fig proliférer

music ['mjuːzɪk] musique f; in written form partition f; **musical 1** adj musical; person musicien **2** n comédie f musicale; musician musicien(ne) m(f)

mussel ['mʌsl] moule f

must [mʌst] **1** v/aux ⊳ necessity devoir; **I ~ be on time** je dois être à l'heure, il faut que je sois (subj) à l'heure; **I ⌐n't be late** je ne dois pas être en retard, il ne faut pas que je sois en retard

⊳ probability devoir; **it ~ be about 6 o'clock** il doit être environ six heures

mustache [mə'stæʃ] moustache f

mustard ['mʌstərd] moutarde f

musty ['mʌsti] *room* qui sent le renfermé; *smell* de renfermé

mutilate ['mjuːtɪleɪt] mutiler

mutiny ['mjuːtɪnɪ] 1 *n* mutinerie *f* 2 *v/i* se mutiner

mutter ['mʌtər] marmonner

mutual ['mjuːtʃʊəl] *(reciprocal)* mutuel; *(common)* commun

muzzle ['mʌzl] 1 *n* of animal museau *m*; *for dog* muselière *f* 2 *v/t*: ~ **the press** bâillonner la presse

my [maɪ] mon *m*, ma *f*; *pl* mes; **myself** moi-même; *reflexive* me; *before vowel* m'; *after prep* moi; **I hurt** ~ je me suis blessé

mysterious [mɪ'stɪrɪəs] mystérieux; **mysteriously** mystérieusement; **mystery** mystère *m*; **mystify** rendre perplexe; *of tricks* mystifier

myth [mɪθ] *also fig* mythe *m*; **mythical** mythique

N

nag [næg] 1 *v/i of person* faire des remarques continuelles 2 *v/t* harceler; **nagging** *pain* obsédant; **I have this** ~ **doubt that** ... je n'arrive pas à m'empêcher de penser que ...

nail [neɪl] *for wood* clou *m*; *on finger, toe* ongle *m*; **nail polish** vernis *m* à ongles; **nail polish remover** dissolvant *m*; **naive** [naɪ'iːv] naïf

naked ['neɪkɪd] nu

name [neɪm] 1 *n* nom *m*; **what's your** ~? comment vous appelez-vous? 2 *v/t* appeler; **namely** à savoir; **namesake** homonyme *m/f*

nanny ['nænɪ] nurse *f*

nap [næp] sieste *f*

napkin ['næpkɪn] *(table)* serviette *f* (de table); *(sanitary* ~) serviette *f* hygiénique

narcotic [nɑːr'kɑːtɪk] stupéfiant *m*

narrate [nə'reɪt] raconter; **narrative** 1 *adj poem, style* narratif 2 *n* *(story)* récit *m*; **narrator** narrateur(-trice) *m(f)*

narrow ['nærəʊ] étroit; *victory* serré; **narrowly** *win* de justesse; *escape* de peu; **narrow-minded** étroit d'esprit

nasty ['næstɪ] *person, thing to say* méchant; *smell* nauséabond; *weather, cut, wound, disease* mauvais

nation ['neɪʃn] nation *f*; **national** 1 *adj* national 2 *n* national *m*, ressortissant *m*; **national anthem** hymne *m* national; **national debt** dette *f* publique; **nationalism** nationalisme *m*; **nationality** nationalité *f*; **nationalize** in-

dustry etc nationaliser
native ['neitiv] **1** *adj* natal **2** *n* natif(-ive) *m(f)*; (*tribesman*) indigène *m*; **Native American 1** *adj* amérindien **2** *n* Amérindien(ne) *m(f)*
NATO ['neitou] (= *North Atlantic Treaty Organization*) OTAN *f* (= Organisation du traité de l'Atlantique Nord)
natural ['nætʃrəl] naturel; **naturalist** naturaliste *m/f*; **naturalize**: *become* **~d** se faire naturaliser; **naturally** (*of course*) bien entendu; *behave, speak* naturellement, avec naturel; (*by nature*) de nature; **nature** nature *f*; **nature reserve** réserve *f* naturelle
naughty ['nɔːti] vilain; *photograph , word etc* coquin
nausea ['nɔːziə] nausée *f*; **nauseate** (*of*) écœurer; **nauseating** écœurant; **nauseous**: *feel* **~** avoir la nausée
nautical ['nɔːtikl] nautique, marin
naval ['neivl] naval, maritime; *history* de la marine
navel ['neivl] nombril *m*
navigate ['nævigeit] *also* COMPUT naviguer; *in car* diriger; **navigation** navigation *f*; *in car* indications *fpl*; **navigator** navigateur *m*
navy ['neivi] marine *f*; **navy blue 1** *adj* bleu marine *inv* **2** *n* bleu *m* marine

near [nir] **1** *adv* près; *come* **~er** approche-toi **2** *prep* près de **3** *adj* proche; *in the* **~** *future* dans un proche avenir; **nearby** tout près; **nearly** presque; *I* **~** *lost it* j'ai failli le perdre; **near-sighted** myope
neat [niːt] *room, desk* bien rangé; *person* ordonné; *in appearance* soigné; *whiskey etc* sec; *solution* ingénieux; *F* (*terrific*) super *inv* F
necessarily ['nesəserəli] nécessairement, forcément; **necessary** nécessaire; *it is* **~** *to …* il faut …; **necessity** nécessité *f*
neck [nek] cou *m*; *of clothing* col *m*; **necklace** collier *m*; **neckline** *of dress* encolure *f*; **necktie** cravate *f*
née [nei] née
need [niːd] **1** *n* besoin *m*; *if* **~** *be* si besoin est; *in* **~** dans le besoin **2** *v/t* avoir besoin de; *you don't* **~** *to wait* vous n'êtes pas obligés d'attendre; *I* **~** *to talk to you* il faut que je te parle
needle ['niːdl] aiguille *f*; **needlework** travaux *mpl* d'aiguille
needy ['niːdi] nécessiteux
negative ['negətiv] négatif
neglect [ni'glekt] **1** *n* négligence *f*; *state* abandon *m* **2** *v/t* négliger; **neglected** négligé
negligence ['neglidʒəns] né-

gligence f; **negligent** négligent; **negligible** quantity négligeable

negotiable [nɪˈɡəʊʃəbl] négociable; **negotiate 1** v/i négocier **2** v/t deal négocier; obstacles franchir; bend in road négocier, prendre; **negotiation** négociation f; **negotiator** [ɡəʊʃɪeɪtər] négociateur(-trice) m(f)

neighbor [ˈneɪbər] voisin(e) m(f); **neighborhood** in town quartier m; **neighboring** house, state voisin; **neighborly** aimable

neighbour etc Br → **neighbor** etc

neither [ˈniːðər] **1** adj: ~ player aucun(e) des deux joueurs **2** pron ni l'un ni l'autre **3** adv: ~ ... **nor** ... ni ... ni ... **4** conj: ~ **do/can I** moi non plus

neon light [ˈniːɑːn] néon m

nephew [ˈnefjuː] neveu m

nerve [nɜːrv] nerf m; (courage) courage m; (impudence) culot m F; **nerve-racking** angoissant, éprouvant; **nervous** nerveux; **nervous breakdown** dépression f nerveuse; **nervousness** nervosité f; **nervy** (fresh) effronté, culotté F

nest [nest] nid m

net¹ [net] n for fishing, tennis etc filet m; Internet Net m

net² [net] adj price etc net

nettle [ˈnetl] ortie f

'network also COMPUT réseau m

neurologist [nʊˈrɑːlədʒɪst] neurologue m/f

neurosis [nʊˈrəʊsɪs] névrose f; **neurotic** névrosé, obsédé

neuter [ˈnuːtər] animal castrer; **neutral 1** adj neutre **2** n gear point m mort; **neutrality** neutralité f; **neutralize** neutraliser

never [ˈnevər] jamais; **I've been to New York** je ne suis jamais allé à New York; **nevertheless** néanmoins

new [nuː] nouveau; (not used) neuf; **newborn** nouveau-né; **newcomer** nouveau venu m, nouvelle venue f; **newly** (recently) récemment; nouvellement; **newly-weds** jeunes mariés mpl

news [nuːz] nouvelle(s) f(pl); on TV, radio informations fpl; **newscast** TV journal m télévisé; **newscaster** TV présentateur(-trice) m(f); **news flash** flash m d'information; **newspaper** journal m; **newsreader** TV etc présentateur(-trice) m(f); **news report** reportage m; **newsstand** kiosque m à journaux; **newsvendor** vendeur(-euse) m(f) de journaux

'New Year nouvel an m; **Happy ~!** Bonne année!; **New Year's Day** jour m de l'an; **New Year's Eve** la Saint-Sylvestre

next [nekst] **1** adj prochain; **the ~ month** le mois suivant

2 *adv (after)* ensuite, après; **~ to** à côté de; **next-door 1** *adj* **neighbor** d'à côté **2** *adv* **live** à côté; **next of kin** parent *m* le plus proche

nibble ['nɪbl] *cheese* grignoter; *ear* mordiller

nice [naɪs] agréable; *person also* sympathique; *house, hair* beau; **that's very ~ of you** c'est très gentil de votre part; **nicely** *written, presented* bien; *(pleasantly)* agréablement

niche [niːʃ] *in market* créneau *m*; *(special position)* place *f*

nick [nɪk] *(cut)* coupure *f*

nickel ['nɪkl] MIN nickel *m*; *coin* pièce *f* de cinq cents

'nickname surnom *m*

niece [niːs] nièce *f*

night [naɪt] nuit *f*; *(evening)* soir *m*; **11 o'clock at ~** onze heures du soir; **during the ~** pendant la nuit; **good ~** going to bed bonne nuit; leaving office, friends' house etc bonsoir; **nightcap** *drink* boisson *f* du soir; **nightclub** boîte *f* de nuit; **nightdress** chemise *f* de nuit; **night flight** vol *m* de nuit; **nightlife** vie *f* nocturne; **nightly 1** *adj* de toutes les nuits, *in evening* de tous les soirs **2** *adv* toutes les nuits, *in evening* tous les soirs; **nightmare** *also fig* cauchemar *m*; **night porter** gardien *m* de nuit; **night school** cours *mpl* du soir; **night shift**

équipe *f* de nuit; **nightshirt** chemise *f* de nuit (d'homme); **nightspot** boîte *f* (de nuit); **nighttime: at ~, in the ~** la nuit

nimble ['nɪmbl] agile; *mind* vif

nine [naɪn] neuf; **nineteen** dix-neuf; **nineteenth** dix-neuvième; **ninetieth** quatre-vingt-dixième; **ninety** quatre-vingt-dix; **ninth** neuvième

nip [nɪp] *(pinch)* pincement *m*; *(bite)* morsure *f*

nipple ['nɪpl] mamelon *m*

nitrogen ['naɪtrədʒn] azote *m*

no [noʊ] **1** *adv* non **2** *adj* aucun, pas de; **there's ~ coffee left** il ne reste plus de café; **I have ~ money** je n'ai pas d'argent; **~ smoking** défense de fumer

noble ['noʊbl] noble

nobody ['noʊbədɪ] personne; **~ knows** personne ne le sait; **there was ~ at home** il n'y avait personne

no-brainer [noʊ'breɪnər] jeu *m* d'enfant; **the math test was a ~** le devoir de maths était super facile

nod [naːd] **1** *n* signe *m* de tête **2** *v/i* faire un signe de tête

noise [nɔɪz] bruit *m*; **noisy** bruyant; **be ~** of person faire du bruit

nominal ['naːmɪnl] nominal; *(token)* symbolique

nominate ['naːmɪneɪt] *(ap-*

point) nommer; **nomination** *(appointment)* nomination *f*; *(person proposed)* candidat *m*; **nominee** candidat *m*

nonalco'holic non alcoolisé

noncommissioned 'officer ['nɒnkəmɪʃnd] sous-officier *m*

noncommittal [nɑːnkə'mɪtl] évasif

nondescript ['nɑːndɪskrɪpt] quelconque; *color* indéfinissable

none [nʌn] aucun(e); ***there is/ are ~ left*** il n'en reste plus

nonentity [nɑːn'entətɪ] être *m* insignifiant

none'xistent inexistant

non'fiction ouvrages *mpl* non littéraires

noninter'ference non-ingérence *f*

noninter'vention non-intervention *f*

no-'nonsense *approach* pragmatique

non'payment non-paiement *m*

nonpol'luting non polluant

non'resident non-résident *m*; *in hotel* client *m* de passage

nonre'turnable non remboursable

nonsense ['nɑːnsəns] absurdité(s) *f(pl)*; ***don't talk ~*** ne raconte pas n'importe quoi

non'smoker non-fumeur (-euse) *m(f)*

non'standard non standard *inv*; *use of word* impropre

non'stop 1 *adj flight, train* direct; *chatter* incessant **2** *adv fly, travel* sans escale; *chatter, argue* sans arrêt

non'union non syndiqué

non'violence non-violence *f*; **nonviolent** non-violent

noodles ['nuːdlz] nouilles *fpl*

noon [nuːn] midi *m*

no-one → **nobody**

noose [nuːs] nœud *m* coulant

nor [nɔːr] ni; **~ do I** moi non plus

norm [nɔːrm] norme *f*; **normal** normal; **normality** normalité *f*; **normally** normalement

north [nɔːrθ] **1** *n* nord *m* **2** *adj* nord *inv*; *wind* du nord **3** *adv travel* vers le nord; **North America** Amérique *f* du Nord; **North American 1** *adj* nord-américain **2** *n* Nord-Américain(e) *m(f)*; **northeast** nord-est *m*; **northerly** *wind* du nord; *direction* vers le nord; **northern** du nord; **northerner** habitant *m* du Nord; **North Korea** Corée *f* du Nord; **North Korean 1** *adj* nord-coréen **2** *n* Nord-Coréen(ne) *m(f)*; **North Pole** pôle *m* Nord; **northward** *travel* vers le nord; **northwest** nord-ouest *m*

nose [nouz] nez *m*

◆ **nose around** F fouiner

nostalgia [nɑː'stældʒə] nostalgie *f*; **nostalgic** nostalgique

nostril ['nɑ:strəl] narine *f*

nosy ['nouzɪ] F curieux

not [nɑ:t] pas; **~ now** maintenant; **~ there** pas là; **~ a lot** pas beaucoup *with verbs* ne … pas; **it's ~ allowed** ce n'est pas permis; **he didn't help** il n'a pas aidé

notable ['noutəbl] notable

notch [nɑ:tʃ] entaille *f*

note [nout] MUS, *written* note *f*; (*short letter*) mot *m*; **notebook** carnet *m*; COMPUT ordinateur *m* bloc-notes; **noted** célèbre; **notepad** bloc-notes *m*; **notepaper** papier *m* à lettres

nothing ['nʌθɪŋ] rien; **she said ~** elle n'a rien dit; **~ but** rien que; **~ much** pas grand-chose; **for ~** (*for free*) gratuitement; (*for no reason*) pour un rien

notice ['noutɪs] **1** *n on bulletin board, in street* affiche *f*; (*advance warning*) préavis *m*; *in newspaper* avis *m*; **to leave job** démission *f*; *to leave house* préavis *m*; **at short ~** dans un délai très court; **until further ~** jusqu'à nouvel ordre; **hand in one's ~** *to employer* donner sa démission; **take no ~ of** ne pas faire attention à **2** *v/t* remarquer; **noticeable** visible

notify ['noutɪfaɪ]: **~ s.o. of sth** signaler qch à qn

notion ['noufn] idée *f*

notorious [nou'tɔːrɪəs] notoire

noun [naun] substantif *m*, nom *m*

nourishing ['nʌrɪʃɪŋ] nourrissant; **nourishment** nourriture *f*

novel ['nɑːvl] roman *m*; **novelist** romancier(-ière) *m(f)*; **novelty** nouveauté *f*

November [nou'vembər] novembre *m*

novice ['nɑːvɪs] (*beginner*) novice *m*, débutant *m*

now [nau] maintenant; **~ and again**, **~ and then** de temps à autre; **~ by ~** maintenant; **nowadays** aujourd'hui, de nos jours

nowhere ['nouwer] nulle part; **it's ~ near finished** c'est loin d'être fini

nuclear ['nuːklɪər] nucléaire; **nuclear energy** énergie *f* nucléaire; **nuclear power** énergie *f* nucléaire; POL puissance *f* nucléaire; **nuclear power station** centrale *f* nucléaire; **nuclear reactor** réacteur *m* nucléaire; **nude** [nuːd] **1** *adj* nu **2** *n painting* nu *m*; **in the ~** tout nu

nudge [nʌdʒ] *person* donner un coup de coude à; *parked car* pousser (un peu)

nudist ['nuːdɪst] nudiste *m/f*

nuisance ['nuːsns] peste *f*, plaie *f*; *event, task* ennui *m*; **make a ~ of o.s.** être embêtant F

null and 'void [nʌl] nul et non
avenu

numb [nʌm] engourdi; *emotionally* insensible

number ['nʌmbər] **1** *n* nombre *m*; *symbol* chiffre *m*; *of
hotel room, phone ~ etc* nu-
méro *m* **2** *v/t* (*put a ~ on*) numéroter

numeral ['nu:mərəl] chiffre *m*

numerous ['nu:mərəs] nombreux

nun [nʌn] religieuse *f*

nurse [nɜːrs] infirmier(-ière)
m(f); **nursery** maternelle *f*;
for plants pépinière *f*; **nurs-**
ery rhyme comptine *f*; **nursery school** école *f* maternelle; **nursing** profession *f*
d'infirmier; **nursing home**
for old people maison *f* de retraite

nut [nʌt] (*walnut*) noix *f*; (*Brazil*) noix *f* du Brésil; (*hazelnut*) noisette *f*; (*peanut*) cacahuète *f*; *for bolt* écrou *m*;
nutcrackers casse-noisettes
m inv

nutrient ['nu:trɪənt] élément
m nutritif; **nutrition** nutrition *f*; **nutritious** nutritif

nuts [nʌts] F (*crazy*) fou

O

oar [ɔːr] aviron *m*, rame *f*

oasis [ouˈeɪsɪs] *also fig* oasis *f*

oath [ouθ] LAW serment *m*;
(*swearword*) juron *m*

oats [outs] *npl* avoine *f*

obedience [ouˈbiːdɪəns]
obéissance *f*; **obedient**
obéissant; **obediently** doci-
lement

obese [ouˈbiːs] obèse; **obesity** obésité *f*

obey [ouˈbeɪ] obéir à

obituary [ouˈbɪtʃuerɪ] nécro-
logie *f*

object¹ ['ɑːbdʒɪkt] *n* (*thing*)
objet *m*; (*aim*) objectif *m*;
GRAM complément *m* d'objet

object² [əbˈdʒekt] *v/i* protester; *if nobody ~s* si personne
n'y voit d'objection

objection [əbˈdʒekʃn] objection *f*; **objectionable** (*unpleasant*) désagréable; **objective 1** *adj* objectif *m* 2
n objectif *m*; **objectively** objecti-
vement; **objectivity** objectivité *f*

obligation [ɑːblɪˈɡeɪʃn] obligation *f*; **obligatory** obligatoire; **obliging** serviable,
obligeant

oblique [əˈbliːk] **1** *adj* reference indirect; *line* oblique **2**
n in punctuation barre *f* oblique

obliterate [əˈblɪtəreɪt] *city* détruire; *memory* effacer

oblivion [əˈblɪvɪən] oubli *m*

oblong ['ɑːblɔːŋ] **1** *adj* oblong
2 *n* rectangle *m*

obscene [ɑːbˈsiːn] obscène; *salary, poverty* scandaleux; **obscenity** obscénité *f*

obscure [əbˈskjʊr] obscur; *village* inconnu; **obscurity** obscurité *f*

observant [əbˈzɜːrvənt] observateur; **observation** observation *f*; **observe** observer; **observer** observateur(-trice) *m(f)*

obsess [əbˈses]: **be ~ed with** être obsédé par; **obsession** obsession *f* (**with** de)

obsolete [ˈɑːbsəliːt] obsolète

obstacle [ˈɑːbstəkl] *also fig* obstacle *m*

obstetrician [ɑːbstəˈtrɪʃn] obstétricien(ne) *m(f)*; **obstetrics** obstétrique *f*

obstinacy [ˈɑːbstɪnəsɪ] entêtement *m*, obstination *f*; **obstinate** obstiné

obstruct [əbˈstrʌkt] *road* bloquer, obstruer; *investigation* entraver; *police* gêner; **obstruction** *on road etc* obstacle *m*; **obstructive** *behavior* qui met des bâtons dans les roues; *tactics* obstructionniste

obtain [əbˈteɪn] obtenir; **obtainable** *products* disponible

obtuse [əbˈtuːs] *fig* obtus

obvious [ˈɑːbvɪəs] évident, manifeste; **obviously** manifestement; **~!** évidemment!

occasion [əˈkeɪʒn] occasion *f*; **occasional** occasionnel; **occasionally** de temps en temps, occasionnellement

occupant [ˈɑːkjʊpənt] occupant(e) *m(f)*; **occupation** (*job*) métier *m*; *of country* occupation *f*; **occupy** occuper

occur [əˈkɜːr] avoir lieu, se produire; **occurrence** (*event*) fait *m*

ocean [ˈoʊʃn] océan *m*

o'clock [əˈklɑːk]: **at five ~** à cinq heures

October [ɑːkˈtoʊbər] octobre *m*

odd [ɑːd] (*strange*) bizarre; (*not even*) impair; **oddball** F original *m*; **odds and ends** petites choses *fpl*, bricoles *fpl*; **odds-on: the ~ favorite** le grand favori

odometer [oʊˈdɑːmətər] odomètre *m*

odor, *Br* **odour** [ˈoʊdər] odeur *f*

of [ɑːv] de; **the name ~ the street/hotel** le nom de la rue/de l'hôtel; **the color ~ the paper** la couleur du papier; **five minutes ~ ten** dix heures moins cinq; **die ~ cancer** mourir d'un cancer; **love ~ money** l'amour de l'argent

off [ɑːf] **1** *prep*: **~ the main road** *away from* en retrait de la route principale; *near* près de la route principale; **$20 ~ the price** 20 dollars de réduction **2** *adv*: **be ~** *of light, TV, machine* être éteint; *of brake* être desserré; *of lid* ne pas être mis; *not at* work ne pas être là; *canceled* être annulé; **we're ~ tomorrow** *leaving* nous partons demain; **take a day ~** prendre un jour de congé; **it's 3 miles ~** c'est à 3 miles; **it's a long way ~** c'est loin 3 *adj:* **the ~ switch** le bouton d'arrêt

offence *Br* → **offense**

offend [ə'fend] (*insult*) offenser; **offender** LAW délinquant(e) *m(f)*; **offense** LAW *minor* infraction *f*; *serious* délit *m*; **take ~ at sth** s'offenser de qch; **offensive 1** *adj behavior, remark* offensant; *smell* repoussant **2** *n* MIL offensive *f*

offer ['ɑ:fər] **1** *n* offre *f* **2** *v/t* offrir

off'hand *attitude* désinvolte

office ['ɑ:fɪs] bureau *m*; (*position*) fonction *f*; **officer** MIL officier *m*; *in police* agent *m* de police; **official 1** *adj* officiel **2** *n* *civil servant etc* fonctionnaire *m/f*; **officially** officiellement; (*strictly speaking*) en théorie; **officious** trop zélé

'off-line *work* hors connexion; **go ~** se déconnecter

'off-peak *rates* en période creuse

'off-season basse saison *f*

'offset *losses* compenser

'offshore offshore

'offside SP hors jeu

'offspring progéniture *f*

'off-the-record officieux

often ['ɑ:fn] souvent; **how ~ do you go there?** vous y allez tous les combien?

oil [ɔɪl] **1** *n* huile *f*; *petroleum* pétrole *m* **2** *v/t* lubrifier, huiler; **oil change** vidange *f*; **oil company** compagnie *f* pétrolière; **oilfield** champ *m* pétrolifère; **oil painting** peinture *f* à l'huile; **oil refinery** raffinerie *f* de pétrole; **oil rig** *at sea* plate-forme *f* de forage; *on land* tour *f* de forage; **oil slick** marée *f* noire; **oil tanker** *ship* pétrolier *m*; **oil well** puits *m* de pétrole; **oily** graisseux

ointment ['ɔɪntmənt] pommade *f*

ok [oʊ'keɪ]: **can I?** **~** je peux? – d'accord; **is it ~ with you if ...?** ça te dérange si ...?; **does that look ~?** est-ce que ça va?; **that's ~ by me** ça me va; **are you ~?** (*well, not hurt*) ça va?

old [oʊld] vieux; (*previous*) ancien; **how ~ is he?** quel âge a-t-il?; **old age** vieillesse *f*; **old-fashioned** démodé

olive ['ɑ:lɪv] olive *f*; **olive oil** huile *f* d'olive

Olympic Games Jeux *mpl* Olympiques

omelet, *Br* **omelette** ['ɑ:mlət] omelette *f*

ominous ['ɑ:mɪnəs] inquiétant

omission [ou'mɪʃn] omission *f*; **omit** [ou'mɪt] omettre
on [ɑːn] **1** *prep* sur; ~ *the table* sur la table; ~ *the bus* dans le bus; ~ *the third floor* au deuxième étage; ~ *TV* à la télé; ~ *Sunday* dimanche; ~ *Sundays* le dimanche; *the 1st of ...* le premier...; *this is* ~ *me* (*I'm paying*) c'est moi qui paie; *have you any money* ~ *you?* as-tu de l'argent sur toi?; ~ *his arrival* à son arrivée; ~ *his departure* au moment de son départ; ~ *hearing this* en entendant ceci **2** *adv:* *be* ~ *of light, TV, computer etc* être allumé; *of brake* être serré; *of lid* être mis; *of program: being broadcast* passer; *of meeting: be scheduled to happen* avoir lieu; *what's* ~ *tonight?* on *TV etc* qu'est-ce qu'il y a ce soir?; (*what's planned?*) qu'est-ce qu'on fait ce soir?; *you're* ~ (*I accept*) c'est d'accord; ~ *you go* (*go ahead*) vas-y; *talk* ~ continuer à parler; *and so* ~ et ainsi de suite; *and* ~ *talk etc* pendant des heures **3** *adj:* *the* ~ *switch* le bouton marche

once [wʌns] **1** *adv* (*one time*) une fois; (*formerly*) autrefois; ~ *again,* ~ *more* encore une fois; *at* ~ (*immediately*) tout de suite **2** *conj* une fois que; ~ *you have finished*

une fois que tu auras terminé
one [wʌn] **1** *number* un *m* **2** *adj* un(e); ~ *day* un jour **3** *pron:* ~ *is bigger than the other* l'un(e) est plus grand(e) que l'autre; *which* ~*?* lequel/laquelle?; ~ *by* ~ enter, deal with un(e) à la fois; *the little* ~*s* les petits *mpl*; *I for* ~ pour ma part; *what can I* ~ *say?* qu'est-ce qu'on peut dire?; *one-parent family* famille *f* monoparentale; *oneself:* *hurt* ~ se faire mal; *for* ~ pour soi ou soi-même; *do sth by* ~ faire qch tout seul; *one-way street* rue *f* à sens unique; *one-way ticket* aller *m* simple
onion ['ʌnjən] oignon *m*
on-line en ligne; *go* ~ *to* se connecter à; *on-line banking* (services *mpl* de) banque *f* en ligne; *on-line dating* rencontres *fpl* en ligne; *on-line shopping* shopping *m* en ligne
onlooker ['ɑːnlʊkər] spectateur(-trice) *m(f)*
only ['ounlɪ] **1** *adv* seulement; *he's* ~ *six* il n'a que six ans **2** *adj* unique
onset début *m*
on-the-job 'training formation *f* sur le tas
opaque [ou'peɪk] *glass* opaque
open ['oupən] **1** *adj* ouvert; *in the* ~ *air* en plein air **2** *v/t* ouvrir **3** *v/i of shop, flower* s'ou-

vrir; *open-air meeting, concert* en plein air; *pool* découvert; **open day** *journée f* portes ouvertes; **open-ended** *contract* etc flexible; **opening** *in wall* etc ouverture *f*; *of film, novel* etc début *m*; *(job)* poste *m* (vacant); **openly** (*honestly, frankly*) ouvertement; **open-minded** à l'esprit ouvert, ouvert; **open ticket** billet *m* open

opera ['ɒpərə] opéra *m*; **opera house** opéra *m*; **opera singer** chanteur(-euse) *m(f)* d'opéra

operate ['ɒpəreɪt] **1** *v/i of company* opérer; *of airline, bus service* circuler; *of machine* fonctionner; MED opérer **2** *v/t machine* faire marcher

♦ **operate on** MED opérer

'operating room MED salle *f* d'opération; **operating system** COMPUT système *m* d'exploitation; **operation** MED opération *f* (chirurgicale); *of machine* fonctionnement *m*; **have an ~** MED se faire opérer; **operator** *of machine* opérateur(-trice) *m(f)*; *(tour ~)* tour-opérateur *m*, voyagiste *m*; TELEC standardiste *m/f*

opinion [ə'pɪnjən] opinion *f*; **opinion poll** sondage *m* d'opinion

opponent [ə'pəʊnənt] adversaire *m/f*

opportunist [ɑːpər'tuːnɪst] opportuniste *m/f*; **opportunity** occasion *f*

oppose [ə'pəʊz] s'opposer à; **be ~d to** être opposé à

opposite ['ɑːpəzɪt] **1** *adj* opposé; *meaning* contraire **2** *adv* en face; **the house ~** la maison d'en face **3** *prep* en face de; **opposite 'number** homologue *m/f*

opposition [ɑːpə'zɪʃn] opposition *f*

oppress [ə'pres] *people* opprimer; **oppressive** *rule* oppressif; *weather* oppressant

optician [ɑːp'tɪʃn] opticien (-ne) *m(f)*

optimism ['ɑːptɪmɪzəm] optimisme *m*; **optimist** optimiste *m/f*; **optimistic** optimiste; **optimistically** avec optimisme

optimum ['ɑːptɪməm] optimal

option ['ɑːpʃn] option *f*; **optional** facultatif

or [ɔːr] ou; **~ else!** sinon ...

oral ['ɔːrəl] *exam* oral; *hygiene* dentaire

orange ['ɔːrɪndʒ] **1** *adj color* orange *inv* **2** *n fruit* orange *f*; *color* orange *m*; **orange juice** jus *m* d'orange

orator ['ɔːrətər] orateur(-trice) *m(f)*

orbit ['ɔːrbɪt] **1** *n of earth* orbite *f* **2** *v/t the earth* décrire une orbite autour de

orchard ['ɔːrtʃərd] verger *m*

ourselves

orchestra [ˈɔːrkəstrə] orchestre *m*

orchid [ˈɔːrkɪd] orchidée *f*

ordain [ɔːrˈdeɪn] ordonner

ordeal [ɔːrˈdiːl] épreuve *f*

order [ˈɔːrdər] **1** *n* ordre *m*; *for goods, in restaurant* commande *f*; **an ~ of fries** une portion de frites; **in ~ to** pour; **out of ~** (*not functioning*) hors service; **out of ~** (*not in sequence*) pas dans l'ordre **2** *v/t* (*put in sequence, proper layout*) ranger; *goods, meal* commander; **~ s.o. to do sth** ordonner à qn de faire qch **3** *v/i* commander; *orderly* **1** *adj life-style* bien réglé **2** *n in hospital* aide-soignant *m*

ordinarily [ɔːrdɪˈnerɪlɪ] (*as a rule*) d'habitude; **ordinary** ordinaire

ore [ɔːr] minerai *m*

organ [ˈɔːrgən] ANAT organe *m*; MUS orgue *m*; **organic** *food, fertilizer* biologique; **organically** *grown* biologiquement; **organism** organisme *m*

organization [ɔːrgənaɪˈzeɪʃn] organisation *f*; **organize** organiser; **organizer** *person* organisateur(-trice) *m(f)*

Orient [ˈɔːrɪənt] Orient *m*; **Oriental** oriental

origin [ˈɑːrɪdʒɪn] origine *f*; **original 1** *adj* (*not copied*) original; (*first*) d'origine, initial **2** *n painting etc* original

m; **originality** originalité *f*; **originally** à l'origine; (*at first*) au départ; **originate 1** *v/t idea* être à l'origine de **2** *v/i of idea, belief* émaner (**from** de); *of family* être originaire (**from** de)

ornamental [ɔːrnəˈmentl] décoratif

ornate [ɔːrˈneɪt] *architecture* chargé; *prose style* fleuri

orphan [ˈɔːrfn] orphelin(e) *m(f)*

orthodox [ˈɔːrθədɑːks] orthodoxe

orthopedic [ɔːrθəˈpiːdɪk] orthopédique

ostensibly [ɑːˈstensəblɪ] en apparence

ostentatious [ɑːstenˈteɪʃəs] prétentieux, tape-à-l'œil *inv*

ostracize [ˈɑːstrəsaɪz] frapper d'ostracisme

other [ˈʌðər] **1** *adj* autre; **the ~ day** (*recently*) l'autre jour; **every ~ day** un jour sur deux; **~ people** d'autres **2** *n*: **the ~** l'autre *m/f*

otherwise [ˈʌðərwaɪz] **1** *conj* sinon **2** *adv* (*differently*) autrement

ought [ɔːt]: **I/you ~ to know** je/tu devrais le savoir; **you ~ to have done it** tu aurais dû le faire

ounce [aʊns] once *f*

our [ˈaʊər] notre; *pl* nos; **ours** le nôtre, la nôtre; *pl* les nôtres; **it's ~** c'est à nous; **ourselves** nous-mêmes; *reflex-*

ive nous; *after prep* nous; *we enjoyed* nous nous sommes amusé(e)s

oust [aʊst] *from office* évincer

out [aʊt]: *be*~ *of light, fire* être éteint; *of flower* être en fleur; *of sun* briller; *(not at home, not in building)* être sorti; *of calculations* être faux; *(be published)* être sorti; *of secret* être connu; *(no longer in competition)* être éliminé; *(no longer in fashion)* être passé de mode; ~ *here in Dallas*: **(get)** ~*!* dehors!; **(get)** ~ *of my room!* sors de ma chambre!; *that's* ~*!* (~ *of the question)* hors de question!; *he's* ~ *to win* (*fully intends to*) il est bien décidé à gagner; **outbreak** *of war* déclenchement *m*; *of violence* éruption *f*

'**outcast** exclu(e) *m(f)*
'**outcome** résultat *m*
'**outcry** tollé *m*
out'dated démodé
out'do surpasser
'**outdoor** *activities* de plein air; *life* au grand air; *toilet* extérieur; **outdoors** dehors
outer ['aʊtər] *wall etc* extérieur

'**outfit** *(clothes)* tenue *f*, ensemble *m*; *(company, organization)* boîte *f* F
out'last durer plus longtemps que
'**outlet** *of pipe* sortie *f*; *for sales point m* de vente; ELEC prise *f* de courant
'**outline 1** *n* silhouette *f*; *of plan, novel* esquisse *f* **2** *v/t plans* ébaucher
out'live survivre à
'**outlook** *(prospects)* perspective *f*
out'number être plus nombreux que
out of ◇ *motion* de, hors de; **run** ~ *the house* sortir de la maison en courant
◇ *position:* **20 miles** ~ **Detroit** à 32 kilomètres de Détroit
◇ *cause* par; ~ *jealousy* par jalousie
◇ *without: we're* ~ *gas* nous n'avons plus d'essence
◇ *from a group* sur; **5** ~ **10** 5 sur 10
'**out-of-date** dépassé; *(expired)* périmé
'**output 1** *n of factory* production *f*, rendement *m*; COMPUT sortie *f* **2** *v/t (produce)* produire
'**outrage 1** *n feeling* indignation *f*; *act* outrage *m* **2** *v/t* faire outrage à; **outrageous** *acts* révoltant; *prices* scandaleux
'**outright 1** *adj* expérience incontesté **2** *adv kill* sur le coup; *refuse* catégoriquement
'**outset** début *m*
out'shine éclipser
out'side 1 *adj* extérieur **2** *adv* dehors, à l'extérieur **3** *prep* à

l'extérieur de; (*apart from*) en dehors de **4** *n of building, case etc* extérieur *m*

'out**size** *clothing* grande taille

'out**skirts** *of town* banlieue *f*

out'**smart** → **outwit**

'out**source** externaliser

out'**standing** exceptionnel, remarquable; FIN impayé

outstretched ['aʊtstretʃt] *hands* tendu

out**ward** ['aʊtwəd] *appearance* extérieur; ~ *journey* voyage *m* aller; **outwardly** en apparence

out'**weigh** l'emporter sur

out'**wit** se montrer plus malin que

oval ['əʊvl] ovale

oven ['ʌvn] four *m*

over ['əʊvər] **1** *prep* (*above*) au-dessus de; (*across*) de l'autre côté de; (*more than*) plus de; (*during*) pendant; *she walked ~ the street* elle traversa la rue; *travel all ~ Brazil* voyager à travers le Brésil; *we're ~ the worst* le pire est passé; ~ *and above* en plus de **2** *adv*: *be* ~ (*finished*) être fini; (*left*) rester; *there were just 6* ~ il n'en restait que 6; ~ *in Japan* au Japon; ~ *here* ici; ~ *there* là-bas; *it hurts all* ~ ça fait mal partout; *painted white all* ~ peint tout en blanc; *it's all* ~ c'est fini; ~ *and again* maintes et maintes fois; *do sth* ~ (*again*) refaire

qch; **overall** *measure* en tout; (*in general*) dans l'ensemble; **overalls** bleu *m* de travail

over'**awe** impressionner, intimider

over'**balance** *of person* perdre l'équilibre

over'**bearing** dominateur

'over**cast** *sky* couvert

over'**charge** faire payer trop cher à

'over**coat** pardessus *m*

over'**come** *difficulties* surmonter

over'**crowded** *city* surpeuplé; *train* bondé

over'**do** (*exaggerate*) exagérer; *in cooking* trop cuire; **over-'done** *meat* trop cuit

'over**dose** overdose *f*

'over**draft** découvert *m*; *have an* ~ être à découvert; **over-'draw** *account* mettre à découvert

over**dressed** trop habillé

over'**estimate** surestimer

overex'**pose** surexposer

'over**flow**[1] *n pipe* trop-plein *m inv*

over'**flow**[2] *v/i of water* déborder

over'**haul** *engine etc* remettre à neuf; *plans* remanier

over**head 1** *adj* au-dessus *m* **2** *n* FIN frais *mpl* généraux

over'**hear** entendre (*par hasard*)

over'**heated** *room* surchauffé; *engine* qui chauffe

over**joyed** [əʊvər'dʒɔɪd] ravi,

enchanté

'overland 1 *adj transport* par terre **2** *adv travel* par voie de terre

over'lap *of tiles, periods etc* se chevaucher; *of theories* se recouper

over'load surcharger

over'look *of tall building etc* surplomber, dominer; *of window* donner sur; (*not see*) laisser passer

overly ['ouvǝrlɪ] trop

'overnight *travel* la nuit; *fig: change etc* du jour au lendemain

'overpass pont *m*

over'power *physically* maîtriser

overpriced [ouvǝr'praɪst] trop cher

overrated [ouvǝ'reɪtɪd] surfait

over'ride *decision etc* annuler; *technically* forcer; **overriding** *concern* principal

over'rule *decision* annuler

over'seas à l'étranger

over'see superviser

over'shadow *fig* éclipser

'oversight omission *f*

over'sleep se réveiller en retard

over'state exagérer; **overstatement** exagération *f*

over'take *also Br* MOT dépasser

over'throw[1] *v/t government* renverser

'overthrow[2] *n of government* renversement *m*

'overtime 1 *n* SP temps *m* supplémentaire **2** *adv*: **work ~** faire des heures supplémentaires

over'turn 1 *v/t also government* renverser **2** *v/i of vehicle* se retourner

'overview *n* vue *f* d'ensemble

overwhelming [ouvǝr'welmɪŋ] *feeling* irrépressible; *relief* énorme; *majority* écrasant

over'work *n* surmenage *m* **2** *v/i* se surmener

owe [ou] devoir (*s.o.* à qn); **owing to** à cause de

owl [aul] hibou *m*, chouette *f*

own[1] [oun] *v/t* posséder

own[2] [oun] *pron*: **an apartment of my ~** un appartement à moi; **on my/his ~** tout seul

◆ **own up** avouer

owner ['ounǝr] propriétaire *m/f*; **ownership** possession *f*, propriété *f*

oxygen ['ɑːksɪdʒǝn] oxygène *m*

oyster ['ɔɪstǝr] huître *f*

ozone ['ouzoun] ozone *m*; **ozone layer** couche *f* d'ozone

P

PA [piː'eɪ] (= *personal assistant*) secrétaire *m/f*

pace [peɪs] (*step*) pas *m*; (*speed*) allure *f*; **pacemaker** MED stimulateur *m* cardiaque, pacemaker *m*; SP lièvre *m*

Pacific [pə'sɪfɪk]: **the ~** (**Ocean**) le Pacifique, l'océan *m* Pacifique

pacifier ['pæsɪfaɪər] for baby sucette *f*; **pacifism** pacifisme *m*; **pacifist** pacifiste *m/f*; **pacify** calmer, apaiser

pack [pæk] **1** *n* (*back~*) sac *m* à dos; *of cereal, cigarettes etc* paquet *m*; *of cards* jeu *m* **2** *v/t* *item of clothing etc* mettre dans ses bagages; *goods* emballer; **~ one's bag** faire sa valise **3** *v/i* faire ses bagages; **package 1** *n* (*parcel*) paquet *m*; *of offers etc* forfait *m* **2** *v/t* *in packs* conditionner; *idea, project* présenter; **packaging** *of product* conditionnement *m*; *material* emballage *m*; *of idea* présentation *f*; **packet** paquet *m*

pact [pækt] pacte *m*

pad¹ [pæd] **1** *n* *protective* tampon *m* de protection; *over wound* tampon *m*; *for writing* bloc *m* **2** *v/t* *with material* rembourrer; *speech, report* délayer

pad² [pæd] *v/i* (*move quietly*) marcher à pas feutrés

padding ['pædɪŋ] *material* rembourrage *m*; *in speech etc* remplissage *m*

paddle ['pædl] **1** *n* *in canoe* pagaie *f* **2** *v/i* *in canoe* pagayer

paddock ['pædək] paddock *m*

padlock ['pædlɑːk] cadenas *m*

page¹ [peɪdʒ] *n* *of book etc* page *f*

page² [peɪdʒ] (*call*) (faire) appeler

pager ['peɪdʒər] pager *m*, radiomessageur *m*; *for doctor* bip *m*

paid em'ployment travail *m* rémunéré

pain [peɪn] douleur *f*; **be in ~** souffrir; **painful** *arm, leg etc* douloureux; (*distressing*) pénible; (*laborious*) difficile; **painfully** (*extremely, acutely*) terriblement; **painkiller** analgésique *m*; **painstaking** minutieux

paint [peɪnt] **1** *n* peinture *f* **2** *v/t* peindre; **paintbrush** pinceau *m*; **painter** peintre *m*; **painting** *activity* peinture *f*; *picture* tableau *m*; **paintwork** peinture *f*

pair [per] paire *f*; *of people, animals* couple *m*; **a ~ of pants** un pantalon

pajamas [pəˈdʒɑːməz] pyjama *m*

Pakistan [pækɪˈstɑːn] Pakistan *m*; **Pakistani 1** *adj* pakistanais *m* **2** *n* Pakistanais(e) *m(f)*

pal [pæl] F *(friend)* copain *m*, copine *f*

palace [ˈpælɪs] palais *m*

palate [ˈpælət] ANAT, *fig* palais *m*

palatial [pəˈleɪʃl] somptueux

pale [peɪl] pâle; **go ~** pâlir

Palestine [ˈpæləstaɪn] Palestine *f*; **Palestinian 1** *adj* palestinien **2** *n* Palestinien(ne) *m(f)*

pallet [ˈpælɪt] palette *f*

pallor [ˈpælər] pâleur *f*

palm [pɑːm] *of hand* paume *f*

palm tree palmier *m*

paltry [ˈpɔːltrɪ] dérisoire

pamper [ˈpæmpər] gâter

pamphlet [ˈpæmflɪt] *for information* brochure *f*; *political* tract *m*

pan [pæn] casserole *f*; *for frying* poêle *f*

pancake [ˈpænkeɪk] crêpe *f*

pandemonium [pændɪˈmounɪəm] désordre *m*

pane [peɪn]: **a ~ of glass** un carreau

panel [ˈpænl] panneau *m*; *people* comité *m*; *on TV program* invités *mpl*

paneling, *Br* **panelling** lambris *m*

panic [ˈpænɪk] **1** *n* panique *f* **2** *v/i* paniquer; **panic-stricken**

affolé, pris de panique

panorama [pænəˈrɑːmə] panorama *m*; **panoramic** panoramique

pant [pænt] *of person* haleter

panties [ˈpæntɪz] culotte *f*

pantihose → **pantyhose**

pants [pænts] pantalon *m*

pantyhose [ˈpæntɪhouz] collant *m*

papal [ˈpeɪpəl] papal

paparazzi [pæpəˈrætsiː] paparazzi *m/f*

paper [ˈpeɪpər] **1** *n* papier *m*; *(news~)* journal *m*; *(wall~)* papier *m* peint; *academic article m*, exposé *m*; *(examination ~)* épreuve *f*; **~s** *(documents)* documents *mpl*; *(identity ~s)* papiers *mpl* **2** *adj (made of ~)* en papier **3** *v/t room* tapisser; **paperback** livre *m* de poche; **paper clip** trombone *m*; **paperwork** tâches *fpl* administratives

parachute [ˈpærəʃuːt] **1** *n* parachute *m* **2** *v/i* sauter en parachute **3** *v/t troops, supplies* parachuter

parade [pəˈreɪd] **1** *n (procession)* défilé *m* **2** *v/i of soldiers* défiler; *showing off* parader

paradise [ˈpærədaɪs] REL, *fig* paradis *m*

paradox [ˈpærədɑːks] paradoxe *m*; **paradoxical** paradoxal; **paradoxically** paradoxalement

paragraph [ˈpærəgræf] para

graphe *m*

parallel ['pærəlel] **1** *n* parallèle *f*; GEOG, *fig* parallèle *m* **2** *adj also fig* parallèle **3** *v/t* (*match*) égaler

paralysis [pə'ræləsɪs] *also fig* paralysie *f*; paralyze paralyser

paramedic [pærə'medɪk] auxiliaire *m/f* médical(e)

parameter [pə'ræmɪtər] paramètre *m*

paramilitary [pærə'mɪlɪterɪ] **1** *adj* paramilitaire **2** *n* membre *m* d'une organisation paramilitaire

paranoia [pærə'nɔɪə] paranoïa *f*; paranoid paranoïaque

paraphrase ['pærəfreɪz] paraphraser

parasite ['pærəsaɪt] *also fig* parasite *m*

parasol ['pærəsɔːl] parasol *m*

paratrooper ['pærətruːpər] parachutiste *m*, para *m* F

parcel ['pɑːrsl] colis *m*, paquet *m*

pardon ['pɑːrdn] **1** *n* LAW grâce *f*; *I beg your ~?* (*what did you say?*) comment?; (*I'm sorry*) je vous demande pardon **2** *v/t* pardonner; LAW gracier; *~ me?* pardon?

parent ['perənt] père *m*; mère *f*; *my ~s* mes parents; parental parental; parent company société *f* mère

parent-'teacher association association *f* de parents

d'élèves

parish ['pærɪʃ] paroisse *f*

park¹ [pɑːrk] *n* parc *m*

park² [pɑːrk] MOT **1** *v/t* garer **2** *v/i* stationner, se garer; parking MOT stationnement *m*; parking brake frein *m* à main; parking garage parking *m* couvert; parking lot parking *m*; parking meter parcmètre *m*; parking ticket contravention *f*

parliament ['pɑːrləmənt] parlement *m*

parole [pə'roʊl] **1** *n* libération *f* conditionnelle **2** *v/t* mettre en liberté conditionnelle

parrot ['pærət] perroquet *m*

part [pɑːrt] **1** *n* partie *f*; *of machine* pièce *f*; *in movie* rôle *m*; *in hair* raie *f*; *take ~ in* participer à, prendre part à **2** *adv* (*partly*) en partie **3** *v/i of two people* se quitter, se séparer; partial (*incomplete*) partiel; partially partiellement

participant [pɑːr'tɪsɪpənt] participant(e) *m(f)*; participate participer (*in* à); participation participation *f*

particular [pər'tɪkjələr] particulier; (*fussy*) à cheval (*about* sur), exigeant; particularly particulièrement

partition [pɑːr'tɪʃn] (*screen*) cloison *f*; *of country* partage *m*, division *f*

partly ['pɑːrtlɪ] en partie

partner ['pɑːrtnər] partenaire

m; COM associé *m*; *in relationship* compagnon(ne) *m(f)*; **partnership** COM, *in relationship* association *f*; *in particular activity* partenariat *m*

'**part-time** à temps partiel

party ['pɑːtɪ] **1** *n* (*celebration*) fête *f*; *for adults in the evening also* soirée *f*; POL parti *m*; (*group of people*) groupe *m* **2** *v/i* F faire la fête

pass [pæs] **1** *n for entry* laissez-passer *m inv*; SP passe *f*; *in mountains* col *m* **2** *v/t* (*go past*) passer devant; *another car* doubler, dépasser; *competitor* dépasser; (*go beyond*); (*approve*) approuver; ~ *an exam* réussir (à) un examen **3** *v/i of time* passer; *in exam* être reçu; SP *in exam* faire une passe; (*go away*) passer

◆ **pass away** (*euph: die*) s'éteindre

◆ **pass on 1** *v/t information*, *book* passer **2** *v/i* (*euph: die*) s'éteindre

◆ **pass out** (*faint*) s'évanouir

◆ **pass up** *opportunity* laisser passer

passable ['pæsəbl] *road* praticable; (*acceptable*) passable

passage ['pæsɪdʒ] (*corridor*) couloir *m*; *from book, of time* passage *m*

passenger ['pæsɪndʒər] passager(-ère) *m(f)*

passer-by [pæsər'baɪ] passant(e) *m(f)*

passion ['pæʃn] passion *f*;

passionate *lover* passionné; (*fervent*) fervent, véhément

passive ['pæsɪv] **1** *adj* passif **2** *n* GRAM passif *m*; **passive smoking** tabagisme *m* passif

'**passport** passeport *m*; **passport control** contrôle *m* des passeport; **password** mot *m* de passe

past [pæst] **1** *adj* (*former*) passé; *the ~ few days* ces derniers jours **2** *n* passé *m*; *in the ~* autrefois **3** *prep* après; *it's ~ 7 o'clock* il est plus de 7 heures; *it's half ~ two* il est deux heures et demie **4** *adv*: **run ~** passer en courant

pasta ['pæstə] pâtes *fpl*

paste [peɪst] **1** *n* (*adhesive*) colle *f* **2** *v/t* (*stick*) coller

'**pastime** ['pæstaɪm] passe-temps *m inv*

past par'ticiple GRAM participe *m* passé

pastry ['peɪstrɪ] *for pie* pâte *f*; *small cake* pâtisserie *f*

'**past tense** GRAM passé *m*

pasty ['peɪstɪ] *complexion* blafard

pat [pæt] **1** *n* petite tape *f* **2** *v/t* tapoter

patch [pætʃ] **1** *n on clothing* pièce *f*; (*period of time*) période *f*; (*area*) tache *f*; **go through a bad ~** traverser une mauvaise passe **2** *v/t clothing* rapiécer

◆ **patch up** (*repair*) rafistoler F; *quarrel* régler

patchy ['pætʃɪ] inégal

patent ['peɪtnt] **1** adj (obvious) manifeste **2** n for invention brevet m **3** v/t invention breveter

paternal [pə'tɜːrnl] paternel; **paternalism** paternalisme m; **paternalistic** paternaliste; **paternity** paternité f

path [pæθ] chemin m; surfaced allée f; fig voie f

pathetic [pə'θetɪk] touchant; F (very bad) pathétique

pathological [pæθə'lɑːdʒɪkl] pathologique

patience ['peɪʃns] patience f; **patient 1** adj patient **2** n patient m; **patiently** patiemment

patio ['pætɪoʊ] patio m

patriot ['peɪtrɪət] patriote m/f; **patriotic** person patriote; song patriotique; **patriotism** patriotisme m

patrol [pə'troʊl] **1** n patrouille f **2** v/t streets, border patrouiller dans/à; **patrol car** voiture f de police; **patrolman** agent m de police; **patrol wagon** fourgon m cellulaire

patron ['peɪtrən] of store, movie theater client(e) m(f); of artist, charity etc protecteur(-trice) m(f); **patronize** person traiter avec condescendance; **patronizing** condescendant; **patron saint** patron(ne) m(f)

pattern ['pætərn] on fabric motif m; for sewing patron

m; (model) modèle m; in events scénario m

paunch [pɔːntʃ] ventre m

pause [pɔːz] **1** n pause f **2** v/i faire une pause **3** v/t tape mettre en mode pause

pave [peɪv] paver; **pavement** (roadway) chaussée f; Br (sidewalk) trottoir m

paw [pɔː] **1** n patte f **2** v/t F tripoter

pawn [pɔːn] in chess, fig pion m

pay [peɪ] **1** n paye f, salaire m **2** v/t payer; **~ attention** attention f; **3** v/i payer; (be profitable) être rentable; **~ for** purchase payer

◆ **pay back** rembourser; (get revenge on) faire payer à

◆ **pay off 1** v/t debt rembourser; corrupt official acheter **2** v/i (be profitable) être rentable

◆ **pay up** payer

payable ['peɪəbl] payable; **pay check**, Br **pay cheque** chèque m de paie; **payday** jour m de paie; **payee** bénéficiaire m/f; **payment** paiement m; **pay phone** téléphone m public

PC [piː'siː] (= **personal computer**) P.C. m; (= **politically correct**) politiquement correct

pea [piː] petit pois m

peace [piːs] paix f; **peaceful** paisible, tranquille; demonstration pacifique; **peace-**

fully paisiblement

peach [piːtʃ] pêche f

peak [piːk] **1** n of mountain pic m; fig apogée f **2** v/i culminer; **peak hours** of electricity consumption heures fpl pleines; of traffic heures fpl de pointe

peanut ['piːnʌt] cacahuète f; **get paid ~s** F être payé trois fois rien; **peanut butter** beurre m de cacahuètes

pear [per] poire f

pearl [pɜːrl] perle f

pecan ['piːkən] pécan m

peck [pek] **1** n (bite) coup m de bec; (kiss) bise f (rapide) **2** v/t (bite) donner un coup de bec à; (kiss) embrasser rapidement

peculiar [pɪˈkjuːljər] (strange) bizarre; **peculiarity** bizarrerie f; (special feature) particularité f

pedal ['pedl] **1** n of bike pédale f **2** v/i pédaler; **he ~ed off home** il est rentré chez lui à vélo

peddle ['pedl] drugs faire du trafic de

pedestrian [pɪˈdestrɪən] piéton(ne) m(f)

pediatric [piːdɪˈætrɪk] pédiatrique; **pediatrician** pédiatre m/f; **pediatrics** pédiatrie f

pedicure ['pedɪkjur] soins mpl des pieds

pedigree ['pedɪgriː] **1** adj avec pedigree **2** n of dog, racehorse pedigree m; of person

arbre m généalogique

pee [piː] F faire pipi F

peek [piːk] **1** n coup m d'œil (furtif) **2** v/i jeter un coup d'œil, regarder furtivement

peel [piːl] **1** n peau f **2** v/t fruit, vegetables éplucher, peler **3** v/i of nose, shoulders peler; of paint s'écailler

peep [piːp] → **peek**

'peephole judas m

peer[1] [pɪr] n (equal) pair m; of same age group personne f du même âge

peer[2] [pɪr] v/i regarder

peg [peg] for hat, coat patère f; for tent piquet m; **off the ~** de confection

pejorative [pɪˈdʒɑːrətɪv] péjoratif

pellet ['pelɪt] boulette f; for gun plomb m

pen[1] [pen] stylo m

pen[2] [pen] (enclosure) enclos m

pen[3] [pen] → **penitentiary**

penalize ['piːnəlaɪz] pénaliser

penalty ['penltɪ] sanction f; JUR peine f; fine amende f; SP pénalisation f; soccer penalty m; **penalty area** soccer surface f de réparation; **penalty clause** LAW clause f pénale; **penalty kick** soccer penalty m

pencil ['pensl] crayon m (de bois); **pencil sharpener** taille-crayon m inv

pendant ['pendənt] necklace pendentif m

penetrate ['penɪtreɪt] pénétrer; **penetration** pénétra-
tion f
penguin ['peŋgwɪn] manchot
m
penicillin [penɪ'sɪlɪn] pénicilline f
peninsula [pə'nɪnsjʊlə] presqu'île f
penitence ['penɪtəns] pénitence f, repentir m; **penitentiary** pénitencier m
'pen name nom m de plume
pennant ['penənt] fanion m
penniless ['penɪlɪs] sans le
sou
'pen pal correspondant(e)
m(f)
pension ['penʃn] retraite f,
pension f
◆ **pension off** mettre à la retraite
pensive ['pensɪv] pensif
Pentagon ['pentəgɑːn]: **the ~**
le Pentagone
pentathlon [pen'tæθlən] pentathlon m
penthouse ['penthaʊs] penthouse m, appartement m
luxueux (édifié sur le toit
d'un immeuble)
pent-up ['pentʌp] refoulé
penultimate [pe'nʌltɪmət]
avant-dernier
people ['piːpl] gens mpl;
(race, tribe) peuple m; **10 ~**
10 personnes; **the ~** le peuple; **~ say ...** on dit...
pepper ['pepər] spice poivre
m; vegetable poivron m; pep-

permint candy bonbon m à
la menthe; flavoring menthe
f poivrée
per [pɜːr] par; **~ annum** par an
perceive [pər'siːv] percevoir
percent [pər'sent] pour cent;
percentage pourcentage m
perceptible [pər'septəbl] perceptible; **perceptibly** sensiblement; **perception** perception f; (insight) perspicacité f; **perceptive** perspicace
percolate ['pɜːrkəleɪt] of coffee passer; **percolator** cafetière f à pression
perfect 1 ['pɜːrfɪkt] adj parfait 2 ['pɜːrfɪkt] n GRAM passé
m composé 3 [pər'fekt] v/t
perfectionner; **perfection**
perfection f; **perfectionist**
perfectionniste m/f; **perfect-
ly** parfaitement; (totally)
tout à fait
perforated ['pɜːrfəreɪtɪd] per-
foré; **~ line** pointillé m
perform [pər'fɔːrm] 1 v/t (carry out) exécuter; of actor etc
jouer 2 v/i of actor, musician,
dancer jouer; of machine
fonctionner; **performance**
by actor, musician etc interprétation f; (event) représentation f; of employee, company etc résultats mpl; of machine performances fpl, rendement m; **performer** interprète m/f
perfume ['pɜːrfjuːm] parfum
m
perfunctory [pər'fʌŋktərɪ]

sommaire

perhaps [pər'hæps] peut-être

peril ['perəl] péril *m*

perimeter [pə'rɪmɪtər] périmètre *m*

period ['pɪrɪəd] période *f*; *(menstruation)* règles *fpl*; *punctuation mark* point *m*; **periodic** périodique; **periodical** périodique *m*

peripheral [pə'rɪfərəl] **1** *adj (not crucial)* secondaire **2** *n* COMPUT périphérique *m*; **periphery** périphérie *f*

perish ['perɪʃ] *of rubber* se détériorer; *of person* périr; **perishable** *food* périssable

perjure ['pɜːrdʒər]: ~ *o.s.* faire un faux témoignage; **perjury** faux témoignage *m*

perm [pɜːrm] **1** *n* permanente *f* **2** *v/t*: **have one's hair ~ed** se faire faire une permanente

permanent ['pɜːrmənənt] permanent; *address* fixe; **permanently** en permanence

permeate ['pɜːrmɪeɪt] *also fig* imprégner

permissible [pər'mɪsəbl] permis; **permission** permission *f*; **permissive** permissif; **permit 1** *n* permis *m* **2** *v/t* permettre (*s.o. to do* à qn de faire)

perpendicular [pɜːrpən'dɪkjulər] perpendiculaire

perpetual [pər'petʃuəl] perpétuel; **perpetually** perpétuellement

perplex [pər'pleks] laisser perplexe; **perplexity** perplexité *f*

persecute ['pɜːrsɪkjuːt] persécuter; **persecution** persécution *f*; **persecutor** persécuteur(-trice) *m(f)*

perseverance [pɜːrsɪ'vɪrəns] persévérance *f*; **persevere** persévérer

persist [pər'sɪst] persister; **persistent** *person* tenace, têtu; *questions* incessant; *rain, unemployment etc* persistant; **persistently** *(continually)* continuellement

person ['pɜːrsn] personne *f*; **personal** personnel; **personal computer** ordinateur *m* individuel; **personality** personnalité *f*; **personally** personnellement; *come, intervene* en personne; **personal organizer** organiseur *m*, agenda *m* électronique; *in book form* agenda *m*; **personal stereo** baladeur *m*; **personify** *of person* personnifier

personnel [pɜːrsə'nel] *(employees)* personnel *m*; *department* service *m* du personnel

perspective [pər'spektɪv] *in art* perspective *f*; **get sth into** ~ relativiser qch

perspiration [pɜːrspɪ'reɪʃn] transpiration *f*; **perspire** transpirer

persuade [pər'sweɪd] *person*

persuader; **persuasion** persuasion *f*; **persuasive** *person* persuasif; *argument* convaincant

perturb [pər'tɜːrb] perturber; **perturbing** perturbant

pervasive [pər'veɪsɪv] *influence, ideas* envahissant

perversion [pər'vɜːrʃn] *sexual* perversion *f*; **pervert** *sexual* pervers(e) *m(f)*

pessimism ['pesɪmɪzm] pessimisme *m*; **pessimist** pessimiste *m/f*; **pessimistic** pessimiste

pest [pest] parasite *m*; F *person* peste *f*

pester ['pestər] harceler

pesticide ['pestɪsaɪd] pesticide *m*

pet [pet] **1** *n animal* animal *m* domestique; *(favorite)* chouchou *m* F **2** *adj* préféré, favori **3** *v/t animal* caresser **4** *v/i of couple* se peloter F

petite [pə'tiːt] menu

petition [pə'tɪʃn] pétition *f*

petrify ['petrɪfaɪ] pétrifier

petrochemical [petrou'kemɪkl] pétrochimique

petrol ['petrl] *Br* essence *f*

petroleum [pɪ'trouliəm] pétrole *m*

petting ['petɪŋ] pelotage *m* F

petty ['petɪ] *person, behavior* mesquin; *details* insignifiant

pew [pjuː] banc *m* d'église

pharmaceutical [fɑːrmə'suːtɪkl] pharmaceutique; **pharmaceuticals** produits **mpl** pharmaceutiques

pharmacist ['fɑːrməsɪst] pharmacien(ne) *m(f)*; **pharmacy** *store* pharmacie *f*

phase [feɪz] phase *f*

phenomenal [fə'nɑːmɪnl] phénoménal; **phenomenon** phénomène *m*

philanthropic [fɪlən'θrɑːpɪk] *person* philanthrope; *action* philanthropique; **philanthropist** philanthrope *m/f*; **philanthropy** philanthropie *f*

Philippines ['fɪlɪpiːnz]: *the ~* les Philippines *fpl*

philosopher [fɪ'lɑːsəfər] philosophe *m/f*; **philosophical** philosophique; *attitude etc* philosophe; **philosophy** philosophie *f*

phobia ['foubɪə] phobie *f* (*about* de)

phone [foun] **1** *n* téléphone *m* **2** *v/t* téléphoner à **3** *v/i* téléphoner; **phone book** annuaire *m*; **phone booth** cabine *f* téléphonique; **phone-call** coup *m* de fil *or* de téléphone; **phone card** télécarte *f*; **phone number** numéro *m* de téléphone

phon(e)y ['founɪ] F faux

photo ['foutou] photo *f*; **photocopier** photocopieuse *f*; **photocopy 1** *n* photocopie *f* **2** *v/t* photocopier; **photogenic** photogénique; **photograph 1** *n* photographie *f* **2** *v/t* photographier; **photog-**

rapher photographe *m/f*;
photography photographie *f*

phrase [freɪz] **1** *n* expression *f*; *in grammar* syntagme *m* **2** *v/t* formuler

physical ['fɪzɪkl] **1** *adj* physique **2** *n* MED visite *f* médicale; **physically** physiquement

physician [fɪ'zɪʃn] médecin *m*

physicist ['fɪzɪsɪst] physicien(ne) *m(f)*; **physics** physique *f*

physiotherapist [fɪzɪoʊ'θerəpɪst] kinésithérapeute *m/f*; **physiotherapy** kinésithérapie *f*

physique [fɪ'ziːk] physique *m*

pianist ['pɪənɪst] pianiste *m/f*; **piano** piano *m*

pick [pɪk] (*choose*) choisir; *flowers*, *fruit* cueillir

♦ **pick up 1** *v/t* prendre; *phone* décrocher; *from ground* ramasser; (*collect*) passer prendre; *information* recueillir; *in car* prendre; *in sexual sense* lever F; *language*, *skill* apprendre; *illness* attraper; (*buy*) acheter **2** *v/i of business*, *economy* reprendre; *of weather* s'améliorer

picket ['pɪkɪt] **1** *n of strikers* piquet *m* de grève **2** *v/t*: ~ **a factory** faire le piquet de grève devant une usine

'**pickpocket** voleur *m* à la tire,

pickpocket *m*

pick-up (truck) ['pɪkʌp] pick-up *m*, camionnette *f*

picky ['pɪkɪ] F difficile

picnic ['pɪknɪk] **1** *n* pique-nique *m* **2** *v/i* pique-niquer

picture ['pɪktʃər] **1** *n* (*photo*) photo *f*; (*painting*) tableau *m*; (*illustration*) image *f*; (*movie*) film *m* **2** *v/t* imaginer

picturesque [pɪktʃə'resk] pittoresque

pie [paɪ] tarte *f*; *with top* tourte *f*

piece [piːs] morceau *m*; (*component*) pièce *f*; *in board game* pion *m*; **a ~ of advice** un conseil; **take to ~s** démonter

♦ **piece together** *broken plate* recoller; *evidence* regrouper

piecemeal ['piːsmiːl] petit à petit

pier [pɪr] *Br at seaside* jetée *f*

pierce [pɪrs] (*penetrate*) transpercer; *ears* percer; **piercing** *noise*, *eyes* perçant; *wind* pénétrant

pig [pɪg] cochon *m*, porc *m*; (*unpleasant person*) porc *m*

pigeon ['pɪdʒɪn] pigeon *m*; **pigeonhole** casier *m*

pigheaded ['pɪghedɪd] obstiné; **pigpen** *also fig* porcherie *f*

pile [paɪl] *of books*, *plates etc* pile *f*; *of sand etc* tas *m*; **a ~ of work** F un tas de boulot *m*

♦ **pile up 1** *v/i of work*, *bills*

s'accumuler **2** v/t empiler

'pile-up MOT carambolage m

pilfering ['pɪlfərɪŋ] chapardage m F

pill [pɪl] pilule f

pillar ['pɪlər] pilier m

pillow ['pɪləʊ] oreiller m; **pillowcase** taie f d'oreiller

pilot ['paɪlət] **1** n AVIA, NAUT pilote m **2** v/t airplane piloter

pimp [pɪmp] maquereau m, proxénète m

pimple ['pɪmpl] bouton m

PIN [pɪn] (= **personal identification number**) code m confidentiel

pin [pɪn] **1** n for sewing épingle f; in bowling quille f; (badge) badge m; (fiche f **2** v/t (hold down) clouer; (attach) épingler

◆ pin up notice accrocher

pincers ['pɪnsərz] of crab pinces fpl; tool tenailles fpl

pinch [pɪntʃ] **1** n pincement m; of salt etc pincée f **2** v/t pincer **3** v/i of shoes serrer

pine [paɪn] tree, wood pin m; **pineapple** ananas m

pink [pɪŋk] rose

pinnacle ['pɪnəkl] fig apogée f

'pinpoint indiquer précisément; find identifier; **pins and needles** fourmillements mpl; **pin-up** (girl) pin-up f inv

pioneer [paɪə'nɪr] **1** n fig pionnier(-ière) m(f) **2** v/t lancer; **pioneering** work innovateur

pious ['paɪəs] pieux

pip [pɪp] Br of fruit pépin m

pipe [paɪp] **1** n tuyau m; for smoking pipe f **2** v/t transporter par tuyau; **pipeline** for oil oléoduc m; for gas gazoduc m

pirate ['paɪrət] **1** n pirate m **2** v/t software pirater

pissed [pɪst] P (annoyed) en rogne F; Br P (drunk) bourré

pistol ['pɪstl] pistolet m

piston ['pɪstən] piston m

pit [pɪt] (hole) fosse f; (coal-mine) mine f

pitch¹ [pɪtʃ] n ton m

pitch² [pɪtʃ] **1** v/i in baseball lancer **2** v/t tent planter; ball lancer

pitcher¹ ['pɪtʃər] in baseball lanceur m

pitcher² ['pɪtʃər] container pichet m

pitfall ['pɪtfɔːl] piège m

pitiful ['pɪtɪfl] pitoyable; **pitiless** impitoyable

pittance ['pɪtns] somme f dérisoire

pity ['pɪtɪ] **1** n pitié f; **what a ~!** quel dommage! **2** v/t person avoir pitié de

pizza ['piːtsə] pizza f

placard ['plækɑːrd] pancarte f

place [pleɪs] **1** n endroit m; in race, competition place f; (seat) place f; **at my/his ~** chez moi/lui; **in ~** of à la place de; **take ~** avoir lieu **2** v/t (put) mettre, poser; order passer

placid ['plæsɪd] placide

plagiarism ['pleɪdʒərɪzm] plagiat *m*; **plagiarize** plagier

plain¹ [pleɪn] *n* plaine *f*

plain² [pleɪn] **1** *adj* (*clear, obvious*) clair, évident; (*not ornate*) simple; (*not patterned*) uni; (*not pretty*) ordinaire; (*blunt*) franc **2** *adv* tout simplement; **plainly** (*clearly*) manifestement; (*bluntly*) franchement; (*simply*) simplement; **plain-spoken** simple, direct

plaintive ['pleɪntɪv] plaintif

plan [plæn] **1** *n* plan *m*, projet *m*; (*drawing*) plan *m* **2** *v/t* (*prepare*) organiser, planifier; (*design*) concevoir **3** *v/i* faire des projets

plane¹ [pleɪn] AVIA avion *m*

plane² [pleɪn] *tool* rabot *m*

planet ['plænɪt] planète *f*

plank [plæŋk] *of wood* planche *f*; *fig: of policy* point *m*

planning ['plænɪŋ] organisation *f*, planification *f*

plant¹ [plænt] **1** *n* BOT plante *f* **2** *v/t* planter

plant² [plænt] (*factory*) usine *f*; (*equipment*) installation *f*, matériel *m*

plantation [plæn'teɪʃn] plantation *f*

plaque [plæk] *on wall* plaque *f*; *on teeth* plaque *f* dentaire

plaster ['plɑːstər] **1** *n* plâtre *m* **2** *v/t wall, ceiling* plâtrer

plastic ['plæstɪk] **1** *adj* en plastique **2** *n* plastique *m*;

plastic money cartes *fpl* de crédit; **plastic surgeon** spécialiste *m* en chirurgie esthétique; **plastic surgery** chirurgie *f* esthétique

plate [pleɪt] *for food* assiette *f*; (*sheet of metal*) plaque *f*

plateau ['plætəu] plateau *m*

platform ['plætfɔːrm] (*stage*) estrade *f*; *of railroad station* quai *m*; *fig: political* plateforme *f*

platinum ['plætɪnəm] **1** *adj* en platine **2** *n* platine *m*

platonic [plə'tɒnɪk] platonique

platoon [plə'tuːn] *of soldiers* section *f*

plausible ['plɔːzəbl] plausible

play [pleɪ] **1** *n* jeu *m*; *in theater, on TV* pièce *f* **2** *v/i* jouer **3** *v/t musical instrument* jouer de; *piece of music* jouer; *game* jouer à; *opponent* jouer contre; (*perform: Macbeth etc*) jouer

◆ **play around** F (*be unfaithful*) coucher à droite et à gauche

◆ **play down** minimiser

player ['pleɪr] SP joueur(-euse) *m(f)*; (*musician*) musicien (-ne) *m(f)*; (*actor*) acteur (-trice) *m(f)*; **playful** enjoué; **playground** aire *f* de jeu; **playing card** carte *f* à jouer; **playwright** dramaturge *m/f*

plaza ['plɑːzə] *for shopping* centre *m* commercial

plc [piːel'siː] *Br* (= *public lim-*

ited company S.A. *f* (= société anonyme)

plea [pliː] appel

plead [pliːd]: *~ guilty/not guilty* plaider coupable/non coupable; *~ with* supplier

pleasant ['pleznt] agréable

please [pliːz] **1** *adv* s'il vous plaît, s'il te plaît; *~ do* je vous en prie **2** *v/t* plaire à; *~ yourself* comme tu veux; **pleased** content, heureux; *~ to meet you* enchanté; **pleasing** agréable; **pleasure** plaisir *m*; *with* avec plaisir

pleat [pliːt] *in skirt* pli *m*

pledge [pledʒ] **1** *n* (*promise*) promesse *f*; *as guarantee* gage *m*; *Pledge of Allegiance* serment *m* d'allégeance **2** *v/t* (*promise*) promettre; *money* mettre en gage

plentiful ['plentɪfl] abondant; *be ~* abonder; **plenty** (*abundance*) abondance *f*; *~ of* beaucoup de

pliable ['plaɪəbl] flexible

pliers ['plaɪərz] pinces *fpl*

plight [plaɪt] détresse *f*

plod [plɒd] (*walk*) marcher d'un pas lourd

plot[1] [plɒt] *of land* parcelle *f*

plot[2] [plɒt] **1** *n* (*conspiracy*) complot *m*; *of novel* intrigue *f* **2** *v/t & v/i* comploter

plotter ['plɒtər] conspirateur(-trice) *m(f)*; COMPUT traceur *m*

plow, *Br* **plough** [plaʊ] **1** *n* charrue *f* **2** *v/t & v/i* labourer

♦ **plow back** *profits* réinvestir

pluck [plʌk] *chicken* plumer; *~ one's eyebrows* s'épiler les sourcils

plug [plʌg] **1** *n for sink, bath* bouchon *m*; *electrical* prise *f*; (*spark ~*) bougie *f* **2** *v/t hole* boucher; *new book etc* faire de la pub pour F

♦ **plug in** brancher

plumage ['pluːmɪdʒ] plumage *m*

plumber ['plʌmər] plombier *m*; **plumbing** plomberie *f*

plummet ['plʌmɪt] *of airplane* plonger, piquer; *of share prices* dégringoler

plump [plʌmp] *person, chicken* dodu; *hands, feet* potelé; *face, cheek* rond

plunge [plʌndʒ] **1** *n* plongeon *m*; *in prices* chute *f* **2** *v/i* tomber; *of prices* chuter **3** *v/t* plonger; *knife* enfoncer; **plunging** *neckline* plongeant

plural ['plʊərəl] pluriel *m*

plus [plʌs] **1** *prep* plus **2** *adj* plus de **3** *n sign* signe *m* plus; (*advantage*) plus *m* **4** *conj* (*moreover, in addition*) en plus

plush [plʌʃ] luxueux

plywood ['plaɪwʊd] contreplaqué *m*

PM [piː'em] *Br* (= *Prime Minister*) Premier ministre

p.m. [piː'em] (= *post meridiem*) *afternoon* de l'après-midi; *evening* du soir

pneumonia [nuːˈmoʊnɪə] pneumonie f

poach¹ [poʊtʃ] cook pocher

poach² [poʊtʃ] salmon etc braconner

poached egg [poʊtʃtˈeg] œuf m poché

P.O. Box [piːˈoʊbɑːks] boîte f postale, B. P. f

pocket [ˈpɑːkɪt] **1** n poche f **2** adj (miniature) de poche **3** v/t empocher; **pocketbook** purse pochette f; (billfold) portefeuille m; book livre m de poche; **pocket calculator** calculatrice f de poche

podium [ˈpoʊdɪəm] estrade f; for winner podium m

poem [ˈpoʊɪm] poème m; **poet** poète m, poétesse f; **poetic** poétique; **poetry** poésie f

poignant [ˈpɔɪnjənt] poignant

point [pɔɪnt] **1** n of pencil, knife pointe f; in competition, exam point m; (purpose) objet m; (moment) moment m; in argument, discussion point m; in decimals virgule f; **that's beside the ~** il n'est pas la question; **be on the ~ of doing sth** être sur le point de faire qch; **get to the ~** en venir au fait; **the ~ is ...** le fait est (que)...; **there's no ~ in waiting** ça ne sert à rien d'attendre **2** v/i montrer (du doigt)

◆ **point out** sights montrer; advantages etc faire remarquer

◆ **point to** with finger montrer du doig; fig (indicate) indiquer

pointed [ˈpɔɪntɪd] remark acerbe, mordant; **pointer** for teacher baguette f; (hint) conseil m; (sign, indication) indice m; **pointless** inutile; **point of view** point m de vue

poise [pɔɪz] assurance f, aplomb m; **poised** person posé

poison [ˈpɔɪzn] **1** n poison m **2** v/t empoisonner; **poisonous** snake, spider venimeux; plant vénéneux

poke [poʊk] **1** n coup m **2** v/t (prod) pousser; (stick) enfoncer

◆ **poke around** F fouiner F

poker [ˈpoʊkər] card game poker m

polar [ˈpoʊlər] polaire

pole¹ [poʊl] of wood, metal perche f

pole² [poʊl] of earth pôle m

police [pəˈliːs] police f; **police car** voiture f de police; **policeman** gendarme m; criminal policier m; **police state** État m policier; **police station** gendarmerie f; for criminal matters commissariat m; **policewoman** femme f gendarme; criminal femme f policier

policy¹ [ˈpɑːləsɪ] politique f

policy² [ˈpɑːləsɪ] (insurance ~) police f (d'assurance)

polio [ˈpoʊlɪoʊ] polio f

polish ['pɑ:lɪʃ] **1** *n for furniture* cire *f; for shoes* cirage *m; for metal* produit *m* lustrant; *(nail ~)* vernis *m* (à ongles) **2** *v/t* faire briller, lustrer; *shoes* cirer; *speech* parfaire; **polished** *performance* impeccable

polite [pə'laɪt] poli; **politely** poliment; **politeness** politesse *f*

political [pə'lɪtɪkl] politique; **politically correct** politiquement correct; **politician** politicien *m,* homme *m/femme f* politique; **politics** politique *f*

poll [poʊl] **1** *n (survey)* sondage *m;* **go to the ~s** *(vote)* aller aux urnes **2** *v/t people* faire un sondage auprès de; *votes* obtenir

pollen ['pɑ:lən] pollen *m*

pollster ['pɑ:lstər] sondeur *m*

pollutant [pə'lu:tənt] polluant *m;* **pollute** polluer; **pollution** pollution *f*

'polo shirt polo *m*

polyester [pɑ:lɪ'estər] polyester *m*

polystyrene [pɑ:lɪ'staɪri:n] polystyrène *m*

polyunsaturated [pɑ:lʌn-'sætʃəreɪtɪd] polyinsaturé

pond [pɑ:nd] étang *m;* *artificial* bassin *m*

pontiff ['pɑ:ntɪf] pontife *m*

pony ['poʊnɪ] poney *m;* **ponytail** queue *f* de cheval

pool¹ [pu:l] *(swimming ~)* piscine *f; of water, blood* flaque *f*

pool² [pu:l] *game* billard *m* américain

pool³ [pu:l] **1** *n (common fund)* caisse *f* commune **2** *v/t resources* mettre en commun

'pool hall salle *f* de billard; **pool table** table *f* de billard

poop [pu:p] F caca *m* F

pooped [pu:pt] F crevé F

poor [pʊr] **1** *adj pauvre; quality etc* médiocre, mauvais **2** *npl:* **the ~** les pauvres *mpl;* **poorly 1** *adj (unwell)* malade **2** *adv* mal

pop¹ [pɑ:p] MUS pop *f*

pop² [pɑ:p] F *(father)* papa *m*

'popcorn pop-corn *m*

pope [poʊp] pape *m*

Popsicle® ['pɑ:psɪkl] glace *f* à l'eau

popular ['pɑ:pjələr] populaire; **popularity** popularité *f;* **populate** ['pɑ:pjəleɪt] peupler; **population** population *f*

porch [pɔ:rtʃ] porche *m*

pork [pɔ:rk] porc *m*

porn [pɔ:rn] F porno F; **pornographic** pornographique; **pornography** pornographie *f*

port¹ [pɔ:rt] *n* port *m*

port² [pɔ:rt] *adj (left-hand)* de bâbord

portable [pɔ:rtəbl] **1** *adj* portable, portatif **2** *n* COMPUT portable *m; TV* téléviseur *m* portable *or* portatif

porter ['pɔːrtər] (*doorman*)
portier *m*

portion ['pɔːrʃn] partie *f*, part
f; *of food* portion *f*

portrait ['pɔːrtreɪt] **1** *n* portrait *m* **2** *adv* print en mode
portrait, à la française; **portray** *of artist* représenter; *of actor* interpréter; *of author*
décrire

Portugal ['pɔːrtʃəgl] le Portugal; **Portuguese 1** *adj* portugais **2** *n person* Portugais(e)
m(f); *language* portugais *m*

pose [pouz] **1** *n* attitude *f* **2** *v/i*
for artist poser; ~ **as** se faire
passer pour **3** *v/t problem* poser; *threat* constituer

position [pə'zɪʃn] **1** *n* position
f **2** *v/t* placer

positive ['pɑːzətɪv] positif;
be ~ (*sure*) être sûr; **positively** vraiment

possess [pə'zes] posséder;
possession possession *f*;
possessive possessif

possibility [pɑːsə'bɪlətɪ] possibilité *f*; **possible** possible;
possibly (*perhaps*) peut-être

post¹ [poust] **1** *n of wood,
metal* poteau *m* **2** *v/t notice*
afficher; *profits* enregistrer

post² [poust] *n* (*place of duty*) poste *m* **2** *v/t soldier, employee* affecter; *guards* poster

post³ [poust] *Br* **1** *n* (*mail*)
courrier *m* **2** *v/t letter* poster

postage ['poustɪdʒ] affran-

chissement *m*; **postage
stamp** *fml* timbre *m*; **postal**
postal; **postcard** carte *f* postale; **postdate** postdater

poster ['poustər] poster *m*, affiche *f*

postgraduate ['poustgrædʒuət] étudiant(e) *m(f)* de troisième cycle

posthumous ['pɑːstʃəməs]
posthume

posting ['poustɪŋ] (*assignment*) affectation *f*

'**postmark** cachet *m* de la poste

post-mortem [poust'mɔːrtəm] autopsie *f*

'**post office** poste *f*

postpone [poust'poun] remettre (à plus tard), reporter; **postponement** report *m*

pot¹ [pɑːt] *for cooking* casserole *f*; *for coffee* cafetière *f*;
for tea théière *f*; *for plant*
pot *m*

pot² [pɑːt] F (*marijuana*) herbe *f*

potato [pə'teɪtou] pomme *f*
de terre; **potato chips**, *Br*
potato crisps chips *fpl*

potent ['poutənt] puissant

potential [pə'tenʃl] **1** *adj* potentiel **2** *n* potentiel *m*; **potentially** potentiellement

'**pothole** *in road* nid-de-poule
m

potter ['pɑːtər] potier(-ière)
m(f); **pottery** poterie *f*; *items*
poteries *fpl*

pouch [pautʃ] *bag* petit sac *m*

poultry ['pəʊltrɪ] volaille f

pound¹ [paʊnd] *weight* livre f (0,453kg)

pound² [paʊnd] n *for strays, cars* fourrière f

pound³ [paʊnd] v/i *of heart* battre (la chamade)

pour [pɔːr] 1 v/t *liquid* verser 2 v/i: **it's ~ing (with rain)** il pleut à verse

◆ **pour out** *liquid* verser; *troubles* déballer F

poverty ['pɑːvərtɪ] pauvreté f

powder ['paʊdər] 1 n poudre f 2 v/t: **~ one's face** se poudrer le visage

power ['paʊər] 1 n *(strength)* puissance f, force f; *(authority)* pouvoir m; *(energy)* énergie f; *(electricity)* courant m; **power drill** perceuse f; **power failure** panne f d'électricité; **powerful** puissant; **powerless** impuissant; **power line** ligne f électrique; **power outage** coupure f de courant; **power station** centrale f électrique; **power steering** direction f assistée

PR [piː'ɑːr] (= **public relations**) relations fpl publiques

practical ['præktɪkl] pratique; **practically** d'une manière pratique; *(almost)* pratiquement

practice ['præktɪs] 1 n pratique f; *training also* entraînement m; *(rehearsal)* répétition f; *(custom)* coutume f 2 v/i s'entraîner 3 v/t travail-

ler; *law, medicine* exercer

practise Br → **practice** v/i & v/t

prairie ['preərɪ] prairie f

praise [preɪz] 1 n louange f, éloge m 2 v/t louer; **praiseworthy** méritoire, louable

pray [preɪ] prier; **prayer** prière f

preach [priːtʃ] prêcher; **preacher** pasteur m

precaution [prɪ'kɔːʃn] précaution f; **precautionary measure** préventif, de précaution

precede [prɪ'siːd] précéder; **precedent** précédent m; **preceding** précédent

precious ['preʃəs] précieux

precise [prɪ'saɪs] précis; **precisely** précisément; **precision** précision f

preconceived ['priːkənsiːvd] *idea* préconçu

precondition [priːkən'dɪʃn] condition f requise

predator ['predətər] prédateur m; **predatory** prédateur

predecessor ['priːdɪsesər] prédécesseur m

predicament [prɪ'dɪkəmənt] situation f délicate

predict [prɪ'dɪkt] prédire, prévoir; **prediction** prédiction f

predominant [prɪ'dɑːmɪnənt] prédominant; **predominantly** principalement

prefabricated [priː'fæbrɪkeɪtɪd] préfabriqué

preface ['prefɪs] préface f

prefer [prɪ'fɜːr] préférer; **preferable** préférable; **preferably** de préférence; **preference** préférence f; **preferential** préférentiel

pregnancy ['pregnənsɪ] grossesse f; **pregnant** enceinte; *animal* pleine

prehistoric [priːhɪs'tɒrɪk] *also fig* préhistorique

prejudice ['predʒʊdɪs] **1** n (*bias*) préjugé m **2** v/t *person* influencer; *chances* compromettre; **prejudiced** partial

preliminary [prɪ'lɪmɪnerɪ] préliminaire

premarital [priː'mærɪtl] *sex* avant le mariage

premature [prɪ'məʊtʊr] prématuré

premier ['premɪr] POL Premier ministre m

première ['premɪr] première f

premises ['premɪsɪz] locaux mpl

premium ['priːmɪəm] *in insurance* prime f

prenatal [priː'neɪtl] prénatal

preoccupied [priː'ɑːkjʊpaɪd] préoccupé

preparation [prepə'reɪʃn] préparation f; **~s** préparatifs mpl; **prepare** [prɪ'per] **1** v/t préparer; **be ~d to do sth** willing, ready être prêt à faire qch **2** v/i se préparer

preposition [prepə'zɪʃn] préposition f

prerequisite [priː'rekwɪzɪt]

condition f préalable

prescribe [prɪ'skraɪb] *of doctor* prescrire; **prescription** MED ordonnance f

presence ['prezns] présence f; **in the ~ of** en présence de

present¹ ['preznt] **1** *adj* (*current*) actuel; **be ~** être présent **2** n: **the ~** *also* GRAM le présent

present² ['preznt] n (*gift*) cadeau m

present³ [prɪ'zent] v/t *award, bouquet* remettre; *program* présenter

presentation [prezn'teɪʃn] présentation f; **present-day** actuel; **presenter** présentateur(-trice) m(f); **presently** (*at the moment*) à présent; (*soon*) bientôt

preservative [prɪ'zɜːrvətɪv] conservateur m; **preserve 1** n (*domain*) domaine m **2** v/t *standards, peace etc* maintenir; *wood etc* préserver; *food* conserver

preside [prɪ'zaɪd] *at meeting* présider; **presidency** présidence f; **president** POL président(e) m(f); *of company* président-directeur m général, PDG m; **presidential** présidentiel

press [pres] **1** n: **the ~** la presse **2** v/t *button* appuyer sur; *hand* serrer; *grapes, olives* presser; *clothes* repasser; **pressing** pressant; **pressure 1** n pression f **2** v/t faire pression sur

prestige [pre'sti:ʒ] prestige *m*; **prestigious** prestigieux

presumably [prɪ'zu:məblɪ] sans doute; **presume** présumer; **presumption** *of innocence, guilt* présomption *f*

presuppose [pri:sə'pəʊz] présupposer

pre-tax ['pri:tæks] avant impôts

pretence Br → **pretense**

pretend [prɪ'tend] **1** *v/t* prétendre **2** *v/i* faire semblant; **pretense** semblant *m*; **under the ~ of cooperation** sous prétexte de coopération; **pretentious** prétentieux

pretext ['pri:tekst] prétexte *m*

pretty ['prɪtɪ] **1** *adj* joli **2** *adv* (*quite*) assez

prevail [prɪ'veɪl] (*triumph*) prévaloir, l'emporter; **prevailing** *wind* dominant; *opinion* prédominant; (*current*) actuel

prevent [prɪ'vent] empêcher; *disease* prévenir; **~ s.o. (from) doing sth** empêcher qn de faire qch; **prevention** prévention *f*; **preventive** préventif

preview ['pri:vju:] **1** *n* avant-première *f* **2** *v/t* voir en avant-première

previous ['pri:vɪəs] (*earlier*) antérieur; (*the one before*) précédent; **previously** auparavant, avant

prey [preɪ] proie *f*

price [praɪs] **1** *n* prix *m* **2** *v/t* com fixer le prix de; **priceless** sans prix

prick[1] [prɪk] **1** *n* pain piqûre *f* **2** *v/t* (*jab*) piquer

prick[2] [prɪk] V (*penis*) bite *f* V; *person* con *m* F

prickle ['prɪkl] *on plant* épine *f*, piquant *m*; **prickly** *beard, plant* piquant *m*; (*irritable*) irritable

pride [praɪd] fierté *f*; (*self-respect*) amour-propre *m*, orgueil *m*

priest [pri:st] prêtre *m*

primarily [praɪ'merɪlɪ] principalement; **primary 1** *adj* principal **2** *n* POL (*élection f*) primaire *f*

prime 'minister Premier ministre *m*

primitive ['prɪmɪtɪv] primitif; *conditions* rudimentaire

prince [prɪns] prince *m*; **princess** princesse *f*

principal ['prɪnsəpl] **1** *adj* principal **2** *n of school* directeur(-trice) *m(f)*; **principally** principalement

principle ['prɪnsəpl] principe *m*; **on ~** par principe; **in ~** en principe

print [prɪnt] **1** *n in book etc* texte *m*, (*photograph*) épreuve *f*; **out of ~** épuisé **2** *v/t* imprimer; (*use block capitals*) écrire en majuscules; **printer** ['prɪntər] *person* imprimeur *m*; *machine* imprimante *f*; **printout** impression *f*

prior ['praɪr] **1** adj préalable, antérieur **2** prep: **~ to** avant

prioritize (put in order of priority) donner un ordre de priorité à; (give priority to) donner la priorité à; **priority** priorité f

prison ['prɪzn] prison f; **prisoner** prisonnier(-ère) m(f); **take s.o.** ~ faire qn prisonnier; **prisoner of war** prisonnier(-ière) m(f) de guerre

privacy ['praɪvəsɪ] intimité f; **private 1** adj privé; letter personnel; secretary particulier **2** n MIL simple soldat m; **privately talk to s.o.** en privé; (inwardly) intérieurement; **~ owned** privé

privilege ['prɪvəlɪdʒ] privilège m; **privileged** privilégié

prize [praɪz] **1** n prix m **2** v/t priser, faire (grand) cas de; **prizewinner** gagnant m; **prizewinning** gagnant

probability [prɑːbə'bɪlətɪ] probabilité f; **probable** probable; **probably** probablement

probation [prə'beɪʃn] in job période f d'essai; LAW probation f

probe [proʊb] **1** n (investigation) enquête f; scientific sonde f v/t sonder; (investigate) enquêter sur

problem ['prɑːbləm] problème m; **no ~** pas de problème; it doesn't worry me c'est pas grave

procedure [prə'siːdʒər] procédure f; **proceed** (go: of people) se rendre; (of work etc) avancer, se dérouler; **proceedings** (events) événements mpl; **proceeds** bénéfices mpl

process ['prɑːses] **1** n processus m **2** v/t food, raw materials transformer; data, application traiter; **procession** procession f; **processor** processeur m

prod [prɑːd] **1** n (petit) coup m **2** v/t donner un (petit) coup à, pousser

prodigy ['prɑːdɪʒɪ] prodige m; (child) ~ enfant m/f prodige

produce[1] ['prɑːduːs] n produits mpl (agricoles)

produce[2] [prə'duːs] v/t produire; (bring about) provoquer; (bring out) sortir

producer [prə'duːsər] producteur m; of play, movie, TV program producteur m; **product** produit m; **production** production f; **productive** productif; **productivity** productivité f

profess [prə'fes] prétendre; **profession** profession f; **professional 1** adj professionnel **2** n (doctor, lawyer etc) personne f qui exerce une profession libérale; not amateur professionnel(le) m(f); **professionally** play sport professionnellement (*well, skillfully*) de manière professionnelle

professor [prə'fesər] professeur *m*

proficient [prə'fɪʃnt] excellent, compétent

profile ['prəʊfaɪl] profil *m*

profit ['prɑːfɪt] **1** *n* bénéfice *m*, profit *m* **2** *v/i*: **~ from** profiter de; **profitability** rentabilité *f*; **profitable** rentable

profound [prə'faʊnd] profond

prognosis [prɑːg'nəʊsɪs] MED pronostic *m*

program ['prəʊgræm] **1** *n* programme *m*; *on radio, TV* émission *f* **2** *v/t* programmer; **programme** *Br* → **program**; **programmer** programmeur(-euse) *m(f)*

progress ['prɑːgres] *n* progrès *m(pl)* **2** [prə'gres] *v/i* (*in time*) avancer; (*move on*) passer à; (*make ~*) faire des progrès, progresser; **progressive** (*enlightened*) progressiste; (*which progresses*) progressif; **progressively** progressivement

prohibit [prə'hɪbɪt] défendre, interdire; **prohibitive** *prices* prohibitif

project¹ ['prɑːdʒekt] *n* projet *m*; EDU étude *f*; (*housing area*) cité *f* (H.L.M.)

project² [prə'dʒekt] **1** *v/t* *figures, sales* prévoir; *movie* projeter **2** *v/i* (*stick out*) faire saillie

projection [prə'dʒekʃn] (*forecast*) projection *f*, prévision *f*; **projector** *for slides* projecteur *m*

prolog, *Br* **prologue** ['prəʊlɑːg] prologue *m*

prolong [prə'lɒŋ] prolonger

prominent ['prɑːmɪnənt] *nose, chin* proéminent; *visually* voyant; (*significant*) important

promiscuity [prɑːmɪ'skjuːətɪ] promiscuité *f*; **promiscuous** dévergondé

promise ['prɑːmɪs] **1** *n* promesse *f* **2** *v/t & v/i* promettre; **promising** prometteur

promote [prə'məʊt] *employee, idea* promouvoir; COM *also* faire la promotion de; **promoter** *of sports event* organisateur *m*; **promotion** promotion *f*

prompt [prɑːmpt] **1** *adj* (*on time*) ponctuel; (*speedy*) prompt **2** *v/t* (*cause*) provoquer; *actor* souffler à; **promptly** (*on time*) ponctuellement; (*immediately*) immédiatement

prone [prəʊn]: **be ~ to** être sujet à

pronoun ['prəʊnaʊn] pronom *m*

pronounce [prə'naʊns] prononcer

pronto ['prɑːntəʊ] F illico (presto) F

pronunciation [prənʌnsɪ'eɪʃn] prononciation *f*

proof [pruːf] preuve f; *of book* épreuve f

prop [prɒp] THEA accessoire m

♦ **prop up** soutenir

propaganda [prɒpəˈɡændə] propagande f

propel [prəˈpel] (*real*) vrai; **propeller** hélice f

proper [ˈprɒpər] (*real*) vrai; (*correct*) bon, correct; (*fitting*) convenable; **properly** (*correctly*) correctement; (*fittingly also*) convenablement; **property** propriété f

proportion [prəˈpɔːrʃn] proportion f; **proportional** proportionnel

proposal [prəˈpəʊzl] proposition f; *of marriage* demande f en mariage; **propose 1** v/t (*suggest*) proposer; **~ to do sth** (*plan*) se proposer de faire qch 2 v/i (*make offer of marriage*) faire sa demande en mariage; **proposition 1** n proposition f 2 v/t *woman* faire des avances à

proprietor [prəˈpraɪətər] propriétaire m

prosecute [ˈprɒsɪkjuːt] LAW poursuivre (en justice); **prosecution** LAW poursuites fpl (judiciaires); *lawyers* accusation f

prospect [ˈprɒspekt] (*chance, likelihood*) chance(s) f(pl); (*thought of something in the future*) perspective f; **~s** perspectives fpl

(*d'avenir*); **prospective** potentiel

prosper [ˈprɒspər] prospérer; **prosperity** prospérité f; **prosperous** prospère

prostitute [ˈprɒstɪtuːt] prostituée f; **male ~** prostitué m; **prostitution** prostitution f

protect [prəˈtekt] protéger; **protection** protection f; **protective** protecteur; **protector** protecteur(-trice) m(f)

protein [ˈprəʊtiːn] protéine f

protest [ˈprəʊtest] 1 (*protest*) protestation f; (*demonstration*) manifestation f 2 [prəˈtest] v/t (*object to*) protester contre 3 [prəˈtest] v/i protester; (*demonstrate*) manifester

Protestant [ˈprɒtɪstənt] 1 adj protestant 2 n protestant(e) m(f)

protester [prəˈtestər] manifestant(e) m(f)

prototype [ˈprəʊtətaɪp] prototype m

protrude [prəˈtruːd] *of eyes, ear* être saillant; *from pocket etc* sortir; **protruding** *ears* décollé; *chin* avancé; *teeth* en avant

proud [praʊd] fier; **proudly** fièrement, avec fierté

prove [pruːv] prouver

proverb [ˈprɒvɜːrb] proverbe m

provide [prəˈvaɪd] fournir; **~d that** (*on condition that*) pourvu que (+*subj*), à condition que (+*subj*)

province ['prɒvɪns] province *f*; **provincial** [prə'vɪnʃl] *also pej* provincial; *city* de province

provision [prə'vɪʒn] (*supply*) fourniture *f*; *of services* prestation *f*; *in a law, contract* disposition *f*; **provisional** provisoire

provocation [prɒvə'keɪʃn] provocation *f*; **provocative** [prə'vɒkətɪv] provocant; **provoke** provoquer

prowl [praʊl] *of tiger etc* chasser; *of burglar* rôder; **prowler** rôdeur(-euse) *m(f)*

proximity [prɒk'sɪmətɪ] proximité *f*

proxy ['prɒksɪ] (*authority*) procuration *f*; *person* mandataire *m/f*

prudence ['pru:dns] prudence *f*; **prudent** prudent

pry [praɪ] être indiscret

PS ['pi:es] (= *postscript*) P.-S. *m*

pseudonym ['su:dənɪm] pseudonyme *m*

psychiatric [saɪkɪ'ætrɪk] psychiatrique; **psychiatrist** psychiatre *m/f*; **psychiatry** psychiatrie *f*

psychoanalysis [saɪkəʊən'æləsɪs] psychanalyse *f*; **psychoanalyst** psychanalyste *m/f*; **psychoanalyze** psychanalyser

psychological [saɪkə'lɒdʒ-ɪkl] psychologique; **psychol-** ogist psychologue *m/f*

psychology psychologie *f*

psychopath ['saɪkəʊpæθ] psychopathe *m/f*

psychosomatic [saɪkəʊsə'mætɪk] psychosomatique

pub [pʌb] *Br* pub *m*

public ['pʌblɪk] **1** *adj* public **2** *n*: **the ~** le public

publication [pʌblɪ'keɪʃn] publication *f*

public 'holiday jour *m* férié

publicity [pʌb'lɪsətɪ] publicité *f*; **publicize** (*make known*) faire connaître, rendre public; сом faire de la publicité pour

publicly ['pʌblɪklɪ] en public, publiquement

'public school école *f* publique; *Br* école privée (du secondaire)

publish ['pʌblɪʃ] publier; **publisher** éditeur(-trice) *m(f)*; maison *f* d'édition; **publishing** édition *f*; **publishing company** maison *f* d'édition

puff [pʌf] **1** *n of wind* bourrasque *f*; *of smoke* bouffée *f* **2** *v/i* (*pant*) souffler, haleter; **puffy** *eyes, face* bouffi

pull [pʊl] **1** *n on rope* coup *m*; F (*appeal*) attrait *m*; F (*influence*) influence *f* **2** *v/t* tirer; *tooth* arracher; *muscle* se déchirer **3** *v/i* tirer

♦ **pull ahead** *in race, competition* prendre la tête

◆ **pull down** (*lower*) baisser; (*demolish*) démolir

◆ **pull in** *of bus, train* arriver

◆ **pull up 1** *v/t* (*raise*) remonter; *plant* arracher **2** *v/i of car etc* s'arrêter

pulley ['pʊlɪ] poulie *f*

pulsate [pʌl'seɪt] *of heart, blood* battre, *of rhythm* vibrer

pulse [pʌls] pouls *m*

pulverize ['pʌlvəraɪz] pulvériser

pump [pʌmp] **1** *n* pompe *f* **2** *v/t* pomper

pumpkin ['pʌmpkɪn] potiron *m*

pun [pʌn] jeu *m* de mots

punch [pʌntʃ] **1** *n blow* coup *m* de poing; *implement* perforeuse *f* **2** *v/t with fist* donner un coup de poing à; *hole* percer; *ticket* composter

punctual ['pʌŋktʃʊəl] ponctuel; **punctuality** ponctualité *f*

punctuation [pʌŋktʃu'eɪʃn] ponctuation *f*

puncture ['pʌŋktʃər] **1** *n* piqûre *f* **2** *v/t* percer, perforer

punish ['pʌnɪʃ] punir; **punishing** *pace, schedule* éprouvant, épuisant; **punishment** punition *f*

puny ['pju:nɪ] *person* chétif

pup [pʌp] chiot *m*

pupil[1] ['pju:pl] *of eye* pupille *f*

pupil[2] ['pju:pl] (*student*) élève *m/f*

puppet ['pʌpɪt] *also fig* marionnette *f*

purchase[1] ['pɜːrtʃəs] **1** *n* achat *m* **2** *v/t* acheter

purchase[2] ['pɜːrtʃəs] *n* (*grip*) prise *f*

purchaser ['pɜːrtʃəsər] acheteur(-euse) *m(f)*

pure [pjʊr] pur; *white* immaculé; **purely** purement

purge [pɜːrdʒ] **1** *n* POL purge *f* **2** *v/t* POL épurer

purify ['pjʊrɪfaɪ] *water* épurer

puritan ['pjʊrɪtən] puritain(e) *m(f)*

purity ['pjʊrɪtɪ] pureté *f*

purpose ['pɜːrpəs] (*aim, object*) but *m*; **on ∼** exprès; **purposely** exprès

purr [pɜːr] *of cat* ronronner

purse [pɜːrs] (*pocketbook*) sac *m* à main; *Br for money* porte-monnaie *m inv*

pursue [pər'suː] poursuivre; **pursuer** poursuivant(e) *m(f)*; **pursuit** poursuite *f*; (*activity*) activité *f*

push [pʊʃ] **1** *n* (*shove*) poussée *f* **2** *v/t* (*shove, pressure*) pousser; *button* appuyer sur; F *drugs* revendre, trafiquer **3** *v/i* pousser; **pusher** F *of drugs* dealer(-euse) *m(f)*; **push-up**: **do ∼s** faire des pompes; **pushy** F qui se met en avant

puss, pussy (*cat*) [pʊs, 'pʊsɪ (kæt)] F minou *m*

put [pʊt] mettre; *question* poser; **∼ the cost at** estimer le prix à

◆ **put across** *idea etc* faire comprendre
◆ **put aside** *money, work* mettre de côté
◆ **put away** *in closet etc* ranger; *in institution* enfermer; *in prison* emprisonner; F (*consume*) s'enfiler F; *animal* faire piquer
◆ **put back** (*replace*) remettre
◆ **put down** poser; *deposit* verser; *rebellion* réprimer; (*belittle*) rabaisser
◆ **put forward** *idea etc* soumettre, suggérer
◆ **put in for** (*apply for*) demander
◆ **put off** *light, TV* éteindre; (*postpone*) repousser; (*deter*) dissuader; (*repel*) dégoûter
◆ **put on** *light, TV* allumer; *music, jacket etc* mettre; (*perform*) monter; *accent*

etc prendre
◆ **put out** *hand* tendre; *fire, light* éteindre
◆ **put together** (*assemble*) monter; (*organize*) organiser
◆ **put up** *hand* lever; *person* héberger; (*erect*) ériger; *prices* augmenter; *poster* accrocher; *money* fournir
◆ **put up with** supporter, tolérer

putty ['pʌtɪ] mastic *m*
puzzle ['pʌzl] **1** *n* (*mystery*) énigme *f*, mystère *m*; *game* jeu *m*, casse-tête *m*; (*jigsaw* ~) puzzle *m* **2** *v/t* laisser perplexe; **puzzling** curieux
PVC [piːviːˈsiː] (= *polyvinyl chloride*) P.V.C. *m* (= polychlorure de vinyle)
pyjamas *Br* → **pajamas**
pylon ['paɪlən] pylône *m*

Q

quadrangle ['kwɒdræŋgl] *figure* quadrilatère *m*; *courtyard* cour *f*
quadruped ['kwɒdruped] quadrupède *m*
quail [kweɪl] flancher
quaint [kweɪnt] *cottage* pittoresque; (*eccentric: ideas etc*) curieux
quake [kweɪk] **1** *n* (*earthquake*) tremblement *m* de terre **2** *v/i* of earth, with fear tremble

qualification [kwɒlɪfɪˈkeɪʃn] *from university etc* diplôme *m*; **qualified** *doctor, engineer etc* qualifié; (*restricted*) restreint; **qualify 1** *v/t of degree, course etc* qualifier; *remark etc* nuancer **2** *v/i* (*get degree etc*) obtenir son diplôme; *in competition* se qualifier
quality ['kwɒlətɪ] qualité *f*; **quality control** contrôle *m* de qualité
quandary ['kwɒndərɪ] di-

lemme *m*

quantify ['kwɒntɪfaɪ] quantifier

quantity ['kwɒntətɪ] quantité *f*

quarantine ['kwɒrəntiːn] quarantaine *f*

quarrel ['kwɒrəl] **1** *n* dispute *f*, querelle *f* **2** *v/i* se disputer

quarry[1] ['kwɒrɪ] *in hunt* gibier *m*

quarry[2] ['kwɒrɪ] *for mining* carrière *f*

quart [kwɔːrt] quart *m* de gallon *(0,946 litre)*

quarter ['kwɔːrtər] quart *m*; *25 cents* vingt-cinq cents *mpl*; *part of town* quartier *m*; **a ~ of an hour** un quart d'heure; **a ~ of 5** cinq heures moins le quart; **a ~ after 5** cinq heures et quart; **quarterfinal** quart *m* de finale; **quarterfinalist** quart-finaliste *m*, quart-finalise *m*; **quarterly 1** *adj* trimestriel **2** *adv* trimestriellement; **quarters** MIL quartiers *mpl*; **quartet** MUS quatuor *m*

quartz [kwɒrts] quartz *m*

quash [kwɒʃ] *rebellion* réprimer, écraser; *court decision* casser, annuler

quaver ['kweɪvər] **1** *n* *in voice* tremblement *m* **2** *v/i* *of voice* trembler

queasy ['kwiːzɪ] nauséeux; **feel ~** avoir la nausée

queen [kwiːn] reine *f*

queer [kwɪr] *(peculiar)* bizar-

re

quell [kwel] réprimer

quench [kwentʃ] *thirst* étancher, assouvir; *flames* éteindre

query ['kwɪrɪ] **1** *n* question *f* **2** *v/t* *(express doubt about)* mettre en doute; *(check)* vérifier

quest [kwest] quête *f*

question ['kwestʃn] **1** *n* question *f* **2** *v/t* *person* questionner, interroger; *(doubt)* mettre en question; **questionable** contestable; **questioning 1** *adj look* interrogateur **2** *n* interrogatoire *m*; **question mark** point *m* d'interrogation; **questionnaire** questionnaire *m*

queue [kjuː] *Br* **1** *n* queue *f* **2** *v/i* faire la queue

quibble ['kwɪbl] chipoter, chercher la petite bête

quick [kwɪk] rapide; **be ~!** fais vite!; **quickly** vite, rapidement; **quickwitted** à l'esprit vif

quiet ['kwaɪət] *street, life* tranquille; *music* doux; *engine* silencieux; *voice* bas; **~!** silence!; **quietly** doucement, sans bruit; *(unassumingly, peacefully)* tranquillement; **quietness** calme *m*, tranquillité *f*

quilt [kwɪlt] *on bed* couette *f*

quinine ['kwɪniːn] quinine *f*

quip [kwɪp] **1** *n* trait *m* d'esprit **2** *v/i* plaisanter

quirk [kwɜːrk] manie *f*, lubie

f; **quirky** bizarre, excentrique

quit [kwɪt] **1** v/t job quitter **2** v/i (leave job) démissionner; COMPUT quitter

quite [kwaɪt] (fairly) assez; (completely) tout à fait; **~ a lot** pas mal, beaucoup

quiver ['kwɪvər] trembler

quiz [kwɪz] **1** n on TV jeu m télévisé; on radio jeu m radiophonique; at school interrogation f **2** v/t interroger

quota ['kwoʊtə] quota m

quotation [kwoʊ'teɪʃn] from author citation f; price devis m; **quotation marks** guillemets mpl; **quote 1** n from author citation f; price devis m; (quotation mark) guillemet m; **in ~s** entre guillemets **2** v/t text citer; price proposer

R

rabbit ['ræbɪt] lapin m

rabble ['ræbl] cohue f, foule f; **rabble-rouser** agitateur(-trice) m(f)

rabies ['reɪbiːz] rage f

raccoon [rə'kuːn] raton m laveur

race[1] [reɪs] n of people race f

race[2] [reɪs] **1** n SP course f **2** v/i (run fast) courir à toute vitesse **3** v/t: **I'll ~ you** je le premier arrivé a gagné

'racecourse champ m de courses, hippodrome m; **racehorse** cheval m de course; **race riot** émeute f raciale; **racetrack** for cars circuit m, piste f; for horses hippodrome m

racial ['reɪʃl] racial

racing ['reɪsɪŋ] course f

racism ['reɪsɪzm] racisme m; **racist 1** adj raciste **2** n raciste m/f

rack [ræk] **1** n for bags on train

porte-bagages m inv; for CDs range-CD m inv **2** v/t: **~ one's brains** se creuser la tête

racket[1] ['rækɪt] SP raquette f

racket[2] ['rækɪt] (noise) vacarme m; criminal activity escroquerie f

radar ['reɪdɑːr] radar m

radiance ['reɪdɪəns] éclat m; **radiant** smile radieux; **radiate** of heat, light irradier, rayonner; **radiation** nuclear radiation f; **radiator** radiateur m

radical ['rædɪkl] **1** adj radical **2** n POL radical(e) m(f); **radicalism** POL radicalisme m; **radically** radicalement

radio ['reɪdɪoʊ] radio f; **radioactive** radioactif; **radioactivity** radioactivité f; **radio alarm** radio-réveil m; **radiographer** radiologue m/f; **radiography** radiographie f;

radio station station *f* de radio

radius ['reɪdɪəs] rayon *m*

raft [rɑːft] radeau *m*

rafter ['rɑːftər] chevron *m*

rag [ræg] *for cleaning etc* chiffon *m*

rage [reɪdʒ] **1** *n* colère *f*, rage *f* **2** *v/i of storm* faire rage

ragged ['rægɪd] *edge* irrégulier; *appearance* négligé; *clothes* en loques

raid [reɪd] **1** *n by troops*, FIN raid *m*; *by police* descente *f*; *by robbers* hold-up *m* **2** *v/t of troops* attaquer; *of police* faire une descente dans; *of robbers* attaquer; *fridge* faire une razzia dans; **raider** (*robber*) voleur *m*

rail [reɪl] *on track* rail *m*; (*hand~*) rampe *f*; *for towel* porte-serviettes *m inv*; **by ~** en train; **railings** *around park etc* grille *f*; **railroad** chemin *m* de fer; *track* voie *f* ferrée; **railroad station** gare *f*; **railway** *Br* chemin *m* de fer; *track* voie *f* ferrée

rain [reɪn] **1** *n* pluie *f* **2** *v/i* pleuvoir; **it's ~ing** il pleut; **raincheck**: *can I take a ~ on that?* F peut-on remettre cela à plus tard?; **raincoat** imperméable *m*; **raindrop** goutte *f* de pluie; **rainfall** précipitations *fpl*; **rain forest** forêt *f* tropicale (humide); **rainproof** *fabric* imperméable; **rainstorm** pluie *f* torrentielle; **rainy** pluvieux

raise [reɪz] **1** *n in salary* augmentation *f* (de salaire) **2** *v/t shelf etc* surélever; *offer* augmenter; *children* élever; *question* soulever; *money* rassembler

rake [reɪk] *for garden* râteau *m*

rally ['rælɪ] (*meeting, reunion*) rassemblement *m*; MOT rallye *m*; *in tennis* échange *m*

RAM [ræm] COMPUT (= *random access memory*) RAM *f*, mémoire *f* vive

ram [ræm] **1** *n* bélier *m* **2** *v/t ship, car* heurter, percuter

ramble ['ræmbl] **1** *n walk* randonnée *f* **2** *v/i walk* faire de la randonnée; (*when speaking*) discourir; (*talk incoherently*) divaguer; **rambling 1** *adj speech* décousu *f in walking* randonnée *f*; *in speech* digression *f*

ramp [ræmp] rampe *f* (d'accès), passerelle *f*; *for raising vehicle* pont *m* élévateur

rampant ['ræmpənt] *inflation* galopant

rampart ['ræmpɑːrt] rempart *m*

ramshackle ['ræmʃækl] délabré

ranch [ræntʃ] ranch *m*; **rancher** propriétaire *m/f* de ranch; **ranchhand** employé *m* de ranch

rancid ['rænsɪd] rance

rancor, *Br* **rancour** ['ræŋkər] rancœur *f*

R & D [ɑːrənˈdiː] (= *research and development*) R&D *f* (= recherche et développement)

random ['rændəm] **1** *adj* aléatoire, au hasard; ~ *sample* échantillon *m* pris au hasard **2** *n*: *at* ~ au hasard

range [reɪndʒ] *n of products* gamme *f*; *of gun* portée *f*; *of airplane* autonomie *f*; *of voice, instrument* registre *m*; *of mountains* chaîne *f*; *at close* ~ de très près **2** *v/i*: ~ *from X to Y* aller de X à Y; **ranger** garde *m* forestier

rank [ræŋk] **1** *n* MIL grade *m*; *in society* rang *m* **2** *v/t* classer

♦ **rank among** compter parmi

ransack ['rænsæk] *searching* fouiller; *plundering* saccager

ransom ['rænsəm] *money* rançon *f*

rap [ræp] **1** *n at door etc* petit coup *m* sec; MUS rap *m* **2** *v/t table etc* taper sur

rape¹ [reɪp] *n* viol *m* **2** *v/t* violer

rape² [reɪp] *n* BOT colza *m*

rapid ['ræpɪd] rapide; **rapidity** [rəˈpɪdətɪ] rapidité *f*; **rapidly** rapidement; **rapids** rapides *mpl*

rapist ['reɪpɪst] violeur *m*

rare [rer] rare; *steak* saignant, bleu; **rarely** rarement; **rarity** rareté *f*

rash¹ [ræʃ] *n* MED éruption *f* (cutanée)

rash² [ræʃ] *adj action*, imprudent, impétueux; **rashly** sans réfléchir

rat [ræt] rat *m*

rate [reɪt] taux *m*; (*price*) tarif *m*; (*speed*) rythme *m*; *at this* ~ (*at this speed*) à ce rythme; (*carrying on like this*) si ça continue comme ça; *at any* ~ en tout cas

rather ['ræðər] (*fairly, quite*) plutôt; *I would* ~ *stay here* je préférerais rester ici

ratification [rætɪfɪˈkeɪʃn] *of treaty* ratification *f*; **ratify** ratifier

ratings ['reɪtɪŋz] indice *m* d'écoute

ratio ['reɪʃɪoʊ] rapport *m*, proportion *f*

ration ['ræʃn] **1** *n* ration *f* **2** *v/t supplies* rationner

rational ['ræʃənl] rationnel; **rationality** rationalité *f*; **rationalization** rationalisation *f*; **rationalize 1** *v/t* rationaliser **2** *v/i* (se) chercher des excuses; **rationally** rationnellement

rattle ['rætl] **1** *n of bottles, chains* cliquetis *m*; *in engine* bruit *m* de ferraille; *toy* hochet *m* **2** *v/t* chains etc entrechoquer **3** *v/i* faire du bruit; *of engine* faire un bruit de ferraille; *of crates* s'entrechoquer; *of chains* cliqueter; **rattlesnake** serpent *m* à sonnette

raucous ['rɔ:kəs] bruyant

rave [reɪv] **1** n party rave f, rave-party f **2** v/i délirer; **~ about sth** (be very enthusiastic) s'emballer pour qch

ravenous ['rævənəs] affamé

ravine [rə'vi:n] ravin m

raw [rɔ:] meat, vegetable cru; sugar, iron brut; **raw materials** matières fpl premières

ray [reɪ] rayon m

razor ['reɪzər] rasoir m; **razor blade** lame f de rasoir

re [ri:] COM en référence à

reach [ri:tʃ] **1** n: **within ~** à portée; **out of ~** hors de portée **2** v/t atteindre; destination arriver à; decision parvenir à

react [rɪ'ækt] réagir; **reaction** réaction f; **reactionary 1** adj POL réactionnaire **2** n POL réactionnaire m/f; **reactor** nuclear réacteur m

read [ri:d] lire

◆ **read out** aloud lire à haute voix

readable ['ri:dəbl] lisible; **reader** person lecteur(-trice) m(f)

readily ['redɪlɪ] admit, agree volontiers, de bon cœur

reading ['ri:dɪŋ] activity lecture f; from meter etc relevé m

readjust [ri:ə'dʒʌst] **1** v/t régler (de nouveau) **2** v/i to conditions se réadapter (**to** à)

ready ['redɪ] (prepared, willing) prêt; **get sth ~** préparer qch; **ready cash** (argent m)

liquide m; **ready-made** stew etc cuisiné; solution tout trouvé; **ready-to-wear** de confection; **~ clothing** prêt-à-porter m

real [ri:l] not imaginary réel; not fake vrai; **real estate** immobilier m, biens mpl immobiliers; **real estate agent** agent m immobilier; **realism** réalisme m; **realist** réaliste m/f; **realistic** réaliste; **realistically** de façon réaliste; **reality** réalité f; **realize** se rendre compte de; FIN réaliser; **really** vraiment; **real time** COMPUT temps m réel; **real-time** COMPUT en temps réel

realtor ['ri:ltər] agent m immobilier; **realty** immobilier m

reappear [ri:ə'pɪr] réapparaître

reappearance [ri:ə'pɪrəns] réapparition f

rear [rɪr] **1** adj arrière inv, de derrière **2** n arrière m

rearm [ri:'ɑ:rm] réarmer

rearrange [ri:ə'reɪndʒ] flowers réarranger; furniture déplacer; schedule, meetings réorganiser

rear-view 'mirror rétroviseur m, rétro m F

reason ['ri:zn] **1** n (cause), faculty raison f; **reasonable** raisonnable; **reasonably** act, behave raisonnablement; (quite) relativement; **reasoning** raisonnement m

reassure [ri:ə'ʃʊr] rassurer;

reassuring rassurant

rebate ['ri:beɪt] (refund) remboursement m

rebel 1 ['rebl] n rebelle m/f 2 [rɪ'bel] v/i se rebeller; rebellion rébellion f; rebellious rebelle; rebelliousness esprit m de rébellion

rebound [rɪ'baʊnd] of ball etc rebondir

rebuild ['ri:bɪld] reconstruire

recall [rɪ'kɔːl] goods, ambassador rappeler; (remember) se rappeler

recap ['ri:kæp] récapituler

recapture [ri:'kæptʃər] reprendre

recede [rɪ'si:d] of flood waters baisser

receipt [rɪ'si:t] for purchase reçu m (for de), ticket m de caisse; ~s FIN recette f(pl); receive recevoir; receiver TELEC combiné m; for radio (poste m) récepteur m; receivership: be in ~ être en liquidation judiciaire

recent ['ri:snt] récent; recently récemment

reception [rɪ'sepʃn] réception f; (welcome) accueil m; reception desk réception f; receptionist réceptionniste m/f; receptive: be ~ to sth être réceptif à qch

recess ['ri:ses] in wall etc renfoncement m, recoin m; EDU récréation f; of legislature vacances fpl judiciaires; recession economic récession f

recharge [ri:'tʃɑːrdʒ] battery recharger

recipe ['resəpɪ] recette f

recipient [rɪ'sɪpɪənt] of parcel etc destinataire m/f; of payment bénéficiaire m/f

reciprocal [rɪ'sɪprəkl] réciproque

recite [rɪ'saɪt] poem réciter; details, facts énumérer

reckless ['rekləs] imprudent; recklessly imprudemment

reckon ['rekən] (think, consider) penser

◆ reckon on compter sur

reclaim [rɪ'kleɪm] land from sea gagner sur la mer; lost property récupérer

recline [rɪ'klaɪn] s'allonger; recliner chair chaise f longue, relax m

recluse [rɪ'klu:s] reclus m/f

recognition [rekəg'nɪʃn] reconnaissance f; recognizable reconnaissable; recognize reconnaître

recoil [rɪ'kɔɪl] reculer

recollect [rekə'lekt] se souvenir de; recollection souvenir m

recommend [rekə'mend] recommander; recommendation recommandation f

recompense ['rekəmpens] compensation f, dédommagement m

reconcile ['rekənsaɪl] réconcilier; differences concilier; facts faire concorder; reconciliation réconciliation f; of *differences, facts* conciliation f

recondition [riːkənˈdɪʃn] refaire, remettre à neuf

reconnaissance [rɪˈkɑːnɪsəns] MIL reconnaissance f

reconsider [riːkənˈsɪdər] **1** v/t reconsidérer **2** v/i reconsidérer la question

reconstruct [riːkənˈstrʌkt] reconstruire; *crime* reconstituer

record[1] [ˈrekərd] *n* MUS disque m; SP etc record m; *written document etc* rapport m; *in database* article m, enregistrement m; **~s** (*archives*) archives fpl, dossiers mpl; **have a criminal ~** avoir un casier judiciaire

record[2] [rɪˈkɔːrd] v/t *electronically* enregistrer; *in writing* consigner

'record-breaking qui bat tous les records; **record holder** recordman m, recordwoman f

recording [rɪˈkɔːrdɪŋ] enregistrement m

recount [rɪˈkaʊnt] (*tell*) raconter

re-count [ˈriːkaʊnt] **1** *n of votes* recompte m **2** v/t recompter

recoup [rɪˈkuːp] *financial losses* récupérer

recover [rɪˈkʌvər] **1** v/t retrouver **2** v/i *from illness* se remettre; *of business* reprendre; **recovery** *of sth lost* ré-

cupération f; *from illness* rétablissement m

recreation [rekriˈeɪʃn] récréation f; **recreational** *done for pleasure* de loisirs

recruit [rɪˈkruːt] **1** *n* recrue f **2** v/t recruter; **recruitment** recrutement m

rectangle [ˈrektæŋgl] rectangle m; **rectangular** rectangulaire

rectify [ˈrektɪfaɪ] rectifier

recuperate [rɪˈkuːpəreɪt] récupérer

recur [rɪˈkɜːr] *of error, event* se reproduire; *of symptoms* réapparaître; **recurrent** récurrent

recycle [riːˈsaɪkl] recycler; **recycling** recyclage m

red [red] **1** *adj* rouge **2** *n:* **in the ~** FIN dans le rouge; **Red Cross** Croix-Rouge f

redecorate [riːˈdekəreɪt] refaire

redeem [rɪˈdiːm] *debt* rembourser; *sinners* racheter

redevelop [riːdɪˈveləp] *part of town* réaménager

redhead roux m, rousse f; **red light** *for traffic* feu m rouge; **red light district** quartier m chaud; **red meat** viande f rouge; **redneck** F plouc m F; **red tape** F paperasserie f

reduce [rɪˈduːs] réduire; **reduction** réduction f

reek [riːk] empester (**of sth** qch)

reel [riːl] *of film, thread* bobine f

re-e'lect réélire; **re-election** réélection f

re-'entry *of spacecraft* rentrée f

ref [ref] F arbitre m

◆ **refer to** faire allusion à; *dictionary etc* se reporter à

referee [refə'riː] SP arbitre m; *for job:* personne qui fournit des références; **reference** *(allusion)* allusion f; *for job* référence f; *(~ number)* (numéro m de) référence f; **reference book** ouvrage m de référence; **reference number** numéro m de référence

referendum [refə'rendəm] référendum m

refill ['riːfɪl] remplir

refine [rɪ'faɪn] *oil, sugar* raffiner; *technique* affiner; **refinement** *to process, machine* perfectionnement m; **refinery** raffinerie f

reflect [rɪ'flekt] **1** *v/t* refléter **2** *v/i* *(think)* réfléchir; **reflection** *also fig* reflet m; *(consideration)* réflexion f

reflex ['riːfleks] *in body* réflexe m

reform [rɪ'fɔːrm] **1** *n* réforme f **2** *v/t* réformer; **reformer** réformateur(-trice) m(f)

refresh [rɪ'freʃ] rafraîchir; *of sleep, rest* reposer; *of meal* redonner des forces à; **refreshing** *drink* rafraîchissant; *experience* agréable; **refreshments** rafraîchisse-

ments mpl

refrigerate [rɪ'frɪdʒəreɪt] réfrigérer; **refrigerator** réfrigérateur m

refuel [riː'fjuːəl] **1** *v/t airplane* ravitailler **2** *v/i of airplane* se ravitailler (en carburant)

refuge ['refjuːdʒ] refuge m; **take ~** *from storm etc* se réfugier; **refugee** réfugié m(f)

refund 1 ['riːfʌnd] *n* remboursement m **2** [rɪ'fʌnd] *v/t* rembourser

refusal [rɪ'fjuːzl] refus m; **refuse** refuser; **~ to do sth** refuser de faire qch

regain [rɪ'geɪn] *control, territory, the lead* reprendre; *composure* retrouver

regard [rɪ'gɑːrd] **1** *n:* **with ~ to** en ce qui concerne; *(kind)* **~s** cordialement; **with no ~ for** sans égard pour **2** *v/t:* **~ as** considérer comme; **regarding** en ce qui concerne; **regardless** quand même; **~ of** sans se soucier de

regime [reɪ'ʒiːm] *(government)* régime m

regiment ['redʒɪmənt] régiment m

region ['riːdʒən] région f; **regional** régional

register ['redʒɪstər] **1** *n* registre m **2** *v/t birth, death* déclarer; *vehicle* immatriculer; *letter* recommander; *emotion* exprimer **3** *v/i for a course* s'inscrire; *with police* se déclarer *(with* à); **registered letter lettre f recommandée; **registration** of birth, death déclaration f; of vehicle immatriculation f; for a course inscription f

regret [rɪˈgret] **1** v/t regretter **2** n regret m; **regretful** plein de regrets; **regrettable** regrettable

regular [ˈregjʊlər] **1** adj régulier; (normal) normal **2** n at bar etc habitué(e) m(f); **regularity** régularité f; **regularly** régulièrement

regulate [ˈregjʊleɪt] régler; expenditure contrôler; **regulation** (rule) règlement m

rehabilitate [riːhəˈbɪlɪteɪt] ex--criminal réinsérer; disabled person rééduquer

rehearsal [rɪˈhɜːrsl] répétition f; **rehearse** répéter

reign [reɪn] **1** n règne m **2** v/i régner

reimburse [riːɪmˈbɜːrs] rembourser

reinforce [riːɪnˈfɔːrs] renforcer; argument étayer; **reinforced concrete** béton m armé; **reinforcements** MIL renforts mpl

reinstate [riːɪnˈsteɪt] person in office réintégrer, rétablir dans ses fonctions; paragraph etc réintroduire

reject [rɪˈdʒekt] rejeter; **rejection** rejet m

relapse [ˈriːlæps] MED rechute f

related [rɪˈleɪtɪd] by family

apparenté; events, ideas etc associé; relation in family parent(e) m(f); (connection) rapport m, relation f; **relationship** relation f; sexual liaison f; relative **1** adj relatif **2** n parent(e) m(f); **relatively** relativement

relax [rɪˈlæks] **1** v/i se détendre; ~! du calme! **2** v/t muscle relâcher; **relaxation** détente f, relaxation f; **relaxed** détendu, décontracté; **relaxing** reposant, relaxant

relay [rɪˈleɪ] v/t message transmettre; radio, TV signals relayer, retransmettre **2** n [ˈriːleɪ]: ~ race (course f de) relais m

release [rɪˈliːs] **1** n from prison libération f; of CD, movie etc sortie f; CD, record nouveauté f **2** v/t prisoner libérer; CD, record, movie sortir; parking brake desserrer; information communiquer

relegate [ˈreləgeɪt] reléguer

relent [rɪˈlent] se calmer; of person s'adoucir; **relentless** (determined) acharné; rain etc incessant

relevance [ˈreləvəns] pertinence f; **relevant** pertinent

reliability [rɪlaɪəˈbɪlətɪ] fiabilité f; **reliable** fiable; **reliance** confiance f (on en); on equipment dépendance f (on vis-à-vis de)

relic [ˈrelɪk] relique f

relief [rɪˈliːf] soulagement m;

relieve *pain* soulager; *(take over from)* relayer, relever

religion [rɪˈlɪdʒən] religion f; religious religieux; *person* croyant

relinquish [rɪˈlɪŋkwɪʃ] abandonner

relish [ˈrelɪʃ] **1** *n sauce* relish f; *(enjoyment)* délectation f **2** *v/t idea, prospect* se réjouir de

relive [riːˈlɪv] *event* revivre

relocate [riːləˈkeɪt] *of business* se réimplanter; *of employee* déménager

reluctance [rɪˈlʌktəns] réticence f; reluctant réticent; **be ~ to do sth** hésiter à faire qch

♦ rely on [rɪˈlaɪ] compter sur; **rely on s.o. to do sth** compter sur qn pour faire qch

remain [rɪˈmeɪn] rester; **~ silent** garder le silence; remainder *also* MATH reste m; remaining restant; **the ~ refugees** le reste des réfugiés; remains *of body* restes *mpl*

remake [ˈriːmeɪk] *of movie* remake m, nouvelle version f

remark [rɪˈmɑːrk] **1** *n* remarque f **2** *v/t (comment)* faire remarquer; remarkable remarquable; remarkably remarquablement

remarry [riːˈmærɪ] se remarier

remedy [ˈremədɪ] MED, *fig* remède m

remember [rɪˈmembər] **1** *v/t* se souvenir de, se rappeler

2 *v/i* se souvenir

remind [rɪˈmaɪnd]: **~ s.o. to do sth** rappeler à qn de faire qch; **~ X of Y** rappeler Y à X; **~ s.o. of sth** *(bring to their attention)* rappeler qch à qn; reminder rappel m

reminisce [remɪˈnɪs] évoquer le passé

remission [rɪˈmɪʃn] MED rémission f; **go into ~** *of patient* être en sursis

remnant [ˈremnənt] vestige m, reste m

remorse [rɪˈmɔːrs] remords m; remorseless impitoyable; *demands* incessant

remote [rɪˈmout] *village* isolé; *possibility* vague; *ancestor* lointain; **remote control** télécommande f; remotely *related, connected* vaguement

removable [rɪˈmuːvəbl] amovible; removal enlèvement m; *of demonstrators* expulsion f; *of doubt* dissipation f; remove enlever; *demonstrators* expulser; *doubt* dissiper

rename [riːˈneɪm] rebaptiser; *file* renommer

rendez-vous [ˈrɑːndeɪvuː] rendez-vous m

renew [rɪˈnuː] *contract* renouveler; *discussion* reprendre; renewal *of contract etc* renouvellement m; *of discussion* reprise f

renounce [rɪˈnauns] renoncer à

renovate ['renəveɪt] rénover; **renovation** rénovation f

rent [rent] **1** n loyer m; **for ~** à louer **2** v/t louer; **rental** for apartment loyer m; for TV, car location f; **rental car** voiture f de location; **rent-free** sans payer de loyer

reopen [ri:'oupn] **1** v/t rouvrir; negotiations reprendre **2** v/i of store etc rouvrir

reorganization [ri:ɔːrgənaɪ-'zeɪʃn] réorganisation f; **reorganize** réorganiser

repaint [ri:'peɪnt] repeindre

repair [rɪ'per] **1** v/t réparer **2** n réparation f; **repairman** réparateur m

repatriate [ri:'pætrɪeɪt] rapatrier; **repatriation** rapatriement m

repay [ri:'peɪ] rembourser; **repayment** remboursement m

repeal [rɪ'piːl] law abroger

repeat [rɪ'piːt] **1** v/t répéter **2** n TV program etc rediffusion f; **repeatedly** à plusieurs reprises

repel [rɪ'pel] repousser (disgust) dégoûter; **repellent 1** adj repoussant, répugnant **2** n (insect ~) répulsif m

repercussions [riːpərˈkʌʃnz] répercussions fpl

repertoire ['repərtwɑːr] répertoire m

repetition [repɪ'tɪʃn] répétition f; **repetitive** répétitif

replace [rɪ'pleɪs] (put back)

remettre; (take the place of) remplacer; **replacement** person remplaçant m; product produit m de remplacement; **replacement part** pièce f de rechange

replay ['riːpleɪ] **1** n recording relecture f, replay m; match nouvelle rencontre f, replay m **2** v/t match rejouer

replenish [rɪ'plenɪʃ] container remplir (de nouveau); supplies refaire

replica ['replɪkə] réplique f

reply [rɪ'plaɪ] **1** n réponse f **2** v/t & v/i répondre

report [rɪ'pɔːrt] **1** n (account) rapport m, compte-rendu m; in newspaper bulletin m **2** v/t facts rapporter; to authorities déclarer **3** v/i (present o.s.) se présenter; **reporter** reporter m/f

repossess [riːpə'zes] COM reprendre possession de

represent [reprɪ'zent] représenter; **representative 1** adj (typical) représentatif **2** n représentant(e) m(f)

repress [rɪ'pres] réprimer; **repression** POL répression f; **repressive** POL répressif

reprieve [rɪ'priːv] **1** n LAW sursis m; fig also répit m **2** v/t prisoner accorder un sursis à

reprimand ['reprɪmænd] réprimander

reprint ['riːprɪnt] **1** n réimpression f **2** v/t réimprimer

reprisal [rɪ'praɪzl] représailles

fpl

reproach [rɪ'prəʊtʃ] **1** *n* reproche *m* **2** *v/t:* ~ **s.o. for sth** reprocher qch à qn; **reproachful** réprobateur

reproduce [riːprə'djuːs] **1** *v/t* reproduire **2** *v/i* BIO se reproduire; **reproduction** reproduction *f*

reproductive reproducteur

reptile ['reptaɪl] reptile *m*

republic [rɪ'pʌblɪk] république *f*; **Republican 1** *adj* républicain **2** *n* Républicain(e) *m(f)*

repulsive [rɪ'pʌlsɪv] repoussant

reputable ['repjʊtəbl] de bonne réputation; **reputation** réputation *f*

request [rɪ'kwest] **1** *n* demande *f*; **on** ~ sur demande **2** *v/t* demander

require [rɪ'kwaɪr] (*need*) avoir besoin de; **required** (*necessary*) requis; **requirement** (*need*) besoin *m*, exigence *f*; (*condition*) condition *f* (requise)

requisition [rekwɪ'zɪʃn] réquisitionner

re-route [riː'ruːt] *airplane etc* dérouter

rerun ['riːrʌn] **1** *n of TV program* rediffusion *f* **2** *v/t tape* repasser

reschedule [riː'skedjuːl] changer l'heure/la date de

rescue ['reskjuː] **1** *n* sauvetage *m* **2** *v/t* sauver, secourir

research [rɪ'sɜːtʃ] recherche *f*; **research and development** recherche *f* et développement; **researcher** chercheur(-euse) *m(f)*

resemblance [rɪ'zembləns] ressemblance *f*; **resemble** ressembler à

resent [rɪ'zent] ne pas aimer; *person also* en vouloir à; **resentful** plein de ressentiment; **resentment** ressentiment *m* (*of* par rapport à)

reservation [rezər'veɪʃn] réservation *f*; *mental, (special area)* réserve *f*; **reserve 1** *n (store, aloofness)* réserve *f*; SP remplaçant(e) *m(f)* **2** *v/t seat, judgment* réserver; **reserved** *table, manner* réservé

reservoir ['rezərvwɑːr] *for water* réservoir *m*

residence ['rezɪdəns] *fml: house etc* résidence *f*; (*stay*) séjour *m*; **resident** résident(e) *m(f)*; *on street* riverain(e) *m(f)*; *in hotel* client(e) *m(f)*; **residential** résidentiel

residue ['rezɪdjuː] résidu *m*

resign [rɪ'zaɪn] **1** *v/t position* démissionner de; ~ **o.s. to** se résigner à **2** *v/i from job* démissionner; **resignation** *from job* démission *f*; *mental* résignation *f*

resilient [rɪ'zɪliənt] *personality* fort; *material* résistant

resist [rɪ'zɪst] **1** *v/t* résister à; *new measures* s'opposer à **2** *v/i* résister; **resistance** résistance f; **resistant** *material* résistant

resolution [rezə'luːʃn] résolution f

resort [ri'zɔːrt] *place* lieu m de vacances; *at seaside* station f balnéaire; *for health cures* station f thermale; **as a last ~** en dernier ressort

◆ **resort to** avoir recours à, recourir à

◆ **resound with** [ri'zaʊnd] résonner de

resounding [ri'zaʊndɪŋ] *success, victory* retentissant

resource [ri'sɔːrs] ressource f; **resourceful** ingénieux

respect [ri'spekt] **1** n respect m; **in this/that ~** à cet égard; **in many ~s** à bien des égards **2** v/t respecter; **respectability** respectabilité f; **respectable** respectable; **respectful** respectueux; **respective** respectif; **respectively** respectivement

respiration [respi'reɪʃn] respiration f; **respirator** MED respirateur m

respond [ri'spɑːnd] répondre; *(react also)* réagir; **response** réponse f; *(reaction also)* réaction f

responsibility [rispɑːnsɪ'bɪlətɪ] responsabilité f; **responsible** responsable (**for** de); **a ~ job** un poste à responsabilités

rest¹ [rest] **1** n repos m; *during walk, work* pause f **2** v/i

se reposer **3** v/t *(lean, balance)* poser

rest² [rest]: **the ~** *objects* le reste; *people* les autres

restaurant ['restərɑːnt] restaurant m

restful ['restfl] reposant; **rest home** maison f de retraite; **restless** agité; **restlessly** nerveusement

restoration [restə'reɪʃn] *of building* restauration f; **restore** *building etc* restaurer; *(bring back)* restituer; *confidence* redonner

restrain [ri'streɪn] retenir; **restraint** *(moderation)* retenue f

restrict [ri'strɪkt] restreindre; **I'll ~ myself to …** je me limiterai à …; **restriction** restriction f

'rest room toilettes fpl

result [ri'zʌlt] résultat m; **as a ~ of this** par conséquent

resume [ri'zuːm] reprendre

résumé ['rezʊmeɪ] *of career* curriculum vitae m inv, C.V. m inv

resumption [ri'zʌmpʃn] reprise f

resurface [riː'sɜːrfɪs] **1** v/t *roads* refaire (le revêtement de) **2** v/i *(reappear)* refaire surface

Resurrection [rezə'rekʃn] REL Résurrection f

retail ['riːteɪl] **1** adv: **sell sth ~** vendre qch au détail **2** v/i: **~ at** se vendre à; **retailer** détaillant(e) *m(f)*

retain [rɪ'teɪn] conserver; **re-tainer** FIN provision *f*

retaliate [rɪ'tælieɪt] riposter, se venger; **retaliation** riposte *f*

rethink [riː'θɪŋk] repenser

reticence ['retɪsns] réserve *f*; **reticent** réservé

retire [rɪ'taɪr] *from work* prendre sa retraite; **retired** à la retraite; **retirement** retraite *f*; **retiring** réservé

retort [rɪ'tɔːrt] **1** *n* réplique *f* **2** *v/t* répliquer

retract [rɪ'trækt] *claws, undercarriage* rentrer; *statement* retirer

're-train se recycler

retreat [rɪ'triːt] **1** *v/i also* MIL battre en retraite **2** *n* MIL, *place* retraite *f*

retrieve [rɪ'triːv] récupérer

retroactive [retrou'æktɪv] *law etc* rétroactif; **retroactively** rétroactivement, par rétroaction

retrograde ['retrəgreɪd] rétrograde

retrospective [retrə'spektɪv] rétrospective *f*

return [rɪ'tɜːrn] **1** *n* retour *m*; (*profit*) bénéfice *m*; ~ (*ticket*) *Br* aller *m* retour; **many happy ~s (of the day)** bon anniversaire; **in ~ for** en échange de; contre **2** *v/t* (*give back*) rendre; (*send back*) renvoyer; (*put back*) remettre **3** *v/i* (*go back*) retourner;

(*come back*) revenir

reunification [riːjuːnɪfɪ'keɪʃn] réunification *f*

reunion [riː'juːnjən] réunion *f*; **reunite** réunir; *country* réunifier

reusable [riː'juːzəbl] réutilisable; **reuse** réutiliser

◆ **rev up** [rev] *engine* emballer

revaluation [riːvæljuˈeɪʃn] réévaluation *f*

reveal [rɪ'viːl] révéler; (*make visible*) dévoiler; **revealing** *remark* révélateur; *dress* suggestif; **revelation** révélation *f*

revenge [rɪ'vendʒ] vengeance *f*; **take one's ~** se venger

revenue ['revənuː] revenu *m*

reverberate [rɪ'vɜːrbəreɪt] *of sound* retentir, résonner

revere [rɪ'vɪr] révérer; **reverence** déférence *f*, respect *m*; **reverent** respectueux

reverse [rɪ'vɜːrs] **1** *adj* *sequence* inverse **2** *n* (*opposite*) contraire *m*; (*back*) verso *m*; MOT *gear* marche *f* arrière **3** *v/i* MOT faire marche arrière

review [rɪ'vjuː] **1** *n* *of book, movie* critique *f*; *of troops* revue *f*; *of situation etc* bilan *m* **2** *v/t* *book, movie* faire la critique de; *troops* passer en revue; *situation etc* faire le bilan de; EDU réviser; **reviewer** *of book, movie* critique *m*

revise [rɪ'vaɪz] *opinion* revenir sur; *text* réviser; **revision**

of text révision f

revival [rɪ'vaɪvl] *of custom, old style* renouveau m; *of patient* rétablissement m; **revive** *v/t custom, old style* faire renaître; *patient* ranimer 2 *v/i of business* reprendre

revoke [rɪ'vouk] *law* abroger; *license* retirer

revolt [rɪ'voult] 1 n révolte f 2 *v/i* se révolter; **revolting** répugnant; **revolution** révolution f; **revolutionary** 1 *adj* révolutionnaire 2 n révolutionnaire m/f; **revolutionize** révolutionner

revolve [rɪ'vɑːlv] tourner (**around** autour de); **revolver** revolver m

revulsion [rɪ'vʌlʃn] répugnance f

reward [rɪ'wɔːrd] 1 n *financial* récompense f; (*benefit derived*) gratification f 2 *v/t financially* récompenser; **rewarding** *experience* gratifiant, valorisant

rewind [riː'waɪnd] *film, tape* rembobiner

rewrite [riː'raɪt] réécrire

rhetoric ['retərɪk] rhétorique f

rhyme [raɪm] 1 n rime f 2 *v/i* rimer (**with** avec)

rhythm ['rɪðm] rythme m

rib [rɪb] ANAT côte f

ribbon ['rɪbən] ruban m

rice [raɪs] riz m

rich [rɪtʃ] 1 *adj person, food* ri-

che 2 *npl*: **the~** les riches *mpl*

ricochet ['rɪkəʃeɪ] ricocher (**off** sur)

rid [rɪd]: **get ~ of** se débarrasser de

ride [raɪd] 1 n *on horse* promenade f (à cheval); *excursion in vehicle* tour m; (*journey*) trajet m; **do you want a ~ into town?** est-ce que tu veux que je t'emmène en ville? 2 *v/t horse* monter; *bike* se déplacer en; **can I ~ your bike?** est-ce que je peux monter sur ton vélo? 3 *v/i on horse* monter à cheval; *on bike* rouler (à vélo); **rider** *on horse* cavalier(-ière) m(f); *on bike* cycliste m/f

ridge [rɪdʒ] (*raised strip*) arête f (saillante); *of mountain* crête f; *of roof* arête f

ridicule ['rɪdɪkjuːl] 1 n ridicule m 2 *v/t* ridiculiser; **ridiculous** ridicule; **ridiculously** ridiculement

riding ['raɪdɪŋ] *on horseback* équitation f

rifle ['raɪfl] fusil m, carabine f

rift [rɪft] *in earth* fissure f; *in party* etc scission f

rig [rɪg] 1 n (*oil ~*) tour f de forage; *at sea* plateforme f de forage; (*truck*) semi-remorque m 2 *v/t elections* truquer

right [raɪt] 1 *adj* bon; *be ~ of answer* être juste; *of person* avoir raison; *of clock* être à l'heure; **it's not ~ to ...** ce n'est pas bien de ...;

put things ~ arranger les choses; **that's ~!** c'est ça!; **that's all ~** (*doesn't matter*) ce n'est pas grave; **when s.o. says thank you** je vous en prie; **it's all ~** (*is acceptable*) ça me va; **I'm all ~** *not hurt* je vais bien; **have enough** ça ira pour moi **2** *adv* (*directly*) directement, juste; (*correctly*) correctement, bien; (*not left*) à droite; **~ now** (*immediately*) tout de suite; (*at the moment*) en ce moment; **it's ~ here** c'est juste là **3** *n* civil, legal droit *m*; (*not left*, *POL*) droite *f*; **be in the ~** avoir raison; **right-angle** angle *m* droit; **rightful** *owner* etc légitime; **right-handed** *person* droitier; **right-hand man** bras *m* droit; **right of way** *in traffic* priorité *f*; *across land* droit *m* de passage; **right wing** POL droite *f*; SP ailier *m* droit; **right-wing** POL de droite

rigid ['rɪdʒɪd] *also* fig rigide

rigor ['rɪgər] *of discipline* rigueur *f*; **rigorous** rigoureux; **rigorously** *check* rigoureusement

rigour Br → **rigor**

rile [raɪl] F agacer

rim [rɪm] *n of wheel* jante *f*; *of cup* bord *m*; *of eyeglasses* monture *f*

ring¹ [rɪŋ] *n* (*circle*) cercle *m*; *on finger* anneau *m*; *in box-*

ing ring *m*; *at circus* piste *f*

ring² [rɪŋ] **1** *n of bell* sonnerie *f*; *of voice* son *m* **2** *v/t bell* (faire) sonner; *Br* TELEC téléphoner à **3** *v/i of bell* sonner, retentir

'ringleader meneur(-euse) *m(f)*; **ring-pull** anneau *m* (d'ouverture)

rink [rɪŋk] patinoire *f*

rinse [rɪns] **1** *n for hair color* rinçage *m* **2** *v/t hair* rincer

riot ['raɪət] **1** *n* émeute *f* **2** *v/i* participer à une émeute; **start to ~** créer une émeute; **rioter** émeutier(-ière) *m(f)*; **riot police** police *f* anti-émeute

rip [rɪp] **1** *n in cloth* etc accroc *m* **2** *v/t cloth* etc déchirer

◆ **rip-off** F *customers* arnaquer *f*

ripe [raɪp] *fruit* mûr; **ripen** *of fruit* mûrir; **ripeness** *of fruit* maturité *f*

'rip-off F arnaque *f*

ripple ['rɪpl] *on water* ride *f*

rise [raɪz] **1** *v/i from chair, bed, of sun* se lever; *of rocket, price, temperature* monter **2** *n in price, temperature* hausse *f*; *in water level* élévation *f*; *Br: in salary* augmentation *f*

risk [rɪsk] **1** *n* risque *m*; **take a ~** prendre un risque **2** *v/t* risquer; **risky** risqué

ritual ['rɪtʊəl] **1** *adj* rituel **2** *n* rituel *m*

rival ['raɪvl] **1** *n* rival(e) *m(f)* **2**

v/t (*match*) égaler; (*compete with*) rivaliser avec; **rivalry** rivalité *f*

river ['rɪvər] rivière *f*; *bigger* fleuve *m*; **riverbank** rive *f*; **riverbed** lit *m* de la rivière/ du fleuve; **riverside 1** *adj* en bord de rivière **2** *n* berge *f*, bord *m* de l'eau

riveting fascinant

road [roʊd] route *f*; *in city* rue *f*; **roadblock** barrage *m* routier; **road-holding** *of vehicle* tenue *f* de route; **road map** carte *f* routière; **road safety** sécurité *f* routière; **roadsign** panneau *m* (de signalisation); **roadway** chaussée *f*; **roadworthy** en état de marche

roam [roʊm] errer

roar [rɔːr] **1** *n* rugissement *m*; *of traffic* grondement *m*; *of engine* vrombissement *m* **2** *v/i* rugir; *of traffic* gronder; *of engine* vrombir

roast [roʊst] **1** *n of beef etc* rôti *m* **2** *v/t* rôtir **3** *v/i of food* rôtir; **roast beef** rosbif *m*

rob [rɑːb] *person* voler, dévaliser; *bank* cambrioler, dévaliser; **robber** voleur(-euse) *m(f)*; **robbery** vol *m*

robe [roʊb] *of judge, priest* robe *f*; (*bath~*) peignoir *m*; (*dressing gown*) robe *f* de chambre

robot ['roʊbɑːt] robot *m*

robust [roʊ'bʌst] robuste

rock [rɑːk] **1** *n* rocher *m*; MUS

rock *m* **2** *v/t baby* bercer; *cradle* balancer; (*surprise*) secouer **3** *v/i on chair, of boat* se balancer; **rock-bottom** *price* le plus bas possible; **rock climber** varappeur(-euse) *m(f)*; **rock climbing** varappe *f*

rocket ['rɑːkɪt] **1** *n* fusée *f* **2** *v/i of prices etc* monter en flèche

rocking chair ['rɑːkɪŋ] rocking-chair *m*; **rock 'n' roll** rock-and-roll *m inv*; **rocky** *beach* rocheux

rod [rɑːd] baguette *f*; *for fishing* canne *f* à pêche

rodent ['roʊdnt] rongeur *m*

rogue [roʊg] vaurien *m*

role [roʊl] rôle *m*; **role model** modèle *m*

roll [roʊl] **1** *n* (*bread ~*) petit pain *m*; *of film* pellicule *f*; (*list, register*) liste *f* **2** *v/i of ball, boat* rouler

◆ **roll over 1** *v/i* se retourner **2** *v/t person, object* tourner; (*renew*) renouveler; (*extend*) prolonger

'roll call appel *m*; **roller** *for hair* rouleau *m*; **roller blade®** roller *m* (en ligne); **roller coaster** montagnes *fpl* russes; **roller skate** patin *m* à roulettes

ROM [rɑːm] COMPUT (= *read only memory*) ROM *f*, mémoire *f* morte

Roman 'Catholic 1 *adj* REL catholique **2** *n* catholique *m/f*

romance ['roʊmæns] (*affair*)

idylle f; *novel, movie* histoire f d'amour; **romantic** romantique

roof [ruːf] toit m; **roof-rack** MOT galerie f

rookie ['rʊkɪ] F bleu m F

room [ruːm] pièce f, salle f; (*bed~*) chambre f; (*space*) place f; **room clerk** réceptionniste m/f; **roommate** *in apartment* colocataire m/f; *in room* camarade m/f de chambre; **room service** service m en chambre; **room temperature** température f ambiante; **roomy** spacieux; *clothes* ample

root [ruːt] racine f

rope [rəʊp] corde f

rosary ['rəʊzərɪ] REL rosaire m, chapelet m

rose [rəʊz] BOT rose f

roster ['rɒstər] tableau m de service

rostrum ['rɒstrəm] estrade f

rosy ['rəʊzɪ] *also fig* rose

rot [rɒt] **1** n pourriture f **2** v/i pourrir

rotate [rəʊ'teɪt] **1** v/i tourner **2** v/t (*turn*) (faire) tourner; *crops* alterner; **rotation** rotation f

rotten ['rɒtn] *also F weather, luck* pourri

rough [rʌf] **1** adj *surface* rugueux; *hands, skin* rêche; *voice* rude; (*violent*) brutal; *crossing, seas* agité; (*approximate*) approximatif; **~ draft** brouillon m **2** n *in golf* rough

m; **roughage** *in food* fibres fpl; **roughly** (*approximately*) environ; (*harshly*) brutalement

roulette [ruː'let] roulette f

round [raʊnd] **1** adj rond **2** n *of mailman, doctor, drinks* tournée f; *of competition* manche f, tour m; *in boxing* round m **3** v/t *corner* tourner **4** adv & prep → **around**

◆ **round up** *figure* arrondir; *suspects* ramasser

roundabout ['raʊndəbaʊt] **1** adj détourné, indirect **2** n *Br: on road* rond-point m; **round-the-world** autour du monde; **round trip** aller-retour m; **round-up** *of cattle* rassemblement m; *of suspects* rafle f; *of news* résumé m

rouse [raʊz] *from sleep* réveiller; *emotions* soulever; **rousing** exaltant

route [ruːt] itinéraire m

routine [ruː'tiːn] **1** adj de routine; *behavior* routinier **2** n routine f

row¹ [rəʊ] n (*line*) rangée f; *of troops* rang m; **5 days in a ~** 5 jours de suite

row² [rəʊ] v/i *in boat* ramer

rowboat ['rəʊbəʊt] bateau m à rames

rowdy ['raʊdɪ] tapageur, bruyant

royal ['rɔɪəl] royal; **royalty** (*membres mpl de*) la famille royale; *on book, recording* droits *mpl* d'auteur

rub [rʌb] frotter

rubber ['rʌbər] **1** *n material* caoutchouc *m* **2** *adj* en caoutchouc; **rubber band** élastique *m*

rubble ['rʌbl] *from building* gravats *mpl*, décombres *mpl*

ruby ['ru:bɪ] *jewel* rubis *m*

rudder ['rʌdər] gouvernail *m*

ruddy ['rʌdɪ] *complexion* coloré

rude [ru:d] impoli; *language, gesture* grossier; **rudely** (*impolitely*) impoliment; **rudeness** impolitesse *f*

rudimentary [ru:dɪ'mentərɪ] rudimentaire; **rudiments** rudiments *mpl*

rueful ['ru:fl] contrit, résigné; **ruefully** avec regret; *smile* d'un air contrit

ruffian ['rʌfɪən] voyou *m*, brute *f*

ruffle ['rʌfl] **1** *n on dress* ruche *f* **2** *v/t hair* ébouriffer; *person* énerver

rug [rʌg] tapis *m*; *blanket* couverture *f*

rugby ['rʌgbɪ] rugby *m*

rugged ['rʌgɪd] *scenery, cliffs* escarpé; *face* aux traits rudes; *resistance* acharné

ruin ['ru:ɪn] **1** *n* ruine *f* **2** *v/t* ruiner; *party, plans* gâcher

rule [ru:l] **1** *n* règle *f*; *of monarch* règne *m*; **as a** ~ en règle générale **2** *v/t country* gouverner **3** *v/i of monarch* régner; **ruler** *for measuring* règle *f*; *of state* dirigeant(e) *m(f)*; **ruling 1** *n* décision *f* **2** *adj party* dirigeant, au pouvoir

rum [rʌm] *drink* rhum *m*

rumble ['rʌmbl] *of stomach* gargouiller; *of thunder* gronder

rumor, *Br* **rumour** ['ru:mər] **1** *n* bruit *m*, rumeur *f* **2** *v/t*: **it is** ~ed that ... le bruit court que ...

rump [rʌmp] *of animal* croupe *f*

rumple ['rʌmpl] *clothes, paper* froisser

'rumpsteak rumsteck *m*

run [rʌn] **1** *n on foot* course *f*; *in pantyhose* échelle *f*; **go for a** ~ *for exercise* aller courir; **in the short/long** ~ à court/ long terme **2** *v/i of river, paint, makeup* couler; *of trains, buses* passer, circuler; *of play* être à l'affiche; *of engine, machine* marcher, tourner; *of software* fonctionner; *in election* se présenter; ~ **for President** être candidat à la présidence **3** *v/t race* courir; *business, hotel etc* diriger; *software* exécuter, faire tourner; *car* entretenir

◆ **run away** s'enfuir; *from home for a while* faire une fugue; *for good* s'enfuir de chez soi

◆ **run down 1** *v/t* (*knock down*) renverser; (*criticize*)

critiquer; *stocks* diminuer **2** *v/i of battery* se décharger
◆ **run off 1** *v/i* s'enfuir **2** *v/t* (*print off*) tirer
◆ **run out** *of contract* expirer; *of time* s'écouler; *of supplies* s'épuiser
◆ **run out of** ne plus avoir de
◆ **run over 1** *v/t* (*knock down*) renverser **2** *v/i of water etc* déborder
◆ **run up** *debts* accumuler

'**runaway** fugueur(-euse) *m(f)*; **run-down** *person* épuisé; *area* délabré
rung [rʌŋ] *of ladder* barreau *m*
runner ['rʌnər] *athlete* coureur(-euse) *m(f)*; **runner beans** haricots *mpl* d'Espagne; **runner-up** second(e) *m(f)*; **running 1** *n* sp course *f*; *of business* gestion *f* **2** *adj*: *for two days* ~ pendant deux jours de suite; **running water** eau *f* courante; **runny** *substance* liquide; *nose* qui coule; **run-up** sp élan *m*; *in the* ~ *to* pendant la période

qui précède; **runway** AVIA piste *f*
rupture ['rʌptʃər] **1** *n also fig* rupture *f* **2** *v/i of pipe* éclater
rural ['rʊrəl] rural
ruse [ruːz] ruse *f*
rush [rʌʃ] **1** *n* ruée *f*; *do sth in a* ~ faire qch à la hâte; *be in a* ~ être pressé **2** *v/t person* presser; *meal* avaler à toute vitesse; **3** *v/i* se presser; **rush hour** heures *fpl* de pointe
Russia ['rʌʃə] Russie *f*; **Russian** ['rʌʃən] **1** *adj* russe **2** *n* Russe *m/f*; *language* russe *m*
rust [rʌst] **1** *n* rouille *f* **2** *v/i* se rouiller; **rust-proof** antirouille *inv*; **rusty** *also fig* rouillé
rut [rʌt] *in road* ornière *f*; *be in a* ~ *fig* être tombé dans la routine
ruthless ['ruːθlɪs] impitoyable, sans pitié; **ruthlessly** impitoyablement; **ruthlessness** dureté *f* (impitoyable)
rye [raɪ] seigle *m*; **rye bread** pain *m* de seigle

S

sabotage ['sæbətɑːʒ] **1** *n* sabotage *m* **2** *v/t* saboter; **saboteur** saboteur(-euse) *m(f)*
sachet ['sæʃeɪ] sachet *m*
sack [sæk] **1** *n bag* sac *m* **2** *v/t* virer F
sacred ['seɪkrɪd] sacré

sacrifice ['sækrɪfaɪs] **1** *n* sacrifice *m* **2** *v/t also fig* sacrifier
sacrilege ['sækrɪlɪdʒ] REL, *fig* sacrilège *m*
sad [sæd] triste
saddle ['sædl] **1** *n* selle *f* **2** *v/t*

horse seller

sadism ['seɪdɪzm] sadisme *m*; **sadist** sadique *m/f*; **sadistic** sadique

sadly ['sædlɪ] tristement; (*regrettably*) malheureusement; **sadness** tristesse *f*

safe [seɪf] **1** *adj* (*not dangerous*) pas dangereux; *driver* prudent; (*not in danger*) en sécurité **2** *n* coffre-fort *m*; **safeguard 1** *n*: **as a ~ against** par mesure de protection contre **2** *v/t* protéger; **safely** *arrive, drive, assume* sans risque; **safety** sécurité *f*; *of investment, prediction* sûreté *f*; **safety pin** épingle *f* de nourrice

sag [sæg] *of ceiling* s'affaisser; *of rope* se détendre; *fig: of output* fléchir

saga ['sɑːɡə] saga *f*

sage [seɪdʒ] *herb* sauge *f*

sail [seɪl] **1** *n of boat* voile *f*; *trip* voyage *m* (en mer) **2** *v/i* faire de la voile; (*depart*) partir; **sailboard 1** *n* planche *f* à voile **2** *v/i* faire de la planche à voile; **sailboarding** planche *f* à voile; **sailboat** bateau *m* à voiles; **sailing** *sp* voile *f*; **sailor** marin *m*

saint [seɪnt] saint(e) *m(f)*

sake [seɪk]: **for my ~** pour moi

salad ['sæləd] salade *f*

salary ['sælərɪ] salaire *m*

sale [seɪl] **1** *n*; *reduced prices* soldes *mpl*; **for ~** *sign* à vendre; **be on ~** être en

vente; *at reduced prices* être en solde; **sales department** vente *f*; **sales clerk** *in store* vendeur(-euse) *m(f)*; **sales figures** chiffre *m* d'affaires; **salesman** vendeur *m*; (*rep*) représentant *m*; **saleswoman** vendeuse *f*

salient ['seɪlɪənt] marquant

saliva [sə'laɪvə] salive *f*

salmon ['sæmən] saumon *m*

saloon [sə'luːn] (*bar*) bar *m*; *Br* MOT berline *f*

salt [sɔːlt] sel *m*; **salty** salé

salute [sə'luːt] **1** *n* MIL salut *m* **2** *v/t* MIL saluer **3** *v/i* MIL faire un salut

salvage ['sælvɪdʒ] *from wreck* sauver

salvation [sæl'veɪʃn] *also fig* salut *m*

same [seɪm] **1** *adj* même **2** *pron*: **the ~** le/la même; *pl* **the ~** les mêmes; **Happy New Year – the ~ to you** Bonne année – à vous aussi; **all the ~** (*even so*) quand même **3** *adv*: **look/sound the ~** se ressembler, être pareil

sample ['sæmpl] *of work, cloth* échantillon *m*; *of blood* prélèvement *m*

sanction ['sæŋkʃn] **1** *n* (*approval*) approbation *f*; (*penalty*) sanction *f* **2** *v/t* (*approve*) approuver

sand [sænd] **1** *n* sable *m* **2** *v/t* *with sandpaper* poncer au papier de verre

sandal ['sændl] sandale *f*

'sandbag sac m de sable;
sand dune dune f; sander
tool ponçeuse f; sandpaper
1 n papier m de verre 2 v/t
poncer au papier de verre
sandwich ['sænwɪtʃ] sand-
wich m
sandy ['sændɪ] beach de sable; soil sablonneux; feet,
towel plein de sable; hair
blond roux
sane [seɪn] sain (d'esprit)
sanitarium [sænɪ'terɪəm] sa-
natorium m
sanitary ['sænɪterɪ] sanitaire;
(clean) hygiénique; sanitary
napkin serviette f hygiénique; sanitation installations
fpl sanitaires; (removal of
waste) système m sanitaire
sanity ['sænətɪ] santé f mentale
Santa Claus ['sæntəklɔːz] le
Père Noël
sap [sæp] 1 n in tree sève f 2 v/t
s.o.'s energy saper
sapphire ['sæfaɪr] saphir m
sarcasm ['sɑːrkæzm] sarcasme m; sarcastic sarcastique;
sarcastically sarcastique-
ment
sardine [sɑːr'diːn] sardine f
sardonic [sɑːr'dɑːnɪk] sardonique
satellite ['sætəlaɪt] satellite
m; satellite dish antenne f
parabolique; satellite TV télévision f par satellite
satin ['sætɪn] satin m
satire ['sætaɪr] satire f; satiri-

cal satirique; satirize satiri-
ser
satisfaction [sætɪs'fækʃn] satisfaction f; satisfactory
satisfaisant; (just good enough)
convenable; satisfy satisfaire; conditions remplir
Saturday ['sætərdeɪ] samedi
m
sauce [sɔːs] sauce f; sauce-
pan casserole f; saucer soucoupe f
Saudi Arabia [saʊdɪə'reɪbɪə]
Arabie f saoudite; Saudi
Arabian 1 adj saoudien 2 n
Saoudien(ne) m(f)
sausage ['sɔːsɪdʒ] saucisse f;
dried saucisson m
savage ['sævɪdʒ] 1 adj féroce
2 n sauvage m/f; savagery
férocité f
save [seɪv] 1 v/t (rescue), SP
sauver; (economize, put
aside) économiser; (collect)
faire collection de; COMPUT
sauvegarder 2 v/i (put money
aside) faire des économies; SP
arrêter le ballon 3 n SP arrêt
m; saver person (-euse) m(f); savings économies fpl; savings account
compte m d'épargne; sav-
ings and loan caisse f
d'épargne-logement; sav-
ings bank caisse f d'épargne
savior, Br saviour ['seɪvjər]
REL sauveur m
savor ['seɪvər] savourer; sa-
vory not sweet salé
savour etc Br → savor etc

saw [sɔː] **1** n tool scie f **2** v/t scier; **sawdust** sciure f

saxophone ['sæksəfəʊn] saxophone m

say [seɪ] dire; **that is to ~** c'est-à-dire; **saying** dicton m

scab [skæb] on wound croûte f

scaffolding ['skæfəldɪŋ] échafaudage m

scald [skɔːld] ébouillanter

scale[1] [skeɪl] n on fish écaille f

scale[2] [skeɪl] **1** n of project, map etc, on thermometer échelle f; MUS gamme f **2** v/t cliffs etc escalader

scales [skeɪlz] for weighing balance f

scallop ['skæləp] shellfish coquille f Saint-Jacques

scalp [skælp] n cuir m chevelu

scalpel ['skælpl] scalpel m

scam [skæm] F arnaque m F

scampi ['skæmpɪ] scampi m

scan [skæn] **1** n MED scanner m; during pregnancy échographie f **2** v/t horizon, page parcourir du regard; COMPUT faire un scanner de; COMPUT scanner m

◆ scan in COMPUT scanner

scandal ['skændl] scandale m; **scandalize** scandaliser; **scandalous** scandaleux

scanner ['skænər] MED, COMPUT scanner m

scanty ['skæntɪ] dress réduit au minimum

scapegoat ['skeɪpgəʊt] bouc

m émissaire

scar [skɑːr] **1** n cicatrice f **2** v/t marquer d'une cicatrice

scarce [skers] rare; **scarcely** ['skerslɪ] à peine; **~ anything** presque rien; **scarcity** manque m

scare [sker] **1** v/t faire peur à; **be ~d of** avoir peur de **2** n (panic, alarm) rumeurs fpl alarmantes; **scaremonger** alarmiste m/f

scarf [skɑːrf] around neck écharpe f; over head foulard m

scarlet ['skɑːrlət] écarlate

scary ['skerɪ] effrayant

scathing ['skeɪðɪŋ] cinglant

scatter ['skætər] **1** v/t leaflets, seed éparpiller **2** v/i of people se disperser; **scattered** showers intermittent; **villages** éparpillé

scavenge ['skævɪndʒ] **~ for sth** fouiller pour trouver qch; **scavenger** charognard m; person fouilleur(euse) m(f)

scenario [sɪˈnɑːrɪəʊ] scénario m

scene [siːn] scène f; of accident, crime etc lieu m; **make a ~** faire une scène; **behind the ~s** dans les coulisses; **scenery** paysage m; THEA décor(s) m(pl)

scent [sent] odeur f; Br (perfume) parfum m

sceptic etc Br → **skeptic** etc

schedule ['skedjuːl] **1** n of

events calendrier *m; for trains* horaire *m; of lessons, work* programme *m; **be on ~ of work, workers** être dans les temps; *of train* être à l'heure; **be behind ~** être en retard *v/t* (*put on ~*) prévoir; **scheduled flight** vol *m* régulier

scheme [skiːm] **1** *n* plan *m* **2** *v/i* (*plot*) comploter; **scheming** intrigant

schizophrenia [skɪtsə'friːnɪə] schizophrénie *f;* **schizophrenic 1** *adj* schizophrène **2** *n* schizophrène *m/f*

scholar ['skɑːlər] érudit(e) *m(f);* **scholarly** savant, érudit; **scholarship** (*learning*) érudition *f; financial award* bourse *f*

school [skuːl] école *f;* (*university*) université *f;* **school bag** cartable *m;* **schoolchildren** écoliers *mpl*

science ['saɪəns] science *f;* **scientific** scientifique; **scientist** scientifique *m/f*

scissors ['sɪzərz] ciseaux *mpl*

scoff[1] [skɑːf] *food* engloutir

scoff[2] [skɑːf] (*mock*) se moquer

scold [skoʊld] réprimander

scoop [skuːp] *for ice-cream* cuiller *f* à glace; *of ice cream* boule *f; story* scoop *m*

scooter ['skuːtər] *with motor* scooter *m; child's* trottinette *f*

scope [skoʊp] ampleur *f;* (*freedom, opportunity*) possibilités *fpl*

scorch [skɔːrtʃ] brûler; **scorching** très chaud

score [skɔːr] **1** *n* SP score *m;* (*written music*) partition *f; of movie etc* musique *f* **2** *v/t goal, point* marquer; (*cut: line*) rayer **3** *v/i* SP marquer; (*keep the ~*) marquer les points; **scoreboard** tableau *m* des scores; **scorer** marqueur(-euse) *m(f)*

scorn [skɔːrn] **1** *n* mépris *m* **2** *v/t idea* mépriser; **scornful** méprisant; **scornfully** avec mépris

Scot [skɑːt] Écossais(e) *m(f);* **Scotch** *whiskey* scotch *m;* **Scotch tape**® scotch *m;* **Scotland** Écosse *f;* **Scottish** écossais

scoundrel ['skaʊndrəl] gredin *m*

scour ['skaʊər] (*search*) fouiller

scowl [skaʊl] **1** *n* air *m* renfrogné **2** *v/i* se renfrogner

scramble ['skræmbl] **1** *n* (*rush*) course *f* folle **2** *v/t message* brouiller **3** *v/i:* **he ~d to his feet** il se releva d'un bond; **scrambled eggs** œufs *mpl* brouillés

scrap [skræp] **1** *n metal* ferraille *f;* (*fight*) bagarre *f; of food, paper* bout *m* **2** *v/t idea, plan* abandonner

scrape [skreɪp] **1** *n on paint, skin* éraflure *f* **2** *v/t paint-*

work, arm etc érafler
'scrap metal ferraille *f*
scrappy ['skræpɪ] *work, essay* décousu
scratch [skrætʃ] **1** *n* mark égratignure *f*; **start from ~** partir de zéro; **not up to ~** pas à la hauteur **2** *v/t* (*mark: skin, paint*) égratigner; *of cat* griffer; *because of itch* se gratter **3** *v/i* of cat griffer
scrawl [skrɔːl] **1** *n* gribouillis *m* **2** *v/t* gribouiller
scrawny ['skrɔːnɪ] décharné
scream [skriːm] **1** *n* cri *m* **2** *v/i* pousser un cri
screech [skriːtʃ] **1** *n of tires* crissement *m*; (*scream*) cri *m* strident **2** *v/i of tires* crisser; (*scream*) pousser un cri strident
screen [skriːn] **1** *n of room, hospital* paravent *m*; *in movie theater, of TV, computer* écran *m* **2** *v/t* (*protect, hide*) cacher; *movie* projeter; *for security reasons* passer au crible; **screenplay** scénario *m*; **screen saver** économiseur *m* d'écran; **screen test** *for movie* bout *m* d'essai
screw [skruː] **1** *n* vis *m* **2** *v/t attach* visser (**to** à); F (*cheat*) rouler F; V (*have sex with*) baiser V; **screwdriver** tournevis *m*; **screwed up** F *psychologically* paumé F; **screwy** F déjanté F
scribble ['skrɪbl] **1** *n* griffonnage *m* **2** *v/t* (*write quickly*)

griffonner **3** *v/i* gribouiller
script [skrɪpt] *for movie* scénario *m*; *for play* texte *m*; *form of writing* script *m*; Scripture: **the (Holy) ~s** les Saintes Écritures *fpl*; **scriptwriter** scénariste *m/f*

◆ **scroll down** [skrəʊl] COMPUT faire défiler vers le bas

◆ **scroll up** COMPUT faire défiler vers le haut

scrounge [skraʊndʒ] se faire offrir; **scrounger** profiteur(-euse) *m(f)*
scrub [skrʌb] *floor* laver à la brosse
scruples ['skruːplz] scrupules *mpl*; **scrupulous** *morally*, (*thorough*) scrupuleux; **scrupulously** (*meticulously*) scrupuleusement
scrutinize ['skruːtɪnaɪz] (*examine closely*) scruter; **scrutiny** examen *m* minutieux
scuba diving ['skuːbə] plongée *f* sous-marine autonome
scuffle ['skʌfl] bagarre *f*
sculptor ['skʌlptər] sculpteur(-trice) *m(f)*; **sculpture** sculpture *f*
scum [skʌm] *on liquid* écume *f*; *pej: people* bande *f* d'ordures F
sea [siː] mer *f*; **seabird** oiseau *m* de mer; **seafood** fruits *mpl* de mer; **seagull** mouette *f*
seal [siːl] *n animal* phoque *m*
seal² [siːl] **1** *n on document*

sceau *m*; TECH étanchéité *f* **2** *v/t container* sceller

'sea level: *above/below* ~ -dessus/au-dessous du niveau de la mer

seam [siːm] *on garment* couture *f*; *of ore* veine *f*

'seaman [ˈsɜːrʃ] marin *m*; **seaport** port *m* maritime

search [sɜːrʃ] **1** *n* recherche *f* (*for* de) **2** *v/t* chercher dans ◆ **search for** chercher

searching [ˈsɜːrʃɪŋ] *look, question* pénétrant; **search- light** projecteur *m*

'seashore plage *f*; **seasick: *get* ~** avoir le mal de mer; **seaside: *at the* ~** au bord de la mer

season [siːzn] saison *f*; **sea- sonal** *vegetables, employ- ment* saisonnier; **seasoned** *wood, traveler, cam- paigner* expérimenté; **sea- soning** assaisonnement *m*; **season ticket** carte *f* d'abonnement

seat [siːt] place *f*; *chair* siège *m*; *of pants* fond *m*; **please take a ~** veuillez vous asseoir; **seat belt** ceinture *f* de sécurité

'seaweed algues *fpl*

secluded [sɪˈkluːdɪd] retiré

second [ˈsekənd] **1** *n of time* seconde *f* **2** *adj* deuxième **3** *adv come in* deuxième **4** *v/t motion* appuyer; **secondary** secondaire; **second floor** premier étage *m*, *Br* deuxiè-

me étage *m*; **second-hand** d'occasion;   **secondly** deuxièmement;   **second- -rate** de second ordre

secrecy [ˈsiːkrəsɪ] secret *m*; **secret 1** *n* secret *m* **2** *adj* secret

secretarial [sekrəˈterɪəl] *job* de secrétariat; **secretary** se- crétaire *m/f*; POL ministre *m/f*; **Secretary of State** se- crétaire *m/f* d'État

secretive [ˈsiːkrətɪv] secret; **secretly** en secret

sect [sekt] secte *f*

section [ˈsekʃn] section *f*

sector [ˈsektər] secteur *m*

secular [ˈsekjʊlər] séculier

secure [sɪˈkjʊr] **1** *adj shelf etc* bien fixé; *job, contract* sûr **2** *v/t shelf etc* fixer; *s.o.'s help, finances* se procurer; **securi- ties market** FIN marché *m* des valeurs; **security** sécuri- té *f*; *for investment* garantie *f*; **security alert** alerte *f* de sécurité; **security forces** for- ces *fpl* de sécurité; **security guard** garde *m* de sécurité; **security risk** menace poten- tielle à la sécurité de l'État ou d'une organisation

sedan [sɪˈdæn] MOT berline *f*

sedate [sɪˈdeɪt] donner un calmant à; **sedative** calmant *m*

sedentary [ˈsedənterɪ] *job* sé- dentaire

sediment [ˈsedɪmənt] sédi- ment *m*

seduce [sɪ'duːs] séduire; seduction séduction f; seduc-
tive dress, offer séduisant

see [siː] with eyes, (understand) voir; ~ you! F à plus! F
◆ see off at airport etc raccompagner; (chase away)
chasser

seed [siːd] single graine f; collective graines fpl; of fruit pépin m; in tennis tête f de série; seedy miteux

seeing 'eye dog chien m
d'aveugle; seeing (that)
étant donné que

seek [siːk] chercher

seem [siːm] sembler; seem-
ingly apparemment

seesaw ['siːsɔː] bascule f

'see-through transparent

segment ['segmənt] segment
m; of orange morceau m

segregate ['segrɪgeɪt] séparer; segregation ségréga-
tion f; of sexes séparation f

seismology [saɪz'mɑːlədʒɪ]
sismologie f

seize [siːz] opportunity, arm,
of police etc saisir; power
s'emparer de; seizure MED
crise f; of drugs etc saisie f

seldom ['seldəm] rarement

select [sɪ'lekt] 1 v/t sélection-
ner 2 adj group of people
choisi; hotel etc chic inv; selection sélection f; selective
sélectif

self [self] moi m; self-assur-
ance confiance f en soi;
self-assured sûr de soi;

self-centered, Br self-cen-
tred égocentrique; self-confidence confiance en soi;
self-confident sûr de soi;
self-conscious intimidé;
about sth gêné (about par);
self-consciousness timidité f; about sth gêne f (about
par rapport à); self-control
contrôle m de soi; self-defense, Br self-defence autodéfense f; LAW légitime défense f; self-employed indépendant; self-evident évident; self-expression ex-
pression f; self-government
autonomie f; self-interest
intérêt m (personnel); selfish égoïste; selfless désinte-
ressé; self-made man self-
-made man m; self-pity api-
toiement m sur soi-même;
self-portrait autoportrait m;
self-reliant autonome; self-
-respect respect m de soi;
self-satisfied pej suffisant;
self-service libre-service;
self-service restaurant self
m; self-taught autodidacte

sell [sel] 1 v/t vendre 2 v/i of
products se vendre; sell-by
date date f limite de vente;
seller vendeur(-euse) m(f);
selling com vente f; selling
point COM point m fort

Sellotape® ['seləteɪp] Br
scotch m

semester [sɪ'mestər] semestre m

semi ['semɪ] truck semi-re-

morque *f*; **semicircle** demi-
-cercle *m*; **semiconductor**
ELEC semi-conducteur *m*;
semifinal demi-finale *f*;
semifinalist demi-finaliste
m/f

seminar ['semɪnɑːr] séminaire *m*

semi'skilled *worker* spéciali-
sé

senate ['senət] Sénat *m*; **senator** sénateur(-trice) *m(f)*

send [send] envoyer (**to** à)
♦ **send back** renvoyer
♦ **send for** *doctor* faire venir;
help envoyer chercher
sender ['sendər] *of letter* ex-
péditeur(-trice) *m(f)*

senile ['siːnaɪl] sénile; **senil-
ity** sénilité *f*

senior ['siːnjər] (*older*) plus
âgé; *in rank* supérieur; **seni-
or citizen** personne *f* âgée;
seniority *in job* ancienneté *f*

sensation [sen'seɪʃn] sensation *f*; **sensational** sensationnel

sense [sens] **1** *n* sens *m*; (*common* ~) bon sens *m*; (*feeling*)
sentiment *m*; **come to one's
~s** revenir à la raison; **it
doesn't make** ~ cela n'a
pas de sens **2** *v/t* sentir;
senseless (*pointless*) stupide

sensible ['sensɪbl] sensé;
clothes, *shoes* pratique; **sen-
sibly** raisonnablement

sensitive ['sensətɪv] sensible;
sensitivity sensibilité *f*

sensor ['sensər] détecteur *m*

sensual ['senʃʊəl] sensuel;
sensuality sensualité *f*

sensuous ['senʃʊəs] voluptueux

sentence ['sentəns] **1** *n* GRAM
phrase *f*; LAW peine *f* **2** *v/t*
LAW condamner

sentiment ['sentɪmənt] (*senti-
mentality*) sentimentalité *f*;
(*opinion*) sentiment *m*; **sentimental** sentimental; **senti-
mentality** sentimentalité *f*

sentry ['sentrɪ] sentinelle *f*

separate 1 ['sepərət] *adj* séparé **2** ['sepəreɪt] *v/t* séparer
(**from** de) **3** *v/i* *of couple* se
séparer; **separated** *couple*
séparé; **separately** séparément; **separation** séparation
f

September [sep'tembər] septembre *m*

septic ['septɪk] septique

sequel ['siːkwəl] suite *f*

sequence ['siːkwəns] ordre
m

serene [sɪ'riːn] serein

sergeant ['sɑːrdʒənt] sergent
m

serial ['sɪrɪəl] feuilleton *m*;
serialize *novel on TV* adapter en feuilleton; **serial number** *of product* numéro *m* de
série

series ['sɪriːz] série *f*

serious ['sɪrɪəs] *person*, *company* sérieux; *illness*, *situation*, *damage* grave; **seriously** *injured* gravement; *under-*

staffed sérieusement; **take s.o.** ~ prendre qn au sérieux; **seriousness** *of person, situation, illness etc* gravité *f*

sermon ['sɜːmən] sermon *m*

servant ['sɜːrvənt] domestique *m/f*

serve [sɜːrv] **1** *n in tennis* service *m* **2** *v/t & v/i* servir; **server** *in tennis* serveur(-euse) *m(f)*; COMPUT serveur *m*; **service 1** *n also in tennis* service *m*; *for vehicle, machine* entretien *m*; **~s** services *mpl* **2** *v/t vehicle, machine* entretenir; **service charge** service *m*; **serviceman** MIL militaire *m*; **service station** station-service *f*; **serving** *of food* portion *f*

session ['seʃn] session *f*; *meeting, talk* discussion *f*

set [set] **1** *n (collection)* série *f*; *(group of people)* groupe *m*; MATH ensemble *m*; THEA *(scenery)* décor *m*; *for movie* plateau *m*; *in tennis* set *m* **2** *v/t (place)* poser; *movie, novel etc* situer; *date, time, limit* fixer; *alarm* mettre; *broken limb* remettre en place; *jewel* sertir; ~ **the table** mettre la table **3** *v/i of sun* se coucher; *of glue* durcir **4** *adj ideas* arrêté; *(ready)* prêt

◆ **set off 1** *v/i on journey* partir **2** *v/t alarm etc* déclencher

◆ **set out 1** *v/i on journey* partir **2** *v/t ideas, goods* exposer

◆ **set up 1** *v/t company,*

equipment, machine monter; *market stall* installer; *meeting* arranger; F *(frame)* faire un coup à **2** *v/i in business* s'établir

'setback revers *m*

settee [se'tiː] *Br (couch, sofa)* canapé *m*

setting ['setɪŋ] *of novel, play, house* cadre *m*

settle ['setl] **1** *v/i of bird* se poser; *of dust* se déposer; *of building* se tasser; *to live* s'installer **2** *v/t dispute, issue, debts* régler; *nerves, stomach* calmer; *that* ~*s it!* ça règle la question!

◆ **settle down** *(stop being noisy)* se calmer; *(stop wild living)* se ranger; *(in an area)* s'installer

◆ **settle for** *(accept)* accepter

settled ['setld] *weather* stable; **settlement** *of claim, debt, dispute, (payment)* règlement *m*; *of building* tassement *m*; **settler** *in new country* colon *m*

'set-up *(structure)* organisation *f*; *(relationship)* relation *f*; F *(frame-up)* coup *m* monté

seven ['sevn] sept; **seventeen** dix-sept; **seventeenth** dix-septième; **seventh** septième; **seventieth** soixante-dixième; **seventy** soixante-dix

sever ['sevər] sectionner; *relations* rompre

sharpen

several ['sevrl] plusieurs

severe [sɪ'vɪr] *illness* grave; *penalty* lourd; *winter, weather* rigoureux; *teacher* sévère;

severely *punish, speak* sévèrement; *injured* grièvement; *disrupted* fortement; **severity** *of illness* gravité *f*; *of penalty* lourdeur *f*; *of winter* rigueur *f*; *of teacher* sévérité *f*

sew [sou] coudre

sewage ['su:ɪdʒ] eaux *fpl* d'égouts; **sewer** égout *m*

sewing ['souɪŋ] *skill* couture *f*; *(that being sewn)* ouvrage *m*

sex [seks] sexe *m*; **have ~ with** coucher avec; **sexist 1** *adj* sexiste **2** *n* sexiste *m/f*; **sexual** sexuel; **sexuality** sexualité *f*; **sexually** sexuellement; **sexy** sexy *inv*

shabbily ['ʃæbɪlɪ] *dressed* pauvrement; *treat* mesquinement; **shabby** *coat etc* usé; *treatment* mesquin

shack [ʃæk] cabane *f*

shade [ʃeɪd] **1** *n for lamp* abat-jour *m*; *of color* nuance *f*; *on window* store *m*; **in the ~ 1** à l'ombre **2** *v/t from sun* protéger du soleil; *from light* protéger de la lumière

shadow ['ʃædou] ombre *f*

shady ['ʃeɪdɪ] *spot* ombragé; *character* louche

shaft [ʃæft] *of axle* arbre *m*; *of mine* puits *m*

shake [ʃeɪk] **1** *n*: **give sth a good ~** bien agiter qch **2**

v/t bottle agiter; *emotionally* bouleverser; **~ one's head** *in refusal* dire non de la tête; **~ hands with s.o.** serrer la main à qn **3** *v/i of hands, voice, building* trembler; **shaken** *emotionally* bouleversé; **shake-up** remaniement *m*; **shaky** *table etc* branlant; *after illness, shock* faible; *voice, hand* tremblant; *grasp of sth, grammar etc* incertain

shall [ʃæl] ◇ *future:* **I ~ do my best** je ferai de mon mieux ◇ *suggesting:* **~ we go now?** si nous y allions maintenant?

shallow ['ʃælou] *water* peu profond; *person* superficiel

shame [ʃeɪm] **1** *n* honte *f*; **what a ~!** quel dommage! **2** *v/t* faire honte à; **shameful** honteux; **shameless** effronté

shampoo [ʃæm'pu:] shampo(o)ing *m*

shape [ʃeɪp] **1** *n* forme *f* **2** *v/t clay, character* façonner; *the future* influencer; **shapeless** *dress etc* informe; **shapely** *figure* bien fait

share [ʃer] **1** *n* part *f*; FIN action *f* **2** *v/t & v/i* partager; **shareholder** actionnaire *m/f*

shark [ʃɑːrk] requin *m*

sharp [ʃɑːrp] **1** *adj knife* tranchant; *mind, pain* vif; *taste* piquant **2** *adv* MUS haut; **at 3 o'clock** à 3 heures pile; **sharpen** *knife, skills* aiguiser

shatter ['ʃætər] **1** v/t glass, illusions briser **2** v/i of glass se briser; **shattered** ['ʃætərd] F (exhausted) crevé F; F (very upset) bouleversant; **shattering** news bouleversant

shave [ʃeɪv] **1** v/t raser **2** v/i se raser **3** n: **have a ~** se raser; **shaven** head rasé; **shaver** rasoir m électrique

shawl [ʃɔːl] châle m

she [ʃiː] elle; **there ~ is** la voilà

sheath [ʃiːθ] for knife étui m; contraceptive préservatif m

shed[1] [ʃed] v/t blood, tears verser; leaves perdre

shed[2] [ʃed] n abri m

sheep [ʃiːp] mouton m; **sheepdog** chien m de berger; **sheepish** penaud

sheer [ʃɪr] pur; cliffs abrupt

sheet [ʃiːt] drap m; of paper, metal, glass feuille f

shelf [ʃelf] étagère f; **shelves** set of shelves étagère(s) f(pl)

shell [ʃel] **1** n of mussel, egg coquille f; of tortoise carapace f; MIL obus m **2** v/t peas écosser; MIL bombarder; **shellfire** bombardements mpl; **shellfish** fruits mpl de mer

shelter ['ʃeltər] **1** n abri m **2** v/i s'abriter (**from** de) **3** v/t (protect) protéger; **sheltered** place protégé; **lead a ~ life** mener une vie protégée

shelve [ʃelv] fig mettre en suspens

shepherd ['ʃepərd] berger (-ère) m(f)

sheriff ['ʃerɪf] shérif m

shield [ʃiːld] **1** n MIL bouclier m; sports trophy plaque f; badge: of policeman plaque f **2** v/t (protect) protéger

shift [ʃɪft] **1** n (change) changement m; (move, switchover) passage m (**to** à); at work poste m; people équipe f **2** v/t (move) déplacer; production, employee transférer; stains etc faire partir **3** v/i (move) se déplacer; in attitude virer; **shifty** pej: person louche; eyes fuyant

shin [ʃɪn] tibia m

shine [ʃaɪn] **1** v/i briller; fig: of student etc être brillant (**at**, **in** en) **2** n on shoes etc brillant m; **shiny** brillant

ship [ʃɪp] **1** n bateau m, navire m **2** v/t (send) expédier **3** v/i of new product être lancé (sur le marché); **shipment** envoi m; **shipowner** armateur m; **shipping** sea traffic navigation f; (sending) expédition f; **shipwreck** naufrage m; **shipyard** chantier m naval

shirt [ʃɜːrt] chemise f

shit [ʃɪt] **1** n P merde f P **2** v/i P chier P **3** int P merde P; **shitty** F dégueulasse F

shiver ['ʃɪvər] trembler

shock [ʃɑːk] **1** n choc m; ELEC décharge f; **be in ~** MED être en état de choc **2** v/t choquer

shock absorber MOT amortisseur *m*; **shocking** choquant; F (*very bad*) épouvantable

shoddy ['ʃɑːdɪ] *goods* de mauvaise qualité; *behavior* mesquin

shoe [ʃuː] chaussure *f*, soulier *m*; **shoelace** lacet *m*; **shoemaker** cordonnier(-ière) *m(f)*; **shoe mender** cordonnier(-ière) *m(f)*; **shoestore** magasin *m* de chaussures

shoot [ʃuːt] **1** *n* BOT pousse *f* **2** *v/t* tirer sur; *and kill* tuer d'un coup de feu; *movie* tourner **3** *v/i* tirer

◆ **shoot down** *airplane* abattre; *fig: suggestion* descendre

◆ **shoot up** *of prices* monter en flèche; *of children, new buildings etc* grandir

shooting star ['ʃuːtɪŋ] étoile *f* filante

shop [ʃɑːp] **1** *n* magasin *m* **2** *v/i* faire ses courses; **go ~ping** faire les courses; **shopkeeper** commerçant *m*,-ante *f*; **shoplifter** voleur(-euse) *m(f)* à l'étalage; **shoplifting** vol *m* à l'étalage

shopping *items* courses *fpl*; **go ~** faire les courses; **shopping bag** sac *m* à provisions; **shopping list** liste *f* de commissions; **shopping mall** centre *m* commercial

shore [ʃɔːr] rivage *m*; **on ~** *not at sea* à terre

short [ʃɔːrt] **1** *adj* court; *in*

height petit; **be ~ of** manquer de **2** *adv*: **cut ~** abréger; **go ~ of** se priver de; **in ~** bref; **shortage** manque *m*; **shortcoming** défaut *m*; **shortcut** raccourci *m*; **shorten** raccourcir; **shortfall** déficit *m*; **short-lived** de courte durée; **shortly** (*soon*) bientôt; **~ before/after that** peu avant/après; **shortness** *of visit* brièveté *f*; *in height* petite taille *f*; **shorts** short *m*; *underwear* caleçon *m*; **short-sighted** myope; *fig* peu perspicace; **short-sleeved** à manches courtes; **short-tempered** *by nature* d'un caractère emporté; *at a particular time* de mauvaise humeur; **short-term** à court terme

shot [ʃɑːt] *from gun* coup *m* de feu; (*photograph*) photo *f*; (*injection*) piqûre *f*; **shotgun** fusil *m* de chasse

should [ʃʊd]: *what ~ I do?* que dois-je faire?; *you ~n't do that* tu ne devrais pas faire ça; *you ~ have heard him* tu aurais dû l'entendre

shoulder ['ʃoʊldər] épaule *f*

shout [ʃaʊt] **1** *n* cri *m* **2** *v/t & v/i* crier; **shouting** cris *mpl*

shove [ʃʌv] **1** *n*: **give s.o. a ~** pousser qn **2** *v/t & v/i* pousser

shovel ['ʃʌvl] pelle *f*

show [ʃoʊ] **1** *n* THEA, TV spectacle *m*; (*display*) démonstration *f* **2** *v/t* montrer; *at exhibition* présenter; *movie* projeter 3 v/i (*be visible*) se voir; *of movie* passer

◆ **show in** faire entrer
◆ **show off 1** v/t *skills* faire étalage de 2 v/i *pej* crâner
◆ **show up 1** v/t *shortcomings etc* faire ressortir 2 v/i (*arrive, turn up*) se pointer F; (*be visible*) se voir

'**show business** monde *m* du spectacle; **showcase** *also fig* vitrine *f*; **showdown** confrontation *f*

shower [ʃauər] **1** n *of rain* averse *f*; *to wash* douche *f*; *party*: petite fête avant un mariage ou un accouchement à laquelle tout le monde apporte un cadeau; **take a ~** prendre une douche 2 v/i prendre une douche

'**show-off** *pej* prétentieux (-euse) *m(f)*; **showroom** salle *f* d'exposition; **showy** voyant

shred [ʃred] **1** n *of paper etc* lambeau *m*; *of meat etc* morceau *m* 2 v/t *documents* déchiqueter; *in cooking* râper; **shredder** *for documents* déchiqueteuse *f*

shrewd [ʃruːd] perspicace; **shrewdness** perspicacité *f*

shriek [ʃriːk] **1** n cri *m* aigu 2 v/i pousser un cri aigu

shrill [ʃrɪl] perçant

shrimp [ʃrɪmp] crevette *f*

shrine [ʃraɪn] lieu *m* saint

shrink¹ [ʃrɪŋk] v/i *of material* rétrécir; *of support* diminuer

shrink² [ʃrɪŋk] n F (*psychiatrist*) psy *m* F

shrivel [ˈʃrɪvl] se flétrir

shrub [ʃrʌb] arbuste *m*; **shrubbery** massif *m* d'arbustes

shrug [ʃrʌɡ]: **~ (one's shoulders**) hausser les épaules

shudder [ˈʃʌdər] **1** n *of fear, disgust* frisson *m*; *of earth* vibration *f* 2 v/i *with fear, disgust* frissonner; *of earth* vibrer

shuffle [ˈʃʌfl] v/t *cards* battre

shun [ʃʌn] fuir

shut [ʃʌt] **1** v/t fermer 2 v/i *of door, box* se fermer; *of store* fermer

◆ **shut down 1** v/t *business* fermer; *computer* éteindre 2 v/i *of business* fermer ses portes; *of computer* s'éteindre

◆ **shut up** F (*be quiet*) se taire; **shut up!** tais-toi!

shutter [ˈʃʌtər] *on window* volet *m*; PHOT obturateur *m*

shuttle bus [ˈʃʌtl] *at airport* navette *f*

shy [ʃaɪ] timide; **shyness** timidité *f*

sick [sɪk] malade; *sense of humor* noir; **be ~** *Br* (*vomit*) vomir; **sicken 1** v/t (*disgust*) écœurer; (*make ill*) rendre malade 2 v/i: **be ...ing for** couver; **sickening** écœurant; **sick leave** congé *m* de maladie; **sickness** maladie *f*; (*vomiting*) vomissements *mpl*

side [saɪd] **1** *n* côté *m*; SP équipe *f*; **take ~s** (*favor one ~*) prendre parti; **~ by ~** côte à côte; **side effect** effet *m* secondaire; **sidestep** éviter; *fig also* contourner; **side street** rue *f* transversale; **sidewalk** trottoir *m*; **sideways** de côté

siege [siːdʒ] siège *m*

sieve [sɪv] *for flour* tamis *m*

sift [sɪft] tamiser; *data* passer en revue

sigh [saɪ] **1** *n* soupir *m* **2** *v/i* soupirer

sight [saɪt] spectacle *m*; (*power of seeing*) vue *f*; **~s** *of city* monuments *mpl*; **know by ~** connaître de vue; **sightseeing: go ~** faire du tourisme; **sightseer** touriste *m/f*

sign [saɪn] **1** *n* signe *m*; (*road~*) panneau *m*; *outside shop* enseigne *f* **2** *v/t & v/i* signer

signal ['sɪɡnl] **1** *n* signal *m* **2** *v/i* of driver mettre son clignotant

signatory ['sɪɡnətɔːrɪ] signataire *m/f*

signature ['sɪɡnətʃər] signature *f*

significance [sɪɡ'nɪfɪkəns] importance *f*; **significant** *event, sum of money, improvement etc* important; **significantly** *larger, more expensive* nettement

signify ['sɪɡnɪfaɪ] signifier

'sign language langage *m* des signes; **signpost** poteau *m* indicateur

silence ['saɪləns] **1** *n* silence *m* **2** *v/t* faire taire; **silent** silencieux

silhouette [sɪluː'et] silhouette *f*

silicon ['sɪlɪkən] silicium *m*

silk [sɪlk] **1** *adj* shirt etc en soie **2** *n* soie *f*; **silky** soyeux

silliness ['sɪlɪnɪs] stupidité *f*; **silly** bête

silo ['saɪloʊ] silo *m*

silver ['sɪlvər] **1** *adj* ring en argent; hair argenté **2** *n* argent *m*; **silverware** argenterie *f*

similar ['sɪmɪlər] semblable (**to** à); **similarity** ressemblance *f*; **similarly** de la même façon

simple ['sɪmpl] simple; **simple-minded** *pej* simple, simplet; **simplicity** simplicité *f*; **simplify** simplifier; **simplistic** simpliste; **simply** (*absolutely*) absolument; (*in a simple way*) simplement

simultaneous [saɪməl'teɪnɪəs] simultané; **simultaneously** simultanément

sin [sɪn] **1** *n* péché *m* **2** *v/i* pécher

since [sɪns] **1** *prep & adv* depuis; **I've been here ~ last week** je suis là depuis la semaine dernière **2** *conj in expressions of time* depuis que; (*seeing that*) puisque

sincere [sɪn'sɪr] sincère; **sincerely** sincèrement; **Sincerely yours** Je vous prie d'agréer, Madame/Monsieur, l'expression de mes sentiments les meilleurs; **sincerity** sincérité f

sinful ['sɪnful] *deeds* honteux; **~ person** pécheur m, pécheresse f

sing [sɪŋ] chanter

singe [sɪndʒ] brûler légèrement

singer ['sɪŋər] chanteur(-euse) m(f)

single ['sɪŋgl] **1** *adj* (*sole*) seul; (*not double*) simple; *bed* à une place; (*not married*) célibataire **2** n MUS single m; (~ *room*) chambre f à un lit; *person* personne f seule; **~s** in *tennis* simple m; **single-handed** seul; **single-minded** résolu; **single parent** mère/père qui élève ses enfants tout seul; **single parent family** famille f monoparentale; **single room** chambre f à un lit

singular ['sɪŋgjələr] GRAM **1** *adj* au singulier **2** n singulier m

sinister ['sɪnɪstər] sinistre

sink [sɪŋk] **1** n évier m **2** v/i of *ship*, *object* couler; of *sun* descendre; of *interest rates etc* baisser **3** v/t *ship* couler; *money* investir

sinner ['sɪnər] pécheur m, pécheresse f

sip [sɪp] **1** n petite gorgée f **2** v/t boire à petites gorgées

sir [sɜːr] monsieur m

siren ['saɪrən] sirène f

sirloin ['sɜːrlɔɪn] aloyau m

sister ['sɪstər] sœur f; **sister-in-law** belle-sœur f

sit [sɪt] (~ *down*) s'asseoir; **she was sitting** elle était assise

◆ **sit down** s'asseoir

sitcom ['sɪtkɑːm] sitcom m

site [saɪt] **1** n emplacement m; of *battle* site m **2** v/t *new offices etc* situer

sitting ['sɪtɪŋ] of *committee*, *court*, *for artist* séance f; *for meals* service m; **sitting room** salon m

situated ['sɪtueɪtɪd] situé; **situation** situation f; of *building etc* emplacement m

six [sɪks] six; **sixteen** seize; **sixteenth** seizième; **sixth** sixième; **sixtieth** soixantième; **sixty** soixante

size [saɪz] of *room*, *jacket* taille f; of *shoes* pointure f; of *loan* montant m; of *shoes* pointure f; **sizeable** *meal*, *house* assez grand; *order*, *amount* assez important

skate [skeɪt] **1** n patin m **2** v/i patiner; **skateboard** skateboard m; **skateboarding** skateboard m; **skater** patineur(-euse) m(f); **skating** patinage f; **skating rink** patinoire f

skeleton ['skelɪtn] squelette m

m

skeptic ['skeptɪk] sceptique *m/f*; **skeptical** sceptique; **skepticism** scepticisme *m*

sketch [sketʃ] **1** *n* croquis *m*; THEA sketch *m* **2** *v/t* esquisser; **sketchy** *knowledge etc* sommaire

ski [ski:] **1** *n* ski *m* **2** *v/i* faire du ski

skid [skɪd] **1** *n* dérapage *m* **2** *v/i* déraper

skier ['ski:ər] skieur(-euse) *m(f)*; **skiing** ski *m*

skilful *etc Br* → **skillful**

skill [skɪl] technique *f*; **~s** compétences *fpl*; **skilled** habile; **skillful** habile; **skillfully** habilement

skim [skɪm] *surface* effleurer

skimpy ['skɪmpɪ] *account etc* sommaire; *dress* étriqué

skin [skɪn] **1** *n* peau *f* **2** *v/t animal* écorcher; *tomato* peler; **skin diving** plongée *f* sous-marine autonome; **skinny** maigre; **skin-tight** moulant

skip [skɪp] **1** *n* (*little jump*) saut *m* **2** *v/i* sautiller **3** *v/t* (*omit*) sauter; **skipper** capitaine *m/f*

skirt [skɜːrt] jupe *f*

skull [skʌl] crâne *m*

skunk [skʌŋk] mouffette *f*

sky [skaɪ] ciel *m*; **skylight** lucarne *f*; **skyline** silhouette *f*; **skyscraper** gratte-ciel *m inv*

slab [slæb] *of stone, butter* plaque *f*; *of cake* grosse tranche *f*

slack [slæk] *rope* mal tendu; *work* négligé; *period* creux; *pace* ralentir; **slacks** pantalon *m*

slacken *rope* détendre; *pace* ralentir; **slacks** pantalon *m*

slam [slæm] claquer

slander ['slændər] **1** *n* calomnie *f* **2** *v/t* calomnier; **slanderous** calomnieux

slang [slæŋ] *also of a specific group* argot *m*

slant [slænt] **1** *v/i* pencher **2** *n* inclinaison *f*; *given to a story* perspective *f*; **slanting** *roof* en pente; *eyes* bridé

slap [slæp] **1** *n* (*blow*) claque *f* **2** *v/t* donner une claque à

slash [slæʃ] **1** *n* *cut* entaille *f*; *in punctuation* barre *f* oblique **2** *v/t painting, skin* entailler; *prices* réduire radicalement

slaughter ['slɔːtər] **1** *n* *of animals* abattage *m*; *of people, troops* massacre *m* **2** *v/t animals* abattre; *people, troops* massacrer; **slaughterhouse** abattoir *m*

slave [sleɪv] esclave *m/f*

slay [sleɪ] tuer; **slaying** (*murder*) meurtre *m*

sleaze [sliːz] POL corruption *f*; **sleazy** *bar, character* louche

sleep [sliːp] **1** *n* sommeil *m*; **go to ~** s'endormir **2** *v/i* dormir

◆ **sleep with** (*have sex with*) coucher avec

'sleeping bag sac *m* de couchage; **sleeping car** RAIL wagon-lit *m*; **sleeping pill** som-

---

nifère m; **sleepwalker** somnambule m/f; **sleepwalking** somnambulisme m; **sleepy** person qui a envie de dormir; yawn, town endormi; **I'm ~** j'ai sommeil

sleet [sliːt] neige f fondue

sleeve [sliːv] of jacket etc manche f; **sleeveless** sans manches

slender ['slendər] mince; chance, margin faible

slice [slaɪs] **1** n of bread, pie tranche f; fig: of profits part f **2** v/t loaf etc couper en tranches

slick [slɪk] **1** adj performance habile; pej (cunning) rusé **2** n of oil marée f noire

slide [slaɪd] **1** n for kids toboggan m; PHOT diapositive f **2** v/i (decrease) of exchange rate etc baisser **3** v/t item of furniture faire glisser

slight [slaɪt] person, figure frêle; (small) léger; **no, not in the ~est** pas le moins du monde; **slightly** légèrement

slim [slɪm] person mince; chance faible

slime [slaɪm] (mud) vase f; of slug etc bave f; **slimy** liquid etc vaseux

sling [slɪŋ] **1** n for arm écharpe f **2** v/t F (throw) lancer

slip [slɪp] **1** n (mistake) erreur f **2** v/i glisser; in quality, quantity baisser

◆ **slip up** (make a mistake) faire une gaffe

slipped 'disc [slɪpt] hernie f discale

slipper ['slɪpər] chausson m

slippery ['slɪpəri] glissant

'slip-up (mistake) gaffe f

slit [slɪt] **1** n (tear) déchirure f; (hole), in skirt fente f **2** v/t ouvrir, fendre

sliver ['slɪvər] petit morceau m; of wood, glass éclat m

slob [slɑːb] pej rustaud(e) m(f)

slog [slɑːg] long walk trajet m pénible; hard work corvée f

slogan ['slougən] slogan m

slop [slɑːp] (spill) renverser

slope [sloup] **1** n inclinaison f; of mountain côté m **2** v/i être incliné

sloppy ['slɑːpi] F work, in dress négligé; (too sentimental) gnangnan F

slot [slɑːt] fente f; in schedule créneau m; **slot machine** for vending distributeur m (automatique); for gambling machine f à sous

slovenly ['slʌvnli] négligé

slow [slou] lent; **be ~** of clock retarder

◆ **slow down 1** v/t ralentir **2** v/i ralentir; in life faire moins de choses

'slowdown in production ralentissement m; **slowly** lentement; **slowness** lenteur f

sluggish ['slʌgɪʃ] lent; river à cours lent

slum [slʌm] area quartier m

pauvre; *house* taudis *m*

slump [slʌmp] **1** *n in trade* effondrement *m* **2** *v/i of economy* s'effondrer; *of person* s'affaisser

slur [slɜːr] **1** *on character* tache *f* **2** *v/t words* mal articuler

slush [slʌʃ] neige *f* fondue; *pej (sentimental stuff)* sensiblerie *f*; **slush fund** caisse *f* noire

slut [slʌt] *pej* pute *f* F

sly [slaɪ] *(furtive)* sournois; *(crafty)* rusé

small [smɔːl] petit

smart[1] [smɑːrt] *adj* élégant; *(intelligent)* intelligent; *pace* vif

smart[2] [smɑːrt] *v/i (hurt)* brûler

'smart card carte *f* à puce; **smartly** *dressed* avec élégance

smash [smæʃ] **1** *n noise* fracas *m*; *(car crash)* accident *m*; *in tennis* smash *m* **2** *v/t break* fracasser; *(hit hard)* frapper **3** *v/i break* se fracasser

smattering ['smætərɪŋ]: **have a ~ of Chinese** savoir un peu de chinois

smear [smɪr] **1** *n of ink etc* tache *f*; *Br* MED frottis *m*; *on character* diffamation *f* **2** *v/t character* entacher

smell [smel] **1** *n* odeur *f*; **sense of ~** sens *m* de l'odorat **2** *v/t* sentir **3** *v/i unpleasantly* sentir mauvais; *(sniff)* renifler; **smelly** qui sent mauvais

smile [smaɪl] **1** *n* sourire *m* **2** *v/i* sourire

smirk [smɜːrk] petit sourire *m* narquois

smoke [smouk] **1** *n* fumée *f* **2** *v/t also food* fumer **3** *v/i of person* fumer; **smoker** fumeur(-euse) *m(f)*; **smoke- -free** non-fumeur *inv*; **smoking: no ~** défense de fumer; **smoky** enfumé

smolder ['smouldər] *of fire* couver

smooth [smuːð] **1** *adj surface, skin, sea* lisse; *ride, flight, crossing* bon; *pej: person* mielleux **2** *v/t hair* lisser; **smoothly** *without any problems* sans problème

smother ['smʌðər] *person, flames* étouffer

smoulder *Br* → **smolder**

smudge [smʌdʒ] **1** *n* tache *f* **2** *v/t paint* faire des traces sur; *ink, mascara* étaler

smug [smʌg] suffisant

smuggle ['smʌgl] passer en contrebande; **smuggler** contrebandier(-ière) *m(f)*; **smuggling** contrebande *f*

smutty ['smʌtɪ] *joke* grossier

snack [snæk] en-cas *m*

snag [snæg] *(problem)* hic *m* F

snake [sneɪk] serpent *m*

snap [snæp] **1** *n sound* bruit *m* sec; PHOT instantané *m* **2** *v/t break* casser **3** *v/i break* se casser net **4** *adj decision, judgement* rapide, subit;

snappy *person, mood* cassant; *decision* prompt; **be a ~ dresser** s'habiller chic; **snapshot** photo *f*

snarl [snɑːrl] **1** *n* of dog grondement **2** *v/i* of dog gronder en montrant les dents

snatch [snætʃ] (*grab*) saisir; ⊦ (*steal*) voler; ⊦ (*kidnap*) enlever

snazzy ['snæzɪ] F *necktie* etc qui tape F

sneakers ['sniːkərz] tennis *mpl*

sneaky ['sniːkɪ] F (*under-handed*) sournois

sneer [snɪr] **1** *n* ricanement *m* **2** *v/i* ricaner

sneeze [sniːz] **1** *n* éternuement *m* **2** *v/i* éternuer

snicker ['snɪkər] pouffer de rire

sniff [snɪf] renifler

sniper ['snaɪpər] tireur *m* embusqué

snitch [snɪtʃ] **1** *n* (*telltale*) mouchard(e) *m(f)* F **2** *v/i* (*tell tales*) vendre la mèche

snivel ['snɪvl] pleurnicher

snob [snɑːb] snob *m/f*; **snobbery** snobisme *m*; **snobbish** snob *inv*

◆ **snoop around** [snuːp] fourrer le nez partout

snooty ['snuːtɪ] arrogant

snooze [snuːz] **1** *n* petit somme *m* **2** *v/i* roupiller F

snore [snɔːr] ronfler; **snoring** ronflement *m*

snorkel ['snɔːrkl] tuba *m*

snort [snɔːrt] *of bull, horse* s'ébrouer; *of person* grogner

snow [snoʊ] **1** *n* neige *f* **2** *v/i* neiger; **snowball** boule *f* de neige; **snowdrift** amoncellement *m* de neige; **snowman** bonhomme *m* de neige; **snowplow** chasse-neige *m inv*; **snowstorm** tempête *f* de neige; **snowy** *weather* neigeux; *roads, hills* enneigé

snub [snʌb] **1** *n* rebuffade *f* **2** *v/t* snober; **snub-nosed** au nez retroussé

snug [snʌg] bien au chaud; (*tight-fitting*) bien ajusté

so [soʊ] **1** *adv* si, tellement; **~ kind** tellement gentil; *not ~ much for me* pas autant pour moi; **~ much easier** tellement plus facile; *drink ~ much* tellement boire; **~ many people** tellement de gens; *I miss you ~* tu me manques tellement; **~ am/do I** moi aussi; **~ is/does she** elle aussi; **~ and ~** et ainsi de suite **2** *pron*: *I hope ~* je l'espère bien; *I think ~* je pense que oui; *50 or ~* une cinquantaine, à peu près cinquante **3** *conj* (*for that reason*) donc; (*in order that*) pour que (+*subj*); **~ (that) I could come too** pour que je puisse moi aussi venir; **~ what?** F et alors?

soak [soʊk] (*steep*) faire tremper; *of water* tremper; **soaked** trempé

solution

soap [soʊp] *for washing* savon *m*; soap (**opera**) feuilleton *m*; soapy savonneux

soar [sɔːr] *of rocket, prices etc* monter en flèche

sob [sɑːb] **1** *n* sanglot *m* **2** *v/i* sangloter

sober ['soʊbər] en état de sobriété; (*serious*) sérieux

so-'called (*referred to as*) comme on le/la/les appelle; (*incorrectly referred to as*) soi-disant *inv*

soccer ['sɑːkər] football *m*

sociable ['soʊʃəbl] sociable

social ['soʊʃl] social; (*recreational*) mondain; **social democrat** social-démocrate *m/f*; **socialism** socialisme *m*; **socialist 1** *adj* socialiste **2** *n* socialiste *m/f*; **socialize** fréquenter des gens; **social worker** assistant sociale *m*, assistante sociale *f*

society [sə'saɪətɪ] société *f*

sociologist [soʊsɪ'ɑːlədʒɪst] sociologue *m/f*; **sociology** sociologie *f*

sock¹ [sɑːk] *n for wearing* chaussette *f*

sock² [sɑːk] *v/t* (*punch*) donner un coup de poing à

socket ['sɑːkɪt] ELEC *for light bulb* douille *f*; Br (*wall* ~) prise *f* de courant; *of eye* orbite *f*

soda ['soʊdə] (~ *water*) eau *f* gazeuse; (*soft drink*) soda *m*; (*ice-cream* ~) soda *m* à la crème glacée

sofa ['soʊfə] canapé *m*

soft [sɑːft] doux; (*lenient*) gentil; **soften** *position* assouplir; *impact, blow* adoucir; **softly** doucement; **software** logiciel *m*

soggy ['sɑːgɪ] *soil* détrempé; *pastry* pâteux

soil [sɔɪl] **1** *n* (*earth*) terre *f* **2** *v/t* salir

solar energy ['soʊlər] énergie *f* solaire

soldier ['soʊldʒər] soldat *m*

sole¹ [soʊl] *n of foot* plante *f*; *of shoe* semelle *f*

sole² [soʊl] *adj* seul; *responsibility* exclusif

solely ['soʊlɪ] exclusivement

solemn ['sɑːləm] solennel; **solemnity** solennité *f*; **solemnly** solennellement

solicit [sə'lɪsɪt] *of prostitute* racoler

solid ['sɑːlɪd] (*hard*) dur; (*without holes*) compact; *gold, silver etc, support* massif; **solidarity** solidarité *f*; **solidify** se solidifier; **solidly** *built* solidement; *in favor of* massivement

solitaire [sɑːlɪ'ter] *card game* réussite *f*

solitary ['sɑːlɪterɪ] *life, activity* solitaire; (*single*) isolé; **solitude** solitude *f*

solo ['soʊloʊ] **1** *adj* en solo **2** *n* MUS solo *m*; **soloist** soliste *m/f*

soluble ['sɑːljʊbl] *substance, problem* soluble; **solution** *also mixture* solution *f*

solve [sɑːlv] résoudre; **solvent** *financially* solvable

somber, *Br* **sombre** ['sɒmbər] sombre

some [sʌm] **1** *adj:* ~ *cream/chocolate/cookies* de la crème/du chocolat/des biscuits; ~ *people say that ...* certains disent que ... **2** *pron:* ~ *of the money* une partie de l'argent; ~ *of the group* certaines personnes du groupe; *would you like ~?* est-ce que vous en voulez?; *give me ~* donnez-m'en peu (*a bit*) un peu; **somebody** quelqu'un; **someday** un jour; **somehow** (*one means or another*) d'une manière ou d'une autre; (*for some unknown reason*) sans savoir pourquoi; **someone** → **somebody**; **someplace** → **somewhere**

somersault ['sʌmərsɔːlt] **1** *n* roulade *f*; *by vehicle* tonneau *m* **2** *v/i of vehicle* faire un tonneau

'**something** quelque chose; **sometime** un de ces jours; ~ *last year* dans le courant de l'année dernière; **sometimes** parfois; **somewhat** quelque peu; **somewhere 1** *adv* quelque part **2** *pron:* *let's go* ~ *quiet* allons dans un endroit calme; ~ *to park* un endroit où se garer

son [sʌn] fils *m*

song [sɑːŋ] chanson *f*

'**son-in-law** beau-fils *m*; **son of a bitch** V fils *m* de pute V

soon [suːn] (*in a short while*) bientôt; (*quickly*) vite; (*early*) tôt; *how~?* dans combien de temps?; *as ~ as* dès que; *as ~ as possible* le plus tôt possible; ~*er or later* tôt ou tard; *the ~er the better* le plus tôt sera le mieux

soothe [suːð] calmer

sophisticated [sə'fɪstɪkeɪtɪd] sophistiqué; **sophistication** sophistication *f*

sophomore ['sɑːfəmɔːr] étudiant(e) *m(f)* de deuxième année

soprano [sə'prɑːnoʊ] soprano *m/f*

sordid ['sɔːrdɪd] sordide

sore [sɔːr] **1** *adj* F (*angry*) fâché; (*painful*): *is it ~?* ça vous fait mal? **2** *n* plaie *f*

sorrow ['sɑːroʊ] chagrin *m*

sorry ['sɑːrɪ] *day* triste; *sight* misérable; (*I'm*) ~! (*apologizing*) pardon!; *be* ~ être désolé

sort [sɔːrt] **1** *n* sorte *f*; ~ *of ...* F plutôt **2** *v/t also* COMPUT trier

SOS [esoʊ'es] S.O.S. *m; fig:* *plea for help* appel *m* à l'aide

so-'so F comme ci comme ça

soul [soʊl] *also fig* âme *f*

sound¹ [saʊnd] **1** *adj* (*sensible*) judicieux; *judgment* solide; (*healthy*) en bonne santé; *sleep* profond **2** *adv:* *be* ~

asleep être profondément endormi

sound² [saʊnd] **1** *n* son *m*; *(noise)* bruit *m* **2** *v/i: that ~s interesting* ça a l'air intéressant

soundly ['saʊndlɪ] *sleep* profondément; *beaten* à plates coutures; **soundproof** insonorisé; **soundtrack** bande *f* sonore

soup [su:p] soupe *f*

sour ['saʊər] *apple, milk* aigre; *comment* désobligeant

source [sɔːrs] *of river, information etc* source *f*

south [saʊθ] **1** *n* sud *m*; *the South of France* le Midi **2** *adj* sud *inv*; *wind* du sud **3** *adv travel* vers le sud; **South Africa** Afrique *f* du sud; **South African 1** *adj* sud-africain **2** *n* Sud-Africain *m*, Sud-Africaine *f*; **South America** Amérique *f* du sud; **South American 1** *adj* sud-américain **2** *n* Sud-Américain(e) *m(f)*; **southeast 1** *n* sud-est *m* **2** *adj* sud-est *inv* **3** *adv travel* vers le sud-est; **southeastern** sud-est *inv*; **southerly** *wind* du sud; *direction* vers le sud; **southern** du Sud; **southerner** habitant(e) *m(f)* du Sud; **southernmost** le plus au sud; **South Pole** pôle *m* Sud; **southward** vers le sud; **southwest 1** *n* sud-ouest *m* **2** *adj* sud-ouest *inv* **3** *adv* vers

le sud-ouest; **southwestern** sud-ouest *inv*

souvenir [su:vəˈnɪr] souvenir *m*

sovereign ['sɑːvrɪn] *state* souverain

sow¹ [saʊ] *n (female pig)* truie *f*

sow² [soʊ] *v/t seeds* semer

space [speɪs] espace *m*; *(room)* place *f*; **space shuttle** navette *f* spatiale; **space station** station *f* spatiale; **spacious** spacieux

spade [speɪd] *for digging* bêche *f*; *~s in card game* pique *m*

spaghetti [spəˈgetɪ] spaghetti *mpl*

Spain [speɪn] Espagne *f*

spam (mail) [spæm] spam *m*

span [spæn] *(cover)* recouvrir; *of bridge* traverser

Spaniard ['spænjərd] Espagnol *m*, Espagnole *f*; **Spanish 1** *adj* espagnol **2** *n language* espagnol *m*; *the ~* les Espagnols

spanner ['spænər] *Br* clef *f*

spare [sper] **1** *v/t time* accorder; *(lend: money)* prêter; *(do without)* se passer de; *can you ~ the time?* est-ce que vous pouvez trouver un moment? **2** *adj (extra) cash* en trop; *pair of glasses, clothes* de rechange **3** *n* pièce *f* de rechange; **spare part** pièce *f* de rechange; **spare ribs** côtelette *f* de porc dans l'échine; **spare room** chambre *f* d'ami; **spare time** temps *m* libre; **spare wheel** roue *f* de secours; **sparing**: *be ~ with* économiser; **sparingly** en petite quantité

spark [spɑːrk] étincelle *f*

sparkle ['spɑːrkl] étinceler; **sparkling wine** vin *m* mousseux

'spark plug bougie *f*

sparse [spɑːrs] *vegetation* épars

spartan ['spɑːrtn] *room* spartiate

spasmodic [spæz'mɑːdɪk] intermittent; *conversation* saccadé

spate [speɪt] *fig* série *f*, avalanche *f*

spatial ['speɪʃl] spatial

speak [spiːk] **1** *v/i* parler (*to, with* à); **~ing** TELEC lui-même, elle-même **2** *v/t foreign language* parler; **speaker** *at conference* intervenant(e) *m(f)*; (*orator*) orateur(-trice) *m(f)*; *of sound system* haut-parleur *m*; **French/Spanish ~** francophone *m/f* / hispanophone *m/f*

special ['speʃl] spécial; *effort, day etc* exceptionnel; **specialist** spécialiste *m/f*; **specialize** se spécialiser (*in* en, dans); **specially** → **especially**; **specialty** spécialité *f*

species ['spiːʃiːz] espèce *f*

specific [spə'sɪfɪk] spécifique; **specifically** spécifique-

ment; **specifications** *of machine etc* spécifications *fpl*; **specify** préciser

specimen ['spesɪmən] *of work* spécimen *m*; *of blood, urine* prélèvement *m*

spectacular [spek'tækjʊlər] spectaculaire

spectator [spek'teɪtər] spectateur(-trice) *m(f)*

spectrum ['spektrəm] *fig* éventail *m*

speculate ['spekjʊleɪt] *also* FIN spéculer; **speculation** spéculations *fpl*; FIN spéculation *f*; **speculator** FIN spéculateur(-trice) *m(f)*

speech [spiːtʃ] discours *m*; (*ability to speak*) parole *f*; (*way of speaking*) élocution *f*; **speechless** *with shock, surprise* sans voix

speed [spiːd] **1** *n* vitesse *f* **2** *v/i* (*go quickly*) se précipiter; *of vehicle* foncer; *drive too quickly* faire de la vitesse; **speedboat** vedette *f*; *with outboard motor* hors-bord *m* inv; **speed bump** dos d'âne *m*, ralentisseur *m*; **speed-dial button** bouton *m* de numérotation abrégée; **speedily** rapidement; **speeding** *when driving* excès *m* de vitesse; **speed limit** limitation *f* de vitesse; **speedometer** compteur *m* de vitesse; **speedy** rapide

spell¹ [spel] **1** *v/t word* écrire, épeler; *how do you ~ it?*

comment ça s'écrit? **2** v/i: **he can/can't ~** il a une bonne/mauvaise orthographe

spell² n of time période f

spelling ['spelɪŋ] orthographe f

spend [spend] money dépenser; time passer; **spendthrift** pej dépensier(-ière) m(f)

sperm [spɜːrm] spermatozoïde m; (semen) sperme m

sphere [sfɪr] also fig sphère f

spice [spaɪs] (seasoning) épice f; **spicy** food épicé

spider ['spaɪdər] araignée f; **spiderweb** toile f d'araignée

spike [spaɪk] pointe f; on plant, animal piquant m

spill [spɪl] **1** v/t renverser **2** v/i se répandre **3** n of oil déversement m accidentel

spin¹ [spɪn] **1** n (turn) tour m **2** v/t faire tourner **3** v/i of wheel tourner

spin² v/t wool etc filer; web tisser

spinach ['spɪnɪdʒ] épinards mpl

spinal ['spaɪnl] de vertèbres; **spinal column** colonne f vertébrale; **spinal cord** moelle f épinière; **spine** colonne f vertébrale; of book dos m; on plant, hedgehog épine f; **spineless** (cowardly) lâche

'spin-off retombée f

spiny ['spaɪnɪ] épineux

spiral ['spaɪrəl] **1** n spirale f **2** v/i rise quickly monter en spirale

spire ['spaɪr] of church flèche f

spirit ['spɪrɪt] esprit m; (courage) courage m; **spirited** (energetic) énergique; **spirits** (alcohol) spiritueux mpl; (morale) moral m; **be in good/poor ~** avoir/ne pas avoir le moral; **spiritual** spirituel

spit [spɪt] of person cracher

spite [spaɪt] malveillance f; **in ~ of** en dépit de; **spiteful** malveillant; **spitefully** avec malveillance

splash [splæʃ] **1** n noise plouf m; small amount of liquid goutte f; of color tache f **2** v/t person éclabousser; water, mud asperger **3** v/i of person patauger; **~ against sth** of waves s'écraser contre qch; **splashdown** amerrissage m

splendid ['splendɪd] magnifique; **splendor**, Br **splendour** splendeur f

splint [splɪnt] MED attelle f

splinter ['splɪntər] **1** n of wood, glass éclat m; in finger écharde f **2** v/i se briser

split [splɪt] **1** n damage fente f; (disagreement) division f; (of profits etc) partage m; (share) part f **2** v/t wood fendre; log fendre en deux; (cause disagreement in, divide) diviser **3** v/i of wood etc se fendre; (disagree) se diviser

◆ **split up** *of couple* se séparer

spoil [spɔɪl] *child* gâter; *surprise, party* gâcher; **spoilsport** F rabat-joie *m/f*; **spoilt** *child* gâté

spoke [spəʊk] *of wheel* rayon *m*

spokesperson ['spəʊkspɜːrsən] porte-parole *m/f*

sponge [spʌndʒ] éponge *f*; **sponger** F parasite *m/f*

sponsor ['spɒnsər] **1** *n for club membership* parrain *m*, marraine *f*; RAD, TV, SP sponsor *m/f* **2** *v/t for club membership* parrainer; RAD, TV, SP sponsoriser; **sponsorship** RAD, TV, SP sponsorisation *f*

spontaneous [spɒn'teɪnɪəs] spontané; **spontaneously** spontanément

spool [spuːl] bobine *f*

spoon [spuːn] cuillère *f*; **spoonful** cuillerée *f*

sporadic [spə'rædɪk] intermittent

sport [spɔːrt] sport *m*; **sporting** *event* sportif; *(fair, generous)* chic *inv*; **sports car** voiture *f* de sport; **sportsman** sportif *m*; **sportswoman** sportive *f*; **sporty** sportif

spot[1] [spɒt] *n on skin* bouton *m*; *in pattern* pois *m*

spot[2] *n (place)* endroit *m*

spot[3] *v/t (notice, identify)* re-

pérer

'**spot check** contrôle *m* au hasard; **spotless** impeccable; **spotlight** *beam* feu *m* de projecteur; *device* projecteur *m*; **spotty** *with pimples* boutonneux

spouse [spaʊs] *fml* époux *m*, épouse *f*

spout [spaʊt] **1** *n* bec *m* **2** *v/i of liquid* jaillir **3** *v/t* F débiter

sprain [spreɪn] **1** *n* foulure *f*; *serious* entorse *f* **2** *v/t ankle, wrist* se fouler; *seriously* se faire une entorse à

sprawl [sprɔːl] s'affaler; *of city* s'étendre; **sprawling** tentaculaire

spray [spreɪ] **1** *n of sea water* embruns *mpl*; *from fountain* gouttes *fpl* d'eau; *for hair* laque *f*; *container* atomiseur *m* **2** *v/t perfume, lacquer* vaporiser; *paint, weed-killer etc* pulvériser; **~ graffiti on sth** peindre des graffitis à la bombe sur qch; **spraygun** pulvérisateur *m*

spread [spred] **1** *n of disease, religion etc* propagation *f*; F *(big meal)* festin *m* **2** *v/t (lay)* butter étaler; *news, rumor, disease* répandre; *arms, legs* étendre **3** *v/i* se répandre; **spreadsheet** COMPUT feuille *f* de calcul; *program* tableur *m*

sprightly ['spraɪtlɪ] alerte

spring[1] [sprɪŋ] *n season* printemps *m*

spring² [sprɪŋ] *n* device ressort *m*

spring³ [sprɪŋ] **1** *n (jump)* bond *m*; *(stream)* source *f* **2** *v/i* bondir

'springboard tremplin *m*; **springtime** printemps *m*

sprinkle ['sprɪŋkl] saupoudrer; **sprinkler** *for garden* arroseur *m*; *in ceiling* extincteur *m*

sprint [sprɪnt] **1** *n* sprint *m* **2** *v/i* SP sprinter; *fig* piquer un sprint F; **sprinter** SP sprinteur(-euse) *m(f)*

spy [spaɪ] **1** *n* espion(ne) *m(f)* **2** *v/i* faire de l'espionnage **3** *v/t (see)* apercevoir

◆ **spy on** espionner

squabble ['skwɑːbl] **1** *n* querelle *f* **2** *v/i* se quereller

squalid ['skwɒlɪd] sordide; **squalor** misère *f*

squander ['skwɒndər] gaspiller

square [skwer] **1** *adj in shape* carré; **~ mile** mile carré **2** *n in shape*, MATH carré *m*; *in town* place *f*; *in board game* case *f*

squash¹ [skwɑːʃ] *n vegetable* courge *f*

squash² [skwɑːʃ] *n game* squash *m*

squash³ [skwɑːʃ] *v/t (crush)* écraser

squat [skwɑːt] **1** *adj in shape* ramassé **2** *v/i sit* s'accroupir; *illegally* squatter

squeak [skwiːk] **1** *n of mouse* couinement *m*; *of hinge* grin-

cement *m* **2** *v/i of mouse* couiner; *of hinge* grincer

squeal [skwiːl] **1** *n* cri *m* aigu; *of brakes* grincement *m* **2** *v/i* pousser des cris aigus; *of brakes* grincer

squeamish ['skwiːmɪʃ] trop sensible

squeeze [skwiːz] *hand* serrer; *shoulder*, *(remove juice from)* presser; *fruit*, *parcel* palper

squid [skwɪd] calmar *m*

squirm [skwɜːrm] se tortiller

squirt [skwɜːrt]

St (= *saint*) St(e) (= saint(e)); (= *street*) rue

stab [stæb] poignarder

stability [stə'bɪlətɪ] stabilité *f*; **stabilize** **1** *v/t* stabiliser **2** *v/i* se stabiliser; **stable** **1** *adj* stable **2** *n for horses* écurie *f*

stack [stæk] **1** *n (pile)* pile *f* **2** *v/t* empiler

stadium ['steɪdɪəm] stade *m*

staff [stæf] *(employees)* personnel *m*; *(teachers)* personnel *m* enseignant

stage¹ [steɪdʒ] *n in project etc* étape *f*

stage² [steɪdʒ] **1** *n* THEA scène *f* **2** *v/t play* mettre en scène; *demonstration* organiser

stagger ['stægər] **1** *v/i* tituber **2** *v/t (amaze)* ébahir; *coffee breaks etc* échelonner; **staggering** stupéfiant

stagnant ['stægnənt] *water*, *economy* stagnant; **stagnate** *fig* stagner

'stag party enterrement *m* de

vie de garçon

stain [steɪn] **1** n (*dirty mark*) tache f; for wood teinture f **2** v/t (*dirty*) tacher; wood teindre; **stained-glass window** vitrail m; **stainless steel** acier m inoxydable

stair [ster] marche f; **the ~s** l'escalier m; **staircase** escalier m

stake [steɪk] **1** n of wood pieu m; when gambling enjeu m; (*investment*) investissements mpl; **be at ~** être en jeu **2** v/t tree soutenir avec un pieu; money jouer; person financer

stale [steɪl] bread rassis; air empesté; fig: news plus très frais

stalk¹ [stɔːk] n of fruit, plant tige f

stalk² [stɔːk] v/t animal, person traquer

stall¹ [stɔːl] n at market étalage m; for cow, horse stalle f

stall² [stɔːl] **1** v/i of vehicle, engine caler; (*play for time*) chercher à gagner du temps **2** v/t engine caler; person faire attendre

stalls [stɔːlz] THEA orchestre m

stalwart ['stɔːlwərt] supporter fidèle

stamina ['stæmɪnə] endurance f

stammer ['stæmər] **1** n bégaiement m **2** v/i bégayer

stamp¹ [stæmp] **1** n for letter timbre m; device, mark tampon m **2** v/t letter timbrer; passport tamponner

stamp² [stæmp] v/t: **~ one's foot** taper du pied

stance [stæns] position f

stand [stænd] **1** n at exhibition stand m; (*witness*) ~ barre f des témoins; (*support, base*) support m; take the ~ LAW venir à la barre **2** v/i (be situated) se trouver; (as opposed to sit) rester debout; (rise) se lever **3** v/t (tolerate) supporter; (put) mettre

◆ **stand by** v/i (not take action) rester là sans rien faire; (be ready) se tenir prêt **2** v/t person soutenir; decision s'en tenir à

◆ **stand down** (withdraw) se retirer

◆ **stand for** (tolerate) supporter; (represent) représenter

◆ **stand out** be visible ressortir

◆ **stand up** **1** v/i se lever **2** v/t F poser un lapin à

◆ **stand up for** défendre

◆ **stand up to** (face) tenir tête à

standard ['stændərd] **1** adj procedure etc normal; ~ **practice** pratique f courante **2** n (level) niveau m; moral critère m; TECH norme f; **standardize** normaliser; **standard of living** niveau m de vie

'**standby** fly en stand-by;

standing *in society* position *f* sociale; (*repute*) réputation *f*; **standoffish** distant; **standpoint** point *m* de vue; **standstill**: *be at a ~* être paralysé; *bring to a ~* paralyser

staple¹ ['steɪpl] *n foodstuff* aliment *m* de base

staple² ['steɪpl] **1** *n fastener* agrafe *f* **2** *v/t* agrafer

stapler ['steɪplər] agrafeuse *f*

star [stɑːr] **1** *n in sky* étoile *f*; *fig also* vedette *f* **2** *v/t of movie* avoir comme vedette(s); **starboard** de tribord

stare [ster]: *~ into space* regarder dans le vide; *it's rude to ~* ce n'est pas poli de fixer les gens

stark [stɑːrk] **1** *adj landscape, color* austère; *reminder, contrast etc* brutal **2** *adv: ~ naked* complètement nu

starry ['stɑːrɪ] *night* étoilé; **Stars and Stripes** bannière *f* étoilée

start [stɑːrt] **1** *n* début *m* **2** *v/i* commencer; *of engine, car* démarrer; *~ing from tomorrow* à partir de demain **3** *v/t* commencer; *engine, car* mettre en marche; *business* monter; **starter** *of meal* entrée *f*; *of car* démarreur *m*

startle ['stɑːrtl] effrayer; **startling** surprenant

starvation [stɑːr'veɪʃn] inanition *f*; **starve** souffrir de la faim; *I'm starving* F je meurs de faim F

state¹ [steɪt] **1** *n* (*condition, country, part of country*) état *m*; *the States* les États-Unis *mpl* **2** *adj capital, police etc* d'état; *banquet, occasion etc* officiel

state² [steɪt] *v/t* déclarer; *name and address* décliner

'**State Department** Département *m* d'État (américain); **statement** *to police* déclaration *f*; (*announcement*) communiqué *m*; (*bank ~*) relevé *m* de compte; **state of emergency** état *m* d'urgence; **state-of-the-art** de pointe; **statesman** homme *m* d'État

static (**electricity**) ['stætɪk] électricité *f* statique

station ['steɪʃn] **1** *n* RAIL gare *f*; *of subway, RAD* station *f*; *TV* chaîne *f* **2** *v/t guard etc* placer; **stationary** immobile

stationery ['steɪʃənərɪ] papeterie *f*

'**station wagon** break *m*

statistical [stə'tɪstɪkl] statistique; **statistically** statistiquement; **statistician** statisticien(ne) *m(f)*; **statistics** *science* statistique *f* *figures* statistiques *fpl*

statue ['stætʃuː] statue *f*; **Statue of Liberty** Statue *f* de la Liberté

status ['steɪtəs] statut *m*; (*prestige*) prestige *m*; **status symbol** signe *m* extérieur de richesse

statute ['stætʃuːt] loi *f*

staunch [stɔːntʃ] *supporter* fervent

stay [steɪ] **1** *n* séjour *m* **2** *v/i* rester; **~ in a hotel** descendre dans un hôtel; **~ right there!** tenez-vous là!

◆ **stay behind** rester; ~ *in school* rester après la classe

◆ **stay up** (*not go to bed*) rester debout

steadily ['stedɪlɪ] *improve etc* de façon régulière; **steady 1** *adj hand* ferme; *voice* posé; (*regular*) régulier; (*continuous*) continu **2** *adv*: **~ of couple** sortir ensemble **3** *v/t person* soutenir; *voice* raffermir

steak [steɪk] bifteck *m*

steal [stiːl] **1** *v/t* voler **2** *v/i* (*be a thief*) voler; **~ in/out** entrer/sortir à pas feutrés

stealthy ['stelθɪ] furtif

steam [stiːm] **1** *n* vapeur *f* **2** *v/t food* cuire à la vapeur; **steamed up** F fou de rage; **steamer** *for cooking* cuiseur *m* à vapeur

steel [stiːl] **1** *adj* (*made of* ~) en acier **2** *n* acier *m*; **steelworker** ouvrier(-ière) *m(f)* de l'industrie sidérurgique

steep¹ [stiːp] *adj hill etc* raide; F *prices* excessif

steep² [stiːp] *v/t* (*soak*) faire tremper

steer¹ [stɪr] *n animal* bœuf *m*

steer² [stɪr] *v/t* diriger

steering ['stɪrɪŋ] MOT direction *f*; **steering wheel** volant

stem¹ [stem] *n of plant* tige *f*; *of glass* pied *m*; *of word* racine *f*

stem² [stem] *v/t* (*block*) enrayer

stench [stentʃ] odeur *f* nauséabonde

stencil ['stensɪl] **1** *n* pochoir *m*; *pattern* peinture *f* au pochoir **2** *v/t pattern* peindre au pochoir

step [step] **1** *n* (*pace*) pas *m*; (*stair*) marche *f*; (*measure*) mesure *f* **2** *v/i*: **~ forward/back** faire un pas en avant/en arrière

◆ **step down** *from post etc* se retirer

◆ **step up** (*increase*) augmenter

'**stepbrother** demi-frère *m*; **stepdaughter** belle-fille *f*; **stepfather** beau-père *m*; **stepladder** escabeau *m*; **stepmother** belle-mère *f*; **stepsister** demi-sœur *f*; **stepson** beau-fils *m*

stereo ['sterɪəʊ] (*sound system*) chaîne *f* stéréo; **stereotype** stéréotype *m*

sterile ['steraɪl] stérile; **sterilize** stériliser

sterling ['stɜːlɪŋ] FIN sterling *m*

stern¹ [stɜːrn] *adj* sévère

stern² [stɜːrn] *n* NAUT arrière *m*

sternly ['stɜːrnlɪ] sévèrement

steroids ['sterɔɪdz] stéroïdes *m*

mpl

stew [stuː] ragoût *m*

steward ['stjuːəd] *on plane, ship* steward *m*; *at demonstration, meeting* membre *m* du service d'ordre; **stewardess** *on plane, ship* hôtesse *f*

stick¹ [stɪk] *n* morceau *m* de bois; *of policeman* bâton *m*; *(walking)* canne *f*

stick² [stɪk] **1** *v/t with adhesive* coller (*to* à); F *(put)* mettre **2** *v/i (jam)* se coincer; *(adhere)* adhérer

◆ **stick by** F ne pas abandonner

◆ **stick to** *(adhere to)* coller à; F *(keep to)* s'en tenir à; *(follow)* suivre

◆ **stick up for** F défendre

sticker ['stɪkər] autocollant *m*; **stick-in-the-mud** F encroûté(e) *m(f)*; **sticky** gluant; *label* collant

stiff [stɪf] *brush, cardboard, mixture etc* dur; *muscle, body* raide; *in manner* guindé; *drink* bien tassé; *competition* acharné; *fine* sévère; **stiffness** *of muscles* raideur *f*; *in manner* aspect *m* guindé

stifle ['staɪfl] étouffer; **stifling** étouffant

stigma ['stɪgmə] honte *f*

still¹ [stɪl] **1** *adj* calme **2** *adv*: **keep ~!** reste tranquille!; **stand ~!** ne bouge pas!

still² [stɪl] *adv (yet)* encore, toujours; *(nevertheless)* quand même

'stillborn: **be ~** être mort à sa naissance; **still life** nature *f* morte

stilted ['stɪltɪd] guindé

stimulant ['stɪmjʊlənt] stimulant *m*; **stimulate** stimuler; **stimulating** stimulant; **stimulation** stimulation *f*; **stimulus** *(incentive)* stimulation *f*

sting [stɪŋ] **1** *n from bee, jellyfish* piqûre *f* **2** *v/t & v/i* piquer; **stinging** *criticism* blessant

stink [stɪŋk] **1** *n (bad smell)* puanteur *f*; F *(fuss)* grabuge *m* F **2** *v/i (smell bad)* puer; *(be very bad)* être nul

stipulate ['stɪpjʊleɪt] stipuler; **stipulation** condition *f*; *of will, contract* stipulation *f*

stir [stɜːr] **1** *v/t* remuer **2** *v/i of sleeping person* bouger; **stirring** *music, speech* émouvant

stitch [stɪtʃ] **1** *n* point *m*; **~es** MED points *mpl* de suture **2** *v/t (sew)* coudre; **stitching** *(stitches)* couture *f*

stock [staːk] **1** *n (reserve)* réserves *fpl*; COM *of store* stock *m*; *animals* bétail *m*; FIN actions *fpl*; *for soup etc* bouillon *m*; **be in/out of ~** être en stock/épuisé **2** *v/t* COM avoir (en stock)

'stockbreeder éleveur *m*; **stockbroker** agent *m* de change; **stock exchange** bourse *f*; **stockholder** actionnaire *m/f*; **stockist** revendeur *m*; **stock market**

marché *m* boursier; **stock-pile 1** *n* of food, weapons stocks *mpl* de réserve **2** *v/t* faire des stocks de

stocky ['stɑːkɪ] trapu

stodgy ['stɑːdʒɪ] food bourratif

stoical ['stəʊɪkl] stoïque; **stoicism** stoïcisme *m*

stomach ['stʌmək] **1** *n* (insides) estomac *m*; (abdomen) ventre *m* **2** *v/t* (tolerate) supporter

stone [stəʊn] pierre *f*; (pebble) caillou *m*; **stoned** F on drugs défoncé F

stool [stuːl] seat tabouret *m*

stoop¹ [stuːp] *v/i* (bend down) se pencher

stoop² [stuːp] *n* (porch) perron *m*

stop [stɑːp] **1** *n* for train, bus arrêt *m* **2** *v/t* arrêter; (prevent) empêcher; check faire opposition à; **~ doing sth** arrêter de faire qch **3** *v/i* s'arrêter

◆ **stop over** faire escale

'stopgap bouche-trou *m*; **stoplight** (traffic light) feu *m* rouge; (brake light) stop *m*; **stopover** étape *f*; **stopper** for bottle bouchon *m*; **stop sign** stop *m*; **stopwatch** chronomètre *m*

storage ['stɔːrɪdʒ] *com* emmagasinage *m*; in house rangement *m*; **store 1** *n* magasin *m*; (stock) provision *f*; (~house) entrepôt *m* **2** *v/t* en-

treposer; COMPUT stocker; **storefront** devanture *f* de magasin; **storekeeper** commerçant(e) *m(f)*

storey Br → **story²**

storm [stɔːrm] with rain, wind tempête *f*; (thunder~) orage *m*; **stormy** orageux

story¹ ['stɔːrɪ] (tale, account, F: lie) histoire *f*; (newspaper article) article *m*

story² ['stɔːrɪ] of building étage *m*

stout [staʊt] person corpulent, costaud

stove [stəʊv] for cooking cuisinière *f*; for heating poêle *m*

stow [stəʊ] ranger

◆ **stow away** s'embarquer clandestinement

'stowaway passager clandestin *m*, passagère clandestine *f*

straight [streɪt] **1** *adj* line, back, knees droit; hair raide; (honest, direct) franc; (not criminal) honnête; whiskey etc sec; (tidy) en ordre; (conservative) sérieux; (not homosexual) hétéro F **2** *adv* (in a straight line) droit; (directly, immediately) directement; **go ~** F of criminal revenir dans le droit chemin; **~ ahead** tout droit; **~ away**, **~ off** tout de suite; **~ out** très clairement; **~ up** without ice sans glace; **straighten** redresser; **straightforward** (honest, direct) direct; (sim-

strictly

ple) simple

strain¹ [streɪn] **1** n *on rope, engine* tension f; *on heart* pression f; **suffer from ~** souffrir de tension nerveuse **2** v/t *back* se fouler; *eyes* s'abîmer; *finances* grever

strain² [streɪn] v/t *vegetables* faire égoutter; *oil, fat etc* filtrer

strained [streɪnd] *relations* tendu; **strainer** *for vegetables etc* passoire f

strait [streɪt] détroit m; **straitlaced** collet monté *inv*

strange [streɪndʒ] *(odd, curious)* étrange, bizarre; *(unknown, foreign)* inconnu; **strangely** *(oddly)* bizarrement; **~ enough,** ... c'est bizarre, mais ...; **stranger** étranger(-ère) m (f); **he's a complete ~** je ne le connais pas du tout; **I'm a ~ here myself** moi non plus je ne suis pas d'ici

strangle ['stræŋgl] étrangler

strap [stræp] *of purse, shoe* lanière f; *of brassiere, dress* bretelle f; *of watch* bracelet m; **strapless** sans bretelles

strategic [strə'tiːdʒɪk] stratégique; **strategy** stratégie f

straw [strɔː] *material, for drink* paille f; **strawberry** fraise f

stray [streɪ] **1** *adj animal, bullet* perdu **2** n *animal* m errant **3** v/i *of animal* vagabonder; *of child* s'égarer; *fig: of eyes,*

thoughts errer (**to** vers)

streak [striːk] **1** n *of dirt, paint* traînée f; *in hair* mèche f; *fig: of nastiness etc* pointe f **2** v/i *move quickly* filer

stream [striːm] ruisseau m; *fig: of people* flot m; **streamline** *fig* rationaliser; **streamlined** *car, plane* caréné; *organization* rationalisé

street [striːt] rue f; **streetcar** tramway m; **streetlight** réverbère m; **street people** sans-abri *mpl*; **street value** *of drugs* prix m à la revente; **strength** [streŋθ] force f; *(strong point)* point m fort; **strengthen** **1** v/t *body* fortifier; *bridge, currency, bonds etc* consolider **2** v/i se consolider

strenuous ['strenjuəs] fatigant; **strenuously** *deny* vigoureusement

stress [stres] **1** n *(emphasis)* accent m; *(tension)* stress m **2** v/t *syllable* accentuer; *importance etc* souligner; **stressed out** F stressé F; **stressful** stressant

stretch [stretʃ] **1** n *of land, water* étendue f; *of road* partie f **2** *adj fabric* extensible **3** v/t *material* tendre; *small income* tirer le maximum de; F *rules* assouplir **4** v/i *to relax muscles, to reach sth* s'étirer; *(spread)* s'étendre; **stretcher** brancard m

strict [strɪkt] strict; **strictly**

strictement; *it is ~ forbidden*
c'est strictement défendu
stride [straɪd] **1** *n* (grand) pas
m **2** *v/i* marcher à grandes en-
jambées
strident ['straɪdnt] strident;
demands véhément
strike [straɪk] **1** *n of workers*
grève *f*; *in baseball* balle *f*
manquée; *be on ~* être en grève **2**
v/i of workers faire grève; (*attack: of wild animal*) attaquer; *of killer* frapper; *of disaster* arriver; *of clock* sonner
3 *v/t also fig* frapper; *match*
allumer; *oil* découvrir
♦ **strike out** *delete* rayer
strikebreaker ['straɪkbreɪk-
ər] briseur(-euse) *m(f)* de
grève; **striker** (*person on
strike*) gréviste *m/f*; *in soccer*
buteur *m*; **striking** (*marked,
eye-catching*) frappant
string [strɪŋ] ficelle *f*; *of violin, tennis racket* corde *f*;
stringed instrument instrument *m* à cordes
stringent ['strɪndʒnt] rigoureux
strip [strɪp] **1** *n* bande *f*; (*comic ~*) bande *f* dessinée **2** *v/t*
(*remove*) enlever; (*undress*)
déshabiller **3** *v/i* (*undress*)
se déshabiller; *of stripper* faire du strip-tease; **strip club**
boîte *f* de strip-tease
stripe [straɪp] rayure *f*; MIL galon *m*; **striped** rayé
stripper ['strɪpər] strip-tea-

seuse *f*; *male ~* strip-teaseur
m; **striptease** strip-tease *m*
stroke [strouk] **1** *n* MED attaque *f*; *when painting* coup
m de pinceau; *of swim-
ming* nage *f* **2** *v/t* caresser
stroll [stroul] **1** *n* balade *f* **2** *v/i*
flâner; **stroller** *for baby*
poussette *f*
strong [strɒŋ] fort; *structure*
solide; *candidate* sérieux;
support, supporter vigoureux; **strongly** fortement;
strong-minded: *be ~* avoir
de la volonté; **strong point**
point *m* fort; **strongroom**
chambre *f* forte; **strong-
-willed** qui sait ce qu'il/elle
veut
structural ['strʌktʃərəl] *damage* de structure; *fault, problems* de construction; **structure 1** *n* (*something built*)
construction *f*; *of novel, poem etc* structure *f* **2** *v/t* struc-
turer
struggle ['strʌgl] **1** *n* lutte *f* **2**
v/i with a person se battre; *~
to do sth* avoir du mal à faire
qch
strut [strʌt] se pavaner
stub [stʌb] *of cigarette* mégot
m; *of check, ticket* souche
f
stubborn ['stʌbərn] *person,
refusal etc* entêté; *defense* farouche
stubby ['stʌbɪ] boudiné
stuck [stʌk] F: *be ~ on s.o.*
être fou de qn

student ['stu:dnt] *at high school* élève m/f; *at college, university* étudiant(e) m(f)

studio ['stu:dɪəʊ] studio m; *of artist* atelier m

studious ['stu:dɪəs] studieux; **study 1** n *room* bureau m; (*learning*) études fpl; (*investigation*) étude f **2** v/t & v/i étudier

stuff [stʌf] **1** n (*things*) trucs mpl; *substance, powder etc* truc m; (*belongings*) affaires fpl **2** v/t *turkey* farcir; **~ sth into sth** fourrer qch dans qch; **stuffing** *for turkey* farce f; *in chair, toy* rembourrage m; **stuffy** *room* mal aéré; *person* vieux jeu inv

stumble ['stʌmbl] trébucher; **stumbling block** pierre f d'achoppement

stump [stʌmp] **1** n *of tree* souche f **2** v/t: **I'm ~ed** je colle F

stun [stʌn] étourdir; *animal* assommer; *fig* (*shock*) abasourdir; **stunning** (*amazing*) stupéfiant; (*very beautiful*) épatant

stunt [stʌnt] *for publicity* coup m de publicité; *in movie* cascade f; **stuntman** *in movie* cascadeur m

stupefy ['stu:pɪfaɪ] stupéfier

stupendous [stu:'pendəs] prodigieux

stupid ['stu:pɪd] stupide; **stupidity** stupidité f

sturdy ['stɜ:rdɪ] robuste

stutter ['stʌtər] bégayer

style [staɪl] (*method, manner*) style m; (*fashion*) mode f; (*fashionable elegance*) classe f; **stylish** qui a de la classe; **stylist** (*hair ~*) styliste m/f

subcommittee ['sʌbkəmɪtɪ] sous-comité m

subconscious [sʌb'kɑ:nʃəs] subconscient; **subconsciously** subconsciemment

subcontract [sʌbkən'trækt] sous-traiter; **subcontractor** sous-traitant m

subdivide [sʌbdɪ'vaɪd] sous-diviser

subdue [səb'du:] contenir

subheading ['sʌbhedɪŋ] sous-titre m

subhuman [sʌb'hju:mən] sous-humain

subject 1 ['sʌbdʒɪkt] n *of country*, GRAM, (*topic*) sujet m; (*branch of learning*) matière f **2** ['sʌbdʒɪkt] adj: **be ~ to** être sujet à **3** [səb'dʒekt] v/t soumettre (**to** à); **subjective** subjectif

sublet ['sʌblet] sous-louer

submachine gun [sʌbmə-'ʃi:ngʌn] mitraillette f

submarine ['sʌbməri:n] sous-marin m

submission [səb'mɪʃn] (*surrender*), *to committee etc* soumission f; **submissive** soumis; **submit 1** v/t *plan* soumettre **2** v/i se soumettre

subordinate [sə'bɔ:rdɪnət] **1** adj *position* subalterne **2** n subordonné(e) m(f)

subpoena

subpoena [səˈpiːnə] LAW **1** *n* assignation *f* **2** *v/t person* assigner à comparaître

◆ **subscribe to** [səbˈskraɪb] *magazine etc* s'abonner à; *theory* souscrire à

subscriber [səbˈskraɪbər] *to magazine* abonné(e) *m(f)*; **subscription** abonnement *m*

subsequent [ˈsʌbsɪkwənt] ultérieur

subside [səbˈsaɪd] *of waters* baisser; *of winds* se calmer; *of building* s'affaisser; *of fears* s'apaiser

subsidiary [səbˈsɪdɪrɪ] filiale *f*

subsidize [ˈsʌbsɪdaɪz] subventionner; **subsidy** subvention *f*

substance [ˈsʌbstəns] substance *f*

substandard [sʌbˈstændərd] de qualité inférieure

substantial [səbˈstænʃl] considérable; *meal* consistant; **substantially** (*considerably*) considérablement; (*in essence*) de manière générale

substantive [səbˈstæntɪv] réel

substitute [ˈsʌbstɪtuːt] **1** *n* substitut *m* (*for* de); SP remplaçant(e) *m(f)* (*for* de) **2** *v/t* remplacer; ~ *X for Y* remplacer Y par X; **substitution** remplacement *m*

subtitle [ˈsʌbtaɪtl] sous-titre *m*

subtle [ˈsʌtl] subtil

subtract [səbˈtrækt] soustraire

suburb [ˈsʌbɜːrb] banlieue *f*; **the** ~**s** la banlieue; **suburban** typique de la banlieue; *attitudes etc* de banlieusards

subversive [səbˈvɜːrsɪv] **1** *adj* subversif **2** *n* personne *f* subversive

subway [ˈsʌbweɪ] métro *m*

succeed [səkˈsiːd] **1** *v/i* réussir; *to throne* succéder à; ~ **in doing sth** réussir à faire qch **2** *v/t* (*come after*) succéder à; **success** réussite *f*; **be a** ~ avoir du succès; **successful** *person* qui a réussi; *talks, operation* réussi; **be** ~ **in doing sth** réussir à faire qch; **successfully** avec succès; **successive** successif; *on three* ~ **days** trois jours de suite; **successor** successeur *m*

succinct [səkˈsɪŋkt] succinct

succumb [səˈkʌm] (*give in*) succomber

such [sʌtʃ] **1** *adj*: ~ **a** (*so much of a*) un tel, une telle; *it was* ~ **a surprise** c'était une telle surprise; (*of that kind*): ~ **as** tel/telle que; *there is no* ~ *word as...* le mot ... n'existe pas **2** *adv* tellement; ~ **an easy question** une question tellement facile

suck [sʌk] **1** *v/t candy etc* sucer **2** *v/i* P: *it* ~**s** c'est merdique P; **sucker** F *person* niais(e) *m(f)*; F (*lollipop*) sucette *f*; **suction** succion *f*

sudden ['sʌdn] soudain; **suddenly** tout à coup, soudain

sue [su:] poursuivre en justice

suede [sweɪd] daim *m*

suffer ['sʌfər] **1** *v/i* souffrir **2** *v/t experience* subir; **suffering** souffrance *f*

sufficient [sə'fɪʃnt] suffisant; **not ~ funds** pas assez d'argent; **sufficiently** suffisamment

suffocate ['sʌfəkeɪt] **1** *v/i* s'étouffer **2** *v/t* étouffer; **suffocation** étouffement *m*

sugar ['ʃʊgər] **1** *n* sucre *m* **2** *v/t* sucrer

suggest [sə'dʒest] suggérer; **suggestion** suggestion *f*

suicide ['su:ɪsaɪd] suicide *m*

suit [su:t] **1** *n for man* costume *m*; *for woman* tailleur *m*; *in cards* couleur *f* **2** *v/t of clothes, color* aller à; **suitable** approprié, convenable; **suitably** convenablement; **suitcase** valise *f*

suite [swi:t] *of rooms* suite *f*; *furniture* salon *m* trois pièces; MUS suite *m*

sulk [sʌlk] bouder; **sulky** bouder

sullen ['sʌlən] maussade

sultry ['sʌltrɪ] *climate* lourd; *sexually* sulfureux

sum [sʌm] *(total, amount)* somme *f*; *in arithmetic* calcul *m*

◆ **sum up 1** *v/t (summarize)* résumer; *(assess)* se faire

une idée de **2** *v/i* LAW résumer les débats

summarize ['sʌməraɪz] résumer; **summary** résumé *m*

summer ['sʌmər] été *f*

summit ['sʌmɪt] *also* POL sommet *m*

summon ['sʌmən] *staff, meeting* convoquer; **summons** LAW assignation *f* (à comparaître)

sun [sʌn] soleil *m*; **sunbathe** prendre un bain de soleil; **sunbed** lit *m* à ultraviolets; **sunblock** écran *m* solaire; **sunburn** coup *m* de soleil; **sunburnt: be ~** avoir des coups de soleil; **Sunday** dimanche *m*; **sunglasses** lunettes *fpl* de soleil; **sunny** *day* ensoleillé; *disposition* gai; **it's ~** il y a du soleil; **sunrise** lever *m* du soleil; **sunset** coucher *m* du soleil; **sunshade** *handheld* ombrelle *f*; *over table* parasol *m*; **sunshine** soleil *m*; **sunstroke** insolation *f*; **suntan** bronzage *m*; **get a ~** bronzer

super ['su:pər] **1** *adj* F super *inv* F **2** *n (janitor)* concierge *m/f*

superb [sʊ'pɜːrb] excellent

superficial [su:pər'fɪʃl] superficiel

superfluous [sʊ'pɜːrfluəs] superflu

superintendent [su:pərɪn'tendənt] *of apartment block* concierge *m/f*

superior [suː'pɪrɪər] **1** *adj* supérieur **2** *n in organization* supérieur *m*

superlative [suː'pɜːrlətɪv] **1** *adj* (superb) excellent **2** *n* GRAM superlatif *m*

supermarket supermarché *m*

'superpower POL superpuissance *f*

supersonic [suːpər'sɑːnɪk] supersonique

superstition [suːpər'stɪʃn] superstition *f*; **superstitious** superstitieux

supervise [suː'pərvaɪz] *children activities etc* surveiller; *workers* superviser; **supervisor** *at work* superviseur *m*

supper ['sʌpər] dîner *m*

supplement ['sʌplɪmənt] (extra payment) supplément *m*

supplier [sə'plaɪr] COM fournisseur(-euse) *m(f)*; **supply 1** *n of electricity, water etc* alimentation *f* (of en); **~ and demand** l'offre et la demande; **supplies** of food provisions *fpl* **2** *v/t goods* fournir

support [sə'pɔːrt] **1** *n for structure* support *m*; (backing) soutien *m* **2** *v/t structure* supporter; *financially* entretenir; (back) soutenir; **supporter** *of politician, football etc team* supporter(-trice) *m(f)*; *of theory* partisan(e) *m(f)*; **supportive** *attitude* de soutien; **be very ~ of s.o.** beaucoup soutenir qn

suppose [sə'pouz] (imagine)

supposer; **be ~d to do sth** (be meant to, said to) être censé faire qch; **supposing ... (et) si ...;** **supposedly** apparemment

suppress [sə'pres] réprimer; **suppression** répression *f*

supremacy [suː'preməsɪ] suprématie *f*; **supreme** suprême; **Supreme Court** Cour *f* suprême

surcharge ['sɜːrtʃɑːrdʒ] surcharge *f*

sure [ʃʊr] **1** *adj* sûr; **make ~ that ...** s'assurer que ... **2** *adv*: **~ enough** en effet; **it ~ is hot today** F il fait vraiment chaud aujourd'hui; **~!** F mais oui, bien sûr!; **surety** *for loan* garant(e) *m(f)*

surf [sɜːrf] **1** *n on sea* écume *f* **2** *v/t the Net* surfer sur

surface ['sɜːrfɪs] **1** *n* surface *f* **2** *v/i from water* faire surface; (appear) refaire surface; **surface mail** courrier *m* par voie terrestre ou maritime

'surfboard planche *f* de surf; **surfer** surfeur(-euse) *m(f)*; **surfing** surf *m*; **go ~** aller faire du surf

surge [sɜːrdʒ] *in electric current* surtension *f*; *in demand etc* poussée *f*

surgeon ['sɜːrdʒən] chirurgien *m(f)*; **surgery** chirurgie *f*; **surgical** chirurgical; **surgically** *remove* par opération chirurgicale

surly ['sɜːrlɪ] revêche

surmount [sər'maʊnt] *difficulties* surmonter

surname ['sɜːrneɪm] nom *m* de famille

surpass [sər'pæs] dépasser

surplus ['sɜːrpləs] **1** *n* surplus *m* **2** *adj* en surplus

surprise [sər'praɪz] **1** *n* surprise *f* **2** *v/t* étonner; **be/look ~d** être/avoir l'air surpris; **surprising** étonnant; **surprisingly** étonnamment

surrender [sə'rendər] **1** *v/i of army* se rendre **2** *v/t weapons etc* rendre **3** *n* capitulation *f*; *(handing in)* reddition *f*

surrogate mother ['sʌrəgət] mère *f* porteuse

surround [sə'raʊnd] **1** *v/t* entourer **2** *n of picture etc* bordure *f*; **surrounding** environnant; **surroundings** environs *mpl*; *setting* cadre *m*

survey 1 ['sɜːrveɪ] *n of modern literature etc* étude *f*; *Br of building* inspection *f*; *(poll)* sondage *m* **2** [sər'veɪ] *v/t (look at)* contempler; *Br building* inspecter; **surveyor** *Br* expert *m*

survival [sər'vaɪvl] survie *f*; **survive 1** *v/i* survivre **2** *v/t accident, (outlive)* survivre à; **survivor** survivant(e) *m(f)*

suspect 1 ['sʌspekt] *n* suspect(e) *m(f)* **2** [sə'spekt] *v/t person* soupçonner; *(suppose)* croire; **suspected** *murderer* soupçonné; *cause, heart attack etc* présumé

suspend [sə'spend] *(hang)*, *from office* suspendre; **suspenders** *for pants* bretelles *fpl*; *Br* porte-jarretelles *m*

suspense [sə'spens] suspense *m*; **suspension** *in vehicle, from duty* suspension *f*

suspicion [sə'spɪʃn] soupçon *m*; **suspicious** *(causing suspicion)* suspect; *(feeling suspicion)* méfiant; **be ~ of s.o.** se méfier de qn; **suspiciously** *behave* de manière suspecte; *ask* avec méfiance

sustain [sə'steɪn] soutenir; **sustainable** durable

SUV [esjuː'viː] (= *sports utility vehicle*) véhicule *m* utilitaire

swab [swɑːb] tampon *m*

swallow¹ ['swɑːloʊ] *v/t & v/i* avaler

swallow² ['swɑːloʊ] *n bird* hirondelle *f*

swamp [swɑːmp] **1** *n* marécage *m* **2** *v/t*: **be ~ed with** être submergé de; **swampy** marécageux

swap [swɑːp] échanger (**for** contre)

swarm [swɔːrm] **1** *n of bees* essaim *m* **2** *v/i*: **the town was ~ing with ...** la ville grouillait de ...

swarthy ['swɔːrðɪ] basané

swat [swɑːt] *insect* écraser

sway [sweɪ] **1** *n (influence, power)* emprise *f* **2** *v/i in wind* se balancer; *because drunk, ill* tituber

swear [swer] **1** v/i (use swear-word) jurer; **~ at s.o.** injurier qn **2** v/t LAW, (promise) jurer
◆ **swear in** witnesses etc faire prêter serment à
'swearword juron m

sweat [swet] **1** n sueur f **2** v/i transpirer, suer; **sweat band** bandeau m en éponge; **sweater** pull m; **sweatshirt** sweat(-shirt) m; **sweaty** plein de sueur

sweep [swi:p] **1** v/t floor, leaves balayer **2** n (long curve) courbe f; **sweeping** statement hâtif; changes radical

sweet [swi:t] taste, tea sucré; F (kind) gentil; F (cute) mignon; **sweetcorn** maïs m; **sweeten** sucrer; **sweetheart** amoureux(-euse) m(f)

swell [swel] **1** v/i of wound, limb enfler **2** adj F (good) super F inv **3** n of the sea houle f; **swelling** MED enflure f

swerve [swɜːrv] of driver, car s'écarter brusquement

swift [swift] rapide

swim [swim] **1** v/i nager **2** n baignade f; **go for a ~** aller se baigner; **swimmer** nageur(-euse) m(f); **swimming** natation f; **swimming pool** piscine f; **swimsuit** maillot m de bain

swindle [swindl] **1** n escroquerie f **2** v/t escroquer; **~ s.o. out of sth** escroquer qch à qn

swing [swiŋ] **1** n oscillation f; for child balançoire f; **~ to the Democrats** revirement m d'opinion en faveur des démocrates **2** v/t object in hand, hips balancer **3** v/i se balancer; (turn) tourner; of public opinion etc virer

Swiss [swis] **1** adj suisse **2** n person Suisse m/f; **the ~** les Suisses mpl

switch [switʃ] **1** n for light bouton m; (change) changement m **2** v/t (change) changer de **3** v/i (change) passer
◆ **switch off** lights, engine, PC éteindre; engine arrêter
◆ **switch on** lights, engine, PC allumer; engine démarrer

Switzerland ['switsərlənd] Suisse f

swivel ['swivl] pivoter

swollen ['swoulən] stomach ballonné; ankles, face enflé

syllabus ['siləbəs] programme m

symbol ['simbəl] symbole m; **symbolic** symbolique; **symbolism** symbolisme m; **symbolist** symboliste m/f; **symbolize** symboliser

symmetrical [si'metrikl] symétrique; **symmetry** symétrie

sympathetic [simpə'θetik] (showing pity) compatissant; (understanding) compréhensif
◆ **sympathize with** ['simpə-

θaɪz] *person* compatir avec; *views* avoir des sympathies pour

sympathizer ['sɪmpəθaɪzər] POL sympathisant(e) *m(f)*;

sympathy *(pity)* compassion *f*; *(understanding)* compréhension *f* (**for** de)

symphony ['sɪmfənɪ] symphonie *f*

symptom ['sɪmptəm] MED, *fig* symptôme *m*

synchronize ['sɪŋkrənaɪz] synchroniser

synonym ['sɪnənɪm] synonyme *m*; **synonymous** synonyme

synthesizer ['sɪnθəsaɪzər]

MUS synthétiseur *m*; **synthetic** synthétique

syphilis ['sɪfɪlɪs] syphilis *f*

Syria ['sɪrɪə] Syrie *f*; **Syrian 1** *adj* syrien **2** *n* Syrien(ne) *m(f)*

syringe [sɪ'rɪndʒ] seringue *f*

syrup ['sɪrəp] sirop *m*

system ['sɪstəm] système *m*; *(orderliness)* ordre *m*; *(computer)* ordinateur *m*; **systematic** systématique; **systematically** systématiquement

systems analyst COMPUT analyste-programmeur(-euse) *m(f)*

T

table ['teɪbl] table *f*; *of figures* tableau *m*; **tablecloth** nappe *f*; **table lamp** petite lampe *f*; **table of contents** table *f* des matières; **tablespoon** cuillère *f* à soupe

tablet ['tæblɪt] MED comprimé *m*

tabloid ['tæblɔɪd] *newspaper* journal *m* à sensation

taboo [tə'buː] tabou *inv m* à feminine

tacit ['tæsɪt] tacite

tack [tæk] **1** *n* nail clou *m* **2** *v/t in sewing* bâtir **3** *v/i of yacht* louvoyer

tackle ['tækl] **1** *n (equipment)* attirail *m*; SP tacle *m*; *in rug-*

by plaquage *m* **2** *v/t* SP tacler; *in rugby* plaquer; *problem* s'attaquer à; *(confront)* confronter; *physically* s'opposer à

tacky ['tækɪ] *paint, glue* collant; F *(cheap, poor quality)* minable F

tact [tækt] tact *m*; **tactful** diplomate; **tactfully** avec tact

tactical ['tæktɪkl] tactique; **tactics** tactique *f*

tactless ['tæktlɪs] qui manque de tact, peu délicat

tag [tæg] *(label)* étiquette *f*

tail [teɪl] queue *f*; **tail light** feu *m* arrière

tailor ['teɪlər] tailleur *m*; **tai-**

lor-made *also fig* fait sur mesure

'tail pipe *of car* tuyau *m* d'échappement

take [teɪk] prendre; (*transport, accompany*) amener; *subject at school, photograph, photocopy, stroll* faire; (*exam*) passer; (*endure*) supporter; (*require; courage etc*) demander; **how long will it ~ you to ...?** combien de temps est-ce que tu vas mettre pour ...?

◆ **take after** ressembler à

◆ **take away** *object* enlever; *pain* faire disparaître; MATH soustraire (**from** de)

◆ **take back** *object* rapporter; *person to a place* ramener; **she wouldn't take him back** *husband* elle ne voulait pas qu'il revienne

◆ **take down** *from shelf* enlever; *scaffolding* démonter; *pants* baisser; (*write down*) noter

◆ **take in** (*take indoors*) rentrer; (*give accommodation to*) héberger; (*make narrower*) reprendre; (*deceive*) duper; (*include*) inclure

◆ **take off** *v/t clothes, hat* enlever; *10% etc* faire une réduction de; (*mimic*) imiter **2** *v/i of airplane* décoller; (*become popular*) réussir

◆ **take on** *job* accepter; *staff* embaucher

◆ **take out** *from bag, pocket* sortir (**from** de); *tooth, word from text* enlever; *money from bank* retirer; *to dinner, theater etc* emmener; *insurance policy* souscrire à

◆ **take over 1** *v/t company etc* reprendre **2** *v/i* POL arriver au pouvoir; *of new director* prendre ses fonctions; (*do sth in s.o.'s place*) prendre la relève

◆ **take up** *carpet etc* enlever; (*carry up*) monter; *dress etc* raccourcir; *judo, Spanish etc* se mettre à; *new job* commencer; *space, time* prendre; *offer* accepter

'takeoff *of airplane* décollage *m*; (*impersonation*) imitation *f*; **takeover** *com* rachat *m*; **takeover bid** offre *f* publique d'achat, OPA *f*; **takings** recette *f*

tale [teɪl] histoire *f*

talent ['tælənt] talent *m*; **talented** doué; **talent scout** dénicheur(-euse) *m(f)* de talents

talk [tɔːk] **1** *v/t & v/i* parler; **~ business** parler affaires **2** *n* (*conversation*) conversation *f*; (*lecture*) exposé *m*; **~s** pourparlers *mpl*

◆ **talk back** répondre

talkative ['tɔːkətɪv] bavard; **talk show** talk-show *m*

tall [tɔːl] grand

tally ['tælɪ] **1** *n* compte *m* **2** *v/i* correspondre; *of stories* concorder

tame [teɪm] apprivoisé; *not wild* pas sauvage; *joke etc* fade

◆ **tamper with** ['tæmpər] toucher à

tampon ['tæmpɑːn] tampon *m*

tan [tæn] **1** *n from sun* bronzage; *color* marron *m* clair **2** *v/i in sun* bronzer **3** *v/t leather* tanner

tangent ['tændʒənt] MATH tangente *f*

tangible ['tændʒɪbl] tangible

tangle ['tæŋgl] enchevêtrement *m*

tango ['tæŋgou] tango *m*

tank [tæŋk] MOT, *for water* réservoir *m*; *for fish* aquarium *m*; MIL char *m*; *for skin diver* bonbonne *f* d'oxygène; **tanker** (*oil ~*) pétrolier *m*; *truck* camion-citerne *m*

tanned [tænd] bronzé

tantalizing ['tæntəlaɪzɪŋ] alléchant

tantrum ['tæntrəm] caprice *m*

tap [tæp] **1** *n Br* (*faucet*) robinet *m* **2** *v/t* (*knock*) taper; *phone* mettre sur écoute

tape [teɪp] **1** *n for recording* bande *f*; *recording* cassette *f*; *sticky* ruban *m* adhésif **2** *v/t conversation etc* enregistrer; *with sticky tape* scotcher; **tape deck** platine *f* cassettes; **tape drive** COMPUT lecteur *m* de bandes; **tape measure** mètre *m* ruban

taper ['teɪpər] *of stick* s'effi-

ler; *of column, pant legs* se rétrécir

'**tape recorder** magnétophone *m*; **tape recording** enregistrement *m*

tar [tɑːr] goudron *m*

tardy ['tɑːrdɪ] tardif

target ['tɑːrgɪt] **1** *n in shooting* cible *f*; *fig* objectif *m* **2** *v/t market* cibler

'**target audience** public *m* cible; **target date** date *f* visée; **target market** marché *m* cible

tariff ['tærɪf] (*customs ~*) taxe *f*; (*prices*) tarif *m*

tarmac ['tɑːrmæk] *at airport* tarmac *m*

tarnish ['tɑːrnɪʃ] ternir

tarpaulin [tɑːr'pɔːlɪn] bâche *f*

tart [tɑːrt] tarte *f*

task [tæsk] tâche *f*; **task force** commission *f*; MIL corps *m* expéditionnaire

taste [teɪst] **1** *n* goût *m* **2** *v/t* goûter; (*perceive taste of*) sentir; *try, fig* goûter à **3** *v/i: it~s like ...* ça a (un) goût de ...; **tasteful** de bon goût; **tastefully** avec goût; **tasteless** *food* fade; *remark, décor* de mauvais goût; **tasting** *of wine* dégustation *f*; **tasty** délicieux

tattered ['tætərd] en lambeaux

tattoo [tə'tuː] tatouage *m*

taunt [tɔːnt] **1** *n* raillerie *f* **2** *v/t* se moquer de

taut [tɔːt] tendu

tax [tæks] **1** *n* on income impôt *m*; on goods, services taxe *f* **2** *v/t* income imposer; goods, services taxer; **taxable income** revenu *m* imposable; **taxation** act imposition *f*; *(taxes)* charges *fpl* fiscales; **tax bracket** fourchette *f* d'impôts; **tax-deductible** déductible des impôts; **tax evasion** fraude *f* fiscale; **tax-free** hors taxe; **tax haven** paradis *m* fiscal

taxi ['tæksɪ] taxi *m*; **taxi driver** chauffeur *m* de taxi

taxing ['tæksɪŋ] exténuant

'**taxi stand**, *Br* '**taxi rank** station *f* de taxis

'**taxpayer** contribuable *m/f*; **tax return** déclaration *f* d'impôts; **tax year** année *f* fiscale

TB [tiː'biː] (= *tuberculosis*) tuberculose *f*

tea [tiː] *drink* thé *m*; **teabag** sachet *m* de thé

teach [tiːtʃ] enseigner; *person* enseigner à; **teacher** professeur *m/f*; *in elementary school* instituteur(-trice) *m(f)*; **teaching** *profession* enseignement *m*

'**teacup** tasse *f* à thé

teak [tiːk] tek *m*

team [tiːm] équipe *f*; **team spirit** esprit *m* d'équipe; **teamster** camionneur(-euse) *m(f)*; **teamwork** travail *m* d'équipe

'**teapot** ['tiːpɒt] théière *f*

tear¹ [ter] **1** *n* in cloth etc déchirure *f* **2** *v/t* paper, cloth déchirer **3** *v/i* (run fast, drive fast): **she tore down the street** elle a descendu la rue en trombe

◆ **tear down** poster arracher; building démolir

◆ **tear out** page arracher

◆ **tear up** déchirer; contract etc annuler

tear² [tɪr] *n* in eye larme *f*; **be in ~s** être en larmes; **tearful** look plein de larmes; **tear gas** gaz *m* lacrymogène

tease [tiːz] taquiner

'**teaspoon** cuillère *f* à café

technical ['teknɪkl] technique; **technically** *(strictly speaking)* en théorie; **technician** technicien(ne) *m(f)*; **technique** technique *f*

technological [teknə'lɒdʒɪkl] technologique; **technology** technologie *f*; **technophobia** technophobie *f*

teddy bear ['tedɪber] ours *m* en peluche

tedious ['tiːdɪəs] ennuyeux

tee [tiː] *in golf* tee *m*

teenage ['tiːneɪdʒ] fashion pour adolescents; **teenager** adolescent(e) *m(f)*

teens [tiːnz] adolescence *f*

teeny ['tiːnɪ] F *tout petit*

teeth [tiːθ] *pl* → **tooth**

teethe [tiːð] faire ses dents

telecommunications [telɪkəmjuːnɪ'keɪʃnz] télécommunications *fpl*

telegraph pole ['telɪgræfpool] *Br* poteau *m* télégraphique

telepathic [telɪ'pæθɪk] télépathique; **telepathy** télépathie *f*

telephone ['telɪfoun] **1** *n* téléphone *m*; *on the ~ (speak) on the* ~ *person* être au téléphone à 3 *v/i* téléphoner; **telephone book** annuaire *m*; **telephone booth** cabine *f* téléphonique; **telephone call** appel *m* téléphonique; **telephone conversation** conversation *f* téléphonique; **telephone directory** annuaire *m*; **telephone number** numéro *m* de téléphone

telephoto lens [telɪ'foutoulenz] téléobjectif *m*

telesales ['telɪseɪlz] télévente *f*

telescope ['telɪskoup] télescope *m*

televise ['telɪvaɪz] téléviser

television ['telɪvɪʒn] *also set* télévision *f*; *on* ~ à la télévision; **television program**, *Br* **television programme** émission *f* télévisée; **television studio** studio *m* de télévision

tell [tel] **1** *v/t story* raconter; *lie* dire; *I can't* ~ *the difference* je n'arrive pas à faire la différence; ~ *s.o. sth* dire qch à qn; ~ *s.o. to do sth* dire à qn de faire qch **2** *v/i* (*have effect*) se faire sentir; *teller in bank* guichetier(-ière) *m(f)*; **telling off**: *get a* ~ se faire re-

monter les bretelles F; **telltale 1** *adj signs* révélateur *f* **2** *n* rapporteur(-euse) *m(f)*

temp [temp] **1** *n* employee intérimaire *m/f* **2** *v/i* faire de l'intérim

temper ['tempər] (*bad* ~) mauvaise humeur *f*; *lose one's* ~ se mettre en colère

temperament ['tempramənt] tempérament *m*; **temperamental** (*moody*) capricieux

temperate ['tempərət] tempéré

temperature ['temprətʃər] température *f*

temple¹ ['templ] REL temple *m*

temple² ['templ] ANAT tempe *f*

tempo ['tempou] MUS tempo *m*

temporarily [tempə'rerɪlɪ] temporairement; **temporary** ['tempərerɪ] temporaire

tempt [tempt] tenter; **temptation** tentation *f*; **tempting** tentant

ten [ten] dix

tenacious [tɪ'neɪʃəs] tenace; **tenacity** ténacité *f*

tenant ['tenənt] locataire *m/f*

tend¹ [tend] *v/t lawn* entretenir; *sheep* garder; *the sick* soigner

tend² [tend] *v/i*: ~ *to do sth* avoir tendance à faire qch

tendency ['tendənsɪ] tendance *f*

tender¹ ['tendər] *adj* (*sore*) sensible; (*affectionate*), *steak* tendre

tender[2] ['tendər] n COM offre f

tenderness ['tendənɪs] of kiss etc tendresse f; of steak tendreté f

tendon ['tendən] tendon m

tennic ['tenɪs] tennis m; **tennis ball** balle f de tennis; **tennis court** court m de tennis; **tennis player** joueur(-euse) m(f) de tennis

tenor ['tenər] MUS ténor m

tense[1] [tens] n GRAM temps m

tense[2] [tens] adj tendu

tension ['tenʃn] tension f

tent [tent] tente f

tentative ['tentətɪv] smile, steps hésitant; conclusion, offer provisoire

tenth [tenθ] dixième

tepid ['tepɪd] also fig tiède

term [tɜːrm] (period, word) terme m; Br EDU trimestre m; (condition) condition f; **be on good/bad ~s with s.o.** être en bons/mauvais termes avec qn; **in the long/short ~** à long/court terme

terminal ['tɜːrmɪnl] n 1 at airport aérogare m; for buses terminus m; for containers, COMPUT terminal m; ELEC borne f **2** adj illness incurable; **terminally: ~ ill** en phase terminale; **terminate 1** v/t mettre fin à; pregnancy interrompre **2** v/i se terminer; **termination** of contract résiliation f; in pregnancy interrup-

tion f volontaire de grossesse

terminus ['tɜːrmɪnəs] terminus m

terrace ['terəs] terrasse f

terrain [te'reɪn] terrain m

terrible ['terəbl] horrible, affreux; **terribly** (very) très

terrific [tə'rɪfɪk] génial; **terrifically** (very) extrêmement, vachement F

terrify ['terɪfaɪ] terrifier; **terrifying** terrifiant

territorial [terə'tɔːrɪəl] territorial; **territory** territoire m; fig domaine m

terror ['terər] terreur f; **terrorism** terrorisme m; **terrorist** terroriste m/f; **terrorist attack** attentat m terroriste; **terrorize** terroriser

terse [tɜːrs] laconique

test [test] n 1 in scientific, technical test m; academic, for driving examen m **2** v/t tester, mettre à l'épreuve; **test-drive** car essayer

testicle ['testɪkl] testicule m

testify ['testɪfaɪ] LAW témoigner

testimony ['testɪmənɪ] LAW témoignage m

testy ['testɪ] irritable

tetanus ['tetənəs] tétanos m

text [tekst] n 1 texte m; message texto m **2** v/t envoyer un texto à; **textbook** manuel m; **text-message** texto m, SMS m

textile ['tekstaɪl] textile m

texture ['tekstʃər] texture f

than [ðæn] que; *with numbers* de; *faster ~ me* plus rapide que moi

thank [θæŋk] remercier; *~ you* merci; *no ~ you* (non) merci; **thankful** reconnaissant; **thankfully** (*luckily*) heureusement; **thankless** *task* ingrat; **thanks** remerciements *mpl*; *~!* merci!; *~ to* grâce à; **Thanksgiving (Day)** jour *m* de l'action de grâces, Thanksgiving *m*

that [ðæt] **1** *adj* ce, cette; *masculine before vowel* cet; *~ one* celui-là, celle-là **2** *pron* cela, ça; *give me ~* donne-moi ça; *~'s tea* c'est du thé; *what is ~?* qu'est-ce que c'est que ça?; *who is ~?* qui est-ce? **3** *rel pron* que; *the car ~ you see* la voiture que vous voyez **4** *adv* (*so*) aussi; *~ expensive* aussi cher **5** *conj* que; *I think ~ ...* je pense que ...

thaw [θɔː] *of snow* fondre; *of frozen food* se décongeler

the [ðə] le, la; *pl* les; *to the station/theater* à la gare/au théâtre; *~ more I try* plus j'essaie

theater, *Br* **theatre** ['θɪətər] théâtre *m*; **theatrical** *also fig* théâtral

theft [θeft] vol *m*

their [ðer] leur; *pl* leurs; (*his or her*) son, sa; *pl* ses; *it's ~* c'est à eux/elles

them [ðem] *object* les; *indirect object* leur; *with prep* eux, elles; *I know ~* je les connais; *I gave ~ a dollar* je leur ai donné un dollar; *this is for ~* c'est pour eux/elles; *who? ~ ~* qui? - eux/elles

theme [θiːm] thème *m*; **theme park** parc *m* à thème

themselves [ðem'selvz] eux-mêmes, elles-mêmes; *reflexive* se; *after prep* eux, elles; *they gave ~ a holiday* ils se sont offerts des vacances

then [ðen] (*at that time*) à l'époque; (*after that*) ensuite; *deducing* alors; *by ~* alors

theoretical [θɪə'retɪkl] théorique; **theoretically** en théorie; **theory** théorie *f*

therapeutic [θerə'pjuːtɪk] thérapeutique; **therapist** thérapeute *m/f*; **therapy** thérapie *f*

there [ðer] là; *over ~/down ~* là-bas; *~ is/are ...* il y a ...; *~ is/are ...?* est-ce qu'il y a ...?, y a-t-il ...?; *~ is/are not ...* il n'y a pas ...; *~ you are* voilà; *~ and back* aller et retour; *~ he is!* le voilà!; *~, ~!* allons, allons; *we went ~ yesterday* nous y sommes allés hier; *thereabouts*: *$500 or ~* environ 500 $; *therefore* donc

thermometer [θər'mɑːmɪtər] thermomètre *m*

thermos flask ['θɜːrməsflæsk] thermos *m*

these [ðiːz] **1** adj ces **2** pron ceux-ci, celles-ci

thesis ['θiːsɪs] thèse f

they [ðeɪ] ils, elles; (he or she) il; **there ~ are** les voilà; **~ say that ...** on dit que ...

thick [θɪk] épais; F (stupid) lourd; **it's 3 cm ~** ça fait 3 cm d'épaisseur; **thicken** sauce épaissir; **thick-skinned** fig qui a la peau dure

thief [θiːf] voleur(-euse) m(f)

thigh [θaɪ] cuisse f

thin [θɪn] material léger, fin; layer mince; person maigre; line fin; soup liquide

thing [θɪŋ] chose f; **~s** (belongings) affaires fpl

think [θɪŋk] penser; **I ~ so** je pense que oui; **I don't ~ so** je ne pense pas; **I'll ~ about it** offer je vais y réfléchir

♦ **think over** réfléchir à

♦ **think through** bien examiner

♦ **think up** plan concevoir

'think tank comité m d'experts

thin-skinned ['θɪnskɪnd] fig susceptible

third [θɜːrd] **1** adj troisième **2** n troisième m/f; **thirdly** troisièmement; **third-party** tiers m; **third-party insurance** Br assurance f au tiers; **Third World** Tiers-Monde m

thirst [θɜːrst] soif f; **thirsty** assoiffé; **be ~** avoir soif

thirteen [θɜːrˈtiːn] treize; thir-

teenth treizième; **thirtieth** trentième; **thirty** trente

this [ðɪs] **1** adj ce, cette; masculine before vowel cet; **~ one** celui-ci, celle-ci **2** pron cela, ça; **~ is good** c'est bien; **~ is ...** c'est ...; introducing s.o. je vous présente ... **3** adv: **~ high** haut comme ça

thorn [θɔːrn] épine f; **thorny** also fig épineux

thorough ['θɜːroʊ] search, knowledge approfondi; person méticuleux; **thoroughbred** horse pur-sang m; **thoroughly** complètement; clean, search for, know à fond

those [ðoʊz] **1** adj ces **2** pron ceux-là, celles-là

though [ðoʊ] **1** conj (although) bien que (+subj), quoique (+subj); **as ~** comme si **2** adv pourtant

thought [θɔːt] pensée f; thoughtful pensif; book profond; (considerate) attentionné; **thoughtless** inconsidéré

thousand ['θaʊznd] mille m; **~s of** des milliers mpl de; **thousandth 1** adj millième **2** n millième m/f

thrash [θræʃ] rouer de coups; sp battre à plates coutures

♦ **thrash out** solution parvenir à

thrashing volée f de coups; **get a ~** sp se faire battre à plates coutures

thread [θred] **1** *n* fil *m*; *of screw* filetage *m* **2** *v/t needle, beads* enfiler; **threadbare** usé jusqu'à la corde

threat [θret] menace *f*; **threaten** menacer; **threatening** menaçant

three [θri:] trois; **three-quarters** les trois-quarts *mpl*

threshold ['θreʃhəʊld] *of house, new era* seuil *m*

thrifty ['θrɪftɪ] économe

thrill [θrɪl] **1** *n* frisson *m* **2** *v/t*: **be ~ed** être ravi; **thriller** thriller *m*; **thrilling** palpitant

thrive [θraɪv] *of plants* bien pousser; *of business* prospérer

throat [θrəʊt] gorge *f*; **throat lozenge** pastille *f* pour la gorge

throb [θrɒb] **1** *n of heart* pulsation *f*; *of music* vibration *f* **2** *v/i of heart* battre fort; *of music* vibrer

throne [θrəʊn] trône *m*

throttle ['θrɒtl] **1** *n on motorbike, boat* papillon *m* des gaz **2** *v/t (strangle)* étrangler

through [θru:] **1** *prep* ◇ *(across)* à travers; **go ~ the city** traverser la ville ◇ *(during)* pendant; **all ~ the night** toute la nuit; **Monday ~ Friday** du lundi au vendredi (inclus) ◇ *(by means of)* par **2** *adv*: **wet ~** mouillé jusqu'aux os **3** *adj*: **be ~** *(have arrived, of news etc)* être parvenu; **we're**

~ of couple c'est fini entre nous; **be ~ with s.o./sth** en avoir fini avec qn/qch; **throughout 1** *prep* tout au long de, pendant tout(e) **2** *adv (in all parts)* partout

throw [θrəʊ] **1** *v/t* jeter, lancer; *of horse* désarçonner; *(disconcert)* déconcerter; *party* organiser **2** *n* jet *m*; **it's your ~** c'est à toi de lancer
- **throw away** jeter
- **throw out** *old things* jeter; *from bar, home* jeter dehors, mettre à la porte; *from country* expulser; *plan* rejeter
- **throw up 1** *v/t ball* jeter en l'air **2** *v/i (vomit)* vomir

throw-away ['θrəʊəweɪ] *(disposable)* jetable; *remark* en l'air; **throw-in** SP remise *f* en jeu

thru [θru:] → **through**

thrust [θrʌst] *(push hard)* enfoncer

thud [θʌd] bruit *m* sourd

thug [θʌg] brute *f*

thumb [θʌm] **1** *n* pouce *m* **2** *v/t*: **~ a ride** faire de l'auto-stop; **thumbtack** punaise *f*

thunder ['θʌndər] tonnerre *m*; **thunderous** *applause* tonitruant; **thunderstorm** orage *m*; **thunderstruck** abasourdi; **thundery** *weather* orageux

Thursday ['θɜ:rzdeɪ] jeudi *m*

thus [ðʌs] ainsi

thwart [θwɔ:rt] contrarier

tick [tɪk] **1** *n of clock* tic-tac *m*

Br (*checkmark*) coche *f* **2** *v/i* faire tic-tac

ticket ['tɪkɪt] *for bus, museum* ticket *m*; *for train, airplane, theater, concert, lottery* billet *m*; *for speeding, illegal parking* P.V. *m*; **ticket machine** distributeur *m* de billets; **ticket office** billetterie *f*

ticking ['tɪkɪŋ] *noise* tic-tac *m*

tickle ['tɪkl] chatouiller

tidal wave ['taɪdlweɪv] raz-de-marée *m*

tide [taɪd] marée *f*

tidiness ['taɪdɪnɪs] ordre *m*; **tidy** *person, habits* ordonné; *room, house, desk* en ordre

◆ **tidy up** *v/t room, shelves* ranger; **tidy o.s. up** remettre de l'ordre dans sa tenue **2** *v/i* ranger

tie [taɪ] **1** *n* (*necktie*) cravate *f*; *SP* (*even result*) match *m* à égalité; **he doesn't have any ~s** il n'a aucune attache **2** *v/t laces* nouer; *knot* faire; *hands* lier **3** *v/i of teams* faire match nul; *of runner* finir ex æquo

◆ **tie down** attacher; *fig* (*restrict*) restreindre

◆ **tie up** *hair* attacher; *person* ligoter; *boat* amarrer

tier [tɪr] *of hierarchy* niveau *m*; *of seats* gradin *m*

tight [taɪt] **1** *adj clothes, knot, screw* serré; *shoes* trop petit; (*properly shut*) bien fermé; *not leaving much time* juste; *security* strict; F (*drunk*)

bourré F **2** *adv hold* fort; *shut* bien; **tighten** *control, security* renforcer; *screw* serrer; (*make tighter*) resserrer; **tight-fisted** radin; **tightly** *adv* → **tight** *adv*; **tightrope** corde *f* raide; **tights** *Br* collant *m*

tile [taɪl] *on floor, wall* carreau *m*; *on roof* tuile *f*

till¹ [tɪl] → **until**

till² [tɪl] (*cash register*) caisse *f*

tilt [tɪlt] pencher

timber ['tɪmbər] bois *m*

time [taɪm] *n* temps *m*; (*occasion*) fois *f*; **have a good ~** bien s'amuser; **what's the ~?** quelle heure est-il?; **the first ~** la première fois; **all the ~** pendant tout ce temps; **at the same ~** *speak, reply etc*, (*however*) en même temps; **in ~** à temps; **on ~** à l'heure **2** *v/t* chronométrer; **time bomb** bombe *f* à retardement; **time difference** décalage *m* horaire; **time-lag** laps *m* de temps; **time limit** limite *f* dans le temps; **timely** opportun; **time out** *SP* temps *m* mort; **timer** *device* minuteur *m*; **timesaving** économie *f* de temps; **timescale** *of project* durée *f*; **time switch** minuterie *f*; **time zone** fuseau *m* horaire

timid ['tɪmɪd] timide

tin [tɪn] *metal* étain *m*; **tinfoil** papier *m* aluminium

tinge [tɪndʒ] soupçon *m*

tingle ['tɪŋgl] picoter

tinkle ['tɪŋkl] *of bell* tintement *m*

tinsel ['tɪnsl] guirlandes *fpl* de Noël

tint [tɪnt] **1** *n of color* teinte *f; for hair* couleur *f* **2** *v/t:* ~ **one's hair** se faire une coloration; **tinted** *glasses* teinté; *paper* de couleur pastel

tiny ['taɪnɪ] minuscule

tip¹ [tɪp] *n (end)* bout *m*

tip² [tɪp] *n* **1** *advice* conseil *m; money* pourboire *m* **2** *v/t waiter etc* donner un pourboire à

◆ **tip off** informer

'tip-off renseignement *m*, tuyau *m* F

tipped [tɪpt] *cigarettes* à bout filtre

tippy-toe ['tɪpɪtoʊ]: *on* ~ sur la pointe des pieds

tipsy ['tɪpsɪ] éméché

tire¹ ['taɪr] *n* pneu *m*

tire² ['taɪr] **1** *v/t* fatiguer **2** *v/i* se fatiguer

tired ['taɪrd] fatigué; **tiredness** fatigue *f;* **tireless** *efforts* infatigable; **tiresome** *(annoying)* fatigant; **tiring** fatigant

tissue ['tɪʃuː] ANAT tissu *m; handkerchief* mouchoir *m* en papier; **tissue paper** papier *m* de soie

title ['taɪtl] *of novel, person etc* titre *m;* LAW titre *m* de propriété *f* (*to* de); **titleholder** SP tenant(e) *m(f)* du titre

to [tuː] **1** *prep* à; ~ *Japan* au Japon; ~ *Chicago* à Chicago; ~ *my place* chez moi; ~ *the north of* au nord de; *give sth* ~ *s.o.* donner qch à qn **2** *with verbs:* ~ *speak,* ~ *shout* parler, crier; *learn* ~ *drive* apprendre à conduire; *too heavy* ~ *carry* trop lourd à porter **3** *adv:* ~ *and fro* walk, pace de long en large

toast [toʊst] **1** *n for eating* pain *m* grillé; *when drinking* toast *m;* **propose a** ~ *to s.o.* porter un toast à qn **2** *v/t when drinking* porter un toast à

toaster grille-pain *m inv*

tobacco [tə'bækoʊ] tabac *m*

today [tə'deɪ] aujourd'hui

toddler ['tɒdlər] jeune enfant *m*

to-do [tə'duː] F remue-ménage *m*

toe [toʊ] orteil *m; of sock, shoe* bout *m;* **toenail** ongle *m* de pied

together [tə'geðər] ensemble; *(at the same time)* en même temps

toilet ['tɔɪlɪt] toilettes *fpl;* **toilet paper** papier *m* hygiénique; **toiletries** articles *mpl* de toilette

token ['toʊkən] *sign* témoignage *m;* Br *(gift* ~) bon *m* d'achat; *instead of coin* jeton *m*

tolerable ['tɒlərəbl] *pain etc* tolérable; *(quite good)* acceptable; **tolerance** tolérance *f;* **tolerant** tolérant; **tolerate** tolérer

toll¹ [toul] *v/i* of bell sonner

toll² [toul] *n* (deaths) bilan *m*

toll³ [toul] *n* for bridge, road péage *m*

'**toll booth** poste *m* de péage; **~-free** TELEC gratuit; **~ number** numéro *m* gratuit

tomato [təˈmeɪtou] tomate *f;* **tomato ketchup** ketchup *m*

tomb [tuːm] tombe *f;* **tombstone** pierre *f* tombale

tomcat [ˈtɑːmkæt] matou *m*

tomorrow [təˈmɔːrou] demain; **the day after ~** après-demain; **~ morning** demain matin

ton [tʌn] tonne *f* courte (=907 kg)

tone [toun] of color, conversation ton *m;* of musical instrument timbre *m;* of neighborhood classe *f;* **~ of voice** ton *m;* **toner** toner *m*

tongue [tʌŋ] langue *f*

tonic [ˈtɑːnɪk] MED fortifiant *m;* **tonic (water)** Schweppes® *m,* tonic *m*

tonight [təˈnaɪt] ce soir; *sleep* cette nuit

too [tuː] (also) aussi, (excessively) trop; **me ~** moi aussi; **~ much rice** trop de riz

tool [tuːl] outil *m*

tooth [tuːθ] dent *f;* **toothache** mal *m* de dents; **toothbrush** brosse *f* à dents; **toothpaste** dentifrice *m;* **toothpick** cure-

dents *m*

top [tɑːp] **1** *n* also clothing haut *m;* (lid: of bottle etc) bouchon *m;* of pen capuchon *m;* of the class, league premier(-ère) *m(f);* MOT: gear quatrième *f*/cinquième *f;* **on ~** of sur; **be at the ~ of** être en haut de; **be at the ~ of** league être premier de; **get to the ~** of company, mountain être arriver au sommet **2** adj branches du haut; floor dernier; player etc meilleur; speed maximum; note le plus élevé; **~ official** haut fonctionnaire *m*

topic [ˈtɑːpɪk] sujet *m;* **topical** d'actualité

topless [ˈtɑːplɪs] aux seins nus; **topmost** branch le plus haut; floor dernier; **topping** on pizza garniture *f*

topple [ˈtɑːpl] **1** *v/i* s'écrouler **2** *v/t* government renverser

top 'secret top secret *inv*

topsy-turvy [tɑːpsɪˈtɜːrvɪ] sens dessus dessous

torment 1 [ˈtɔːrment] *n* tourment *m* **2** [tɔːrˈment] *v/t* person, animal harceler

tornado [tɔːrˈneɪdou] tornade *f*

torpedo [tɔːrˈpiːdou] **1** *n* torpille *f* **2** *v/t* also fig torpiller

torrent [ˈtɑːrənt] also fig torrent *m*

torture [ˈtɔːrtʃər] **1** *n* torture *f* **2** *v/t* torturer

toss [tɑːs] **1** *v/t* ball lancer;

rider désarçonner; *salad re-muer*

total [ˈtoʊtl] **1** *adj* total; *disaster* complet; *idiot* fini; **he's a ~ stranger** c'est un parfait inconnu **2** *n* total *m*; **totalitarian** totalitaire; **totally** totalement

totter [ˈtɑːtər] tituber

touch [tʌʃ] **1** *n sense* toucher *m*; **lose ~ with s.o.** perdre contact avec qn; **in ~** SP en touche **2** *v/t also emotionally* toucher; *exhibits etc* toucher à **3** *v/i of two things* se toucher

◆ **touch down** *of airplane* atterrir; SP faire un touché-en-but

touchdown *of airplane* atterrissage *m*; SP touché-en-but; **touching** touchant; **touchline** SP ligne *f* de touche; **touch screen** écran *m* tactile; **touchy** *person* susceptible

tough [tʌf] *person, material* résistant; *meat, question, exam, punishment* dur

tour [tʊr] **1** *n* visite *f*; *as part of package* circuit *m* (**of** dans); *of band etc* tournée *f* **2** *v/t area* visiter **3** *v/i of tourist* faire du tourisme; *of band* être en tournée; **tour guide** accompagnateur(-trice) *m(f)*; **tourism** tourisme; **tourist** touriste *m/f*; **tourist industry** industrie *f* touristique; **tourist information office** office *m*

de tourisme

tournament [ˈtʊrnəmənt] tournoi *m*

tour operator tour-opérateur *m*, voyagiste *m*

tow [toʊ] remorquer

◆ **tow away** *car* emmener à la fourrière

toward [tɔːrd] *vers*; *with attitude, feelings etc* envers

towel [taʊl] serviette *f*

tower [ˈtaʊər] tour *f*

town [taʊn] ville *f*; **town center**, *Br* **town centre** centre-ville *m*; **town council** conseil *m* municipal; **town hall** hôtel *m* de ville

toxic [ˈtɑːksɪk] toxique; **toxin** toxine *f*

toy [tɔɪ] jouet *m*

trace [treɪs] **1** *n of substance* trace *f* **2** *v/t* (*find*) retrouver; *draw* tracer

track [træk] *path*, (*racecourse*) piste *f*; *motor racing* circuit *m*; *on record*, *CD* morceau *m*; RAIL voie *f* (ferrée); **~ 10** RAIL voie 10; **keep ~ of sth** suivre qch

◆ **track down** *person* retrouver; *criminal* dépister; *object* dénicher

tracksuit *Br* survêtement *m*

tractor [ˈtræktər] tracteur *m*

trade [treɪd] **1** *n* commerce *m*; (*profession, craft*) métier *m* **2** *v/i* (*do business*) faire du commerce **3** *v/t* (*exchange*) échanger (**for** contre); **trade fair** foire *f* commerciale;

trademark marque f de commerce; **trade mission** mission f commerciale; **trader** commerçant(e) m(f)

tradition [trəˈdɪʃn] tradition f; **traditional** traditionnel; **traditionally** traditionnellement

traffic [ˈtræfɪk] circulation f; *at airport, in drugs* trafic m
♦ **traffic in** *drugs* faire du trafic de

'**traffic circle** rond-point m; **traffic cop** F agent m de la circulation; **traffic jam** embouteillage m; **traffic light** feux mpl de signalisation; **traffic sign** panneau m de signalisation

tragedy [ˈtrædʒədɪ] tragédie f; **tragic** tragique

trail [treɪl] **1** n (path) sentier m; *of blood* traînée f **2** v/t (follow) suivre à la trace; (tow) remorquer **3** v/i (lag behind) traîner; **trailer** *pulled by vehicle* remorque f; *(mobile home)* caravane f; *of movie* bande-annonce f

train[1] [treɪn] n train m

train[2] [treɪn] **1** v/t entraîner; *dog* dresser; *employee* former **2** v/i *of team, athlete* s'entraîner; *of teacher etc* faire sa formation

trainee stagiaire m/f; **trainer** SP entraîneur(-euse) m(f); *of dog* dresseur(-euse) m(f); **~s** Br: *shoes* tennis mpl; **training** *of new staff* for-

mation f; SP entraînement m

'**train station** gare f

traitor [ˈtreɪtər] traître m, traîtresse f

♦ **trample on** piétiner

trampoline [ˈtræmpəliːn] trampoline m

tranquil [ˈtræŋkwɪl] tranquille; **tranquility**, *Br* **tranquillity** tranquillité f; **tranquilizer**, *Br* **tranquillizer** tranquillisant m

transaction [trænˈzækʃn] *of business* conduite f; *piece of business* transaction f

transatlantic [trænzətˈlæntɪk] transatlantique

transcript [ˈtrænskrɪpt] transcription f

transfer 1 [trænsˈfɜːr] v/t transférer **2** [trænsˈfɜːr] v/i *when traveling* changer; *in job* être muté (**to** à) **3** [ˈtrænsfɜːr] n transfert m; **transferable** *ticket* transférable; **transfer fee** *for sportsman* prix m de transfert

transform [trænsˈfɔːrm] transformer; **transformation** transformation f; **transformer** ELEC transformateur m

transfusion [trænsˈfjuːʒn] transfusion f

transit [ˈtrænzɪt]: **in ~** en transit; **transition** transition f; **transitional** de transition; **transit lounge** *at airport* salle f de transit; **transit pas-**

senger passager(-ère) *m(f)* en transit

translate [træns'leɪt] traduire; **translation** traduction *f*; **translator** traducteur(-trice) *m(f)*

transmission [trænz'mɪʃn] TV, AUT transmission *f*; **transmit** news, program diffuser; disease transmettre; **transmitter** RAD, TV émetteur *m*

transparency [træns'pærənsɪ] PHOT diapositive *f*; **transparent** transparent; (obvious) évident

transplant MED **1** ['trænsplænt] transplantation *n f*; organ transplanted transplant *m* **2** [træns'plænt] *v/t* transplanter

transport 1 ['trænspɔːrt] *n* transport *m* **2** [træns'pɔːrt] *v/t* transporter; **transportation** of goods, people transport *m*

transvestite [træns'vestaɪt] travesti *m*

trap [træp] **1** *n* also fig piège *m* **2** *v/t* also fig piéger; **trappings** of power signes extérieurs *mpl*

trash [træʃ] (garbage) ordures *fpl*; F goods etc camelote *f* F; fig: person vermine *f*; **trash can** poubelle *f*; **trashy** goods de pacotille; novel de bas étage

traumatic [trɔː'mætɪk] traumatisant; **traumatize** traumatiser

travel ['trævl] **1** *n* voyages *mpl* **2** *v/i* voyager **3** *v/t* miles parcourir; **travel agency** agence *f* de voyages; **travel agent** agent *m* de voyages; **traveler**, Br **traveller** voyageur(-euse) *m(f)*; **traveler's check**, Br **traveller's cheque** chèque--voyage *m*; **travel expenses** frais *mpl* de déplacement; **travel insurance** assurance--voyage *f*

trawler ['trɔːlər] chalutier *m*

tray [treɪ] for food, photocopier plateau *m*; to go in oven plaque *f*

treacherous ['tretʃərəs] traître; **treachery** traîtrise *f*

tread [tred] **1** *n* pas *m*; of staircase dessus *m* des marches; of tire bande *f* de roulement **2** *v/i* marcher

treason ['triːzn] trahison *f*

treasure ['treʒər] **1** *n* trésor *m* **2** *v/t* gift etc chérir; **treasurer** trésorier(-ière) *m(f)*; **Treasury Department** ministère *m* des Finances

treat [triːt] **1** *n* plaisir *m*; **it's my ~** (I'm paying) c'est moi qui paie **2** *v/t* traiter; **~ s.o. to sth** offrir qch à qn; **treatment** traitement *m*

treaty ['triːtɪ] traité *m*

treble ['trebl] **1** adv: **~ the price** le triple du prix **2** *v/i* tripler

tree [triː] arbre *m*

tremble ['trembl] trembler

tremendous [trɪ'mendəs]

(very good) formidable; *(enormous)* énorme; **tremendously** *(very)* extrêmement; *(a lot)* énormément

tremor ['tremər] *of earth* secousse *f* (sismique)

trench [trentʃ] tranchée *f*

trend [trend] tendance *f*; *(fashion)* mode *f*; **trendy** branché

trespass ['trespəs] entrer sans autorisation; **no ~ing** défense d'entrer; **trespasser** *personne qui viole la propriété d'une autre*

trial ['traɪəl] LAW procès *m*; *of equipment* essai *m*; **be on ~** LAW passer en justice

triangle ['traɪæŋgl] triangle *m*; **triangular** triangulaire

tribe [traɪb] tribu *f*

tribunal [traɪ'bjuːnl] tribunal *m*

tributary ['trɪbjʊterɪ] *of river* affluent *m*

trick [trɪk] **1** *n to deceive* tour *m*; *(knack)* truc *m* **2** *v/t* rouler; **trickery** tromperie *f*

trickle ['trɪkl] **1** *n* filet *m*; *fig* tout petit peu *m* **2** *v/i* couler goutte à goutte

tricky ['trɪkɪ] *(difficult)* délicat

trifling ['traɪflɪŋ] insignifiant

trigger ['trɪgər] *on gun* détente *f*

♦ **trigger off** *v/t* déclencher

trim [trɪm] **1** *adj (neat)* bien entretenu; *figure* svelte **2** *v/t hair* couper un peu; *hedge* tailler; *costs* réduire; *(deco-*

rate; dress) garnir **3** *n* cut taille *f*

trinket ['trɪŋkɪt] babiole *f*

trip [trɪp] **1** *n (journey)* voyage *m*; *(outing)* excursion *f* **2** *v/i (stumble)* trébucher **3** *v/t (make fall)* faire un croche-pied à

♦ **trip up 1** *v/t (make fall)* faire un croche-pied à; *(cause to go wrong)* faire trébucher **2** *v/i (stumble)* trébucher; *(make a mistake)* faire une erreur

triple ['trɪpl] → **treble**

trite [traɪt] banal

triumph ['traɪʌmf] triomphe *m*

trivial ['trɪvɪəl] insignifiant; **triviality** banalité *f*

trolley ['trɑːlɪ] *(streetcar)* tramway *m*

troops [truːps] troupes *fpl*

trophy ['troʊfɪ] trophée *m*

tropic ['trɑːpɪk] GEOG tropique *m*; **tropical** tropical; **tropics** tropiques *mpl*

trot [trɑːt] trotter

trouble ['trʌbl] **1** *n (difficulties)* problèmes *mpl*; *(inconvenience)* dérangement *m*; *(disturbance)* affrontements *mpl*; **get into ~** s'attirer des ennuis **2** *v/t (worry)* inquiéter; *(bother, disturb)* déranger; *of back, liver etc* faire souffrir; **troublemaker** fauteur(-trice) *m(f)* de troubles; **troubleshooting** dépannage *m*; **troublesome** pénible

trousers ['traʊzərz] Br pantalon m

trout [traʊt] truite f

truant ['truːənt]: **play ~** faire l'école buissonnière

truce [truːs] trêve f

truck [trʌk] camion m; **truck driver** camionneur(-euse) m(f); **truck stop** routier m

trudge [trʌdʒ] **1** v/i se traîner **2** n marche f pénible

true [truː] vrai; *friend, American* véritable; **come ~** of hopes, dream se réaliser; **truly** vraiment; **Yours ~** je vous prie d'agréer mes sentiments distingués

trumpet ['trʌmpɪt] trompette f

trunk [trʌŋk] of tree, body tronc m; of elephant trompe f; of car coffre m

trust [trʌst] **1** n confiance f; FIN fidéicommis m **2** v/t faire confiance à; **trusted** éprouvé; **trustee** fidéicommissaire m/f; **trustful, trusting** confiant; **trustworthy** fiable

truth [truːθ] vérité f; **truthful** honnête

try [traɪ] **1** v/t & v/i essayer; LAW juger; **~ to do sth** essayer de faire qch; **you must ~ harder** tu dois faire plus d'efforts **2** n rugby essai m; **trying** (annoying) éprouvant

T-shirt ['tiːʃɜːrt] tee-shirt m

tub [tʌb] (bath) baignoire f for liquid bac m; for yoghurt pot

m; **tubby** boulot

tube [tuːb] (pipe) tuyau m; of toothpaste tube m; **tubeless** tire sans chambre à air

Tuesday ['tuːzdeɪ] mardi m

tuft [tʌft] touffe f

tug [tʌg] **1** n NAUT remorqueur m **2** v/t tirer

tuition [tuː'ɪʃn] cours mpl

tumble ['tʌmbl] tomber; **tumbledown** qui tombe en ruines; **tumbler** for drink verre m; in circus acrobate m/f

tummy ['tʌmɪ] F ventre m; **tummy ache** mal m de ventre

tumor, Br **tumour** tumeur f

tumult ['tuːmʌlt] tumulte m; **tumultuous** tumultueux

tuna ['tuːnə] thon m

tune [tuːn] **1** n air m **2** v/t instrument accorder

♦ **tune up** v/i of orchestra s'accorder **2** v/t engine régler

tuneful ['tuːnfl] harmonieux; **tune-up** of engine règlement m

tunnel ['tʌnl] tunnel m

turbine ['tɜːrbaɪn] turbine f

turbulence ['tɜːrbjələns] in air travel turbulences fpl; **turbulent** agité

turf [tɜːrf] gazon m; piece motte f de gazon

turkey ['tɜːrkɪ] dinde f

turmoil ['tɜːrmɔɪl] confusion f

turn [tɜːrn] **1** n (rotation) tour m; in road virage m; in vaudeville numéro m; **take ~s doing sth** faire qch à tour

de rôle; *it's my* ~ c'est à moi 2
v/t wheel tourner; ~ *the corner* tourner au coin de la rue
3 *v/i of driver, car, wheel*
tourner; *of person* se retourner; *it has* ~ed *cold* le temps
s'est refroidi

◆ **turn around 1** *v/t object*
tourner; *company* remettre
sur pied; COM *order* traiter
2 *v/i* se retourner; *with a
car* faire demi-tour

◆ **turn away 1** *v/t (send away)*
renvoyer 2 *v/i (walk away)*
s'en aller; *(look away)* détourner le regard

◆ **turn back 1** *v/t edges, sheets*
replier 2 *v/i of walkers, in
course of action* faire demi-
tour

◆ **turn down** *offer* rejeter;
volume, heating baisser; *edge*
replier

◆ **turn off 1** *v/t TV, heater*
éteindre; *faucet* fermer; *engine* arrêter 2 *v/i of car, driver* tourner; *of machine*
s'éteindre

◆ **turn on 1** *v/t TV, heater* allumer; *faucet* ouvrir; *engine*
mettre en marche; F *sexually*
exciter 2 *v/i of machine* s'allumer

◆ **turn over 1** *v/i in bed* se retourner; *of vehicle* se renverser 2 *v/t (put upside down)*
renverser; *page* tourner; FIN
avoir un chiffre d'affaires de

◆ **turn up 1** *v/t collar* remonter; *volume* augmenter; *heat-*

ing monter 2 *v/i (arrive)* arriver, se pointer F

turning ['tɜːrnɪŋ] *in road* virage; **turning point** tournant
m; **turnout** *at game etc* nombre *m* de spectateurs; **turnover** FIN chiffre *m* d'affaires;
turnpike autoroute *f*
payante; **turn signal** MOT clignotant *m*

turquoise ['tɜːrkwɔɪz] turquoise

turtle ['tɜːrtl] tortue *f* de mer;
turtleneck sweater pull *m* à
col cheminée

tusk [tʌsk] défense *f*

tutor ['tuːtər] *at university*
professeur *m/f*; *(private)* ~
professeur *m* particulier

tuxedo [tʌkˈsiːdoʊ] smoking
m

TV [tiːˈviː] télé *f*; *on* ~ à la télé;
TV dinner plateau-repas *m*;
TV guide guide *m* de télé;
TV program, *Br* **TV pro-
gramme** programme *m* télé

twang [twæŋ] **1** *n in voice* accent *m* nasillard 2 *v/t guitar
string* pincer

tweezers ['twiːzərz] pince *f* à
épiler

twelfth [twelfθ] douzième;
twelve douze

twentieth ['twentɪθ] vingtième; **twenty** vingt

twice [twaɪs] deux fois; ~ *as
much* deux fois plus

twig [twɪg] brindille *f*

twilight ['twaɪlaɪt] crépuscule
m

twin [twɪn] jumeau *m*, jumelle *f*; **twin beds** lits *mpl* jumeaux

twinge [twɪndʒ] *of pain* élancement *m*

twinkle ['twɪŋkl] scintiller

'twin room chambre *f* à lits jumeaux

twirl [twɜːrl] **1** *v/t* faire tourbillonner; *mustache* tortiller **2** *n of cream etc* spirale *f*

twist [twɪst] **1** *v/t* tordre; **~ one's ankle** se tordre la cheville **2** *v/i of road* faire des méandres; *of river* faire des lacets **3** *n in rope* entortillement *m*; *in road* lacet *m*; *in plot* dénouement *m* inattendu; **twisty** *road* qui fait des lacets

twitch [twɪtʃ] *nervous* tic *m*

twitter ['twɪtər] *of birds* gazouiller

two [tuː] deux; **the ~ of them** les deux

tycoon [taɪ'kuːn] magnat *m*

type [taɪp] **1** *n* (*sort*) type *m* **2** *v/i* (*use a keyboard*) taper **3** *v/t with a typewriter* taper à la machine

typhoon [taɪ'fuːn] typhon *m*

typhus ['taɪfəs] typhus *m*

typical ['tɪpɪkl] typique; **that's ~ of you!** c'est bien de vous!; **typically** typiquement

typist ['taɪpɪst] dactylo *m/f*

tyrannical [tɪ'rænɪkl] tyrannique; **tyrannize** tyranniser; **tyranny** tyrannie *f*; **tyrant** tyran *m*

tyre *Br* → **tire**[1]

U

ugly ['ʌglɪ] laid

UK [juː'keɪ] (= *United Kingdom*) R.-U. *m* (= Royaume-Uni)

ulcer ['ʌlsər] ulcère *m*

ultimate ['ʌltɪmət] (*best, definitive*) meilleur possible; (*final*) final; (*fundamental*) fondamental; **ultimately** (*in the end*) en fin de compte

ultimatum [ʌltɪ'meɪtəm] ultimatum *m*

ultrasound ['ʌltrəsaʊnd] MED ultrason *m*

ultraviolet [ʌltrə'vaɪələt] ultraviolet

umbrella [ʌm'brelə] parapluie *m*

umpire ['ʌmpaɪr] arbitre *m/f*

UN [juː'en] (= *United Nations*) O.N.U. *f* (= Organisation des Nations unies)

unable [ʌn'eɪbl]: **be ~ to do sth** *not know how to* ne pas savoir faire qch; *not be in a position to* ne pas pouvoir faire qch

unacceptable [ʌnək'septəbl] inacceptable

unaccountable [ʌnə-

'kauntəbl] inexplicable

un-American [ʌnə'merɪkən] (*not fitting*) antiaméricain

unanimous [juːˈnænɪməs] *verdict* unanime; **unanimously** à l'unanimité

unapproachable [ʌnə'prəutʃəbl] *person* d'un abord difficile

unarmed [ʌn'ɑːrmd] *person* non armé

unassuming [ʌnə'suːmɪŋ] modeste

unattached [ʌnə'tætʃt] *without a partner* sans attaches

unattended [ʌnə'tendɪd] laissé sans surveillance

unauthorized [ʌn'ɔːθəraɪzd] non autorisé

unavoidable [ʌnə'vɔɪdəbl] inévitable

unbalanced [ʌn'bælənst] *also* PSYCH déséquilibré

unbearable [ʌn'berəbl] insupportable

unbeatable [ʌn'biːtəbl] imbattable

unbeaten [ʌn'biːtn] *team* invaincu

unbelievable [ʌnbɪ'liːvəbl] *also* F incroyable

unbias(s)ed [ʌn'baɪəst] impartial

unblock [ʌn'blɑːk] *pipe* déboucher

unbreakable [ʌn'breɪkəbl] incassable

unbutton [ʌn'bʌtn] déboutonner

uncanny [ʌn'kæni] étrange,

mystérieux

unceasing [ʌn'siːsɪŋ] incessant

uncertain [ʌn'sɜːrtn] incertain; **uncertainty** *of the future* caractère *m* incertain; **there is still ~ about** des incertitudes demeurent quant à …

uncle ['ʌŋkl] oncle *m*

uncomfortable [ʌn'kʌmftəbl] inconfortable

uncommon [ʌn'kɑːmən] inhabituel

uncompromising [ʌn'kɑːmprəmaɪzɪŋ] intransigeant

unconditional [ʌnkən'dɪʃnl] sans conditions

unconscious [ʌn'kɑːnʃəs] MED, PSYCH inconscient

uncontrollable [ʌnkən'trəʊləbl] incontrôlable

unconventional [ʌnkən'venʃnl] non conventionnel

uncooperative [ʌnkoʊ'ɑːpərətɪv] peu coopératif

uncover [ʌn'kʌvər] découvrir

undamaged [ʌn'dæmɪdʒd] intact

undecided [ʌndɪ'saɪdɪd] *question* laissé en suspens; **be ~ about** être indécis à propos de

undeniable [ʌndɪ'naɪəbl] indéniable

under ['ʌndər] sous; (*less than*) moins de; **it is ~ investigation** cela fait l'objet d'une enquête 'under**carriage** train *m* d'atterrissage

'under**cover** clandestin; ~ **agent** agent *m* secret

under**cut** com: ~ **the competition** vendre moins cher que la concurrence

under**done** *meat* pas trop cuit; *pej* pas assez cuit

under**estimate** sous-estimer

under**fed** mal nourri

under**go** subir

under**graduate** *Br* étudiant(e) (de D.E.U.G. ou de licence)

'under**ground 1** *adj* souterrain; POL clandestin **2** *adv* **work** sous terre

under**hand** (*devious*) sournois

under**line** *text* souligner

under**lying** sous-jacent

under**mine** saper

under**neath** [ʌndərˈniːθ] **1** *prep* sous **2** *adv* dessous

'under**pants** slip *m*

'under**pass** *for pedestrians* passage *m* souterrain

under**privileged** [ʌndərˈprɪvɪlɪdʒd] défavorisé

under**rate** sous-estimer

under**staffed** [ʌndərˈstæft] en manque de personnel

under**stand** comprendre; **understandable** compréhensible; **understandably** naturellement; **understanding 1** *adj person* compréhensif **2** *n* compréhension *f*;

(*agreement*) accord *m*

under**take** *task* entreprendre; ~ **to do sth** (*agree to*) s'engager à faire qch; **undertaking** (*enterprise*) entreprise *f*; (*promise*) engagement *m*

under**value** sous-estimer

'under**wear** sous-vêtements *mpl*

'under**world** *criminal* monde *m* du crime organisé

under**write** FIN souscrire

unde**served** [ʌndɪˈzɜːrvd] non mérité

unde**sirable** [ʌndɪˈzaɪrəbl] indésirable

undis**puted** [ʌndɪˈspjuːtɪd] *champion* incontestable

undo [ʌnˈduː] défaire

undoubtedly [ʌnˈdaʊtɪdlɪ] à n'en pas douter

undress [ʌnˈdres] **1** *v/t* déshabiller; **get ~ed** se déshabiller **2** *v/i* se déshabiller

undue [ʌnˈduː] excessif; **unduly** (*excessively*) excessivement

unearth [ʌnˈɜːrθ] *also fig* déterrer

uneasy [ʌnˈiːzɪ] *relationship*, *peace* incertain vouloir signer cela

uneatable [ʌnˈiːtəbl] immangeable

uneconomic [ʌniːkəˈnɑːmɪk] pas rentable

uneducated [ʌnˈedʒəketɪd] sans instruction

unemployed [ʌnɪmˈplɔɪd] **1** *adj* au chômage **2** *npl*: **the**

~ les chômeurs(-euses); **unemployment** chômage *m*

unequal [ʌnˈiːkwəl] inégal

unerring [ʌnˈɜːrɪŋ] *judgment, instinct* infaillible

uneven [ʌnˈiːvn] *surface, ground* irrégulier

uneventful [ʌnɪˈventfl] *day, journey* sans événement

unexpected [ʌnɪkˈspektɪd] inattendu; **unexpectedly** inopinément

unfair [ʌnˈfer] injuste

unfaithful [ʌnˈfeɪθfl] *husband, wife* infidèle; **be ~ to s.o.** tromper qn

unfamiliar [ʌnfəˈmɪljər] peu familier

unfasten [ʌnˈfæsn] *belt* défaire

unfavorable [ʌnˈfeɪvərəbl] défavorable

unfinished [ʌnˈfɪnɪʃt] inachevé

unfold [ʌnˈfould] **1** *v/t letter* déplier; *arms* ouvrir **2** *v/i of story etc* se dérouler; *of view* se déployer

unforeseen [ʌnfɔːrˈsiːn] imprévu

unforgettable [ʌnfərˈgetəbl] inoubliable

unforgivable [ʌnfərˈgɪvəbl] impardonnable

unfortunate [ʌnˈfɔːrtʃənət] malheureux; **unfortunately** malheureusement

unfounded [ʌnˈfaundɪd] non fondé

unfriendly [ʌnˈfrendlɪ] *per-*

son, welcome, hotel froid

ungrateful [ʌnˈgreɪtfl] ingrat

unhappiness [ʌnˈhæpɪnɪs] chagrin *m*; **unhappy** malheureux; *customers etc* mécontent (**with** de)

unharmed [ʌnˈhɑːrmd] indemne

unhealthy [ʌnˈhelθɪ] *person* en mauvaise santé; *food, atmosphere* malsain; *economy* qui se porte mal

unheard-of [ʌnˈhɜːrdəv]: **be ~** ne s'être jamais vu

unhygienic [ʌnhaɪˈdʒiːnɪk] insalubre

unification [juːnɪfɪˈkeɪʃn] unification *f*

uniform [ˈjuːnɪfɔːrm] **1** *n* uniforme *m* **2** *adj* uniforme

unify [ˈjuːnɪfaɪ] unifier

unilateral [juːnɪˈlætərəl] unilatéral

unimaginable [ʌnɪˈmædʒɪnəbl] inimaginable

unimaginative [ʌnɪˈmædʒɪnətɪv] qui manque d'imagination

unimportant [ʌnɪmˈpɔːrtənt] sans importance

uninhabitable [ʌnɪnˈhæbɪtəbl] inhabitable; **uninhabited** inhabitée

unintentional [ʌnɪnˈtenʃnl] non intentionnel; **unintentionally** sans le vouloir

uninteresting [ʌnˈɪntrəstɪŋ] inintéressant

uninterrupted [ʌnɪntəˈrʌptɪd] ininterrompu

union ['juːnjən] POL union f; (labor ~) syndicat m

unique [juːˈniːk] unique

unit ['juːnɪt] unité f

unite [juːˈnaɪt] **1** v/t unir **2** v/i s'unir; **united** uni; **efforts** conjoint; **United Kingdom** Royaume-Uni m; **United Nations** Nations fpl Unies

United States (of America) États-Unis mpl (d'Amérique)

unity ['juːnətɪ] unité f

universal [juːnɪˈvɜːsl] universel; **universe** univers m

university [juːnɪˈvɜːsətɪ] université f

unjust [ʌnˈdʒʌst] injuste

unkind [ʌnˈkaɪnd] méchant, désagréable

unknown [ʌnˈnəʊn] inconnu

unleaded [ʌnˈledɪd] gas sans plomb

unless [ən'les] à moins que (+subj)

unlikely [ʌnˈlaɪklɪ] improbable

unlimited [ʌnˈlɪmɪtɪd] illimité

unload [ʌnˈləʊd] décharger

unlock [ʌnˈlɒk] ouvrir

unluckily [ʌnˈlʌkɪlɪ] malheureusement; **unlucky** day de malchance; **choice** malheureux; **person** malchanceux; **that was so ~ for you!** tu n'as vraiment pas eu de chance!

unmanned [ʌnˈmænd] spacecraft sans équipage

unmarried [ʌnˈmærɪd] non marié

unmistakable [ʌnmɪˈsteɪkəbl] reconnaissable entre mille

unnatural [ʌnˈnætʃrəl] contre-nature

unnecessary [ʌnˈnesəsərɪ] non nécessaire

unnerving [ʌnˈnɜːrvɪŋ] déstabilisant

unobtainable [ʌnəbˈteɪnəbl] goods qu'on ne peut se procurer; TELEC hors service

unobtrusive [ʌnəbˈtruːsɪv] discret

unoccupied [ʌnˈɒkjupaɪd] (empty) vide; position vacant; person désœuvré

unofficial [ʌnəˈfɪʃl] non officiel; **unofficially** non officiellement

unorthodox [ʌnˈɔːθədɒks] peu orthodoxe

unpack [ʌnˈpæk] **1** v/t case défaire **2** v/i défaire sa valise

unpaid [ʌnˈpeɪd] work non rémunéré

unpleasant [ʌnˈpleznt] désagréable

unplug [ʌnˈplʌg] TV, computer débrancher

unpopular [ʌnˈpɑːpjələr] impopulaire

unprecedented [ʌnˈpresɪdentɪd] sans précédent

unpredictable [ʌnprɪˈdɪktəbl] imprévisible

unpretentious [ʌnprɪˈtenʃəs] modeste

unproductive [ʌnprəˈdʌktɪv]

meeting, discussion, land improductif

unprofessional [ʌnprə'feʃnl] non professionnel; *workmanship* peu professionnel

unprofitable [ʌn'prɒfɪtəbl] non profitable

unprovoked [ʌnprə'vəʊkt] *attack* non provoqué

unqualified [ʌn'kwɒlɪfaɪd] non qualifié

unquestionably [ʌn'kwestʃnəblɪ] sans aucun doute; **unquestioning** *attitude* aveugle

unreadable [ʌn'riːdəbl] *book* illisible

unrealistic [ʌnrɪə'lɪstɪk] irréaliste

unreasonable [ʌn'riːznəbl] déraisonnable

unrelated [ʌnrɪ'leɪtɪd] sans relation (**to** avec)

unrelenting [ʌnrɪ'lentɪŋ] incessant

unreliable [ʌnrɪ'laɪəbl] pas fiable

unrest [ʌn'rest] agitation *f*

unrestrained [ʌnrɪ'streɪnd] *emotions* non contenu

unroll [ʌn'rəʊl] *carpet* dérouler

unruly [ʌn'ruːlɪ] indiscipliné

unsanitary [ʌnsætɪs'fæktərɪ] *conditions, drains* insalubre

unsatisfactory [ʌnsætɪs'fæktərɪ] insatisfaisant; (*unacceptable*) inacceptable

unscathed [ʌn'skeɪðd] (*not injured*) indemne; (*not dam-*

aged) intact

unscrew [ʌn'skruː] *sth screwed on* dévisser; *top* décapsuler

unscrupulous [ʌn'skruːpjələs] peu scrupuleux

unselfish [ʌn'selfɪʃ] désintéressé

unsettled [ʌn'setld] incertain; *lifestyle* instable; *bills* non réglé; *issue* non décidé

unshaven [ʌn'ʃeɪvn] mal rasé

unskilled [ʌn'skɪld] *worker* non qualifié

unsophisticated [ʌnsə'fɪstɪkeɪtɪd] peu sophistiqué

unstable [ʌn'steɪbl] instable

unsteady [ʌn'stedɪ] *on feet* chancelant; *ladder* branlant

unsuccessful [ʌnsək'sesfl] *attempt* infructueux; *writer* qui n'a pas de succès; *candidate, marriage* malheureux; **unsuccessfully** sans succès

unsuitable [ʌn'suːtəbl] inapproprié

unswerving [ʌn'swɜːrvɪŋ] *loyalty* inébranlable

unthinkable [ʌn'θɪŋkəbl] impensable

untidy [ʌn'taɪdɪ] en désordre

untie [ʌn'taɪ] *knot* défaire; *prisoner, hands* détacher

until [ən'tɪl] **1** *prep* jusqu'à; *from Monday ~ Friday* de lundi à vendredi; *not ~ Friday* pas avant vendredi **2** *conj* jusqu'à ce que; *can you wait ~ I'm ready?* est-ce que vous pouvez attendre que je sois prêt?

untiring [ʌn'taɪrɪŋ] *efforts* infatigable

untold [ʌn'toʊld] *riches, suffering* inouï; *story* inédit

untrue [ʌn'truː] faux

unused [ʌn'juːzd] *goods* non utilisé

unusual [ʌn'juːʒl] inhabituel; *(strange)* bizarre; **unusually** anormalement, exceptionnellement

unveil [ʌn'veɪl] *statue etc* dévoiler

unwell [ʌn'wel] malade

unwilling [ʌn'wɪlɪŋ]: **be ~ to do** refuser de faire; **unwillingly** à contre-cœur

unwind [ʌn'waɪnd] **1** *v/t tape* dérouler **2** *v/i* of *tape, story* se dérouler; *(relax)* se détendre

unwise [ʌn'waɪz] malavisé

unwrap [ʌn'ræp] déballer

unzip [ʌn'zɪp] *dress etc* descendre la fermeture-éclair de; COMPUT décompresser

up [ʌp] **1** *adv*: **~ in the sky/on the roof** dans le ciel/sur le toit; **~ here** ici; **~ there** là-haut; **be ~** *(out of bed)* être debout; *of sun* être levé; *of temperature* avoir augmenté; *(have expired)* être expiré; **what's ~?** F qu'est-ce qu'il y a?; **~ to 1989** jusqu'à 1989; **he came ~ to me** il s'est approché de moi; **what are you ~ to these days?** qu'est-ce que tu fais en ce

moment?; **be ~ to something (bad)** être sur un mauvais coup; **I don't feel ~ to it** je ne m'en sens pas le courage; **it's ~ to you** c'est toi qui décides; **it's ~ to them to solve it** c'est à eux de le résoudre **2** *prep*: **further ~ the mountain** un peu plus haut sur la montagne; **they ran ~ the street** ils ont remonté la rue en courant; **we traveled ~ to Paris** nous sommes montés à Paris **3** *n*: **~s and downs** hauts *mpl* et bas

'upbringing éducation *f*

up'date *file* mettre à jour

up'grade moderniser; *ticket* surclasser

upheaval [ʌp'hiːvl] bouleversement *m*

up'hold *rights* maintenir

'upkeep maintien *m*

'upload COMPUT transférer

up'market *Br restaurant, hotel* chic; *product* haut de gamme

upon [ə'pɑːn] → **on**

upper ['ʌpər] supérieur

'upright 1 *adj citizen* droit **2** *adv sit* (bien) droit; **upright piano** piano *f* droit

'uprising soulèvement *m*

'uproar vacarme *m*; *fig* protestations *fpl*

up'set 1 *v/t* renverser; *emotionally* contrarier **2** *adj emotionally* contrarié, vexé; **upsetting** contrariant

upside 'down à l'envers; *car* renversé

up'stairs 1 *adv* en haut; ~ **from us** au-dessus de chez nous **2** *adj* **room** d'en haut

up'stream en remontant le courant

up'tight F (*nervous*) tendu; (*inhibited*) coincé

up-to-'date à jour

'upturn *in economy* reprise *f*

upward ['ʌpwəd]: *move sth* ~ élever qch; ~ *of 100* au-delà de 100

uranium [ju'reɪnɪəm] uranium *m*

urban ['ɜːrbən] urbain

urge [ɜːrdʒ] **1** *n* (forte) envie *f* **2** *v/t*: ~ *s.o. to do sth* encourager qn à faire qch; **urgency** urgence *f*; **urgent** urgent

urinate ['jʊrəneɪt] uriner; **urine** urine *f*

US [juː'es] (= *United States*) USA *mpl*

us [ʌs] nous

USA [juːes'eɪ] (= *United States of America*) USA *mpl*

usage ['juːzɪdʒ] usage *m*

use 1 [juːz] *v/t also pej*: *person* utiliser **2** [juːs] *n* utilisation *f*; *it's no* ~ *waiting* ce n'est pas la peine d'attendre

♦ **use up** épuiser

used¹ [juːzd] *car etc* d'occasion

used² [juːst]: *be* ~ *to* être habitué à; *get* ~ *to* s'habituer à

used³ [juːst]: *I* ~ *to work there* je travaillais là-bas avant; *I* ~ *to know him well* je l'ai bien connu autrefois

useful ['juːsfəl] utile; **usefulness** utilité *f*; **useless** inutile; F (*no good*) nul F; **user** *of product* utilisateur(-trice) *m(f)*; **user-friendly** facile à utiliser; COMPUT convivial

usual ['juːʒʊəl] habituel; *as* ~ comme d'habitude; **usually** d'habitude

utensil [juː'tensl] ustensile *m*

utilize ['juːtɪlaɪz] utiliser

utter ['ʌtər] **1** *adj* total **2** *v/t* *sound* prononcer; **utterly** totalement

V

vacant ['veɪkənt] *building* inoccupé; *look* vide, absent; *Br: position* vacant; **vacantly** *stare* d'un air absent; **vacate** *room* libérer

vacation [veɪ'keɪʃn] vacances *fpl*; *be on* ~ être en vacances

vaccinate ['væksɪneɪt] vacciner; **vaccination** vaccination *f*; **vaccine** vaccin *m*

vacuum ['vækjʊəm] **1** *n* vide *m* **2** *v/t* *floors* passer l'aspirateur sur

vagrant ['veɪgrənt] vagabond *m*

vague [veɪg] vague; **vaguely**

vending machine

vaguement

vain [veɪn] **1** *adj person* vaniteux; *hope* vain **2** *n*: **in ~** en vain

valiant ['væljənt] vaillant

valid ['vælɪd] valable; *validate with official stamp* valider; *theory* confirmer; **validity** validité *f*; *of argument* justesse *f*; *of claim* bien-fondé *m*

valley ['vælɪ] vallée *f*

valuable ['væljubl] **1** *adj* de valeur; *colleague, help, advice* précieux **2** *npl*: **~s** objets *mpl* de valeur; **valuation** estimation *f*, expertise *f*; **value 1** *n* valeur *f* **2** *v/t* tenir à, attacher un grand prix à

valve [vælv] *of engine* soupape *f*, valve *f*; *in heart* valvule *f*

van [væn] *small* camionnette *f*; *large* fourgon *m*

vandal ['vændl] vandale *m*; **vandalism** vandalisme *m*; **vandalize** vandaliser

vanilla [və'nɪlə] **1** *n* vanille *f* **2** *adj* à la vanille

vanish ['vænɪʃ] disparaître *f*; *of clouds, sadness* se dissiper

vanity ['vænətɪ] *of person* vanité *f*

vapor ['veɪpər] vapeur *f*; **vaporize** *of atomic bomb, explosion* pulvériser; **vapour** *Br* → **vapor**

variable [və'nɪlə] **1** *adj* variable; *moods* changeant **2** *n* MATH, COMPUT variable *f*; **variant** variante *f*; **variation** va-

riation *f*; **varied** varié; **variety** variété *f*; **various** (*several*) divers, plusieurs; (*different*) divers, différent

varnish ['vɑːrnɪʃ] **1** *n* vernis *m* **2** *v/t* vernir

vary ['verɪ] varier; *it varies* ça dépend

vase [veɪz] vase *m*

vast [væst] vaste; *improvement* considérable; **vastly** *improve etc* considérablement; *different* complètement

Vatican ['vætɪkən]: **the ~** le Vatican

vault[1] [vɔːlt] *n in roof* voûte *f*; **~s** *of bank* salle *f* des coffres

vault[2] [vɔːlt] **1** *n* SP saut *m* **2** *v/t beam etc* sauter

VCR [viːsiːˈɑːr] (= **video cassette recorder**) magnétoscope *m*

veal [viːl] veau *m*

veer [vɪr] virer; *of wind* tourner

vegetable ['vedʒtəbl] légume *m*; **vegetarian 1** *n* végétarien(ne) *m(f)* **2** *adj* végétarien; **vegetation** végétation *f*

vehement ['viːəmənt] véhément

vehicle ['viːɪkl] véhicule *m*

veil [veɪl] voile *m*

vein [veɪn] ANAT veine *f*

velocity [vɪˈlɑːsətɪ] vélocité *f*

velvet ['velvɪt] velours *m*

vendetta [ven'detə] vendetta *f*

vending machine ['vendɪŋ

distributeur *m* automatique; **vendor** LAW vendeur(-euse) *m(f)*

veneer [vəˈnɪr] placage *m*; *of politeness* vernis *m*

venerable [ˈvenərəbl] vénérable; **veneration** vénération *f*

venereal disease [vəˈniːʃn] M.S.T. *f*, maladie *f* sexuellement transmissible

venetian blind [vəˈniːʃn] store *m* vénitien

venom [ˈvenəm] venin *m*

ventilate [ˈventɪleɪt] ventiler; **ventilation** ventilation *f*; **ventilator** ventilateur *m*; MED respirateur *m*

venture [ˈventʃər] **1** *n (undertaking)* entreprise *f*; COM tentative *f* **2** *v/i* s'aventurer

venue [ˈvenjuː] *for meeting, concert etc* lieu *m*; *hall also* salle *f*

veranda [vəˈrændə] véranda *f*

verb [vɜːrb] verbe *m*; **verbal** *(spoken)* oral, verbal; **verbally** oralement, verbalement

verdict [ˈvɜːrdɪkt] LAW verdict *m*; *(opinion, judgment)* avis *m*, jugement *m*

verge [vɜːrdʒ] *of road* accotement *m*, bas-côté *m*; **be on the ~ of ...** être au bord de...

verification [verɪfɪˈkeɪʃn] *(check)* vérification *f*; **verify** *(check)* vérifier, contrôler; *(confirm)* confirmer

vermin [ˈvɜːrmɪn] *(insects)* vermine *f*, parasites *mpl*; *(rats etc)* animaux *mpl* nuisibles

vermouth [vərˈmuːθ] vermouth *m*

versatile [ˈvɜːrsətəl] *person* plein de ressources, polyvalent; *piece of equipment* multiusages; **versatility** *of person* adaptabilité *f*, polyvalence *f*; *of piece of equipment* souplesse *f* d'emploi

verse [vɜːrs] *(poetry)* vers *mpl*, poésie *f*; *of poem* strophe *f*; *of song* couplet *m*

version [ˈvɜːrʃn] version *f*

versus [ˈvɜːrsəs] contre

vertical [ˈvɜːrtɪkl] vertical

vertigo [ˈvɜːrtɪɡoʊ] vertige *m*

very [ˈveri] **1** *adv* très; **was it cold? – not ~** faisait-il froid? – non, pas tellement; **the ~ best** le meilleur **2** *adj* même; **at that ~ moment** à cet instant même, à ce moment précis; **that's the ~ thing I need** c'est exactement ce dont j'ai besoin

vessel [ˈvesl] NAUT bateau *m*, navire *m*

vest [vest] gilet *m*; *Br: undershirt* maillot *m* (de corps)

vestige [ˈvestɪdʒ] vestige *m*; *fig* once *f*

vet¹ [vet] *n (veterinarian)* vétérinaire *m/f*, véto *m/f*

vet² [vet] *v/t applicants etc* examiner

vet³ [vet] *n* MIL F ancien combattant *m*

veteran [ˈvetərən] **1** *n* vétéran *m* **2** *adj (old)* antique; *(old* *and experienced*) aguerri, chevronné

veterinarian [vetərə'neriən] vétérinaire *m/f*

veto ['vi:təʊ] **1** *n* veto *m inv* **2** *v/t* opposer son veto à

via ['vaɪə] par

viable ['vaɪəbl] viable

vibrate [vaɪ'breɪt] vibrer; **vibration** vibration *f*

vice[1] [vaɪs] *n* vice *m*

vice[2] [vaɪs] *Br* → **vise**

vice 'president vice-président *m*

vice versa [vaɪs'vɜːrsə] vice versa

vicious ['vɪʃəs] vicieux; *dog* méchant; *person, temper* cruel; *attack* brutal; **viciously** brutalement

victim ['vɪktɪm] victime *f*; **victimize** persécuter

victorious [vɪk'tɔːrɪəs] victorieux; **victory** victoire *f*

video ['vɪdɪəʊ] **1** *n* vidéo *f*; *actual object* cassette *f* vidéo **2** *v/t* filmer; *tape off TV* enregistrer; **video camera** caméra *f* vidéo; **video cassette** cassette *f* vidéo; **video recorder** magnétoscope *m*; **videotape** bande *f* vidéo

vie [vaɪ] rivaliser

Vietnam [vɪet'næm] Vietnam *m*; **Vietnamese 1** *adj* vietnamien **2** *n* Vietnamien(ne) *m(f)*; *language* vietnamien *m*

view [vjuː] **1** *n* vue *f*; (*assessment, opinion*) opinion *f*, avis

m; **in** ~ **of** compte tenu de, étant donné **2** *v/t* considérer, envisager **3** *v/i* (*watch TV*) regarder la télévision; **viewer** TV téléspectateur(-trice) *m(f)*; **viewpoint** point *m* de vue

vigor ['vɪgər] vigueur *f*; **vigorous** vigoureux; **vigorously** vigoureusement; **vigour** *Br* → **vigor**

village ['vɪlɪdʒ] village *m*; **villager** villageois(e) *m(f)*

villain ['vɪlən] escroc *m*; *in drama* méchant *m*

vindicate ['vɪndɪkeɪt] (*prove correct*) confirmer, justifier; (*prove innocent*) innocenter

vindictive [vɪn'dɪktɪv] vindicatif

vine [vaɪn] vigne *f*

vinegar ['vɪnɪgər] vinaigre *m*

vineyard ['vɪnjɑːrd] vignoble *m*

vintage ['vɪntɪdʒ] **1** *n of wine* millésime *m* **2** *adj* (*classic*) classique

violate ['vaɪəleɪt] violer; **violation** violation *f*; (*traffic ~*) infraction *f* au code de la route

violence ['vaɪələns] violence *f*; **violent** violent

violin [vaɪə'lɪn] violon *m*; **violinist** violoniste *m/f*

VIP [viːaɪ'piː] (= *very important person*) V.I.P. *m*

viral ['vaɪrəl] viral

virgin ['vɜːrdʒɪn] vierge *f*;

male puceau *m* F; **virginity** virginité *f*

virile ['vɪraɪl] viril; **virility** virilité *f*

virtual ['vɜːrtʃʊəl] quasi-; **virtually** (*almost*) pratiquement, presque

virtue ['vɜːrtʃuː] vertu *f*; **virtuous** vertueux

virus ['vaɪrəs] virus *m*

visa ['viːzə] visa *m*

vise [vaɪz] étau *m*

visibility [vɪzə'bɪlɪti] visibilité *f*; **visible** visible

vision ['vɪʒn] (*eyesight*) vue *f*; REL vision *f*

visit ['vɪzɪt] **1** *n* visite *f*; (*stay*) séjour *m* **2** *v/t* rendre visite à; *doctor, dentist* aller voir; *city, country* aller à; *castle, museum* visiter; *website* consulter; (*guest*) invité *m*; (*tourist*) visiteur *m*

visor ['vaɪzər] visière *f*

visual ['vɪʒʊəl] visuel; **visualize** (*imagine*) (s')imaginer; (*foresee*) envisager, prévoir; **visually** visuellement

vital ['vaɪtl] (*essential*) vital, essentiel; **vitality** vitalité *f*; **vitally**: ~ **important** d'une importance capitale

vitamin ['vaɪtəmɪn] vitamine *f*; **vitamin pill** comprimé *m* de vitamines

vivacious [vɪ'veɪʃəs] plein de vivacité, vif; **vivacity** vivacité *f*

vivid ['vɪvɪd] vif; *description* vivant; **vividly** vivement; *re-*

member clairement; *describe* de façon vivante

V-neck ['viːnek] col *m* en V

vocabulary [vou'kæbjʊlərɪ] vocabulaire *m*; (*list of words*) glossaire *m*

vocal ['voukl] vocal; **vocalist** MUS chanteur(-euse) *m(f)*

vocation [və'keɪʃn] vocation *f*; **vocational** *guidance* professionnel

vodka ['vɑːdkə] vodka *f*

vogue [voug] vogue *f*; **be in ~** être en vogue

voice [vɔɪs] **1** *n* voix *f* **2** *v/t* *opinions* exprimer; **voicemail** messagerie *f* vocale

volcano [vɑːl'keɪnou] volcan *m*

volley ['vɑːlɪ] volée *f*

volt [voult] volt *m*; **voltage** tension *f*

volume ['vɑːljəm] volume *m*

voluntarily [vɑːlən'terɪlɪ] de son plein gré, volontairement; **voluntary** volontaire; *work* bénévole; **volunteer 1** *n* volontaire *m/f*; (*unpaid worker*) bénévole *m/f* **2** *v/i* se porter volontaire

vomit ['vɑːmɪt] **1** *n* vomi *m*, vomissure *f* **2** *v/i* vomir

voracious [və'reɪʃəs] vorace; *reader* avide

vote [vout] **1** *n* vote *m* **2** *v/i* POL voter (*for* pour; *against* contre); **voter** POL électeur *m*; **voting** POL vote *m*

♦ **vouch for** [vautʃ] *truth, person* se porter garant de

vow [vaʊ] **1** n vœu m, serment m **2** v/t: **~ to do** jurer de faire
vowel [vaʊl] voyelle f
voyage ['vɔɪdʒ] voyage m

vulgar ['vʌlgər] vulgaire
vulnerable ['vʌlnərəbl] vulnérable
vulture ['vʌltʃər] vautour m

W

waddle ['wɑːdl] se dandiner
wade [weɪd] patauger
wafer ['weɪfər] cookie gaufrette f; REL hostie f
waffle ['wɑːfl] te eat gaufre f
wag [wæg] remuer
wages ['weɪdʒɪz] salaire m
waggle ['wægl] remuer
wail [weɪl] hurler
waist [weɪst] taille f
wait [weɪt] **1** n attente f **2** v/i attendre
◆ **wait for** attendre
◆ **wait on** (serve) servir
◆ **wait up**: **don't wait up (for me)** ne m'attends pas pour aller te coucher
waiter ['weɪtər] serveur m; **~!** garçon!; **waiting list** liste f d'attente; **waiting room** salle f d'attente; **waitress** serveuse f
waive [weɪv] renoncer à
wake [weɪk] **1** v/i: **~ (up)** se réveiller **2** v/t person réveiller
walk [wɔːk] **1** n marche f; (path) allée f; **go for a ~** aller se promener **2** v/i marcher; as opposed to driving aller à pied; (hike) faire de la marche **3** v/t dog promener
◆ **walk out** of spouse prendre

la porte; from theater etc partir; (go on strike) se mettre en grève
walker ['wɔːkər] (hiker) randonneur(-euse) m(f); for baby trotte-bébé m; for old person déambulateur m; **walking** (hiking) randonnée f; **walkout** (strike) grève f; **walkover** (easy win) victoire f facile
wall [wɔːl] mur m
wallet ['wɑːlɪt] (billfold) portefeuille m
'**wallpaper 1** n also COMPUT papier m peint **2** v/t tapisser; **wall-to-wall carpet** moquette f
waltz [wɔːlts] valse f
wan [wɑːn] face pâlot
wander ['wɑːndər] (roam) errer; (stray) s'égarer
wangle ['wæŋgl] F réussir à obtenir (par une combine)
want [wɑːnt] **1** n: **for ~ of** par manque de, faute de **2** v/t vouloir; (need) avoir besoin de; **~ to do sth** vouloir faire qch; **I ~ to stay here** je veux rester ici; **she ~s you to go back** elle veut que tu reviennes (subj) **3** v/i: **~ for nothing**

ne manquer de rien; **wanted by police** recherché

war [wɔːr] guerre *f*; *fig* lutte *f*

ward [wɔːrd] *Br: in hospital* salle *f*; *child* pupille *m/f*

◆ **ward off** éviter

warden ['wɔːrdn] *of prison* gardien (ne) *m(f)*; *Br: of hostel* directeur (-trice) *m (f)*

'**wardrobe** *for clothes* armoire *f*; *(clothes)* garde-robe *f*

warehouse ['werhaʊs] entrepôt *m*

'**warfare** guerre *f*; **warhead** ogive *f*

warily ['werɪlɪ] avec méfiance

warm [wɔːrm] chaud; *welcome, smile* chaleureux

◆ **warm up 1** *v/t* réchauffer **2** *v/i* se réchauffer; *of athlete etc* s'échauffer

warmly ['wɔːrmlɪ] *dress* chaudement; *welcome, smile* chaleureusement; **warmth** *also fig* chaleur *f*; **warm-up** SP échauffement *m*

warn [wɔːrn] prévenir; **warning** avertissement *m*

warp [wɔːrp] *of wood* gauchir; **warped** *fig* tordu

warrant ['wɔːrənt] **1** *n* mandat *m* **2** *v/t* justifier; **warranty** garantie *f*

warrior ['wɔːrɪər] guerrier (-ière) *m(f)*

wart [wɔːrt] verrue *f*

wary ['werɪ] méfiant; **be ~ of** se méfier de

wash [wɑːʃ] **1** *n*: **have a ~** se laver **2** *v/t clothes, dishes* laver **3** *v/i* se laver

◆ **wash up** *(wash one's hands and face)* se débarbouiller

washable ['wɑːʃəbl] lavable; **washbasin, washbowl** lavabo *m*; **washcloth** gant *m* de toilette; **washed out** *(tired)* usé; **washer** *for faucet etc* rondelle *f*; **washing** lessive *f*; **do the ~** faire la lessive; **washing machine** machine *f* à laver; **washroom** toilettes *fpl*

wasp [wɑːsp] guêpe *f*

waste [weɪst] **1** *n* gaspillage *m*; *from industrial process* déchets *mpl*; **it's a ~ of time/money** c'est une perte de temps/d'argent **2** *adj* non utilisé **3** *v/t* gaspiller; **waste basket** corbeille *f* à papier; **waste disposal (unit)** broyeur *m* d'ordures; **wasteful** gaspilleur; **wasteland** désert *m*; **wastepaper** papier(s) *m(pl)* (jeté(s) à la poubelle)

watch [wɑːtʃ] **1** *n timepiece* montre *f*; **keep ~** monter la garde *f*; *(look after)* surveiller **3** *v/i* regarder; **watchful** vigilant

water ['wɔːtər] **1** *n* eau *f* **2** *v/t plant* arroser **3** *v/i*: **my mouth is ~ing** j'ai l'eau à la bouche; **watercolor**, *Br* **watercolour** aquarelle *f*; **watered down** *fig* atténué; **waterfall** chute *f* d'eau; **waterline** ligne *f* de flottaison; **waterlogged** détrempé; *boat* plein d'eau; **watermelon** pastèque *f*; **waterproof** imperméable; **terside** bord *m* de l'eau; **waterskiing** ski *m* nautique; **watertight** *compartment* étanche; *fig: alibi* parfait; **waterway** voie *f* d'eau; **watery** *soup* trop clair; *coffee* trop léger

watt [wɑːt] watt *m*

wave¹ [weɪv] *n in sea* vague *f*

wave² [weɪv] **1** *n of hand* signe *m* **2** *v/i with hand* saluer; *of flag* flotter **3** *v/t flag ein* agiter

'wavelength RAD longueur *f* d'onde; **be on the same ~** *fig* être sur la même longueur d'onde

waver ['weɪvər] hésiter

wavy ['weɪvɪ] ondulé

wax [wæks] cire *f*

way [weɪ] (*method, manner*) façon *f*; (*route*) chemin *m* (**to** de); **this ~** (*like this*) comme ça; (*in this direction*) par ici; **by the ~** (*incidentally*) au fait; **in a ~** (*in certain respects*) d'une certaine façon; **lose one's ~** se perdre; **be in the ~** (*be an obstruction*) gêner le passage; *disturb*) gêner; **no ~!** pas question!; **way in** entrée *f*; **way of life** mode *m* de vie; **way out** sortie *f*; *fig* issue *f*

we [wiː] nous

weak [wiːk] faible; *tea, coffee* léger; **weaken 1** *v/t* affaiblir

2 *v/i* s'affaiblir; *in negotiation etc* faiblir; **weakness** faiblesse *f*

wealth [welθ] richesse *f*; **wealthy** riche

weapon ['wepən] arme *f*

wear [wer] **1** *n:* **~ (and tear)** usure *f* **2** *v/t* (*have on*) porter; (*damage*) user **3** *v/i* (*wear out*) s'user; **~ well** (*last*) faire bon usage

◆ **wear down** user

◆ **wear off** *of effect* se dissiper

◆ **wear out 1** *v/t* (*tire*) épuiser; *shoes, carpet* user **2** *v/i of shoes, carpet* s'user

wearily ['wɪrɪlɪ] avec lassitude; **weary** las

weather ['weðər] **1** *n* temps *m* **2** *v/t crisis* survivre à; **weather-beaten** hâlé; **weather forecast** prévisions météorologiques *fpl*, météo *f*; **weatherman** présentateur *m* météo

weave [wiːv] **1** *v/t cloth* tisser **2** *v/i of cyclist* se faufiler

web [web] *of spider* toile *f*; **the ~** COMPUT le Web; **web page** page *f* de Web; **web site** site *m* Web

wedding ['wedɪŋ] mariage *m*; **wedding anniversary** anniversaire *m* de mariage; **wedding day** jour *m* de mariage; **wedding dress** robe *f* de mariée; **wedding ring** alliance *f*

wedge [wedʒ] *to hold sth in*

place cale *f*; *of cheese etc* morceau *m*

Wednesday ['wenzdeɪ] mercredi *m*

weed [wiːd] **1** *n* mauvaise herbe *f* **2** *v/t* désherber; **weedkiller** herbicide *f*; **weedy** F chétif

week [wiːk] semaine *f*; *a ~ tomorrow* demain en huit; **weekday** jour *m* de la semaine; **weekend** week-end *m*; *on the ~* this one ce week-end; *every one* le week-end; **weekly 1** *adj* hebdomadaire **2** *n* magazine hebdomadaire *m* **3** *adv* be published toutes les semaines; *be paid* à la semaine

weep [wiːp] pleurer

wee-wee ['wiːwiː] F pipi *m* F; *do a ~* faire pipi

weigh [weɪ] peser

◆ **weigh up** (*assess*) juger

weight [weɪt] poids *m*; **weightlessness** apesanteur *f*; **weightlifter** haltérophile *m/f*; **weightlifting** haltérophilie *f*; **weighty** *fig* (*important*) sérieux

weir [wɪr] barrage *m*

weird [wɪrd] bizarre; **weirdo** F cinglé(e) *m(f)* F

welcome ['welkəm] **1** *adj* bienvenu; *you're ~!* je vous en prie! **2** *n* accueil *m* **3** *v/t* accueillir; *fig: news, announcement* se réjouir de; *opportunity* saisir

weld [weld] souder

welfare ['welfer] bien-être *m*; *financial assistance* sécurité *f* sociale; *be on ~* toucher les allocations; **welfare check** chèque *m* d'allocations; **welfare state** État *m* providence; **welfare worker** assistant social *m*, assistante sociale *f*

well[1] [wel] *n* for water, oil puits *m*

well[2] [wel] **1** *adv* bien; *~ done!* bien!; *as ~* (*too*) aussi; *as ~ as* (in addition to) en plus de; *very ~* acknowledging order entendu; reluctantly agreeing très bien; *~, ~!* surprise tiens, tiens!; *~ ... uncertainty, thinking* eh bien ... **2** *adj:* **be ~** aller bien; **well-balanced** équilibré; **well-behaved** bien élevé; **well-being** bien-être *m*; **well-done** *meat* bien cuit; **well-dressed** bien habillé; **well-earned** bien mérité; **well-heeled** F cossu; **well-informed** bien informé; **well-known** connu; **well-meaning** plein de bonnes intentions; **well-off** riche; **well-timed** bien calculé; **well-wisher** personne *f* apportant son soutien

west [west] **1** *n* ouest *m* **2** *adj* ouest *inv*; *wind* d'ouest **3** *adj travel* vers l'ouest; **westerly** *wind* d'ouest; *direction* vers l'ouest; **western 1** *adj* de l'Ouest **2** *n* movie western *m*; **Westerner** occidental(e); **westernized** occidentalisé

West Indian 1 *adj* antillais **2** *n* Antillais(e) *m(f)*; **West Indies: the** ~ les Antilles *fpl*; **westward** vers l'ouest

wet [wet] mouillé; (*rainy*) humide; **wet suit** *for diving* combinaison *f* de plongée

whack [wæk] F (*blow*) coup *m*

whale [weɪl] baleine *f*

what [wɒt] **1** *pron* ◇ : ~? quoi?; ~ **for?** (*why?*) pourquoi?; **so ~?** et alors?
◇ *as object:* ~ **did he say?** qu'est-ce qu'il a dit?, qu'a-t-il dit?; ~ **is that?** qu'est-ce que c'est?; ~ **is it?** (*what do you want?*) qu'est-ce qu'il y a?
◇ *as subject* qu'est-ce qui; ~ **just fell off?** qu'est-ce qui vient de tomber?
◇ *relative as object* ce que; **I did** ~ **I could** j'ai fait ce que j'ai pu
◇ *relative as subject* ce qui; **I didn't see** ~ **happened** je n'ai pas vu ce qui s'est passé
◇ *suggestions:* ~ **about heading home?** et si nous rentrions? **2** *adj* quel, quelle; *pl* quels, quelles; ~ **color is the car?** de quelle couleur est la voiture?

whatever [wɒt'evər]: ~ **the season** quelle que soit la saison; ~ **you do** quoi que tu fasses; **ok,** ~ F ok, si vous le dites

wheat [wiːt] blé *m*

wheel [wiːl] roue *f*; (*steering* ~) volant *m*; **wheelchair** fauteuil *m* roulant; **wheel clamp** *Br* sabot *m* de Denver

wheeze [wiːz] respirer péniblement

when [wen] quand; **on the day** ~ le jour où; **whenever** *each time* chaque fois que; *regardless of when* n'importe quand

where [wer] où; ~ **from?** d'où?; ~ **to?** où?; **this is I used to live** c'est là que j'habitais; **whereas** tandis que; **wherever 1** *conj* partout où; **sit** ~ **you like** assieds-toi où tu veux **2** *adv* où (donc); ~ **can it be?** où peut-il bien être?

whet [wet] *appetite* aiguiser

whether ['weðər] (*if*) si; ~ **you approve or not** que tu sois (*subj*) d'accord ou pas

which [wɪtʃ] **1** *adj* quel, quelle; *pl* quels, quelles **2** *pron* ~ *interrogative* lequel, laquelle; *pl* lesquels, lesquelles; ~ **are your favorites?** lesquels préférez-vous?
◇ *relative: subject* qui; *object* que; *after prep* lequel, laquelle; *pl* lesquels, lesquelles

whiff [wɪf]: **catch a** ~ **of** sentir

while [waɪl] **1** *conj* pendant que; (*although*) bien que (+*subj*) **2** *n*: **a long** ~ longtemps; **for a** ~ pendant un moment

whim [wɪm] caprice *m*

whimper ['wɪmpər] pleurnicher; *of animal* geindre

whine [waɪn] *of dog etc* gémir; F (*complain*) pleurnicher

whip [wɪp] **1** *n* fouet *m* **2** *v/t* (*beat*) fouetter; *cream* battre; F (*defeat*) battre à plates coutures

whirlpool [ˈwɜːrlpuːl] *in river* tourbillon *m*; *for relaxation* bain *m* à remous

whisk [wɪsk] **1** *n* fouet *m* **2** *v/t eggs* battre

whiskey [ˈwɪskɪ] whisky *m*

whisper [ˈwɪspər] chuchoter

whistle [ˈwɪsl] **1** *n sound* sifflement *m*; *device* sifflet *m* **2** *v/t & v/i* siffler

white [waɪt] **1** *n color, of egg* blanc *m*; *person* Blanc *m*, Blanche *f* **2** *adj* blanc; **white-collar worker** col *m* blanc; **White House** Maison *f* Blanche; **white lie** pieux mensonge *m*; **whitewash 1** *n* blanc *m* de chaux; *fig* maquillage *m* de la vérité **2** *v/t* blanchir à la chaux; **white wine** *m* blanc

whittle [ˈwɪtl] *wood* tailler au couteau

◆ **whittle down** réduire

whizzkid [ˈwɪzkɪd] F prodige *m*

who [huː] *interrogative* qui; *relative: subject* qui; *object* que; **the woman ~ you saw** la femme que tu as vue; **whoever** qui que ce soit; **~ gets the right answer** celui/celle qui trouve la bonne réponse

whole [houl] **1** *adj* entier; **the ~ town** toute la ville **2** *n* tout *m*, ensemble *m*; **on the ~** dans l'ensemble; **whole-hearted** inconditionnel; **wholesale** de gros; *fig* en masse; **wholesaler** grossiste *m/f*; **wholesome** sain; **wholly** totalement

whom [huːm] *fml* qui

whore [hɔːr] putain *f*

whose [huːz] *interrogative* à qui; *relative* dont; **~ is this?** à qui c'est?; **a country ~ economy is booming** un pays dont l'économie prospère

why [waɪ] pourquoi

wicked [ˈwɪkɪd] méchant

wicker [ˈwɪkər] osier *m*

wicket [ˈwɪkɪt] *in station, bank* etc guichet *m*

wide [waɪd] *street, field* large; *experience* vaste; **be 12 foot ~** faire 3 mètres et demi de large; **widely** largement; **~ known** très connu; **widen 1** *v/t* élargir **2** *v/i* s'élargir; **wide-open** grand ouvert; **wide-ranging** de vaste portée; **widespread** répandu

widow [ˈwɪdou] veuve *f*; **widower** veuf *m*

width [wɪdθ] largeur *f*

wield [wiːld] *weapon* manier; *power* exercer

wife [waɪf] femme *f*

wig [wɪg] perruque *f*

wiggle [ˈwɪgl] *tooth* etc remuer; *hips* tortiller

winter sports

wild [waɪld] **1** *adj animal,*
flowers sauvage; *teenager* rebelle; *party* fou; *scheme* déli-
rant; *applause* frénétique

wilderness ['wɪldərnɪs] désert *m*

'wildlife faune *f* et flore *f*

wilful *Br* → **willful**

will[1] [wɪl] *n* LAW testament *m*

will[2] [wɪl] *n* (*willpower*) volonté *f*

will[3] [wɪl] *v/aux:* ***I ~ let you***
know tomorrow je vous le
dirai demain; ***the car won't***
start la voiture ne veut pas
démarrer; ***~ you tell her that***
...? est-ce que tu pourrais lui
dire que ...?; ***~ you stop***
that! veux-tu arrêter!

willful ['wɪlful] *person, refusal*
volontaire; *willing helper*
de bonne volonté; ***be ~ to***
do sth être prêt à faire
qch; **willingly** (*with pleasure*)
volontiers; **willingness** empressement *m*; **willpower** volonté *f*

willy-nilly [wɪlɪ'nɪlɪ] (*at ran-*
dom) au petit bonheur la
chance

wilt [wɪlt] *of plant* se faner

wily ['waɪlɪ] rusé

wimp [wɪmp] F poule *f* mouil-
lée

win [wɪn] **1** *n* victoire *f* **2** *v/t &*
v/i gagner; *prize* remporter

wince [wɪns] tressaillir

wind[1] [wɪnd] *n* vent *m*; (*flatu-*
lence) gaz *m*

wind[2] [waɪnd] **1** *v/i of path,*

river serpenter **2** *v/t* enrouler
◆ **wind up 1** *v/t clock, car*
window remonter; *speech*
terminer; *affairs* conclure;
company liquider **2** *v/i* (*fin-*
ish) finir

'wind-bag F moulin *m* à paroles F; **windfall** *fig* aubaine *f*

winding ['waɪndɪŋ] *path* qui
serpente

window ['wɪndou] *also*
COMPUT fenêtre *f*; *of airplane,*
boat hublot *m*; *of store* vitrine *f*; **in the ~** *of store* dans la
vitrine; **window seat** *on*
train place *f* côté fenêtre;
on airplane place côté hublot; **window-shop**: ***go***
~ping faire du lèche-vitrines;
windowsill rebord *m* de fenêtre; **windshield**, *Br* **windscreen** pare-brise *m*; **windshield wiper** essuie-glace
m; **windsurfer** véliplanchiste
m/f; **windsurfing** planche *f* à
voile; **windy** venteux; ***it's so***
~ il y a tellement de vent

wine [waɪn] vin *m*; **wine cellar**
cave *f* (à vin); **wine list** carte *f*
des vins; **winery** établissement *m* viticole

wing [wɪŋ] *of bird, airplane,* SP
aile *f*; **wingspan** envergure *f*

wink [wɪŋk] *of person* cligner
des yeux

winner ['wɪnər] gagnant(e)
m(f); **winning** gagnant; **winning post** poteau *m* d'arrivée; **winnings** gains *mpl*

winter ['wɪntər] hiver *m*; **win-**

ter sports sports *mpl* d'hiver; **wintry** *m* d'hiver

wipe [waɪp] **1** *v/t* essuyer; *tape* effacer; **wiper** ['waɪpər] → **windshield wiper**

wire ['waɪr] fil *m* de fer; *electrical* fil *m* électrique; **wireless phone** téléphone *m* sans fil; **wiring** ELEC installation *f* électrique; **wiry** *person* nerveux

wisdom ['wɪzdəm] sagesse *f*

wise [waɪz] sage; **wisecrack** F vanne *f* F; **wisely** *act* sagement

wish [wɪʃ] **1** *n* vœu *m*; **best ~es** cordialement; *for birthday, Christmas* meilleurs vœux **2** *v/t* souhaiter

♦ **wish for** vouloir

wisp [wɪsp] *of hair* mèche *m*; *of smoke* traînée *f*

wistful ['wɪstfl] nostalgique; **wistfully** avec nostalgie

wit [wɪt] *(humor)* esprit *m*; *person* homme *m*/femme *f* d'esprit

witch [wɪtʃ] sorcière *f*; **witch-hunt** *fig* chasse *f* aux sorcières

with [wɪð] avec; **~ no money** sans argent; *tired* **~** *waiting* fatigué d'attendre; *the woman* **~** *blue eyes* la femme aux yeux bleus; *I live* **~** *my aunt* je vis chez ma tante; *are you* **~** *me?* (*do you understand?*) est-ce que vous me suivez?

withdraw [wɪð'drɔː] **1** *v/t* reti-

rer **2** *v/i* se retire; **withdrawal** retrait *m*; **withdrawal symptoms** (symptômes *mpl* de) manque *m*; **withdrawn** *person* renfermé

with'hold *information, name, payment* retenir; *consent* refuser

with'in (*inside*) dans; *in expressions of time* en moins de; *in expressions of distance* à moins de

with'out sans

with'stand résister à

witness ['wɪtnɪs] **1** *n* témoin *m* **2** *v/t* être témoin de

witticism ['wɪtɪsɪzm] mot *m* d'esprit; **witty** plein d'esprit

wobble ['wɑːbl] osciller; **wobbly** bancal

wolf [wulf] **1** *n* loup *m* **2** *v/t*: **~** (*down*) engloutir

woman ['wumən] femme *f*; **womanizer** coureur *m* de femmes; **womanly** féminin

womb [wuːm] utérus *m*

women ['wɪmɪn] *pl* → **woman**; **women's lib** libération *f* des femmes

wonder ['wʌndər] **1** *n* (*amazement*) émerveillement *m*; **no ~!** pas étonnant! **2** *v/i* se poser des questions; **I ~** *if you could help* je me demandais si vous pouviez m'aider; **wonderful** merveilleux; **wonderfully** (*extremely*) merveilleusement

won't [woʊnt] → **will not**

wood [wʊd] bois *m*; **wooded** boisé; **wooden** *(made of wood)* en bois; **woodpecker** pic *m*; **woodwork** *parts made of wood* charpente *f*; *activity* menuiserie *f*

wool [wʊl] laine *f*; **woolen**, *Br* **woollen 1** *adj* en laine **2** *n* lainage *m*

word [wɜːrd] **1** *n* mot *m*; *of song*, *(promise)* parole *f* **2** *v/t article*, *letter* formuler; **word processor** traitement *m* de texte

work [wɜːrk] **1** *n* travail *m*; *out of* ~ au chômage **2** *v/i of person* travailler; *of machine*, *(succeed)* marcher

♦ **work out 1** *v/t solution*, *(find out)* trouver; *problem* résoudre **2** *v/i at gym* s'entraîner; *of relationship etc* bien marcher

workable ['wɜːrkəbl] *solution* possible; **workaholic** F bourreau *m* de travail; **workday** *(hours of work)* journée *f* de travail; *(not weekend)* jour *m* de travail; **worker** travailleur(-euse) *m(f)*; **workforce** main-d'œuvre; **work hours** heures *fpl* de travail; **working class** classe *f* ouvrière; **working-class** ouvrier; **working hours →** **work hours**; **workload** quantité *f* de travail; **workman** ouvrier *m*; **workmanlike** de professionnel; **workmanship** fabrication *f*; **work**

of art œuvre *f* d'art; **workout** séance *f* d'entraînement; **work permit** permis *m* de travail; **workshop** *also seminar* atelier *m*

world [wɜːrld] monde *m*; **world-class** de niveau mondial; **World Cup** *in soccer* Coupe *f* du monde; **world-famous** mondialement connu; **worldly** du monde; *person* qui a l'expérience du monde; **world record** record *m* mondial; **world war** guerre *f* mondiale; **worldwide 1** *adj* mondial **2** *adv* dans le monde entier

worn-out *shoes*, *carpet* trop usé; *person* éreinté

worried ['wʌrɪd] inquiet; **worry 1** *n* souci *m* **2** *v/t* inquiéter **3** *v/i* s'inquiéter; **worrying** inquiétant

worse [wɜːrs] **1** *adj* pire **2** *adv play*, *perform*, *feel* plus mal; **worsen** empirer

worship ['wɜːrʃɪp] **1** *n* culte *m* **2** *v/t God* honorer; *fig: person*, *money* vénérer

worst [wɜːrst] **1** *adj* pire **2** *adv:* **the areas ~ affected** les régions les plus (gravement) touchées

worth [wɜːrθ] *be ~ ...* valoir; *be ~ it* valoir la peine; **worthwhile** *it's not ~ waiting* cela ne vaut pas la peine d'attendre

worthy ['wɜːrðɪ] *person*, *cause* digne

would [wʊd]: *I ~ help if I could* je vous aiderais si je pouvais; *~ you like to go to the movies?* est-ce que tu voudrais aller au cinéma?; *~ you tell her …?* pourriez-vous lui dire que …?

wound [wuːnd] **1** *n* blessure *f* **2** *v/t with weapon, words* blesser

wow [waʊ] *int* oh là là!

wrap [ræp] *gift* envelopper; *scarf etc* enrouler; **wrapping** emballage *m*; **wrapping paper** papier *m* d'emballage

wrath [ræθ] colère *f*

wreath [riːθ] couronne *f*

wreck [rek] **1** *n of ship* navire *m* naufragé; *of car* épave *f* **2** *v/t* détruire; **wreckage** *of ship* épave *m*; *of airplane* débris *mpl*; *of marriage, career* restes *mpl*; **wrecker** *truck* dépanneuse *f*

wrench [rentʃ] **1** *n tool* clef *f* **2** *v/t* (*pull*) arracher

wrestle ['resl] lutter; **wrestler** lutteur(-euse) *m(f)*; **wrestling** lutte *f*

wriggle ['rɪgl] (*squirm*) se tortiller

wrinkle ['rɪŋkl] *in skin* ride *f*; *in clothes* pli *m*

wrist [rɪst] poignet *m*; **wristwatch** montre *f*

write [raɪt] écrire; *check* faire
◆ **write off** *debt* amortir; *car* bousiller F

writer ['raɪtər] *of letter, book, song* auteur *m/f*; *of book* écrivain *m/f*; **write-up** critique *f*

writhe [raɪð] se tordre

writing ['raɪtɪŋ] (*handwriting, script*) écriture *f*; (*words*) inscription *f*; *in ~* par écrit; **writing paper** papier *m* à lettres

wrong [rɔːŋ] **1** *adj information, decision, side, number* mauvais; *answer also* faux; *be ~ of person* avoir tort; *of answer* être mauvais; *morally* être mal; *get the ~ train* se tromper de train; *what's ~?* qu'est-ce qu'il y a? **2** *adv* mal; *go ~ of person* se tromper; *of marriage, plan etc* mal tourner **3** *n* mal *m*; *injustice* injustice *f*; **wrongful** injuste; **wrongly** à tort

wry [raɪ] ironique

X, Y

xenophobia [zenoʊ'foʊbɪə] xénophobie *f*

X-ray ['eksreɪ] **1** *n* radio *f* **2** *v/t* radiographier

yacht [jɑːt] yacht *m*; **yachting**

voile *f*

Yank [jæŋk] F Ricain(e) *m(f)* F

yank [jæŋk] *v/t* tirer violemment

yard[1] [jɑːrd] *of prison etc* cour *f*; *behind house* jardin *m*; *for storage* dépôt *m*

yard[2] [jɑːrd] *measurement* yard *m*

'yardstick point *m* de référence

yarn [jɑːrn] *(thread)* fil *m*; F *(story)* (longue) histoire *f*

yawn [jɔːn] **1** *n* bâillement *m* **2** *v/i* bâiller

year [jɪr] année *f*; *be six ~s old* avoir six ans; **yearly 1** *adj* annuel **2** *adv* tous les ans

yeast [jiːst] levure *f*

yell [jel] **1** *n* hurlement *m* **2** *v/t & v/i* hurler

yellow ['jeləu] jaune

yelp [jelp] **1** *n of animal* jappement *m*; *of person* glapissement *m* **2** *v/i of animal* japper; *of person* glapir

yes [jes] oui; *after negative question* si; **yes man** *pej* béni-oui-oui *m* F

yesterday ['jestərdeɪ] hier; *the day before ~* avant-hier

yet [jet] **1** *adv*: *the best ~* le meilleur jusqu'ici; *as ~* pour le moment; *have you finished ~?* as-tu (déjà) fini?; *he hasn't arrived ~* il n'est pas encore arrivé; *~ bigger* encore plus grand **2** *conj* (*however*) néanmoins

yield [jiːld] **1** *n from crops, investment etc* rendement *m* **2** *v/t fruit, good harvest* produire; *interest* rapporter **3** *v/i* (*give way*) céder; AUT céder

la priorité

yoga ['jəugə] yoga *m*

yoghurt ['jɔugərt] yaourt *m*

yolk [jəuk] jaune *m* (d'œuf)

you [juː] ◇ *familiar singular: subject* tu; *object* te; *before vowel* t'; *after prep* toi; *he knows ~* il te connaît; *for ~* pour toi

◇ *polite singular, familiar plural and polite plural, all uses* vous

◇ *indefinite* on; *~ never know* on ne sait jamais

young [jʌŋ] jeune; *youngster* jeune *m/f*; *child* petit(e) *m(f)*

your [jʊr] *familiar* ton, ta; *pl* tes; *polite* votre; *pl familiar and polite* vos

yours [jʊrz] *familiar* le tien, la tienne; *pl* les tiens, les tiennes; *polite* le/la vôtre; *pl* les vôtres; *a friend of ~* un(e) de tes ami(e)s; un(e) de vos ami(e)s; *~ at end of letter* amicalement

your'self *familiar* toi-même; *polite* vous-même; *reflexive* te; *after prep* toi; *polite* se; *did you hurt ~?* est-ce que t'es fait mal/ est-ce que vous vous êtes fait mal?

your'selves vous-mêmes; *reflexive* vous; *after prep* vous; *did you hurt ~?* est-ce que vous vous êtes fait mal?

youth [juːθ] jeunesse *f*; (*young man*) jeune homme *m*; (*young people*) jeunes *mpl*; **youth club** centre *m* pour les jeunes; **youthful** juvénile

yuppie ['jʌpɪ] F yuppie *m/f*

Z

zap [zæp] F COMPUT (*delete*) effacer; (*kill*) éliminer; (*hit*) donner un coup à; (*send*) envoyer vite fait

zeal [ziːl] zèle *m*

zero ['zɪrou] zéro *m*

zest [zest] *enjoyment* enthousiasme *m*

zigzag ['zɪgzæg] **1** *n* zigzag *m* **2** *v/i* zigzaguer

zilch [zɪltʃ] F que dalle F

zip [zɪp] *Br* fermeture *f* éclair

♦ **zip up** *dress, jacket* remonter la fermeture éclair de;

COMPUT compresser

'zip code code *m* postal; **zipper** fermeture *f* éclair

zit [zɪt] F *on face* bouton *m*

zone [zoun] zone *f*

zonked [zɑːŋkt] P (*exhausted*) crevé F

zoo [zuː] jardin *m* zoologique

zoology [zuːˈɑːlədʒɪ] zoologie *f*

'zoom lens zoom *m*

zucchini [zuːˈkiːnɪ] courgette *f*

Verbes irréguliers anglais

Vous trouverez ci-après les trois formes principales de chaque verbe : l'infinitif, le prétérit et le participe passé.

arise - arose - arisen

awake - awoke - awoken, awaked

be (am, is, are) - was (were) - been

bear - bore - borne

beat - beat - beaten

become - became - become

begin - began - begun

bend - bent - bent

bet - bet, betted - bet, betted

bid - bid - bid

bind - bound - bound

bite - bit - bitten

bleed - bled - bled

blow - blew - blown

break - broke - broken

breed - bred - bred

bring - brought - brought

broadcast - broadcast - broadcast

build - built - built

burn - burnt, burned - burnt, burned

burst - burst - burst

buy - bought - bought

cast - cast - cast

catch - caught - caught

choose - chose - chosen

cling - clung - clung

come - came - come

cost (*v/i*) - cost - cost

creep - crept - crept

cut - cut - cut

deal - dealt - dealt

dig - dug - dug

dive - dived, dove [douv] (1) - dived

do - did - done

draw - drew - drawn

dream - dreamt, dreamed - dreamt, dreamed

drink - drank - drunk

drive - drove - driven

eat - ate - eaten.

fall - fell - fallen

feed - fed - fed

feel - felt - felt

fight - fought - fought

find - found - found

flee - fled - fled

fling - flung - flung

fly - flew - flown

forbid - forbad(e) - forbidden

forecast - forecast(ed) - forecast(ed)

forget - forgot - forgotten

forgive - forgave - forgiven

freeze - froze - frozen

get - got - got, gotten (2)

give - gave - given

go – went – gone
grind – ground – ground
grow – grew – grown
hang – hung, hanged – hung, hanged (3)
have – had – had
hear – heard – heard
hide – hid – hidden
hit – hit – hit
hold – held – held
hurt – hurt – hurt
keep – kept – kept
kneel – knelt, kneeled – knelt, kneeled
know – knew – known
lay – laid – laid
lead – led – led
lean – leaned, leant – leaned, leant (4)
leap – leaped, leapt – leaped, leapt (4)
learn – learned, learnt – learned, learnt (4)
leave – left – left
lend – lent – lent
let – let – let
lie – lay – lain
light – lighted, lit – lighted, lit
lose – lost – lost
make – made – made
mean – meant – meant
meet – met – met
mow – mowed – mowed, mown

pay – paid – paid
plead – pleaded, pled – pleaded, pled (5)
prove – proved – proved, proven
put – put – put
quit – quit(ted) – quit(ted)
read – read [red] – read [red]
ride – rode – ridden
ring – rang – rung
rise – rose – risen
run – ran – run
saw – sawed – sawn, sawed
say – said – said
see – saw – seen
seek – sought – sought
sell – sold – sold
send – sent – sent
set – set – set
sew – sewed – sewed, sewn
shake – shook – shaken
shed – shed – shed
shine – shone – shone
shit – shit(ted), shat – shit(ted), shat
shoot – shot – shot
show – showed – shown
shrink – shrank – shrunk
shut – shut – shut
sing – sang – sung
sink – sank – sunk
sit – sat – sat
slay – slew – slain
sleep – slept – slept
slide – slid – slid

sling - slung - slung	**stride** - strode - stridden
slit - slit - slit	**strike** - struck - struck
smell - smelt, smelled - smelt, smelled	**swear** - swore - sworn
sow - sowed - sown, sowed	**sweep** - swept - swept
speak - spoke - spoken	**swell** - swelled - swollen
speed - sped, speeded - sped, speeded	**swim** - swam - swum
	swing - swung - swung
spell - spelt, spelled - spelt, spelled (4)	**take** - took - taken
	teach - taught - taught
spend - spent - spent	**tear** - tore - torn
spill - spilt, spilled - spilt, spilled	**tell** - told - told
	think - thought - thought
spin - spun - spun	
spit - spat - spat	**thrive** - throve - thriven, thrived (6)
split - split - split	
spoil - spoiled, spoilt - spoiled, spoilt	**throw** - threw - thrown
	thrust - thrust - thrust
spread - spread - spread	**tread** - trod - trodden
spring - sprang, sprung - sprung	**wake** - woke, waked - woken, waked
stand - stood - stood	**wear** - wore - worn
steal - stole - stolen	**weave** - wove - woven (7)
stick - stuck - stuck	**weep** - wept - wept
sting - stung - stung	**win** - won - won
stink - stunk, stank - stunk	**wind** - wound - wound
	write - wrote - written

(1) **dove** n'est pas utilisé en anglais britannique

(2) **gotten** n'est pas utilisé en anglais britannique

(3) **hung** pour les tableaux mais **hanged** pour les meurtriers

(4) l'anglais américain n'emploie normalement que la forme en **-ed**

(5) **pled** s'emploie en anglais américain ou écossais

(6) la forme **thrived** est plus courante

(7) mais **weaved** au sens de *se faufiler*

Numbers / Les nombres

Cardinal Numbers / Les nombres cardinaux

0	zero, *Br aussi*	14	fourteen *quatorze*
	nought *zéro*	15	fifteen *quinze*
1	one *un*	16	sixteen *seize*
2	two *deux*	17	seventeen *dix-sept*
3	three *trois*	18	eighteen *dix-huit*
4	four *quatre*	19	nineteen *dix-neuf*
5	five *cinq*	20	twenty *vingt*
6	six *six*	21	twenty-one *vingt et un*
7	seven *sept*	22	twenty-two *vingt-deux*
8	eight *huit*	30	thirty *trente*
9	nine *neuf*	31	thirty-one *trente et un*
10	ten *dix*	40	forty *quarante*
11	eleven *onze*	50	fifty *cinquante*
12	twelve *douze*	60	sixty *soixante*
13	thirteen *treize*	70	seventy *soixante-dix*

71	seventy-one *soixante et onze*
72	seventy-two *soixante-douze*
79	seventy-nine *soixante-dix-neuf*
80	eighty *quatre-vingts*
81	eighty-one *quatre-vingt-un*
90	ninety *quatre-vingt-dix*
91	ninety-one *quatre-vingt-onze*
100	a hundred, one hundred *cent*
101	a hundred and one *cent un*
200	two hundred *deux cents*
300	three hundred *trois cents*
324	three hundred and twenty-four *trois cent vingt-quatre*
1000	a thousand, one thousand *mille*
2000	two thousand *deux mille*

1959	one thousand nine hundred and fifty-nine
	mille neuf cent cinquante-neuf
2000	two thousand *deux mille*
1 000 000	a million, one million *un million*
2 000 000	two million *deux millions*
1 000 000 000	a billion, one billion *un milliard*

Notes / Remarques:

i) **vingt** and **cent** take an -s when preceded by another number, except if there is another number following.

ii) If **un** is used with a following noun, then it is the only number to agree (one man **un homme**; one woman **une femme**).

iii) 1.25 (one point two five) = 1,25 (un virgule vingt-cinq)

iv) 1,000,000 (en anglais) = 1 000 000 ou 1.000.000 (in French)

Ordinal Numbers / Les nombres ordinaux

1st first	1er/1ère *premier / première*
2nd second	2e *deuxième*
3rd third	3e *troisième*
4th fourth	4e *quatrième*
5th fifth	5e *cinquième*
6th sixth	6e *sixième*
7th seventh	7e *septième*
8th eighth	8e *huitième*
9th ninth	9e *neuvième*
10th tenth	10e *dixième*
11th eleventh	11e *onzième*
12th twelfth	12e *douzième*
13th thirteenth	13e *treizième*
14th fourteenth	14e *quatorzième*
15th fifteenth	15e *quinzième*

16th	sixteenth	16ᵉ	*seizième*
17th	seventeenth	17ᵉ	*dix-septième*
18th	eighteenth	18ᵉ	*dix-huitième*
19th	nineteenth	19ᵉ	*dix-neuvième*
20th	twentieth	20ᵉ	*vingtième*
21st	twenty-first	21ᵉ	*vingt et unième*
22nd	twenty second	22ᵉ	*vingt-deuxième*
30th	thirtieth	30ᵉ	*trentième*
31st	thirty-first	31ᵉ	*trente et unième*
40th	fortieth	40ᵉ	*quarantième*
50th	fiftieth	50ᵉ	*cinquantième*
60th	sixtieth	60ᵉ	*soixantième*
70th	seventieth	70ᵉ	*soixante-dixième*
71st	seventy-first	71ᵉ	*soixante et onzième*
80th	eightieth	80ᵉ	*quatre-vingtième*
90th	ninetieth	90ᵉ	*quatre-vingt-dixième*
100th	hundredth	100ᵉ	*centième*
101st	hundred and first	101ᵉ	*cent unième*
1000th	thousandth	1000ᵉ	*millième*
2000th	two thousandth	2000ᵉ	*deux millième*
1,000,000th	millionth	1 000 000ᵉ	*millionième*

Dates / Les dates

1996	nineteen ninety-six	*mille neuf cent quatre-vingt-seize*
2005	two thousand (and) five	*deux mille cinq*

November 10/11 (ten, eleven), *Br* **the 10th/11th of November**
le dix/onze novembre

March 1 (first), *Br* **the 1st of March**
le premier mars

French pronunciation

Vowel

a	[a]	valise, déjà	a short sound as in cat, and
	[ɑ]	bas	as in car, mask
		pâte	slightly more closed and drawn out as in pasture, vase
ai	[e]	j'ai	as in make, day
	[ɛ]	bête, exprès	as in plenty, pest
au	[o]	faux, chaud	as in potato
	[ɔ]	Paul	similar to the vowel sound in hot, shot
e	[e]	été, arriver, rendez-vous	a slightly softer version of day, say
	[ɛ]	cher, après fenêtre, mère	like the vowel sound in pet, send
	[ə]	le, que	as in the, a
ei	[ɛ]	peine	like the vowel sound in pet, send
ei	[ɛ̃]	éteindre	as in hand
eil	[ɛj]	bouteille, pareil	as in day, say
eau	[o]	bateau	as in tomato, potato
eu	[ø]	feu	similar to the articles the, a but slightly more drawn out
	[œ]	fleur	as in curtain, bird
i	[i]	cri	as in me, see
		dire	as in pier, clear
o	[o]	pot, hôtel	as in tomato, potato
	[ɔ]	fort	as in law, paw
œu	[ø]	nœud	similar to the articles the, a but slightly more drawn out
	[œ]	œuf	more drawn out when followed by a consonant as in turn

| ou | [u] | goût, soupe | as in **to** |
| **u** | [y] | sûr, mur | no real equivalent in English – the closest would be bl**ue**, men**u**. To make the sound, purse your lips tightly and try saying 'ee', keeping your lips pursed. |

Semi vowels

ieu	[jø]	adieu	like the **byeu** sound in beautiful
oi	[wa]	choisir	pronounced **wa** as in **wa**gon
oui	[wi]	oui	as in **we**
ui	[ɥi]	suite, fuir	no real equivalent in English – the closest would be w**e** with the **w** pronounced with pursed lips

Nasal vowels

In the nasal sound, the air escapes through the nose as well as the mouth, like the **ng** sound in English:

- [ɑ̃] cha**m**bre, cha**n**ter, me**m**bre, ente**n**te
- [ɛ̃] ci**nq**, ti**m**bre, tra**in**, étei**n**dre, ny**m**phe
- [wɛ̃] co**in**, mo**ins**
- [õ] bo**m**be, fo**nd**
- [œ̃] **un**, h**um**ble

Consonant

c	[k]	calcul	a hard vowel sound as in **c**offee, **c**at
	[s]	citron	as in sing
ç	[s]	façon	like the **s** in pasta
ch	[ʃ]	chercher	depending on the word, this is normally pronounced **sh** as in sugar, **sh**oe